THE POLITICAL ECONOMY OF MONOPOLY

Business, Labor and Government Policies

THE POLITICAL ECONOMY OF
MONOPOLY

Business, Labor and Government Policies

by

FRITZ MACHLUP

Baltimore: The Johns Hopkins Press

Books *by* FRITZ MACHLUP

Die Goldkernwährung (1925)
Die neuen Währungen in Europa (1927)
Börsenkredit, Industriekredit and Kapitalbildung (1931)
Führer durch die Krisenpolitik (1934)
Guide à travers les panacées economiques (1938)
The Stock Market, Credit and Capital Formation (1940)
International Trade and the National Income Multiplier
    (1943)
The Basing-Point System (1949)
The Political Economy of Monopoly (1952)
The Economics of Sellers' Competition (1952)

Copyright © 1952 by The Johns Hopkins Press, Baltimore, Md. 21218
Printed in the United States of America
Library of Congress Catalog Card Number 53-6338

Originally published, 1952
Second printing, 1955
Third printing, 1964
Fourth printing, 1967

Author's Preface

I F YOU ARE a student in your first course on economics, I know that you are hard to please: you tend to find many books dull, tough, or condescending. It has been my ambition to avoid all these unloved qualities and to write in a lucid style with a bit of a snap in it. I hope you will like what I have done. Some parts of this book, perhaps, are a little more "abstract" than you are used to. Certain sections in Chapters 9 and 10, on Labor Policies, and in Chapter 12, on Measuring the Degree of Monopoly, are perhaps more technical and "theoretical" than you can stand. But try them anyway.

If you are a "general reader" without any background in economics, you will find the more "descriptive" parts—Chapters 4 to 8—on Business Policies and Government Policies the easiest. But even if the other chapters are harder, I hope you will find them readable and interesting enough to make your reading effort worth while. I can rely on you to know how to skip the more technical sections in Chapter 12 and elsewhere, even without specific advice from me. Incidentally, I should like to know how well or how little I have succeeded in making complicated things intelligible to the general reader. So, please, would you mind writing me about it and telling me which parts in this book you have found clear and interesting, and which parts you have found dull or unintelligible?

If you are a student in a second or third course in economics, I hope the book will be rewarding to you in its entirety. Of course, your chief interest may not be in general economics but in a special field. If it is Labor Economics, I am afraid you will find my Chapters 9 and 10 rather different from the ideas put forth by most other books on the subject of trade-union wage policy; but I trust you will be tolerant of dissenting opinions. If your field is Government Control of Business, or Industrial Organization, you will surely need more illustrative "case" material than is contained here, but the systematic treatment that I have tried to give here of the economic issues involved, may, if I have succeeded, afford you a better perspective and firmer understanding of the field as a whole and of the factual information gained from other sources.

If you are studying the economics of competition and monopoly, this book may provide you with useful background knowledge; but it does not furnish enough of the necessary theoretical analysis. For this you will have to turn to a companion volume, published simultaneously by the Johns Hopkins Press under the title *The Economics of Sellers' Competition: Model Analysis of Sellers' Conduct*, where I present an exposition of the economic theory of competition that will, I hope, provide you with a solid foundation for analytical economic reasoning.

If you are a trained and well-read economist, the present book may interest you mainly for what are, I believe, its somewhat original ways of dealing with issues with which you are familiar. To be sure, you will probably disagree with some of my views and I expect criticism from you, mostly of the really controversial issues of wage theory.

If you are a teacher of economics, I hope you will find that this book is suitable for your students. I wish you would give it a try and let me know how it works.

I expect brickbats on two scores. You may object to the number and length of footnotes; I felt it desirable that the discussion in the text be amplified in a way that permits the reader who does not care for more to skip it without loss of continuity. And you may object to some repetition; but the majority of readers do not finish the book in one sitting, and when reading a chapter, may well have forgotten what was said two or three chapters earlier. Moreover, some repetition is needed if the exposition is to make sense. For example, if business practices evolve in adaptation to changing government policies while government policies are again readjusted to changing business practices, one cannot reasonably avoid discussing each in connection with the other—and this implies repetition.

A few sections of the present book have been published elsewhere. An earlier version of Chapters 1, 2, and 3 has been used in mimeographed form in courses in elementary economics at the University of Buffalo. A portion of Chapter 3 is being published under the title "Monopoly and the Problem of Economic Stability" as one of the papers presented at the conference on *Monopoly and Competition and Their Regulation,* held by the International Economic Association in Talloires, France, in September 1951. A section of Chapter 5 is being published under the title "Characteristics and Types of Price Discrimination" as one of the papers presented at the *Conference on Business Concentration and Price Policy* held by the Universities-National Bureau Committee for Economic Research in Princeton, N.J., in June 1952. A section of Chapter 6 was published as an article entitled "The American Antitrust Laws—Success or Failure?" in the *Schweizerische Zeitschrift für Volkswirtschaft und Statistik,* Vol. 87 (1951), pp. 513–520. Finally, an early version of substantial portions of Chapters 9 and 10 was published under the title "Monopolistic Wage Determination as a Part of the General Problem of Monopoly" in *Wage Determination and the Economics of Liberalism,* Economic Institute of the Chamber of Commerce of the United States (Washington: 1947), pp. 49–82.

I probably should explain that the present book together with the companion volume on *The Economics of Sellers' Competition* take the place of what was previously announced as a forthcoming book "On the Economics of Competition and Monopoly."

I am indebted to numerous friends who have helped me in the preparation of this book. Listing only those who gave me generously of their time, I wish to thank John T. Dunlop, of Harvard University, who assisted me, back in 1939, in writing the first draft of an essay, portions of which are contained in this book; John D. Sumner, of the University of Buffalo, Roy W. Jastram, of the University of California, Emile Benoit-Smullyan, then of the Department of Labor, and Edwin G. Nourse, then of the Brookings Institution in Washington, who gave me friendly criticism of those parts of the manuscript that I had written before 1942; Sigmund Timberg, formerly of the Department of Justice, who made valuable comments on Chapter 6, on "Antitrust Laws"; and Edith Tilton Penrose, of the Johns Hopkins University, whose contribution to this book has been singularly extensive. She discussed with me nearly every problem of analysis and exposition, read and suggested improvements on almost every page, did most of the library research for Part III, on "Government Policies," and furnished a complete draft for Chapter 8. While the credit for many good features of this book should be hers, the responsibility for its shortcomings is of course entirely my own.

I wish to record my gratitude to the Rockefeller Foundation for a grant permitting me to give a whole year—1942–43—to my research on the problem of monopoly, although most of the studies of that year were on the patent system and the results of these studies will eventually go into a monograph on that subject. Financial aid received from the Lessing Rosenthal Fund for Economic Research at the Johns Hopkins University is also gratefully acknowledged; it was used to defray editorial and clerical expenses connected with the preparation of the present book.

Finally, I wish to thank Angela Lavarello, Secretary of the Department of Political Economy at the Johns Hopkins University, who cheerfully assumed the responsibilities connected with the task of getting the manuscript typed.

FRITZ MACHLUP

Baltimore, Maryland, July 1952

Table of Contents

AUTHOR'S PREFACE   V

Chapter

PART I—CONCEPTS, PROBLEMS, APPRAISALS

1. Fundamental Notions and Concepts   3
2. Monopoly: Meanings, Effects, Manifestations   24
3. Monopoly: Economic and Political Appraisals   46

PART II—BUSINESS POLICIES

4. Monopolistic Business Practices: Collusion, Merger, Exclusion   81
5. Monopolistic Business Practices: Price Leadership, Discrimination, Unfair Competition   127

PART III—GOVERNMENT POLICIES

6. Governmental Restraints on Monopoly: Antitrust Laws   181
7. Governmental Aids to Monopoly: Corporation Laws, Taxes, Tariffs, Patents   236
8. Governmental Aids to Monopoly: Licences, Regulation, Price Controls, Labor Law   287

PART IV—LABOR POLICIES

9. Monopolistic Labor Policies: Bargaining Power   333
10. Monopolistic Labor Policies: Wage Rates and Income   380

PART V—FACTS, THEORIES, MEASUREMENTS

11. Economic Fact and Theory   439
12. Measuring the Degree of Monopoly   469

INDEX   529

Analytical Table of Contents

Chapter

PART I—CONCEPTS, PROBLEMS, APPRAISALS

1. Fundamental Notions and Concepts   3
Loose Charges and Vague Notions: The Sins of Monopoly and the Virtues of Competition · Vague Notions and Indiscernible Facts

Competition, Pure and Perfect: Perfect Market · Pure Competition · Interview with a Pure Competitor · Non-Pure Competition · Pure Competition as an Ideal · Perfect Competition · The Function of Competitive Prices

2. Monopoly: Meanings, Effects, Manifestations   24
Monopolistic Restrictions of Operations and Entry: Restrictions of the Volume of Operations · Restrictions of Entry · Practices to Tighten Restrictions of Operations · The Economic Effects of Monopolistic Restrictions · Provisos and Reservations

Monopoly in Business, Labor, and Agriculture: Monopolistic Business Policies · Various Meanings of Business Monopoly · Monopsony in Business · Monopolistic Restrictions in Agriculture · Monopolistic Labor Policies

3. Monopoly: Economic and Political Appraisals   46
Inevitability and Desirability of Monopoly: The Cost of Avoidance · Public versus Private Monopoly · Large-Scale Production · Variety of Product · Exploitation of Natural Resources · "Unstable" Industries · Monopolistic Shock-Absorbers and Stable Growth · Monopolistic Brakes and Technological Progress · Monopoly Policies versus Tax Policies

Debits and Credits of Monopolistic Restraints: False Issues and Real · Conflicting Objectives · A Balance Sheet

Monopoly and Democracy: Monopoly and the Road to Serfdom · Democracy in a Planned Economy · Superstition or Prudence?

[xi]

Chapter

PART II—BUSINESS POLICIES

4. Monopolistic Business Practices: Collusion, Merger,
   Exclusion   81
   Meanings and Distinctions: Confusion Worse Confounded ·
   Distinctions and "Reality"

   Cooperation, Collusion, Cartels: Gentlemen's Agreement ·
   Trade Associations, Cost Calculations and Statistics · Delivered-Price Formulas · Cartels with Enforcement Apparatus · The Contents of Cartel Arrangements · Profit
   Pools and Average Price Cartels · Centralized Selling

   Oppression, Domination, Merger, Concentration: Manifold
   Interrelationships, Warfare and Cooperation · Oppressive
   Practices · Domination · The Merger Movement · Integra-
   tion and Conglomeration · Concentration

   Restrictions on Entry: Governmental Barriers · Threats of
   Ruinous Campaigns · Barred Access to Resources · Bigger
   Minimum Size

5. Monopolistic Business Practices: Price Leadership,
   Discrimination, Unfair Competition   127

   Price Leadership: A Background of Merger, Domination,
   Coercion · Conformance without Pressure, Suasion or Collusion · Mutual Understanding between Leader and Followers · Four Types of Price Leadership

   Price Discrimination: Definition · Monopoly Power as a
   Prerequisite · Classifications of Price Discrimination · Personal Discrimination · Group Discrimination · Consumer
   Location · Consumer Status · Product Use · Product Discrimination · Price Discrimination and the Public Interest

   A Digression on Price Uniformity: A Symptom of Collusion
   or of Competition? · Necessary Distinctions · Implications
   of Price Identity and Uniformity

   Unfair Competition: What is Unfair? · The Right to Com-
   pete · Economic Classification · Deception of the Consumer
   · Competition to Reduce Competition · No Harm to the
   Consumer

Chapter

PART III—GOVERNMENT POLICIES

6. Governmental Restraints on Monopoly: Antitrust
   Laws   181
   Interventions against Competition and against Monopoly:
   Interventions against Competition · Interventions against
   Monopoly

   A Chronology of Antimonopoly Policy: Ancient History ·
   English History · American History

   The Antitrust Laws of the United States: The Sherman Act
   · The Clayton Act · The Federal Trade Commision Act ·
   The Robinson-Patman Act · The Celler Anti-Merger Act ·
   Rules and Exceptions

   The Law of Collusion: Juridical Controversies · Unconditional Prohibitions · Certainties and Uncertainties · Observance, Enforcement, Penalties · Collusion through Restrictive Patent Licensing · Exemptions for Labor and Agriculture · Exemptions for Transportation, Banking, and Insurance · Exemptions for Exporters and Retail Distributors
   · "Emergency" Exemptions

   The Law of Monopolization: Vexing Problems · An All Too
   Judicious Judiciary · An Injudicious Legislature · Frustration Continued · Frustration Ended?

   Antitrust Laws—Success or Failure?: Contradictory Appraisals · Stopping the Cartels—a Partial Success · Checking
   the Trusts—a Dismal Failure · Alternative and Complementary Antitrust Policies

7. Governmental Aids to Monopoly: Corporation
   Laws, Taxes, Tariffs, Patents   236
   Corporation Laws: The Privileges of the Body Corporate ·
   Large-Scale Production versus Monopoly Control · Gratui-
   tous Privileges and Lack of Limitations · Limiting the
   Privileges · Federal Incorporation

   Tax Policies: Non-Fiscal versus Fiscal Objectives · Corporation Income Taxes: Why and How? · The Actual Bias
   Against Small Business · Tax-Induced Sales of Small Business Firms · The Potential Bias Against Big Business · Differential Taxes on Retained Earnings · Tax Policy and
   Antimonopoly Policy

Chapter

    Trade Barriers: Import Tariffs · Arguments for Tariff Protection · Pressure Group Politics · Tariffs, Competition, Cartelization · Import Quotas · Foreign Exchange Restrictions · Interstate Trade Barriers

    Patent Laws: Justification of Patent Protection · Extension of the Patent Monopoly · Abolition or Prevention of Abuse?

8. Governmental Aids to Monopoly: Licences, Regulation, Price Controls, Labor Law   287
    Licensing and "Board Regulation": Economic Freedom Gained and Lost Again · The Public Interest and the Private Interests · The Guild System Has Returned

    Public Utilities and Transportation: Protecting Competing Monopolies · Suppression of Competition in Transportation · Competition Prohibited

    Conservation of Natural Resources: Private and Social Costs · Organic Natural Resources · Oil Conservation or Restriction? · Coal Conservation—a Misnomer

    Price Controls: Minimum Prices and Price Supports · Output Control and Surplus Removal · Marketing Programs · International Price Programs · Subsidized Production for Destruction · Minimum-Price Controls · Prohibition of Sales Below Cost · Maximum-Price Legislation · Rent Control

    Labor Legislation: Legislature versus Judiciary · The Power to Organize · The Use of Organized Power · Pruning Back · The Public Interest

PART IV—LABOR POLICIES

9. Monopolistic Labor Policies: Bargaining Power   333
    Labor and Society: The Size of the Group Called "Labor" · "Pro-Labor" Sentiment · Approval of Labor Monopoly · Arguments for Strong Trade Unions · Two Points of Romantic Semantics

    Equalizing the Bargaining Power: The Meaning of Bargaining Power · "Labor—the Most Perishable Commodity" · Workers Must Eat—They Cannot Wait · No Visible Competition for Labor · Conspiracies among Employers · Immobility of Labor · Immobility and Isolated Markets ·

Chapter
Profits at the Expense of Wages · Immobility and General
Unemployment · Immobility and Nonwage Competition ·
Corporations as Combinations of Capital · Redressing the
Balance · Dealing with Isolated Labor Markets · Dealing
with Employers' Collusion · Dealing with "Employer Dif-
ferentiation"

10. Monopolistic Labor Policies: Wage Rates and In-
    come   380
    Correcting Defects of the Labor Market: Wage Differentials
    and Job Evaluation · Incorrect Adjustments to Changes ·
    Upward and Downward Spirals

    Raising the National Income: The Purchasing Power Argu-
    ment · Increasing the Propensity to Consume · Shocking
    the Employers into Increased Efficiency · Energizing the
    Workers into Increased Efficiency

    Redistributing the National Income: Gaining—at Whose
    Expense? · Real Wages and Labor's Relative Share · Wage
    Increases Paid Out of Profits? · Getting a "Cut" in Mono-
    poly Profits · Squeezing all Profits in a Changing Economy
    · Raising Wages as Productivity Rises · The Unorganized
    Majority · There Will Always Be a Short Run

    The Wage Structure: Restricting the Supply · "No Help
    Wanted" · "Natural" and "Artificial" Wage Differentials ·
    Wages in General Are Too Low

    Wages, Employment, Inflation: The Hidden Connection ·
    Wage Policies of Trade Unions · "Full Employment Policy"
    · Political Freedom in Jeopardy · Restraint or Self-Re-
    straint? · Governmental Regulation of Wage Rates · Re-
    ducing the Monopoly Power of Unions · The Problems of
    Poverty and Insecurity · The Wage Problem under Social-
    ism

                    Part V—Facts, Theories, Measurements

11. Economic Fact and Theory   439
    Variations in Method: Conceptual Framework (Part I) ·
    Taxonomic Approach (Part II) · Historical Approach (Part
    III) · Theoretical Approach (Part IV)

    Abstraction, Theory, and Fact: "It's a Fact" · "It's Just a
    Theory" · Facts or Implied Theories?

Chapter

Explanation, Prediction, Evaluation: Prediction versus Explanation · Hypothetical Predictions · Evaluation · Implied
Value Judgments · An Illustration · Conflicting Values

Measurement: "Science is Measurement" · Some Implications of Measurement · Fictitious Accuracy

12. Measuring the Degree of Monopoly   469
    Purposes, Obstacles, Criteria: The Desirability of Measure-
    ment · Degree of Monopoly versus Monopoly Power · The
    Basic Difficulties of Measurement · The Possible Criteria for
    Measurement

    Numbers and Concentration: The Number of Firms · The
    Concentration of Control · Definitions of Firm and Industry
    · The Size of the Market · Competition from Outside the
    Industry · The Index of Divergence

    The Rate of Profit: The Accounting Rate of Profit · An Ad-
    justed Rate of Profit

    Price Inflexibility: The Rigidity of Administered Prices ·
    Frequency and Amplitude of Changes · Comparing the In-
    dexes · Margin Inflexibility

    The Gap Between Marginal Cost and Price: Inequality Be-
    tween Marginal Cost and Price · Objections and Limita-
    tions · Changes in the Degree of Monopoly

    Other Measurement Proposals: Gross Profit Margin and Ag-
    gregate Monopoly Income · Industry Control and the Slope
    Ratios of Demand Curves · Cross-Elasticities of Demand ·
    Penetration and Insulation

    A Monopolist's Self-Analysis

    Conclusion

PART I—CONCEPTS, PROBLEMS, APPRAISALS

CHAPTER 1

Fundamental Notions and Concepts

Loose Charges and Vague Notions: The Sins of Monopoly and the Virtues of Competition · Vague Notions and Indiscernible Facts

Competition, Pure and Perfect: Perfect Market · Pure Competition · Interview with a Pure Competitor · Non-Pure Competition · Pure Competition as an Ideal · Perfect Competition · The Function of Competitive Prices

IN POLITICAL and popular discussions of economic problems the term "monopolistic practices" is often used to mean "evil practices," chiefly of "big business." At the same time many scholarly economists assert that monopolistic forms of competition are typical and normal for all markets of industrial products. Are we then to conclude that all industrial policies are by definition "evil practices"? This is not a very felicitous background for an objective investigation of current economic problems. It would be helpful if politicians, lawyers, economists, and businessmen understood the language of one another better than they actually do.

LOOSE CHARGES AND VAGUE NOTIONS

The Sins of Monopoly and the Virtues of Competition

An impressive list of sins allegedly committed by "the monopolies" is periodically resubmitted. The monopolies, according to the indictment, pick the pockets of the consumers by charging too high prices; cut the throats of small, independent businessmen by ruthless local price-cutting; exploit their workers and suppliers of raw material by iniquitous hiring and buying techniques; reduce the national product through uneconomic allocation and inefficient use of productive resources; jeopardize social stability through concen-

[3]

tration of economic control; use all sorts of pressure to influence governmental policies in behalf of their own interests; prevent possible improvements of the standard of living by suppressing the adoption of superior production techniques; aggravate economic depressions by maintaining inflexible prices in the face of falling costs and falling demand; obstruct sustained recovery by choking revived demand through unwarranted price increases; create permanent unemployment by restricting production and resisting expansion; cause deflationary drains of purchasing power by accumulating idle cash surpluses; and threaten the existence of free enterprise and democratic government.

The charges against "monopoly" are at the same time credits to "competition" inasmuch as the latter is supposed to prevent the evil consequences ascribed to the former. But more specifically, competition is credited with securing lower prices for consumers, improvements in the qualities of the products, the introduction of new products and new services to the consumer, the use of the most efficient methods of production, and the best allocation of the productive resources of the economy.

Not everybody, however, has been using only dark colors for picturing the effects of monopoly and only bright colors for the effects of competition. There are many to whom the word competition suggests—instead of "order and efficiency"—disorder, anarchy, the "law of the jungle," ruthlessness, wastefulness, and hence a state of economic life that is socially undesirable. To them it appears preferable to restrict competition, and substitute for it various schemes of "orderly marketing," "regulated competition" or "cooperation." But somehow the public appeal of the word competition is sufficiently favorable, and that of the word monopoly sufficiently unfavorable, to persuade the advocates of regulation or cooperation to retain the word competition in the descriptions or preambles of their schemes, and to insist that they do not propose to eliminate competition but merely to limit it, to hold it to "healthy" degrees.

There is also the idea that competition is helpful as long as it does not go too far; in other words, that we may have too much competition as well as too little, and that there exists somewhere a dose that is just right and beneficial for the economy. Since we have not yet learned how to measure the *amount* or *degree* of competition, some have proposed that there are good and bad *kinds* of competition. Producers are inclined to dislike price competition, that is, attempts by individual sellers to secure more business by reducing their prices. Most consumers, however, find price competition among sellers more useful than any other kind, and many economists agree with them.

If it is a seller's ambition to secure more business, he can do other things as well as, or instead of, reducing his prices. He may improve the quality of his product; he may provide additional services to his customers; he may attract new customers or win loyalty of his old ones by advertising and other sorts of selling effort; he may deliver his products over great distances without collecting the full cost of transport; he may grant his customers more credit or for longer periods or on better terms; he may lie to his customers about some special qualities of his products; he may disparage the wares of his competitors; he may disturb the business of his competitors and thus divert their customers to himself; he may make it inconvenient for buyers to patronize his competitors; he may reduce the business of his competitors by obstructing their access to certain supplies or services needed for their production; or he may through ruinous price wars force competitors out of business. If all these practices come under the heading of competition, it is certainly impossible to make generalizations about the benefits or evils of "competition." It would be necessary to distinguish socially harmful forms of competition from socially desirable ones. Some economists prefer to call the presumably harmful practices "monopolistic practices" and confine the word competition to those forms which they consider beneficial to society. To fit the definitions to one's prejudices is analytically of no use. It is possible, though, to adopt such a narrow definition of competition that it covers only some idealized situations—which are regarded as socially desirable—and to call all deviations from this construction "monopolistic." This is permissible, but then it is necessary to provide distinctions on the basis of which the various kinds of deviations from the "ideal" competition can be analysed and appraised.

In view of the wholesale condemnation of "monopoly," it is hardly astonishing that from time to time action against the "defendant" is urgently demanded. The difficulty, however, is that it is not known, or certainly not agreed upon, who the defendant really is. Against whom should action be taken—and what action should be taken? Are all industries monopolistic? Which are the more, which the less, monopolistic industries? Should we punish them; break them up; nationalize them; rationalize them; regulate them; prohibit particular practices; apply specific measures to specific situations; use moral suasion; compete with them through public operation of rival establishments; influence them through the placing of government contracts; design special systems of taxes and bounties; reduce certain tariffs; or—should we do nothing?

Vague Notions and Indiscernible Facts

One fundamental difficulty is that there is no agreement as to what should be considered the criterion of monopoly. Not only are the legal concepts of monopoly different from the various economic concepts; but most of the concepts are vague, or to say the least, rarely amenable to demonstration by discernible and measurable facts. Indeed, it can be shown that any attempts to measure the degree of monopoly power by various "reliable symptoms" leads to inconsistent results.[1]

To say that monopoly means *absence of competition* is not of much help. Absence of competition of any sort? Certainly *no* seller has a monopoly in this sense, because he must compete for the consumer's dollar with the thousands of different products that are offered in the market. To say that monopoly means *control over output* is not of much help either. Control over what output? His own? Certainly *every* seller would be a monopolist in this sense, because he has control over his own output—except for the vagaries of nature and the acts of God, State, and foreign or public enemies.

Both these unsuccessful definitions seem to make a little better sense if they incorporate the word *industry:* "absence of competition in the industry" and "control over the output of the whole industry." To those who have not given much thought to these questions, the matter seems rather simple: If there is only one seller

[1] See below Ch. 12.

in the industry, there is a monopoly; if there are many sellers in the industry, there is competition. Alternatively the definitions might incorporate the word *commodity:* "Absence of competition in the sale of a certain commodity" and "control over the output of a certain commodity." But, unfortunately, the concepts of "an industry" and of "a commodity" are both hopelessly vague, one as much as the other. This is not surprising, because an industry is often understood as a group of firms producing the same commodities (although frequently it means a group of firms using the same materials or processes). Hence if we have a hard time deciding whether two similar articles are two different qualities of one commodity or two different commodities, we must have the same difficulty deciding whether their producers belong to the same or to different industries. Are plate glass and flat glass two different commodities? Are plate glass manufacturers and window glass manufacturers in two different industries? You may take your choice. But if this is more or less a matter of taste or convention, there can be no definite meanings to the phrases "competition in an industry" and "control over the supply of a commodity."

Whether there is competition or monopoly in any particular case would thus depend on what we choose to call an industry. If there was only one producer of aluminum, he would be a monopolist in the "aluminum industry," but one of many competitors in the "non-ferrous metals industry." If there were many makers of fountain-pens but only one maker of ball-point pens, the latter would be characterized as having a monopoly or as being in competition depending on whether we decide to distinguish a ball-point pen industry or to include it in the fountain-pen industry.

Many people have recognized that it makes little sense to take the number of firms in an industry as the criterion, because one or two out of a very large number of firms may be so big and powerful that they practically control the industry. The conclusion was drawn, quite correctly, that the degree of *concentration of control* within the industry was much more significant than the *number of firms.* For example, it may not mean much that there are sixty firms in a certain industry if one or two of them own a high proportion of the industry's assets and transact the bulk of its sales. But still, as long as one may arbitrarily delimit the industry and can choose between narrow or extensive boundaries, the degree of concentration in such an arbitrarily defined industry may not be indicative of the competitive situation. If we define industry and commodity very narrowly, the degree of concentration will be high, but there may be plenty of competition between the firms of this industry and firms in other industries. Their products, although called different commodities, may be highly substitutable for one another and thus compete vigorously with one another in the markets. On the other hand, we may define industry and commodity rather broadly and may then find that some firms in that industry, despite its low degree of concentration, enjoy a very sheltered position, *a degree of control over the price of their products* which one cannot help characterizing as monopoly power.

These arguments suggest that the customary lines drawn between industries may not be the ones that are relevant for the degree of competition prevailing among firms. Products offered by firms regarded as being in different industries may be more substitutable for each other than products offered by firms in the same industry. But how can we ascertain the substitutability between goods? We know that it is not the physical similarity that counts. The substitutability between physically identical goods may be zero if they are at different places very far apart. Physically very different products may be close substitutes for one another and thus compete heavily for the favor of the consumer. (Just think of fuel oil, coal, coke, natural gas, electricity, etc., which may all compete for the same use.) Sometimes there is a possibility of comparing physical efficiencies of competing materials or products (for example, through caloric contents). But often the decisive element is nothing but the "appeal" that the competing goods have to the buyers. It is the consumer who ultimately decides what he wants to buy and how easily he will switch from one product or one product quality to another.

The greater the readiness of buyers to substitute other products for the product of a particular firm, the smaller will be that firm's control over its selling prices. As the characteristic of monopoly power, control over price is much less ambiguous than control over output, although one still has the problem of finding criteria and measurements for the *degree* of control over price. Various measures have been suggested to express the "buyers' readiness to switch." The two expressions most relevant for our purposes are the *price-elasticity of demand* and the *cross-elasticity of demand*. Both relate the quantities demanded to prices charged: the former relates them to the prices of the product itself, the latter to the prices of other products in the market. Thus, they indicate what would happen to the sales of a product if its price were changed, and what would happen if the price of another product were changed.[2]

There is little chance of obtaining the information needed for actual estimates of these elasticities. The cross-elasticities are particularly hopeless unknowns. The price-elasticities or, as they are usually called more briefly, the elasticities of demand, are not quite so far beyond our reach. But we must realize that these elasticities are nothing but hypothetical propositions. They tell, for example, how much more of a product could be sold *if* its price were lowered by a certain percentage. These hypothetical judgments are conjectures about people's *inclinations*. To be sure, many businessmen think that they have a pretty good idea of the responsiveness of their market, but, if they have, their idea will hardly be formulated in any exact terms and, in any case, such matters are regularly treated as business secrets. Thus, unable to measure the buyers' inclinations, we cannot even ascertain the sellers' conjectures about these inclinations. At best we may try to infer something about the sellers' conjectures by observing what policies they pursue. But these are indirect and unreliable clues indeed.

Elasticities of demand certainly have something to do with monopoly, whether we can measure them or not. A seller does not have much leeway in his price policy if he believes that customers would respond very sensitively to small changes in his price:—a

---

[2] The price-elasticity of demand for good A is the relative change in the quantity of A demanded, divided by the relative change in the price of A charged. The cross-elasticity of demand for good A with respect to good B is the relative change in the quantity of A demanded, divided by the relative change in the price of B charged. (A more complicated measure of the substitutability between the two goods is the elasticity of substitution. It is the relative change in the ratio of the quantities of A and B demanded, divided by the relative change in the prices of A and B charged.)

small increase in price, and he would have practically no takers for his product; a small reduction in price, and there would be so many takers that he could not meet the demand. A seller faced with a demand as elastic as this has little "control" over price. On the other hand, a seller facing a less elastic demand has a much greater choice of possible selling prices. To be sure, he may feel that his current price is the most profitable one—that is, he may not care to raise his price, although he would still expect to make substantial sales at a higher price; and he may not wish to lower it, expecting that not much more could be sold at a lower price. He may not in fact experiment with higher and lower prices, but he will probably feel that he has a greater leeway in his price policy. Thus, he has more "control" over price in the sense that the price he will charge depends more on his *judgment* and less on the dictates of the market.

Sellers often *endeavor to reduce the elasticity of demand* for their product. Advertising, for example, not only serves to increase the demand but also to reduce its elasticity. For it may attach customers more faithfully to the particular seller or his product, thus allowing him to keep their patronage in spite of a rise (or a refused reduction) of the selling price. Frequently sellers pursue all sorts of policies to distinguish their products more effectively from rival products; the more different they become in the eyes of the customers, the less substitutable other products seem to be for theirs, the less likely will the sellers lose custom when they put up the price or refuse to lower it.

Collusion among rival sellers, long known as a way of reducing the degree of competition and increasing the chances for charging "monopoly prices," can also be explained in terms of demand elasticity. In the absence of collusion each seller is chary of raising his price, fearing that he would lose customers to his competitors; and many a seller is tempted to cut his price, hoping that he would attract much business away from his competitors. Collusion among sellers can "remedy" this situation. For example, if a seller knows that his competitors will follow his lead, his fear that any price increase would drive his customers to rival sellers is allayed, and his temptation to steal customers from them is gone because he knows that any price cut would be immediately followed. Price leadership, of course, is only one of many manifestations of collusion. Incidentally, though, whether or not price leadership necessarily implies collusion is a very controversial issue. The whole problem of collusion is full of controversy, because the law in the United States has made collusion among competitors an illegal restraint of trade and, therefore, businessmen are wary and direct evidence of collusive practices is hard to obtain. If collusion must be largely inferred, it cannot well be used as a criterion of monopoly—apart from the fact that one cannot be sure that collusion always creates or increases monopoly power.

Merger with a competing firm is a rather obvious way of reducing competition. The fusion of previous competitors reduces the elasticity of demand for the products of the united firm. No more stealing of customers between them, less temptation to cut prices, less fear of losing customers at raised prices. But, again, we have no way of "proving," in concrete cases, in quantitative terms the increase in monopoly power that results from merger, no way of measuring the reduction in the degree of competition.

We have said nothing thus far about *monopoly profits*. Is not the presence of monopoly profits a good indication of the presence of monopoly power? Probably so. But how can monopoly profits be distinguished from ordinary profits? Should any profit rate above some "normal rate" be attributed to the exercise of monopoly power? The vagueness of the concept of profit would make an affirmative answer to the last question rather rash. There is an abundance of arbitrariness in the calculation of profits, what with the wide-open problems of valuation of fixed assets, depreciation allowances, comparative risks and uncertainties, differential talents, and so forth. Moreover, there is the argument, most persuasive, that absence of monopoly profits need not imply absence of monopoly power, or even absence of the actual exercise of monopoly power.

Price inflexibility has sometimes been suggested as an indication of the presence of monopolistic control. But this is no less elusive a piece of circumstantial evidence of monopoly power than the others. Monopoly does not always result in inflexible prices, and inflexible prices are not always attributable to monopoly. This is not to deny that there may be a strong correlation between price inflexibility and the exercise of monopoly power.

After this superficial survey of some notions closely associated with monopoly, we cannot help being impressed with the inordinate degree of vagueness surrounding almost all these concepts and relationships, or with their indiscernibleness in the real world of the facts the concepts are supposed to cover. Tired of the fuzzy ideas and anxious to find some clear and stable point of reference, economists escape with relief to the construction of an abstract model of *pure and perfect competition in a perfect market,* a model which, however unrealistic it may be, has the advantage of being definite and relatively unambiguous.

Competition, Pure and Perfect

The model of competition can be taken apart into three pieces, to which some people have given the names "perfect market," "pure competition," and "perfect competition." But since these terms have not been generally accepted, there exists much terminological confusion, despite conceptual clarity.[3] The labels on the concepts sometimes get interchanged; and especially the shuffling between "pure" and "perfect" may involve the uninitiated in a comedy of errors. Since the terminological tug-of-war between the "purists" and the "perfectionists" seems to drag on without there being much chance of a decision, and since its entertainment value is slight, I have elsewhere proposed different terms for both. Here, however, I shall avoid the use of new terms and I propose an agreement with the reader on the following designations: "Pure competition" shall mean perfectly elastic demand for a seller's product; "perfect competition" shall stand for perfectly free entry into his field; and "perfect market" shall refer to a market organization which secures to each seller and buyer full knowledge of all bids and offers, free access to each other, and complete freedom as to the prices and quantities for which they may contract.

[3] For a survey of the terminologies of various authors, see Fritz Machlup, *The Economics of Sellers' Competition: Model Analysis of Sellers' Conduct* (Baltimore: Johns Hopkins Press, 1952), Ch. 4.

Perfect Market

The concept of the perfect market is designed to rule out such things as a buyer remaining ignorant of an opportunity to purchase at a lower price, or being barred from purchasing at the price at which others are served, or being prohibited from paying a price that he would be willing to pay; or such things as a seller having to accept a lower price because he has failed to hear about buyers who were paying more, or being unable to reach them, or being forbidden by governmental control measures to accept the higher price the buyers are offering or to sell them the quantities they wish to buy.

Thus, three institutional conditions must be fulfilled if a market is to be called perfect: (1) All buyers and sellers have complete knowledge of prices and price offers; (2) every buyer can buy from any seller, and every seller can buy from any buyer, without discrimination; and (3) no restrictions are imposed upon sellers or buyers as to the prices which they may accept or as to the quantities for which they may contract. To these institutional conditions we must add a "psychological" condition generally made in economics: that people prefer more income to less, or in particular that sellers prefer to make more money rather than less and that buyers prefer to get more for their money rather than less.

If a perfectly homogeneous commodity is traded in a perfect market, it cannot be traded at different prices at the same time. For, obviously, with the "full knowledge" and the "free access" that are implied in the perfection of the market, no seller would want to accept a lower price than others are getting and no buyer would want to pay a higher price than others are paying. Moreover, no sellers would be left with any unsold quantities that they had been ready to sell at the price that was actually paid for the commodity; and no buyers would be left with any unsatisfied demand which they had been ready to satisfy by paying the price that was asked for the commodity. This implies that the bidding and asking in a perfect market must result in the emergence of a price at which the quantity supplied and the quantity demanded are equal.

In reality few markets are perfect, but a good many markets come more or less close to being perfect. Even if a large number of markets are far from perfect, we cannot understand what is going on in such markets except by making comparisons with the ideal model of a perfect market. In other words, the model helps us to make sense out of the observed "market processes," market prices, and volumes traded, and out of the presumed "market forces" such as supply and demand.

A market may be perfect even if competition is neither pure nor perfect. In other words, sellers and buyers may have full knowledge of all prices, price bids and offers; free access to each other; absolute freedom to sell or buy any quantities they like and to take or pay any price they find acceptable; a strong ambition never to take less than they can get; but none of these things—which constitute "perfection of the market"—presupposes or entails that sellers are in positions of pure competition and under the pressure of perfect competition.

Pure Competition

Pure competition exists if a seller thinks that at the market price he could sell as much as he wanted while at a higher price he could sell nothing at all. He has no difficulty selling his goods at the given price and sees no difficulty selling larger quantities at the same price if he cared to do so; but he would expect to lose all his sales if he charged a higher price. This clearly defined situation certainly implies absence of control over price. At a higher price no sales could be made, and a lower price would constitute a needless sacrifice on the part of the seller.

It is possible that the situation depicted in this model is approximated, if not actually realized, in the markets for certain agricultural products. No single cotton or wheat grower may think himself capable of influencing the market price of his product. He may have his ideas as to the future changes of prices, but he will not think that the relatively small quantities which he might sell can affect the price in the least. He is such a trivial part of the total market that the commodity exchange would neither become firmer if he withheld some of his produce nor become weaker if he sold larger quantities.

What are the preconditions for a state of pure competition?

Only a seller who offers relatively small quantities of a standardized product, undifferentiated from the product of a very large number of other sellers, can be in a position of pure competition. That the products are identical in quality means, not that there cannot be various grades of the commodity, but only that within each grade all units are so nearly homogeneous that there is no preference on the part of buyers for the product of a particular seller. Nor must there be any other reasons why buyers should prefer one seller to another—for example, better service, greater convenience and the like. If there should exist any differences between sellers, they must not be worth even a penny to the customer: the loyalty of a customer to particular sellers must not cost him anything; or, more correctly, there must not be any loyalty which would enable the seller to keep a customer in spite of charging more than other sellers.

Identity of quality and of service are not sufficient to ensure absence of customers' preferences for particular sellers; location may make a significant difference. Location need not interfere with pure competition if sellers in various locations ship their entire output to a central market where only one price rules at any one time. But if a seller serves different customers at different distances from his location, his sales possibilities begin to look very different. The different transportation costs, either in money or in convenience, which the buyer has to incur with respect to differently located sellers, would create for most of these sellers some degree of control over price. A slightly higher selling price (f.o.b. at the shipper's place) would involve the loss of only the more distant customers; and on the other hand, the quantities salable at a given price are definitely limited so that only a reduction of his price would enable the seller to reach more distant customers. Hence, the sales volume would depend on the price which the seller charged, that is, competition would not be "pure."

Interview with a Pure Competitor

The more we examine the concept of pure competition, the more convinced shall we be that the concept does not fit the situation prevailing in industry. To make this absolutely clear we may

present here a short questionnaire, or a report on an imaginary
hearing, with the answers which a "purely competitive" seller
would have to give.

Q. Do you believe that you might get a higher price for your
   product if you reduced your output or withheld part of it from
   the market?
A. No. My output does not count. If the others go on selling the
   same quantities, nobody would notice that I sell less and I
   would not get a higher price.
Q. Do you believe that you might depress the selling price of
   your product if you tried to sell more?
A. No, not unless the others tried to do the same. The small quantities which I can sell do not make any difference to the market.
Q. How many other producers are there selling the same product
   which you sell?
A. I don't know. There are hundreds of them.
Q. Do you ever try to take a customer away from one of the others?
A. No, that is not necessary. I have no difficulty selling my output
   to the same or to other customers.
Q. Is your product better or inferior in comparison with the
   product of most of the others?
A. It is the same. You cannot distinguish them. My first quality is
   the same as anybody else's first, and my second quality is the
   same as anybody else's second.
Q. Are your customers very loyal to you?
A. I don't care. If the one did not come, another would come along.
Q. Could you not get a higher price from customers who are loyal
   to you?
A. No, nobody would buy from me if he had to pay me more than
   the market price.
Q. You would lose all customers if you asked a higher price?
A. Yes, I could not sell anything if I did not accept the market
   price.
Q. Do you advertise?
A. No. Why should I?
Q. Could you not sell more if you advertised?
A. I can sell any quantity I care to sell without advertising if I
   accept the current price.

Q. If you are able to sell more, why don't you do it?
A. I can sell all I produce.
Q. But could you not produce more?
A. Yes, I could, but it would not pay me to produce more at the present price.

Non-Pure Competition

It does not take much imagination to recognize that with few exceptions the answers would be very different if the questions were put to representatives of most industries. Among the rare cases which come close to the "ideal type" of pure competition are the producers of percale (a certain type of gray goods), the most standardized product of the cotton textile industry. In one inquiry into the policies of a firm in that industry it was found that "prices of both raw materials and gray goods are market-determined and the company has no control over them." [4] This is not, however, a typical situation in industry, and our imaginary interview would elicit quite different answers from most American industrialists.

The difference would become especially striking with respect to the question "why don't you produce more?" To this question we might expect either of two answers from the majority of industrial representatives: one, "We would not be able to sell more"; the other, "We would not be able to sell more except at unbearably low prices." Precisely these answers are considered by many economists to be the essence of the monopolistic element in market positions, regardless of how many traits of competitive selling may be present in these markets.

To the businessman most forms of non-pure competition appear much more competitive than the model of pure competition. Nothing particularly competitive is seen in the behavior of our pure competitor. He does not try to win customers from his rivals; he does not try to advertise; he does not claim any superiority of the quality of his product; he does not care about, and still less compete for, the loyalty of his customers; and he does not worry about what his competitors might do or think about his own ac-

[4] *Industrial Wage Rates, Labor Costs and Price Policies. Monograph No. 5.* Temporary National Economic Committee (Washington, 1940), p. 50.

tions. A feeling of rivalry towards his competitors is foreign to that "pure competitor." It may sound paradoxical that pure competition should exclude everything that resembles the businessman's idea of competitive actions and real rivalry among sellers. What most businessmen would consider the *essence* of heavy competition—price cutting and underselling, quality boasting, advertising, stealing one another's customers—is claimed by the economists as evidence of the *absence* of pure competition and of the presence of monopolistic elements. Thus one can easily understand why the businessman is amazed at the peculiar conceptions of the economist.

Pure Competition as an Ideal

The economists have good reasons for not scrapping the model of pure competition although it clearly does not fit many actual cases and the underlying assumptions seem so utterly unrealistic to the practical man. The model is useful as a standard of comparison and as a standard of performance. As a standard of comparison the model has explanatory value, just as the model of a perfect vacuum has explanatory value in physics even if masses never move in a perfect vacuum. As a standard of performance the model is used in judgments of welfare economics and in the evaluation of economic policy, although it can be used only in combination with a number of additional assumptions. Certain results that can be deduced from such a combination appear so happy and desirable to most economists that they like to regard pure competition not only as an "ideal type"—an abstract construction for analytical purposes—but also as an "ideal"—a state of affairs to which they wish reality would conform as much as possible.

The additional assumptions to be combined with the model of pure competition are perhaps not quite so unrealistic, although opinion on this point is divided. One assumption is that businessmen know their technological possibilities and their cost conditions, know how to calculate, and attempt to make as much profit as possible—in short, that businessmen are *sensible and money-minded.* In addition it is assumed that they have their eyes and ears open, find out quickly about any new opportunities for making money, and try to take advantage of such opportunities—in short, that businessmen are *enterprising*. A final assumption is that the social and legal institutions are such that any businessman at any time is free to take up the business that he chooses and can gain *free entry* to any trade that seems attractive. These assumptions may be put together into a model of the alert, profit-seeking and freely moving entrepreneur. If this model is combined with the model of pure competition, results can be deduced which are widely regarded as the best possible arrangement of the economic resources at the disposal of society.

The condition of perfectly free entry into any field or branch of business has been regarded by some as the chief criterion of *perfect* competition, and its absence as the quintessence of monopoly.

Perfect Competition

Perfect competition requires that everybody is free to move unlimited amounts of productive resources into any field that looks promising to him, and that there are no man-made obstacles to the movement of factors of production into and out of particular employments.

Free mobility of resources, free access to all occupations and free entry into all industries do not imply that each and every unit of any kind of resources should be willing and able to move or be moved at the slightest provocation. It is sufficient if some small fraction of the factors of production in any occupation or at any place have such mobility. If wage rates at one place or in one occupation rise, the assumption of mobility and free access does not mean that all qualified workers should rush in at the same time from all sides. If profits rise in an industry, the assumption of free entry does not require that at one stroke hundreds of new enterprises take up that business. Such movements, rather, are supposed to be gradual. The chief points are that there must not be any man-made obstacles obstructing or delaying the movements, and that these movements tend to equalize the prices of homogeneous factors of production, including the rates of return of investible funds and the earnings of enterprise.[5]

The condition of perfectly free entry into any field of economic activity is certainly not satisfied in reality. There are thousands of barriers keeping out newcomers from particular occupations, trades or industries at particular places. Most of these barriers have been erected at the instigation of insiders seeking protection against "overcrowding." Some of the barriers are the work of private organizations, others are the work of public institutions set up under the laws of the land by national, state, or local government.

But, again, the assumption of perfectly free entry is useful, despite its lack of realism, in the analysis of reality as well as in the derivation of propositions of welfare economics. Let us now take a look at the welfare implications of the combined model of pure and perfect competition in perfect markets.

The Function of Competitive Prices

The functioning of the price system is evaluated according to its efficiency in steering the available resources—natural (land), human (labor), and man-made (capital)—into those uses which yield the most urgently demanded products and services. The allocation of resources must be regarded as uneconomic if it is possible through a shift of resources from one use to another to improve the well-being of any one without reducing the well-being of anyone else. It is also uneconomic—that is, it implies that society takes less than the best it could have—if a shift of resources could be found by which somebody's well-being is improved and someone else is hurt, but the former would still be better off than before even after paying full compensation to all that are hurt by the change. It is convenient to separate in one's thinking the problem of compensation payments by those who gain to those who lose through a reallocation of resources, and indeed to separate the

[5] This tendency refers only to homogeneous factors. Liquid funds seeking only gilt-edged investment and liquid funds disposable as venture capital are no more homogeneous (i.e., interchangeable) than white-collar labor and the labor of steeple-jacks. That capital goods in their specific form must not be regarded as homogeneous with liquid capital funds should be obvious. It is odd that people should have made the error of lumping them all as "capital," seemingly substitutable for one another without difficulty.

whole problem of income distribution from the problem of the efficiency of national production, that is, the problem of total national income.[6] With any given distribution of income the most economic allocation of productive resources is then achieved when no shift of resources could produce a net increase in national income. In plain language, we have the best when nothing better can be had. This optimum allocation can be achieved only if consumers and producers can make their choices on the basis of prices which truly reflect the cost of products and services—cost in the sense of the most desirable alternative uses of the resources, the "foregone opportunities," which society is sacrificing in devoting the resources to any particular use.

There are so-called "external" repercussions which do not usually enter into the price system: for example, the dissatisfaction caused by the smoke that a factory "furnishes" to the neighborhood as an undesirable by-product of its output; or the satisfaction caused to the community by the good-looking houses whose value expresses only the satisfaction of the individual buyers. Apart from these deviations of private benefits and costs from social benefits and costs—deviations for which governments sometimes try to compensate, and often overcompensate, through some sort of intervention—the price system would reflect social benefits and costs, as appraised with the given distribution of incomes, provided there were no artificial restraints in the movement of resources and no self-imposed restrictions in the use of factors or in the output of products with a view to influencing their prices. Both types of restraints and restrictions are called "monopolistic." They may cause prices of factors and products to be above or below their "competitive" values, that is, above or below the values they would have if used entirely for the most heavily demanded of all competing uses they could serve. If one regards it as the function of the price system to effect the allocation of resources among alternative uses, one may conclude that competitive prices result in the "optimum allocation." [7]

[6] Logically the separation can never be complete, because the values by which efficiency and national income are measured reflect buyers' preferences under a given distribution of income. See below Chapter 11.

[7] More should be said about the relevance which the distribution of income may have for the notion of the optimum allocation of resources. Since

The price of a factor of production employed for a certain use is above its competitive level if further quantities of the factor equally suitable and available for the same use are not employed in that use but for other uses at lower prices (or are not employed at all). The price of a product is above its competitive level if it exceeds the added cost at which an increased quantity of the product could be produced, that is, if it more than covers the prices of the additional factors of production required for producing more output.

Pure and perfect competition would prevent factor and product prices from staying above or below competitive levels. *Perfect competition*—free entry of enterprise and resources into all fields —would prevent factor prices from staying higher in some uses than in others and would prevent product prices from staying higher than the cost of the factors required for the product. *Pure competition*—perfect elasticities of selling and buying opportunities and, thus, absence of sellers' and buyers' control over prices— would prevent production from remaining at volumes below those for which additional cost of production would equal the product prices. Thus one may make the statement, subject to certain quali-

---

prices are based on consumers' demand, and demand, in turn, on the consumers' expected satisfactions, each weighted by the individual consumer's purchasing power, the distribution of income is obviously reflected in any free system of prices. If we should dislike the given distribution of income, are we still to call an "optimum" allocation of resources one that corresponds to competitive prices reflecting the *given* income distribution? The answer is that there is only one way of judging the allocation of resources and this is through a system of economic indicators of relative importance and scarcity, called prices. Anyone who dislikes the given distribution of income can advocate its redistribution through taxes and transfer payments (although he should take into account the effects which such a redistribution may have upon the total productivity of the economy). But if the advocate of redistribution attempts to achieve his objective by distorting the relations between prices, he will have no way of judging the results of his interference. He will not even know whether the allocation of resources which he engineers comes closer to what he would like best; it may just as easily be inferior, at the expense of the majority of people concerned.

We conclude that any allocation of resources can be optimal only with reference to *some* distribution of income, whether it be one which includes large incomes from inherited wealth and big differentials due to differential opportunities, or one which results from a system of drastic inheritance and income taxes.

fications, that pure and perfect competition would lead to the most economic utilization of available productive capacity, because producers would strive to make unit costs of production as low as they could possibly be, that is, lower than if volumes of output were either greater or smaller; and that consequently the combination of the abstract models of pure and perfect competition can be useful as a "standard of performance" for the economic processes of the real world, and perhaps also for an examination of the possibilities of creating in the real world *conditions* that come closer to (or deviate less widely from) the assumptions made in the idealized models or, where this seems impossible, of bringing about *results* that approximate those of the workings of the models.

CHAPTER 2

Monopoly: Meanings, Effects, Manifestations

Monopolistic Restrictions of Operations and Entry: Restrictions of the Volume of Operations · Restrictions of Entry · Practices to Tighten Restrictions of Operations · The Economic Effects of Monopolistic Restrictions · Provisos and Reservations

Monopoly in Business, Labor, and Agriculture: Monopolistic Business Policies · Various Meanings of Business Monopoly · Monopsony in Business · Monopolistic Restrictions in Agriculture · Monopolistic Labor Policies

THE IDEAL constructions of pure and perfect competition serve as a convenient frame of reference for specifying the meaning or meanings of monopoly as well as for distinguishing its various manifestations. The economic effects of monopolistic restrictions, likewise, can best be demonstrated with the aid of these analytic models.

MONOPOLISTIC RESTRICTIONS OF OPERATIONS AND ENTRY

Deviations from competitive price can be divided for analytical purposes into two kinds: those connected with restrictions of input and output on the part of insiders operating in a field of activity, and those connected with restrictions upon outsiders, preventing them from entering a particular field of activity. This division derives logically from the main parts of the model of competition, pure and perfect. The absence of pure competition causes firms in a field to restrict their operations because of anticipated effects on factor prices paid and product prices received. The absence of free entry keeps potential newcomers—productive factors and new enterprise—away from the field.

Restrictions of the Volume of Operations

Under pure competition there is only one reason why a firm will not expand its operations: technological or organizational efficiency would so suffer from an increase in the volume of production that production cost would be too high for the given level of selling prices. The seller, without any choice as to the height of the selling price but able to sell at the given price as much as he cares to sell, would clearly produce as much as it would pay him to produce at that price. For as long as the additional cost of additional output would fall short of the selling price, he could increase his profit by increasing his output, and nothing would keep him from doing so. This situation is radically changed if competition is not pure. Now the seller cannot sell at one given price any amount of output that he might care to sell. At a given price his sales opportunities are limited. He may be able to sell more, but only if he lowers the price, and this it may not pay him to do. On the other hand, he may be able to raise the price and still sell a substantial quantity, and this he may find to be the best proposition.

If a seller thinks he can sell at a given price all he cares to sell, his production will certainly be larger than if he thinks he could sell more only at lower prices or not at all. The knowledge that more can be sold only at reduced prices, if at all, is an efficient check on increased production; in other words, this knowledge is effective in restricting the operations of the firm. The production volume, therefore, is not only limited by the technological and organizational conditions under which the firm produces, but also by its conjectures concerning the elasticity of the demand for its output. If these conjectures change, the firm will be inclined to change its selling prices and its production volume. For example, if a revised view includes the anticipation that demand would respond to price adjustments more sensitively than was previously thought, prices may be reduced by the firm. On the other hand, if a smaller response is anticipated, the firm may find it best to raise its prices. The prices which the firm charges will of course determine its actual sales. Hence, the anticipated elasticity of demand is a major factor in determining the output of the firm. The smaller the elasticity of demand as seen by the seller, the more drastic will be the restriction of his operations.

Although economists speak of these restrictions of operations as "monopolistic" restrictions, the firms in question, or their managers, may not even realize that they restrict their output. As a rule, they satisfy the entire demand that is effective át the announced price, and would be more than glad to expand production if the market could absorb more. The charge of output restriction appears to them as unfair and surely contrary to fact. To the question "Why don't you produce more?" they would· answer: "We could not sell more," or "The market could not absorb more." In all probability these would be truthful answers. But "output restriction" does not mean refusal to sell all that is demanded at the given prices; instead, it may mean merely maintenance of prices which were set precisely because the seller recognized the limitations of the market. Thus, another possible answer to the question might be: "The market would only take more at prices lower than we could afford." Sometimes it might be franker to answer: "We could not sell more unless we cut our prices and this would reduce our profit." In not a few instances, however, the answer would be: "We could not sell more except by unfair price cutting"—which implies the existence of an understanding of what price is considered "fair" by the trade and is therefore tantamount to the existence of implicit collusion among the competitors.

Restrictions of Entry

While monopolistic restrictions associated with imperfect elasticity of demand have recently received the greater share of attention by theoretical economists, monopolistic restrictions associated with imperfect freedom of entry used to be the focus of interest in the monopoly discussion. Perhaps this was because, in the era of liberalization from governmental regimentation of industry, public interferences with entry had aroused strong popular opposition; and private interferences with entry had often been rather spectacular and had led to the American trust-busting era. As time went on, the private interferences have become less blatant and the public interferences have regained popular support.

Private barriers of the spectacular type have included open threats of cut-throat competition against newcomers and harassing patent suits so costly as to ruin a competitor even if he won, a practice which besides putting existing competitors out of business creates a climate that keeps potential competitors away. Less ostentatious private barriers are the withholding of financial aid to potential competitors by cooperating banking institutions, the denial to newcomers of the existing channels of distribution, the use of discriminatory pricing techniques jeopardizing the profitability of industries at new locations, closed-shop agreements between labor organizations and employers in conjunction with high initiation fees or the refusal of union cards to job-seeking laborers, and many other techniques of giving protection or security to insiders against the competition from outsiders.

Public barriers have included franchises, provisions for certificates of convenience and necessity, other municipal licences, a large variety of international or interstate trade barriers, exclusive patent grants preventing competitors from making certain products or using certain processes or machines, and hundreds of less conspicuous ordinances and regulations designed to protect vested interests against newcomers' competition.

Differences in earnings between insiders and outsiders are not incidental effects but are the very objective of the institutional barriers against the entry of additional factors or new enterprise into the fields deemed "worthy" of protection. In some instances the restrictive measures include the direct fixing of minimum prices for the services or products in the field in question. At these prices the demand is limited and there are no takers for the additional supply. In such cases restrictions of entry are not immediately apparent as the causes of the higher-than-competitive prices (or wage rates), although as a rule overt restrictions will still be necessary in order to make the prices (wage rates) hold up against the onrush of competition "from the outside."

Practices to Tighten Restrictions of Operations

Restrictions of entry are the intended results of conscious measures or policies of interest groups or of government acting on their behalf. The restrictions of the operations within existing firms, as we have described them above, are not fundamentally the results of consciously restrictive practices or policies. They are merely incidental to the setting of selling prices by sellers who know the limitations of the market and therefore will neither expand their outputs as they anticipate too large a decrease in price nor reduce their prices as they anticipate too small an increase in sales. There are, however, a number of practices and policies which firms may pursue for the purpose of increasing the awareness of each firm of the effects its actions are likely to have upon the prices received by it along with the rest of the industry. In other words, where the elasticity of demand for the product of each firm acting independently would be so high that the firm would be apt to underrate the effects of its isolated actions upon the whole market, movements for the development of increased "industry-consciousness" of the competing firms will be set afoot. Two kinds of policy can further this objective: collusion and merger. The former aims at greater unity in spirit (and action), the latter at unity in corporate body.

Collusive practices may impose direct output restrictions upon the competing members of the group. For example, the firms may agree on absolute production quotas, or on fixed relative shares of aggregate sales. But only a small part of all collusive arrangements are of this type. A much larger part relate to limitations of price competition, division of markets or fields of operations, etc. Hence, the effects of these arrangements—often merely tacit understandings—are only indirectly restrictive of the production volumes of the individual firms. The direct effects are merely to make price reductions less attractive (or price increases more attractive) to the individual sellers.

Understandings among competitors attempting or effecting regulation or limitation of competition are called cartels. Cartelization of an industry composed of a very large number of small firms is difficult to achieve without the help of the government. If combination and consolidation of small firms through merger can reduce the number of competitors in the industry, or if some strong merger-born firms attain dominance in the industry, cartelization will be greatly facilitated. Thus, extensive mergers are doubly effective: first of all, they lead to larger units which, because their share in the market is substantial, will find self-imposed output restriction, or self-restraint in price cutting, to be the best principle for their conduct; secondly, they reduce the number of firms and increase the strength of some, and thereby promote the development of a climate in which the competing firms are inclined to act in concert and conform to standards of conduct, which results in turn in further restrictions of the volumes of operation.

The Economic Effects of Monopolistic Restrictions

All these types of restriction—restrictions of entry, restrictions of operations by cooperating firms, restrictions of operations by merger-grown firms, and restrictions of operations without collusion or merger—have in common that the use of productive resources for a particular purpose falls short of the level called for by the "competitive norm." It is perhaps a confusing use of words if every deviation of prices from their "competitive" level, or everything which results in restrictions of output below its "competitive" level, is said to be "monopolistic." It certainly cannot be said that all such restrictions are the consequence of "monopoly" in the traditional sense or in the legal sense or even in the sense which I have adopted elsewhere to classify market positions of particular sellers. Yet there is no use trying to stop trends in the dynamics of language. The adjective "monopolistic" has expanded in meaning and its contents have grown far beyond those of the original noun "monopoly." The words "monopolistic," "monopoly power" and "degree of monopoly" are now generally used with reference to firms which no one would contend enjoy monopoly positions or act as monopolists.[1]

---

[1] Some economists go further and use also the noun "monopoly" for the position of a seller whose product is only slightly different from those of his competitors. E.g., "Heterogeneity as between producers is synonymous with the presence of monopoly." Edward H. Chamberlin, "Product Heterogeneity and Public Policy," *American Economic Review,* Supplement, Vol. XL (1950), p. 86.—On the other hand, the fashion of seeing monopoly or a defect of competition in the simple fact of product differences has been severely

In discussing the economic effects of monopolistic restrictions one should carefully separate the effects on particular groups within the economy from the effect upon the economy as a whole. For example, there is little doubt that restrictions of entry are highly beneficial for insiders thereby protected. There may be some doubt about the long-run benefits to the participants of collusive restrictions, but very often these benefits are real and lasting. To jump, however, to the conclusion that what's good for an industry must be good for the entire economy would be utterly wrong. There will always be some who are harmed by the restrictions, and indeed there is a presumption that the net effect on the economy as a whole is harmful.

Concerning this net effect on the whole economy, that is, the effect on the total national product, a distinction between static and dynamic analysis may be in order. Statements that seem to be unquestionable on the basis of static analysis, assuming given resources, given technology and given money supply, become open to question in an analysis of growth and progress and in an analysis of deflationary movements. However, we are not permitted to skip static reasoning on the ground that it *may* turn out to be subject to qualifications or corrections when the additional assumptions appropriate to a dynamic analysis are introduced. We shall, therefore, defer our comments regarding the effects of monopolistic restrictions on economic progress, and regarding their relationship to the problem of deflation, until we have seen what static analysis has to say about the effects of monopolistic restrictions on the economic allocation of productive resources.

As we have seen before, the main function of prices in a rational economic system is to steer productive resources into the production of the most urgently demanded commodities. This implies that one purpose of high prices is to discourage consumers from buying a commodity, or larger quantities of a commodity, the production of which would require factors of production that are more urgently demanded for other things. Where the requisite

criticized: "The talk about the defects of competition when we are in fact talking about the necessary differences between commodities and services conceals a very real confusion and leads on occasion to absurd conclusions." Friedrich A. Hayek, "The Meaning of Competition," in *Individualism and Economic Order* (Chicago: University of Chicago Press, 1948), p. 97.

factors are available the function of prices is to encourage the purchase of the product. This function is disturbed if a product is overpriced, which may happen in two ways: (1) the factor prices may be too high relative to the values of the factors in competing employment; and (2) the product price may be too high relative to the factor prices. In both cases the purchase of the product is discouraged although there are no equally urgent alternative uses competing for the resources.

The first disturbance refers, thus, to the *prices of productive resources,* primarily labor. Monopolistic wage fixing can severely restrict the employment of labor. Industries that have to pay monopolistic wage rates will ordinarily employ less labor than they would at competitive wage levels. Workers, willing and able to work but unable to find employment in these industries, are compelled to look for other employment. Some will crowd into other occupations and fields, in which access is not restricted, and will thereby depress the wage rates in these occupations and fields. Others will remain unemployed. (That is to say, "full-time leisure" may be the only alternative "use" of their labor power. Only if unemployment were voluntary on the part of the "worker" could full-time leisure be regarded as the preferred alternative use of his time.)

The second disturbance of the economic allocation of resources refers to the *prices of products.* Sellers can set prices so high as to restrict the purchase of products to an output level at which additional production would cause an addition to total cost of production that could still be more than covered by the prices at which the added output would sell. The productive resources which remain unused for the industry concerned as a result of its smaller output would either remain unemployed or they might find employment for uses less desired than the one from which they were excluded. The alternative employment might be in industries where producers are not in a position to foresee the price falls which go with increased output; or, in more technical terms, the factors of production may find in more competitive industries the employment which they were refused by more monopolistic industries.

The fact that product prices are higher than the additional cost at which additional output could be produced, may thus have two results: an "uneconomical allocation of resources" among various lines of production; and an "uneconomical rate of utilization of resources" for production in general. "Not used for the right things" —is the one result; "not used at all"—is the other. While the former may be said to spring from the fact that the degree of control over prices is different in different industries, the latter can be attributed to the existence of monopoly prices in general—except, of course, when other considerations, particularly shrinkages in total effective demand, become more important.

Provisos and Reservations

The economic effects of monopolistic restrictions, according to this analysis, are expressed and evaluated in terms of a sacrifice of potential national income: the wasteful use of productive resources resulting from the restrictions makes the total income smaller than it would be in the absence of the restrictions. Resources used for less urgently demanded products, resources used less efficiently, and resources remaining entirely unused—these are the economic consequences of monopolistic restrictions.

One must be on guard against the widespread misunderstanding that the effects of monopoly power are always visible in the form of "exorbitant prices" being charged to buyers. Several brief comments on this issue may be helpful. (1) If a price is called exorbitant when it includes a large profit margin over production costs as shown by customary accounting methods, one should bear in mind that the difference between historical cost, based on book values, and economic cost, based on alternative-opportunity values, may be substantial and may completely distort the test. (2) Where the monopolistic restrictions lead to inefficient use of resources, it may be the economic costs that are excessive, not the profit margin. (3) Where resources are relatively underemployed in a certain field, their relative oversupply to unrestricted fields may lead there to inordinately low prices. The price relationships are what matters, not individual prices or the average level of prices. (4) Not infrequently firms with monopoly power choose for strategic reasons to keep the selling prices of their products temporarily below rather than above their competitive values based on factor prices, which (although the buyers of the particular products may like it well) involves a wasteful allocation of resources. (To avoid it, prices must be allowed to rise in accordance with the relative scarcity of the resources allocated to the production.) (5) Monopolistic firms, pursuing for certain periods such a policy of keeping prices below competitive values, may not be able to satisfy the demand effective at these low prices and may therefore resort to some private systems of consumer rationing with the result that the products are not allocated according to economic principles.

A qualification must be stipulated concerning the generality of the conclusion which sees wasteful use of resources in every kind of deviation from pure competition. Homogeneity of products was listed among the prerequisites of pure competition. But consumers may like variety, heterogeneity of products; indeed they may prefer more expensive heterogeneous goods to cheaper homogeneous ones. If this is so, it would be illegitimate to conclude that the restrictions of output by each of the heterogeneous producers constitute a sacrifice of national income. To be sure, since the production of homogeneous products would be more efficient, people might be able to obtain more product if they did not insist on product variety; but insofar as they do, they must accept the "restricted output volumes" as an unavoidable consequence.

A reservation must be made concerning the long-run effects of certain restrictions of entry. For example, one may argue that some restrictions (such as patents) increase national income in the long run because of induced changes in technology. The short-run losses of national income that result from restrictions of entry are probably undeniable. But if these restrictions induce the development of technologies which would not emerge otherwise, it may be possible that the short-run losses would be worth taking in anticipation of later, but lasting, gains. Tariff protection for infant industries as well as patents on inventions have been justified by such arguments. These issues will call for further discussion in the next chapter.

Similar claims of long-run advantages more than compensating for short-run sacrifices are made by advocates of cartel restrictions and similar monopolistic devices. Their contention is that these restrictions allow certain sensitive parts of the economy to build up greater resistance to cyclical fluctuations and thus to increase the "economic security" of large numbers of people and indirectly of the whole economy. These contentions are not convincing to those who believe that increased security of some is likely to involve reduced security to others and no more stability to the economy as a whole. The answer to the problem of the business cycle and of monetary deflation is to be found in more enlightened monetary and fiscal policies as well as in policies designed to give greater stability to aggregate private investment, not in policies of restriction of competition with the resulting restrictions of production.[2]

A comment of a different nature concerns the unequal distribution of monopoly power in the economy. If relative prices are the significant thing in the economic allocation of resources and if deviations of the competitive price relationships are the causes of misallocation, would not matters be improved by measures to equalize all monopolistic (bargaining) power? Would not relative prices then be more nearly the same as relative prices under universal competition? In other words, if the nation cannot reach its full economic potential when it is half monopolistic and half competitive, and if it is apparently too difficult to "demonopolize" the monopolistic half, would it not be the best solution to monopolize the competitive half? This idea of solving or alleviating the monopoly problem, not by reducing existing monopoly power, but by creating monopoly power where none exists or strengthening it where it is weak, may appeal to those who have not studied the theory of "bilateral monopoly." Those who have know that the relative prices and the corresponding resource allocation in an economy where almost all sellers have monopoly power and almost all buyers have monopsony power will not even faintly resemble the relative prices and resource allocation in a competitive economy. The idea of equalizing monopoly power in order

---

[2] K. E. Boulding argues that "the drive towards monopoly is not only the result of . . . human selfishness, but is also a desperate and rather misguided attempt to solve . . . the problem of deflation." See "In Defense of Monopoly," *Quarterly Journal of Economics*, Vol. LIX (1945), p. 524.

to approach more closely the results of competition is poor economics—and political dynamite.

Monopoly in Business, Labor, and Agriculture

To divide monopolistic restrictions into two kinds—restrictions of operations and restrictions of entry, the one relating to existing firms and their lines of product, the other relating to newcomers (additional resources and new enterprise) to particular fields of production—may satisfy the strict logic of the monopoly problem. But this lumps too many things together. For an applied analysis it is useful to distinguish between monopoly in business, in labor, and in agriculture, and then to subdivide monopoly in business according to the type of practices employed in the creation, maintenance, increase, or exploitation of monopoly power.

Monopolistic Business Policies

The subdivision of monopolistic business policies is complicated because the business aspects, the legal aspects, and the economic aspects must be given some sort of simultaneous consideration in spite of the fact that they are very different from one another. Moreover, the types of techniques and practices employed by business are too numerous to be conveniently packed away in a few conceptual boxes. But since, for the beginning at least, a simple classification is more useful than a detailed and exhaustive one, we propose to distinguish the following four categories of monopolistic business policies:

I. Policies by which an individual firm, not acting in concert with others, determines its selling prices, product qualities, selling efforts, and production volumes in such a manner as to take account of the limitations, and to make the most of the elasticities, of its sales possibilities as it sees them, or also in such a manner as to reduce the existing limitations and elasticities by influencing the buying propensities of the consumers.[3]

---

[3] In order to avoid a more cumbersome formulation we have confined ourselves to the output and selling side of the business. The definition of the analogous policies on the input and purchasing side of the business calls for

II. Policies by which two or more firms act under some implicit or explicit understanding concerning pricing or marketing and which reduce their freedom or weaken their inclination to use all the means at their disposal to compete for more business and a larger share in the market.[4]

III. Policies by which an individual firm attempts to reduce competition in its markets and to increase its influence over prices by constraining, blocking, or controlling competing firms or eliminating them as independent sellers through merger or otherwise.

IV. Policies by which one or more firms, through their own acts or by promoting or inducing acts of third parties including trade associations, pressure groups, and governments, create or maintain obstacles to the entry of new firms into particular fields of economic activity or to the movement of productive resources— labor, land, materials, capital—into particular occupations, fields or methods of production.

There is an essential difference between the first category and the other three. In contrast to the others, the first category does not include policies designed to reduce competition through actions directed at actual or potential competitors or to achieve or maintain cooperation among competitors. It is true that by adopting policies of the first category a seller may succeed in reducing the substitutability of rival products for his own products, thus reducing the elasticity of demand and increasing his control over his prices. But this is done through actions directed only toward his consumers, for ex-

---

distinctions between buying, hiring, renting, and borrowing. Omitting the last two, that is, concentrating only on materials and labor, the monopsonistic business policies of this first category may be described as policies by which an individual firm, not acting in concert with others, determines its purchasing prices (wage rates), specifications (job qualifications), purchasing terms (hiring techniques and working conditions) and quantities (employment volumes) in such a manner as to take account of the limitations, and to make the most of the elasticities, of its buying (hiring) possibilities as it sees them, or also in such a manner as to reduce the existing limitations and elasticities by influencing the selling (working) propensities of the suppliers (workers).

[4] The analogous policies on the input side—confined to materials and labor —can be described as policies by which two or more firms act under some implicit or explicit understanding concerning purchasing prices (wage rates) and sources of supply (recruiting and hiring) and which reduce their freedom or weaken their inclination to use all the means at their disposal to compete for larger quantities (for a larger work force).

ample, through promotional efforts or improvements in quality or service. It is also true that the policies of the first category may include discriminatory pricing. But, if so, the discrimination is practiced, not as part of a cooperative pricing scheme (which would belong in the second category) and not as part of a plan to weaken or eliminate a competitor (which would belong in the third category), but rather as a method of exploiting existing differences in the customers' eagerness to buy and ability to pay or as a method of developing a larger clientele. Finally, it is true that policies of the first category may become subject to governmental attention, supervision, or interference. But this will be the case only if the firm in question or its service is regarded as a "public utility."

How broad our four categories are will be appreciated when one realizes that the first category includes all types of sellers: small heterogeneous sellers serving only insignificant fractions of a large market; sellers in close competition with only a few rivals; sellers without any direct competitors. The second category includes all sorts of conduct by which competitors may try to coordinate their actions or cooperate in the market: implicit understandings, compliance with an "ethical code" of the trade, tacit or explicit collusion, resulting in peaceful market sharing, division of the market, common use of pricing formulas, or elaborate cartel arrangements. All these and many other schemes may be voluntary or imposed, temporary or lasting, fully complied with or frequently violated, lawful or unlawful.

The following synoptic tabulation may serve to point up the main differences between the four categories of monopolistic business policies:

Category II: Cooperation, Collusion, Cartelization.
Category III: Oppression, Domination, Merger, Concentration.
Category IV: Exclusion, Barriers, Licences, Protection.
Category I: Ordinary business operation, non-collusive, non-oppressive, non-empire-building, non-exclusive, unprotected, but with some control over prices.

Various Meanings of Business Monopoly

From our discussion it has become more than apparent that monopoly is a word with many meanings. Even the narrower concept of business monopoly has several different meanings. It might be convenient if we could all agree on one meaning only and then select other words for the meanings deprived of their name. Yet there is no chance of agreement. Thus we shall go on using monopoly in all its conventional meanings, leaving it to the reader to decide which one is relevant in the particular context. But it may be worth while to attempt definitions for the meanings most frequently referred to.

Our discussion of pure and perfect competition will now stand us in good stead: at least three of the definitions that we shall offer are derived from it. Monopoly is defined as

(1) any deviation from the model of pure and perfect competition;

(2) the market position of a seller with limited sales possibilities—quantity sold depending on selling price (and selling effort), or price received depending on quantity disposed of—who therefore has a choice in determining his price or output policies;

(3) the market position of a seller protected by barriers against potential competition from new enterprise, additional resources, or rival products entering his field or market;

(4) the market position of a seller who does not consider any products of others as direct substitutes for his own product, nor regards the prices and marketing policies of other sellers as affecting his own sales possibilities, nor anticipates the appearance of such other sellers in the market in consequence of his own policies;

(5) the market position of the sellers in an industry who, having recognized the reciprocal effects of their individual competitive actions, the avoidability of a competitive depression of selling prices, and the mutual advantages of greater coordination in their marketing policies, pursue a common course of action in the market, based on implicit understanding or explicit agreement;

(6) the market position of a seller who through expansion by merger or otherwise has acquired such a dominant position in his industry that he can impose his will upon his competitors or can influence them sufficiently to achieve some measure of coordination in their selling policies.

It will be noted that deviation from pure competition is the essential characteristic in the second definition, and deviation from perfect competition is the essential characteristic in the third one. Many other variations of these themes have been advanced, some in terms of the logically implied relationships between costs and prices.[5] The fourth definition combines three criteria which I have carefully examined elsewhere as part of a "model analysis" of sellers' conduct.[6] The fifth definition centers on collusiveness, the sixth on concentration and domination. Many more definitions could be added to this selection, but they would constitute for the most part merely different combinations of the characteristics employed in the ones presented.

In discussions of the general economic effects of "monopoly" upon the output of the nation and, in particular, upon the use of its productive resources, the first definition is relevant. In the model analysis of sellers' conduct, where several fine distinctions must be made and different ideal types of behavior constructed, the fourth definition of monopoly comes into its rights. For discussions of economic policy and development, of political charges against and defenses of "monopoly," of the role of government and its attitudes toward "monopoly," the first definition is too wide, the fourth too narrow, the second too general to be relevant. Only such aspects of "monopoly" about which something can be done—conceivably at least—are relevant for such discussions. Hence, the reference here will be to the third, fifth and sixth definitions, emphasizing barriers to entry, collusion, concentration, domination, and similar matters possibly subject to governmental control.

[5] The second definition could be reformulated as
  (2a) the power of a producer to sell his product at a price above its marginal cost and at the same time make marginal cost equal (or nearly equal) to marginal revenue.
The third definition could be reformulated as
  (3a) the power of producer to sell his product for a long period at an economic profit, that is, at a price exceeding the economic average cost, which is the sum of the current prices or opportunity costs (whichever are lower) of all productive services needed for the production of the product, divided by the quantity produced.

[6] Fritz Machlup, *The Economics of Sellers' Competition: Model Analysis of Sellers' Conduct* (Baltimore: Johns Hopkins Press, 1952), Chapters 4 and 17.

Monopsony in Business

In its most general meaning "monopoly" includes not only the selling side but also the buying side of the business. The definitions and discussions here presented are mostly so phrased as to refer only to sellers. But it should not be too hard for the reader to formulate for himself the definitions and propositions as they would apply to buyers and their control over the prices of the things they purchase (hire, rent, borrow).

In its literal meaning the word monopoly, according to its Greek roots, refers only to selling. For a long time writers used the words "buyer's monopoly" when they spoke of the buyer's control over the prices of the goods or services demanded. Now we have a separate word for it: monopsony. Thus, we have also the terminological counterparts to all ideas pertaining to monopoly. We can speak of monopsony power and of monopsonistic business practices, of collusive monopsony, and of monopsony based merely on the heterogeneity of the buyers and the elasticity of supply that confronts them as a consequence.

One must not think that a firm having some degree of monopoly regarding its products will necessarily also have some degree of monopsony regarding its means of production. There is nothing in the logic of things or in the reality of economic conditions that necessarily makes a monopolist also a monopsonist. His position as a seller and his position as a buyer are independent of each other. He may be the sole producer of some new gadget for which there is no close substitute on the market. But he need not for that reason be the only buyer, or even an important buyer, of labor in his area, or of steel or plastics, bolts and screws, fuel and oil, cartons and tape. On the other hand, a producer of a commodity, say percale, that is sold under conditions of almost pure competition, may conceivably be located in an area where he is the only employer of labor. Or a producer of an industrial material with little control over his selling prices may have substantially more control over the price of some raw material that is produced in the vicinity of his plant.

There are also, of course, many instances where ·monopoly power and monopsony power are combined. The small number of large producers of national brands of cigarettes have undoubtedly a substantial degree of monopsony in the markets for tobacco leaf as well as a considerable degree of monopoly in the sale of cigarettes. (Compared with them, a small producer of cigars, or of cigarettes of an unadvertised brand, has very little monopoly power and probably no monopsony power at all.)

Although there is no presumption that any particular business firm simultaneously possesses both monopoly and monopsony power, the inclination to believe that "business" has that double power to exploit is understandable. For, according to a widely used set of definitions, business is the only group of economic units (or "organisms") that both buy and sell for profit. "Consumers" buy only; "workers," "land owners," and "capitalists" sell only; "business firms" buy and sell. Hence, only business can be able to exercise control over both buying and selling prices. Such tautological reasoning may easily mislead in questions of applied economics. For example, it would force us to lump agriculture with business, because farmers ordinarily have to buy (hire, rent, borrow) some of their means of production. For many purposes, however, it is necessary to separate agriculture from other forms of business, just as it may be necessary to keep trade (in the narrow sense) apart from industry (in the narrow sense), or mining from manufacturing. This, of course, leaves the exact contents of the concept of "business" rather indefinite, and generalizations about monopoly and monopsony in "business" must be applied with extreme caution.

Monopolistic Restrictions in Agriculture

One hears very little of monopoly in agriculture. There are good reasons for this: in agricultural production private monopoly is rare unless it is directly aided and fostered by government.

In most fields of agriculture, especially in the so-called staple crops, the number of producers is extremely large, their individual size is small in relation to the total market, their product is fairly standardized. Thus, the single firm, or farmer, has no control over price. The probability of all farmers getting together to agree on coordinated marketing or fixed selling prices is small because there are too many of them to make agreement possible or to permit supervision of compliance or enforcement against "individualists." Nor is it likely that a few of them become sufficiently strong to coerce the others to conform. Under these circumstances the chances of monopolistic policies in agricultural staple products are slight—except under governmental programs.

Agricultural programs by governments are, as a rule, monopolistic arrangements in one of the senses defined before: they are designed to keep prices received by producers above the competitive level and they attempt to achieve this through restricting operations by existing producers or distribution of the produced output or entry of available additional resources into production or entry of competing suppliers into the market—or through a combination of these restrictions.

Nevertheless, for historical reasons, agricultural "monopoly arrangements" of the government are not normally called by that name because habitually one thinks more of "private" monopolists. The early English popular movements against monopoly were against privileges granted to private firms, not against state-operated monopolies. The American political antimonopoly campaigns were against "the trusts" and "big business." Governmental prosecution of monopoly was against private restraints of trade. To be sure, the governmental measures designed to raise agricultural prices above competitive levels and to restrict supplies of agricultural products below competitive levels were often criticized and opposed; but the difference in the political situation, more impressive than the similarity of the economic nature of the policies, apparently has prevented critics from using the term "monopolistic" to characterize the agricultural programs of the government. Economic analysis, however, and economic welfare evaluation may conveniently deal with these programs in terms of monopoly restrictions and monopoly prices, regardless of what terminology is employed.

Not all agricultural monopoly is confined to government programs. Other forms of organization can be used for the execution of monopolistic policies concerning non-staple produce. For example, in dairy farming and fruit growing the formation of strong cooperatives has been a successful instrument of monopolistic policy, although even here direct intervention by the government was often required for the enforcement of the "agreements" against producers who would not agree. Aided by the coercive power of the state, collusive monopoly has achieved an "enviable record of success" in several fields of agricultural production—enviable from the point of view of some industrial producers whose attempts at cooperation with their competitors have been only moderately successful and frequently short-lived.

There will not be much discussion of agricultural monopoly in this book. Chapter 8, on "Governmental Aids to Monopoly," contains a sketchy account of some farm programs in the United States. Beyond that, the word "agriculture" will not often occur in the discussions of monopolistic practices or of monopoly power. But failure to mention the word agriculture does not imply inapplicability or irrelevance of the analysis to agriculture. The firm and the seller whose conduct is analysed may be a farmer just as well as an industrialist or merchant. An industrial producer as a member of a "selling cartel" or "syndicate" and an agricultural producer as a member of a marketing cooperative may behave very similarly in several respects and the same analytical model may apply to both. And that the analysis of the small, undifferentiated seller of homogeneous products may fit the agricultural producer of staple products better than most industrial producers has already been said.

Thus, as far as the competitive or monopolistic conduct of the individual farmer is concerned—rather than the execution of monopolistic farm policies of the government—much of the "theory of the firm" may be found to relate to agriculture no less than to other forms of business. As far as the general monopoly problem and its significance in the economy is concerned, many of the general observations of these chapters are as pertinent to agricultural restrictions as to any others.

Monopolistic Labor Policies

To what extent will the applicability of most general observations about the effects of monopoly extend to labor and monopolistic labor policies? And to what extent will the analysis of sellers'

conduct fit the case of the sale of labor effort? Our answer to the
first question is: "to a very great extent," but: "hardly at all," to
the second.

Neither an individual worker selling his labor to an employer
nor a labor union bargaining about the price at which labor may
be bought by an employer, can be usefully regarded as a firm selling its products or services. The analysis of the conduct of a business firm as a seller of its output has little to offer for the explanation of the conduct of a worker or a labor union. There may be
some similarity between the considerations of a syndicate or the
council of a cartel and the executives of a labor union, the former
pondering what prices, the latter what wage rates, their members
should obtain. But how far this similarity goes and to what extent
the same model can be helpful in the analysis of both cartel price
and union wage determination are open questions. It is not suggested here that the model analysis of sellers' conduct is applicable
to the problem of wage determination.

It is suggested, however, that the *effects* of union wage determination can and should be analysed in terms of monopoly
prices and monopolistic restrictions. Wage rate making through
collective bargaining by large national unions can hardly result
in a competitive wage structure, nor is it intended to do so. The
substitution of collective bargaining for the individual bargain has
the very purpose of eliminating wage-depressing competition
among job seekers, and to the extent that this purpose is attained
the resulting wage determination must be regarded as monopolistic. Wage rates thus set above the competitive level restrict the volume of employment in the firms or industries concerned. And since
the presence of a large supply of unemployed eligible candidates
for the same jobs may make it difficult to obtain and maintain these
monopolistic wage rates, policies of restricting entry into the union,
into the occupation, or into the region may be pursued as valuable
or necessary supports for the wage policies. These restrictions of
entry are, of course, no more and no less monopolistic than the
various barriers to the entry of new enterprise in industry. Both
are designed to protect the earnings of the insiders against newcomers' competition.

Some sensitive advocates of strong labor unionism have objected to the phrase "labor monopoly" and consider it to be a slur on the objectives of the labor movement. There are historical reasons for this disinclination to treat combinations of workers in the same language as combinations of businessmen. For there was a time when workers were prohibited from forming combinations while business combinations went unchallenged. Some employers' coalitions had the explicit purpose of keeping wage rates down— they were, technically speaking, collusive monopsonies. Even after the legal bans against labor coalitions were lifted, it took them considerable time to attain substantial "bargaining power," that is, monopoly power. With understandable sympathy for the under-dog, the lawmakers in the United States then completed the swing of the pendulum and wrote explicit exemptions for labor into the antimonopoly laws. With this history behind the development of labor organizations one may understand the protestations of their advocates that "there is no such thing as a labor monopoly."

It is peculiar that one should have to quarrel about the "justi-fication" for using the term "monopoly" in connection with labor organization when the purpose is neither legal nor political but entirely analytical. It is reminiscent of the fight of the trade asso-ciations against the use of the word monopoly applied to their activities in connection with the pricing techniques of their mem-bers. From the legal point of view their protestations were under-standable. Analytically they were specious and irrelevant. Trade unions and trade associations, to the extent that they are concerned with wages and prices and with collective or cooperative methods of determining them or influencing their determination, unques-tionably invite the use of the same models or tools of analysis, at least with respect to the effects of their activities on relative prices and the allocation of productive resources.

CHAPTER 3

Monopoly: Economic and Political Appraisals

Inevitability and Desirability of Monopoly: The Cost of Avoidance ·
Public versus Private Monopoly · Large-Scale Production · Variety of
Product · Exploitation of Natural Resources · "Unstable" Industries ·
Monopolistic Shock-Absorbers and Stable Growth · Monopolistic Brakes
and Technological Progress · Monopoly Policies versus Tax Policies

Debits and Credits of Monopolistic Restraints: False Issues and Real ·
Conflicting Objectives · A Balance Sheet

Monopoly and Democracy: Monopoly and the Road to Serfdom · Democracy in a Planned Economy · Superstition or Prudence?

T HERE ARE those who think that monopoly has one thing in
common with the weather: you may complain but you cannot do anything about it. A few do not even complain about
monopoly, but find many good things to say about it. On the other
side are those who are in a constant state of agitation about the
evils of monopoly and call for a mobilization of all political forces
against it. In the middle are the judicious ones, together with the
meek, the placid, and the indolent.

But monopoly is not an indivisible whole. It is a variety of ingredients, separable and inseparable, in the "ragout" of the national economy, some of which can be fished out to great advantage while others cannot. The real issue is not about "monopoly
as a whole," but about bigger or smaller individual lumps of
monopoly, and the question of whether they *can* and *should* be
gotten rid of.

INEVITABILITY AND DESIRABILITY OF MONOPOLY

For each separate lump of monopoly the question of its avoidability and desirability should be asked separately. There are ba-

sically four different answers: any particular element of monopoly may be (a) unavoidable and desirable; (b) avoidable but desirable; (c) undesirable but unavoidable; (d) undesirable and avoidable. If there were agreement about which of the answers was correct in a particular instance, there could be no doubt that we should do nothing to combat monopoly in each of the first three cases. And in the fourth, before "doing something" one would have to ask two further questions: "just *how* undesirable?" and "avoidable *at what cost?*"

The Cost of Avoidance

Only seldom is it possible to answer the question whether some particular lump of monopoly is "unavoidable" with an unqualified yes. It can nearly always be turned into a question of the cost of avoidance. For example, if monopoly in telephone service is definitely inherent in the technology of the thing, one might still eliminate this monopoly by doing without telephone service at all. Most people will undoubtedly agree that this would be too high a cost to pay for the removal of this particular lump of monopoly. The meaning of avoiding monopoly power, of course, need not imply a choice between all or none but rather between more monopoly or less. It is, for example, technologically possible to have several competing companies furnish telephone service in one city. The cost of the service under this set-up would probably be higher and the convenience to the public would be considerably reduced. Depending on whether "inevitability" is to mean that monopoly power cannot be *eliminated* (except by eliminating the entire production of the good or service) or that it cannot be *reduced,* we should find the answers (a) or (b) appropriate in this instance. With respect to the quality of the service, the telephone is an obvious example of a field in which monopoly is desirable.

In other instances the cost of reducing monopoly power and the relative desirability of monopoly seem to merge into one question. Take the case of streetcar systems in large cities. We have known cities with competing tramway companies, serving parallel streets and operating four tracks in wider streets. The disadvantage of having more streets cut up by car-tracks, the advantage of more people being closer to a car line, the disadvantage of no transfer between competing lines, the advantage of quality competition (if it exists), all these considerations are so mixed up with the comparative cost of the service that it is hard to consider them separately. (Incidentally, it should be said that the existence of "duopoly" rather than monopoly in the narrow sense of the word rarely involves a reduction in the "degree of monopoly" and any closer approximation to the state of "pure competition." On the other hand, even a streetcar "monopoly" may have to compete with several other means of transportation, such as elevated and underground railways, bus lines and taxi cab companies.) The consensus seems to be in favor of monopoly in the streetcar service of a city, although the considerations behind this view need not support monopoly in bus service.

The relative inevitability of monopoly in the provision of a community with water, gas, and electricity is well recognized. It lies in the technology of distributing these utilities to the consumer: the mains, pipes and cable lines could not economically be duplicated and certainly not multiplied. These are "natural" monopolies. The cost of reducing—to say nothing about avoiding—monopoly in these fields would be so enormous that one is entitled to say that monopoly here is practically inevitable.

Public versus Private Monopoly

Where monopoly is inevitable or, more correctly, where its avoidance is too costly, the question of *public* versus *private* monopoly arises. In favor of public, and against private, monopoly the following arguments have been advanced:

1. If someone has to have power, it is less intolerable if vested in the state rather than in private persons.

2. The state may be assumed to be more responsible in the exercise of monopoly power than private persons.

3. The state is executor of the public will and guardian of the public interest, whereas private persons look out for their own interests; hence, consumers and workers will fare better under public than under private monopolies.

4. It may be desirable to have the products of certain monopo-

lies furnished at prices below average cost; for example, where enterprises must operate under decreasing marginal cost—which may happen precisely where monopoly cannot reasonably be avoided—marginal cost pricing would imply selling below cost; public ownership of the monopolies, with the state covering the deficits out of general funds, is preferable to any system of government subsidies for private monopolies.

The case against public and for private monopoly has been argued as follows:

1. The managements of private monopolies, since they are always suspected of operating against the public interest, will be more carefully watched; the managements of public monopolies, supposed to have the public interest at heart, are not *prima facie* suspect, and therefore will be less suspiciously watched.

2. Private managements are afraid of the government and are more careful to avoid cause for discontent than public managements who regard themselves as part of the government.

3. Private monopolies can attract more competent men for their management than can public monopolies, where "politics" is apt to dominate the selection of personnel.

4. Private monopolies must protect their liquidity more carefully than public monopolies, which may fall back on "general funds"; hence, costs and efficiency are likely to be watched more closely under private management.

5. Public monopolies are more exposed to pressures of organized interest groups, such as trade unions or special consumer groups.

6. If there is dissatisfaction with the conduct of private monopolies, the people have an appeal to the government, which may start to "discipline" the monopolies; if the people are dissatisfied with the government operation of monopolies they cannot carry their appeal to anybody but the government itself.

7. If as a result of changes connected with the growth of the economy—especially with technological progress—a more competitive organization of the industry should become practical, there is some chance that competition, direct or through newly developed substitutes, will eventually emerge and end the rule of private monopolies; but if monopolies are public, entry of newcomers

will probably be outlawed and competition by new substitutes prevented.

Many more arguments exist on each side; only the more respectable ones were here enumerated. We should note that the nationalization of inevitably monopolistic industries is not always a socialist demand, but is sometimes proposed by antisocialist advocates of a free-enterprise economy.[1] On the other hand, some of the arguments against public monopolies are sometimes given strong support by socialist writers who favor nationalization but recognize, and wish to guard against, the dangers incident to public operation of nationalized industries.[2]

[1] Henry C. Simons, *A Positive Program for Laissez-Faire: Some Proposals for a Liberal Economic Policy* (Chicago: University of Chicago Press, 1934). Reprinted in Henry C. Simons, *Economic Policy for a Free Society* (Chicago: University of Chicago Press, 1948). Simons states that "the case for a liberal-conservative policy must stand or fall on the . . . abolition of private monopoly. . . . It implies that every industry should be either effectively competitive or socialized and that government should plan definitely on socialization . . . of every industry where competitive conditions cannot be preserved" (pp. 57–58).

[2] W. Arthur Lewis, "Recent British Experience of Nationalization as an Alternative to Monopoly Control." Paper presented to the Round Table on *Monopoly and Competition and Their Regulation*, International Economic Association (Talloires, September 6, 1951). The following quotations from this objective account may serve as illustrations for some of the arguments listed in the text. "The appointing of public directors to manage an undertaking is not sufficient public control." "Parliament is handicapped in controlling corporations by its lack of time. . . . Neither have Members of Parliament the competence to supervise these great industries. . . . Parliament is further handicapped . . . by paucity of information . . . for example, less information is now published about the railways than was available before they were nationalized." "Except in the case of transport, the British government has resisted proposals that public corporations should be treated in the same way [as private monopolies], with the result that the consumer is formally less well protected vis-a-vis public corporations than he was vis-a-vis private firms operating public utilities." "The [public] corporation's Board, though publicly appointed, has many loyalties in addition to its loyalty to the public. It has also a loyalty to itself, and to its own staff, which may well conflict with the interest of the consumer." "Public corporations have not found it easy to dismiss redundant workers, or even to close down inefficient units or to expand more efficient units in some other place (e.g., railways, mines). It may well turn out that public corporations are less able to promote this kind of efficiency than are private corporations, in the British atmosphere of tenderness towards established sources of income."

Large-Scale Production

There may be industrial products of which the entire demand can be met by the output of a single establishment. Where the capacity of the productive establishment of "optimum size" is very large in relation to the total demand for the product, competition cannot exist or cannot endure. The fact that the technological developments of the last century have resulted in conspicuous economies of large-scale production has frequently been interpreted as evidence of the *technological inevitability of monopoly*.

Those who offer such an interpretation overlook the fact that the growth of markets and of total demand has usually kept pace, and often more than kept pace, with the growth of the efficient plant size.[3] That the size of industrial firms has grown as much as it has and the number of independent firms in many industries has decreased during the last fifty years was not solely or chiefly the consequence of technological developments. To say this is not to deny that there may be certain products for which highly monopolistic supply conditions are practically unavoidable for technological reasons. (That is to say, to make these products in separate plants operated by separate firms—so that there would be a larger number of firms—might cost so enormously much more than to make them in one single plant that people would refuse to consider it as a practical possibility.) But this, surely, can be only an exception, not the rule. Ordinarily the economies of large-scale production in manufacturing industry can be fully utilized if the total output is produced in a relatively large number of plants. If these many plants are operated by only a small number of firms, each running several plants, one cannot point to technology as the explanation of monopoly.

Besides technological economies, however, there may be organizational or managerial economies of large-scale operation, making it cheaper if several separate plants are centrally managed by a single firm. There may be savings through the possibility of

[3] Without technological changes the increase in total demand might have resulted in a parallel increase in the number of firms of unchanged size. If technology has changed and the size of the individual plant of optimum efficiency has grown apace with total demand, the number of firms could have remained unchanged.

avoiding duplication of systems of records and supervision required by each firm, of employing systems of control, research or engineering development which small firms could not afford, of regularizing the flows of inputs and outputs. No convincing evidence of such economies has been presented, but it cannot be denied that they may exist. One can hardly believe, however, that they are great,[4] certainly not great enough to warrant statements to the effect that independent operation would be impractical. Thus, it is probably safe to make the generalization that in the case of the vast majority of all standardized products total demand is sufficiently large to permit the existence of a large number of establishments, each fully taking advantage of the technological economies and of most of the organizational economies of large-scale production and each operated by an independent firm in competition with all the other independent firms. This would rarely mean "pure" competition, but the "degree of monopoly" of each of these firms could not be substantial.

That so many industries producing highly standardized products in a considerable number of separate plants are nevertheless controlled by a very few large corporations is primarily the result of the unchecked merger movement. A large percentage of the industrial establishments now operated by giant companies were once operated by independent firms; these firms have been absorbed in the course of time by "empire-building" corporations bent upon control of a large portion of the industry. The accumulation of formerly independent establishments in the hands of corporate giants is a matter of public record. There may be real and substantial economic benefits connected with such concentration of industrial control, although I do not see them.[5] But one thing

---

[4] There are offsetting diseconomies of large-scale central management: "One of these is inflexibility—the difficulty that any far-flung enterprise experiences in adjusting itself to varying circumstances. Another is red tape—the tendency to avoid incoherence and confusion by excessively rigid rules and meticulous observance of hierarchical lines of authority. A third is internal conflict—the tendency of members of a large organization to intrigue against one another for power by devices that partially thwart each in the performance of his assigned duties." Corwin D. Edwards, *Maintaining Competition: Requisites of a Governmental Policy* (New York: McGraw-Hill, 1949), p. 115.

[5] In many cases, "central-office functions are likely to be limited to such matters as pricing, litigation, lobbying, and maintenance of satisfactory pub-

seems certain: neither the growth of the firms nor the economic advantages supposedly connected with it can properly be attributed to technological developments.

The strong element of monopoly prevalent in most industries manufacturing standardized industrial products cannot be said to be unavoidable. It may be claimed, however, that it is desirable. These claims we shall presently discuss. But before we do we turn to another argument for the inevitability of monopoly.

Variety of Product

While the thesis of the technological inevitability of monopoly in the production of most standardized industrial products is only a legend, the argument that monopoly is unavoidable in the production of differentiated products rests on firmer ground.[6] If each of many producers, no matter how many they are, is, in the eyes of the consumers, a little different from all the others—because the product quality, the service, the location, or the personality of the seller are different—each of these producers will have "monopoly power." This element of monopoly is inevitable so long as the heterogeneity of the producers continues.

It may in many instances be possible through governmental intervention to eliminate the heterogeneity and with it the monopoly power of the producers. But where the heterogeneity is the result of differences in the quality of the product it is frequently considered desirable. The wider scope for choice on the part of the consumer may be considered to be a positive contribution to the economic welfare of the nation. Where, on the other hand, the heterogeneity of the producers is the result of differences in plant location, the cost of making them all alike for enough consumers in order to eliminate the monopoly power of the producers may be forbidding. In this sense, the element of monopoly in the pro-

---

lic relations. However advantageous the enterprise may find such projects, there is no public advantage in private accretions of power for such purposes." *Ibid.*, p. 115.

[6] This presupposes that the expanded meaning of "monopoly" is accepted. To those who favor a narrower meaning the argument that product differences imply "monopoly" is untenable. See Hayek's comment quoted above in footnote 1, p. 29.

duction of these products is inevitable. Let us illustrate these points.

What kind of governmental measures could succeed in "homogenizing" a qualitatively heterogeneous product? Imagine for a moment that there are forty cigarette factories in the country, that each is operated by a separate firm selling its own brand. Each firm, being the sole seller of its brand, will have a modest degree of monopoly. The government then decrees that all proprietary names be abolished and that there be no more than four, completely standardized qualities, each corresponding to very exact specifications, conformance to which is strictly enforced. All producers, losing their "identity," lose the small monopoly power they have had. And consumers lose the opportunity of choosing among forty varieties. They can now choose among only four. If the larger variety of product is desirable, the monopoly power that goes with it cannot well be deemed undesirable.

What measures can be taken to "homogenize" a locationally heterogeneous product? Imagine for a moment that there are 200 cement factories widely dispersed over the country, that each is operated by a separate firm, that each makes exactly the same standard quality cement, and sells f.o.b. from its own factory, that is, from a location different from that of all the others. Each firm, being the sole seller in its areas, will have a modest degree of monopoly. The government then decrees that there be no more than twenty central cement markets in the country, each with large warehouse facilities, and that all cement must first be shipped to these warehouses, rather than directly to consumers or local building supply stores. All producers, losing their regional freight advantages, lose the small monopoly power they have had. And the cost of cement to the consumers will be very much higher than before because of the serious waste of cross-hauling the cement from the neighborhood factory to the (possible distant) warehouse and back to the place where it is needed. If this waste is considered intolerable, as it well might be, society will not stand for such an extravagant scheme and will consider the locational heterogeneity and the monopoly power that it involves as unavoidable.[7]

[7] Lest anyone fall into grievous error, we repeat that the monopoly power

If it is then granted that the element of monopoly inherent in the heterogeneity of producers may be desirable or practically unavoidable, how serious is the monopoly power involved? Where the number of producers is large, where the size of the individual producer is not large relatively to the total market, and where no restrictions are placed in the way of potential newcomers to the field, the monopoly power of the producers is likely to be trivial. Where the monopoly power is substantial, it is in all probability derived, not from the heterogeneity of the producers of their product, but from reduction in their number and increases in their size achieved mostly through merger, from collusive arrangements, or from barriers protecting them from newcomers' competition. These are the sources of that monopoly power which is really strong—and avoidable.

Exploitation of Natural Resources

It is frequently contended that the private competitive exploitation of natural resources results in such wastes that restriction or regulation of competition is called for in the public interest. From this it is a short step to the advocacy of government-supported monopolistic arrangements regarding the exploitations of these resources, the advocates of course insisting that they are

---

which rests on the heterogeneity of many small producers is relatively small, and that the fantastic schemes described in the text and rejected as undesirable or excessively costly, had the objective of *eliminating* that small monopoly power. They must not be confused with similar private schemes of quality standardization and freight equalization which, however, have the effect of drastically *increasing* the monopoly power of the producers. For example, assume that the four "standardized qualities" of cigarettes are given brand names, each owned and exclusively used by a large firm which operates numerous factories. As a result the monopoly power of each of these four firms will be immensely greater than in the case of the forty varieties. Assume that the twenty "central markets" for cement are not used as actual storage and distribution centers but merely as industry-wide basing points for base-price determination and freight calculation, and that all cement producers quote identical delivered prices on that basis. As a result the monopoly power of all these producers, participating in a common pricing scheme, will be far greater than in the case of the two hundred regional monopolies. This is not the place to give detailed explanations of the differences between the cases described. The danger of the snare and the difficulty of extricating oneself from it will probably be appreciated by the reader.

merely trying to protect the public welfare. It is, however, clearly a confusion of thought to argue that because natural resources can be and have been wastefully exploited under private competition the only method of conserving them is to establish monopolistic exploitation.

The confusion arises because of the failure to recognize that it is possible, and indeed necessary, to separate the question of whether there shall be competition among producers from the question of whether producers shall be free to adopt any method of exploitation they desire. It is certainly true that the reckless cutting of trees, the careless ploughing of the soil, the stripping of oyster beds and fishing grounds without regard for their re-placement may forever deprive society of these resources and have many serious ramifications in other directions. It is equally true, however, that regulations may be imposed on producers requiring them to adopt approved practices without interfering in the least with a competitive market. In very special cases, for example, the exploitation of an oil pool, it may be necessary to im-pose some restrictions on competitive exploitation. But the so-called "conservation" measures actually adopted in this as in other cases go far beyond anything required in the interests of true conservation and in some cases are themselves productive of waste-ful monopolistic exploitation.[8]

"Unstable" Industries

It is frequently alleged that for a large number of commodities the supply and demand conditions are such that under unregu-lated competition prices fluctuate excessively, creating undesirable and unjustified instability in the industry. Particular reference is usually made to certain primary commodities, e.g., tin, coal, wheat, sugar, coffee, tea, rubber, cotton, copper, vegetable oils. Although similar allegations are also made by advocates of cartels for manu-factured commodities, the problems are usually seen in a more extreme form in agriculture and mining.

The case for monopolistic regulations affecting agriculture and

[8] A more extensive discussion of government measures undertaken in the name of conservation of natural resources will be offered in Ch. 8.

mining is frequently made on general grounds, but there are in fact several different types of "instability" that must be distinguished. For when careful distinctions are made, it becomes clear that in few, if any, cases do monopolistic restrictions on output assist in removing the basic difficulties and in many cases they can be expected to aggravate them.

1. *Cyclically fluctuating demand and inelastic supply.* The demand for some commodities is very inelastic with respect to price but highly elastic with respect to income. When, therefore, the income of consumers falls, demand falls precipitously, and a reduction in price will do little to encourage consumption. If at the same time supply is inelastic and production, therefore, fails to contract until the price has been forced down to very low levels, severe losses will be inflicted on all producers. Certain raw materials widely used in industry, e.g., rubber, are affected this way by cyclical fluctuations in income of the manufacturing countries. Two types of proposals, to be used singly or in combination, have been made to "correct" this situation: Severe restrictions on output through quota regulations, and price support through buffer stock purchases.

Let us deal with the last proposal first. If buffer stock operations were so conducted that no net accumulation of stocks took place over the period of the business cycle, and if there were no controls on output, it would mean that the average price was the "right" one, i.e., approximated the price that would just call forth a supply equal to the amount demanded at that price during the period. Under such conditions, buffer stock operations need not be regarded as monopolistic regulations tending to distort the allocation of resources. Unfortunately, no buffer stock has ever been operated so wisely and, indeed, the uncertainties regarding the "right" price and the relevant cyclical period are so great that such operation would require a remarkable degree of omniscience. Were it carried out in good faith, there might be something to be said for the attempt, but the chances are great of the arrangement breaking down because of mistakes and mismanagement and in particular because of the pressure of vested producer interests who always consider prices too low.

Output control is the more favored proposal, especially by the more powerful producer groups, because by this device excess stocks, which would depress prices, are prevented from emerging while at the same time quota systems always give the largest producers the largest quotas. By means of production or export quotas production is reduced as demand falls. Prices may conceivably be prevented from dropping appreciably, but the reduction in total income cannot be prevented. The reduction in output results, of course, in a reduction of employment and, consequently, since it is the very purpose of the restriction scheme to reduce output more severely than it would have been reduced in response to a drastic price fall, the income of the area may shrink more drastically than it would have under unrestricted competition.[9]

If the objective of output restrictions is to make consumers pay more money for less goods, the first part of the scheme—more money—may be justified in severe depressions; but the second part—less goods—cannot be defended. The scheme is clearly a means of reducing the hardships that the fall in demand works on producers; it is a sort of concealed subsidy paid to the producers by other elements in society. If the subsidy could be obtained without the output restriction, society would accept an income transfer but would suffer no income loss. The monopolistic output restrictions do nothing to remove the basic cause of the trouble—the fall in demand—and are thus only a palliative which, like many palliatives, may in the long run aggravate the illness. Vested interests in the maintenance of controls are created, pressures for using them to exploit consumers long after the cyclical "crisis" is past always emerge and, even if one looks at the matter from the producers' point of view alone, it is doubtful whether in most cases all producers, or even the majority, are benefited. One of the chief drawbacks of output regulation is the arbitrary allocation of the permitted output among producers. Quotas are usually set on the basis of past output. Hence, high-cost producers

[9] The total proceeds from exports would be larger (because we assumed demand to be relatively inelastic), but since output and employment are smaller, total wages would be lower and profits higher. Total area income would immediately be smaller in the case of absentee ownership. But even with domestic ownership total area income may eventually shrink further if the propensities to spend out of profits are much smaller than the propensities to spend out of wages.

are frequently protected against low-cost producers, which is another way of saying that low-cost producers are discriminated against in favor of high-cost producers, and the total cost of the smaller output is higher than it need be.

2. *Fluctuating crop yields.* The supply of some commodities fluctuates appreciably as a result of weather, pests and other conditions not within the producers' control. This is the case of many annual crops, e.g., wheat. For the most part the crop must be disposed of for what it will bring and, if demand is relatively inelastic with respect to price, a large crop will have to be sold at a very low price and the total income of the producers will be smaller. The lower price is not a signal that too many resources have been devoted to the production of the commodity, for in the following year yields may be poor and with the same resources a very small crop may be produced. Price will then rise and the producers will have a "good year." The fluctuations in prices and incomes as a result of fluctuations in crop yields are widely considered undesirable and buffer stocks or other "support price" devices have been proposed to eliminate them. The remarks with respect to buffer stocks made above are equally applicable in this case. Correctly managed, buffer stock operations might introduce a useful element of stability both from the point of view of agriculture and of industry. It should be noted, however, that if the crop does not have to be carried too long and can be reasonably easily stored, and if there is any element of predictability in the cycle of changing yields, the operations of ordinary market speculators can be expected to smooth out some of the price fluctuations. There is, however, clearly no case to be made for monopolistic controls if fluctuating crop yields are the only cause of price instability.

3. *"Cobweb" cycles.* The price of some commodities is alleged to fluctuate excessively because producers never learn from past mistakes and are always doing the wrong thing. Such is supposed to be part of the explanation of the price "cycles" of certain agricultural commodities where the producers plan on the basis of the current market price. If this price is high they think it will stay high and plan for a large output. When eventually the output comes on the market, prices fall drastically. Producers then think

that the price is now going to stay low and they plan for a very small output. When this comes to the market the price goes up again. The cycle is thereupon repeated indefinitely. This type of instability (if in fact it exists, and it could only exist under very special conditions and in the absence of effective speculation) could clearly be reduced or eliminated without monopolistic controls over output by an efficient program of education and information, perhaps supplemented by an improvement of credit facilities.

4. *Backward rising supply curve.* Another type of instability is alleged to occur when a commodity is produced by small peasant producers who respond to price falls by producing more in an attempt to maintain a given total income. Thus as prices fall, production increases, prices fall even further and the producers become progressively worse off. It has never been clearly demonstrated that any appreciable number of producers do act in this way. But even if they do, attempts to restrict their output would not improve their lot if they were in competition with any other groups of producers whose output was unrestricted. Thus, apart from the fact that it is next to impossible to impose restrictions on large numbers of small producers who are unwilling to cooperate, output controls would have to cover all competitive groups and be very rigidly enforced if the groups for whose benefit the controls were introduced were not to be placed in an even worse position than they were before.

5. *Instability due to excess capacity.* By far the largest source of so-called instability is the existence of excess productive capacity of producers whose output is not saleable at a price that would cover their costs but who nevertheless continue to produce. Monopolistic regulations are therefore demanded to prevent "disorganization" of the industry and "cut-throat" competition,[10] i.e., to protect producers who would be ruined by competition. In such situations it is very common to find that the existence of "excess capacity" in the industry is accompanied by a tendency to expand capacity. This merely indicates that low-cost producers find it

---

[10] This is, in my opinion, a misuse of the term cut-throat competition, which was originally meant to refer to deliberate acts by a seller to eliminate a rival.

profitable to increase their production at the same time that high-cost producers find it unprofitable to produce with existing capacity. Protection of the high-cost producers is then clearly at the expense of low-cost producers as well as of consumers and would seem unjustified both economically and ethically. Indeed, in many cases the demand for monopolistic regulations is merely a demand from a special group for favors at the expense of the rest of society.

In other cases, however, especially where a very large part of existing capacity would have to be scrapped if prices were permitted to descend to competitive levels, it is argued that the required transfer of resources is so extensive and so difficult that severe hardships would be worked not only on producers but on the economy of whole regions and sometimes of whole countries if it had to be done very rapidly. In addition, if producers are very hard to force out of production, as is commonly the case where alternative occupations are few ("one-crop economies") there is the likelihood that a price sufficiently low to force out enough producers would force out too many so that excessively low prices would be replaced by excessively high ones and a long period of "disorganization" would follow.

Under these circumstances, existing high-cost producers, who are very frequently the more powerful ones, demand permanent output controls. These demands are economically indefensible. Certain economists, however, have argued that *temporary* output controls should be permitted for the purpose of facilitating the necessary adjustments and slowing down the transition. If the control scheme were carried out by disinterested economists, it *might* have some merit,[11] but it will always in fact be carried out by interested producer groups and their governments. Furthermore, the advocates of such policies always overestimate the difficulties of making changes in the economic system and underestimate the flexibility of the system. The introduction of monopolistic controls is the introduction of a further element of

[11] The chief condition to be satisfied is that the shift of productive resources from the industry with excess capacity into alternative employment is not merely talked about but actually carried out, and without favoritism.

rigidity and it is extremely unlikely that it will increase the adaptability of the economy.[12]

Monopolistic Shock-Absorbers and Stable Growth

Monopolistic restrictions have often been credited with performing the useful function of "stabilizers" in the economic system. The relationship between stability and monopoly is not simple and at least three different issues have been referred to in these terms. Two of them have already been taken up in this chapter.

There is first the issue just discussed, the prevention of abnormal price fluctuations in particular industries, basically unstable because of the peculiar conditions under which they operate. Monopolistic restrictions are advocated for these industries in order to stabilize the prices of their products.

There is, second, the prevention of deflationary reductions in average price levels and aggregate income levels in the economy as a whole, whose instability is allegedly increased by highly flexible prices of factors and products.[13] Monopolistic restrictions are advocated, especially for labor, in order to create a price inflexibility that will put a floor to declines in general prices and incomes.[14] As we have said before (p. 34), however, there is no evidence for the claim that increased price stability in selected sectors of the economy will increase the income stability of the economy as a whole. It may just as well reduce it. Answers to the problem of fluctuations of the aggregate income of the nation must

[12] The rejection of monopolistic controls as "solutions" for the various problems of instability should not mean that these problems cannot or need not be solved.

[13] "In fact, when people talk and write about the 'evils of competition,' what they are usually referring to, all unconsciously, is the process of deflation." K. E. Boulding, "In Defense of Monopoly," *Quarterly Journal of Economics*, Vol. LIX (1945), p. 534.

[14] "It is becoming apparent that 'price flexibility,' far from being the golden recipe for prosperity, may lead us into disastrous and even bottomless deflation . . . It is only the inflexibilities in the system, however, that prevent such a bottomless deflation. . . ." Boulding, *op. cit.*, p. 531. Perhaps it should be mentioned that Boulding includes among the "inflexibilities" the fact that the money supply cannot run down without limit.

be sought in other measures than monopolistic actions for price maintenance.

It is the third issue that now calls for our attention: the prevention of especially drastic reductions in the profits of industries requiring an abundant flow of private investment funds in the long run that would be discouraged through excessive depression losses. Monopolistic restrictions are advocated in order to prevent competition from being too discouraging to investors.

Should monopolistic restrictions be regarded as useful props under the capital structure of industries which under unrestricted competition would in bad times suffer such losses that the flow of investment funds needed for its long-run growth would be impaired? In an economy with rapid change, unlimited competition is said to be too rough, too ruthless, too discouraging to investors. A dose of monopoly has, according to some, a balancing, steadying effect, permitting the economy to progress less erratically, more steadily and, as a net result, faster than under unlimited competition. If a mechanical analogy may be used, monopolistic devices may act as shock-absorbers without which investors would not dare to travel the rough and bumpy roads to higher levels of national production.

The argument is persuasive. The flow of funds into investment is certainly a prerequisite of the growth of the economy. In a private enterprise system the flow of funds depends on the confidence of investors. Few risks to the value of investments are greater than those arising from unrestricted competition among rival producers fighting for larger shares in temporarily declining markets. The elimination or reduction of these risks by means of monopolistic devices can do much to bolster the confidence of investors and thus to make them devote their funds to the expansion of productive capacity.

This argument for monopolistic restrictions as "shock-absorbers" necessary for the confidence of investors financing the *growth of capacity* is very similar to the argument for monopolistic restrictions as "brakes" necessary for the confidence of investors financing *the development and use of new technology*. The role of monopoly as a brake on innovation in order to promote technological progress will now be analysed: the conclusions arrived at will apply with equal validity to the question of the role of monopoly as a shock-absorber.

Monopolistic Brakes and Technological Progress

The contention is that unrestricted competition, by denying innovators enough time to enjoy the profits of their new ventures, would discourage innovation and retard technological progress. Comparing on this score the performance of perfectly competitive capitalism with that of monopoly capitalism, the advocate of the latter comes to the conclusion that "perfect competition is not only impossible but inferior." [15]

Perfect competition, according to this view, is inferior because it creates a climate inimical to technological innovation. Investors in technological research and development and investors in such untried ventures as the introduction of new products or new processes must be granted some measure of protection against the speedy emergence of profit-removing competition. Innovators would tend to hold back if they feared that imitators would quickly follow their lead and deprive them of the fruits of their courage and ingenuity, or if they feared that a steady stream of further innovation would render their large investments obsolete long before the investments had paid for themselves.

There is, however, the opposite view, to the effect that barriers against newcomers, against imitation, and against the introduction of improvements, retard innovation and restrict the utilization of new technology not only temporarily but also in the long run. It is held that the use of old techniques is kept profitable by protective barriers against newcomers and, in the absence of a constant threat that others may come forth with improved techniques, the firms in the sheltered positions lack the incentive to develop better products and better ways of making them or even

---

[15] Joseph A. Schumpeter, *Capitalism, Socialism and Democracy* (New York: Harper, 1943), p. 106. It was Schumpeter who used the metaphor of the monopolistic "brake" necessary to speed up progress. This was his statement: ". . . restrictions of this type are, in the conditions of the perennial gale, incidents, often unavoidable incidents of a long-run process of expansion which they protect rather than impede. There is no more of paradox in this than there is in saying that motorcars are traveling faster than they otherwise would because they are provided with brakes."

to exploit technologies that would look promising to one who had a good chance of breaking into the field. In addition, the new technologies that are introduced are not utilized to the extent to which they would have been under unrestricted competition, because the newly discovered paths remain closed to general use, and thus the actual contribution to the nation's income that is made by successful pioneering falls far short of its potential contribution.

These, it will be noted, are the customary arguments for and against strong patent protection. Without the monopolies which patents grant to innovators, investment in innovating ventures will not pay sufficiently and the necessary venture capital will not be forthcoming. (The development of the chemical industry is often attributed to the protection which it has enjoyed in the monopolistic exploitation of its new inventions.) With strong patent monopolies, on the other hand, industrial development will be retarded by making it rather hopeless for the barred outsider and unnecessary for the sheltered insider to press forward on the road to progress. (The development of the automobile industry is often attributed to the fact that the courts sided with Henry Ford when he contested the validity of early patents granting exclusivity for motorcar production.)

What is true concerning patent protection may hold equally well for other monopolistic restraints. Not all types of inventions are patentable, and not all innovations in industrial production are based on inventions. The execution of the innovation, rather than the discovery or invention, is the thing that really counts in this respect and for which the protection from competition may be needed. Is innovation encouraged or discouraged by restrictions of entry into an industry? No proof is possible for one contention or the other. Is expansion furthered or retarded by the existence of price agreements or other cartel practices limiting competition in an industry? No experiment can verify or disprove one theory or the other. We are left to rely on our "considered judgment" in deciding where the weight of argument lies.

References to historical facts are not conclusive in this question. It is true that instances of deliberate suppression of inventions have been found only in industries in which there is a high degree of monopoly. But perhaps these inventions would not have been

made in the first place if these industries had been more competitive. It is true that certain typically competitive industries
have shown comparatively little progress in technology and organization, while some highly monopolistic industries have shown
remarkable advance. But this does not indicate that these industries have been stagnant or dynamic because they were competitive
or monopolistic, respectively. In many instances, for example, it
was chiefly the technological advance itself which, with the aid
of patent protection, was responsible for the development of dominating monopolies. Cause and effect would thus be reversed: technological progress under existing institutions would make for monopoly positions rather than monopoly for progress.

Even if it were clearly established that monopoly in certain
industries promoted faster technological progress, it could not be
concluded that the speed of technological progress in society as a
whole was accelerated by monopolistic restraints. The concentration of technological progress in these industries might instead
indicate that innovating talents and efforts had merely been diverted to them from other fields by the higher rewards the monopoly offered.

It is probably true that "monopolization may increase the
sphere of influence of the better brains." [16] But this neither means
that monopolization creates these brains nor that without monopolization there would be no appropriate use for them. The inventive genius, the contriving instinct, the organizational talent,
the venturous drive, the gambling spirit, the dynamic personality,
all these requisites of progress are not dependent on opportunities to monopolize any field and could find ample scope for innovation in competitive industries. The giant corporation with its
rich resources and secure monopoly power can attract the researchers, inventors, organizers, and enterprising talents by letting them share in its monopoly profits, paying higher salaries than
competitive industry can afford. They would certainly not be idle
if industries were without monopoly power; they would merely
be distributed over other fields of activity.

It can hardly be said with any assurance that progress would
be slower if it were not concentrated in firms or fields where patent

[16] Schumpeter, *op. cit.*, p. 101.

protection makes it most lucrative. More assuredly it may be said that without concentration progress would be more balanced. And in all probability, it would be faster if the new paths broken or opened by industrial pioneers were not closed to others by monopolistic barriers, but remained open for general use. This is not an argument against reasonable "toll charges" exacted by the path-finders under a well-devised patent system; but it is an argument against the tight restrictions which industry can set up under the present patent system and by many other methods available under present institutions.

Monopoly Policies versus Tax Policies

In our brief examination of the role of monopoly as a brake designed for safe traveling on the road of technological progress we have concluded that full utilization of imaginativeness, talent and drive probably does not depend on monopolistic protection of innovators. But there still remains the question of full utilization of investible funds. It is with regard to this question that the monopolistic brake and the monopolistic shock-absorber may have analogous effects. An adequate volume of investment is regarded as a major requirement for the maintenance of a high level of employment in the economy. Sufficient incentives to invest are, therefore, of paramount importance. The argument that unrestricted competition will weaken or kill the investment incentives, while monopolistic devices will strengthen them, needs additional attention.[17]

Investments in ventures with novel products and novel techniques are exceedingly risky. A chance of high profits acts as "bait" for the investor who is to take the risk of losing most or all of his capital in his venture. If successful, the risk-taker may be rewarded by a high profit. The success, however, will attract others to take up the business which has proved so profitable and no longer involves large risks. Thus, profits will soon disappear under the pressure of competition. But it is surely safer to make invest-

[17] The reasoning in this section follows closely the arguments which I presented in my chapter "Summary and Analysis" in *Financing American Prosperity*, ed. by P. T. Homan and F. Machlup (New York: Twentieth Century Fund, 1945), pp. 424 ff.

ments as a "follower" rather than as a "leader." Yet if everyone
chooses to wait for others to lead and to show him the good investment opportunities, no investment will be forthcoming.

This reasoning suggests that most people will be willing to
undertake new ventures only if their lead can be secured by monopolistic devices. The longer the time during which competitors
are kept away, the greater will be the profits of the innovator. But
who can tell how much of a lead is appropriate? If we foster investment by "leaders" through restricting investment by "followers," can we know whether investment on balance will not be more
restricted than encouraged?

The pioneer knows that others will come after him if his ventures meet with success. The innovator reckons with the eventual
emergence of competitors; a jump ahead of them, he needs the
expectation of making enough money while he is in the lead. If the
gain which he expects to make in the meantime, until competitors
catch up with him, is sufficiently attractive, he will go ahead. But
this attractiveness depends, among other things, on the tax system. High taxes on the income from enterprise may act as a deterrent of investment. Is it wise for society to create this deterrent
and then to rely on the effects of a compensating "sop" for investors in the form of monopolistic devices?

We recognize here a peculiar relationship between two very
distinct fields of governmental activities: tax policy and monopoly
policy. The alternatives seem to be whether to deal with high
profits from enterprise by taxing them away regularly or by allowing competition to wipe them out as fast as it can work; whether
to secure investment incentives by lower taxes on income from
enterprise or by monopolistic restraints of competition. There can
be little doubt that, instead of erecting barriers to competition in
order to increase the pioneer's or insider's gain, it is simpler and
safer to increase it by letting him keep more of it—that is, by taking less through taxes.[18]

The greater the slice the government takes from the returns to

[18] This should not be understood as an argument for lower income taxes
in general. There can be differential tax rates for different types of income.
This is the proposal made by Sumner H. Slichter, in his chapter "Public Policies and Postwar Employment," in *Financing American Prosperity, op. cit.,*
p. 318.

venture capital, the more "necessary" does it become to "bribe" capital into new ventures by permitting monopolistic devices to fence off any competing investments. The result is an artificial plugging of outlets for masses of investible funds in order to channel a small portion of them into well-protected "investment opportunities." If innovators are permitted to keep more of their gains they will be attracted to new ventures despite the probability that "the gravy" will soon be gone owing to the unrestricted stream of competing investments that will follow them into the new fields.

Insecurity is a serious deterrent to the maintenance of an adequate flow of funds into productive investment. But it is not a sound policy to reduce insecurity of investment by creating "security from competition." For, although there are certain risks to investment which can be reduced or eliminated in order to increase the total flow of funds into investment, a reduction of the "risk of competition" is apt to have the opposite effect. If it succeeds in encouraging one investment, it usually does so by restricting another.

DEBITS AND CREDITS OF MONOPOLISTIC RESTRAINTS

It is not easy to find one's way through this maze of claims and counterclaims and to assess their validity and significance. Validity *and* significance—because some arguments may be perfectly valid but relatively insignificant, others would be highly significant but may be of doubtful validity. The confusion is increased by the manifold meanings of monopoly, by the indiscriminate application of highly abstract concepts on a level of concreteness for which they are inappropriate, and by attempts to discredit the opponent's arguments by giving his terms other meanings than those he had intended. On top of all this we may find serious clashes between the objectives which different "experts" elect to regard as the ultimate goals of society.

False Issues and Real

The proponents of anti-monopoly policies are often criticized. A favorite sport of the critics is to demonstrate the impossibility of pure and perfect competition in the real world. If every deviation from pure and perfect competition is monopoly, no policy can succeed in eliminating monopoly. From this it seems plausible to jump to the conclusion that anti-monopoly policies are futile and, hence, undesirable.[19]

There is an element of monopoly in the situation in which sellers are somewhat different from one another. Is this a reason for condoning cartel arrangements or other forms of cooperation among them? There may be an element of monopoly in the fact that it takes time for new enterprise to move into a profitable line of business. Does this make it good policy to aid insiders in prolonging this period? One may define perfect competition so narrowly that it would require newcomers to appear on the scene a few minutes after new profit expectations are aroused by changes in demand or by new technical knowledge. Under such circumstances, of course, there could be no profit in costly research, development and innovation. Must one conclude from this that technological progress is impossible under perfect competition, and monopoly is a prerequisite of progress? Alternatively, one may define perfect competition to allow the existence of normal frictions and delays and, hence, of a period of undisturbed profits, before newcomers' competition becomes effective. Monopoly, then, would be only the artificial prolongation of the period of protection from newcomers' competition. And the real question would be whether or not the extra stimulation which the extra profits from the lengthened period of protection may provide for innovating ventures are worth the cost of the delayed full exploitation of the new technology— which is a legitimate question and one that must be analysed before one can have a well-founded opinion about the kind of protection that society should accord to those who introduce new inventions.

[19] "Indeed, far from competition being beneficial only when it is 'perfect,' I am inclined to argue that the need for competition is nowhere greater than in fields in which the nature of the commodities or services makes it impossible that it ever should create a perfect market in the theoretical sense. The inevitable actual imperfections of competition are as little an argument against competition as . . . imperfect health is an argument against health." Friedrich A. Hayek, "The Meaning of Competition," in *Individualism and Economic Order* (Chicago: University of Chicago Press, 1948), pp. 103–104.

In any event, the controversy about the role of government in aiding or restraining competition and in aiding or restraining monopoly is not concerned with those elements of monopoly which are practically inevitable. The controversy is confined to "avoidable monopoly," to monopolistic practices that can be prevented, to monopolistic barriers that can be removed, to monopoly-promoting institutions that can be abolished. More concretely, the controversy about the "monopoly problem" turns on such questions as whether all forms of collusion should be prosecuted, whether mergers of competing firms should be prohibited, whether trade unions should have closed-shop agreements and industry-wide collective bargaining, whether the patent system should be reformed to make it less restrictive, whether building ordinances by municipal governments should exclude new materials or protect local producers, whether states should limit operation in various fields to holders of certificates of convenience and necessity, whether the nation should maintain a high protective tariff, whether the government should force fruit growers to conform with marketing arrangements drafted by cooperatives to which they do not belong, whether storekeepers should be fined if they sell tooth paste and baby oil below the list price, whether local labor unions should have the right to exclude out-of-towners working in their profession, whether large corporations should be permitted to resort to local price-cutting in order to force smaller competitors out of business, whether truckers should be forbidden to haul goods at rates below the officially approved ones, and so on and so forth. Pages could be filled merely listing the concrete questions of policy concerning "the monopoly problem."

Conflicting Objectives

It can be shown that maximum total income, maximum total employment, maximum progress, maximum stability, maximum security, and maximum freedom are social goals which are not fully compatible with one another. They go together to a certain extent, but beyond it they conflict with each other. People differ in the compromises they would prefer. Some would sacrifice more of current income than others would to secure a rapid rate of progress. Some would do with less progress if it could be had only at the price of considerable instability. Some would insist on a guarantee of full employment even if it should jeopardize freedom. Some put the economic security of workers and producers above the realization of higher incomes and greater freedom.[20]

If people disagree on the ultimate goals, we cannot expect them to agree on particular policies. We shall not attempt here to analyse the relationships of competition and monopoly to each of the alternative social goals, especially since monopoly, as we have previously shown, is not an indivisible whole and different elements or phases of monopoly may bear different relationships to particular objectives. (For example, a strong patent system probably has more to do with "progress," a closed-shop agreement or a municipal licensing ordinance more with "security.") Thus we cannot expect that experts will *consistently* incline toward the competitive or the monopolistic answers to the many questions which constitute the monopoly problem. Only those who place the "income" and "freedom" goals decidedly ahead of the others may show a conspicuous bias in favor of competition and against monopoly in almost all avoidable forms. Even this presupposes, in addition to the consensus on the hierarchy of ultimate social goals, a consensus on what are in fact the probable effects of particular policies and institutions.

A Balance Sheet

It may be helpful to construct a list of charges and counter-charges in the form of a balance sheet of "debits and credits" in the account of monopolistic restrictions. The monopoly elements charged with harmful or credited with beneficial effects include governmental restraints of competition as well as restrictive busi-

[20] "It seems quite possible that a society arranged for the maximum security of producers based upon powerful monopolies—including union monopolies of workmen—would satisfy men better than one arranged to get the maximum freedom of consumers' choice and workers' mobility." C. Sutton, "The Relation between Economic Theory and Economic Policy," *The Economic Journal*, Vol. XLVII (1937), p. 52.

ness or labor practices, public as well as private barriers to the movement of resources into economic uses.[21]

Monopolistic Restraints of Competition

Debits	Credits
(1) They result in uneconomic allocation of productive resources.	(1) They result in a more economic allocation of productive resources in a dynamic economy.
(2) They give rise to extortion of the consumer through higher prices and lower qualities of products.	(2) They benefit the consumer in the long run through lower prices and better qualities.
(3) They permit exploitation of workers through lower wages and poorer working conditions.	(3) They avoid competitive reductions of wages and deterioration of working conditions under competitive pressures.
(4) They eliminate the penalty which competition involves for inefficiency and inertia, and thus entail inefficient management and operation.	(4) They make superior methods available, including scientific research and use for better brains.
(5) They remove incentives to technological innovations and reduce the flow of investment.	(5) They permit long-range investment and encourage innovations.
(6) They prevent full utilization of productive capacity.	(6) They allow greater expansion of productive capacity in the long run.

[21] The charges are taken from the "indictment of monopoly" which Clair Wilcox compiled for his useful study *Competition and Monopoly in American Industry, Monograph No. 21,* Temporary National Economic Committee (Washington, 1940), pp. 16–18. The credits are taken chiefly from the defense of monopoly which Joseph A. Schumpeter presented in his eminently original and provocative book cited on p. 64 above. The arrangement of all debit and credit items, in particular the omission of a credit item balancing the tenth debit item, is my own contrivance. This was done for expositional purposes, as will become apparent later in the text.

Monopolistic Restraints of Competition

Debits	Credits
(7) They obstruct adjustment to economic change, e.g., through rigid prices, and thus contribute to general industrial instability.	(7) They alleviate depressions, provide effective remedies for set-backs, and thus facilitate steadier industrial expansion.
(8) They retard improvements in the standard of living.	(8) They promote improvements in the standard of living in the long run.
(9) They aggravate the existing inequality in the distribution of income through excessive profits and concentration of wealth.	(9) They give rise occasionally to abnormal profits, which function as bait for other investors, making most capitalists work for nothing.
(10) They threaten the existence of free private enterprise and representative government.	

Monopoly and Democracy

The balance sheet which was presented above to give account of the charges and credits to monopolistic restraints did not exactly balance. While the accounting may have been faulty in general and several items on either side may have been omitted, the items that were entered showed a definite debit balance. For one particular item on the debit side no offsetting entry appears on the credit side. This item related not to economic but to political consequences of monopoly.

Monopoly and the Road to Serfdom

The charge in question contends that monopoly "threatens the existence of free private enterprise and representative government." [22] The contention that monopoly constitutes a serious threat

[22] Wilcox, *op. cit.*, p. 18. The Federal Trade Commission, in a report submitted in 1939 to the Temporary National Economic Committee, stated: "The capitalist system of free initiative is not immortal, but is capable of dying

to democracy is frequently advanced without explanation. Whatever the explanation, the charge certainly does not mean that the demise of democracy from an overdose of monopoly is predicted as an inevitable and immediate occurrence, but merely as a threatened and gradual development. This development may take several different forms, some of which may be sketched here:

(1) Monopolistic restraints in industrial, agricultural and labor markets prevent the capitalist system from working satisfactorily and lead to increasing government regulation of economic life; the larger the scope of regimentation and the greater the responsibilities of government in the economic sphere, the less satisfactorily can democracy operate; after a succession of serious economic and political crises, democratic government will give way to an authoritarian regime.

(2) Monopolistic restrictions of production and employment may so badly sabotage the working of the private enterprise economy that a dissatisfied majority or a desperate minority may (through peaceful means or violent overthrow, respectively) establish a government committed to a system of a centrally planned economy. Efficient management of such a system will call for authoritarian rule.

(3) Monopolistic groups in industry, agriculture and labor acquire and exercise so much political power that their influence upon government becomes intolerable and paralyses the democratic machinery; in defense against the strong pressure groups, democracy is "suspended," and a strong-arm government is set up along authoritarian lines.

(4) Monopolistic groups acquire and exercise so much economic power that the conflicts among them (through bargaining, strikes, shutdowns, boycotts) assume the character of economic warfare; eventually, following a series of paralysing strikes with outbreaks of violence and mass disorder, government finds itself compelled to establish order through authoritarian methods (pos-

---

and of dragging down with it the system of democratic government. Monopoly constitutes the death of capitalism and the genesis of authoritarian government." *Hearings of the Temporary National Economic Committee,* Part 5 (Washington: 1939), p. 2200. Innumerable other statements in the same vein could be quoted.

sibly after government has been "taken over" by one of the monopolistic groups in an attempt to suppress the others).

Democracy in a Planned Economy

The number of these "models" can be easily multiplied through
slight variations and combinations of their different elements, but
they all picture the end of democracy. Agreement or disagreement
on this issue is, however, a precarious matter because "democracy"
can mean so many different things. To know what it means is especially important in the controversial question whether a centrally
planned economy is or is not compatible with democratic government.

In one of its many meanings, democracy implies opportunity of
the people to accept or refuse the men who are to govern, whereby
this opportunity must be afforded through "free competition among
would-be leaders for the vote of the electorate." [23] Provided that
these are the only criteria of "democracy," and nothing else is required, democratic government can *conceivably* endure if it is
saddled with the responsibility of planning and running the economic system; but it is not very *likely* to endure under such conditions.

Even if democracy in a merely formal sense could be maintained in an economy planned and operated by the government,
it would be highly questionable how "free" such a "democratic"
society would be. "Democratic control may prevent power from
becoming arbitrary, but it does not do so by its mere existence. If
democracy resolves on a task which necessarily involves the use
of power which cannot be guided by fixed rules, it must become
arbitrary power." [24] Economic decisions are matters of judgment
rather than of application of fixed rules. As long as economic power
is so widely dispersed that those who make economic decisions
lack any large amount of power, and as long as the decisions of the
state are chiefly on matters that can be decided by applying fixed

[23] Schumpeter, *op. cit.*, p. 285. It should be noted that the exact contents of these criteria will depend on the meaning of "free competition" among
politicians for votes.

[24] F. A. Hayek, *The Road to Serfdom* (Chicago: University of Chicago
Press, 1944), p. 71.

rules, society can operate without excessive exercise of arbitrary power. The concentration of economic power, however, and its fusion with political power is apt to be fatal to *free* society—regardless of whether or not it is called "democratic" according to the letter (rather than spirit) of a definition which stresses only the empty forms of political institutions. The more criteria of *not merely formal* character are included in the definition of democracy, the smaller becomes the probability that the government of a government-planned economy can in the long run remain democratic.[25] And the probability that a government-planned economy will be the successor of an economy directed or misdirected by powerful private monopolies becomes increasingly threatening.

If competition is so weakened and restrained that the "automatic controls" by which anonymous market forces steer the economic system are removed, the establishment of "direct controls," handled by a central power, becomes necessary. "A Community which fails to preserve the discipline of competition exposes itself to the discipline of absolute authority." [26]

Superstition or Prudence?

The foregoing warnings against the dire consequences of monopolistic practices to society may sound too dramatic. It is possible that our fears are exaggerated. But there is always the difficulty of evaluating the seriousness of a danger. Who can say whether any particular warning is due to overcautiousness, timidity or even superstition or, on the other hand, to prudence and foresight?

There is the view that we have come to hold "a wildly exaggerated opinion of the amount of monopoly power possessed and exercised by producers . . . ," and that the explanation can be found "in a well-recognized trait of human nature, the urge to ex-

[25] According to Hayek, whose views on this issue are often regarded as too pessimistic, "the clash between planning and democracy arises simply from the fact that the latter is an obstacle to the suppression of freedom which the direction of economic activity requires." *The Road to Serfdom*, p. 70.

[26] Henry C. Simons, "Some Reflections on Syndicalism," *Journal of Political Economy*, Vol. LII (1944), p. 5.

plain any supposed evil by finding an 'enemy' and to deal with it by 'liquidating' somebody." [27]

It is, of course, possible that "monopoly" is merely a bugbear frightening the believers in free enterprise and free society; but it is equally possible that we have underestimated the acuteness of the danger and have allowed the situation to deteriorate to such a degree that only a very radical effort can still save our social and political system.

[27] Frank H. Knight, "Anthropology and Economics," *Journal of Political Economy*, Vol. XLIX (1941), p. 264.

PART II—BUSINESS POLICIES

Monopolistic Business Practices: Collusion, Merger, Exclusion

Meanings and Distinctions: Confusion Worse Confounded · Distinctions and "Reality"

Cooperation, Collusion, Cartels: Gentlemen's Agreement · Trade Associations, Cost Calculations and Statistics · Delivered-Price Formulas · Cartels with Enforcement Apparatus · The Contents of Cartel Arrangements · Profit Pools and Average Price Cartels · Centralized Selling

Oppression, Domination, Merger, Concentration: Manifold Interrelationships, Warfare and Cooperation · Oppressive Practices · Domination · The Merger Movement · Integration and Conglomeration · Concentration

Restrictions on Entry: Governmental Barriers · Threats and Ruinous Campaigns · Barred Access to Resources · Bigger Minimum Size

T HE NEATEST definitions and clearest classifications of business monopoly and the soundest analyses of its economic effects will not tell us what we are really talking about unless we have some knowledge of actual business practices. Hence, a more descriptive discussion of monopolistic business practices is called for. A couple of chapters devoted to this purpose are, however, a very imperfect substitute for books of case studies. Those who have never read historical works on trusts and cartels, price policies and business concentration are urgently advised to do so. They will find them interesting reading, some of them even exciting, almost like detective stories. Certain trust and antitrust stories, such as the Standard Oil case, the Tobacco case, the United States Steel case, are significant parts of American history and, thus, of the education of every American. Studies of more recent developments in corporate policies and industrial concentration reveal important economic and political aspects of the present American scene.[1] We shall not undertake in these chapters to present large amounts of case material on monopolistic business practices, because it would not be possible to do justice to such material within that short compass. But we shall offer a generally descriptive discussion.

MEANINGS AND DISTINCTIONS

A descriptive discussion of monopolistic business practices calls for a reminder about the expansion that has taken place in the meaning of the term "monopolistic."

Confusion Worse Confounded

As was pointed out before, economists frequently speak of a monopoly even where there are many sellers offering practically the same product or service and where there are no restraints of trade, no cartels or other elements of collusion, no large firms dominating the market, no trusts, no history or expectation of merg-

[1] There are many good books available on these subjects. The best writing will be found in Frank A. Fetter, *The Masquerade of Monopoly* (New York: Harcourt, Brace and Co., 1931), discussing chiefly the oil and steel cases. Other works to be recommended include Arthur Robert Burns, *The Decline of Competition* (New York: McGraw-Hill, 1936); Walton H. Hamilton and Associates, *Price and Price Policies* (New York: McGraw-Hill, 1938); Thurman W. Arnold, *The Bottlenecks of Business* (New York: Reynal and Hitchcock, 1940); Clair Wilcox, *Competition and Monopoly in American Industry*, Monograph No. 21, Temporary National Economic Committee (Washington, 1941); Harry L. Purdy, Martin L. Lindahl, and William A. Carter, *Corporate Concentration and Public Policy* (New York: Prentice-Hall, 1942); Corwin D. Edwards, *Economic and Political Aspects of International Cartels*, Monograph No. 1, Senate Subcommittee on War Mobilization of the Committee on Military Affairs, 78th Congress, 2nd Session (Washington, 1944); David Lynch, *Concentration of Economic Power* (New York: Columbia University Press, 1946); George W. Stocking and Myron W. Watkins, *Cartels in Action* (New York: Twentieth Century Fund, 1946); Vernon A. Mund, *Open Markets: An Essential of Free Enterprise* (New York: Harper, 1948); Walter Adams, ed., *The Structure of American Industry* (New York: Macmillan, 1950). Beyond the compass of the American scene, one of the most useful studies of monopolistic business practices is the small book by E. A. G. Robinson, *Monopoly* (Cambridge: University Press, 1941), which in a most engaging manner succeeds in combining theoretical insight and factual case material.

ers, no private or governmental barriers to the entry of new resources. The mere fact that a firm *could* sell some of its product at a higher price than it actually does indicates that it has a *choice*, and this is enough to characterize its market position as "monopolistic." The mere fact that a firm finds its sales *limited by the market*, that is, by the demand for its products, is sufficient to characterize its prices as "monopoly prices."

Indeed, in this wide sense in which the word is now used, one may say that *any price policy whatsoever is a monopolistic policy by definition.* For price "policy" clearly implies that the firm or organization in question can choose between possible prices and, perhaps, can influence the range of prices from which it can choose. This involves some sort of "monopolistic position." In this sense almost every business in manufacturing and in retailing, from the smallest grocery store up to the Aluminum Corporation, is some sort of a monopoly, the difference being one of degree and not of principle.

It is admittedly confusing that economists—including the present writer—should condone such an expansion of the concept of monopoly that almost every man becomes a monopolist and "monopoly" is thus turned into a politically neutral concept, and should nevertheless continue to use it also in the narrower sense in which monopoly is possibly an unlawful and probably a socially harmful thing against which the forces of the state should be mobilized.[2] One can only hope that repeated warnings of the multiplicity of meaning will avert or reduce the danger of confusion.

Lawyers may scoff at the ambiguities introduced into the dis-

[2] There are those who habitually look for sinister motives behind every terminological decision of a writer. It happens that the widening of the monopoly concept which has made monopoly so pervasive and universal in our economic system could be ascribed to two very different political purposes. (1) The socialist critic of the capitalist order can use the semantic trick for deriving the following inference: "Since monopoly is socially harmful and since almost every seller in our economic system necessarily possesses monopoly power, the system is bad and must be abolished." (2) The conservative critic of antitrust prosecutions can use the same trick for this conclusion: "Since it makes no sense fighting the inevitable, and since monopoly is inherent in almost every kind of business, antitrust prosecutions are useless and should be stopped." I cannot deny that both types of inferences have been made by partisans of the respective attitudes.

cussion because of the inability of economists to agree on a clear
meaning of the word. But the legal concept is equally ambiguous.
Lawyers in the United States have for many years protested the
vagueness of the antitrust laws and the impossibility of "predicting" the legality or illegality of particular business practices. It
would be of no help if economists were to attempt to adopt legal
definitions of monopoly and monopolistic practices. Apart from
the difficulty of determining what the legal definitions are and what
the legal status of certain business practices is under the American
antimonopoly laws, one must not forget that the law is different
in different countries and the same sort of business practice is legal
in some countries and illegal in others. Hence, the economic concept of monopoly must be independent of the legal one. A general
survey of monopolistic business practices cannot, therefore, be
based on their legal status. We shall, however, wherever it seems
appropriate, include references to the legal situation in the United
States.

Distinctions and "Reality"

One may attempt to distinguish monopolistic business actions according to whether they serve to *create*, to *maintain*, to
strengthen, or to *exploit* a monopolistic position. These distinctions, like many others, are not easily applied to concrete situations.
First of all, it is difficult to ascertain either the intended or the
actual results of any action. Neither of them can be conclusively
proved. Intentions are highly subjective matters and can at best
be introspectively recognized or reconstructed by the actor or inferred by the observer. Actual results can only be shown to be
"probably so" on the basis of accepted theory. There cannot be
certainty about causal relationships.[3]

It is further difficult to determine to what extent an action
which strengthens a monopolistic position may at the same time
help to maintain it, or to what extent an action which exploits a
monopoly position contributes also to its maintenance. In ideal

[3] The best we can ever expect to have by way of "proof" is a "reasonable"
conformance of observations with a "plausible" model (or mental construction) of links between hypothetical causes and hypothetical effects.

cases a separation may be possible. But as soon as we deal with real cases rather than ideal ones, the separation becomes as a rule impracticable. Nevertheless, in certain instances it may be revealing to ask whether particular actions are more likely designed to create, to maintain, to strengthen, or to exploit a monopolistic position.

Four categories of monopolistic business policies were distinguished in Chapter 2. These distinctions do not provide, however, a suitable framework for the organization of a full discussion of monopolistic business practices, because purpose and form were two of the chief bases of classification when we set up these categories, and particular practices can be used for many different purposes and in many different forms.[4] Nevertheless it is still useful to consider together certain practices that clearly are related to questions of "cooperation, collusion, and cartels"—the labels used for our second category—to "oppression, domination, merger, and concentration"—the labels for the third category—and finally to the fourth, restrictions on entry. Several larger complexes of monopolistic business practices, however, which cut across these categories but are more conveniently discussed under headings of their own will be taken up in the subsequent chapter.

COOPERATION, COLLUSION, CARTELS

No lines, certainly no clear lines, can be drawn between cooperation, collusion, and cartelization.[5] For purely informal, self-

---

[4] In using the words business *actions, behavior, conduct, practices,* and *policies* without formal definitions I have assumed that their meanings are clear without semantic exercises. There are writers who make careful distinctions between some of these terms. Sociologists, for example, have pointed out that the word "conduct" has a strong connotation of rationality, which may not be intended by the word "behavior." Emphasis on the typical or habitual is usually intended when one speaks of "practices," and long-term consistency and purposefulness are part of the meaning conveyed by the word "policies." To be sure, different kinds of practices may serve one kind of policy, and one kind of practice may serve different kinds of policies. Moreover, while practices can often be observed by an outside-observer, policies can only be inferred.

[5] I have defined cartels as "business arrangements which have the purpose or effect of reducing or regulating competition." See my chapter on "The Nature of the International Cartel Problem," in *A Cartel Policy for the United*

imposed restraints on competitive conduct without any direct or indirect communication among competitors and without any set pattern for pricing or selling practices the term *cooperation* may be most fitting. For less informal limitations in competitive conduct, involving direct or indirect communication among competitors or compliance with a set pattern of pricing or selling, the term *collusion* may be more appropriate. For arrangements involving more frequent communication among competitors or some sort of permanent organization such as a trade association, an "institute," a statistical bureau, periodic circulars or published notices the term *cartel* may be most suitable. Since there is an air of suspicion and illegality attached to the terms "collusion" and "cartel"—in the United States at least—"cooperation" is the widely preferred term for all forms of restraint or non-aggressiveness in competition. It is not easy in the United States for a businessman to participate in collusive activities or cartels and yet have the same good conscience that one has who merely "cooperates" with his fellow men—or fellow sellers. However, neither pangs of conscience nor court convictions are relevant for economic distinctions. As the economics of the three things is the same, attempts to keep them apart result in distinctions without differences.

Gentlemen's Agreement

Among the better known forms of collusion the gentlemen's agreement is usually given a prominent place. A gentlemen's agreement is an unwritten agreement among competitors. That such agreements are oral rather than in writing is of no importance from an economic point of view but is of great practical importance in the United States, because a written document might be found by an agent of the Attorney General's office in the files of one of the parties to the agreement and might be used as evidence of a violation of the antitrust laws. In some other countries businessmen avoid putting their agreements in the form of written contracts because this would make them liable to stamp taxes. But

Nations by Corwin D. Edwards and others (New York: Columbia University Press, 1945), p. 3. Essentially the same definition applies to cooperation and collusion among competing sellers.

whether they are notarized compacts, witnessed and signed contracts, exchange of correspondence, unsigned memoranda, oral undertakings before witnesses, oral agreements confirmed by solemn handshakes, casual nods, telephonic okays, or merely implicit consensus shown by compliance makes little difference for their economic effects. Indeed, when we speak of the effects of an agreement we usually mean the effects of the performance which it conditions. Compliance is not dependent on the form of the agreement. An oral, or even tacit, understanding may be more faithfully complied with than the most formal contract.[6] The degree of compliance depends on a number of circumstances, such as the number of participants and the rate of change of external conditions. In comparison with these circumstances the form of the agreement weighs little.

The gentlemen's agreement holds its special place in the history of collusion chiefly for two reasons. One is the famous statement made by Adam Smith in 1776 and quoted with great regularity in all discussions of this kind. He said: "People of the same trade seldom meet together even for merriment and diversion, but the conversation ends in a conspiracy against the public, or on some contrivance to raise prices." [7] The other reason is the fame of one of the best known American examples of such gentlemen's conversations, the so-called Gary Dinners, where the leaders of the steel industry met from time to time, during the years 1907–1911, to discuss—for "merriment and diversion"—by way of after-dinner speeches, the market situation and the most appropriate prices for their products. Since price-fixing agreements were unlawful in the United States, those gentlemen believed themselves to be within the law when they avoided formal agreements. But if the main speaker submitted that the market situation warranted,

[6] Judge Gary of the United States Steel Corporation once explained that "close communication and contact" among the members of his industry had created such mutual "respect and affectionate regard" that they regarded themselves as honor-bound to protect one another and that each felt that this moral obligation was "more binding on him than any written or verbal contract." *United States* v. *United States Steel Corporation, Brief for the United States,* II, p. 989.

[7] Adam Smith, *An Inquiry into the Nature and Causes of the Wealth of Nations* (publ. 1776, Routledge ed. 1903), p. 102.

in his humble opinion, a price of so and so many dollars, and if the next speakers expressed their belief that the main speaker, who incidentally was usually the biggest steel boss, had shown perfect understanding of the situation and that they saw eye to eye with him, the dinner party was likely to be a lasting success (giving indigestion only to the non-invited public).

Trade Associations, Cost Calculations and Statistics

Price agreements can be couched in such terms that no agreement is voiced and no price is mentioned. The "correct" price can be computed from some announced basic formulas containing assumed "average" cost figures, "customary" charges, "regular" percentages for overhead and profit. The whole scheme is then offered as a code to sell at "cost plus fair profit," which is represented as the only "fair," indeed the only "ethical," thing to do. These "cost" figures are, of course, mere conventions. Trade associations often consider it their duty to help their members in the observance of "ethics" and in the calculation of the "cost," and they supply them with all the necessary information, keys and instructions. These thinly concealed forms of collusion are very widespread, almost ubiquitous, and in public opinion as well as in the practice of the courts they are regarded as reasonable and fair policies.[8]

Apart from the guidance that trade associations give their members in the "fair" calculation of cost, they may influence members' price and production policies through some meaningful "statistical" services. In at least one case a "Statistical Committee" of a trade association was abolished by court action, and the association and its members were enjoined from distributing statistical information on production, sales, orders, and prices as part of a scheme to reduce competition among the firms.[9] Statistical services of this sort are by no means rare in trade associations.

[8] Thurman W. Arnold, then Assistant Attorney General in charge of the Antitrust Division, said in his 1942 testimony before the Senate Committee on Patents: "That idea of a fair cost is one of the most frequent things we find in American industry. . . . It is a typical cartel agreement. They want to be sure that no one really competes." *Hearings of the Senate Committee on Patents on S. 2303*, Part 2 (Washington, 1942), p. 974.

[9] The Court enjoined the Glass Container Association and its members

A special type of trade association, praised as something like a stream-lined model of fairness in competition, is the *open-price association*.[10] The official aim of open-price associations is the fullest publicity for prices and transactions. Each member reports its prices and transactions to the association, which in turn disseminates this important information to all members. This practice purportedly permits the perfect knowledge of the market that is said to be a prerequisite of a perfectly competitive market; in actual fact it is singularly adapted to achieve "concerted action with respect to prices" [11] on the part of the "competing" members of the association. The similarity between price-fixing agreements and open-price agreements is particularly obvious in cases where "waiting periods" are provided, binding each competitor to maintain his old price until a certain time after he announces openly a new price. Thus each seller can be confident that none of his competitors will get the jump on him and they all will maintain their prices and resist downward pressure with greater assurance.[12]

But even without waiting periods the open-price system is very effective in lowering the degree of competition, especially if the participating firms are honest and trust one another. If each firm is confident that its competitors do not grant secret discounts or refunds (and do not count thirteen pieces as a dozen or 2100 pounds as a ton, and do not call their first quality second, etc.)

---

from agreeing "to collect, compile, analyse, or distribute data concerning the production, sales, orders, shipments, deliveries, costs, or prices of glassware or of machinery used in the manufacture of glassware, where there is a disclosure of data concerning any particular manufacturer or where the purpose or effect is to coerce or intentionally persuade any manufacturer to limit or control production or to fix, raise, or maintain the price of glassware or of such machinery." *United States* v. *Hartford-Empire Company et al.* (Northern District of Ohio), 46 F. Supp. 541 (1942). See also Supreme Court 323 U.S. 392 (1945).

[10] First advocated by Arthur Jerome Eddy, *The New Competition* (Chicago: A. C. McClury & Co., 1913).

[11] These are the words used by the Supreme Court in 1925 in its decision in the case *Maple Flooring Manufacturers Association* v. *United States* (268 U.S. 563, 586). In this decision, however, the Court paradoxically held that the open-price system would not result in concerted action.

[12] The Federal Trade Commission in its Report on *Open-Price Associations* (Senate Document 226, 70th Congress, 2nd session, 1929) reported on no less than 1103 such associations, of which 975 were interstate.

they will all firmly stick to their announced prices and see their sales volume shrink rather than start "chiseling."

Delivered-Price Formulas

The most effective reduction, or elimination, of price competition can be achieved if the products of rival manufacturers are standardized and are offered at identical delivered prices, regardless of the location of the individual manufacturer. Where freight costs are small relative to the value of the goods, the manufacturers can absorb these costs and offer the product at a uniform price all over the country. Where freight costs are more important, the producers may agree on *zone-prices*. Under such a system all producers charge identical delivered prices, not uniform for the whole country but uniform for all destinations within the same zone. (The agreement, of course, need not be formal. It is enough if all sellers follow automatically the price announcements of a leader.)

Where the freight costs are a very substantial part of the price, zone prices become inconvenient. It is then better to have a separate price for each destination. But how can it be arranged that all sellers always quote an identical price, as is required if price competition is to be eliminated? That they communicate with one another on every order for which they are invited to bid would not be practicable (nor would it be advisable under the antitrust laws). The solution for this problem was the so-called *basing-point system*. "The basing-point technique of pricing makes it possible for any number of sellers, no matter where they are located and without any communication with each other, to quote identical delivered prices for any quantity of the product in standardized qualities and specifications, going to any of the 60,000 or more possible destinations in the United States. It is only necessary that one or a few 'base prices' governing the entire industry be announced. All competitors can then use the formula 'applicable base price *plus* specified extra charge *plus* applicable railroad freight.' Depending on whether it is a 'single basing-point system,' a 'multiple basing-point system,' or a 'plenary basing-point system,' there will be either one basing-point for deliveries to all destinations or a number of basing-points of which the one 'governing' a particular destination can be found by a simple rule." [13]

It should be mentioned that some such pricing schemes as the basing-point system work best if the manufacturers exclude dealers and middlemen and sell directly to the consumers. If there were wholesale dealers with large stocks, it might be difficult to supervise the delivered prices and avoid frequent "outbreaks" of price competition.

Cartels with Enforcement Apparatus

Formal price-fixing agreements, informal gentlemen's agreements, price recommendations and "cost calculations" of trade associations and institutes, open-price associations, delivered-price systems, and similar collusive arrangements often work without any enforcement mechanism. The conditions of success for these schemes—success for the sellers, of course, at the expense of consumers—are not present in all lines of industry and trade. One of the conditions is that the members of the industry be reasonably reliable and observe the "ethical code" of their business, for if there is too much cheating and chiseling, the fixed or recommended prices will not be maintained. Another condition is that the production volume in the industry be currently adjusted to the inflow of orders, for if production is not "to order" or not geared to the volume of orders which come to hand at the fixed prices,

[13] Fritz Machlup, *The Basing-Point System* (Philadelphia: The Blakiston Company, 1949), p. 7. Many defenders of the basing-point system have denied that it is necessarily a collusive scheme. They are right. "It is conceivable, for example, that a firm might devise such a formula for use by its own employees in its sales department even though no other firm was making use of the same formula. For example, a firm may have several plants located in different regions. The price list of the firm may indicate that delivered prices are calculated by adding to the listed base prices the lowest freight from any of the establishments of the firm to the destination. These delivered prices may apply no matter from which plant delivery is made. The firm, finding that the closest plant cannot fill the order at the particular time, may assign delivery of the order to one of its other plants. This is, in a sense, a basing-point method of pricing. But if it is only used in one firm and not by any of its competitors, the practice is not part of a plan or scheme generally used within the industry for the purpose of quoting identical delivered prices" (*Ibid.*, pp. 19–20). But "if the system is used by competitors with mutual knowledge, it constitutes a cartel, a scheme to limit or eliminate price competition among the participants." *Ibid.*, p. 20.

these prices will not stand up against the pressure of accumulating
unsold stocks.

If the first of these two conditions is absent, a strict control of
all sales or sometimes even a centralized selling organization will
be needed for the maintenance of the monopoly price. If the second condition is absent, a control of sales quota or of production
volumes or both will be needed. Certain pools and cartels provide
for these controls, that is, in the favorite language of the advocates
of monopoly, they include the necessary devices to secure "orderly
marketing" in an otherwise "chaotic" industry.[14] The kind of apparatus for checking on compliance and providing for enforcement
and sanctions depends of course on the laws of the country.
"Straight" cartel agreements were most customary in Germany,
where they were legal and enforceable, and even fostered by the
government.[15] In countries where the courts would not enforce
cartel agreements, the agreements usually provided for private
arbitration of all disputes and for the potential forfeit of blocked
deposits held by trustees to secure payment of penalties for con-
traventions. In countries where straight agreements in restraint
of trade were unlawful, subterfuges had to be found. Patent agreements were the most efficient instruments of cartels. *Patent licence contracts* could be most conveniently used for stipulating

[14] Some writers distinguish between pools and cartels. Perhaps a difference can be found to exist in the time element: the cartel is usually intended to
be a long-term affair while the pool may not have such high ambitions. But
few writers accept this distinction. Until some ten years ago many organizations would be called pools if they were in America or England, and cartels
if they were on the European continent. In the meantime, however, the word
cartel has become more widely accepted in the English-speaking world in professional as well as in popular literature. A few writers have used the word
cartel only for international business agreements. There is no reason for this
narrow use of the word. In smaller countries perhaps the larger number of
business agreements among competitors include foreign members and are
therefore international cartels. But in larger countries domestic cartels will be
more numerous than international cartels, although the economic significance
of the latter is considerable. For recent studies on international cartels see
George W. Stocking and Myron W. Watkins, *Cartels or Competition* (New
York: Twentieth Century Fund, 1948) and Corwin Edwards' monograph
cited above in footnote 1 on page 82.

[15] As early as 1901 there existed 450 cartels in Germany. See *Hearings of
the Senate Committee on Patents on S. 2303, Part 3* (Washington, 1942),
p. 1274.

all sorts of restrictions relating to selling prices, markets and marketing channels, output qualities and output volumes, and many other matters.

Cartel arrangements in the form of restricted patent licences are popular not only in countries where cartels by straight agreement are against the law but also in countries where such agreements are legal but not enforced by the courts. It is relatively simple to sue for infringement of a patent. If the cartel agreement is in the form of a patent licence, the licensee has acknowledged the validity of the patent and he becomes automatically an "infringer" when the patent licence is terminated because of his failure to perform in accordance with all its provisions.[16] Industries which do not make any patentable products and do not use any patentable processes must resort to other forms of cartelization. For instance, *trade-mark agreements* have been used as the instrument of international cartel arrangements concerning branded goods, especially where territorial divisions of markets were desired, and the trade-mark laws for the enforcement of the arrangements.

Great difficulties of supervision and enforcement have long beset cartel agreements in retailing, especially in countries where price fixing is illegal. In the retailing of branded articles the difficulties are reduced if the producer is willing to fix and insist on uniform resale prices and if the law is changed to make *resale price maintenance* legally permissible and enforceable. This has been done in the United States. Back in 1922 the Supreme Court of the United States declared that retail price fixing by agreement between manufacturer and distributor, then known as the "Beechnut system of merchandising," was illegal because it suppressed competition and hence violated the antitrust laws.[17] But then, under the organized pressure of distributor groups, aided by some manufacturers, the legislatures in 43 of the 48 states and, with respect to interstate commerce, the Congress of the United States, saw fit to permit, by enacting resale-price-maintenance laws, the abolition of price competition among retail dealers of brand-named or trade-marked goods.

[16] Cf. my chapter on "The Nature of the International Cartel Problem," in *A Cartel Policy for the United Nations*, p. 8.

[17] *Beechnut Packing Company* v. *United States,* 257 U.S. 441.

For these laws, which in plain language must be called "price-fixing laws," the legislators chose the euphemistic name "fair-trade laws."[18] Under these laws a manufacturer or wholesale distributor may fix minimum resale prices, discounts, and mark-ups for branded or trade-marked goods by a contract with the retailer. Indeed such price agreements are enforceable even against retailers who have not directly agreed: the manufacturer's contract with one distributor applies automatically to all of them.[19] No matter whether the cost of distribution is high or low—and it can certainly not be equal everywhere—the retail price fixed by the manufacturer must be maintained by all retailers under threat of penalties imposed by the courts.[20] Thus, the government has taken over the enforcement of these retailers' cartel agreements for branded articles.

The Contents of Cartel Arrangements

The more modest cartel agreements are confined to the *terms of sale*, such as discount, credit terms, cancellation rights. For the greater part, however, cartels are concerned with *prices*. Price cartels will rarely require the consent of all members of the cartel for each separate price change. Ordinarily this question is left to the decision of a small committee or of one price leader. Some-

[18] In the Hearings before the Temporary National Economic Committee, Mr. Wendell Berge, member of the Committee and Special Assistant to the Attorney General, stated that "through a vertical agreement [as legalized by the Fair Trade Act] in an industry you can accomplish what is forbidden [by anti-trust laws] if attempted horizontally." T.N.E.C. *Hearings,* Part 5 (Washington, D.C., 1939), p. 1763. The Federal Trade Commission has repeatedly expressed its opposition to this legislation for retail price fixing. See its Report on *Resale Price Maintenance,* transmitted to the House of Representatives, January 30, 1939.

[19] In 1951 the Supreme Court declared that the Federal law did not extend to state enforcement of price fixing agreements against price-cutting retailers who had not signed the agreements. But in 1952 Congress amended the law and legalized state enforcement of the price fixing schemes.

[20] It may be well to explain that if for many years you paid only 39 cents for a 50-cent tube of tooth paste you were not buying at a cut rate. The minimum contract price was "list price minus 20 per cent minus 1 cent." A cut rate, below 39 cents, would have been in violation of the contract and, thus, of the fair-trade law.

times different firms act as price leaders for particular types or qualities of product or for particular markets.

In less formal price cartels without "organs" and enforcement apparatus, the sanctions for underbidding may consist merely in the "social disapproval" of the "unethical conduct" by the offender; where the group contains financially stronger members, sanctions may be imposed in the form of retaliatory measures. In more formal price cartels, with secretariats, staff, committees, or separate agents, the advisory, supervisory, and enforcement functions may be much more elaborate.

By *dividing the markets* among the "would-not-be competitors," giving each relatively free reign in his own sheltered territory, price agreements may be rendered unnecessary, or less necessary. Each "competitor" becomes a monopolist in the narrower sense of the word—or almost such a monopolist—in his territory.

Division of the markets may be geographical, functional, or technological. Geographical division is most frequent in international cartels. Functional division is accomplished if each cartel member is allowed to serve only particular categories of customers. Technological division of the market refers chiefly to restrictions upon the field in or purpose for which the products or processes of production may be used by each concern. This method, especially adapted to patent licensing contracts, sometimes operates to reduce existing competition, but more often to forestall potential competition.

In some instances of territorial division of the market each member has his own territory to himself, with no "overlapping" and sharing; in other cases there may be a distinction between "reserve territories," "free territories" (into which all members are free to sell) and "pay territories" (into which all members may sell upon payment of certain commissions or "duties" into a general fund to be distributed periodically among all or particular members).[21] The division of territories, which eliminates or dimin-

---

[21] For illustrations of all sorts of pools by actual cases in American industries see Charles S. Tippetts and Shaw Livermore, *Business Organization and Control* (New York: D. Van Nostrand Company, 1932), pp. 300–307.

ishes competition in each of the regional markets, may be used either as a substitute for price agreements or as a method of supplementing and reenforcing price agreements and of preventing "reckless" unrestricted production. Where the producer is wide-awake to the limitations of the demand for his product he will not underestimate the effect his unrestricted output may have on the market situation and he will be more likely to try to hold his production down to the rate at which orders at the fixed price come to hand.

More direct output controls are exercised by quota cartels or "output syndicates." The member firms are allotted quotas constituting the maximum output volumes permissible, either in absolute or in relative figures. Although absolute production quotas might often work more reliably, relative quotas, e.g. percentage shares in the total sales of the industry, are more readily accepted by the members when they, after vigorous struggles for large shares in the market, join the restriction scheme. Sanctions may be provided for firms whose sales exceed their quota; usually these firms have to pay penalties for their excess sales into a fund which is distributed among those whose sales fall short of their quotas.

In some cases cartel quotas are transferable among members, so that firms wishing to operate on a larger scale may purchase the quotas of members who decide to close down temporarily. Sometimes the members of the syndicate may decide to pay curtailment subsidies or "shut-down compensations" to firms which are prepared to reduce their production or to close down for a time, thereby allowing the other producers to work at a higher per cent of their capacity. (Since such practices would constitute unlawful restraint of trade in the United States, American industrialists have accomplished the same objective by buying up whole plants or firms rather than by buying their abstinence from production. On the European continent shut-down compensations have been quite common.)

Profit Pools and Average Price Cartels

There are too many types of pools and cartels to permit of anything approaching a complete survey here. A few more types, however, though not frequent, are interesting. The *profits pool,* which provides that all net-earnings be paid into a general fund to be redistributed among the members according to a predetermined plan, is sometimes a device adopted in order to win over to the cartel idea some stubborn producers who have qualms that they might be at a disadvantage against other firms in the pool or cartel. Another purpose served by profits pools may be the "just" distribution of the excess income from price discrimination. If the pool abolishes competition for the orders from customers who could afford to pay higher prices, and so makes the exaction of these higher prices possible, a method of avoiding jealousy among the members over their shares in the high-price business will prove necessary. Pooling the profits may prevent jealousies which could easily disrupt the whole organization.

The same objective—to avoid jealousy and to distribute good orders and less satisfactory business equitably among the members—can be accomplished by *average price cartels.* Skilful exploitation of the market calls for price discrimination and, in order to avoid a struggle for the better orders, the members may agree to pool all receipts, to compute a weighted average of prices and remunerate every producer on the basis of the resulting average price. This averaging of all obtained prices is useful also when the cartel finds it expedient to change selling prices during the year. Assumed that prices had to be lowered in the second half of the year, firms which were ahead in their sales quota would get a greater share of the better-priced business than firms who caught up only during the latter part of the year. An annual averaging can take care of both price discrimination and price fluctuation through time. Schemes of this sort, however, have proved to be rather intricate and prolific of quarrels and dissatisfaction among the participants.[22]

[22] The writer was at one time in charge of the average price computation of a cartel in Austria. The experiences with this scheme were not altogether happy. Among better known examples of average-price cartels were the coal, iron, and steel syndicates in Germany: Rheinisch Westfälisches Kohlensyndikat (started in 1893), Oberschlesisches Roheisensyndikat (1901), Stahlwerksverband A.G., Düsseldorf (1901).

Centralized Selling

In all of the forms of pools, cartels or syndicates mentioned the firms may do their selling individually and independently or they may do it through a common sales agency. Where a common sales agency is established by formal agreement, one speaks of a selling cartel or syndicate. If the formation of a common or united sales agency implies that all firms must give up their own sales organizations, there will usually be considerable resistance on the part of producers who are afraid of losing valuable market connections, difficult and costly to recover later in the event the cartel should eventually fail. On the other hand, the single sales agency for the whole group will be almost a necessary condition for the lasting success of a cartel if the industry produces a standardized material and consists of a large number of small firms whose so-called business "ethics" is not high and who are without powerful leaders.

OPPRESSION, DOMINATION, MERGER, CONCENTRATION

The relationship between our second and third categories of monopolistic policies (p. 37) is not entirely one of contrast and substitutability but partly one of commixture and complementarity. In plain language, it is not always "either one or the other," but often "one with the other." In some instances the choice "cartel or trust," or "cartel or merger," may aptly characterize the historical development, but "cartel among merger-grown corporations" is often the formula that better fits the facts. In some instances "voluntary cooperation among equals" and "domination of the giant over the weak" may be true opposites, but more often cooperation develops into domination or domination into cooperation, and in most industries the two coexist in various blends.

Manifold Interrelationships, Warfare and Cooperation

Even within the compass of our third category the relationships are somewhat complicated. The four words in our label of the category—oppression, domination, merger, concentration—need not indicate either alternatives or complements; there may be all sorts of causal and historical relationships among them. Oppressive practices may be used by a firm *vis-à-vis* its competitors for several years, leading to a period of peaceful cooperation among the firms with one of them holding a dominating position; eventually weaker firms may be merged with the stronger, and this results in a high degree of concentration of control in the industry. Or the oppressive practices may lead directly to merger, the merger-grown corporations acquiring enough control to dominate other firms in the industry. Oppressive practices may or may not continue after domination is achieved. Or oppressive practices may be no part of the picture at any time, cooperation being initiated without prior struggle; this cooperation may lead to domination with or without eventual mergers, or to mergers with or without eventual domination over the remaining independent firms in the industry. It is also possible that neither oppression, nor domination by one of the competitors, nor cooperation among the competitors exists in the beginning and that instead outside-operators, such as financial groups, initiate a number of mergers, and a high degree of concentration of control in the industry results.

We recall the distinction between the uses of monopolistic practices for the creation, increase, maintenance, or exploitation of monopolistic power. Contrary to the opinion of some lawmakers, there can be no oppressive or predatory practices to "create" monopoly power, because no one who does not already have some such power could do anything oppressive to others. A modicum of monopoly power is needed before any action of an individual firm can have appreciable effects upon others. The general aims of oppressive business practices are to maintain existing monopoly positions and to strengthen them.

Lawyers who have not yet arrived at a "relative" concept of monopoly—as something which can exist in various degrees, ranging from very low to very high—have stressed, almost to the exclusion of other aspects, the importance of predatory practices for the "creation" of a monopoly. Price discrimination in the form of local price cutting, deliberate "cut-throat competition," was for many years regarded as the very prototype of monopolistic practice. This was probably due to the fact that early public discussion and court proceedings directed the limelight of legal and economic monopoly investigations in the United States toward the then-notorious monopolistic practices of the oil and tobacco industries.

The facts in the Standard Oil case go back to the period from 1870 to 1901; the court proceedings to the period from 1892 to 1911; but in most textbook discussions of "monopoly" the Standard case has remained the standard case ever since. Cut-throat competition was the main weapon in the "creation" (correctly: "strengthening") of monopoly in the oil case; the local price cutting, which was to ruin the small independent companies or to force them to terms, was practiced by the big company itself or, in order to deceive the public and the law, through "bogus independents." The practice was successful if the competing company was forced out of business or forced to conclude a price agreement or forced to follow the leader's price policy or forced to enter a still closer combination with the large concern—selling out to it or merging with it by joining a "trust" or by being absorbed in a holding company.

These violent practices were not the essence of the monopoly positions which they helped create. The early history of American monopoly was a history of *economic warfare*. For this reason the American public failed to recognize the old song when the words changed and monopoly became largely a matter of *economic co-operation*. Price agreements, selling pools, trusts, mergers and all the rest need not be different in effect whether they are the result of force, threat, persuasion, mutual interest, voluntary cooperation or professional ethics. The substitution of peaceful monopolization for belligerent monopolization makes little difference to the consuming public. Indeed, the public may have been worse off when the periods of "wars of extermination" were followed by periods of gentle "follow-the-leader" or "live-and-let-live" policies; as an eminent student of the monopoly problem once said, "monopoly had learned to 'say it with flowers' and make the public pay the florist's bill." [23]

[23] Frank A. Fetter, *The Masquerade of Monopoly*, p. 53.

Oppressive Practices

A firm resorting to oppressive practices *vis-à-vis* its competitors in order to strengthen its monopolistic position may have its sights on a variety of objectives. For example, it may attempt to

(a) reduce the competitors' business volume absolutely,

(b) keep competitors from growing, or from growing faster, and thus reduce their relative shares in the total business,

(c) favor some firms at the expense of others, thereby promoting a balance of power facilitating greater control over prices and output,

(d) coerce competitors to accept its price leads and to desist from price cutting,

(e) impress competitors with the futility of vigorous competition and the desirability of cooperation,

(f) induce competitors to sell either their corporate control or assets,

(g) force competitors out of business.

The first three aims merely concern a change in the balance of power within the industry, either for the sake of attaining a greater freedom of choice in price and marketing decisions or for the sake of preparing the ground from which to launch further attacks. The next two aims (d and e) are restrained competition and collusive arrangements. Here we see a close connection between monopolistic practices of the third category, oppressive in this case, and those of the second category, involving cooperation and cartel activities. It is the pattern of "a war to end all wars" or of predatory competition to replace vigorous competition by restrained competition. The last two aims (f and g) are to remove competitors from the scene, either by absorbing or by eliminating their productive capacity.

It is very hard in practice to set up and apply criteria to distinguish vigorous competition from oppressive or predatory competitive practices. Thus, if a struggle between competitors ends with the complete elimination of one of them, it is difficult to establish whether he succumbed to superior efficiency or to an expensive assault with intent to kill. If, however, a competitive struggle ends with a merger between the rival firms and with continued operation of their productive facilities, the presumption that it was a cut-throat battle of oppression rather than a forthright battle of efficiency is stronger. In other words, where the productive capacity of one of the firms is eliminated the contention that it was too inefficient is more plausible than in instances where it is taken over by another firm which thereby increases its control over prices and output. To put it in somewhat frivolous terms, a shot-gun marriage between competitors smells more strongly of monopolistic practice than a shot-gun killing.

What makes competitive actions "oppressive practices"? What test is there for us to say whether competition is vigorous (a Good thing) or predatory (a Bad thing) in a particular case? In the absence of a book of rules, how can we decide whether the fight is fair or foul? The loser is always inclined to shout "foul" and the winner to have an air of self-righteousness. How can competition be refereed and by what standards?

We shall defer most of the discussion of these questions until the next chapter when we talk about "Unfair Competition." But the fundamental principle of the answers can be given here. We have seen that the basic "merits" of competition lie in its contribution to economic efficiency (optimum allocation of productive resources) and dispersion of power. Competition resulting in the elimination of firms because they are less efficient serves one of the functions assigned to it. Competition leading to greater concentration of control without an increase in efficiency does not. Ideally, competition benefits the consumer in all its phases; during the competitors' struggle as well as after the disappearance of the inefficient and the expansion of the efficient producer. Not so if a financially stronger firm drives a financially weaker competitor out of business by "competitive" practices without being economically more efficient in the sense that it can make more output with given resources. This stronger firm finances its competitive campaign out of its capital (or out of its earnings from other activities); it succeeds not because it is more efficient in producing the goods and services with which it competes, but merely because it commands overwhelming financial strength. This is the kind of competition that is called oppressive or predatory and injurious to the public interest.

The trouble is that it is hard to find conclusive evidence of the predatory nature of competitive actions. Mere "selling below cost" need not be in the least oppressive in intent or character. With regard to certain types of price discrimination oppressiveness can be presumed, though the presumption is refutable. As the lawyers concerned with the provisions of the Clayton and Robinson-Patman Acts well know, these are matters defying definition. It is impossible to write into the law prohibitions which would not prohibit desirable kinds of competitive practices, and exemptions which would not exempt undesirable kinds of practices. With regard to a very large number of business practices, we are almost without any practical test evaluating their competitive or monopolistic character. The courts have struggled valiantly with these issues. We shall, in the section on Unfair Competition, present a long list of practices which at one time or other were declared illegal by the court because of their oppressive character. It is even uncertain whether the prohibitions of predatory competition have done more good or harm to the economy, because many firms, allegedly or actually afraid of the sanctions of the law, resort to "soft" or restrained competition in order to avoid charges of cut-throat competition, and therefore spare the inefficient competitors whose elimination would be justified in the interests of a more efficient economy.

One thing is certain: "injury to a competitor" or "injury to competitors" must not be mistaken for "injury to competition." Indeed, competition which is really beneficial to the public will as a rule be injurious to some, if not all, competitors. Unfortunately many legislators have allowed themselves to be persuaded to the erroneous belief that what is injurious to competitors is apt to be injurious to competition.

A clear case of injury to the public is that of a firm gaining a "competitive advantage" over its rivals by maliciously creating obstacles to their operations. The resulting increase in the procurement, production or selling costs of the competitors entails that society will get less product from given resources, a result exactly opposite to that traditionally ascribed to competition. "Competitive" practices designed to reduce the efficiency and increase the cost of the rivals are regarded by some economists as "monopolis-

tic" practices *par excellence*. Indeed there are some who see the
criterion of monopoly in the creation of artificially high cost to all
actual or potential competitors.

Domination

That a firm "dominates" an industry may mean no more and no
less than that it possesses a large degree of monopoly. In other
words, "domination" and "monopoly power" are sometimes so defined that they become synonyms. This is a waste of words, particularly since a word is needed to denote the relationship among
firms when one or more of them have a strong influence upon the
conduct of the others. Domination in this sense exists if a firm has
the power to impose its will upon others in the pricing and marketing of their products and services.

Monopoly power need not imply domination in this sense. The
"monopolist" in the narrowest sense of the word has no competitor
whom he can dominate. The so-called "monopolistic competitor"
has too insignificant a position in the market to dominate others.
Typically domination will occur in situations of "oligopoly," but
need not occur even there. This does not mean that it is a rare occurrence. Indeed, there are indications that domination exists in
a very large number of industries.

Two connotations which the word domination has to many,
the existence of a feeling of antagonism between dominating and
dominated firms and, still more, the existence of violence or struggle, must be rejected. There may or may not be a history of violence—oppressive practices—behind the dominating position of
a firm; in any case the domination, once achieved, may be perfectly peaceful, benign, or even friendly. More often than not, the
dominated firms feel that they are "protected" rather than "abused,"
and they are willing to support the dominating firms when the latter are under political attack.[24]

Peaceful and friendly domination contains of course a large
dose of collusion. Price leadership, the practice of one firm initiating price changes and others following suit, combines cooperation

[24] For an example, see my book on *The Basing-Point System,* p. 168.

and domination in different mixtures, depending on the motivations which the followers have for their continuing compliance. We shall come back to this in the next chapter.

Domination by outside-operators should again be mentioned. Such domination may be achieved by a holder of patents under which all firms in the industry must be licensed, by the lessor of machinery which is indispensable to producers in the field, by the supplier of a monopolistically controlled material needed by all processors, or by a financial institution exercising control over all or most corporations in the industry. Instances of all these types of outside domination have become well known through court cases and congressional investigations.

The Merger Movement

The often repeated statement that the monopolization of industry was accomplished in Europe through cartels and in the United States through mergers is probably exaggerated in that it underestimates the degree to which collusive practices are common among American business firms. (The underestimation is understandable since most of the collusive arrangements are secret or skilfully camouflaged.) But there can be no doubt about the fact that the merger movement has been relatively much more important in the United States than in Europe.

The chief reason for this was unquestionably the one-sidedness of the antitrust laws, which were relatively effective in prohibiting "loose-knit combinations"—agreements in restraint of trade—but entirely ineffective in preventing "close-knit combinations" in the form of mergers.[25] Additional reasons were in the corporation laws and in the tax systems. The corporate form of business facilitates changes in ownership and control, but because of peculiarities in the corporation laws and because of considerable differences in

[25] A classic example of this absurd legal situation is the Addyston Pipe and Steel case. In that case—*Addyston Pipe and Steel Co.* v. *U.S.* 175 U.S. 211 (1899)—six companies were enjoined from conspiring to fix prices in the sale of cast iron pipe. Subsequently they merged and became the largest manufacturer of cast iron pressure pipe in the country. See *Report of the Federal Trade Commission on the Merger Movement* (Washington, 1948), pp. 8–9.

the tax rates the development of the corporation in continental
Europe was hampered in comparison with its development in the
United States.

In any event, the merger movement in the United States was
phenomenal in its dimensions. Several tidal waves of mergers were
observed: the first from 1890 to 1904, a second between 1919 and
1921, a third between 1926 and 1929, and the most recent after
the close of World War II.[26] The methods by which the mergers
were accomplished changed over the years, chiefly in adjustment
to changes in the law and its judicial interpretation.

One early method of accomplishing a quick combination of
several independent firms was so much talked about that its name
became the name of the whole movement. The so-called trustee
device, the *trust agreement* by which in 1882 some forty different
oil companies were brought under a unified control, started the
nomenclature according to which trust-making and trust-busting
became almost identical with creating and breaking up monopoly
positions. The idea of the trust agreement was that stockholders of
corporations, the unified control of which was intended, turned
over their stock to trustees, receiving a trust certificate in return.
With the control over the companies in the hands of the trustees,
price policies, production policies and investment policies could
be wisely planned and perfectly coordinated.

When the courts in several cases declared that trust agreements
of the described sort were illegal, new forms of combination and
coordination were resorted to. *Interlocking of directorates* became
a very popular device for achieving coordination of policies on the
part of separate corporations. If the same men give instructions or
advice in several "competing" companies, competition among these
companies is not likely to be very vigorous. It should be noted,
however, that membership on the board of directors does not always involve a really "directing" function and that names sometimes appear on directorates for not much more than decorative

---

[26] Between 1940 and 1947 "more than 2,450 formerly independent manufacturing and mining companies have disappeared as a result of mergers and
acquisitions. . . . The asset value of these 2,450 firms amounted to $5.2 bil-
lion, or roughly 5.5 percent of the total of all manufacturing corporations in
the country during the wartime year of 1943." *Report of the Federal Trade
Commission on the Merger Movement*, p. 17.

purposes. The interlocking of directorates may involve, but need not involve, practices affecting the market control of the industry concerned.

The simplest, and at one time most popular, method of combining the control over several corporations is the *holding company*, a corporation whose chief assets are blocks of shares, sufficiently large to assure control, of other corporations. Here again the oil industry has played the role of the pioneer. It was in 1899 that the Standard Oil Company of New Jersey was founded, a holding company controlling the stock of over forty petroleum companies. Many industries followed Standard's example. The American Tobacco Company included over sixty concerns. The United States Steel Corporation, founded in 1901, welded twelve combinations, each composed of a number of formerly separate firms, into one organization, which thus comprised what once had been approximately two hundred independent managements operating more than 400 separate plants.[27]

[27] "In 1898 the Federal Steel Co. was incorporated as a consolidation of the Illinois Steel Co., the Lorain Steel Co., and the Minnesota Iron Co., the latter being one of the largest iron-ore concerns in the Lake Superior region with important rail and lake transportation facilities. At that time Federal Steel operated about 15 percent of the Nation's ingot capacity. In the following year, 1899, the National Steel Co. acquired several important steel-producing companies and had about 12 percent of the country's ingot capacity. Finally, in March 1900, the Carnegie Co. (New Jersey) was formed to take over the original Carnegie Steel Co., Ltd. and the H. C. Frick Coke Co. This consolidation operated about 18 percent of the country's ingot capacity. These three companies, each resulting from previous mergers, and together owning 45 percent of the ingot capacity of the Nation, were united in 1901 to form the United States Steel Corp. Together with these three steel ingot producers other fabricating firms were also merged. These included: (1) the American Tin Plate Co. which in itself was the merger of 36 companies in 1898 and operated about 75 percent of the Nation's tin plate capacity; (2) the American Steel & Wire Co. which was a merger of 19 companies in 1898 and operated about 80 percent of the Nation's wire and wire-products capacity; (3) the National Tube Co. which was a merger of 21 companies in 1899, operating about 85 percent of the production of iron and steel tubing; (4) the American Steel Hoop Co. which was a merger of 9 companies in 1899; (5) the American Sheet Co. which was a merger of 26 companies in 1900, producing flat rolled products; (6) the American Bridge Co. which merged 27 companies in 1900 and was reported to have held about 50 percent of the structural fabricating capacity of the country; and (7) the Shelby Steel Tube Co. which operated about two-thirds of the output of seamless tubing. Finally the United States Steel Corp. in the year of its inception also acquired the

There are of course several other methods of corporate combination. A merger between corporation A and corporation B can be accomplished by A acquiring B, by B acquiring A, or by both being acquired by C, the latter being either a holding company or also an operating company. For legal, financial and tax purposes it may make a serious difference whether the control over productive facilities is exercised by direct ownership or by holding enough shares of another corporation that owns the facilities, or perhaps by holding shares of a corporation that holds shares of a corporation that holds shares of a corporation that owns the real assets. But for the price and output effects of the combined control over productive assets the method by which it is achieved and maintained are less relevant.

The great significance of stock acquisitions by corporations lies in the relative ease with which combinations can be effected by this means. This device makes it unnecessary for a corporation which desires to acquire another corporation to buy up the whole firm; it can obtain full control by buying a portion of the corporate stock. It may have to acquire 51 per cent of the stock, but where not all the stock is "voting stock," or where the stock is fairly widely distributed, a much smaller percentage may secure control.[28] Often no liquid capital is needed for the stock purchase, for the seller may be willing to dispose of his shares in exchange for shares in the acquiring company.

The Sherman Antitrust law in the United States might have stopped the merger movement had the courts not allowed themselves to be persuaded that merger among competitors is per-

Lake Superior Consolidated Iron Mines Co. which owned the bulk of the Mesabi iron range." *The Iron and Steel Industry. Report of the Subcommittee on Study of Monopoly Power of the Committee on the Judiciary, House of Representatives.* Eighty-first Congress, Second Session, December 19, 1950. (Washington: 1950), pp. 45–6. (Misprints in the Report garbling the information on National Tube Co. are corrected here after consultation with the Department of Commerce.)

[28] A merger by which a corporation acquires 100 percent or close to 100 percent of the stock of another company is often called consolidation. This term is used also for the accounting practice of treating the assets and liabilities of a fully owned subsidiary as assets and liabilities of the parent company. In a third use consolidation means the legal acquisition of the assets and liquidation of the subsidiary corporation.

missible as long as it is "reasonable" and does not create a monopoly "in and of itself." [29] The Clayton Act later (1914) gave the Government power to forbid stock acquisitions where the effect may be "to substantially lessen competition" between the merged firms. But the result was merely that other methods of accomplishing mergers became more popular. Whereas in the early years of the merger movement the bulk of all mergers were in the form of *stock* acquisitions, later more mergers took the form of *asset* acquisitions.

Merger through asset acquisition is not quite as easy as through stock acquisition. That the managements of both corporations agree on the desirability of the transfer of the assets is not enough; to sell all its property a firm needs the consent of its stockholders. Where this is hard to obtain it may be necessary for the would-be buyer first to acquire enough stock to control the firm. But since, because of the prohibition of merger by stock acquisition, it was legally unsafe to leave it at that, the control was quickly used to accomplish the sale of the assets of the firm. This was the "*stock-first, assets-later*" method of merger. Corporations acquired the stock of other corporations even where this apparently violated the legal prohibition and then they voted the stock so as to accomplish merger of assets. The courts held that under the law (prior to the 1950 amendment) the Government had no power to order a "divestiture" of assets even if these assets had been acquired by way of an illegal acquisition of stock. This method was therefore a convenient detour around the obstacle which the law had meant to put in the way of mergers between competitors. But even this detour was not often necessary, because the "*completely-by-assets*" method, permissible because of the loophole in the law, was not always so difficult as it seemed. [30]

[29] The quoted words are famous phrases from Supreme Court decisions. The "rule of reason," pronounced in 1911 in the Standard Oil case but going back to an old common law case, confines illegality only to "unreasonable" restraint of trade. That a large combination is illegal if it is not "in and of itself" a monopoly, that is, if enough independent competitors are left, is a statement of the 1920 decision in the United States Steel case.

[30] The Department of Justice examined most of the mergers and acquisitions which took place in manufacturing industries during 1946–47; out of the several hundred mergers examined, it found that in less than ten percent of the cases was it essential for the acquiring company to buy the stock as a

Integration and Conglomeration

Mergers between competitors do not constitute the bulk of all corporate mergers; nor are they the only kind that is relevant to the problem of monopoly and competition. Three directions of expansion are usually distinguished in discussions of the growth of the business firm: horizontal integration, vertical integration, and diversification.

Integration of firms or establishments means different things to different people. It may mean technological integration, where the productive facilities are brought into physical contiguity, if not under the same roof; or administrative integration; or merely a loose coordination of financial control. Some who insist on using the term only in the narrowest—physical—sense, object to its use for mere combinations of management or control.[31] But in its most common use the term denotes the unification of administrative functions; this may or may not include technological integration.

Horizontal integration is the unification of the management of establishments producing the same products. Vertical integration unifies the management of establishments of which one uses (processes, fabricates, distributes) the products of the other. Diversification adds new lines of business to the production program of a firm. If the new product is so different from those previously produced that it is classified as belonging to a different industry—which is admittedly very arbitrary—one frequently speaks of the corporation as having become a "conglomerate." Acquisition of several firms engaged in very diverse industries is sometimes referred to as an "agglomeration."

If former competitors are brought together under unified corporate control, it is obvious that competition between them is reduced or eliminated. But not every case of horizontal integration is a case of merging former competitors. If a bread factory in Boston and a bread factory in San Francisco are merged, competition

necessary step in securing the assets. *Report of the Federal Trade Commission on the Merger Movement*, p. 6.

[31] Cf. Frank A. Fetter, *The Masquerade of Monopoly*, p. 354. Fetter contemptuously spoke of "integration without integrity" when he referred to people who gave technological illustrations for cases which in fact were only combinations of managerial or proprietary control. *Ibid.*, p. 88.

is not reduced, because there could not have been competition between them. A holding company controlling the street car systems of Philadelphia and of Buffalo may serve several purposes, proper or improper, but reduction of competition in the sale of their services cannot be among them. In many instances, however, horizontal integration involves reduction or elimination of competition in the markets in question.

Where corporate mergers effect vertical integration, how do they affect competition in the markets? In what ways may the merging of processors, fabricators or distributors with their sources of supply influence the degree of competition? In some instances there may be no effect at all, although there is a presumption that the market for the materials or products in question will become thinner and more sensitive if a part of the supply will not pass through it but will be assigned by administrative decision to a particular user. In other instances the administrative channeling of a part of the flow of supplies, the by-passing of the market, may severely affect other users' access to such supplies. If these supplies (or facilities or services) have been available to all comers, but after the merger are denied to competing users or offered to them only in a discriminatory fashion, the vertical integration may be instrumental in securing a dominating position for the concern.[32] Firms that are competitors of the integrated concern in the sale of the end product may be its customers as purchasers of necessary materials, services or intermediate products and they may become quite dependent on its good graces. The integrated concern through its influence upon prices in the different stages of production may be able to control "the operating margins of its customer-competitors"[33] and to squeeze them when they do not "behave."

Diversifying mergers may reduce competition in the markets

[32] Often the purpose of vertical integration may be "to assure the continued supply of parts, but the effect is to squeeze out those concerns unable to buy up their suppliers, and to concentrate the business in the hands of fewer integrated companies." Answers by the Attorney General to questions submitted by a Congressional committee. *United States versus Economic Concentration and Monopoly*. A Staff Report to the Monopoly Subcommittee of the Committee on Small Business, House of Representatives, 79th Congress (Washington, 1946), p. 250.

[33] Corwin D. Edwards, *Maintaining Competition: Requisites of a Governmental Policy* (New York: McGraw-Hill, 1949), p. 98.

for some products by linking the distribution of these products with others, in which the concern is in a stronger position. To be sure, tying arrangements and full-line forcing, devices by which the supply of certain products—in which the concern has a more or less monopolistic position—is restricted to those faithful customers who also patronize the concern as a supplier of other products—in the sale of which it would have to compete with other suppliers—may be attacked in court if they can be shown to reduce competition substantially. But the appearance of "compulsion" or "coercion" can be easily avoided; things can be arranged in a more subtle fashion and it may become a matter of "convenience" and "expediency" for most buyers to obtain all the products in question from the concern that can supply them together; thus, competitors not carrying the full line may be squeezed out of the market. There are also other methods, for example, exclusive-dealer arrangements, through which a diversified concern may gain competitive advantages over less diversified firms—advantages which are in no way connected with efficiency in the use of productive resources in the production and distribution of output.

Conglomerating mergers bringing together, under unified control, a variety of lines of business not connected by any technological or distributive links may affect the market position of the concern only by way of the increase in power that goes with the increase in size. Even if the concern, on the strength of its own share in the markets in which it buys or sells, should have no great influence over prices and other terms, it may acquire such influence as an adjunct of the power generated by sheer bigness. Some of this power comes from the special advantages which the big business concern has "in litigation, politics, public relations, and finance." [34] And by effectively exploiting its power the "giant en-

---

[34] Edwards explains this as follows: "The large concern has an advantage in the law courts because it can afford to use litigation systematically as a competitive weapon, not only where it stands to win the suits, but also where the costs and delays of litigation will embarrass its less powerful rivals. It can acquire unusual influence in politics through personal contacts and campaign contributions and through unremitting attention to the detail of all political matters which affect it. It can do much to manufacture its own reputation by large expenditures for direct and indirect advertising under the guidance of public relations counsel. It can attain a substantial degree of control over the sources of credit, for through affiliation with one or more great commercial

terprise can sap the vigor and attenuate the usefulness of competition" in many of the markets in which it deals.[35]

The United States Congress has recently (1950) closed two loopholes in the anti-merger provisions of the Clayton Act: the original provisions covered only merger by stock acquisition and only merger between firms in substantial competition with each other. Now mergers by asset acquisition and mergers between any two or more corporations can also be prevented if they may effect a substantial reduction of competition in any line of business in any section of the country. It is doubtful that the courts will interpret a mere increase in size of a corporate combine as likely to effect a substantial reduction of competition. How the potential effects of vertical integration will be judged is still an open question.[36] And what if a firm, looking toward vertical or horizontal integration, absorbs other firms one by one and if competition each time is only slightly reduced, although the eventual cumulative effect may be substantial? Moreover, it should not be impossible for ingenious businessmen and lawyers to invent new methods of achieving intercorporate control without corporate merger.[37]

---

banks it may have preferential access to funds and be protected against the calling of its loans when credit is overextended or its own position has become precarious; and through affiliation with one or more great investment banks it may command sympathetic underwriting service. Such financial affiliations may also be useful in imposing a handicap upon inconvenient rivals; for the affiliated bank is unlikely to extend or continue loans to competitors whose market policies are regarded as dangerous to the large enterprise, and the affiliated investment bank is unlikely to encourage security flotations by such rivals." *Ibid.*, pp. 102–104.

[35] *Ibid.*, p. 105.

[36] However, the Report of the House Judiciary Committee which accompanied the bill amending the Clayton Act referred specifically to vertical and conglomerate mergers as potential threats to competition: "If, for example, one or a number of raw-material producers purchases firms in a fabricating field (i.e., a 'forward vertical' acquisition), and if as a result thereof competition in that fabricating field is substantially lessened in any section of the country, the law would be violated, even though there did not exist any competition between the acquiring (raw material) and the acquired (fabricating) firms.

"The same principles would, of course, apply to backward vertical and conglomerate acquisitions and mergers." Report No. 1191, To accompany H.R. 2734, House of Representatives, 81st Congress, 1st Session, (August 4, 1949).

[37] Loan arrangements may figure among the possibilities: a firm may grant

Concentration

Prohibition of future mergers will not undo the mergers of the past or reverse their effects. The degree of concentration of control [38] that has resulted in particular industries from the unchecked merger activity between 1890 and 1950 will not be quickly affected by checks upon further mergers.

We must guard against the impression that the concentration of control is entirely the result of mergers. There is no *necessary* association between merger and concentration. If we refer to the concentration of control in particular industries, narrowly defined according to specific product classes, we must realize that only horizontal combinations contribute to such concentration, while vertical combinations and diversifications do not.[39] And just as there may be merger which does not result in concentration, there may be concentration which is not the result of merger. For if some firms grow by "internal expansion," i.e., by new construction of

a large loan, coupled with cash considerations, to another firm with the option of receiving payment of interest and principal in kind in the form of the debtor's product. There are probably many other methods of achieving results which used to be obtained through merger.

[38] Degree of concentration, it should be noted, is not easily defined and still less easily measured. The greatest difficulties lie in delimiting the industry whose total capacity (assets, sales, output, or employment) is to be examined and in obtaining the necessary data. But even if we were sure how to delimit the industry and if we were able to obtain all the data we want, there would still be the question of constructing a numerical index by which the concentration of control in the industry could be expressed in an unambiguous way. The customary indexes state the percentages of the industry totals (of assets, sales, output, or employment) that are accounted for by the largest four and the largest eight firms in the industry. Now, what will these measures show if the second largest four firms grow relatively faster than the four largest and also faster than most of the smaller firms? The largest four firms may then account for a smaller percentage, while the largest eight firms may account for a larger percentage of the industry than they did before this change occurred. "Concentration" will have increased and decreased at the same time, depending on how we look at it.

For measurements of the degrees of concentration in many industries and for a discussion of the main issues involved see below, Chapter 12.

[39] Unfortunately, an index measuring concentration in such an industry will still show an increase if it is computed on the basis of total assets, value added, or employment. Only if it is based on sales of output in the same stage of fabrication will the concentration index be unaffected by vertical integration.

productive facilities, while other firms fail to grow, or go out of business, the degree of concentration will become greater without any "external expansion," i.e., without any acquisition of existing productive facilities.

The part of the growth of individual firms that has been due to internal expansion and the part due to external expansion can be roughly calculated. But this does not imply that the causes for an increase in the degree of concentration of control in particular industries can be determined. Even if all expansion had been horizontal and without diversification—which is hardly ever true—a "calculation" of the increase in concentration attributable to merger could be made only on the basis of highly arbitrary assumptions. One would have to assume, for example, that all the firms that were absorbed by others would have survived as independent entities if they had not been absorbed, and would have neither grown nor declined. The result of a calculation on this basis would overestimate the role that merger has played in the increase in concentration if the absorbed companies, contrary to the assumption, would have disappeared in any case, or at least declined. On the other hand, the part that merger has played would be underestimated by the same procedure if the absorbed companies would themselves have grown relatively to the rest of the industry had they remained independent. Thus, the historian cannot say much about the actual "results" of past mergers that does not rest on judgments of a hypothetical nature, namely, on judgments as to what would have happened in the absence of the mergers.[40]

[40] Such judgment may be well founded. For example, the history of the concentration in the steel industry may be safely interpreted as a history of merger. For the early mergers see footnote 27 on p. 107. In 1945, the three largest companies owned 58.9 percent of the steel ingot capacity of the country. *Report of the Federal Trade Commission on the Concentration of Productive Facilities, 1947.* (Washington: 1949), p. 23. An analysis of the growth of fixed assets of these three companies, with a breakdown according to internal growth (new construction) and external growth (acquisition of assets of other firms), showed that such acquisitions (including initial acquisitions at the foundation of the companies) amounted to 20 percent of the total fixed assets of the United States Steel Corporation, to 30.4 percent of the Bethlehem Steel Corporation, and to 43 percent of the Republic Steel Corporation. (These figures were calculated by Gertrude Guyton Schroeder in her study "The Growth of the Major Basic Steel Companies, 1900–1948," which is part of a project financed by the Merrill Foundation and directed jointly by G. H.

The implications of the degree of concentration for the degree of competition are rather obvious. Given all other conditions, especially with regard to competition from products of other industries and competition from foreign products, an increase in the concentration of control in a particular industry implies a reduction of competition in the sale of its products. This is so for several reasons. First, the larger the percentage of capacity controlled by the largest firms the greater the dependence of the customers upon these firms; the customers cannot switch their patronage, because the rest of the firms in the industry could not take care of their needs. Second, the larger the degree of concentration the easier the conclusion and maintenance of informal alliances and tacit understandings among the largest producers. Third, the larger the degree of concentration the smaller the incentive of the small producers to pursue independent policies and to engage in price competition.

It has long been fashionable to explain the high degree of concentration of control in many industries by allegedly large economies of horizontal integration. These economies may relate to production, distribution, or administration. There is no evidence that merely administrative integration of separate establishments can effect large economies in manufacturing industry. (See above, Chapter 3, pp. 51 ff.) Economies of large-scale distribution apply only to a few industries. Can the existence of significant economies

---

Evans, Jr., and myself.) According to a computation of the Federal Trade Commission of the growth of steel companies between 1915 and 1945, 33.4 percent of the total increment in net assets of the Bethlehem Steel Corporation was due to acquisitions, while the corresponding figure for Republic Steel Corporation was no less than 63.8 percent. *Report of the Federal Trade Commission on the Merger Movement* (Washington: 1948), p. 72. Of course, the expansion of these concerns was for a large part vertical in direction and hence not always relevant to the final concentration of steel production capacity.

According to Professor George Stigler's testimony "all the largest steel firms . . . are the product of merger. Not one steel company has been able to add to its relative size as much as 4 percent of the ingot capacity of the industry in 50 years by attracting customers. Every firm that has gained four or more percent of the industry's capacity in this half century has done so by merger." *The Iron and Steel Industry. Hearings before the Subcommittee on Study of Monopoly Power*, Committee on the Judiciary, House of Representatives, 81st Congress, 2nd Session, Serial No. 14, Part 4B (Washington: 1950), p. 996.

of horizontal technological integration explain the high degrees of concentration attained in many industries?

Additional productive facilities newly constructed by an existing company may be technologically integrated with the previously existing facilities or they may be actually or potentially separate from them. The significant question (for the evaluation of the growth of firms and concentration of industry) is whether there is a sort of symbiosis between the productive facilities of a firm, in the sense that their "togetherness" makes them more productive, or whether they could just as well, without serious loss of efficiency, be completely apart or separately operated. In other words, the question is whether or not firms big enough to realize all advantages of large-scale production would have to be so big that a few of them could satisfy the entire demand for the product. If so, a high degree of concentration in such an industry would be fully explained as a requirement of technology.

Conditions of this sort seem to exist in a few industries, for example in the manufacturing of computing machines or of aircraft engines. Apparently they do not exist in a large number of industries in which the degree of concentration is extraordinarily high.

No matter whether high concentration is technologically conditioned or not, it certainly spells domination. And concentration is extremely high in American industry. According to recent studies, one third (measured by value) of all manufactured products in the United States is produced in industries in which four or less producers control 75 to 100 percent of production.[41]

RESTRICTIONS ON ENTRY

There are essentially four ways in which businessmen can restrict entry into the field of their operations. The insiders can keep out potential newcomers by

    (i) using the government to exclude them,
    (ii) discouraging them by threats of ruinous campaigns,

[41] *Competition and Monopoly in American Industry.* Monograph No. 21, prepared by Clair Wilcox, Temporary National Economic Committee (Washington: 1940), p. 116.

(iii) restricting their access to needed resources,
(iv) increasing the minimum size of the efficient unit of operation.

Governmental Barriers

The use of the power of the state to restrict entry into a market, industry, trade or profession raises problems over which economists have long been at loggerheads. Is it a matter for "economics,"
"sociology," or "politics" that certain groups within the economy
can get the government to undertake the protection of their special interests? Assuming that this protection is found upon critical
evaluation to be injurious to "general welfare" and the "public
interest," should one "blame" the *government* for the objectionable policies, or the particular economic *group* for prevailing upon
the government to intervene on their behalf, or the *people* at large
for their stupidity in tolerating such government policies? [42] No
attempt is made here to elaborate on these problems, although the
fact that separate chapters will be devoted to governmental policies may reveal some of the analytical inclinations of the writer.

The "practices" by which men in certain occupations, businessmen in certain industries, attempt to influence government to intervene in their behalf and protect them from newcomers' competition may, from some points of view, be regarded as "monopolistic
business practices." The financing and organizing of lobbies in the
legislatures, the pressures upon representatives and senators, the
distribution of "educational" literature, the attention to "public
relations," especially the creation and maintenance of sympathetic
attitudes of the press, and similar tasks may be counted among
monopolistic business practices inasmuch as they may be prerequisites, in a democratic country, for getting the government to under-

---

[42] For Marxian theorists the answer is clear: "capitalism" implies for them
that government is an instrument in the hands of the capitalists for the suppression of the masses. Hence, Marxians reject in their economic analysis
separation of business (read: bourgeois) and government. Libertarian economists, on the other hand, are inclined to separate the political problem of
what the government does from the economic problem of how businessmen
take advantage of it and from the sociological problem of how the people can
be befuddled about what is good for them.

take the acts by which competition is restricted. The protective measures taken by the government ordinarily prohibit entry except after onerous conditions are satisfied, dues, fees, or duties are paid, or special permits, certificates or licences are obtained. Numerous examples of governmental barriers against the entry of markets, industries, trades or occupations will be given in Chapters 7 and 8.

Monopolistic business practices in a more direct sense than in the case of business *getting* government to restrict competition are those practices by which business *uses* existing governmental institutions beyond the scope for which they were intended by government. The most obvious examples of such unduly extensive uses of exclusive devices are connected with patents for inventions. The use of the patent privilege beyond the intended scope of the patent monopoly granted by the government may be in three directions: as instrument of collusion, as instrument of domination, and as instrument for the exclusion of newcomers to the industry. The actual practices involved will often serve more than one of the purposes. For example, a patent pooling agreement which through its restrictive provisions achieves cartelization of its members may be closed to newcomers and therefore achieve effective protection of the insiders against any ambitions of others to break into the industry. Or, the accumulation of most of the fundamental patents in an industry in the hands of one firm may not only give that firm domination over all other members of the industry but it may also effectively insulate it against outsiders. Again, the use of patents, basic or not basic, of unquestionable or of doubtful validity, for harassing litigation may not only be a means of oppressing, subduing or eliminating financially weaker competitors, but at the same time constitute a powerful discouragement to anyone desirous of going into the same business.[43]

[43] "In reviewing the role that patents have played in radio development, one cannot help being depressed by the excessive litigation involved. The high cost of patent suits has played into the hands of the large corporations: the great electrical firms have operated patent factories in which a field is blanketed with applications, and suits are pressed aggressively against infringers." W. Rupert Maclaurin, *Invention and Innovation in the Radio Industry* (New York: Macmillan, 1949), p. 256.

Threats of Ruinous Campaigns

The last example, in which legal exclusive privileges are used chiefly for the purpose of causing unbearable expenses to weaker competitors, may be mentioned under more than one heading. Harassing litigation, on patents or otherwise, within an industry works as a warning to potential newcomers. The threat of ruinous campaigns of costly litigation may be enough to keep the most venturous would-be entrants away from the industry.

Harassing litigation, however, is not the only method of discouraging potential competitors. Periodic price wars, if they are sufficiently destructive, may serve the same purpose. This is not to say that every firm initiating a costly price war against weaker competitors actually thinks of the value which its campaign may have for it as a deterrent to any possible invaders of the field. Price wars are often more a matter of emotions than of rational deliberations with calculated risks and estimated chances of success. But there probably are instances of cut-throat competition where a strong competitor does pursue fairly definite aims and considers the effectiveness of his price policy as a deterrent to potential competitors along with its direct objective of weakening his existing competitors.

Even the "normal" pricing techniques that are practiced in an industry may be such as to involve inherent threats of ruin to entrepreneurs weighing the prospects of entering. The basing-point system is a case in point. Under this system the locational advantages of producers close to their customers are largely neutralized through so-called freight-equalization and no one can count on his regional business or is able to fight for it through price competition. Distant competitors, powerful concerns not minding the expense of large freight absorption, may go out to take as much as possible of the business in the natural market of a weaker competitor, forcing thereby the latter to seek unprofitable business in remote markets. This risk is a serious discouragement to outsiders considering entry into an industry using a basing-point system.[44]

[44] "The power of the large concerns to use the basing-point system of pricing and the inherent discriminatory selection of market territories for depressing, or even destroying, the profits of their small competitors must unquestionably act as a barrier to entry. No matter how promising the es-

The most drastic of all threats to potential newcomers is the threat of violence, the threat of physical damage to productive facilities and of personal injury to their operators. If this is included in a survey of monopolistic business practices, it is done so with the qualification that the initiative for these schemes of violence, in the instances of which I know, did not come from the businessmen in the trade but from racketeers organizing the "protection" of the businessmen for purposes of extortion. The "protective organizations" enforced compliance with price fixing schemes by dealing roughly with "chiselers" and newcomers and they "levied" heavy dues, sometimes in the form of participations in gross sales or profits, upon the members in good standing. The laundry and cleaning industries, the barber shop and shoe shine operators, and similar service trades in some regions of the United States have at times been known to operate under such monopolistic schemes imposed by gangs and rackets. Illegal trades, such as bootlegging, gambling and prostitution, are the more usual "victims" of these practices, with the government or police sometimes providing the double boon of official prohibition and unofficial protection.

Barred Access to Resources

There are usually some resources or services that are indispensable for producers in an industry. If it is possible to deny these resources or services to newcomers, insiders can thereby secure their own protection. Newcomers' access to strategic materials, machinery, transportation services, distribution channels, or financial accommodation may either be entirely barred or seriously hindered through discriminatory practices, often stemming from conspiratorial arrangements between the sources of supply and the insiders attempting to exclude new competitors.

---

tablishment of a new firm would look to enterprising outsiders on the basis of prospective costs and prevailing selling prices in the chosen territory, the possibility that the existing large concerns may at any time pay special attention to that territory and 'meet the competition' of the newcomer, leaving him only the chance of seeking business that calls for forbidding amounts of freight absorption, must ruin the best prospects." Machlup, *The Basing-Point System*, p. 167.

Complaints about barred access to strategic materials have frequently been publicized. At the end of the last century the printing type trust, for example, cornered the entire American supply of strip brass to make printers' rule, forcing an outsider to send to Germany for some of the material.[45] Where such practices involve conspiracy they are obviously unlawful—at least in normal times. Under war-emergency regulations, however, when direct controls are used, allocations of scarce materials are quite officially made in such a way that new competitors are excluded.

Cases in which machinery was refused to potential newcomers were known in the steel industry. Manufacturers of tin-plate had contracts with machine makers under which large cash subsidies were paid to the latter for their commitment not to supply any competitors. The annual subsidies became more expensive when new firms started to make machinery and also had to be paid off to keep them from equipping competitors.[46]

The most famous case in this category is the freight rate discrimination favoring the old Standard Oil Company at the expense of independent oil refiners. By playing one railroad against another, the oil trust got them to agree to pay large rebates on the freight bills of the trust as well as of the competitors—but to pay all these rebates to the trust. Under these circumstances, existing independents had a slim chance to survive, and newcomers no incentive to take up the business.[47]

Instances in which the use of the existing channels of distribution were denied to weaker competitors and to new competitors have been known in several industries, such as cigarettes,[48] newspapers, motion pictures, and dress patterns.[49] Needless to say, if it is known that a newcomer to an industry cannot count on having

---

[45] George L. Bolen, *The Plain Facts as to the Trusts and the Tariff* (New York: Macmillan, 1902), p. 36.

[46] *Ibid.*

[47] John Moody, *The Truth about the Trusts* (New York: Moody Publishing Co., 1904), p. 114.—I learn from Aaron Director of the University of Chicago that this story, though repeated in a host of books, cannot be substantiated by the available evidence.

[48] *Report of the Industrial Commission on Trusts and Industrial Combinations* (Washington: 1901), Vol. XIII, pp. 333–37.

[49] *Standard Fashion Co.* v. *Magrane-Houston Co.,* 258 U.S. 346 (1922).

access to the services of the wholesale or retail distributors in the field, there will be few newcomers—or none.

Denial of funds to newcomers is another method by which insiders in an industry or trade, in conspiracy with investment bankers and commercial bankers, have attempted to prevent new competition.

Bigger Minimum Size

Industries in which the smallest productive unit that can still be efficiently operated is very large are not readily entered by newcomers. This is so for several reasons: it takes enormous amounts of capital to put up a new unit; the establishment of a new unit may mean such a large addition to the existing capacity of the industry that the effect upon total supply may be more than the market can be expected to absorb without drastic price reductions; and the uncertainties involved in all this may appear forbidding. Thus, a large minimum size, or large optimum size, may be seen to be a sort of "natural" barrier to entry. This, however, is not always quite so natural as it may appear; it certainly is not always a requirement of technology. Some organizational features of an industry may increase the optimum size of the single firm far beyond technological requirements, and these organizational features may be gratuitous in the sense that the goods and services in question could be produced and distributed just as well (or almost as well) without them.

Some of the "institutions" of industry—trade practices, selling methods, etc.—have grown up without having been consciously devised by any individual member of the industry; others are the result of deliberate decisions, but even if they later proved to have monopolistic effects, they need not have been designed with these in mind. One may therefore hesitate to call practices monopolistic when only their incidental effects have turned out to be so. Yet, where no censures or accusations are implied, a discussion that fails to include unintentionally monopolistic business practices would be incomplete. Hence we call attention to some business practices which have had the effect of increasing the optimum size of

the individual firm in an industry far beyond technological requirements and, thus, of increasing the difficulties of newcomers
attempting to enter the field.

National advertising is one of these practices. There are many
products that can be made in small plants just as efficiently as in
large plants—or perhaps even more efficiently if account is taken
of transportation costs—but for which advertising expenses are so
heavy that it becomes practically impossible for small firms to
undertake them or for new firms to risk incurring them. The cost
of advertising a certain brand of a product on a nationwide scale
may be so high that only giant corporations with huge volumes of
output can take the risk. If the public taste after years of "condi-
tioning" becomes so dependent on advertising appeal that unadvertised brands, or little advertised brands, stand little chance with
the consumer, it becomes almost impossible for a new firm to enter
the field. The necessary investment in advertising becomes forbidding.

For a series of years the advertising expenditures of the three
biggest cigarette manufacturers were over $40,000,000 a year.[50]
"Such tremendous advertising," according to the Supreme Court,
is "a widely published warning that these companies possess and
know how to use a powerful offensive and defensive weapon
against new competition. New competition dare not enter such a
field, unless it be well supported by comparable national advertising. . . . Prevention of all potential competition is the natural
program for maintaining a monopoly here, rather than any program of actual exclusion."[51]

One of the most conspicuous methods of increasing the minimum size of the efficient business unit is the integration of the *distribution machinery* with the production apparatus. Small firms may
be fully as efficient as large firms as far as the physical production

---

[50] From 1935 to 1939 total advertising outlays of the three principal
tobacco companies were consistently over 40 million dollars. This "large-scale
advertising . . . has principally served as a means of achieving control over
prices and monopoly profits, while in turn protecting these prices and profits
against serious inroads from new firms . . . We may conclude that the key
to the monopoly problem in the cigarette industry is advertising." William H.
Nicholls, *Price Policies in the Cigarette Industry* (Nashville: Vanderbilt University Press, 1951), pp. 200–201.

[51] *American Tobacco Co.* v. *United States*, 328 U.S. 781, 797 (1946).

of merchandise is concerned, but if it is "necessary" for each firm to have its own distribution machinery with exclusive retail outlets in hundreds, or thousands, or even hundreds of thousands of localities, the possibility of small firms in such industries is effectively eliminated. This method of restricting newcomers' competition was tried unsuccessfully in some industries, while others have used it with full success. Attempts failed where the intent of exclusion was too obvious and the government intervened on behalf of unrestricted competition. A case in point was the attempt of a big Chicago newspaper to transform all newspaper vendors into their exclusive agents so that a competing paper would have to create its own distribution system. This scheme was stopped by the antitrust enforcement agencies. But in other industries the intent of the integration was either not obvious or originally not of a restrictive nature and the government allowed the system of exclusive selling outlets to develop into effective barriers against newcomers' competition.

The integration of retail distribution and production need not take the form of direct ownership or of corporate affiliation with the retail firms. Contractual arrangements may do the trick. If the existing producers have exclusive contracts with all dealers and agents in the business, no new producer can enter the field unless he is prepared to set up a complete organization for retailing his product. It may take a very large firm to do this, although apart from this a small firm could be a most efficient producer in this industry.

The increase of the optimum size through the practice of "integrating" retail distribution with production is sometimes accompanied by similar arrangements concerning the *servicing and repair work* for branded durable goods. If a product is sold over a wide territory, has to be periodically or occasionally serviced or repaired, and cannot conveniently and cheaply be returned for such work to the producing plant, a separate service and repair business must exist. To the extent to which the existing service and repair firms are either affiliated or contractually tied up with the existing producers, no new producer can enter the field without creating a whole new network of firms that can service and repair his product. Even where the minimum size of an efficient producing unit would be small enough to make it easy for new firms to be established, the task of setting up the organization for servicing and repairing their products may be so formidable that newcomers are practically barred from the industry.[52]

[52] The automobile industry is probably a good example for the issues under discussion, because all three factors mentioned as contributing to the increase of the minimum size of the efficient firm are prevalent there. In the physical production of automobiles a firm of relatively small size—relative to the large firms now in the industry—need not be less efficient than some of the biggest. Among the greatest difficulties confronting a newcomer in the industry— there has been only one surviving newcomer in the last thirty years—are the problems of national advertising, retail distribution and service and repair work.

To point to the monopolistic consequences of these business practices is not to contend that they are on balance injurious to the public interest and that "there ought to be a law against them." There are surely great advantages for the traveling automobilist in the fact that he finds an "authorized" repair station with parts and accessories for his make of car in almost every town or city through which he passes. Whether or not equally competent service could be had under a system without exclusive dealer arrangements I do not feel qualified to say.

CHAPTER 5

Monopolistic Business Practices:
Price Leadership, Discrimination,
Unfair Competition

Price Leadership: A Background of Merger, Domination, Coercion · Conformance without Pressure, Suasion or Collusion · Mutual Understanding between Leader and Followers · Four Types of Price Leadership

Price Discrimination: Definition · Monopoly Power as a Prerequisite · Classifications of Price Discrimination · Personal Discrimination · Group Discrimination · Consumer Location · Consumer Status · Product Use · Product Discrimination · Price Discrimination and the Public Interest

A Digression on Price Uniformity: A Symptom of Collusion or of Competition? · Necessary Distinctions · Implications of Price Identity and Uniformity

Unfair Competition: What is Unfair? · The Right to Compete · Economic Classification · Deception of the Consumer · Competition to Reduce Competition · No Harm to the Consumer

IN THE PRECEDING chapter numerous monopolistic business practices were described under headings corresponding to a classification attempted on an earlier page. Large complexes of monopolistic business practices which cut across the categories distinguished in that classification were reserved for discussion in the present chapter. These are the practices conveniently grouped under the headings "Price Leadership," "Price Discrimination" and "Unfair Competition." A digression on the implications of price uniformity will also be included in this chapter.

PRICE LEADERSHIP

A witness before an investigating committee of the Government once warned of "one of the most dangerous types of monopoly, the price-leader-type of monopoly. This type of monopoly is often beyond the pale of existing law, because you can't find any evidence of conspiracy or collusion." [1] He traced its development chiefly to "unrestricted merger" and to the dominant positions thereby acquired by large concerns in the industry. In any case it is clear that price leadership, which of course implies the existence of firms who follow the leader, can be a result of collusion among competitors as well as of domination by a strong concern.

A Background of Merger, Domination, Coercion

In most discussions leadership in certain fields is closely linked with domination of industries by merger-grown giant corporations and of coercive practices employed by them. There is, however, no reason for confining one's attention to those price-leadership positions which have grown out of the merger movement. After all, (1) firms can grow large without merger; and (2) firms can be price leaders without being large in terms of dollars of capital or carloads produced or men employed.

In connection with the first point it should be clear that a firm which has expanded only by adding newly constructed capacity can be just as large and just as powerful as a firm which has grown by acquiring existing capacity through merger and combination. Of course, one may wish to erect legal obstacles to growth through merger of existing firms, without opposing growth through creation of new plant capacity. But it should be understood that internal as well as external expansion can lead to the emergence of giant concerns, to concentration of market control and to positions of price leadership.

With regard to the second point—possible price leadership by small firms—the relativity of size should be borne in mind. Where the market is limited, territorially or otherwise, a small firm—small in terms of capital or other "objective" measures—may enjoy a dominant position. Thus, neither expansion nor merger nor growth of any sort need have been among the factors responsible for the

---

[1] *Investigation in the Concentration of Economic Power, Hearings before the Temporary National Economic Committee,* Part 5a (Washington, 1939), p. 1771, Testimony of W. J. Ballinger, Economic Advisor to the Federal Trade Commission.

monopolistic position and, in particular, for the leadership role of a firm.

Historically, to be sure,—and this is the reason for the usual color of the pictures presented—most cases of price leadership that have through court action or congressional investigation come to the attention of the public involved large-sized firms and, indeed, merger-grown firms.

Price leadership invites particular disapprobation if the "leader" enforces his will upon the "followers" by force, threat and intimidation. There are even cases, mostly in local trades, where the "forceful influences" are extra-economic, such as social boycott and similar sorts of moral suasion or acts of violence committed or threatened by racketeers and "protective societies." In larger industries the pressures, if there are any, are more likely to be threats of price wars, harassing litigation, and the like.

About the maintenance of price leadership in the steel industry with its basing-point prices the Federal Trade Commission has said: "The potential punishment for any serious attempt to violate the basing-point price system is price raiding, that soon brings the rebels to terms." [2] Although the existence of price leadership was admitted by the steel producers, the statement that "price raiding" or similar methods of punishment were used by the leaders in order to hold the followers in line has not remained unprotested. But even if someone were to prove that there was no determination on the part of the leaders to punish the bad boys who failed to obey, he could not prove that the good boys who did obey were free from fear of punishment for disobedience. It is a matter of record that punitive actions and threats of punitive action against recalcitrant members have occurred in several industries where price leadership existed and there is good evidence that price followers have operated under the impression that they would be harshly dealt with if they failed to "play the game 100 per cent." [3]

[2] Federal Trade Commission, "Monopoly and Competition in Steel," a report submitted to the Temporary National Economic Committee, in *Hearings before the Temporary National Economic Committee*, Part 5 (Washington, 1939), p. 2198.

[3] This phrase is part of the Supreme Court's description of price enforcement procedures employed by the leaders in the cement industry. *Federal Trade Commission* v. *The Cement Institute*, 333 U.S. 683 (1948).

Threats of patent litigation may be highly effective in securing compliance with the price scheme of the leader. In earlier years the Government prosecuted cases of patent-protected price leadership only if they were based on "bogus patents." For example, in the first cement case, in 1910, a bogus patent that had been employed for purposes of price enforcement was disallowed. It was only in 1940, after an envigorated Antitrust Division had attacked the use of *bona fide* patents on gasoline production for the enforcement of prices set by the leader, that the Supreme Court decided that the patent licensing device must not be used to suppress competition in marketing the product.[4]

Conformance without Pressure, Suasion or Collusion

The fact that price leadership has often been aided by enforcement schemes should not mislead us into believing that pressure upon the followers is necessary for the existence of price leadership. In many cases the "little fellows" pursue a follow-the-leader policy because this is in their own interest and secures them the highest possible net earnings quite apart from any punishment for non-conformance. Compliance with the leader's price policy, just as compliance with trade association rules or with "fair cost" rules, frequently becomes a matter of "business ethics"—which should be considered as one of the most popular cartel supports. This was recognized by the Supreme Court when it stated "that the phrase 'business ethics' is used to denote compliance with 'marketing policies and prevailing prices' of the . . . industry, which are the 'marketing policies and posted prices of the major . . . companies or the market leaders among them.' " [5]

"Enforced compliance" may be necessary during brief periods when there is—perhaps during a recession—a temporary temptation for the little fellow to step out on the leader; but normally acceptance of the prices set by the leader is to the small seller not only the most profitable but also the most natural thing to do. Indeed, there are industries where the small producer is in a position of quasi-pure competition: he is unable to sell anything at a

[4] *Ethyl Gasoline Corporation v. United States,* 309 U.S. 436 (1940).
[5] *Ethyl Gasoline Corporation v. United States,* 309 U.S. 436 (1940).

higher price but he can sell at the given price any quantity that he can produce with his capacity. He accepts the "market price" as beyond his control and it makes little difference to his position that this market price is not the result of the impersonal forces of "supply and demand" but the result of the price policy of one or two large producers in the industry.

This picture, however, fits only situations in which the leaders are very big and the followers very small. The individual follower, to correspond to this model, must be conscious of his own insignificance; if he thinks that an increase in his sales might hurt the business or the pride of the leader, he is no longer unconcerned about the reactions of the leader and the considerations behind his business decisions assume a different character. Where the size of the leader compared with that of his followers is not like that of a giant compared with dwarfs, the motives of the followers are likely to include a conscious desire to avoid price competition, and their decisions are probably made in deliberate compliance with a mutual understanding or a common course of action.

Mutual Understanding between Leader and Followers

That the petroleum industry for decades followed the Standard Oil companies in the purchase price of crude oil and in the selling price of gasoline; that the agricultural machine manufacturers for several years followed the price lead of the International Harvester Company; that the anthracite coal industry accepted for many years the prices set by the Philadelphia and Reading Company; that the prices of corn products were consistently the same as those set by the Corn Products Refining Company; that the price of newsprint in the Pacific Coast area followed the quotations of the Crown Zellerbach Corporation and in the rest of the United States the quotations of the International Paper Company; that fertilizer in the South was sold according to the price list of the Virginia-Carolina Chemical Company and in the North according to the price list of the American Agricultural Chemical Company; that the price of industrial alcohol conformed to the price announcements of the United States Industrial Alcohol Company; and that similar situations existed in the markets for non-ferrous metals, lead, crackers, canned salmon, and many other products,[6] can be satisfactorily explained only in terms of implicit or explicit understandings.[7] In some instances the existence of a mutual understanding between leader and follower can be clearly inferred from statements by parties involved; in other instances from the fact that periodic conferences were held between leaders and followers in order to "exchange information." [8]

For many years the firms concerned did not deny the existence of price leadership, indeed they were anxious to admit it in order that the identical price quotations by allegedly competing firms would not be attributed to outright price agreements. At that time the parties relied on the Supreme Court decision that "the fact that competitors may see proper in the exercise of their own judgment to follow the prices of another manufacturer does not establish any suppression of competition or show any sinister domination," [9] and on the hope that evidence of explicit understandings between the competitors would not be detected. The situation changed considerably when the Supreme Court decided that "the fixing of

[6] For case material on all of the above mentioned instances of price leadership see Chapter III of Arthur Robert Burns, *The Decline of Competition* (New York: McGraw-Hill, 1936), pp. 76–145.

[7] "The idea that the leader has had no intention of being followed, and the followers did not feel under the least obligation to follow his price leads, but merely found it most convenient to do so; the idea that the leader-follower relationship developed without any concerted action, never aided by moral suasion, never by threats, never by mutual understanding; the idea that out of such a casual relationship emerged the basing-point system with all its trimmings is just too absurd to be taken seriously." Fritz Machlup, *The Basing-Point System* (Philadelphia: Blakiston, 1949), pp. 129–30. It should be stated that most of the industries enumerated as examples of price leadership practiced more or less developed basing-point systems of delivered pricing.

[8] As an example of a revealing statement one may cite the observation made by the president of the National Petroleum Marketers Association to the effect that the Standard Oil Company was the "logical organization to take the initiative in making intelligent and constructive markets to conform properly with the laws of supply and demand," and the exclamation by an officer of the American Oil Men's Association that "It is God's blessing to the industry that they have a Standard Oil Company to set the price." Quoted from Federal Trade Commission, *Petroleum Industry; Prices, Profits, and Competition.* Senate, 70th Congress, 1st Session (Washington, 1928), pp. 230 and 231.

[9] *United States* v. *International Harvester Company,* 274 U.S. 693 (1927).

prices by one member of a group, pursuant to express delegation, acquiescence, or understanding, is just as illegal as the fixing of prices by direct, joint action." [10] There was still the possibility that direct evidence for the "express delegation" or for the "understanding" would be required before price leadership would be held an illegal combination. But then the Supreme Court stated that "It is enough to warrant a finding of a 'combination' within the meaning of the Sherman Act, if there is evidence that persons, with knowledge that concerted action was contemplated and invited, give adherence to and then participate in a scheme." [11] This sharply pointed up the collusive nature of most cases of price leadership.

This change in the legal standing of price leadership made it expedient for companies to deny the existence of price leadership in their field. The usual ways of "proving" or "disproving" that price leadership has existed in a particular field are peculiar in that each side tries to support its case by the same evidence: those who claim that price leadership has prevailed would point to the fact that, say, in 80 percent of all price changes one particular company had taken the initiative, while those who claim that no price leadership has existed would point to the fact that in 20 percent of all price changes firms other than the alleged leader had taken the lead. This "evidence" of course supports neither of the two claims unless it is supplemented by information on several other points. For example, if price changes were frequent—say, several times a week—and entirely anonymous [12] or at least not openly announced, and a count over a one-year period showed that the changes originated in twenty out of one hundred instances with various firms alleged to be followers, one would be inclined to question the allegation of price leadership. On the other hand, if prices had remained stable over long periods, with changes few and far between, and if the finding of the 80:20 ratio referred to a period of several years, one could take this as warranting a pre-

[10] *United States* v. *Masonite Corporation*, 316 U.S. 265, 276 (1942).

[11] *Federal Trade Commission* v. *Cement Institute*, 333 U.S. 683, 716 (1948).

[12] The anonymity must be real, as on the stock exchange. For if it were generally understood that, for example, the opening bid or offer each market day was normally made by the same firm, the conclusion of collusive price leadership would be inescapable.

sumption of leadership. The 20 percent might then be the exceptions that proved the rule. The very fact that prices remained stable over long periods would suggest that most of the members of the industry "hesitated" to take the lead, probably because they "normally" accepted the leadership of a particular firm, which chose to maintain its prices. A very "orderly market" without erratic fluctuations is usually the result of a collusive system.[13]

Four Types of Price Leadership

The legal significance of price leadership depends partly on the relation between the leader and his followers. Four types of relationship may be distinguished:

(1) The followers are very small producers who have no choice of prices; they cannot sell anything at prices above the price set by the leader (or above a price differing from it by a certain margin) but they can sell at this price all they care to produce; hence, they would never think of selling at a lower price.

(2) The followers have a choice of prices in the sense that they would lose some sales, but not all sales, by raising prices above the level set by the leader, and might gain some business by lowering prices below that level; yet, in spite of the immediate attractiveness of underselling the leader, they must refrain from doing so or invite punishment through smashing price raids, costly patent law suits or other harassing tactics.

(3) The followers have the same choice of prices as in type (2), but refrain from underselling the leader not from fear of punishment by the latter but because they expect that the "leader" would turn around, accept the "lead" of the audacious competitor and meet his lowered price; this would all but nullify the effect of the move of the for-once-leading "follower" and would turn a smart and profitable move into a stupid and costly one: in view of these considerations the followers abstain from experiments in leadership and leave the initiative to their bigger brethren.

(4) The followers have a choice of prices but—having learned

[13] Price stability can exist in a truly competitive market only in the sense of fluctuations being relatively small. It would be the (rather unexpected) result of constant "pulling and pushing."

that independent pricing allows the buyers to play off one seller against the other, results in generally lower prices and is in the long run less lucrative than concerted action—they have secretly or tacitly agreed to proceed in unison, letting a stronger or smarter member of the industry act as leader of the concert.

In these four situations we find four different motives for accepting and maintaining the prices set by the leader. In case (1) the small firm does not think of price cutting, because it sells all it cares to sell anyhow. In case (2) the small firm does not dare cut prices, because it fears punishment. In case (3) the small firm abstains from cutting its prices because the big firm would surely meet the lower prices and nullify their effects. In case (4) the small firm prefers not to cut prices, because it knows that in the long run it pays well to stick to its agreement with its competitors.

The differences are significant chiefly for the appraisal of the legal implications under the American antitrust laws. A "conservative" lawyer would see nothing illegal in the first or in the third situations, while in the second situation he might look into the question of coercion and oppressive domination, and in the fourth he might want to search for direct evidence of the price fixing agreement. A more "progressive" lawyer would be satisfied with inferential evidence of concerted price setting in the fourth case. He would also go into the third case and seek to find why the followers expected that the leader would "surely" meet their lowered prices; if this expectation were based on the systematic use of particular pricing techniques, a scheme to which the members of the industry generally adhered, the lawyer would infer the existence of unlawful collusion. The first case appears to be beyond the pale of the law—unless the leader had acquired his dominant position in the industry by illegal methods—for "mere size is no offense."

PRICE DISCRIMINATION

The business practices forming the large complex called "price discrimination" are of such a variety that there are few generalizations holding for all of them. These practices cut across all four of the categories of monopolistic policies we have distinguished: some types of price discrimination are employed in order to exploit existing market positions without any collusive or oppressive elements; other types are practiced under collusive arrangements; certain types have oppressive purposes, for example, to force a weaker competitor to terms; and there is also the possibility of using discriminatory pricing to keep newcomers out of an industry.

Definition

Comprehensive definitions of price discrimination will always be clumsy because they must include price making by buyers as well as price making by sellers and they must refer not only to discriminatory price differentials for the same goods and services but also to discriminatory price uniformities or price similarities for different goods and services. For in most practical cases the goods and services subject to discriminatory treatment are not homogeneous and the discrimination can be demonstrated only by comparing their prices with what they cost the seller or what they are worth to the buyer.

We shall avoid some of the complications by confining the discussion to discriminatory selling and by letting the word "products" comprise goods and services. But we cannot simplify the account by speaking only of price differentials for the *same* products; this would leave out some of the most important instances of discrimination. To sell different qualities at the same price may be just as discriminatory as to sell the same quality at different prices. It is the comparison of price differentials with cost differentials which counts. The different prices which a seller may charge to different customers are not discriminatory if they correspond to differences in cost. A seller practices price discrimination if the relative prices which he charges for his different products or to his different customers are not in line with the relative costs of making these products or serving these customers.

Monopoly Power as a Prerequisite

The fact that price discrimination has at times been used by strong concerns to kill off weaker rivals, or at least to prevent their growth, has lead to the widespread belief that discrimination is essentially a method used "to create a monopoly." To believe that price discrimination could create monopoly power where none had existed before is to overlook the fact that it is the existence of monopoly—of some degree of monopoly (in the wider sense of the word)—that makes discrimination possible. Even in the simplest cases of price discrimination the basic fact is that the seller accepts orders that leave him different net prices; [14] some prices are satisfactory to him, others are less so or are even unsatisfactory, being made perhaps only to spite a rival. A higher degree of competition would make every seller run after the good orders and refuse the bad ones—until the good ones would be less good and the bad ones better. Where this does not happen the market is "imperfectly competitive," that is, "monopolistic."

A seller can of course make special prices to his friends or to poor people even if he is in a position of pure competition. But is there any use speaking of "price discrimination" if a farmer gives away some of his eggs or milk to poor children in the village? Acts of friendship, charity, patriotism, etc., may take the form of special pricing, but we may omit them in this discussion of the "economics" of a business practice which is essentially monopolistic even where, by some standards, it may not be judged to be injurious to the public interest or where it may make the selling more competitive than it would be otherwise.[15]

Classifications of Price Discrimination

Neither an analysis nor even an elementary description of price discrimination can do without some classification. For economic analysis a classification according to the *purposes* for which sellers practice price discrimination, another according to the *techniques*

---

[14] A businessman selling to different places with different transport costs, in different kinds of packing, with different discounts, etc. can compare these prices only by deducting the differential expenses, that is, by reducing them to a common basis. Thus he computes his "net prices."

[15] In theoretical analysis comparisons are made between the price and output decisions made (a) under discriminating monopoly, (b) under nondiscriminating monopoly, and (c) under pure competition. The results under (a) are hardly ever regarded as more favorable to the public than those under (c)—if (c) is possible—but they are often less unfavorable than those under (b)—which may be the only practical alternative.

they use, and a third according to the *degree of discriminating power* are most helpful. This is, however, too much for this survey.[16] We shall attempt here to describe more than twenty types of price discrimination, grouped according to techniques employed, but distinguished also by purposes served, effects achieved, or special conditions required. For the selected types names will be chosen that convey their character through the use of suggestive catchwords.

The techniques of price discrimination are grouped into three main classes: Personal Discrimination, Group Discrimination, and Product Discrimination.[17] Personal discrimination makes differences between individual customers the basis for extending differential treatment to them. Group discrimination differentiates not between individuals as such but between categories or classes of customers. Product discrimination selects neither individual customers nor customer groups for different treatment but allows customers to choose freely among different products (qualities) offered at discriminatory prices.

Personal Discrimination

With one important exception, personal discrimination is by its very nature an unsystematic form of discrimination. Prices may be differentiated according to the seller's appraisal of the individual customer's bargaining strength, of his eagerness to buy, of his income, or of the use he intends to make of the product and the consequent earning power it may have for him.

An extreme example of this class is the *haggle-every-time* type which only appears in a relatively unorganized market. The buyers are not regular customers with constantly recurring demand but are a fluctuating group of varying composition. The seller tries to size up each buyer's ability to pay, urgency of demand and knowledge of the market, and then drives as hard a bargain as he can. This type of discrimination is interesting more for the art of personnel selection and for studies in buyer psychology than for

[16] A much more comprehensive classification and analysis will be included in a separate volume on the Economics of Price Discrimination.

[17] Ralph Cassady, Jr., "Techniques and Purposes of Price Discrimination," *Journal of Marketing*, Vol. XI (1946), pp. 135–43.

economic analysis. It occurs chiefly in certain types of retail trade, for example in antique dealings, or at times in parts of the automobile market by way of trade-in allowances. But it may occur also in other types of trade or industry. The concessions made to a strong bargainer may be in terms of price or method of payment or in terms of extra costs (freight) assumed by the seller. The seller, while not adopting any systematic policy of discounts or freight absorption, may be influenced in his dealings with a particular customer by the terms upon which this customer claims he can buy the goods from a rival, and bargaining may take place over price, terms, extra services, and delivery costs.

A similar kind of individual bargaining exists also in markets in which the buyers are regular customers with constantly recurring demand. The sellers in considerable number, but none of dominant size, offer a little differentiated product in an unorganized and imperfect market in which transactions are secret and "knowledge of the market" is based chiefly on rumors—so that buyers can play one seller against the other. Each deal is separately negotiated and sellers are sometimes willing to make special concessions in competing for particular hard-to-get orders. This *give-in-if-you-must* type of discrimination is practiced chiefly in a "buyers' market," where business is slack and producers have a difficult time keeping their plants busy. (The theorist who is anxious to fit the case to his given set of tools might discuss the weakness of the seller vis-à-vis the hard-bargaining buyer in terms of a very high elasticity of that separate portion of the demand.)

The *let-him-pay-more* type is a more systematic but not very important type of personal discrimination. Sellers who for the greater part of their business are in a fairly competitive position with little control over price may have a few customers whom they can consistently "overcharge." These may be the "nice" customers who do not take the trouble to shop around, or customers who, although they have free access to a more competitive market, are located so near the particular producer and so far from the central market that they fare better at a high discriminatory price than at the uniform market price. "Let them pay more," thinks the seller and exacts higher prices. To the seller these discriminatory sales are merely some "toothsome morsels," the bulk of his business be-

ing done in a competitive market. (It would be a different type
of discrimination if a larger part of the output could be sold in
the discriminatory fashion.)

The *size-up-his-income* type of discrimination is often practiced by doctors and lawyers. In rendering their bills they ask
themselves how much the particular patients or clients can afford
to pay for their professional services. Doctors may treat impecuni-
ous patients for very much less than they charge their wealthy
patients. To middle-class patients, "moderate" fees are charged
not so much out of kind-heartedness as in consideration of the
greater elasticity of demand for medical treatment of this class of
people. In charging little to the very poor the doctors may be
motivated by sheer philanthropy and generosity. Their ability to
make their rich patients make up for it will depend on their quasi-
monopolistic position in the field, a position supported by the
strict "code of ethics" which effectively reduces competition in
the medical profession.

The *measure-the-use* type of discrimination is, in contrast to
the other types of personal discrimination, a very systematic way
of adjusting the price approximately to the profits which the buyer
makes from using the sold or leased article. The monopolistic position of the seller or lessor in these cases must be well protected,
for example through patents or copyrights. Patented machines are
often leased to users whose rentals are fixed per unit of output produced on the machines or in percentages of sales of fabricated
goods. The exhibitors of motion pictures usually pay for the copy-
righted films on the basis of their actual or prospective box office
success in their theatres. A newspaper usually pays for the use of
syndicated columns, comic strips, and news services in rough proportion to the size of its circulation. The underlying theory of all
these schemes is that the prices charged should be at least roughly
in accordance with the earning power which the acquired rights
provide to the buyer.

Group Discrimination

Group discrimination is in a sense a semi-personal type of discrimination. It depends on differences between different groups

of buyers, and aims at taking advantage of these differences in such a way that the buyers cannot easily evade the discriminatory prices. Prices, for example,[18] may be differentiated according to the age of the customer (half fares for children, children's haircuts); the sex of the customer (reduced admission for ladies at ball games); the military status of the customer (reduced theatre tickets for men in uniform); membership in certain organizations (sales to members of clubs or associations); the public nature of the agency acquiring the item (transportation for the government). Discrimination between functional or occupational categories of buyers is often found in subscription rates for papers and magazines, in selling prices of books (educational rates; trade editions and college editions), and in advertising rates (manufacturers' advertisements in newspapers). Social welfare schemes of public authorities designed to assist specified groups in the community by the use of discriminatory pricing may also come into this category (the Food Stamp Plan).

Techniques for discriminating between different groups of buyers may also be based upon the location of the customer (goods sold at uniform delivered prices in all markets or at different zone prices, or surpluses sporadically "dumped" in a market geographically separated from the seller's regular market); upon the patronage status of the customer (special rates for new customers, or quantity and volume discounts to large ones); and upon the use to which the product is put (fluid milk for fresh consumption and for processing, railroad transportation for high-valued finished goods and for low-valued raw materials, or postal service for letters and for parcels).

The most important types of group discrimination come under the headings just indicated—discrimination according to consumer location, patronage status of the customer, and product use—and we shall select them for more detailed discussion. We shall find, however, that the techniques involved are less significant than the purposes they are intended to serve. For example, several methods of separating different buyer groups serve the purpose of taking advantage of differences in the "squeezability" of the separate

[18] Almost all the examples are taken from Cassady's classification cited in footnote 17, p. 138.

groups—their ability to stand higher prices. Discrimination according to the patronage status of the customer may serve the different purposes of developing new clientele, of rewarding cooperating customers and punishing disobedient ones, or of strengthening strong distributors or fabricators at the expense of weaker ones. Discrimination based upon the consumer's location—"locational" or "geographic" discrimination—may be practiced in order to squeeze more money out of the market, it may be part of a scheme of predatory competition, or it may not have any direct or conscious purpose but be merely an incidental by-product of a particular pricing practice.

Consumer Location

We shall select seven different types of geographic discrimination for brief descriptions in this section. In some of these types the discrimination lies not in price differentials, but rather in price uniformities or price similarities in the face of cost differences. Thus, only comparisons of net prices realized after deducting the costs "absorbed" by the seller can reveal the price discrimination.

The forget-the-cost-difference type of discrimination consists of a failure to adjust selling prices exactly to the existing cost differentials, a failure arising from an inclination "not to bother" or to "forget about it." The cost differentials may be too small in relation to the cost, clerical or other, of differentiating the prices accordingly.

For example, if a retail store charges fifteen cents for local delivery regardless of the distance, this will imply discrimination against nearby customers in favor of more distant customers. It would not pay to calculate delivery charges on the basis of miles and pounds. If goods are delivered without extra charge, the cash-and-carry customers are discriminated against. If the manufacturer of a nationally advertised article finds it desirable to have it sold at the same price everywhere all over the country, he absorbs the freight differences and thus discriminates against the buyers in places near his plant.[19]

[19] It is interesting to observe that delivered prices or "freight allowed" systems (i.e. systems under which the seller absorbs all freight costs) are

By way of digression we may note here that price discrimination through the neglect of small cost differences is not always geographic discrimination: instead of transportation costs some other expenses may be absorbed by the seller. The underlying principle is the same. For example, if charge account sales are made at the same prices as sales to cash customers, the latter pay part of the cost of credit to the former. Or, if in the garment industry large sizes of suits are sold at the same price as smaller sizes, the buyers of the latter are made to pay for some of the extra material that goes into the garments of their taller or stouter fellow men.

In all these instances, the failure to take account of certain cost differentials and to have them reflected in the selling prices may be due to the desire to save the effort or cost of figuring and charging adequate price differentials or to the desire to gain and maintain customer loyalty by avoiding any "annoying" charges.[20] There are other instances, however, in which the seller has altogether different reasons for absorbing cost differences. In several "freight allowed" systems of pricing the seller's purpose is to limit competition among his various wholesale distributors. His motive is no longer characterized by a harmless "forget the cost difference"; it is, instead, to aid in the maintenance of resale prices by a pricing system which discourages interzonal competition among distributors.

Under this *keep-them-in-their-zones* type of price discrimination the seller quotes his prices "f.o.b. factory, freight allowed." This means that the manufacturer will ship the product to the wholesaler's establishment and permit him to deduct the freight

---

often practiced for the nationally advertised brands while they are not practiced for the unadvertised brands of the same commodities. The greater degree of competition in the more standardized commodities makes it unprofitable to practice the geographic price discrimination which is inherent in freight absorptions. For example, unadvertised brands of tea, coffee, cocoa, canned soups, and crackers are sold f.o.b. shipping place without freight absorption. Advertised brands of the same goods are sold at uniform delivered prices or with "freight allowed." See *Price Behavior and Business Policy, Monograph No. 1* of the *Temporary National Economic Committee*, prepared by Saul Nelson and Walter G. Keim (Washington, 1940), pp. 298–300.

[20] A U.S. Circuit Court once concluded that where freight differences were small the charging of uniform prices was considered a practice making for economy and convenience. *United States* v. *Corn Products Refining Co.*, 234 Fed. 994 (1916).

from the bill. What this seller calls his "f.o.b. factory price" is really a delivered price, every distributor getting the product at exactly the same price c.i.f. destination. While the manufacturer thus absorbs the freight to the distributors or to destinations within their zones, any further freights must be paid by the distributors. The distributor in Zone A pays for shipments into his zone the same delivered price that the distributor in Zone B pays for shipments into B. If the Zone A distributor tried to sell in Zone B, a territory not assigned to him, he would have to pay the freight from his zone to the other and the goods would therefore cost him more than they cost the appointed zone distributor. Distributors are thus discouraged from invading each other's territories and the manufacturer avoids what he calls "demoralization" of his market.

The motives of sellers who absorb freight under systematic "freight equalization" schemes are of a different nature. The *match-the-freight* type of price discrimination is practiced if a seller, in an attempt to overcome the competitive disadvantage of being located farther away from a customer than some of his competitors, offers to absorb any excess of the actual freight over the lowest freight from any competitor's plant to the destination. Thus, he matches the freight charges from, but not the price quoted by, competing firms. Delivered prices quoted by competing sellers would be identical if all competitors not only offered to match the lowest freight charges but also to quote identical f.o.b. mill prices or use identical base prices. Freight equalization alone would not, therefore, imply identical delivered prices. Freight equalization—a system of meeting lower freight charges, but not lower prices—is discriminatory in that the seller absorbing a difference in freight costs accepts a lower mill net price; but the scheme does not exclude price competition.

Price competition is excluded under a system where sellers systematically meet the lowest quoted prices as well as freight charges. Such a scheme, ensuring the identity of delivered prices quoted by all firms, is not only inherently discriminatory, because the mill net prices which a seller realizes from sales to buyers in different locations must vary considerably, but is also inherently collusive, because it involves a common course of action with regard to prices. In view of the collective or cooperative character of the pricing scheme we may speak of the *play-the-game* type of price discrimination.[21] The official name of the scheme is basing-point system.

Although a definition of this system was given in the preceding chapter in connection with collusive formula-pricing, a description of how the system works should be given here in order to demonstrate its discriminatory nature. The single-basing point system may be best illustrated by the famous "Pittsburgh Plus" pricing scheme of the steel industry before 1924. Prices of steel were set f.o.b. Pittsburgh. For all deliveries buyers had to pay the Pittsburgh price plus the freight from Pittsburgh to the destination. This would seem reasonable if all steel were first shipped to Pittsburgh. But this was not the case. A steel customer in Chicago had to pay the Pittsburgh price plus the freight from Pittsburgh to Chicago even if the steel was delivered directly from a steel mill at or near Chicago. (This steel mill was thus collecting a so-called "phantom freight.") With a Pittsburgh base price of $30 per ton and the freight Pittsburgh-Chicago of $7.60 per ton, the Chicago steel mill would net $37.60 for steel delivered to the Chicago customers, $30.00 for steel delivered half-way between Chicago and Pittsburgh,[22] and $22.40 for steel delivered to Pittsburgh. Similarly, a Duluth steel mill would net $43.20 for steel delivered to Duluth, $31.00 for steel delivered to Chicago, $25.00 for steel delivered to Detroit, and $22.00 for steel delivered to Cleveland.[23] Thus any mill not located at Pittsburgh realized different net prices for different sales.

[21] The catchwords "play-the-game" (or cooperative) discrimination are borrowed from Frank A. Fetter, *The Masquerade of Monopoly*, p. 310. We ought to distinguish: (1) price agreements which *intend* to secure a certain scheme of discriminatory prices and (2) price agreements which result *incidentally* in a scattering of discriminatory prices. The latter is the type discussed now as the play-the-game type. It results when a geographical pricing scheme is adopted by all firms in the industry and the firms "play-the-game 100%" in order to avoid "tearing down the price structure." These phrases were used by the U.S. Supreme Court in the Second Cement Case. *Federal Trade Commission* v. *The Cement Institute*, 333 U.S. 683 (1948).

[22] The delivered price at the half-way point between Pittsburgh and Chicago would be $30.00 plus $3.80, i.e., $33.80. The Chicago mill would absorb the freight from Chicago to the destination, hence it would net $30.00.

[23] See Fetter, *op. cit.*, 308 ff.

Under the multiple-basing-point system each seller quotes as his delivered price the cheapest combination of any of the announced base prices and the freight costs from basing point to destination. For each bid the seller ascertains which of the basing points is "applicable" for the particular destination point, and adds to the relevant base price the freight from the applicable basing point to the destination. Such a system was adopted by the steel industry in 1924. A mill located at a basing point uses it as a basis for calculating delivered prices only for destinations within what is called its own "natural market territory." For other destinations other base prices are applicable. If four basing points are established for a certain steel product made by twenty different mills in the country, there will be in effect four territories, in each of which all delivered prices are calculated as the sum of the base price announced for the governing basing point and the railroad freight from that basing point to the destination, regardless of the actual point of shipment. A non-base mill located closer to a certain destination than to the basing point, collects unspent freight on its shipments to that point. On its shipments to destinations closer to any of the basing points than to its own location, the non-base mill has to absorb freight, that is, it collects a mill net price lower than the relevant base price. A base mill shipping into areas governed by other basing points collects a mill net price less than its own base price.[24]

If all mills were base mills, that is, if every production point were a basing point, this would not eliminate the discriminatory differentials in mill net prices which each mill would realize from different sales, inasmuch as each mill would serve customers at points governed by different basing points. This would not be so if each mill were to use only its own location as its "basing point" for all its sales—but then the industry would no longer have a basing-point system; it would be under a general f.o.b. mill price system, resulting in uniform net realizations by each firm and not in identical delivered prices quoted by different competitors. It is the very essence of the basing-point system that each seller accepts the base prices announced by his competitors as the basis

[24] The mill net price realized by a base mill will fall short of its own base price by the algebraic sum of freight differential and base price differential.

for his own delivered price quotations in their territories. This may achieve two results: First, it eliminates effective price competition among the sellers and, second, it may allow the powerful firms in the industry to control the sales volumes, and thus check the potential growth, of the smaller firms. Because of these possible effects the basing-point system of pricing—which has been used not only by the steel industry but also by the cement, pulp, sugar, and lead industries among others—has been vigorously attacked as one of the worst forms of monopolistic pricing.

When the play-the-game type of price discrimination is used to hold down smaller firms it becomes a type of local price cutting by giant firms, similar to the *kill-the-rival* type of discrimination. This type achieved greatest notoriety and raised issues which furnished strong arguments for the early trust-busting campaigns in the United States. For the most part it is of lesser interest to the economic theorist than to the economic historian and the lawyer. The kill-the-rival or oppress-the-rival type of discrimination was made unlawful in the United States by the Clayton Act, which (in Section 2) declares it to

> be unlawful . . . to discriminate in prices between different purchases of commodities of like grade and quality . . . where the effect of such discrimination may be substantially to lessen competition. . . .

Competition was indeed lessened if, through local price cutting by the financially powerful concern, smaller competitors were killed off—either forced to close down or to sell out to their stronger opponent. Competition was also lessened when the competitors came to terms, when they stopped ambitious attempts to draw more business from the larger concern, when they became willing to fall into line with the policies of the leader. In these latter cases the rivals were not eliminated as other sources of supply but were eliminated as factors disturbing the exercise of the stronger firm's control over price.

The best-known illustrations of the kill-the-rival type of price discrimination are the cases discussed before the courts in the suits leading up to the dissolution in 1911 of the Standard Oil Company of New Jersey and the American Tobacco Company. In the records of the Standard Oil case we can read that the

defendants have pursued a system of unfair competition against
their competitors, whereby the independent companies selling
and marketing petroleum have either been driven out of business or their business so restricted that the Standard Oil Company
has practically controlled the prices and monopolized the commerce in the products of petroleum in the United States. This
system has taken the form of price cutting in particular localities
while keeping up high prices, or raising them still higher, in other
localities where no competition exists; of paying rebates to customers as a part of said system of price cutting, . . .[25]

While it is easy to describe the kill-the-rival or oppress-the-
rival type of price discrimination, it is difficult to prove that a
particular situation in reality is of this type. Local price cutting
may be practiced for different reasons, and "intent" can rarely be
proved. Hence, one will have to search for criteria by which to distinguish instances of local price discrimination that look alike
but are different in purpose as well as in effect.

The sixth type of geographic discrimination to be included in
this survey is sufficiently different from the others to be clearly set
apart. The *dump-the-surplus* type of price discrimination is characterized by its unsystematic and sporadic nature. In order to move his
surpluses without spoiling his regular market, a seller may dispose
of them in a different territory at lower prices. Such dumping is
often highly disturbing to other sellers whose regular market becomes the occasional dumping ground for goods withheld from
their usual outlets. But in spite of the numerous complaints which
this type of sporadic discrimination arouses in international and
interregional trade, it does not offer difficult problems for economic
analysis.

Permanent dumping—charging lower net prices for exports
than for domestic sales—differs from any of the six types of geographic price discrimination thus far discussed. It is not of the
sporadic nature which characterizes the dump-the-surplus policy.
It is not designed to secure the stability of existing market conditions as are the keep-them-in-their-zones and play-the-game policies. It is not undertaken with the intention of eliminating a
competitor as is the kill-the-rival policy. And it is not as incidental

[25] *United States* v. *Standard Oil Company. Brief for the United States,*
1909, Vol. I, pp. 187–88.

to the techniques of freight-cost absorption as are the forget-the-cost-difference and match-the-freight policies. Its purpose is the exploitation of the differences in elasticity between the demands of different regions or countries in order to squeeze more revenue out of the total market without attempting to influence the existing market conditions. Geographic price discrimination of this sort is one of the cases of discriminatory pricing to which the theoretical model of price determination for the purpose of profit maximization is most directly applicable. (The principle involved resembles closely the principle of charging-what-the-traffic-will-bear that has been employed in discussions of railroad rate setting.) We may call this seventh type of geographic price discrimination the *get-the-most-from-each-region* type of discrimination.

Examples of this type of discrimination could be found in the domestic and export price policies of many large concerns—if information were available. One instance that became known from the congressional investigation of and the court case against the glass container industry is the geographic discrimination in the sale of milk bottles. The combination of protection under restrictive patent licences with the geographic separability of the market allowed a manufacturer to sell his milk bottles to Texas at much higher net prices than elsewhere.[26]

Much illustrative material could probably be found in the files of various European cartels with centralized selling organizations. It is very likely that the price differentials fixed by these cartels for their exports to different countries distinctly reflected the differences in the elasticities of demand that resulted from national tariff policies and domestic competition within the various countries.[27]

[26] *Investigation in the Concentration of Economic Power, Hearings before the Temporary National Economic Committee*, Part 2 (Washington, 1939), pp. 611–12.

[27] The writer was at one time connected with the Austrian cardboard cartel. This cartel practiced geographic price discrimination, charging the highest prices for exports to Turkey and the lowest prices for other overseas exports. All markets except the last were protected by tariffs and by international agreements (sometimes involving concealed preferential tariffs). This case of discrimination was unusual in that the domestic market was not charged the highest price; the elasticities of demand in the Hungarian and Italian markets were lower than that in the domestic Austrian market, and they were therefore charged higher prices. Prior to the formation of the

Customer Status

We have referred to three different purposes for which group discrimination based upon the patronage status of the customer may be practiced. New customers, large customers, or cooperating customers may be the groups selected for more favorable treatment in the seller's pricing policy.

In the *promote-new-custom* type of discrimination, the existing demand which the seller can attract through his discriminatory price cutting does not currently provide enough business to warrant his price policy. But the seller expects that this demand will grow—that people will develop a taste for the product or will acquire complementary appliances needed for additional consumption—and that the new demand (pictured by the economist as a new demand curve) will then provide the business and the profits for which he strives. He may then continue his low price or, more likely, he may raise it. Promotional rates or prices—promotional discrimination—will be needed only for development of the demand, not for its continued service.

On the other hand, the seller may wish to favor groups of especially important old customers. The *favor-the-big-ones* type of price discrimination is best characterized by a quantity discount which is in excess of the economies connected with dealing with large buyers. There are many economies involved in large-quantity business, economies in producing big lots and in selling, handling, transporting, recording and collecting large items. Quantity discounts, rebates, allowances or other forms of price differentials in favor of large buyers do not constitute price discrimination as long as, and to the extent to which, they merely reflect the savings in outlays, risk, or trouble.[28] In actual fact, however, quantity dis-

---

cartel as well as after its dissolution geographic discrimination was impossible because of the sharp competition among the Austrian producers, who thus received the same net prices from sales in the domestic and the various export markets.

[28] When the Goodyear Tire & Rubber Company delivered automobile tires to Sears, Roebuck and Co., under a contract which had been effective from 1926 until 1937, the gross price discrimination as compared with sales to smaller retail sellers varied between 29 and 40 percent. The net price discrimination after due allowance for cost differentials was computed to range from 11 to 22 percent. See Federal Trade Commission "Report on

counts and volume discounts (the latter are allowed on a customer's total purchases over a year regardless of the size of his single orders) are often primarily devices to favor the large and handicap the small customers.

Favoritism shown to large buyers need not always be to the liking of the seller, indeed he may feel that he is being "robbed," a victim of the violence of an important customer. The yielding seller "just could not afford to lose the customer." (Where the discrimination is in favor of an individual buyer, not of large buyers in general, the case is really one of the "give-in-if-you-must" type.) Legislation which prohibits price discrimination may in such cases be welcomed by the seller as a substitute for his lack of strength or backbone.

In contrast to these instances in which the discriminatory scheme in favor of large buyers is imposed upon a weak seller, one can find many other instances in which the favoritism to the large buyers is a deliberate policy of a strong seller trying to improve his monopolistic position by creating a more monopolistic position for his chief customers. The degree of competition that prevails in the market in which his customers have to sell—that is, in the selling market of the distributors or processors of his product —will be reflected in the prices he can obtain in the long run. He may therefore be greatly interested in helping his customers to "improve" their market position by cleaning out "excessive competition" among them. Price discrimination against the "small fry" can be very effective in establishing such an increased degree of monopoly for his favored customers in their respective markets.[29]

Monopolistic Practices in Industries," *Hearings before the Temporary National Economic Committee* (Washington, 1939), Part 5A, pp. 2311–12.

[29] The Federal Trade Commission has made the following statement concerning this type of price discrimination: "The Commission considered that a manufacturer, under the Clayton Act, . . . may not make his bargains according to his own interest by discriminating as he pleases, however honest and justifiable such courses might be from the standpoint of commercial principles. Large industrial companies, through price discrimination, can control competitive business conditions among their customers to the extent of enriching some and ruining others. . . . If it were left to a manufacturer to make the price solely on account of quantity, he could easily make discounts by reason of quantity so high as to be practically open to the largest dealers only, and in that manner might hand over the whole trade in his line of commerce to a few or a single dealer." *Ibid.*, p. 2312.

It was primarily this type of price discrimination which the Robinson-Patman Act of 1936 made unlawful when the effect was "to substantially lessen competition."

Discrimination in favor of customers who obey, and against those who do not obey, the seller's wishes regarding resale price maintenance or similar schemes, may be called the *hold-them-in-line* type of price discrimination. It serves to control policies of the customers, and to enforce price maintenance and compliance with the seller's wishes by granting discounts to those who "behave" and by excluding those who do not. The procedure is either to grant the discount to all buyers except those on a "black list" or to grant the discount exclusively to buyers who are on a "white list." The latter procedure is, from the point of view of legality, much safer and therefore more common. One way of doing this type of business is to give the discount to all buyers who are members in good standing of a certain organization or association; but, of course, there are a good many other ways of doing it; for example—to mention only a couple of practices under this heading —through refunds distributed through the association of the "behaving" customers, or through free services rendered or other forms of preferential treatment accorded to the behaving customers.

Product Use

Discrimination based upon the use made of the product is of all types of group discrimination the most interesting for economic analysis because here the differences in eagerness to buy and ability to pay, and the profits made through exploiting them, are the basis and *raison d'être* of the discriminatory pricing. (All but one of the types of group discrimination thus far discussed have been practiced for different reasons.) A seller's profit will surely be higher if he can squeeze each group to just the right extent, exacting high prices from groups that can stand them and conceding low prices to groups that could not afford to use much of the product at higher prices. The seller will be able to do this if the market can be divided by objective criteria and the buyer groups thus separated respond very differently to various price levels for the product. In other words, the elasticities of demand of the separate groups must be different if price discrimination is to yield increased revenues.

The classical application of this principle has been in the railroad industry. It became known there as the charge-what-the-traffic-will-bear principle of freight rate making and we shall speak therefore of the *charge-what-the-traffic-will-bear* type of price discrimination.

The phrase "charge what the traffic will bear" can easily be misunderstood. First of all, it certainly does not mean that the highest possible price is charged without consideration of its effect on sales. (The highest possible price would be the price at which the smallest volume of output could be sold. Such a price would hardly be to anybody's advantage.) Secondly, if it were taken to mean nothing else but that a maximum net revenue is extracted from the business, then this principle would obviously be applicable to every type of business, not merely to discriminating monopolies. The seller in a purely competitive market will also charge what the "traffic" will bear—but the "traffic" will not bear more than the uniform market price. And, likewise, the seller with great control over the price of his product but without being able to discriminate between his customers will charge what the traffic will bear —but it will be one uniform price, rather than a set of different prices, that will fetch the highest possible net revenue. We prefer, however, to use the phrase not in this all too general sense, but only in connection with the problem of discrimination. Although the phrase is often applied by way of analogy to other industries, we shall reserve it for its original and historical meaning in the discussion of railroad rates.

Traditionally three kinds of discrimination are distinguished in the field of railroad transportation: "personal" discrimination (which was always unlawful), "local" discrimination (one phase of which was prohibited by the famous long-and-short-haul clause) [30] and "commodity" discrimination (which was always regarded as legitimate). "Commodity" discrimination is discrimina-

---

[30] The "long-and-short-haul clause" is a provision of the Interstate Commerce Act of 1887 and of its amendment of 1910, forbidding a greater charge for a short than for a long haul over the same line if circumstances were substantially similar.

tion between groups of users of the transportation service according to the commodities they ship.[31] This kind of discrimination is generally practiced by railroads and is condoned by the regulatory agencies of the government, indeed, it has been considered indispensable for railroad operation on a paying basis.

Thus, while the law—chiefly the Interstate Commerce Act—forbids rate differentials which give particular *shippers* or particular *localities* an "undue" advantage over others, it permits differentials which give particular *industries* substantial advantages over others. Incidentally, it is often overlooked that discriminatory rates for various commodities may imply discriminatory treatment of the different localities or regions in which the different industries are located. The rates for transportation per ton-mile are very much higher for expensive materials like silk than for cheap materials like coal or gravel. ("Expensive" and "cheap" refer here to value per unit of weight.) The rates for copper are higher than the rates for steel, the rates for fluid milk higher than the rates for gasoline. That railroad rates are under government regulation makes it difficult to state whether or not the approved rate structure is really all that the traffic will bear in the opinion of the railroad management. The inflexibility of court decisions and commission rules, the emphasis on the "fair return" theory, and perhaps the insertion of various social and political objectives, make it doubtful that both level and structure of rates conform fully to the principle of maximization of net revenues. The approved rate *levels* are possibly lower in prosperity periods and higher in depression periods than some alert managements would set them if they were entirely free to charge what the traffic could bear. The rate differentials, that is, the essentially discriminatory rate *structure,* probably tally more closely with the managements' views about the relative elasticities of different segments of the demand

---

[31] On first thought one may be inclined to interpret commodity discrimination in transportation as a type of product discrimination instead of a type of group discrimination. Product discrimination, however, refers to different products or product qualities offered by a seller at discriminatory prices. Commodity discrimination in railroad transportation, on the other hand, refers to one product, namely, transportation service, which the railroad offers at discriminatory prices to different groups, namely persons using the service for different commodities.

for transportation than the rate level tallies with their views about the combined elasticities of the total market.

The application of the charge-what-the-traffic-will-bear principle to industries other than transportation may be called the *get-the-most-from-each-group* type of price discrimination. It is often practiced by public utilities (although also modified by public regulation of rate making). Electric current for household consumption is usually sold at much higher rates than the current for users of industrial power. And even these two markets are sometimes subdivided according to the amount or kind of use made of the electricity. In some communities electric current for hot-water heating or space heating in households is cheaper than for lighting; current for very large industrial users, who might find it cheaper to produce their own power, is sometimes cheaper than for small industrial users.

For several reasons we know of relatively few illustrations of the get-the-most-from-each-group type of discrimination for manufactured products. First, discrimination in railroad and utility rates is socially approved and publicly regulated, while discrimination in industrial pricing is usually under suspicion and often in danger of being construed as unlawful. Secondly, it is difficult to divide the market into distinct groups of users, while such separations are easy in utilities and transportation. A domestic household can hardly purchase electric current in the disguise of a factory, and milk cannot very well travel in the disguise of gasoline, whereas in the case of manufactured goods the purchasers who are supposed to buy at higher prices may succeed in securing their supply at the lower price, either by "sneaking in" with the preferred group or by having somebody else do the buying for them. Thirdly, it is almost impossible to discover the presence of discrimination for manufactured products where there are actual or alleged cost differentials. The extra cost of transporting bulky articles, or the differences in the cost of transporting in tank cars, box cars, and platform cars, can be much more easily proved or disproved than cost differences in the production of innumerable varieties of manufactured goods. No public commission digs into the cost accounts of manufacturing companies in order to compare costs with selling prices. Finally, an enduring system of price discrimination requires a degree of monopoly which is not so easily achieved in manufacturing industry, unless the government helps to reduce competition through special legislation, patent and copyright laws, or similar devices.

The examples we have of price discrimination practiced by manufacturing industry in the United States usually come from court cases or congressional hearings. In the glass container industry, under the protection of patents which were used for the organization of a tight cartel through licensing contracts, instances of discrimination between groups of users became notorious. Exactly the same kinds of glass container were sold at higher prices as "domestic fruit jars" than as "packers' ware." [32] The elasticity of demand for jars for household use was apparently smaller.

A case of discrimination between different groups of users that achieved much notoriety related to a chemical product. Manufacturers of plastics, protected by patents and patent license agreements, sold a certain material for use in dentures at a price many times higher than the price they charged for the same material for industrial use.[33] In the dental use the cost of the material was only a negligible fraction of the cost of the complementary highly skilled labor and, therefore, the elasticity of derived demand was so much smaller that it could stand the strikingly increased price. The manufacturers were of course anxious to prevent the material bought at low prices by industrial users from being "diverted" to dental use. In order to make sure that such diversion would not occur they advertised that the material sold to industrial users might contain ingredients injurious to a patient's health.[34] This slight "differentiation" of the product might make us wonder whether the case should not be discussed as one of "product dis-

---

[32] *Investigation in the Concentration of Economic Power, Hearings before the Temporary National Economic Committee,* Part 2 (Washington, D.C., 1939), pp. 572–74, 591.

[33] The price differential was further increased by mark-ups—protected by price maintenance arrangements—of the distributors. "Thus methyl methacrylate when marketed for ordinary commercial purposes sold for 85 cents per pound, but when sold for denture purposes costs the dental profession approximately $50 per pound." *Patents. Hearings before the Committee on Patents,* United States Senate, 77th Congress, 2nd Session, Part 2 (Washington: 1942), p. 719.

[34] *Ibid.,* p. 721.

crimination," rather than group discrimination, since the seller offered two "different products," allowing buyers to choose between a cheap material apparently unfit for dental use and an expensive one that could be so used. The case demonstrates that the lines drawn between "classes" of phenomena are arbitrary and anything but watertight.[35]

Two other examples of cases that might be regarded either as instances of product discrimination or of user group discrimination may be cited. The Aluminum Corporation of America used to sell aluminum ingots at a higher price per pound than it sold aluminum in cable form.[36] Effective competition from copper cables was the obvious reason for the lower price on aluminum cables. This segment of the aluminum market would not stand the higher price that was charged for ingots, the less fabricated product. Similarly, producers of plate glass charged a much higher price per square foot for large pieces than for small pieces, although all plate glass is produced in large sheets. The differential was at times more than 100 percent of the price for small sizes. The elasticity of demand for plate glass in small pieces was high because of the heavy competition of ordinary window glass; in large pieces plate glass had no serious substitutes in its chief uses and the producers took advantage of the lower demand elasticity.[37] Patent protection and patent contracts enabled them to practice this discrimination without disturbance either from insiders' defection or outsiders' invasion.

User group discrimination in the marketing of agricultural products is practiced either under governmental plans or by agricultural cooperatives aided by governments. The scheme of the Surplus Commodities Administration, distributing surplus commodities at reduced prices to relief families (the so-called Food Stamp Plan), was price discrimination with a partly "social" ob-

[35] I chose to discuss the case as one of user group discrimination rather than product discrimination because the differentiation of the product was only a device for preventing the diversion of the substantially identical product from the favored users to those held up for the higher price.

[36] The buyers of aluminum cable had to agree not to melt it. National Recovery Administration, *Report on the Aluminum Industry* (mimeographed, Washington, 1935), p. 14.

[37] Myron W. Watkins, *Industrial Combinations and Public Policy* (Boston: Houghton Mifflin Co., 1927), p. 170.

jective—and thus may not belong to the type under discussion—but conceivably a monopolistic seller of these commodities might, if he could, choose the same system in trying to get the most from each group.

A two-price and sometimes three-price system has been created in the distribution of milk, with very substantial price differentials according to the use to which it is put. The highest price is charged for milk for fluid consumption, a much lower price for milk for manufacturing into cheese, ice cream and other products, and sometimes a medium high price for milk separated as cream. The monopolistic organizations needed for the maintenance of these price differentials were provided by producers' cooperatives and large-scale distributors, but soon it became necessary to give the scheme governmental support. Various governmental laws and regulations prohibit competition in this field in order to secure the operation of the system which enables the producer to collect a high price for fluid milk for direct consumption and to dispose of all surplus milk at lower prices for industrial purposes.[38]

Product Discrimination

Product discrimination does not depend upon a separation of buyers in such a way that they cannot evade the demarcation lines, but upon a differentiation of the products in such a way that the buyers will separate themselves and buy at discriminatory prices. A seller may do this by differentiating his products as to design, label, quality, time of sale, or distribution channel having a different appeal to different consumers.[39]

[38] See below, Chapter 8.

[39] As I mentioned earlier, there is a still wider concept of product discrimination. It concerns the sale of products which are not merely differentiated from each other while still substitutable for the same or similar purposes, but products serving totally different purposes. The prices at which a seller offers these different products may be regarded as discriminatory if the "mark-ups" above their respective marginal costs are different. This get-the-most-for-each-product type of discrimination is practiced by multiproduct firms when they meet heavier competition in the sale of some of their products than of others. We shall discuss here only product discrimination in the narrow sense of discrimination effected through the differentiation of what is essentially the same product.

The *appeal-to-the-classes* type of price discrimination is based on a systematic attempt to divide the market according to the ability (or willingness) to pay of different customer groups, not by discriminating between buyers locally, personally, or through any seller-determined criterion, but merely by offering the good or service in slightly differentiated grades or classes among which the buyers may choose. Cases in point are Grade A and Grade B milk in New York City and many other places (with only a small difference in quality or cost); standard and deluxe models of automobiles (with price differences larger than cost differences); railroad fares in pullman parlor cars and day coaches (with a relatively small difference in the cost of the service); expensive and cheap seats in theatres and concert halls (with no difference in cost to the management); goods in fancy containers and the same goods without containers (with price differences far in excess of the cost of packing); books in deluxe binding and in ordinary or even paper binding (with price differentials greater than cost differentials); dining room service and coffee shop service in the same restaurant (with no or only a trivial difference in the cost of the service); and many other goods which come in high grades and cheaper ones (with no cost differentials accounting for the price differentials).

Most instances of the appeal-to-the-classes type of price discrimination are considered as perfectly legitimate business practices. In some of these instances the service to the buyer who pays the higher price is really superior in quality, even if its short-run marginal cost to the seller is not higher than that of the service sold at lower price. (An orchestra seat at a play is certainly *better* than a seat in the rear section of the balcony.) In other instances the inherent class implication is "worth" its price to the buyer (as in the case of services to people who purchase the distinction which they obtain through paying the higher price).

This relatively unobjectionable type of price discrimination is different from the *make-them-pay-for-the-label* type, where the whole differentiation lies in the brand or label of the article and is designed to deceive the buyer by making him believe he is acquiring a more durable or more hygienic or otherwise technologically superior good.

The Federal Trade Commission reported the case of a feather bed pillow manufacturing company which

> marketed their products under the five brand names "Princess," "Progress," "Washington," "Puritan," and "Ideal." In its advertising the manufacturer represented that these products were of different grades in the order named and correspondingly different prices were charged for each. The Commission found, however, that all these five brands were of the same quality, and that the material price differential between the "Princess" and the "Ideal" brand reflected a difference in the label only.[40]

The make-them-pay-for-the-the-label type of price discrimination is definitely obnoxious when the discrimination is combined with deceptive advertising and misrepresentation (as in the case just described). Where differences in quality are not falsely claimed but merely indirectly suggested through different names or labels, the practice is not so offensive. It has become customary for certain producers to sell the same quality of goods at higher prices under a nationally advertised name or label and at lower prices under other names or labels. Certain chemical substances, cosmetics, toothpastes, etc., are sold under non-proprietary names much more cheaply than under proprietary names.[41] The wholesale price difference for nationally advertised hosiery and the same merchandise under private label was, before 1938, up to $1.25 a dozen.[42]

A seller may also differentiate his product in the *clear-the-stock* type of price discrimination by presenting it at special times or, in the case of retail trade, in special parts of his store. In this type the seller disposes of stock on hand in order to make room for new stock. The best known example occurs in the inventory "sales" of retail stores, where customers may buy regular stock at much reduced prices either at times especially advertised by the seller or in special parts (for example, the basement) of the store.

[40] Quoted from *Price Behavior and Business Policy, Monograph No. 1 of the Temporary National Economic Committee,* prepared by Saul Nelson and Walter G. Keim (Washington, D.C., 1939), p. 80. The case is Docket No. 1129 of the Federal Trade Commission.

[41] According to *Price Behavior and Business Policy,* p. 81, the saving for such purchases under non-proprietary names averaged 76 percent in 1938.

[42] See *Knit Goods Weekly,* January 3, 1938, p. 8.

The "temporal" discrimination which is involved in the clear-the-stock type of price discrimination may be sporadic or periodic. In any event, the seller does not want his bargain sales to encroach to any large extent on his regular sales. The less business is switched from regular prices to bargain prices the more nearly is his objective fulfilled. There is a different type of temporal discrimination which a seller practices precisely in order to switch some of the demand for his services from busy to slack periods during the day, the week, or the year. The *switch-them-to-off-peak-times* type of price discrimination is practiced in public utility rates (rates for off-peak electricity; night-and-Sunday rates for long-distance telephone calls), in street-car fares (lower fares for travel between rush hours), in hotel rates (lower off-season rates in resorts), in theatre tickets (matinee prices in theatres), and probably other instances in which the demand for services tends to be concentrated at particular time intervals, leaving capacity under-utilized at other times. In some of these instances, differential pricing need not be discriminatory pricing. For there would be differentials even if these services were supplied by pure competitors without any control over prices. Price differentials are called discriminatory only if they are "administered" and deviate from those that would have emerged under purely competitive conditions. Of course, in practice such a comparison may not be possible.

In most types of pricing described in this section the exercise of discrimination against some buyers is based upon their own decisions. The "segregation" of the buyers is voluntary, for it is up to each buyer whether to choose the cheaper or the more expensive product or service. In some cases, to be sure, particularly where prices are differentiated according to the time the product or service is acquired, the buyer's choice may not be entirely free. (For example, long-distance business calls can usually be made only during business hours; and certain industrial users of electricity could not possibly confine their operations to off-peak hours.) In other cases, the choice may be a matter of mere convenience; again in others, a matter of comparative costs. Where quality appeal is the basis of the price differential, the buyer's belief in the higher quality of the higher-priced good or service is the reason for his preference. In other instances, it may be discrimination itself for which he deliberately pays: he may want to be in the more exclusive division, in the company of others who choose to distinguish themselves by getting the more expensive variety. (The parlor car passenger pays chiefly for the pleasure of traveling with "better-class" people; the dining-room guest wants to eat in an environment more distinguished than the cheaper coffee shop.) [43]

Price Discrimination and the Public Interest

Discrimination is always "against" some buyers and "in favor of" others. There are no accepted standards for determining whether the buyers who pay the relatively high prices are being "exploited" by the seller or whether the seller is being "exploited" by the buyers who pay the relatively low price. Both complaints may be made at the same time and there is no safe ground on which to decide the issue. In some instances it can be shown that the less-favored buyers are not put to any real disadvantage by the more favorable treatment of others. Indeed, they may even be better off in consequence of the discriminatory policy. For example, the price they have to pay may be high relative to the price paid by others and yet, at the same time, lower than the price they would have had to pay in the absence of discrimination. This may be so because discriminatory price reductions may permit the sale and production of a larger output and economies of large-scale production may permit this increased output to be produced at lower marginal cost. One must not assume, however, that this is a frequent case, although much is made of it even where it cannot possibly apply.

In some of the cases of discrimination which we have seen in

[43] The determination of the most profitable price differentials in cases of product discrimination is an interesting problem in theory as well as in practice. And a difficult one as such, because the elasticities of demand for the separate varieties are interdependent. That is to say, the demand for the separate varieties is not "given" in the sense that it depends only on the price charged for the particular variety. It depends also on the prices charged for the other varieties. Economic theory has very nice solutions for the determination of the optimum set of discriminatory prices under the assumption of independent demand curves. A solution for interdependent demand curves requires a more complicated apparatus than that traditionally employed in geometric price analysis.

our survey the issue is not one of exploitation, nor one of obtaining economies in production through market expansion, but rather of creating handicaps for certain purchasers in their competition with others. In other cases the discrimination is merely incidental to particular systems of distribution and not regarded as onerous by any of the purchasers. Or it may be inherent in a system of price setting which is not intentionally discriminatory, yet in effect discriminatory as well as onerous from the point of view of certain buyers. Again in other cases the discrimination is part of a price war between competing sellers which, while it lasts, may be welcome to some buyers, but threatens to end in a regime of serious monopolistic exploitation. Finally, there are the cases where discrimination is a form of subsidization by the government.

Needless to say, in view of such a variety of effects and implications, it would be unreasonable to pronounce a wholesale condemnation of price discrimination of every kind. Analysis will reach verdicts of social undesirability or impropriety in many instances. The presumption is that discriminatory pricing in most cases results in a less efficient allocation of resources in the economy. And in many instances it serves to increase or maintain monopoly positions of the most undesirable type. On the other hand, there are situations where price discrimination is the only way in which an element of price competition can be introduced in an otherwise monopolistic market regime.

A DIGRESSION ON PRICE UNIFORMITY

Price fixing conspiracies and price leadership may result in "price uniformity" in the sense that different producers charge identical prices for their products. "Price uniformity" may also result from pure competition in the sale of homogeneous goods in a perfect market, not because producers choose to charge the same price, but because they cannot get any higher price however hard they try, and will not consider taking less (since they can sell all they want to sell at the uniform market price). Thus, both the presence of pure competition in a perfect market and the total absence of price competition may result in identical prices being received by different sellers.

A Symptom of Collusion or of Competition?

Under these circumstances one may well understand the bewilderment of lawyers and witnesses in court cases, some trying to present price uniformity as a symptom of collusion among sellers, others as a symptom of competition. Taken by itself, it is a symptom of neither. Only in conjunction with several other factors could the existence of a uniform market price be used as an indication of either collusion or pure competition. On the other hand, there may be collusion with price differentials; and, when there are standardized differences in quality or extra costs, there may be price differentials under pure competition. Finally, it is conceivable that there could be price uniformity without either collusion or pure competition.[44]

Only an analysis of the particular situation can reveal the implications of uniform prices in a given instance. To be sure, if several participants in a sealed-bid competition for a large contract submit identical bids, the presumption of collusion is hardly rebuttable. Or if several producers at different locations quote identical delivered prices to buyers at different places which are not regular markets (prices that differ from place to place, but are for any one place the same from all producers) the presumption of an explicitly or implicitly agreed-upon price system is difficult to refute. No definite and general conclusion, however, can be drawn from the existence of uniform prices as such.

[44] The United States Steel Corporation in its statement prepared for the Temporary National Economic Committee argued: ". . . it is quite erroneous to imply . . . that identity of prices at any given time is necessarily evidence of absence of price competition. Quite the contrary is true. In any competitive market, the price quoted by different producers at any given time for any staple product will naturally tend to be uniform." *T.N.E.C. Papers* (Exhibit 1418), p. 34. In a case before the U.S. Supreme Court— the Hardwood Lumber Case, 257 U.S. 377 (1921)—it was asserted that "when different prices are being charged there are obviously no agreements fixing prices." This naive assertion was made not by the defendant but by the Government prosecutor. *Brief for the United States*, pp. 67–68. Referring to the conflicting expert opinions of Yale and Harvard authorities appearing as witnesses in the Maple Flooring case, 268 U.S. 580 (1925), Frank A. Fetter observed sarcastically: "Yale was trying to prove 'uniformity' as a sign of innocence, and Harvard to disprove 'uniformity,' assuming that it was a sign of guilt." *The Masquerade of Monopoly*, p. 334.

Necessary Distinctions

Some of the confusion about the implications of price uniformity is due to a failure to ascertain whether prices are inclusive or exclusive of transport costs—that is, whether they are delivered prices or mill-net prices—and whether uniformity refers to different buyers or different sellers. It is necessary to distinguish between

(1) uniformity of delivered prices quoted to any one buyer by different sellers (located at different places);

(2) uniformity of delivered prices quoted to different buyers (located at different places) by any one seller;

(3) uniformity of delivered prices quoted to different buyers (located at different places) by different sellers (located at different places);

(4) uniformity of mill-net prices realized by any one seller from sales to different buyers (located at different places);

(5) uniformity of mill-net prices realized by different sellers (located at different places) from sales to any one buyer;

(6) uniformity of mill-net prices realized by different sellers (located at different places) from sales to different buyers (located at different places).

It should be clear that some of these types of price uniformity cannot coexist with some other types because they are logically inconsistent with each other. For example, wherever buyers or sellers are located at different places involving different transportation costs, uniform delivered prices must mean different mill-net prices, and uniform mill-net prices must mean different delivered prices.

We can reduce some confusion if we adopt the practice of some writers and make a difference between the words "uniform" and "identical." We shall speak of "uniform" prices when we refer to the prices quoted by one seller to different buyers, as in cases (2) and (4); we shall speak of "identical" prices when we refer to the prices quoted by different sellers to one buyer, as in cases (1) and (5); in cases (3) and (6) the prices are both uniform and identical.

Implications of Price Identity and Uniformity

The interpretation of case (1) has an interesting economic and judicial history. It was this case that experts before courts and in briefs had in mind when they tried to use the theory of the uniform and identical equilibrium price in a perfectly competitive market in support of the assertion that identical quotations of delivered prices by different sellers were the result of perfect competition.[45] Quite apart from the logical fallacy in the argument that price equality must be the result of price competition because price competition results in price equality, the crux of the matter lies in the innocent or fraudulent confusion between the equal prices eventually emerging from competitive bidding-and-asking in the market place and the equal prices initially quoted by different sellers without any shopping around, without any bargaining, and without any bidding-and-asking. Competition in a perfect market does not mean that all sellers *start* by quoting the same prices; it means merely that those who quote higher prices will not obtain any orders as long as other sellers accept lower prices. And, of course, the uniform and identical market price resulting from competitive bidding-and-asking among potential buyers and sellers refers only to a moment of time and will usually be subject to frequent if not continuous fluctuations; prices identical as well as inflexible over an extended period are hardly possible if active price competition exists. Thus, identity of delivered prices quoted to one buyer by different sellers, if it is not an accidental but rather a regular occurrence, establishes the presumption of an organized elimination of price competition among the sellers.

Case (2)—uniform delivered prices quoted by any one seller to different buyers at different locations—implies price discrimination inasmuch as the seller accepts lower net prices from distant customers than from customers to which transportation charges are less. He would surely not do this under pure competition. Absence of pure competition, however, need not imply the existence of a monopoly position of any great strength. A very high degree of competition would still be compatible with the absorption of

[45] For documented examples see Machlup, *The Basing-Point System*, pp. 76–77, 95–99.

small differentials in delivery cost. If freight differentials are not small, their absorption would not be consistent with the existence of very vigorous competition. For under vigorous competition each seller, trying to secure more of the business that brings higher net prices, would reduce delivered prices for the near-by customers and raise them for more distant customers; in other words, he would not retain the practice of charging uniform delivered prices. But even the absence of vigorous competition, which can be inferred from the fact that a seller charges uniform prices in spite of substantial freight costs, allows no inferences concerning the means by which competition has been restricted, in particular, whether or not collusion exists.

In Case (3)—uniform and identical delivered prices quoted by different sellers to different buyers at different locations—the presumption that an organized relaxation or suppression of price competition exists is much stronger, especially if transportation costs are relatively high. If the case is not one of outright price fixing, it is probably one of price leadership or tacit understanding. Such a presumption is not necessarily warranted if transportation costs are relatively small.

Case (4)—uniform mill-net prices realized by a seller from sales to different buyers at different locations—is the one case that would be consistent with "pure competition." The net prices realized by a pure competitor from all his sales must at any one time be the same. But that the case is consistent with pure competition does not mean that it would be inconsistent with all sorts of monopolistic situations. It is quite conceivable that sellers—perhaps under the pressure of governmental measures—abstain from price discrimination so that each will realize uniform net prices from all his sales, but that these mill-net prices are nevertheless the result of price leadership or outright price fixing schemes. It is more difficult, however, for sellers to suppress price competition for long periods if they are compelled to quote uniform f.o.b. mill prices.

The meaning of Case (5)—identical mill-net prices realized by different sellers at different locations from sales to one buyer— is not immediately clear. If mill-net prices are identical and transport costs different, delivered prices must be different. Normally a buyer selects the cheapest offer and rejects the others. The buyer in Case (5) does not; he pays more for goods from distant sellers than from near-by ones. In other words, he practices price discrimination in purchasing. Obviously he buys also from distant sources because he cannot get all he wants from the closest source. He is in a so-called "monopsonistic" position. In paying identical f.o.b. prices to different producers he discriminates against the near-by suppliers and in favor of the more distant ones.

Case (6) implies that actually consummated sales of goods delivered from a variety of places to a variety of places with different transportation costs yield uniform and identical mill-net prices to every seller. It would take a peculiar price-fixing agreement to accomplish this result; for example, a group of buyers could conspire to pay for a material a fixed price f.o.b. producing place wherever this may be. To be sure, a governmental price regulation can do the trick; for example, a regulation fixing the price of an agricultural produce f.o.b. farm regardless of its location.

UNFAIR COMPETITION

A survey of monopolistic business practices would be sadly incomplete without a discussion of "unfair competition," or of those methods of competition that are called unfair either because they involve techniques, such as deception or bribery, regarded as fouls by standards of common decency, or because they injure not only competitors but also consumers, or because business groups have been trying to persuade us that such methods are bad for them, and what's bad for business must be unfair. Unfair competition under the traditions of the common law, unfair competition under recent pressure-group-sponsored statutes, unfair competition under the norms of some special business ethics,—these are rather different things; and an evaluation of the "unfair" practices from the point of view of the economic welfare of society may differ from the results of applying any of these standards.

What Is Unfair?

A few words ought to be said about the meanings of fair and unfair. Of course, we shall not review the dictionary meanings of fair, ranging from blonde and beautiful to gentle and advantageous. When the modes or results of economic actions are called "fair," the connotation is clearly one of justice, equity and propriety, but with a rather vague, shiftable, and highly subjective standard. What may be fair from your point of view need not be fair from mine. Where there is widespread agreement, it is probably because a state of affairs has long prevailed and people have become accustomed to it. What continues to be as it has "normally" been is often regarded as fair, whereas a deviation from the customary is resented by many as unfair.

But if a deviation from the expected—the customary, the normal—is regarded as unfair by those who are disappointed, one should ask whether they had any right to expect what they expected. Do I have a right to expect to be able to recover my investment? Do I have a right to expect that nobody will imitate my new ideas? Do I have a right to expect to resell with a profit? If I have been given a promise, I have a right to expect it to be kept and I may regard its being broken as unfair. If all my competitors have promised me not to cut prices—though such promises would be illegal—I may call those unfair who break the promise. But if they have not promised price maintenance, an expectation on my part that I shall be able to sell at a profit is only a gamble and I have no right to shout "unfair" if someone starts chiseling. I shall be just out of luck.

There is a difference between being out of luck and being robbed, though many overlook this difference and complain that they are robbed whenever their hopes are frustrated by actions of other people who have a perfect right to do what they do and, indeed, whose actions probably benefit the community as a whole. Of course, it is different if the actions that hurt the complainant are clearly in violation of common rules of ethics—rules, for example, against lying and deceiving—or clearly injurious to the public at large. But injury to competitors must not be confused either with injury to competition or with injury to the public.

Unfair competition under the traditions of common law and conservative legal doctrines does not include such things as competitive price cutting, selling below cost, or imitation of a competitor's ideas, designs or styles. Unfair competition under the

provisions of statutes enacted since the 1930's does extend to price
cutting, and in some states to "selling below cost," in the retail
business. Unfair competition under the codes of ethics of some
special business groups extends to fairly widespread competitive
activities which even accommodating legislatures have thus far
refused to outlaw. Evaluations of any of these practices from the
economic point of view will pay no special attention to vested interests but will consider only the effects on the economy as a whole.
These evaluations will distinguish competitive actions by which a
seller makes his product cheaper, bigger, better, or more appealing to the buyer, from competitive actions by which a seller tries
to make his competitors' products more expensive, less serviceable,
less available, or less appealing to the buyer. There is good sense
in calling competitive actions of the latter, or negative, kind unfair competition—for they are prejudicial to the consumer as well
as to the competitors. But competitive actions of the first kind
are probably beneficial to the public, no matter how much they
may hurt some of the competitors. The disappointment of sellers
unable to sell at a profit may evoke sympathy but will not cause
economists to regard the price cutting that causes such disappointment as unfair competition. Competition that prevents sellers from
making a "fair profit" is not for that reason "unfair."

The Right to Compete

Businessmen have always sought protection from damage by
competitors and have often gone to court for relief. But the common law has usually refused to grant such relief and has generally
upheld the right to compete.[46]

Fortunately for the economic development of society, the conservative legal doctrines of unfair competition have sturdily resisted most of the businessmen's attempts to suppress competition
by calling it "unfair diversions of trade" and "unfair appropriation
of intangible trade values" by competitors. By and large, the courts
have upheld the right to compete even where competition meant

[46] One of the earliest court cases against a competitor was the *Schoolmasters' Case* of 1410. It was brought by two English schoolmasters who
sued a newcomer because his competition had reduced tuition fees. The
court denied recovery of the damages.

appropriation by a newcomer of the "fruits of one's labor, investment, and ingenuity." [47]

Since the great depression of the 1930's a number of statutes have been enacted which restrict the right to compete and extend the range of practices regarded as unfair under the law. For particular industries special interest groups have succeeded in reducing competition through specific legislation enacted in the name of fairness. "Preventing unfairness," if one were to judge from the letter and spirit of a host of state laws and local ordinances passed during the last twenty years, is almost equivalent to "preventing competition." Through successful campaigns against alleged unfairness, monopolistic interests have won many local victories. On the national scene, the biggest offensive against competition in the United States was the National Industrial Recovery Act of 1933, inspired by the mistaken theory that it would help to cure the depression. Almost 900 "codes of fair competition" were formulated during the two years of the N.R.A. This experience taught many people that competition would soon be completely stifled or altogether abolished if the businessmen's ideas of fairness were allowed full scope in delimiting the range of permissible competitive practices. Nevertheless, in the retail field the right to use price competition in the sale of articles with trade-marks or trade-names was well-nigh abrogated in the name of "fair trade."

Economic Classification

From the point of view of economic analysis the competitive practices which are regarded as unfair either under the law (common or statutory) or under the ethical standards of the business community—"unfair" either because of the malicious or predatory intent of the perpetrator or because of injurious effects upon competitors or consumers—may be divided into the following four groups:

1. Competitive practices which tend to confuse, deceive or molest the consuming public and thus to impair the economic function of price competition in the markets.

[47] Milton Handler, "Unfair Competition," *Iowa Law Review*, Vol. XXI (1936), reprinted in *Readings in the Social Control of Industry*, ed. E. M. Hoover, Jr. and J. Dean (Philadelphia: Blakiston, 1942), p. 93.

2. Competitive practices which, employed by firms with superior economic power, tend to weaken the competitive position and jeopardize the survival of smaller firms in the industry and, thereby, to increase or reinforce the monopolistic power of the former.

3. Competitive practices (such as nondeceptive imitation and appropriation of ideas) which, although injurious to competitors and regarded as unethical by most people, tend to lead to effects more often beneficial than harmful to the consuming public.

4. Competitive price cutting which, injurious to competitors but not to competition, regarded as unethical by members of the trade but not by the mass of buyers, is perhaps the most important form of competition and unquestionably beneficial to the community.

The fourth class is listed here only under protest. It does not really belong in the category of unfair competition and, until twenty years ago, no lawyer and no economist would have included it. The one thing unfair in connection with competitive price cutting is the attempt of its opponents to stigmatize it as unfair competition and legislate against it in the name of fairness. No further discussion of this point seems necessary in the present context. The other three classes of unfair competition will now be discussed in turn.

Deception of the Consumer

The origin of the term unfair competition is found in cases dealing with the attempts of one seller to pass off his goods as those of another by putting them on the market under a trademark or trade-name associated in the minds of the public with the products of the other. He may appropriate the mark or name of the other or he may merely imitate it so closely that the public is confused. Through such deceit trade is diverted to the imitator. The rightful owner of the trade-mark can bring an action for "infringement of his copyright"; the originator of the trade-name can bring an action charging "unfair competition."

The protection of trade-marks and trade-names which the law accords to their proprietors has an economic justification which does not hinge on the property rights acquired by the first user or on the investment of effort and money which he may have made in order to get his goods accepted and known by the public under the chosen marks or names. The justification is that intelligent consumption "requires some means of identifying today the articles that pleased or displeased yesterday." [48] The consumer is entitled to protection against confusion and deceit. It has been considered expedient to secure this protection by giving the injured competitor and proprietor of the identifying devices the right to sue the simulator; this method "vicariously avenges the fraud upon consumers." [49] The difficulty inherent in this method is that the protection of the property interests of a competitor against unfair diversion of trade and the protection of the consuming public against deception are not always concurrent. Some lawyers, emphasizing the property aspect of the problem, are too much inclined to restrain competition as unfair where no consumer interests are jeopardized, or to deny relief against serious consumer deception if a competitor cannot prove damages to his property interests. Court decisions in trade-mark cases are full of instances of both these types.

Other practices by which goods of one producer are passed off as those of another include imitation of labels, packages and appearances. Any sort of misrepresentation of origin which may seriously mislead the consumer and injure the competitor comes into this category of unfair competition and may be a cause of court action. The protection of trade-marks, names, labels, brands, etc., does, however, enable established firms to secure a position in the public's esteem which newcomers in the field may have great difficulty overcoming. In other words, new producers producing equally good or better products at cheaper prices may be unable to overcome firmly established public preferences that have been carefully nurtured by advertising and other sales campaigns. Devices to protect the consumer against confusion and deception are dearly paid for if they deprive him of the benefits of newcomers' competition. This is the basic justification for grade labeling and other arrangements which enable the consumer to obtain accurate information as to the quality of the product he is buying irrespective

[48] Handler, *op. cit.*, p. 89.
[49] *Ibid.*

of the name or package in which it is presented. Even more drastic measures might be called for in order to guard against the danger that the protection of exclusive rights in the use of identifying devices virtually close the field to newcomers. The throwing open of a trade-name for use by every seller in the field, if the name has become the generic term for the type of product covered, is a measure to which courts have frequently resorted.

Protection of the consumer is not confined to protection against deception as to the origin of goods, but extends to protection against deception through misrepresentation and misbranding of goods as to quantity, quality and character. Misrepresentation may relate either to the seller's own goods or to the goods of his competitors. False statements by a seller about his own wares, in an attempt to make them more desirable to the consumer, and false statements about his competitors' wares, in an attempt to make them less desirable to the consumer, are surely unfair and obnoxious methods of diverting trade from competitors. It is therefore appropriate that not only consumers deceived by unfair competitive practices but also competitors injured by false advertising, malicious disparagement of their goods or services, and other kinds of gross misrepresentation should be given the right to bring legal action for relief and damages.

There is a question, however, where the line should be drawn between the principle that the law should protect the buyer against deception and the principle that the buyer should protect himself by using prudence and common sense. There exist, especially in retail trade, many simple schemes of misleading a buyer into believing that he is being offered a special bargain where this is not the case. And there are the notorious merchandizing schemes featuring lotteries or including other "attractive" elements of chance. Does it devolve on the law to protect the imprudent buyer?

Molestation and intimidation of customers in order to divert trade from competitors, or physical interference with customers' dealings with competitors, are certainly unlawful. That the law, besides protecting the customer against such assaults, undertook to protect a business against a competitor's assaults upon its customers, is an interesting extension of the law of unfair competition.

In the United States the greater part of existing law against unfair competition of the types discussed—protecting the consuming public against deception and molestation—has developed as common law, but statutory law has made some additions. For example, the mail fraud section of the postal laws prohibits the use of the mails for lotteries and fraudulent selling schemes. The Food and Drug Law, enacted first in 1906 and amended several times since, prohibits misbranding and adulteration of foods and drugs. The Federal Trade Commission was established in 1914 for the purpose of banning "unfair methods of competition," and it was thought that the words unfair competition would be permitted "to grow and broaden and mold themselves to meet circumstances as they arise." [50]

Competition to Reduce Competition

A number of sharp practices against competitors are regarded by the law as unfair and not to be tolerated if they are used by firms with superior economic power against smaller firms and jeopardize the survival of the latter as competitors. If the same practices were used against firms of more equal strength, they would still be "sharp" practices, condemned as unfair under our accepted moral code, but they would neither in the short nor in the long run injure the interests of the consuming public and there would be no firm ground for interference by the legislative, judicial or executive powers of the state.

There are a great variety of practices which strong concerns or combines have employed to run weak competitors out of business and which courts have ruled to be illegal because they constituted attempts to reduce competition or create monopolies. Cutting off the sources of supplies of weaker competitors; closing their channels of trade by tying up all the main retail outlets with exclusive dealing contracts; inducing their customers or suppliers to break contracts; enticing away their most valuable employees; shadowing the competitors' salesmen; selling their products below cost; manufacturing and selling inferior imitations of their products; maintaining bogus independents; intimidating the competitors'

[50] Statement by Senator Cummins, *Congressional Record*, Vol. 51 (1914), p. 14002.

customers by threatening them with suits for alleged patent in-
fringements; weakening the competitors' positions through the use
of commercial bribery and espionage or through harassing litigation; arranging group boycotts against competitors or their customers; coercing competitors through threats of cut-throat competition; these are some of the practices which have become notorious
through court cases dealing with violations of the Sherman Antitrust Act.

Price discrimination and tying clauses are two methods of competition to reduce competition that the Clayton Act singled out for
special treatment. These practices are prohibited only if they are
part of a scheme to reduce competition substantially or to create a
monopoly. Price discrimination of the "kill-the-rival" type, the
"favor-the-big-ones" type, and the "hold-them-in-line" type have
frequently been used as part of schemes to reduce competition.[51]
Tying clauses in sale or lease contracts are clauses which prohibit
the buyer or lessee from using goods supplied by competitors.
Such exclusive-dealing agreements are unlawful where their effect
may be to lessen competition substantially.

No Harm to the Consumer

Industrial espionage, betrayal of trade secrets, piracy of ideas,
imitation of original styles and designs—all these sound like grossly
unfair practices. There is, however, an important difference between them and other unfair methods of competition. Whereas
other unfair practices are, as a rule, injurious to a competitor as well
as to the consuming public, this cannot be said about nondeceptive
imitation and appropriation of ideas. Here no harm to the consumer
is involved. On the contrary, the more extensively good ideas are
appropriated, good products copied and good techniques imitated
by competitors, the greater will be the benefit to the consumer.

Lawyers usually see these things in a different light. They are
inclined to apply the philosophy of the patent law to the law of
trade secrets (and, in addition, to label as morally reprehensible any
actions of a competitor which injure the business of another). Under the patent law inventors of certain types of products are

[51] See above, pp. 147, 150 and 152.

granted protection against imitation for a limited period. In spite of the temporary restraint on the utilization of the invention, the consumer is deemed, under the philosophy of the patent law, to benefit because the patent protection generally offered to inventors promotes invention, research, and investment in developing new ideas. Lawyers sometimes insist that the protection of trade secrets, designs, and other industrial and commercial ideas has a similar justification. But can this seriously be argued?·Ideas of this sort are not the result of tremendous research expenditures nor are they of great fundamental value.[52] Where should the line be drawn?

There may perhaps be other grounds on which espionage and bribery for the betrayal of trade secrets should be prohibited as unfair competition; but since the interest of the consumer certainly does not call for it, we should be very careful how far we permit the law to designate as legally wrong actions which merely enable good ideas to be more widely copied. For example, low price dress manufacturers are referred to in most uncomplimentary terms for copying the dress designs put out by the exclusive houses for the wealthy ladies of fashion.[53] Yet one of the arguments against permitting dress designs to be patented in the United States is that it is desirable that the working girl should be able to dress as fashionably as the Park Avenue debutantes. The consumer's interest is harmed rather than benefited by the protection of any "property" in unpatented ideas. This has been recognized by legal theory concerning the appropriation of ideas which cannot be kept secret. In the United States, original styles may be copied with impunity. Unpatented products, designs, advertising schemes and merchandizing methods may be imitated without any legal obstacles (except in cases of "passing off," i.e., deceiving the consumer about the source of offered goods). Imitation, indeed, is accepted as an integral part of competition. To ban nondeceptive imitation would be to eliminate competition and to leave the consumer at the mercy of monopolies.

[52] The institution of private property has a different meaning with respect to material things, on the one hand, and ideas on the other. See below, Chapter 7, pp. 280–81.

[53] See for example Sylvan Gotschal, *The Pirates Will Get You* (New York: Columbia University Press, 1945).

PART III—GOVERNMENT POLICIES

CHAPTER 6

Governmental Restraints on Monopoly: Antitrust Laws

Interventions against Competition and against Monopoly: Interventions against Competition · Interventions against Monopoly

A Chronology of Antimonopoly Policy: Ancient History · English History · American History

The Antitrust Laws of the United States: The Sherman Act · The Clayton Act · The Federal Trade Commission Act · The Robinson-Patman Act · The Celler Anti-Merger Act · Rules and Exceptions

The Law of Collusion: Juridical Controversies · Unconditional Prohibitions · Certainties and Uncertainties · Observance, Enforcement, Penalties · Collusion through Restrictive Patent Licensing · Exemptions for Labor and Agriculture · Exemptions for Transportation, Banking, and Insurance · Exemptions for Exporters and Retail Distributors · "Emergency" Exemptions

The Law of Monopolization: Vexing Problems · An All Too Judicious Judiciary · An Injudicious Legislature · Frustration Continued · Frustration Ended?

Antitrust Laws—Success or Failure? Contradictory Appraisals · Stopping the Cartels—a Partial Success · Checking the Trusts—a Dismal Failure · Alternative and Complementary Antitrust Policies

T HE PROBLEM OF monopoly and competition is by no means a recent concern of government. Indeed, we know of laws about monopolistic practices written more than 4,000 years ago —in Babylon. A truly Babylonian confusion of governmental attitudes toward the problem can be seen in the histories of most nations: a succession of state interventions restraining monopoly and aiding competition, restraining competition and aiding monopoly.

INTERVENTIONS AGAINST COMPETITION AND AGAINST MONOPOLY

Governments, apparently, have never been able to make up their minds as to which they dislike more, competition or monopoly. This has remained true to our days and will most likely continue in the future. In the United States, antimonopoly sentiment has been especially vocal, but legislative action during the last decades has been more "anticompetitive" in character. Whether government activities, on the basis of the presently existing body of law, are on balance more favorable to monopoly or to competition is controversial. A survey of the laws on the statute books —federal, state and local—gives this writer a strong impression that the net effect is in favor of monopoly.

Interventions against Competition

Since monopoly has a definitely "bad" connotation in the minds of people it is obvious that government action *against* monopoly can state its purpose expressly, whereas government action *in favor* of monopolistic developments is usually taken in the name of some other economic or social objective. In many or perhaps most instances the aid which state intervention gives to monopolistic developments is in fact an *incidental* effect of measures aiming at other, more or less generally accepted, goals. Examples are corporation laws—to enable successful financing and efficient management of large enterprises; patent laws—to encourage progress in the technical arts; labor laws—to prevent hardship among workers and improve their economic status; building ordinances— to avoid dangers to public safety and health; and other state and municipal laws and regulations to protect the people from dangers and hardships of one sort or another.

In certain instances government intervention is aimed *expressly* against competition, if only against allegedly vicious or unfair types. Cases in point are tariff laws—to protect domestic industries from foreign competition; fair-trade laws—to protect the upright, independent retailer from "unfair" competition by cut-rate stores; state laws regulating the supply and distribution of milk and other farm products—to safeguard sanitary conditions and, more frankly, to secure "fair" prices for the producers; laws regulating the rates of long-distance trucking services—to protect carriers from competition by operators able to charge low rates because they (allegedly) neglect proper safety provisions; and many similar laws and regulations to protect "qualified" and licensed operators from competition by the "unqualified" and unlicensed.

All these and other governmental aids to monopoly will be discussed in the subsequent chapters. The present chapter is given to the discussion of governmental restraints of monopoly.

Interventions against Monopoly

The most effective kind of action government can take against monopoly is to stop intervening against competition.

Historically, one of the more conspicuous moves against monopolies, the English Statute of Monopolies (of 1624) was merely a prohibition of monopoly grants by the Crown. The abolition of privileges for the exclusive practice of particular trades, privileges previously created by the state (such as the exclusive rights of craft guilds) ranks high among the few successful government actions against monopoly.

Legal proscriptions of private monopoly and monopolistic practices has always been hampered by the difficulty of defining "monopoly" and "monopolistic." That contracts "in restraint of trade" were considered void and unenforceable by English common law was, of course, of considerable significance, but the distinction between "reasonable" and "unreasonable" restraints of trade left the matter ambiguous and vague. In the United States the antitrust laws, according to some legal opinion, merely codified what had been the law of the land. In the view, however, of William Howard Taft, former Chief Justice of the Supreme Court of the United States, "our antitrust statute . . . makes such (unreasonable) restraints, which were . . . only void and unenforceable at common law, positively and affirmatively illegal, actionable, and indictable." [1] In judging what constitutes "unreasonable" re-

[1] William Howard Taft, *The Anti-Trust Act and the Supreme Court* (New York: Harper & Brothers, 1914), p. 21.

straint of trade, American courts in several respects went beyond English courts, but vagueness and uncertainty due to the impossibility of defining such phrases as "unreasonable" restraint have not disappeared. Only recently it has been observed that "under the 'rule of reason' in the application of the antitrust laws to any given situation there is no 'rule of thumb' to determine the issue." [2]

The effectiveness of the antitrust laws is not easy to evaluate. The historians Charles and Mary Beard said of the Sherman Antitrust Act of 1890: "This act was neither imposing nor effective. For a long time presidents allowed it to sleep in the statute book." [3] They might have added that the courts soon after its enactment proceeded to blunt or pull the teeth that Congress had put into the law, and that Congress failed to appropriate the funds necessary to administer it. There was a period, under Presidents Theodore Roosevelt and William Howard Taft, when the Government instituted some significant antitrust suits, but broadly speaking it was not until the late thirties, almost fifty years after the enactment of the Sherman law, that the Government began vigorously to prosecute antitrust violations. [4]

Whatever effectiveness the antitrust laws may have had in preventing conspiracies and collusion among competitors, they were totally ineffective in preventing combinations of competitors through merger. The merger movement in the United States, which started in the late 1880's, has continued practically unchecked, without any serious interference by the Federal Government, aided by convenient adaptations of corporation laws by the states.

[2] George E. Folk, *Patents and Industrial Progress* (New York: Harper & Brothers, 1942), p. 18.

[3] Charles A. and Mary R. Beard, *A Basic History of the United States* (New York: Doubleday, 1944), p. 329.

[4] In 1940 the Government instituted 114 cases under Federal antitrust law. During the 49 years from 1891 to 1939 it had instituted an average of less than nine cases a year and a maximum of 27 cases a year (in 1913). See *United States Versus Economic Concentration and Monopoly*, A Staff Report to the Monopoly Subcommittee of the Committee on Small Business, House of Representatives (Washington, 1946), Appendix G, pp. 276–89.— Perhaps it should be noted that the bulk of the prosecutions instituted by Assistant Attorney General Thurman Arnold (1938–1943) were directed against collusion cases, whereas several of the prosecutions instituted by Attorney General Wickersham (1909–1913) called for the dissolution of trusts.

A CHRONOLOGY OF ANTIMONOPOLY POLICY

The dramatic and yet feeble attempts of government to intervene against the growth of monopolistic business positions can be
more illuminatingly discussed against the background of a historical survey. For curiosity's sake the following chronology of
government attitudes toward monopoly includes a few items from
ancient times; the first 3,500 years of the chronology, however,
are covered by no more entries than the last ten or twelve years
—which, I suppose, is the appropriate historical perspective.

Ancient History [5]

circa 2100 B.C. Code of Hammurabi, King of Babylon, contains references to monopolistic practices.

347 B.C. The word monopoly is first used in Aristotle's *Politics* in
a discussion of people who cornered the market by buying up all the oil presses and all iron, selling later for a
high profit at a time of urgent demand.

circa 160 B.C. Cato, the Elder, refers to associations between rival
companies to establish monopolistic prices.

circa 30 A.D. Tiberius, Roman Emperor, introduces the word monopoly in Latin in an address before the Senate.

circa 79 A.D. Plinius, the Elder, Roman naturalist, records the frequent complaints of citizens against the exactions of
monopoly.

483 A.D. The Edict of Zeno, Roman Emperor, prohibits all
monopolies, whether created by imperial decree or by
private action, combinations and price agreements.

533 A.D. Code of Justinian, Roman Emperor, contains prohibition of monopolistic practices.

English History

After 1000 Merchant guilds and craft guilds develop as privileged
groups endowed with the exclusive right to practice certain
trades and professions in accordance with regulations.

[5] Most of this information is taken from Frank A. Fetter, *The Masquerade
of Monopoly*, pp. 249 ff., 335 ff. and 457, and from his testimony before the
Temporary National Economic Committee. *Investigation of Concentration of
Economic Power*, Hearings, Part 5 (Washington, D.C., 1939), p. 1658. Some

1285   A statute of Edward I prohibits "forestalling," a crime long illegal under common law. (Forestalling is trading outside, and before the opening, of the organized market, making it possible to buy up the supply of a commodity and to corner the market. Unlawful also are "engrossing," i.e., the buying up of large quantities in order to sell at unreasonable prices, and "regrating," i.e., enhancing prices in reselling goods in the same market.)

1299   In a case against the Candlemakers of Norwich the court decides that price agreements are illegal and punishable.

1415   In *Dier's* case the court declares that "contracts in restraint of trade" are void and unenforceable. (Dier had sued for payment of a sum promised him for retiring from the dyeing business.)

1534   The word monopoly is first used in English by Sir Thomas More, author of *Utopia*.

1547   A statute of Edward VI disendows certain religious fraternities but expressly exempts craft fraternities (guilds).

1562   Territorial monopolies of guilds are abolished.

1560–1603   Queen Elizabeth grants many "monopolies" (i.e., exclusive rights to manufacture or sell certain commodities) to nobles, corporations and Court favorites, as well as to innovators.

1603   In the "Case of Monopolies" (*Darcy* v. *Allin*) a court decision declares a monopoly in playing cards void as against common law because it results in higher prices and lower employment.

1623   Parliament passes the Statute of Monopolies forbidding the granting by the Crown of exclusive rights to trade (excepting, however, certain privileges such as those granted by Parliament, charters to craft guilds, patents for new inventions).

1711   In *Mitchel* v. *Reynolds* the court makes the significant distinction between "reasonable" and "unreasonable" restraint of trade.

1813   The East India Company loses its monopolistic trading privileges in India.

1814   Guilds are definitely abolished.

1892   The House of Lords as highest court in *Mogul Steamship*

information is taken from Theodor Mommsen, *The History of Rome* (New York: C. Scribner's Sons, 1870; Revised ed. 1903).

Company v. *McGregor, Gow et al.* refuses to allow damages to a company excluded from the shipping trade through the policies of a freight pool.

1948 The Monopoly (Inquiry and Control) Act is passed, creating the Monopoly and Restrictive Practices Commission to investigate matters referred to it by the Board of Trade, to report to Parliament and to draft Orders, for issuance by the competent Government department, declaring unlawful such practices as are found to operate against the public interest, each Order becoming effective only after approval by Parliament.

American History

1641 The Massachusetts Colonial legislature decrees "there shall be no monopolies granted or allowed among us but of such new inventions as are profitable to the country, and that for a short time."

1779 A statute of the Province of Massachusetts deals with monopoly and forestalling as the same thing.

1877 A court decision in *Munn* v. *Illinois* broadens the scope of public regulation of businesses which are "affected with a public interest."

1887 The Interstate Commerce Act is passed, creating the Interstate Commerce Commission for the regulation of railroads and other common carriers.

1888 The State of New Jersey adopts a general incorporation law permitting intercorporate stockholding (holding companies).

1890 In *The People of the State of N.Y.* v. *The North River Sugar Refining Company,* a suit brought under common law, the Circuit Court of Appeals annuls the corporate existence of a company which had entered into a trust agreement with other corporations, on the grounds that the company had accepted from the State the gift of corporate life only to disregard the conditions upon which it had been given, and on the grounds that it was a violation of the law for corporations to enter into a partnership with other corporations.

1890 The Sherman Antitrust Act is passed, prohibiting all contracts, combinations and conspiracies in restraint of trade as well as all monopolies and attempts to monopolize.

1895   In *United States* v. *E. C. Knight Co.* the Supreme Court, making a distinction between manufacturing and "interstate commerce," refuses to declare void the contracts by which the American Sugar Refining Company had accomplished, through stock acquisitions, the consolidation of control over 98 percent of the industry.

1898   A Congressional Industrial Commission begins a four-year study of the monopoly problem.

1899   In *Addyston Pipe and Steel Co.* v. *United States* the Supreme Court holds illegal a conspiracy among six companies to maintain prices by avoiding competitive bidding and arranging for division of territories.

1903   The Bureau of Corporations in the Department of Commerce is created to investigate organization, conduct and management of corporations engaged in interstate commerce.

1904   In *Northern Securities Company* v. *United States* the Supreme Court orders dissolution of a holding company which controlled the stock of two railroad companies.

1911   In *Standard Oil Company of New Jersey* v. *United States* the Supreme Court orders dissolution of that holding company, which through predatory acts had acquired control of the stock of over seventy petroleum companies in order to monopolize the trade. The decision contains the famous "rule of reason."

1911   In *United States* v. *American Tobacco Company* the Court orders dissolution of the company, which had acquired the assets of over sixty concerns "by methods devised in order to monopolize the trade."

1914   The Federal Trade Commission Act is passed, creating a permanent commission (replacing the Bureau of Corporations) with the power to investigate the practices of corporations (except banks and common carriers, regulated elsewhere) and to prevent, through "cease-and-desist orders" and, if necessary, through enforcement by the Court of Appeals, "unfair methods of competition."

1914   The Clayton Act is passed, supplementing the Sherman Act by prohibiting price discrimination, tying contracts and the acquisition of stock in competing corporations when the effect may be "to substantially lessen competition," and interlocking directorates in large corporations which compete with each other.

1917   In *United States* v. *United Shoe Machinery Co.* the Supreme Court refuses to declare illegal under the Sherman Act a restriction (tying clause) forbidding the licensed lessees of patented shoe machinery to use it for shoes that were not worked also on complementary machines leased from the same company.

1918   The Webb-Pomerene Act, an "Act to Promote Export Trade," is passed to exempt from the operation of the antitrust laws actions of export associations and their members relating to export trade if such actions do not artificially or intentionally affect prices or substantially lessen competition within the United States.

1920   In *United States* v. *United States Steel Corporation* the Supreme Court refuses to order dissolution of that "combination of combinations by which directly or indirectly 180 independent concerns were brought under one control," because "the law does not make mere size an offense" and the corporation was not a complete monopoly.

1921   The Supreme Court, in *American Column & Lumber Co.* v. *United States,* declares the activities of a trade association, attempting through dissemination of trade statistics and exhortations to limit production by its members, to be unlawful restraints under the Sherman Act.

1922   In the second *United States* v. *United Shoe Machinery Co.* case the Supreme Court declares the tying clause restricting the use of patented and leased shoe machinery to be illegal under the Clayton Act.

1921-25   In four cases against trade associations (*Hardwood Lumber, Linseed Oil, Cement, Maple Flooring*) the Supreme Court arrives at different decisions, declaring open-price associations unlawful in the first two cases, vindicating them in the two other cases.

1924   The Federal Trade Commission orders the United States Steel Corporation to cease and desist from the so-called "Pittsburgh Plus" system of pricing as unlawful price discrimination.

1926   In *United States* v. *General Electric Co.* the Supreme Court refuses to declare illegal a marketing scheme whereby 68,000 retailers were licensed as agents of the patentee to sell the product at the price fixed by him.

1926   In three cases involving orders of the Federal Trade Commission against mergers of competing businesses (*Western Meat Co., Thatcher Manufacturing Co., Swift & Co.*) the Supreme Court decides against the Commission and rules that the acquisition of the assets of competing corporations was not prohibited by the Clayton Act, even though such acquisition involved purchase of the voting stock of the competing corporations in violation of the Clayton Act, provided that the stock was disposed of before the Commission could act.

1927   In *United States* v. *Trenton Potteries Company* the Supreme Court declares price fixing illegal under the Sherman Act no matter how "reasonable" the prices may be.

1927   In *United States* v. *International Harvester Company* the Supreme Court refuses to dissolve the corporation and states that "the existence of unexerted power" is no offense and price leadership no proof of domination.

1931   In *United States* v. *Standard Oil Co. (Indiana)* the Supreme Court holds that patent owners combining in a pool and fixing and sharing the royalties charged on products made by patented processes are not unlawfully restraining trade unless they effectively dominate the industry.

1933   The National Industrial Recovery Act is passed, creating the National Recovery Administration (N.R.A.) providing for industrial cooperation under "codes of fair competition," exempted from the operation of the antitrust laws, to be approved and enforced by the Government and to be administered by Code authorities. (874 codes are approved subsequently, regulating labor conditions, production, investment, prices, selling conditions, etc., in industry.)

1935   In *Schechter Poultry Corporation* v. *United States* the Supreme Court declares the N.R.A. unconstitutional, partly because of excessive delegation of legislative power to administrative authorities.

1936   The Robinson-Patman Act is passed, supplementing the Clayton Act by prohibiting the making as well as the accepting of prices which discriminate in favor of large buyers and distributors, and by placing the burden of proof upon the offender.

1936   In *Sugar Institute* v. *United States* the Supreme Court condemns as illegal many trade association practices, including an open-price plan so far as it sought to compel adherence to prices and terms announced in advance.

1937   The Miller-Tydings Fair Trade Act is passed, amending the Sherman and Federal Trade Commission Acts so as to permit agreements and enforcement of resale price maintenance for trade-marked or branded goods under the Fair-Trade Act of any State.

1938   The Temporary National Economic Committee (T.N.E.C.) begins its three-year investigation of concentration of economic power.

1940   In *Ethyl Gasoline Corporation* v. *United States* the Supreme Court decides that a patent licensing device used to maintain resale prices and to enforce non-competitive methods of marketing products is unlawful.

1941   In *United States* v. *William L. Hutcheson* the Supreme Court declares that the activities of labor unions acting alone and in their own interests are not covered by the Sherman Act even though the activities may restrain competition in the commercial market.

1942   In *United States* v. *Univis Lens Co.* the Supreme Court declares it to be illegal for the patentee to fix the resale prices for the licensed retailers of the patented product.

1942   In *Morton Salt Co.* v. *G. S. Suppiger Co.* the Supreme Court declares that the patentee's attempt to enlarge the scope of the patent monopoly (by licenses which restrict the use of leased patented machines to specified material) deprives him of the aid of the court against an infringing competitor.

1942   In *United States* v. *Masonite Corporation* the Supreme Court declares that price fixing by a member of a group, "pursuant to express delegation, acquiescence, or understanding," is just as illegal as price fixing by joint action.

1944   The Supreme Court in *United States* v. *South Eastern Underwriters Association* declares that the insurance business is commerce in the meaning of the antitrust laws and is covered by it.

1945   The Congress passes the McCarran Act exempting the in-

surance business from the antitrust laws if it is regulated
by the states.

1945   In *United States* v. *Hartford Empire Company* the Supreme
Court declares that domination of an industry by means
of a combination to obtain a monopoly of all patents in a
field is illegal and should be terminated through compulsory licensing of present and future patents to all applicants at reasonable royalty rates and without restrictions.

1945   In *Corn Products Refining Co.* v. *Federal Trade Commission* and *Federal Trade Commission* v. *Staley Manufacturing Co.* the Supreme Court declares the single-basing-point
system of pricing to be an unlawful price discrimination
under the Clayton Act.

1945   In *Georgia* v. *Pennsylvania Railroad Co.* the Supreme
Court declares that the "rate-fixing combinations" of the
railroads "have no immunity from the antitrust laws" and
are unlawful restraints of trade.

1945   In *United States* v. *Aluminum Company of America* the
Court of Appeals declares that the power to fix prices constitutes an unlawful monopoly even if no unlawful practices
are proved.

1946   In *American Tobacco Company* v. *United States* the Supreme Court declares that the material consideration in
determining whether or not a monopoly exists is the existence of the power to raise prices or exclude competition,
even though the power has never been exercised.

1948   The Congress passes, over a Presidential veto, the Reed-
Bulwinkle Act exempting carrier agreements on transportation rates from the antitrust laws if the agreements were
approved by the Interstate Commerce Commission.

1948   In *Federal Trade Commission* v. *Cement Institute* the Supreme Court reverses a lower court and sustains an order of
the Commission prohibiting cement producers from carrying out "any planned common course of action" resulting
in identical prices, and particularly from continuing to
practice a multiple basing-point system of pricing.

1950   The President vetoes a bill passed by Congress to amend
the Clayton and Federal Trade Commission Acts in such a
way as to make the practice of the basing-point system safe
against prosecution by the Government.

1950   Congress passes an Act amending Section 7 of the Clayton

Act to make it unlawful for corporations to acquire the
assets of other corporations where this may substantially
lessen competition in any line of commerce in any section
of the country.

1951　In *Schwegmann Brothers* v. *Calvert Distillers Corporation*
the Supreme Court holds that the exemptions from the
Sherman Act which the Miller-Tydings Amendment provides for price maintenance contracts between manufacturers and retailers in states with Fair Trade laws do not
extend to the enforcement of the fixed prices against retailers who have not signed these contracts.

1952　Congress amends the "Fair Trade" amendment to restore
state enforcement of retail price fixing agreements against
retailers who have not signed the agreements.

THE ANTITRUST LAWS OF THE UNITED STATES

Reading the chronology of American court decisions one can
hardly fail to be impressed with the fact that some fundamental
questions of antitrust law were decided only forty years and more
after the enactment of the Sherman Act; that other fundamental
questions seem still to be undecided after sixty years; and that
several questions that were decided were resolved in favor of
the monopolistic tendencies which the original law was supposed
to check. Was the law so vague or ambiguous that it could not be
applied to fulfill its purpose?

The Sherman Act

An American judge recently supplied an answer to this question when, in a decision in an antitrust case, he observed that in
his opinion "the Sherman Act, properly interpreted and administered, would have remedied all the ills meant to be cured. More
comprehensive language than that found in the Sherman Act is
difficult to conceive." [6]

In an industry in which competition prevails, monopoly power

[6] Judge Lindley of the U.S. District Court of Eastern Illinois, in his decision in *United States* v. *New York Great Atlantic and Pacific Tea Company,*
67 F. Supp. 626, 676 (1946).

can be created (1) by eliminating or reducing competition among the existing firms, or (2) by eliminating existing rival firms by forcing them out of business or absorbing them. The Sherman Anti- trust Act, remarkably enlightened on these matters, proscribed both methods by prohibiting *collusion* (in Section 1) as well as *monopolization* (in Section 2). Section 1 makes illegal "every contract, combination . . . or conspiracy in restraint of trade," Section 2 makes it illegal to "monopolize, or attempt to monopolize, . . . any part of the trade," among the several States or with for- eign nations.[7]

These prohibitions of collusion and monopolization, if enforced, could have been effective against the creation, the maintenance and the exploitation of monopoly power. The Act not merely pro- vided for the punishment of violators (in criminal proceedings) but also (in Section 4) gave the courts jurisdiction to "prevent and restrain" the violations (in civil proceedings).

In the words of the Judge whose opinion was quoted above, "That Congress desired to go to the utmost extent of its constitu- tional power in preventing restraints of trade and attempts to monopolize . . . appears very clear." [8] Congress perhaps underes- timated the cost of properly enforcing the law. The funds appro- priated for enforcement were never sufficient. They allowed, at best, for the investigation and prosecution of a small sample of violations, so small a sample that it took half a century to obtain adjudications of the more important types of offenses against the law of collusion. Moreover, when conservative court decisions gave the law of monopolization such a narrow interpretation that the purposes of the law seemed thwarted, Congress, in writing the Clayton Act, failed to make its will sufficiently clear to achieve its objectives. Eventually, the lawmakers lost their zeal and gave in to politically powerful special interests pressing for exemptions from the law. Thus, it is no grave exaggeration to state, with a recent report to a Congressional Committee, that "the enforce-

---

[7] The official title of the law is "An Act to protect trade and commerce against unlawful restraints and monopolies," Public Law No. 190—51st Congress, 1890 (26 Stat. 209), U.S.C. Title 15, Secs. 1–7, 15.

[8] *United States* v. *The New York Great Atlantic and Pacific Tea Company,* 67 F. Supp. 626, 677 (1946).

ment of the Sherman Act was largely a matter of a policeman
looking the other way." [9]

The Clayton Act

The Clayton Act of 1914 was designed to achieve purposes
the Sherman Act might have achieved if it had been less narrowly
interpreted, but which it failed to achieve because of the way
in which it was in fact interpreted. While existing restraints of trade
(if unreasonable) and existing monopolies (if absolute) were disallowed by the courts under the Sherman Act, action was needed,
in the opinion of Congress, "to arrest the creation of trusts, conspiracies, and monopolies in their incipiency and before consum-
mation." [10]

Four kinds of monopolistic practices were singled out by the
Clayton Act: price discrimination "where the effect of such discrimination may be to substantially lessen competition or tend to
create a monopoly in any line of commerce" (Section 2); the use
of tying clauses in sales or leases "where the effect . . . may be
to substantially lessen competition or tend to create a monopoly
in any line of commerce" (Section 3); acquisition by a corporation
of stock of another corporation "where the effect of such acquisition may be to substantially lessen competition" between the
acquiring and the acquired corporation or "to restrain commerce
in any section or community or tend to create a monopoly of
any line of commerce" (Section 7); and interlocking directorates
among corporations (above a certain size) which are or have been
competitors (Section 8).

Section 2, prohibiting price discrimination potentially injurious to competition, was amended and supplemented by the Robinson-Patman Act of 1936. Section 7, prohibiting corporate merger

[9] *United States Versus Economic Concentration and Monopoly.* A Staff
Report to the Monopoly Subcommittee of the Committee on Small Business,
House of Representatives (Washington, 1946), p. 4.

[10] Senate Committee on the Judiciary, *Senate Report No. 695*, 63rd Congress, 2nd session, July 22, 1914, to accompany H.R. 15657, p. 1. The official
title of the Clayton Act is "An Act to supplement existing laws against unlawful restraints and monopolies, and for other purposes." Public Law No. 212—
63rd Congress, 1914. (38 Stat. 730) U.S.C. Title 15, Secs. 12–27, 44.

through stock acquisition, was amended and supplemented only in 1950 by a prohibition of corporate merger through asset acquisition. The story of the attempts to enforce the prohibition of mergers is one of the most frustrating in the history of law enforcement. We shall recount its highlights later in this chapter.

The Federal Trade Commission Act

Enforcement of the four prohibitions of the Clayton Act was made the responsibility of the Federal Trade Commission,[11] which Congress had created in the same year through the Federal Trade Commission Act.[12]

This Act, besides defining the powers of the new Government agency—particularly the power to investigate "the organization, business, conduct, practices, and management" of corporations—contained an important new prohibition: "unfair methods of competition" were declared unlawful (Section 5). The Act provided for procedures by which the Commission could order violators "to cease and desist from the violations of the law" charged by the Commission, but it did not specify or even give any clue as to what methods of competition might be said to be unfair. The statute left this entirely to the courts and, as we have seen in the preceding Chapter on Monopolistic Business Practices, a fair amount of case law has actually developed over the years.

The most significant of these developments is that the law has been construed as a real supplement to and extension of the Sherman Act: It gives the Government an alternative method of restraining private restraints of competition in that "conduct tending to restrain trade is an unfair method of competition even though the selfsame conduct may also violate the Sherman Act."[13] And it expands the zone of things forbidden in that a practice may

[11] The Interstate Commerce Commission was charged with enforcement with respect to common carriers, the Federal Reserve Board with respect to banks and trust companies.

[12] Public Law No. 203—63rd Congress, 1914. (38 Stat. 717) U.S.C. Title 15, Secs. 41–51.

[13] *Federal Trade Commission* v. *The Cement Institute*, 333 U.S. 683, 693 (1948).

be held to be unfair competition either because it "restrains free competition or is an incipient menace to it." [14]

The Robinson-Patman Act

Section 2 of the Clayton Act, prohibiting price discrimination potentially injurious to competition, had provided that quantity discounts and price discrimination practiced "in good faith to meet competition" were not forbidden. These provisions left the door open for many discriminatory practices which were potentially harmful to competition. To remedy this situation Congress in 1936 passed the Robinson-Patman Act,[15] amending Section 2 of the Clayton Act.

The new act prohibited quantity discounts and other advantages granted to large buyers except to the extent that a lower price could be justified by the lower cost of manufacture, delivery or sale in larger quantities. The act also modified the "good faith" provision by replacing the general justification of price discrimination—"to meet competition"—by a much narrower justification —"to meet *an* equally low price of a competitor." Finally, while the prohibited act of price discrimination were in general only subject to the cease-and-desist orders of the Federal Trade Commission, the new law (in Section 3) declared certain types of discrimination to be criminal offenses.

Because it prohibited discriminatory quantity discounts to large buyers, the Robinson-Patman Act has sometimes been called the "Chain-Store Law." While it is true that most of the support for the law came from small business, especially from the independent retail merchants, its provisions have much wider applications.

The Celler Anti-Merger Act

The latest supplement to the antitrust laws was the Celler Anti-Merger Act, in 1950, to amend Section 7 of the Clayton Act, pro-

[14] *Ibid.*
[15] Public Law No. 692—74th Congress, 1936 (49 Stat. 1526; 52 Stat. 446), U.S.C. Title 15, Sec. 13.

hibiting corporate mergers where they may effect a substantial reduction of competition.[16]

The amendment closed a gap which the original law had inadvertently left open: merger through asset acquisition. (Although the mistake in the original version of Section 7 had become apparent soon after the Clayton Act was enacted, it took Congress thirty-six years to correct it.) The amendment, moreover, extended the coverage of the prohibition: its limitation to mergers between competing corporations was removed. Thus, vertical and conglomerate mergers may become subject to review and attack by the Federal Trade Commission.

Rules and Exceptions

We have gone over five pieces of Federal antitrust legislation: the Sherman Act, the Clayton Act, the Federal Trade Commission Act, the Robinson-Patman Act and the Merger Amendment. This does not constitute the bulk of United States legislation on restraint of trade and attempts to monopolize; but it does constitute all of the legislation *against* collusion and monopolizations. The rest —and there is considerable additional legislation on the subject— consists of statutes providing exceptions to and exemptions from the prohibitions of the antimonopoly laws.

Since most of these statutory exceptions and exemptions were made in response to political pressures when the courts began to enforce the prohibitions of the antitrust laws, and since some exemptions were not statutory but the results of unexpectedly narrow judicial interpretations of the statutes, they can be more intelligently discussed together with the development which the laws have had over the years in the course of their application in the courts. Tradition, following the distinction made by the first two sections of the Sherman Act, divides the discussion into two parts, one on the "law of collusion" (or combinations in restraint of trade) and one on the "law of monopolization" (chiefly concerning merger and consolidation). We shall follow this tradition.[17]

[16] Chapter 1184, Public Law 899.

[17] The division into collusion and merger, or "loose-knit combination" and "close-knit combination," seems to leave no place for a discussion of strong-

THE LAW OF COLLUSION

The development of the law of collusion through judicial interpretations of the statutes was slow, but a substantial body of
law has actually evolved over the years. The evolution has not been
without changes in direction, but looking backward over the sixty
years of interpretation one is impressed by the smallness of the
deviations from the general trend. Despite considerable juridical
controversy over the relationship between "restraint of trade" and
"monopoly" and over the place of the "rule of reason" in cases involving restraints of trade, and despite the oscillations of the Supreme Court because of these controversies, "the great majority
of its rulings do appear to follow a fairly constant pattern." [18]

Juridical Controversies

Section 1 of the Sherman Act deals with "restraint of trade"
while Section 2 deals with "monopoly." What exactly is the difference? There were jurists who denied that there was any difference
and treated the two as synonymous.[19] There were others who saw
a considerable difference between the two concepts. And there is
finally the view, now widely accepted among lawyers that every
monopoly may constitute a restraint of trade, but not every restraint of trade is monopolistic.[20] In general, however, the con-

arm monopolistic practices of a powerful corporation against its weaker
competitors. These practices, however, are usually designed to force a competitor to accept either a pricing scheme or a merger, and consequently are
frequently part of a softening-up process preceding one of the two kinds of
combination.

[18] *A Study of the Construction and Enforcement of the Federal Antitrust
Laws. Monograph No. 38* of the Temporary National Economic Committee,
prepared by Milton Handler (Washington: 1941), p. 8. Much of the discussion in the following pages is based on Handler's clear exposition.

[19] For example Chief Justice White, *Standard Oil Company of New Jersey* v. *United States*, 211 U.S. 1, 53 (1911).

[20] For example Justice Douglas, *United States* v. *Socony-Vacuum Oil
Company*, 310 U.S. 150, 226 (1940). The following note from his opinion
throws much light on the relationship: "The existence or exertion of power
to accomplish the desired objective . . . becomes important only in cases
where the offense charged is the actual monopolizing of any part of trade
or commerce in violation of sec. 2 of the act. An intent and a power to
produce the result which the law condemns are then necessary. . . . But the

cept of restraint of trade has been applied to contracts and understandings, whereas the monopoly concept has been chiefly applied
in legal discussion to cases of merger and consolidation.[21] The
practical significance of the conclusion that every monopoly is a
restraint but not every restraint is monopolistic lies in the support
it gives to the legal construction that the existence of monopoly
power is irrelevant to a finding of restraint of trade. Collusion
among competitors is thus an illegal restraint of trade even if
they have not sufficient power to affect the market for their
products.

The place of the "rule of reason" in the interpretation of the
Sherman Act has given rise to much acrimonious debate.[22] There
were jurists who rejected the idea that it was the business of a
court to determine the "reasonableness" of a restraint of competition.[23] There were others who held that only agreements "which

---

crime under sec. 1 is legally distinct from that under sec. 2 . . . though the
two sections overlap in the sense that a monopoly under sec. 2 is a species
of restraint of trade under sec. 1. . . . Only a confusion between the nature
of the offenses under those two sections . . . would lead to the conclusion
that power to fix prices was necessary for proof of a price-fixing conspiracy
under sec. 1."

[21] T.N.E.C. *Monograph* No. 38, p. 85. Handler speaks of "restraint of
trade" in connection with the "loose-knit confederations" among competitors,
and of "monopoly" in connection with the "close-knit integrations" among
competitors.

[22] The rule of reason says in effect that, since the statute did not specify
what restraints were unlawful (and one could not reasonably assume that *all*
restraints were unlawful), the court must in every instance judge from a thorough examination of all circumstances of the case whether a particular restraint was "unreasonable" and hence unlawful.

[23] Judge (later Justice) Taft in the Circuit Court decision of the *Addyston
Pipe* case, 85 Fed. 271, 281 (1898) made the following statement about the
rule of reason in contracts in restraint of trade under common law: ". . .
where the sole object of both parties in making the contract . . . is merely
to restrain competition . . . it would seem that there was nothing to justify
or excuse the restraint, that it would necessarily have a tendency to monopoly,
and therefore would be void. In such a case there is no measure of what is
necessary to the protection of either party, except the vague and varying
opinion of judges as to how much, on principles of political economy, men
ought to be allowed to restrain competition. . . .

"It is true that there are some cases in which the courts . . . have set
sail on a sea of doubt, and have assumed the power to say, in respect to contracts which have no other purpose . . . than the mutual restraint of the

operated to the prejudice of the public interest by unduly restricting competition . . ." [24] were prohibited by the statute (as well
as under common law). This looks like a fundamental difference
of juridical opinion.[25] Yet in practice the rulings of the courts with
respect to the law of collusion were not seriously affected by the
difference in theory. The opponents of the rule of reason would
say that price fixing was always illegal no matter how reasonable

---

parties, how much restraint of competition is in the public interest, and how
much is not.

"The manifest danger in the administration of justice according to so
shifting, vague, and indeterminate a standard would seem to be a strong
reason against adopting it."

[24] Justice White in *Standard Oil Co. of New Jersey* v. *United States*, 221
U.S. 1 (1911) and in *United States* v. *American Tobacco Co.*, 221 U.S. 106,
179 (1911). One of Justice White's arguments in support of the rule of reason
was as follows: "And as the contracts or acts embraced in the provision were
not expressly defined, since the enumeration addressed itself simply to classes
of acts, those classes being broad enough to embrace every conceivable contract or combination which could be made concerning trade or commerce or
the subjects of such commerce, and thus caused any act done by any of the
enumerated methods anywhere in the whole field of human activity to be illegal if in restraint of trade, it inevitably follows that the provision necessarily
called for the exercise of judgment which required that some standard should
be resorted to for the purpose of determining whether the prohibition contained in the statute had or had not in any given case been violated. Thus
not specifying, but indubitably contemplating and requiring a standard, it
follows that it was intended that the standard of reason which had been
applied at the common law and in this country in dealing with subjects of
the character embraced by the statute was intended to be the measure used
for the purpose of determining whether, in a given case, a particular act had
or had not brought about the wrong against which the statute provided."
Standard Oil Company of New Jersey v. *United States*, 221 U.S. 1, 60
(1911).

[25] Cf. Justice Harlan's dissenting opinion in the Standard Oil case, where
he complained that the majority of the court by adopting the rule of reason
had asserted authority "to insert words in the antitrust act which Congress
did not put there." *Standard Oil Company of New Jersey* v. *United States*,
221 U.S. 1, 106 (1911). While one school of jurists followed this interpretation and considered the underlying difference of opinion as fundamental,
there is another school who find the difference immaterial. They interpret
Justice Taft as saying that all restraints of *competition* are illegal *per se,* but
since not every restraint of *trade* is a restraint of *competition* the court will
have to determine this in each particular case of restraint of trade. Justice
White is interpreted as saying that only *unreasonable* restraints of trade are
illegal and whether in a particular case the restraint is reasonable or not will
have to be determined by the court. (I am indebted to Sigmund Timberg.)

it might be. The friends of the rule of reason would say in effect that price fixing was unreasonable as such and therefore always illegal. The consequences of the judicial adoption of the rule of reason were serious only in the application of the law of monopolization, and that largely because of the obscure language employed.

Unconditional Prohibitions

A large variety of contracts, combinations and conspiracies have over the years been declared to be in illegal restraint of trade. A typical list includes

agreements fixing prices,[26] mark-ups, discounts, terms of sales;

agreements restricting output,[27] productive capacity, or productive processes;

agreements on sharing or dividing markets,[28] allocating customers or types of products;

agreements to exclude competitors from the market or to jeopardize their existence through tying clauses, exclusive dealing arrangements, local price cutting or other discriminatory policies.

The word "agreement," however, must not be taken too literally or it would be impossible nowadays to prosecute successfully any conspiracy in restraint of trade. In the first decades of antitrust prosecution businessmen learned that their understandings about prices and markets must not be in writing, and must not even be referred to, however obliquely, in informal correspondence, lest the Government get hold of such evidence and prove the existence of explicit agreement. Hence the prosecuting agencies of the Government had to adjust themselves to the absence of documentary evidence and rest their cases partly on inferential evidence. The courts after some hesitation recognized this as in accord with

[26] The leading cases are *United States* v. *Trenton Potteries Co.* 273 U.S. 392 (1927) and *United States* v. *Socony Vacuum Oil Co.*, 310 U.S. 150 (1940).

[27] The leading case is *American Column & Lumber Co.* v. *United States,* 257 U.S. 377 (1921).

[28] The leading case is *Addyston Pipe and Steel Co.* v. *United States,* 175 U.S. 211 (1899).

"common sense and the realities of the situation."[29] It is now accepted doctrine that, in the absence of direct evidence of agreement among competitors, the existence of a combination can, in conjunction with other indirect evidence, be inferred from group behavior which cannot be fully explained by anything but a planned common course of action.[30]

This implies that there are many concealed and indirect methods of achieving prohibited objectives. The courts have been repeatedly concerned with the techniques by which trade associations, statistical bureaus and institutes, or casual confederations of the members of an industry have contrived to achieve the concert of action essential for the elimination or restriction of competition. Many of these techniques have been declared unlawful. For example, the reporting, under the guise of statistical information or otherwise, of current or future prices, coupled with a promise, expressed or implied, to adhere to them for a certain time or until further notice, is definitely prohibited as a restraint under the Sherman Act.[31] Or the practice of the basing-point system of quoting identical delivered prices is definitely prohibited as an unfair method of competition under the Federal Trade Commis-

[29] *United States Maltsters Association* v. *Federal Trade Commission*, 152 F. 2d 161, 164 (1945).

[30] "It is not the form of the combination or the particular means used but the result to be achieved that the statute condemns. It is not of importance whether the means used to accomplish the unlawful objectives are in themselves lawful or unlawful. Acts done to give effect to the conspiracy may be in themselves wholly innocent acts. Yet, if they are part of the sum of the acts which are relied upon to effectuate the conspiracy which the statute forbids, they come within its prohibitions. No formal agreement is necessary to constitute an unlawful conspiracy. Often crimes are a matter of inference deduced from the acts of the person accused and done in pursuance of a criminal purpose. . . . The essential combination or conspiracy in violation of the Sherman Act may be found in a course of dealings or other circumstances as well as in any exchange of words. . . . Where the circumstances are such as to warrant a . . . finding that the conspirators had a unity of purpose or a common design and understanding, or a meeting of minds in an unlawful agreement, the conclusion that a conspiracy is established is justified." *American Tobacco Company* v. *United States*, 328 U.S. 781, 809, 810 (1946).

[31] *United States* v. *American Linseed Oil Co.*, 262 U.S. 371 (1923); *Sugar Institute* v. *United States*, 297 U.S. 553 (1936).

sion Act and as a discriminatory practice injurious to competition under the Clayton Act.[32]

Certainties and Uncertainties

Foreign jurists and economists have questioned the wisdom of the unconditional prohibition of price fixing. (No such prohibitions are known in cartel-minded Europe.) Why, they ask, should agreements about prices be illegal even when these prices are fair and reasonable? Why should one condemn trade association activities with regard to prices and output if the prices in question are not excessive and the supply is adequate? Those who ask these questions fail to understand the basic philosophy of the antimonopoly law, which is to avoid governmental judgment, necessarily arbitrary, of what prices or supplies are fair, reasonable or adequate, and to leave the determination of prices wherever possible to the anonymous forces operating in a competitive market, free from monopolistic influence, judicial supervision and administrative regulation and dictation. This point of view was expressed with great clarity by the Supreme Court in the Trenton Pottery case. The court also emphasized another important point, one that might impress those who are not impressed by the dangers of governmental regulation and dictation but are sensitive to the impracticability of constant supervision and day-to-day reexamination. Suppose we knew how to evaluate the reasonableness of price, and suppose the government did it efficiently and correctly, and found the prices fixed by a combination of competitors to be reasonable as of a certain day, the constant flux of economic conditions would continually change the relative appropriateness of these prices. "The reasonable price fixed today may through economic and business changes become the unreasonable price of tomorrow." [33]

[32] *Federal Trade Commission* v. *Cement Institute,* 333 U.S. 683 (1948).

[33] *United States* v. *Trenton Potteries Company,* 273 U.S. 392, 397, 398 (1927). The full paragraph of the opinion reads as follows: "The aim and result of every price-fixing agreement, if effective, is the elimination of one form of competition. The power to fix prices, whether reasonably exercised or not, involves power to control the market and to fix arbitrary and unreasonable prices. The reasonable price fixed today may through economic and business

Businessmen are often in angry opposition to the allegedly extensive interpretations of the law by the Antitrust Division of the Department of Justice and the Federal Trade Commission, which are responsible for the enforcement of the law. But the chief complaint of the business community concerns the large degree of "uncertainty" of the law.[34] Yet, some uncertainty is inevitable because the law can never catch up with the ever-changing methods of business policy. Only prosecution and adjudication can reduce the uncertainty as to what is permitted and what is prohibited.[35] It would not be practicable for the statute or the prosecuting agency to enumerate all unlawful practices and, thus to guarantee to the businessman that any practice not explicitly forbidden was lawful. Smart businessmen could easily devise novel practices to achieve the same restraints of trade that the explicitly prohibited practices had been designed to accomplish. Hence, in order to be at all effective, the statute must be in general terms,

changes become the unreasonable price of tomorrow. Once established, it may be maintained unchanged because of the absence of competition secured by the agreement for a price reasonable when fixed. Agreements which create such potential power may well be held to be in themselves unreasonable or unlawful restraints, without the necessity of minute inquiry whether a particular price is reasonable or unreasonable as fixed and without placing on the government in enforcing the Sherman Law the burden of ascertaining from day to day whether it has become unreasonable through the mere variation of economic conditions. Moreover, in the absence of express legislation requiring it, we should hesitate to adopt a construction making the difference between legal and illegal conduct in the field of business relations depend upon so uncertain a test as whether prices are reasonable—a determination which can be satisfactorily made only after a complete survey of our economic organization and a choice between rival philosophies."

[34] In an "intellectual schizophrenia" the angry businessman "quivers and quails at the relatively occasional uncertainty of what constitutes a restraint of trade. He wants certainty, but no 'strait-jacket.' He desires to avoid regulation, but would like to be told what to do." Sigmund Timberg, "Equitable Relief Under the Sherman Act," *University of Illinois Law Forum*, Vol. 1950, p. 637.

[35] In any event the mere fact that businessmen are uncertain about the legality of certain types of action has no serious economic consequence. This type of uncertainty will rarely have the adverse effects on production that uncertainty due to the vagaries of foreign and domestic policies of governments or to fluctuations in income and employment tend to have. If a businessman is seriously uncertain about the legality of an action, the rule "when in doubt, don't do it" will keep him out of trouble with the law without depriving society of much that might benefit it.

and prosecution and judicial interpretation will always have to be behind the progress of the art of collusion.[36] Of course, the less active the prosecution, the greater the gaps in the established law.

Observance, Enforcement, Penalties

As a matter of fact, businessmen in many industries are much too little concerned about the possible illegality of their practices. Tardy prosecution over several decades and wobbly court decisions in important cases have left considerable scope for collusive business practices. Trade association activities resulting in reduced competition are foremost among the practices which the law of collusion has not yet effectively dealt with.

A major defect of the law is the smallness of the penalties provided. Collusive activities in certain industries may have been going on for many years until complaints reach the enforcement agencies of the Government. Then it takes considerable time to investigate the case and to bring suit against the violators. If the government decides to take civil action, the violators will face, as a rule, a court decree ordering them to discontinue the unlawful practice and, at most, some additional injunctions which make continuance or repetition of the unlawful activities more difficult. This may cause a loss of future profits to the violators, but they pay no fines and can keep the pecuniary gains which they may have made over many years from their collusive and restrictive policies, and usually also retain the advantages gained in their position.[37] On the other hand, if the Government decides on criminal prosecution and succeeds in securing convictions of the guilty parties, the maximum fine which the court can impose is five thousand dollars.[38] This is usually a paltry sum compared with

[36] See Corwin D. Edwards, "An Appraisal of the Antitrust Laws," *American Economic Review. Proceedings*, Vol. XXXVI (1946), p. 177. "Active prosecution of antitrust cases lessens the gap between the established judicial interpretations and the latest inventions of the collusively minded, but some gap will remain so long as business evolves and law-breakers are ingenious."

[37] The Temporary National Economic Committee recommended an amendment of the statute which would impose civil penalties for violations of the Sherman Act.

[38] The alternative punishment of one year imprisonment is not often

the monopoly profits already made. No wonder then that "violation is regarded by businessmen as a good business risk." [39]

Collusion through Restrictive Patent Licensing

Businessmen have long been wise to the possibility of using the patent law to obtain "exemption" from antitrust law. Certain restrictive agreements which would be illegal under the antitrust law are permissible in the form of patent license contracts. Patents are grants of exclusive rights in the use of inventions. If a patentee chooses to let others share in the use of a patented invention, he can affirm that he is relaxing his monopoly privilege even though he imposes on his licensees certain conditions and restrictions which would otherwise be classed as in restraint of trade. Thus, he may insist that a restrictive license under his patent, far from constituting an agreement in restraint of trade and an attempt to lessen competition, was really a means for increasing competition by allowing his competitors to produce and sell under his patent.

If this way of reasoning were always accepted without close examination of the particular case, businessmen with patentable inventions could circumvent the law of collusion so easily that they would be practically exempt from it. Patents could be obtained

---

imposed. From 1890 to 1946 there were only 31 antitrust cases leading to convictions of imprisonment. They were chiefly cases of "racketeering."

[39] Answer of Attorney General Tom C. Clark to a question on "inadequacies in present antitrust laws." *United States* versus *Economic Concentration and Monopoly. A Staff Report to the Monopoly Subcommittee of the Committee on Small Business*, House of Representatives. (Washington: 1946) p. 250. The same report contains (p. 240) the following explanation by the Attorney General of the considerations underlying the Government's decision whether criminal or civil action should be brought in an antitrust case: "There are some cases in which criminal prosecution affords the better remedy and others in which civil relief is the more effective. Where the restrictive practice is one against which the Government can obtain affirmative civil relief—relief in addition to a simple prohibition against continuation of the unlawful activities—the injunctive remedy is often the most satisfactory. However, where the only possible civil relief is an injunction ordering the defendants to cease engaging in certain practices violative of the law, the criminal prosecution is usually the more efficacious. Examples of restrictive practices coming within this category are price fixing, boycott, and the like. In such cases there is no substantial advantage in securing a decree directing the parties to desist; the antitrust laws already do that."

on products, on processes by which to make them, or on machines
or tools with which to make them; the owners of the patents could
then agree to license others under certain restrictive provisions—
provisions which would be prohibited by the Sherman Act as conspiracies in restraint of trade if they were parts of straight agreements. This is a serious contradiction. When should a restrictive
license under a patent be regarded as an unlawful agreement in
restraint of trade?

The relationship between patent law and antitrust law has time
and again occupied the courts of the United States. There was a
large gap in established law due to a conspicuous lag of prosecution by government behind practice by business. Only in the late
thirties did the Antitrust Division embark on a vigorous campaign
against misuse of patents for purposes of restraining trade.[40] Several important decisions were handed down from the courts and
the gap has been substantially narrowed.

Certain fundamental rules have always been beyond doubt
(although their strict enforcement would have called for a degree
of vigilance and alacrity which the prosecuting agencies of the
Government could never afford with the funds made available by
Congress). For example, a patent "must not be used as a mere
subterfuge for price fixing; nor can licensees use the patent as an
excuse for agreeing among themselves to fix prices." [41] But even
with regard to bona fide patents and bona fide licenses certain
types of restrictive provisions in patent licenses have been found
to constitute unlawful extensions of the monopoly privilege
granted through the patent. Thus "it is well settled . . . that,
where a patentee makes the patented article and sells it, he can
exercise no future control over what the purchaser may wish to
do with the article after the purchase. It has passed beyond the
scope of the patentee's rights." [42] Hence, the fixing of resale prices,
and restrictions on the use of the patented article after its sale, are
unlawful. Moreover, "every use of a patent as a means of obtaining a limited monopoly of unpatented material is prohibited. [This

[40] From July 1938 until June 1946 the Antitrust Division filed 84 antitrust
cases involving patents.

[41] George E. Folk, *Patents and Industrial Progress* (New York: Harper
& Brothers, 1942), p. 367.

[42] *United States* v. *General Electric Company*, 272 U.S. 489 (1926).

rule] applies whether the patent be for a machine, a product, or a process. It applies whatever the nature of the device by which the owner of the patent seeks to effect such unauthorized extension of the monopoly." [43]

Evasions of these legal principles through novel business practices were not too difficult. If it was unlawful to restrict the use of a patented machine after its sale, instead of selling it one had merely to lease it and could retain the right to restrict its use. If it was unlawful to fix the price at which a patented article should be sold by the distributors, because this would constitute resale price maintenance, one had merely to appoint the distributors as licensed agents selling for the account of the patentee.[44] It is quite possible that there are still hundreds of patent agreements in force which are little more than schemes of regulating competition among licensees or between licensor and licensees.

The variety of license provisions is so great, the possibilities of misuse are so wide and the chances of detection so slim, that the Antitrust Division of the Department of Justice proposed that all restrictive licensing be outlawed. The Temporary National Economic Committee included this proposal among its recommendations. In explanation, the Final Report of the Committee stated that it had investigated many "cases in which patents have been used as a pretext for unlawful restraints of trade." On the strength of the information obtained the Committee recommended "that the owner of a patent be required to grant unrestricted licenses if he grants licenses at all . . ." [45]

The Congress has not acted upon this recommendation and there is no indication that it will. The opposition to any "radical"

[43] *Leitch Manufacturing Company* v. *Barber Company,* 302 U.S. 458 (1939).

[44] This was the selling method adopted by the General Electric Company and adjudged legal by the Supreme Court in 1926. The same agency device employed in the distribution of patented building materials was declared by the Supreme Court as a subterfuge for resale price fixing and "an enlargement of the limited patent privilege" in violation of the Sherman Act. In this case the "agents" were so-called "delcredere agents" and had previously been competitors of the patentee. *United States* v. *Masonite Corporation,* 316 U.S. 265 (1942).

[45] *Investigation of Concentration of Economic Power. Final Report and Recommendations of the Temporary National Economic Committee,* 77th Congress, 1st Session (Washington: 1941), p. 269.

patent reform—an alliance of patent lawyers, industrialists and engineers—is so strong that no Congressional action may be expected along these lines. Continued prosecution and adjudication may succeed in further narrowing the possibilities of using the patent device for regulating competition in industry. But for all practical purposes the patent law will not soon completely cease to serve cartel-minded businessmen virtually as an exemption from the antitrust laws.[46]

Exemptions for Labor and Agriculture

Special interest groups have brought strong pressure to bear on the Congress to exempt them from the prohibitions of the Sherman Act. Congress has given in to several of these demands and granted a considerable number of exemptions for particular activities or industries.

The broadest of these exemptions refer to organized labor and agriculture. One way of exempting farmer and labor organizations from the antitrust laws was through the annual appropriation laws by which the administrative departments of the Government are given the funds for defraying the expenditures necessary to their operation. Year after year the appropriation of funds "for the enforcement of antitrust laws" contained the provisos "that no part of this money shall be spent in the prosecution of any organization or individual for entering into any combination or agreement having in view the increasing of wages, shortening of hours, or bettering the conditions of labor," and "that no part of this appropriation shall be expended for the prosecution of producers of farm products and associations of farmers who cooperate and organize in an effort to . . . obtain and maintain a fair and reasonable price for their products." [47]

How anxious the Congress was to exempt labor and farmer combinations from the law of collusion can be seen from the fact that these provisions in the appropriation laws were made although a separate section (Section 6) had been included in the Clayton

[46] For further discussion of the patent monopoly see Chapter 7.

[47] Public Law No. 3, 63rd Congress, June 23, 1913. Identical provisions are contained in all subsequent appropriation laws, until 1923. See Public Law No. 377, 67th Congress, January 3, 1923.

Act of 1914 to the effect that labor and farmer organizations shall not "be held or construed to be illegal combinations or conspiracies in restraint of trade under the antitrust laws."

Particular activities of labor organizations might still have been held unlawful despite these statutory exemptions. Through a series of court decisions the scope of exemptions was eventually delimited in a most generous way. No matter what the nature of the activities of labor groups was, no matter what their purposes or their effects, they are exempt from the antitrust laws as long as they act alone and in their own interests. The antitrust laws would apply if labor groups combined, for example, with groups of industrial producers or distributors to control competition in the product market. But if it could be done without collusion with the employers and if it could be shown to be in the interest of the workers, labor unions would even be free to fix prices of products in the industries in which they work, to divide the market among their employers, and to do all the things which their employers cannot lawfully do themselves.[48]

Although the Clayton Act had legalized farmer organizations, it had not clearly exempted their activities, in particular with respect to pricing and selling of agricultural products, from the antitrust laws. Farm groups thereupon succeeded in getting Congress specifically to permit agricultural cooperatives to set prices for their products provided that prices were not "unduly enhanced by reason thereof," the Secretary of Agriculture being given authority to scrutinize prices.[49] Further exemptions for agriculture were made in 1933 when, in order to raise farm income, the Secretary of Agriculture was authorized to make "marketing agreements" with handlers of agricultural products.[50] The legislation was renewed in 1937 and has been continued up to date.[51] The law even provides for cases in which some group of growers, handlers, or

[48] This is the effect of the decision in the case *United States* v. *William L. Hutcheson*, 312 U.S. 219 (1941).

[49] Capper-Volstead Act of 1922, "An Act to Authorize association of producers of agricultural products" (42 Stat. 388), U.S.C. Title 7, Secs. 291–92. Essentially the same exemption was given by the Fishery Cooperative Marketing Act of 1934 to associations of producers of aquatic products.

[50] Agricultural Adjustment Act of 1933 (48 Stat. 31, 34).

[51] Agricultural Marketing Agreement Act of 1937 (50 Stat. 246), U.S.C. Title 7, Sec. 601.

processors should be unwilling to join in such a marketing agreement; in such cases the Secretary of Agriculture may make it binding even on those who do not sign, merely by issuing a "marketing order." The regulation of these agreements is, however, done by the interested parties themselves through "control boards" selected by the Secretary of Agriculture. The control boards determine quantities to be sold, fix prices and report on "violations." These private cartels with public sanctions and exemption from prosecution are independent of, or supplemental to, governmental schemes for price maintenance on agriculture.[52]

Exemptions for Transportation, Banking and Insurance

Agriculture and labor are only the beginning in a long list of exemptions. Several vested interest groups have been able to persuade the Congress that they should be exempt from the antitrust laws because of the special circumstances prevailing in their industries or trades.

An outstanding example of these special exemptions is the transportation industry. With regard to shipping, the Congress recognized the almost universal practice among steamship lines of entering into agreements regulating competition through the fixing of rates, the apportionment of traffic, the pooling of earnings, the allocations of ports and the regulations of sailings, when it passed the Shipping Act of 1916, which exempted all such agreements from the antitrust laws provided that they were filed with and approved by the Shipping Board.[53] Similarly in air transportation, agreements on rates and pooling of earnings are exempt from the antitrust laws if approved by the Civil Aeronautics Board.[54] Railroads had long been left alone by the Antitrust Division, although early Supreme Court decisions, in 1897 and 1898, had declared that their rate-fixing combinations were illegal under the Sherman Act. For decades they had carried on continuous rate-

[52] See Chapter 7.

[53] Shipping Act of 1916, "An Act to Establish a United States Shipping Board for the purpose of encouraging, developing . . . etc." (39 Stat. 728).

[54] Civil Aeronautics Act of 1938 (52 Stat. 973), U.S.E. Title 49, Secs. 401–681.

fixing activities in "rate bureaus" and "carrier-shipper rate conferences." In the 1940's the Government instituted action against
these collusive practices. Moreover, the State of Georgia charged
a group of railroads with collusive activities resulting in discriminatory rates. When the Supreme Court decided that the "rate-
fixing combinations" of the railroads "have no immunity from the
antitrust laws," [55] Congress moved to create such immunity. This
was done through the Reed-Bulwinkle Act of 1948, passed over a
Presidential veto.[56] The Act stated that railroads, truck lines and
inland waterway carriers which were parties to rate-making agreements were "relieved from the operation of the antitrust laws" if
the agreements were approved by the Interstate Commerce Commission.

Banking and insurance are examples of other activities partially or entirely exempt from the antitrust laws. The Federal Reserve Act of 1913 permits banks to act cooperatively with respect
to loan policies and interest rates. The case of insurance is especially interesting because the courts had long held that insurance
was not a part of commerce and hence not covered by the antitrust
laws.[57] During that time collusive rate making on the part of insurance companies was checked only—if at all—by the regulation
under the laws of the separate states. After the Supreme Court
declared that the insurance business was subject to the Federal
antitrust laws,[58] Congress was high-pressured into passing a law
exempting it again for all practical purposes. The insurance companies much preferred the uneven and frequently lax or practically
non-existent regulation of the states to the more vigilant eye of
the Department of Justice. Hence the law that was finally enacted
brought insurance companies within the scope of the antitrust
laws only to "the extent that such business is not regulated by

[55] *Georgia* v. *Pennsylvania Railroad Co.*, 324 U.S. 439, 457 (1945).

[56] "An Act to Amend the Interstate Commerce Act with respect to certain
agreements between carriers." Public Law No. 662, 80th Congress, 2nd Session, 1948 (62 Stat. 472).

[57] For the special case of marine insurance, however, Congress granted
exemption from the antitrust laws to marine insurance companies in the
Merchant Marine Act of 1920 (41 Stat. 988).

[58] *United States* v. *South-Eastern Underwriters Association*, 322 U.S. 533
(1944).

State law." [59] Insurance companies are therefore partially exempt from the antitrust laws.

Exemptions for Exporters and Retail Distributors

An exemption the exact scope of which has not yet become clear is that granted to American exporters organized in export associations under the Webb-Pomerene Act.[60] American businessmen have sometimes interpreted this exemption to mean that they may lawfully join an association (under the formal supervision of the Federal Trade Commission) which could not only fix export prices, determine the quantities of commodities to be exported and divide export markets or export quotas among the members, but also enter into international cartel agreements with producer groups in foreign countries, thereby reducing competition in foreign trade. The Antitrust Division of the Department of Justice holds that the law does not afford such far-reaching exemptions, that it was intended to facilitate American participation in international trade and to increase rather than reduce competition with foreign producers.

Laxity of supervision of the registered export associations by the Federal Trade Commission and delay in investigation and prosecution by the Antitrust Division are responsible for the fact that more than thirty years after enactment of the Webb-Pomerene law its scope is still in doubt.[61] However, its effects are apparent: it undoubtedly has encouraged activities to restrain trade and reduce competition in international markets, and probably has also weakened domestic competition in the industries concerned.[62]

The exemption from the antitrust laws which has probably had

[59] McCarran-Ferguson Act of 1945, "An Act to express the intent of the congress with reference to the regulation of the insurance business" (59 Stat. 33).

[60] "An Act to promote export trade, and for other purposes" (40 Stat. 516), 1918, U.S.C. Title 15, Secs. 61–65.

[61] Some of the doubts were dispelled by the Supreme Court decision in *United States Alkali Export Association v. United States*, 325 U.S. 196 (1945).

[62] See, "Consensus Report on the Webb-Pomerene Act," prepared by a Committee of the American Economic Association. *American Economic Review*, Vol. XXXVII (1947), pp. 848–63.

the greatest effect on prices paid by consumers is the exemption of resale price maintenance contracts—so-called "vertical price fixing contracts"—in the resale of commodities which are identified by trademarks, brands or name of producer or distributor. The first of these "Fair Trade Acts" was passed by California in 1931; by 1941 all but three states and the District of Columbia had passed such laws. The operation of the State laws was, however, seriously hampered by the Sherman Antitrust Act and, largely under pressures from organized druggists, the Congress in 1937 passed the Miller-Tydings amendment to the Sherman Act to exempt contracts made pursuant to the Fair Trade Act of any state from the operation of the Sherman Act (as well as of the Federal Trade Commission Act).[63]

Thus manufacturers of branded or otherwise identifiable commodities may enter into an agreement with retailers fixing the resale price of the commodities. All other sellers of the commodities, if put on notice of the contract, are bound to observe its provisions whether or not they are actually parties to the agreements. The significance of this "can be readily appreciated when it is noted that one resale price maintenance contract within a State is sufficient to establish prices for that State." [64] Anyone who willfully or knowingly sells the commodities subject to fair trade contracts at less than the contract price is guilty of "unfair competition." [65]

[63] The Miller-Tydings Act of 1937 was part of "An Act to provide additional revenue for the District of Columbia, and for other purposes" (50 Stat. 673, 693), U.S.C. Title 15, Sec. 1.

[64] Earl R. Boonstra, "Trade Regulation: State Fair Trade Acts and Supplementary Federal Legislation," *Michigan Law Review*, Vol. 47 (1949), p. 826.

[65] In 1951 the Supreme Court, in a liquor trade case, handed down a decision that for practical purposes nullifies the state "fair trade" laws by prohibiting the application of the laws to those who refuse to sign agreements with the manufacturers. Clearly, if only retailers who sign such agreements are bound by them, then few will sign, since they will be undersold by non-signing competitors. Justice Douglas, writing the majority decision, pointed out that the Miller-Tydings Act only exempted "contracts and agreements" from the antitrust laws. Hence "if a distributor and one or more retailers want to agree, combine, or conspire to fix a minimum price, they can do so if state law permits. Their contract, combination or conspiracy— hitherto illegal—is made lawful. They can fix minimum prices pursuant to their contract or agreement with impunity. When they seek, however, to

"Emergency" Exemptions

In the depression years 1933 to 1935, businesses were exempt
on a mass scale from the antitrust acts. Under the National
Industrial Recovery Act,[66] one of the chief purposes of which was
to raise or at least to maintain prices in the face of falling demand,
trade associations were invited to draw up "codes of fair competition" and these codes, when approved by the National Recovery
Administration and signed by the President, became as binding
as any law. All agreements under the NIRA were specifically exempt from the antitrust laws. Business groups made extensive use
of the exemption granted them and "nearly fifty of the codes filed
by the major industries and given public approval contained price-
fixing provisions which were managed by the industries themselves." [67] Thus at the time when the consumer might be expected
to need the most protection from the monopoly power of business
concerns acting in collusion to fix prices, the Government gave
them very nearly a *carte blanche* to do so.[68]

The second type of emergency exemption relates to war con-

impose price fixing on persons who have not contracted or agreed to the
scheme, the situation is vastly different. That is not price fixing by contract
or agreement; that is price fixing by compulsion. That is not following the
path of consensual agreement; that is resort to coercion . . .

"Contracts or agreements convey the idea of a cooperative arrangement,
not a program whereby recalcitrants are dragged in by the heels and compelled to submit to price fixing." *Schwegmann Brothers* v. *Calvert Distillers
Corporation,* 341 U.S. 384 (1951). This decision was hailed by many retail
stores who were once again free to compete for consumer patronage by
offering branded goods at cheaper prices. But one year later Congress, under
extraordinary pressures from retailer groups all over the country, amended the
Miller-Tydings Act so that the Supreme Court decision was undone and price
fixing by compulsion and with state enforcement was duly covered by the
exemption from the Sherman Act.

[66] "An Act to encourage national industrial recovery, to foster fair competition, and to provide for the construction of certain useful public works,
and for other purposes." (48 Stat. 195), 1933.

[67] Vernon A. Mund, *Government and Business* (New York: Harper &
Bros., 1950), p. 236.

[68] The "code approach" to the regulation of competition survived the
NRA in the Bituminous Coal Act of 1937 (48 Stat. 991), under which boards
elected by producers were empowered to propose minimum prices and producers who subscribed to the code were exempt from the Sherman Act. This
act expired in 1943.

ditions. During the Second World War the Chairman of the War Production Board was given power to exempt businessmen from antitrust prosecution whenever he believed that such exemption would further the war effort.[69] (He was required, however, to consult with the Attorney General.) Under the "certificates of immunity" from prosecution, issued by the WPB, groups of firms were permitted to take collusive action with respect to prices, transportation, production and marketing. The certificates were not directed to permitting narrowly defined acts but gave a general immunity from prosecution to firms engaged in broadly described fields of activity.

THE LAW OF MONOPOLIZATION

"Every person who shall monopolize, or attempt to monopolize, or combine or conspire with any other person or persons, to monopolize any part of the trade or commerce among the several States, or with foreign nations, shall be deemed guilty of a misdemeanor. . . ." Thus reads the statutory prohibition of "monopolization" in Section 2 of the Sherman Act of 1890. It has never become really effective. Appalling as the frustrations in the development, administration and enforcement of the law of collusion have been, they are small in comparison with those concerning the law of monopolization.

Vexing Problems

The comparative success that has been achieved in the enforcement of certain phases of the "law of collusion" was due largely to the fact that the courts, for certain types of restriction, took the existence of a restrictive agreement as conclusive evidence of the violation of the law, regardless of the degree of restraint which it had produced or attempted to produce; conspiracies in restraint of trade were clearly illegal. But what is monopoly? When can it be said that a concern has attempted to monopolize an industry? What is the relation of monopoly to the size of the business firm?

[69] Small Business Mobilization Act of 1942 (56 Stat. 357), U.S.C. Title 50, Sec. 1112.

to the legal rights of corporations to acquire property and to expand in order to improve the efficiency of their operations? to the form of affiliation with or absorption of other business firms? What about the "rights" of investors if existing monopolies are dissolved? A guide to the solution of these and other questions was not provided in the Sherman Act and the courts, when specific cases were brought before them, gave inconsistent and incomplete answers.

There is no "golden thread" running through the court decisions tracing out a consistent development of the law of monopolization. The Sherman Act did little more than lay down a broad policy and the field was open for the courts to develop a body of judicial law determining how this policy was to affect American business, setting out the rules which business would be required to observe and establishing the standards of conduct against which actual business behavior would be judged. The courts have not successfully performed this task. In cases brought before them, they were totally unable to thread their way through the complicated facts, the conflicting allegations and the inconsistent legal and economic philosophies, and arrive at a series of decisions clearly defining and consistently applying the intention of the legislature.

The Congress plainly wanted to stop the *growth* of monopoly in the United States when it passed the antitrust laws, but the courts were not prepared to outlaw anything very short of 100 percent control of an industry as illegal in itself. Hence, although attempts to reduce competition by certain restrictive agreements were considered illegal on the evidence that there was such an agreement, attempts to reduce competition by eliminating a competitor were not considered illegal on the evidence that a competitor had actually been eliminated by the defendants. Where the methods of eliminating a competitor had been militant or "predatory,"—for example, local price cutting—a substantial reduction of competition had to be proved before monopolistic intent would be inferred. When the methods of eliminating a competitor has been peaceful—for example, by acquisition of his corporate stock or assets—the courts would not be satisfied unless an extremely high degree of monopoly control had been achieved.

An All Too Judicious Judiciary

The very first suit under the Sherman Act to reach the Supreme Court ran into an unexpected snag concerning the interpretation of the meaning of "trade or commerce among the several States." The Government had asked for dissolution of the Sugar Trust. The American Sugar Refining Company had through a series of stock acquisitions obtained control over 98 percent of the refining capacity of the country. The Supreme Court, in 1895, refused to declare void the contracts for the exchange of stock by which the merger had been achieved, arguing that "manufacturing" was not interstate commerce.[70] The Court ten years later changed its mind on this point [71]—otherwise the Sherman Act would have been entirely useless from the very beginning—but this first encounter of the new law of monopolization with the highest court of the land presaged a tendency toward extremely narrow interpretation of the statute.

The most notorious decisions, from the point of view of the development of case law, were those in the Standard Oil and Tobacco cases in 1911. The Standard Oil Company of New Jersey had, in the course of alarming deals and with the use of predatory practices and all sorts of pressures, acquired the stock of more than 70 companies controlling about 90 percent of the oil-refining business and many by-products. The American Tobacco Company, through strong-arm policies of the most oppressive type, had acquired the stock or assets of more than sixty firms, controlling some 95 percent of the cigarette business and not much less of other tobacco products. The Supreme Court ordered the dissolution of these combines, but found it unnecessary to condemn as illegal the monopoly power they had succeeded in acquiring. The Court emphasized that the trusts were illegal not because of the "dominion and control" they had attained, but because of the "acts and dealings" they had employed in the process and because of the "intent" and "purpose to acquire dominion and control of the . . . trade." [72]

[70] *United States v. E. C. Knight Co.*, 156 U.S. 1 (1895).
[71] *Swift and Company v. United States*, 196 U.S. 375 (1905).
[72] *Standard Oil Company of New Jersey v. United States*, 221 U.S. 1, 74 (1911) and *United States v. American Tobacco Co.*, 221 U.S. 106, 181, 182 (1911).

In addition, the Court spelled out the "rule of reason"—that all the circumstances of a case must be considered in order to determine whether the result of a combination of business firms constituted "unreasonable" restraint of trade. According to this approach to the problem of monopoly, a large degree of monopoly power was not by itself illegal.

While the Supreme Court ordered dissolution in both the Standard Oil and Tobacco cases, it refused to do so in the Steel case decision of 1920. The United States Steel Corporation had been established as a "combination of combinations" comprising approximately 200 formerly independent companies controlling at least half of the steel ingot capacity of the country and much more of the total output of steel products (e.g., 95 percent of the tin-plate production). The Court held that the Corporation for several years had found it necessary to enter into illegal price fixing arrangements with its competitors, which proved that it lacked monopoly power. In other words, the existence of collusion was regarded as a proof for the nonexistence of monopoly. No "unworthy motives" in the creation of the combine were found to exist and any intent to monopolize that the Corporation might have had apparently had not been carried out with discernible success.[73]

This interpretation of the law of monopolization was confirmed in the Harvester case in 1927, when the "existence of unexerted power" was said not to be an offense "when unaccompanied by unlawful conduct in the exercise" of the power.[74]

Thus, the Government found it impossible, with a few exceptions, to use Section 2 of the Sherman Act, as interpreted by the courts for the first half-century, to check the formation or compel the dissolution of trusts.[75] It would have to prove, first of all, an "intent" to monopolize. The size of the merger was not taken

[73] *United States* v. *United States Steel Corporation*, 251 U.S. 417 (1920).

[74] *United States* v. *International Harvester Company*, 274 U.S. 693, 708 (1927).

[75] In the Steel case decision the enforcement of the Sherman Act received what has been called "the greatest setback in its history"; it "marked the end of an era in antitrust enforcement." J. Howard McGrath, Attorney General of the United States, *Remarks before the New York State Bar Association, Antitrust Section,* January 25, 1950 (mimeographed), pp. 3–4.

as evidence of such intent, especially if the defendants could give other motives, for example, that they wanted to improve efficiency or to take advantage of legitimate business opportunities. The fact that a corporation had used predatory tactics to eliminate competitors might be accepted as evidence of an intent to monopolize, but not necessarily as conclusive evidence. In the absence of such "ungentlemanly" conduct on the part of the corporation, the existence of intent was hard to prove. The Government would also have to prove that the corporation had achieved a well-nigh complete monopoly and had exercised its power. This was a hopeless situation.

An Injudicious Legislature

By 1914 the Congress had realized the limitation on the effectiveness of the Sherman Act in dealing with the growth of monopoly, and in the Clayton Act of that year it attempted to stop the monopolization of an industry before it got well under way. For this purpose it prohibited, in Section 7 of the Clayton Act, a corporation from acquiring stock in another corporation "where the effect of such acquisition may be to substantially lessen competition" between the two corporations.

The fate of this prohibition provides a good example of the difficulties in the way of attempting to legislate against a general result by outlawing merely some specific methods of attaining it. This is like blocking only the best known routes to a forbidden goal and leaving all other routes open. Up to 1914 mergers between corporations were largely effected through stock acquisitions, and the Congress reasoned very simply that to block such acquisitions would be automatically to block mergers. The result of the law was to cause business to abandon the old route and adopt a new one: large mergers, from then on, were effected chiefly through the acquisition of the physical assets of one corporation by another and there was nothing in the law to prevent it.[76]

It is universally conceded that this loophole in the law was a sheer oversight, a case of bad drafting, and that Congress had in-

[76] See the discussion of business practices with regard to merger in Chapter 4.

tended to block all mergers substantially reducing competition.[77] This statutory standard, incidentally, was also defectively formulated in that it referred to the substantial reduction of "competition between the corporation whose stock is so acquired and the corporation making the acquisition." Is it conceivable that a merger between two firms would not substantially lessen competition between them? Since every merger would probably have this effect, the prohibition would apply to *all* mergers through stock acquisition, and this was surely not intended by Congress. It was thus left to the courts to interpret the possible meaning of the phrase, and the interpretation was again rather narrow.

Frustration Continued

The judicial interpretation deprived the provision of most of the effect apparently intended. The courts held that a merger was prohibited only if the combining companies had been in substantial competition with each other before they united and only if the merger would effect a substantial reduction of competition, not merely between the merging firms, but in the industry at large.[78]

Even what was left of the prohibition of merger through stock acquisition was rendered almost completely ineffective by the rulings of the courts. Violations of the Clayton Act were not punishable offenses; the only sanctions were "orders" by the Federal Trade Commission to enforce compliance. But a cease-and-desist order would obviously be meaningless with respect to stock already acquired and an order that the acquiring company divest itself of the stock acquired would be meaningless if the company had already used its control of the stock to merge the physical assets of the acquired business with its own.

Exactly such were the rulings of the courts. In three cases the

[77] In the words of Senator Joseph C. O'Mahoney, Chairman of the Temporary National Economic Committee, "it can be stated . . . that inadequate and inexpert drafting of section 7 resulted in the failure of Congress to make its will effective." *Investigation of Concentration of Economic Power,* Hearings before the Temporary National Economic Committee, Part 5 (Washington, 1939), p. 1781.

[78] *Temple Anthracite Coal Company* v. *Federal Trade Commission,* 51 F. (2d) 656 (1931).

Supreme Court decided that if the stock, though illegally acquired, were used to effect an absorption of the corporate assets before the Commission could file its complaint, the Commission did not have the power to order divestiture of the physical properties.[79] In a fourth case the Commission had filed its complaint in time, before the merger of the physical assets was completed, but while it was pending the holding company transferred its stock to two new holding companies formed for this purpose and then brought about the merger of physical properties. Again, the Supreme Court held that the Commission lacked the power under the Clayton Act to order a divestiture of assets, even though the stock "had been acquired contrary to the Act" and the Commission had filed its complaints before the merger of assets had been effected.[80]

The merger prohibition of the Clayton Act had become a "virtual nullity." [81] Year after year the Federal Trade Commission and the Department of Justice stressed the extent to which this one "leak" seriously reduced the effectiveness of the entire antitrust policy of the country. Numerous bills were introduced in Congress to remedy the situation. But the vested interests had become strong and Congressional zeal to maintain competition in the United States economy had apparently weakened.

Frustration Ended?

It was not until December 1950 that Congress found enough gumption to take the long delayed action: it passed an amendment prohibiting the acquisition of stock or assets "where in any line of commerce in any section of the country the effect of such acquisitions may be substantially to lessen competition."

[79] *Federal Trade Commission* v. *Western Meat Co., Thatcher Manufacturing Co.* v. *Federal Trade Commission; Swift & Co.* v. *Federal Trade Commission,* 272 U.S. 554 (1926).

[80] *Arrow-Hart and Hegeman Electric Co.* v. *Federal Trade Commission,* 291 U.S. 587 (1934). In a minority opinion four Justices of the Supreme Court dissented from the decision and took exception to the fact that "an offender against the Clayton Act, properly brought before the Commission and subject to its orders, can evade its authority and defeat the statute by taking refuge behind a cleverly erected screen of corporate dummies." *Ibid.,* p. 608.

[81] *Annual Report of the Federal Trade Commission for the Year 1934.*

From now on, to determine the legality of a corporate combination of stock or assets, it will be "unnecessary for the Government to speculate as to what is in the 'back of the minds' of those who promote a merger; or to prove that the acquiring firm had engaged in actions which are considered to be unethical or predatory; or to show that as a result of a merger the acquiring firm had already obtained such a degree of control that it possessed the power to destroy or exclude competitors or fix prices." [82] There still remains the problem of preventing a gradual increase of monopolistic power through piecemeal acquisition of other firms by corporations growing in size. Under the Sherman Act it proved impossible to convince the courts that a large corporation buying out a few smaller firms in the same field had "attempted to monopolize" a part of the industry; or that another addition to a large firm's control of industrial capacity would make it "a monopoly" when before the addition it was not. Will it be easier under the Clayton Act, as amended in 1950, to prove that such acquisitions may effect a "substantial reduction of competition" in some line of commerce in some section of the country? The future only will tell.

However, the courts have already shown a considerable change of heart. It seems they have done away with some of the obstacles with which the early decisions surrounded the law against trusts. The most drastic change in interpretation came with the Aluminum case in 1945. The "Alcoa decision" rejected the doctrine that unexerted monopoly power was no offense. It declared that Congress "did not condone 'good trusts' and condemn 'bad' ones; it forbade all." [83] The new interpretation was accepted and reiterated by

[82] *Report No. 1191*, Committee on the Judiciary, House of Representatives, to accompany H.R. 2734, 81st Congress, 1st Session, August 1949.

[83] This decision by Judge Learned Hand of the Circuit Court of Appeals was final, because the Supreme Court, lacking a quorum of justices who would qualify themselves to hear the case, had referred it to the Court of Appeals for decision. *United States* v. *Aluminum Company of America,* 148 F. (2d) 416 (1945). The rejection of the doctrine of unexerted power is expressed as follows: "Starting . . . with the authoritative premise that all contracts fixing prices are unconditionally prohibited, the only possible difference between them and a monopoly is that while a monopoly necessarily involves an equal, or even greater, power to fix prices, its mere existence might be thought not to constitute an exercise of that power. That distinc-

the Supreme Court in 1946 in its opinion on the second Tobacco case, which stated that neither proof "of exertion of the power to exclude . . . competitors" nor the fact "that prices are raised" was essential for the charge of monopolization; the *existence* of such power was sufficient.[84]

But that the new interpretation of the law did not yet have clear sailing was shown in the five-to-four decision of the Supreme Court in the Columbia Steel case in 1948. The Court gave its approving nod to a merger of the assets of the Consolidated Steel Corporation with those of a subsidiary of the United States Steel Corporation. The reasoning was that the restraint of competition that would result from the merger would not be "unreasonable." The minority of the Supreme Court in its dissenting opinion showed that they were exasperated:

> This is the most important antitrust case which has been before the Court in years. It is important because it reveals the way of growth of monopoly power—the precise phenomenon at which the Sherman Act was aimed. Here we have the pattern of the evolution of the great trusts. Little, independent units are gobbled up by bigger ones. At times the independent is driven to the wall and surrenders. At other times any number of 'sound business reasons' appear why the sale to or merger with the trust should be made. If the acquisition were the result of predatory practices or restraints of trade, the trust could be required to disgorge. But the impact on future competition and on the economy is the same though the trust was built in more gentlemanly ways.

---

tion is nevertheless purely formal; it would be valid only so long as the monopoly remained wholly inert; it would disappear as soon as the monopoly began to operate; for, when it did—that is, as soon as it began to sell at all— it must sell at some price and the only price at which it could sell is a price which it itself fixes. Thereafter the power and its exercise must needs coalesce. Indeed it would be absurd to condemn such [price-fixing] contracts unconditionally, and not to extend the condemnation to monopolies; for the contracts are only steps toward that entire control which monopoly confers: they are really partial monopolies." *Ibid.*, p. 427.

[84] "Neither proof of exertion of the power to exclude nor proof of actual exclusion of existing or potential competitors is essential to sustain the charge of monopolization under the Sherman Act . . . The authorities support the view that the material consideration in determining whether a monopoly exists is not that prices are raised and that competition actually is excluded but that power exists to raise prices or to exclude competition when it is desired to do so." *American Tobacco Co.* v. *United States*, 328 U.S. 781, 810, 811 (1946).

We have here the problem of bigness. Its lesson should by now
have been burned into our memory. . . . In final analysis, size in
steel is the measure of the power of a handful of men over our
economy. That power can be utilized with lightning speed. It can
be benign or it can be dangerous. The philosophy of the Sherman
Act is that it should not exist. For all power tends to develop into
a government in itself. Power that controls the economy should be
in the hands of elected representatives of the people, not in the
hands of an industrial oligarchy. Industrial power should be de-
centralized. It should be scattered into many hands so that the
fortunes of the people will not be dependent on the whim or
caprice, the political prejudices, the emotional stability of a few
self-appointed men. The fact that they are not vicious men but
respectable and social minded is irrelevant. That is the philosophy
and the command of the Sherman Act. It is founded on a theory
of hostility to the concentration in private hands of power so great
that only a government of the people should have it.[85]

ANTITRUST LAWS—SUCCESS OR FAILURE?

After sixty years' experience with the American antitrust laws
the record, one should think, ought to be clear enough to permit
an appraisal of their effectiveness. Were they, on the whole, a success or a failure?

Contradictory Appraisals

The record, alas, does not speak for itself, or it would not be
possible for honest and intelligent observers to arrive at so different, and even contradictory appraisals. Indeed, we find all sorts
of appraisals, ranging, so to speak, over the whole color spectrum,
differing with regard to the success or failure of these legal institutions as well as to the reasons for it. Here is a list of some typical
views on the effectiveness of the American antitrust laws:

1. The whole objective is silly; a complex economy, such as
ours, needs orderly marketing and industry planning, not anarchic
competition; hence, attempts to enforce competition can only be
wasteful; fortunately, they have had only small effect on the organization of the economy.

2. The objective—to maintain a maximum of competition and

[85] *United States* v. *Columbia Steel Co.,* 334 U.S. 495, 534–36 (1948).

check the growth of monopoly power—may be excellent but is not attainable; it is unrealistic (naive, romantic) to believe that the trend toward increased concentration of economic control can be halted; hence the laws have not worked and could never work.

3. The objective is fine and also attainable, but not by legal prohibitions; while other methods of preventing the growth of monopoly could have been effective, the antitrust laws have not done the job and could not possibly do so.

4. The objective is fine as well as attainable, and legal prohibition of restraint and monopoly is among the best methods of attaining the objective; unfortunately, however, the laws were not correctly designed for the purpose.

5. The objective is fine and attainable, legal prohibitions could work effectively, and the laws were well designed for the purpose; they have not been successful because of narrow interpretation and lax and incompetent enforcement, hampered by insufficient appropriations.

6. The objective is fine and attainable, and has in fact been attained to a fair degree; the efficacy of the laws has been much greater than is commonly believed; one should certainly not regard the system as a failure, but recognize it as reasonably successful. (No one, of course, claims that the system has been wildly successful.)

This list does not attempt completeness; as a matter of fact, many more views than those enumerated have been expressed. Moreover, while some of the views included in the list contradict each other beyond hope of reconciliation, there is no necessary conflict between some of the others. It is quite possible, for example, to accept parts of the four statements from Nos. 3 to 6. Such a synthesis might look like this:

"The objective is fine and largely attainable, but legal prohibitions alone cannot do the job; many other things must be done besides; the laws could have been worded much better, but even as drawn they would have worked better had they been less narrowly interpreted and more effectively enforced; yet, even with all their deficiencies they have not been without success, but have achieved much if one considers what would have happened in the absence of the laws."

This synthetic statement expresses better than any of those previously listed the views of this writer. But no statement on American antitrust legislation "as a whole" can be very profound. Is there much sense in an appraisal which lumps together the law of collusion and the law of monopolization through merger and concentration of control? Obviously, the latter has not worked at all, unless one is willing—which this writer is not—to applaud the decisions in the oil and tobacco cases of 1911 as a success, or unless one is willing—which, again, this writer is not—to applaud the fact that the law has made firms wary of becoming the *sole* source of supply in a nationwide industry and made them prefer living with one or two so-called competitors. On the other hand, the law of collusion has had a very real influence on the development of the American economy, an influence which becomes fully apparent to those who know the extent of cartelization in most countries of Europe. In view of the difference in their effectiveness separate appraisals must be made of the two sections of the law.

Stopping the Cartels—a Partial Success

In appraising the efficacy of the law of collusion we shall have to take stock on a least five scores: (1) the interpretation of the statute by the courts and the development of case law, (2) the gaps and breaches resulting from exemptions, (3) the extent of enforcement, (4) the adequacy of the penalties imposed and the "relief" obtained as a result of successful prosecution, and (5) the indirect effects of the law on the standards of business conduct.

We have seen that, beginning with the Addyston Pipe case in 1898, the statutory prohibition of agreements in restraint of trade received adequate and effective interpretation by the courts. Cartels based on "straight" agreements were effectively outlawed. The situation was different with regard to the supposedly lawful agreements based on patent rights and the clandestine cartels based on trade practices and trade association activities. For several decades the law of collusion was not applied if the restraint of trade took the form of restrictive patent licenses or was the result of the customs and usages of the trade. The first Cement case and the Maple

Flooring case in 1925 were bad set-backs in the prosecution of collusion through trade association activities; although the Sugar Institute case in 1936 struck down a number of these practices, it was not until 1948—the second Cement case—that this situation was corrected. The General Electric case in 1926 and other cases involving agreements in the form of patent licenses retarded the application of the law of collusion to patent cartels until after the decisions of the Ethyl case in 1940 and the Univis Lens and Morton Salt cases in 1942. In any event, although it took between forty and fifty years from the enactment of the statute, the legal prohibition of cartels in any form is now firmly established.[86]

We have reviewed the important exemptions from the antitrust laws which Congress has granted in the interest of particular groups in the economy. Some of these exemptions are more significant politically—inasmuch as they are the results of pressure group influences upon legislators—than they are economically, because they concern industries in which competition would not be very effective in any event and the results of the collusion (i.e., private regulation) which they permit are often, I am afraid, not so very different from the results of governmental regulation. From an economic point of view, the most important exemption is that of retail trade under the fair-trade acts. This, undoubtedly, is a serious breach in the legal prohibition of restraint of trade, but despite all the exemptions there is still a substantial part of the economy that remains subject to the prohibitions of the antitrust laws.

As far as the enforcement of the law is concerned one cannot help contrasting all the trumpeting about "trust-busting" during the political campaigns of the first decades of this century and the ridiculously small efforts that were actually made to "bust" the trusts.[87] To try to enforce the antitrust laws of the country with a force of twenty attorneys is not much less fantastic than to try to

[86] See the chronological survey above, pp. 187–93, for the major issues decided in the cases mentioned here in the text.

[87] During the administration of President Theodore Roosevelt, when trust busting was put forward as a major economic function of government, the Antitrust Division of the Department of Justice consisted of five attorneys and four stenographers. From 1914 to 1923 the number of attorneys in the Division averaged only 18, and by 1933 it had been reduced to 15. Thurman Arnold, "Antitrust Law Enforcement, Past and Future," *Law and Contemporary Problems*, Vol. VII (1940), p. 5.

enforce the speed laws on all the roads of the country with a force of twenty traffic policemen. Even the 200 attorneys which the Antitrust Division had in 1946 [88] could hardly do much more than, to use Thurman Arnold's words, "dramatize an ideal." Hence, any success that the law of collusion may have had cannot be due to the *direct* effects of its enforcement.

We have had occasion to refer to the penalties which the law provides for offenders. Criminal actions against offenders do nothing to correct the monopolistic situation and have almost no punitive effect as long as the maximum fine is only $5,000. After having paid their fines the companies often go right back to their old practices, perhaps with some immaterial modifications. Civil actions may provide permanent relief—if the right kind of relief is asked by the Government and granted by the court. But here lies one of the greatest difficulties: lawyers who may be most competent in proving the illegality of certain activities are often quite helpless in devising ways of remedying the situation. "The legal problem of 'winning' the case is allowed to take precedence over the economic problem of obtaining adequate remedial action." [89] This is an acute problem not only for the Antitrust Division but for the Federal Trade Commission as well. In one case, for example, the Government had to take action every few years against the same firm and was able to win most of its legal battles, but was never able to secure adequate relief.[90] The inclusion in court decrees [91] of a "Damocles sword clause" which allows the Govern-

---

[88] *United States Versus Economic Concentration and Monopoly.* A Staff Report to the Monopoly Subcommittee of the Committee on Small Business. House of Representatives, 79th Congress (Washington, 1946), p. 252.

[89] *Antitrust Law Enforcement by the Federal Trade Commission and the Antitrust Division, Department of Justice—A Preliminary Report.* Select Committee on Small Business, House of Representatives, Eighty-first Congress (Washington: 1951), p. 65.

[90] The war between the Government and the Corn Products Refining Company from 1913 to 1948 is described in Fritz Machlup, *The Basing-Point System,* pp. 83–90.

[91] Court decrees may be either part of the adjudication of a litigated case or "consent decrees" negotiated and agreed upon between the parties—the Government and the defendant—and approved by the court. According to a recent count "about one out of every two civil cases ends in a victory for the Government by consent." *Antitrust Law Enforcement* etc., *op. cit.,* p. 66.

ment to reopen the case if the relief provided in the decree should prove to be inadequate, may be one way of solving the still unsolved problem of how effectively to control the use of monopoly power. On the other hand, it may prove necessary to remove the source of power by breaking up large business units.[92] Where large business firms are determined to prevent competition, it is extremely difficult for the Government to force it on them so long as the corporate organization involved remains intact.

In view of all these difficulties—the exemptions from the law, its unsatisfactory enforcement, the inadequate relief obtained even when the legal case is won—one might be inclined to belittle the effectiveness of the law of collusion. But one should not overlook the indirect effects of the law upon business. Even if the chances of being *caught* in a violation of the law are small, the chances of being *convicted* even smaller, and the chances of being *forced to reform* almost nil, the very fact that collusive activities among competitors are unlawful is unquestionably an important element of the general atmosphere in which business is conducted in the United States. It makes a great difference whether members of a cartel can think of themselves as patriots contributing to public welfare through stabilizing prices in their industry, or whether they must be aware they may be thought of as criminals whose unlawful deeds may possibly be exposed. Even if thousands of businessmen may have the kind of conscience which easily condones a deviation of their business ethics from the standards of the law, there are large numbers of others, who respect the law and prefer to live within it.[93]

It is in this sense that one is justified in regarding the anticartel law as a partial success. It has succeeded in creating a climate less favorable to cartelization than would exist without it. There is no doubt that business in America is much more "competitive" than in

[92] In a consent decree accepted by Libby-Owens-Ford, producers of flat glass, the Government reserved the right to reopen the case after three years "to petition for dissolution, divorcement, and divestiture [i.e., splitting up the firm] as the sole way to reestablish competition." *Antitrust Law Enforcement* etc., *op. cit.*, p. 67.

[93] Of course, continuous prosecution of selected violations is necessary in order to impress people with the existence of the law.

most other countries partly because of the philosophy which is embodied in the law of collusion and dramatized by its enforcement, sporadic though it has been.

In one direction, however, the law against collusion has promoted the growth of monopoly. Since collusion was effectively prosecuted and "monopolization" was not, the result was that cartels—the looser form of monopolistic organization—were vulnerable while corporate combines were almost invulnerable under the law. The effect, naturally, was to give a fillip to the formation of large corporate combines. The prohibition of temporary alliances among competing firms increased the attractiveness of permanent union through merger and consolidation.

Checking the Trusts—a Dismal Failure

An appraisal of the effectiveness of the law of monopolization produces a grim picture. The mark is "unsatisfactory" on every score, as far as past performance is concerned.

We have seen how the judicial interpretation of the statute and the development of case law in the first fifty years reduced Section 2 of the Sherman Act almost to a dead letter. There was first the ruling in the sugar trust case of 1895, and, after the damage had been repaired, there were the confusing if not disabling doctrines enunciated on the occasion of the dissolution of the oil and tobacco trusts in 1911. With the decision in the steel trust case in 1920 the emasculation of the law was completed. The prohibition of mergers injurious to competition, which Congress in 1914 tried to effect in the Clayton Act, also proved a complete failure. The Federal Trade Commission, finding the prohibition "a virtual nullity," had to give up all efforts to enforce it. The change in the statute through the amendment passed by Congress in 1950 and the change in the interpretation of the Sherman Act through the decisions of the Courts in 1945 and 1946 may make a decisive difference for the future. But this remains to be seen.

Since for practical purposes the prohibitions of trusts and mergers were non-existent, the question of gaps and breaches through special exemptions did not become relevant. Nor did the question of sufficient enforcement. After the courts finished interpreting it, there was no law that could be enforced. Similarly, since there have been so few convictions and injunctions, the question of penalties and relief has not been important in the past. In the two notable decisions under the Sherman Act—the oil and tobacco cases—the relief was utterly inadequate. The trusts were ordered dissolved, but in a hopelessly naive fashion: the stock of the separated companies was owned by the same people. In addition, the separation in the oil case was along regional lines, facilitating a geographic division of the market among the separate companies, and the separation of the business and the brands in the tobacco case secured the large successor firms complete domination of the industry. A few recent cases have demonstrated that neither the Government nor the courts have learned how to provide adequate remedies for the situation under attack.[94]

The indirect effects of the law of monopolization were different in nature from those of the law of collusion. While the latter probably has deterred some businessmen from illegal cartelization and made them more willing to compete, the former by singling out "complete" monopoly for attack, probably has induced some large concerns to coddle their weaker competitors. This, of course, is partly a consequence of those court decisions which insisted that proofs of nearly 100 percent control of the supply and of the absence of any competitors were necessary to sustain the charge of monopoly. Businessmen consequently have believed it wise to avoid acquiring "too much" control, and have preferred to keep alive a few less efficient competitors, whom they could easily have eliminated on the basis of cost differences. In other words, "soft competition" and live-and-let-live policies have been among the indirect effects of the stultified law of monopolization.

Nothing then can be said that would in any way qualify the verdict that the law of monopolization, the prohibition of trusts and mergers, has been a dismal failure.

[94] If the law of monopolization should become operative in the future, one of the most important tasks would be to find better ways of correcting monopolistic situations. As a rule this can be done only through drastic reorganizations of the industry in order to establish the structural prerequisites for vigorous competition. Otherwise the greatest legal victories of the Government will remain economically meaningless. Cf. *Antitrust Law Enforcement* etc., *op. cit.*, pp. 62–69.

Alternative and Complementary Antitrust Policies

To say that the antitrust law in the narrow sense of the word —the law against trusts and mergers—has been a failure does not imply that it had to be so because of the nature of things. The law, appropriately interpreted and enforced, could have been of great value in checking the trusts and the growth of monopoly power. On the other hand, even the most effective antitrust and antimerger law could not have been expected to do the job by itself, without the aid of complementary institutions, legal and administrative.

If the legal and administrative framework can be so devised that the self-interest of individual businessmen will induce them to act in the ways desired by society, the positive incentives thus provided will as a rule be more effective in bringing about a desired state of affairs than will the negative restrictions of legal prohibitions and judicial decrees attempting to thwart an otherwise profitable course of action. The profit motive can often be used to guide men in the direction that society wants. If society abhors concentrations of power in private hands and prefers economic control to be widely dispersed, the most effective way of accomplishing this is to make it less profitable to grow big and powerful, and make it more profitable to stay small. A variety of methods can be employed for this purpose, particularly certain features of corporation law, tax law and patent law. We shall see that in actual fact governmental policies in these and other areas have been designed to aid in the growth of monopoly rather than to restrain it.

What has just been said is applicable also to the problem of "reversing the trend." Prohibitions can help in stopping it, but not in reversing it. The prohibition of mergers injurious to competition would certainly have been of great value in stopping the trend toward concentration at the beginning of this century. Such a prohibition now may help prevent matters from getting worse. However, concentration of economic power has proceeded so far that society may not be satisfied with merely checking further concentration, but may wish to reduce some of the power positions that have been created. Would a stronger antitrust law, a real "trust-busting" law, be the best way toward this end?

Proposals along such lines have been advanced and supported. A recent report of a committee of experts studying the monopoly problem recommended compulsory dissolution wherever size and concentration could not be shown to be in the public interest. "The Sherman Act might be amended to establish a rebuttable presumption that concentration exceeding a specified percentage of the market . . . was prejudicial to the public interest." [95] The market would be defined with reference to any product or related group of products. Enterprises larger than the ceiling permitted would then be forced to prove in court that their largeness was in the public interest—or to dissolve and be split into separate parts.

This may be a practicable way. It is certainly not the only one and probably not the best. Far more effective than is commonly realized would be appropriate changes in corporation law, tax law, patent law, or other public policies, changes that create an incentive for concerns to divest themselves of subsidiaries they do not need for efficient operation, and remove some of the existing restraints on competition which have encouraged monopoly growth in the past and still sustain it. It is to a review of these aspects of the monopoly question that we now turn.

[95] "Report of the Twentieth Century Fund Committee on Cartels and Monopoly," in George W. Stocking and Myron W. Watkins, *Monopoly and Free Enterprise* (New York: Twentieth Century Fund, 1951), p. 553.

CHAPTER 7

Governmental Aids to Monopoly:
Corporation Laws, Taxes, Tariffs, Patents

Corporation Laws: The Privileges of the Body Corporate · Large-Scale Production versus Monopoly Control · Gratuitous Privileges and Lack of Limitations · Limiting the Privileges · Federal Incorporation

Tax Policies: Non-Fiscal versus Fiscal Objectives · Corporation Income Taxes: Why and How? · The Actual Bias Against Small Business · Tax-Induced Sales of Small Business Firms · The Potential Bias Against Big Business · Differential Taxes on Retained Earnings · Tax Policy and Anti-monopoly Policy

Trade Barriers: Import Tariffs · Arguments for Tariff Protection · Pressure Group Politics · Tariffs, Competition, Cartelization · Import Quotas · Foreign Exchange Restrictions · Interstate Trade Barriers

Patent Laws: Justification of Patent Protection · Extension of the Patent Monopoly · Abolition or Prevention of Abuse?

THE ECONOMIC POLICIES of government are far-flung and many-sided. On many fronts, therefore, could government fight for competition and against monopoly if it so desired. It has not seen fit to do so. Instead, on many fronts it has used its power to give aid to monopoly and to restrain competition. How government has done this through its corporation laws, tax system, commercial policy, patent laws, franchise and license requirements, trade "board" regulations, municipal ordinances, regulation of utilities and transportation, conservation policies for natural resources, price controls and labor legislation will be related in this chapter and the next.[1]

_____

[1] That the bulk of all restrictions on competition can be attributed to government policies has often been emphasized by liberal economists. For example: "The great monopoly problem mankind has to face today is not an outgrowth of the operation of the market economy. It is a product of pur-

CORPORATION LAWS

While the antitrust laws were aimed at restraining monopoly power, or eliminating monopoly in certain forms; and while some of the governmental policies that we shall discuss later were frankly directed toward restraining competition or eliminating it in certain areas; the corporation laws were not intended to do either. If they have come to be one of the most important aids to the development of monopolistic concentration, this was not the conscious objective of the legislatures that created them. That the corporation laws are what they are is the haphazard result of an abdication of public control over a publicly granted privilege, an abdication that took place in the wilder days of American business, when the foundations of the great corporate empires of today were being laid. A powerful device for good or evil was placed at the disposal of businessmen to use very much as they saw fit.

The Privileges of the Body Corporate

The life of a corporation is independent of the lives of its owners and it therefore enjoys one privilege not vouchsafed to man—the privilege of immortality. The limits to the accumulation of power in corporations with perpetual charters transcends the

---

posive action on the part of governments." Ludwig von Mises, *Human Action: A Treatise on Economics* (New Haven: Yale University Press, 1949), p. 363.—Or, "the major restrictions preventing effective competition are due directly or indirectly to stupid public policy. . . ." ". . . we may refer to the deliberate granting of patents and copyright . . . ; to the coddling of pressure groups in agriculture and organized labor; also to excessive grants of power to corporations." Frank H. Knight, "Economic and Social Policy in Democratic Society," *Journal of Political Economy*, Vol. LVIII (1950), pp. 519–20.

In referring to these writers as "liberals" I call attention to the different meanings of this label in the United States and in most other countries. In Europe, and in Latin America, the freedom of the individual, which is the essential objective of liberalism, includes, or means above all, freedom from the state, especially from government interferences with the operations of the competitive market economy. In the United States the term "liberal" is often used in the opposite sense, namely, for a reformer favoring a good deal of government intervention in economic affairs; indeed, even some "collectivists" would here call themselves "liberals" and in turn dub the Continental-European liberals as "rugged individualists."

limits to individual accumulations.[2] For this reason, the early attitude toward the corporation was one of watchful caution and the
privilege was granted sparingly by governments. That individuals
should have the right to incorporate their businesses merely by
filling out the appropriate forms and paying the requisite fees and
to operate in the absence of strict governmental supervision would
have seemed most improper to 18th- and early 19th-century legislators.

By 1850, however, the pressures from businesses for corporate
charters were so great that several states had adopted general incorporation laws. Much of this pressure was justified by the
"legitimate" needs of business. It has been said over and over
again that without the institution of the business corporation capitalism could not have developed as rapidly as it has and the productive efficiency of our economy could not have reached its
present level. The corporate form of business organization is regarded as a necessary condition for the development of the large
economic units which alone can achieve the efficient use of resources that comes with the techniques of large-scale production.

In order to make use of the technological advantages of large-
scale production, an agglomeration of such masses of capital was
needed as few individual owners could afford. In order to collect the wealth of many individuals and put it under common
control, the joint-stock company had to be created. In order to
make it an economic unit separate from and relatively independent
of its owners, it was given all the legal privileges of a "person":
it could own property, make contracts, undertake liabilities, bring
suits and be sued. In order to attract the funds of people who were
willing to risk their investments but unwilling to risk their fortunes beyond the sums invested in the collective venture, the
privilege of limited liability was conferred on the owners. Some
countries went still further and added to the privilege of limited
liability the privilege of anonymous ownership of the body cor-

[2] "As legal 'persons' they were given all the privileges of natural persons
but, since they were capable of indefinite growth and were immortal, they
accumulated power which it would have been impossible for a natural person to retain and all but impossible to acquire." Frank D. Graham, *Social
Goals and Economic Institutions* (Princeton: Princeton University Press,
1942), p. 209.

porate, an anonymity that applied even *vis-à-vis* the tax authorities and conveniently enabled the stockholders to evade income taxes on dividends collected.[3]

Large-Scale Production versus Monopoly Control

Some concentration of economic power was obviously necessary for the realization of the technological potentials of mass production. The extent, however, to which that concentration has proceeded is entirely out of proportion to the so-called technological necessities or economies. Most of the growth of corporate empires during the last fifty or sixty years was not a matter of technological integration of production but rather financial integration of control. And this integration and concentration of control in larger and larger corporate units was, of course, directly related to the building up of monopoly positions both in the sense of reducing the number of actual competitors in the field and in the sense of reducing the ease with which potential competitors could enter the field.

The corporation laws have facilitated the concentration of economic control over the industry of the country chiefly in two ways. They have enabled single corporations to grow to enormous size through the acquisition of other corporations wholly or in part; and they have made it possible for "interest groups" to control the large corporations themselves.[4] This second type of control, although of great importance from the point of view of economic organization and the social and political climate prevailing in the nation, is probably less important than the first with respect to the monopolistic control over markets and market policies with which we are here concerned.

[3] To guard this anonymity stockholders in several countries can collect dividends by presenting *incognito*, at the window of a bank, coupons which they clip from a sheet attached to their bearer stock certificates and which are payable to the bearer.

[4] "Interest groups" with strong control over large industrial corporations have included J. P. Morgan & Company, the Rockefellers, Du Ponts, Mellons. According to recent studies, eight interest groups control at least 106 of the 250 largest corporations in the United States. Cf. National Resources Committee, *The Structure of the American Economy* (Washington: 1939), pp. 160–61.

An investigation of the largest corporations in the United
States would readily bear out the contention that their growth was
only in part related to larger establishments, bigger machines,
greater power plants, longer conveyor belts, more elaborate as-
sembly lines, lower inter-plant transportation cost, or other economies of large-scale production. Instead, much of their growth was
related to the construction or acquisition of entirely separate plants,
which many believe could be just as efficiently operated by independent firms, and to the acquisition of whole companies, many
of which had been their competitors, suppliers, or customers.

There was nothing "natural" about this growth of business
firms into corporate giants. It was merely a matter of shortsighted
legislatures and courts, and ingenious lawyers, promoters and
businessmen. On the one hand, the various states in the country
found that the business of incorporating corporations was a lucrative one [5] and that the simpler they made the formalities and the
less restrictive the regulations, the more of this business they could
attract.[6] On the other hand, it was "natural" not only that businessmen should make the most of the opportunities which government
policies and legal institutions provided, but also that they should
try to ensure that these institutions and policies were developed
in their interests.

Gratuitous Privileges and Lack of Limitations

The very existence of the corporate form of business is, as we
have pointed out, a vital aid to the growth of the business unit.
Certain features in the corporation laws, however, can be singled
out as "gratuitous" in the sense that they essentially contribute to
a concentration of control far beyond anything that might be
"necessary" for the realization of all possible economies of large-

[5] In 1929 approximately 42% of the total revenue of the State of Dela-
ware was derived from incorporation fees and corporate franchise taxes. See
R. C. Larcom, *The Delaware Corporation* (Baltimore: The Johns Hopkins
Press, 1937).

[6] Even though some states tried to maintain some control over corporations, one "liberal" state was sufficient to vitiate all such attempts since a
corporation created in one state had to be recognized by all other states under
the "full faith and credit clause" of the Constitution.

scale production and distribution. But if one calls some features of the corporation laws "gratuitous," one invites protests from lawyers and economists who can rightly point to material advantages of the criticized provisions. Moreover, in attributing any "effects" to a particular legal provision one is implying that these effects could be avoided by eliminating the provision entirely or by replacing it by some other. Indeed, sometimes it is possible to correct the effects complained of merely by deleting an existing provision in the law. More often, however, some arrangement must be made and it is impossible to complain of the effects of any specific arrangement unless alternatives are considered. Furthermore, if a law confers rights and powers on individuals or groups, one must examine it as much with reference to what it does not provide as to what it does provide. It is axiomatic that in society all individual rights are limited; yet it is up to the law to define what the limits are, and one can attribute to the law itself the consequences that follow from a failure to impose adequate limits.[7]

There is no doubt that the general incorporation laws have conferred powers on corporations of which they could be sheared without impairing their ability to take advantage of modern technology. There is considerable disagreement as to exactly what powers should be limited and how the limitation should be effected, but the following are some of the criticisms and suggestions that have been made.[8]

First, *the right of a corporation to own stock in another corporation* was probably the most important single device that government contrived to facilitate the development of the industry-

[7] Even the fundamental rights of a democracy, such as freedom of speech, must have limits. It is not possible, for example, for an individual to make obscene speeches, or speeches designed to incite violence, without running afoul of the legal limits placed on free speech.

[8] Many of the criticisms and suggestions have been made by people who are not "experts" in corporation law. Since specialists in a field tend to ignore some of the wider ramifications of their subject while the nonspecialist may have a broader point of view, it would be too bad if the former summarily brushed aside all suggestions from the latter. Many general proposals have ideas in them worth exploring even though the form in which they are presented is manifestly inappropriate.

dominating corporation.[9] It was first introduced into a general incorporation law by the State of New Jersey in 1888, just at the time when the trust device for obtaining monopoly control was being challenged in the courts, and it laid the basis for the holding company, which was to become an even more effective instrument of control than the original form of trust.

Second, the laws allowed the development of *other methods of concentrating or coordinating the decision-making powers* that would otherwise be dispersed over several independent business units. Among the most apparent of these methods are "interlocking office-holding" and the "community of interests." [10]

Third, the virtual *"disenfranchisement"* of the owners of many corporations facilitates a concentration of power in the hands of a few that is gratuitous in many respects. There are several devices by which a small group can obtain control over large corporations and coordinate their policies. Thus, instead of the older one-share-one-vote custom, different types of corporate stock may be issued with different voting rights or with none at all. There may be thousands of "owners" of a corporation, only a minority of whom have any control over the corporation policies. But even if all stock is voting stock, a small concentrated minority ownership may be

---

[9] Walter Lippmann in his *Good Society* (Boston: Little Brown & Company, 1937) said: "Fifty years ago no common law lawyer would have thought it conceivable that one corporation could own stock of another. The business corporation, as we know it, is founded on the fact that legislatures and courts gradually invested incorporated associations with new rights, rights which did not exist a hundred years ago, rights which can, therefore, by no stretch of the imagination be regarded as anything but conditional and subject to alteration" (p. 280).

[10] The antitrust laws made a feeble attempt to get at these devices. But ". . . the present law fails to provide adequate safeguards against communities of interest. It contains no provisions against the development of a working accord among business enterprises through the personal relations of their officers, managers, and principal stockholders; no limitations upon the right to have identical executive officers, lawyers, accountants, banks, and advertising agencies; no legal barrier to prevent a single wealthy man or the members of a single family from owning the controlling stock interest in more than one ostensibly competing company. In summary, there has been no substantial effort to prevent competition from being destroyed by ties of ownership and management which unite ostensibly independent concerns." Corwin D. Edwards, *Maintaining Competition: Requisites of a Governmental Policy* (New York: McGraw-Hill, 1949), p. 142.

able to control the corporation, particularly if it has the cooperation of management to whom the "proxy machinery" is available.[11] Management holds an extremely strategic position in the modern corporation, particularly if ownership is widely dispersed, and in many corporations management has virtually complete control. The term "management" is used to include the directors and the top executive officers of the corporation. Clearly this group has a vested interest in the growth of the corporation, and the larger and more powerful the corporation, the more important and more powerful is their position. Although in theory management runs the business for its owners, it frequently happens that the interests of management and of owners conflict. In this case, management control is likely to be used to protect the position of management to the detriment of owners.

Fourth, one of the most serious conflicts of interest between management and ownership concerns the *distribution or retention of corporate profits.* How much of the profits is distributed to the stockholders and how much is "ploughed back" is in effect decided by management. To a very considerable extent corporate expansion is financed by these "internal" funds and, since these funds never reach the capital market, in which they would be subject to competition from other potential users, and are disposed of largely without consulting the wishes of their real owners, they furnish a most appropriate vehicle for the strengthening of the power of management through reinvestment in the corporation. Expansion may take place for no other reason than that management wishes to extend its sphere of operation or control. This type of reinvestment of corporate earnings not only promotes an undue extension of corporate power but, in withdrawing a significant part of the investment capital of the country from the competition of the capital market, may result in wide deviations from the "optimum" allocation of resources in the economy.[12]

[11] When ownership is widely dispersed, most of the shareholders never attend stockholders meetings and, if they vote at all, vote only by proxy. The machinery through which information is given to stockholders and proxies are secured is usually under the control of management. This puts management in a strategic position with regard to any other group who may wish to oppose the interest of management in the meetings.

[12] It should be noted, however, that after a high degree of concentration

Finally, there are *no limits to the size of a corporation.* Society has provided a foundation upon which a Frankensteinian monster can be created. Corporations may become larger than is consistent with the public welfare, larger than is justified by the primary justification for corporations.[13]

Limiting the Privileges

The first two criticisms concern the power of a dominant corporation under present laws to obtain control over other corporations. The *prohibition of intercorporate stock ownership* has often been suggested as a method for reducing this power. Exceptions would have to be made, however, for investment companies, insurance companies, banks, and similar institutions. The purpose of such a provision would be to prevent concentration of control, and intercorporate stockholding that is unrelated to this purpose could well be permitted.[14] Similarly, a *prohibition of interlocking controls* of other kinds could also be written into the corporation laws, instead of attempting to combat them through special prohibitions, such as the Clayton Act provision against interlocking directorates in large competing corporations (which has never been enforced).

Instead of attacking the "disenfranchisement" of the stockholder or the power of management to retain corporate earnings without limit for financing uncontrolled growth, one may directly *attack the separation of ownership and control* that has occurred

---

has been reached in many industries owing to the spectacular growth of a few corporations, continued freedom to retain earnings may tend to *reduce concentration* of industrial control. For it is an established fact that smaller corporations retain larger percentages of their earnings than the corporate giants are wont to do; and we know that retained earnings are practically the only source of funds available to growing small business firms. Hence, restrictions on the retention of earnings would restrict the growth of smaller corporations more than the growth of larger ones. Inasmuch as the permission to retain earnings allows small firms to grow at a faster rate than large firms, it tends to reduce industry control by the latter.

[13] Society has found it wise to limit the size of buildings in cities, the size of trucks on the roads, etc.

[14] "The first and most obvious change needed . . . is a requirement that every corporation disclose its corporate affiliations and the names of those who hold its securities." Corwin D. Edwards, *op. cit.,* p. 134.

because the laws allow a wide diffusion of ownership and permit corporations to be controlled by boards of directors whose members own only little or nothing of the corporate stock.[15] If it were provided that the members of each board must be beneficial owners of at least 51 percent of the stock of the company, this would make it more likely that the company would be run, and its investments would be decided upon, in the interest of the majority of the owners. (If the executives were not spending other people's money but largely their own, they might be more solicitous about expenses as well as investments.) At the same time this provision would effectively limit the tendency toward giantism because the growth of an enterprise could not be out of proportion to the combined wealth of its board members. Moreover it would be more difficult for individuals to accumulate enormous power over several corporations far in excess of their financial stake in these enterprises. Since the existence of corporate giants may be indispensable in some fields—such as railroad, telephone, or telegraph companies—exemptions would have to be granted where size far beyond the wealth of the control group is clearly in the public interest. Alternatively, in lieu of prohibition and exemptions, a general provision might put all corporations that are not controlled by at least a certain percent of their owners under public control or regulation. The wish to avoid government control of an industrial enterprise may act as an incentive for keeping its growth within the bounds dictated by the financial means of its directors.

The proposal just discussed was based on the proposition that those in control of the corporations should also be the effective owners. This would certainly reduce the size of corporations. But it is strongly urged by some that one of the chief advantages of corporations—the ability to raise equity capital from hundreds of relatively minor sources—would be seriously impaired to the detriment of both efficient industrial organization and the convenience

[15] The officers and directors of a sample of 155 companies, taken from the 200 largest corporations in the country, owned in 1935 a median of 1.74 percent and an average of 5.52 percent of the voting stock of their corporations. (Obviously their holdings were an even smaller share of all common stock outstanding.) R. A. Gordon, "Ownership by Management and Control Groups in the Large Corporation," *Quarterly Journal of Economics*, Vol. LII (1938), p. 371.

and position of the small investor; in other words, that this proposal goes too far. Almost the opposite arrangement has also been suggested: that those who have *minority interests* are guaranteed a more than *proportionate degree of control* over the policies of the corporation. This could be accomplished by one of a variety of modified "proportional representation" voting procedures for directors. For example, if there are 15 members of a board of directors to be elected, each share of voting stock could only be voted for, say, three directors, instead of for the whole slate of fifteen. Thus, those with 51 percent of the stock could still only elect three directors if all their stock were voted as a block.

The corporation laws, instead of permitting the incorporation of firms of any size and permitting them to grow without limit, might include a *limit on size*—in terms of capital, sales, employment, or other measures—beyond which special charters would be required, granted only upon proof that greater size was needed for efficient production and distribution of the products of the enterprise. Or the laws might *limit the number of establishments* operated by any one corporation, or they might provide that no person, natural or legal, may *"control"* any business organization which makes deliveries (for compensation) from more than one "point of delivery," unless "the total of all the employees engaged in and for such organizations is less than one thousand." [16]

[16] This is a provision of the fanciful "Business Limitation Act" drafted by a critic of the present corporation laws who proposes to limit the size of firms and the scope of corporate control by means other than public regulation and not requiring administrative or judicial discretion. The limitations proposed would not affect large-scale production, since the size of the establishment (shipping from "one point of delivery") is not limited; nor would they affect multi-plant operation if the plants are all sufficiently small (employing less than a total of 1000 people); nor would they affect the locating of large establishments at different points if the establishments are vertically so completely integrated that only one of them makes deliveries to buyers; and, since the "point of delivery" is defined as a circle with a ten-mile radius, it would be permissible to have production and warehouse facilities somewhat spread out and not strictly contiguous. What the limitations under this scheme would definitely exclude is the concentration of control over establishments located at such a distance from one another that one may assume that they could just the same be run under independent control. An unusually broad definition of "control" increases the effectiveness of these limitations. "Control" is to include any influence, by contract or otherwise, on the selection of executive employees and on "the selection of any commodity, property

With imagination or diligence we could easily add to the criticisms and suggestions and lengthen the list of what the corporation laws have done to aid the growth of monopoly or have failed to do in order to check it.[17] With regard to the effects of a "charter law" there is, we repeat, no logical difference between positive aids and absence of limitations. The enactment of corporation laws constitutes a positive action of the state conferring privileges that would not exist otherwise. The question is whether these privileges

or service to be purchased or employed. Besides the right to vote a majority of stock, control in this sense comprises all restrictions or incentives provided in the form of tying clauses, full-line forcing, quantity discounts, exclusive selling or buying arrangements, etc." See Fred I. Raymond, *The Limitist* (New York: W. W. Norton & Company, 1947), pp. 110–19.

[17] A comprehensive list of proposals for the reform of incorporation laws was advanced by Henry C. Simons in *A Positive Program for Laissez Faire: Some Proposals for a Liberal Economic Policy.* Public Policy Pamphlet, No. 15 (Chicago: University of Chicago Press, 1934). Reprinted in *Economic Policy for a Free Society* (Chicago: University of Chicago Press, 1948), pp. 58–59. He proposed that the laws provide:

"1. That no corporation which engages in the manufacture or merchandising of commodities or services shall own any securities of any other such corporation

2. Limitation upon the total amount of property which any single corporation may own
   a) A general limitation for all corporations, *and*
   b) A limitation designed to preclude the existence in any industry of a single company large enough to dominate that industry— the principle being stated in legislation, the actual maxima for different industries to be fixed by the Federal Trade Commission

3. That corporations may issue securities only in a small number of simple forms prescribed by law and that no single corporation may employ more than two (or three) of the different forms

4. Incorporation of investment corporations under separate laws, designed to preclude their becoming holding companies or agencies of monopoly control—with limitations on their total property, on percentage holdings of securities of any single operating company, and on total investment in any single industry (again under the immediate control of the Federal Trade Commission)

5. That investment corporations shall hold stock in operating companies without voting rights, and shall be prohibited from exercising influence over such companies with respect to management

6. That no person shall serve as an officer in any two corporations in the same line of business and that no officer of an investment corporation shall serve as an officer of any operating company

7. That corporate earnings shall be taxed to shareholders in such manner as to prevent evasion of personal income tax with respect to undistributed earnings."

should be without limits, with generous limits or with narrow limits. The absence of limits in the rights and privileges granted to "legal persons"—limits with regard to interlocking stock-holding, interlocking office-holding, separation of ownership and control, retention of earnings, size and growth, number of non-contiguous establishments—is equivalent to positive aids to the development of monopoly power.

Federal Incorporation

One cannot expect that adequate limitations will be written into the corporation laws of the individual states. After all, "individual States fear to place themselves at a possible disadvantage by imposing requirements which other States would not lay down." [18] Federal incorporation of large enterprises doing business beyond state boundaries has therefore been considered the only practicable way of accomplishing needed reforms.

The Temporary National Economic Committee in 1941 recommended "national standards for national corporations" [19] and bills have been introduced providing for the Federal licensing or incorporation of corporations engaged in interstate commerce. [20] Such proposals have never succeeded in overcoming the resistance of the business interests who stand to gain from the present lax system of incorporation. To strengthen the opposition to a Federal incorporation system, the advocates of the state systems of unlimited corporation charters have skilfully exploited the strong sentiments of the defenders of "state rights" against the expansion of "Federal control." [21]

[18] *Final Report and Recommendations of the Temporary National Economic Committee*, 77th Congress, 1st Session (Washington: 1941), p. 28.
[19] *Ibid.*, p. 29.
[20] See, e.g., *Federal Licensing of Corporations*, Hearings before a Subcommittee of the Committee on the Judiciary, U.S. Senate, on S. 10. 75th Congress, 1st Session (Washington: 1937).
[21] According to the majority view of the Temporary National Economic Committee the "necessary reforms could be effected by a national charter law without in the slightest degree impairing State sovereignty. Indeed, such provisions would have the very opposite effect because they would abolish the principal means by which the concentration which has undermined local economic sovereignty has been effected." *Final Report*, p. 29.

As the laws now stand, the governmental arrangements concerning the creation and operation of corporate bodies are among the most powerful aids to the development of monopoly power in the United States.[22]

TAX POLICIES

If the power to tax is the power to destroy, taxation, one might think, could have been used for the destruction of monopoly. Perhaps such use would have been undesirable; perhaps it would have been impossible; but one thing is certain: it has not been tried.

Non-Fiscal versus Fiscal Objectives

The use of taxation for other than strictly fiscal purposes has often been attacked as an unwise exercise of governmental power. There are so many things that society wishes to do, so many objectives to achieve. If taxes were devised on a grand scale as deterrents and incentives, meting out penalties for socially undesirable behavior and giving indirect premiums for socially desirable behavior, the danger would be great that the tax system could not fulfill its primary functions, to raise revenue for the government and avoid inflation. The tax structure might be undermined by gradual accretions of non-fiscal taxes serving many different social purposes.[23]

[22] "The principal instrument of the concentration of economic power and wealth has been the corporate charter with unlimited powers—charters which afforded a detour around every principle of fiduciary responsibility; charters which permitted promoters and managers to use the property of others for their own enrichment to the detriment of the real owners; charters which made possible the violation of law without personal liability; charters which omitted every safeguard of individual and public welfare which common sense and experience alike have taught are necessary." *Ibid.*, p. 28.

[23] "The use of taxation for non-fiscal ends should not be summarily condemned on the broad grounds that no non-fiscal purposes are properly admissible . . . As students of public finance, we desire to sound a note of warning against hasty and ill considered proposals to use taxation . . . for the achievement of specific economic results . . . There is a real risk that, through the indiscriminating use of our general taxes for other purposes than the raising of money, we may seriously impair their usefulness for the not unimportant task of alimenting the public fisc." Final Report of the Com-

The purist in public finance who rejects any and all non-fiscal functions of taxation on the ground that they might interfere with the fiscal one apparently has a very narrow view of the governmental agenda. No doubt, he is correct in warning of the social costs that may arise from the damage to a tax system burdened with non-fiscal functions. But he forgets to compare these costs with the costs of attempting to fulfill the same functions by different methods or of failing to fulfill them at all. If an important social objective cannot be attained by other methods, or if it can be attained only at higher costs, one should not let the fact that the tax system might suffer damage as a revenue-raising machine be the overriding consideration. The relative importance of the social objectives, the relative merits and demerits of achieving them in alternative ways, as well as the effects on the tax structure must all be carefully evaluated.

Any tax system has non-fiscal implications. Although taxes may be imposed primarily to raise revenue or as part of an overall fiscal policy, they will always affect such things as the distribution of income, economic incentives, and the availability of capital. Their burden may lie with unequal weight on different size firms or on different types of expansion and thus they incidentally become relevant to the question of monopoly and competition. If the prevention of monopolistic domination of the economy is one of the established policies of government, it is not permissible to neglect the actual effects of the tax system as it is as well as the potential effects of the tax system as it might be.[24]

Corporation Income Taxes: Why and How?

For the most part taxation has little relevance for the problem of monopolistic business practices nor can it be easily used to con-

---

mittee of the National Tax Association on Federal Taxation of Corporations, *National Tax Association Proceedings*, 1939, pp. 517, 572.

[24] "Other things being equal, when a choice is available between alternative revenue measures, the first of which promises to produce economic effects considered desirable by the community, and the second of which involves undesirable economic repercussions, it is intelligent to choose the first . . . Again it seems to us obvious that when a given economic program has been established as accepted public policy, it is desirable that tax statutes be brought into harmony with it." *Ibid.*, p. 572.

trol monopoly as such. Proposals for a direct tax on "monopoly profits" have been made. But as we shall see elsewhere in this book, it is difficult enough to identify profits; to separate monopoly profits from other elements in the net income of a business is impossible. Income taxation can touch monopoly only to the extent that *size* is closely associated with monopoly power.[25] It would be technically possible to tax large corporations out of existence. Or through imposing steeply progressive income taxes upon corporations it would be possible to discourage firms from growing larger and to encourage large firms to split up.

All this presupposes that we have and retain corporation taxes at all. Whether they are economically sound and "desirable" is a highly controversial issue. Many economists maintain that business taxes of any kind—sales and excise taxes, excess profits taxes, corporate income taxes, etc.,—are fundamentally unsound because they influence production policies, pricing policies, investment policies of businessmen, which should be determined exclusively by the demand of consumers and the conditions of production.[26] An excise tax may cause producers to produce less than they would otherwise decide to produce. An excess profits tax discourages efforts to reduce costs, promotes wasteful expenditures and may even cause firms to pay higher prices for productive factors than they would pay in the absence of the tax. A corporation income tax may influence investment decisions of the firm by creating a bias against the more risky investments.[27] In order to avoid all such

[25] "Some people propose that taxes should be used to protect little business against monopolies. But special treatment of corporations not engaged in monopolistic practices, as proposed in a bill introduced in the Senate a few years ago, is a dubious panacea for small business ills. Federal policy is opposed to monopoly and such a differentiation might be basically in accord with that policy. But monopoly is an elusive concept. Size does not prove its existence, nor do interlocking directorships. No doubt there is a connection between size in business and monopoly power, but bigness does not always beget monopolies nor does smallness always mean the absence of monopoly. It is almost impossible to devise any test that would be readily useful for tax purposes." Randolph E. Paul, *Taxation for Prosperity* (New York: Bobbs-Merrill, 1947), p. 384.

[26] Some business taxes, e.g., the chain store taxes in some states, the liquor taxes and wartime taxes on luxury goods are imposed for the specific purpose of influencing investment and production.

[27] This will, of course, depend on the loss offsets permitted in the law.

effects, it is forcefully argued, taxes should not be imposed on business firms but only directly on individuals.[28]

Since individuals must, in the last analysis, bear the taxes anyway, it is also argued on grounds of equity that all taxes be placed directly and openly on the individuals who bear them. Taxes cannot be "borne" by "artificial" persons, i.e., corporations, but always fall on the real individuals who have an interest in the corporation's activities as producers, consumers, or suppliers of capital. Hence an income tax on corporations is ultimately imposed on individuals in a concealed fashion without reference to any principles of equity or ability to pay. There is, therefore, a strong case for placing the taxes directly on individuals in accordance with accepted principles of taxation rather than on the earnings of corporations. Administratively this would be more difficult than the present system, the change would result in considerable upheaval and the squawks of the taxpayers would be intensified. The chief advantage of the corporation income tax is that its incidence is concealed from those who bear it and they can therefore be plucked without excessive pother,—surely a somewhat specious principle of taxation!

These are objections to the principle of corporation taxes. Objections can also be made to the particular way in which they are constructed. In the United States, for example, many economists strongly object to the "double taxation of dividends" which results from the fact that the net income of corporations is fully taxed

---

See Evsey D. Domar and Richard A. Musgrave, "Proportional Income Taxation and Risk-Taking," *Quarterly Journal of Economics,* Vol. LVIII (1944), pp. 388–422.

[28] "It is the business of enterprises to produce goods and to make money. Given proper rules of the game, formal and conventional, and a structure of law designed to facilitate transactions and to analyse them in accordance with the public interest (e.g., away from excessive power concentration and monopoly), enterprises should be free from arbitrary influences on their actions and crucial decisions. In particular, the influence of taxes on production and investment policies should be minimized . . . The impact of taxes should be kept as far away as possible from the concern or enterprise, and from the sphere in which operating and investment decisions are made. This means that taxes should fall on the natural person or family as a consuming and saving unit, where their effect will be concentrated on consumption and saving and largely removed from productive enterprise and management." Henry C. Simons, *Federal Tax Reform* (Chicago: University of Chicago Press, 1950), pp. 17 and 20.

before dividends are distributed and that the dividends are taxed again under the personal income tax when the shareholders receive them. The double taxation discriminates against equity financing and in favor of debt financing, because interest payments, deductible from taxable corporate income, are taxed only once. This discrimination may have harmful economic effects, particularly in downswings of the business cycle, when debt may become dangerously burdensome.

Nonetheless, we have had corporation taxes for a long time and we are likely to have them for a long time in the future. Let us, then, take their existence for granted and examine their relation to an antimonopoly program. Except for a slight graduation in the corporation income tax rates, the accepted policy has been to make taxes "neutral" with respect to large versus small business. Should taxes perhaps be so devised that they discriminate against big business? Have they perhaps, as many say, been so devised that they have in fact discriminated against small business?

The Actual Bias Against Small Business

In one sense it may be said that any business tax whatever—unless it is prohibitively progressive—falls harder on small business than on big. Small businesses depend for their development almost entirely on the reinvestment of their earnings. They do not have the access to the credit and capital markets that large corporations have. Thus a tax on the earnings of business, large or small, reduces the only important source of funds available to small business.

To prevent the tax system from aggravating the difficulty small business faces in raising capital, numerous proposals have been made for completely or partially exempting small firms from the corporation income tax, for a more graduated corporation income tax, for the modification of the special surtax that is levied on profits retained in excess of "reasonable" business needs, for accelerated depreciation allowances for durable assets, and for measures to place incorporated and non-incorporated small business on a more nearly equal basis.[29] This is not the place to discuss these

[29] There are many discussions of the effect of taxation on small busi-

measures. Each of them raises special problems, administrative as well as economic, with regard to efficiency as well as equity.[30]

One particular way in which business income taxes have discriminated against new and small firms concerns the incidence of losses. When large diversified established firms enter new lines of activity, losses made in these lines may be offset for tax purposes against profits made in other lines, so that the taxable income of the firm is reduced by the amount of the losses. Such savings on income tax liability do not exist for the small, new firm, because it has no other departments making profits part of which could become non-taxable on account of the loss offset. The small, new firm is therefore at a distinct disadvantage in any risky enterprise.

This disadvantage is aggravated if income taxes are figured on a strictly annual basis so that losses made in one year cannot be offset against gains in other years. The risk of investing in small firms is thus greater than in large firms and investment in them is discouraged. To remove this bias against small firms the law now provides that net losses in the current year may for tax purposes be "carried back" and set off against income in the two preceding years, and any loss balance still remaining may be "carried forward" against income in the two following years. The carry-back provisions may be very important for small businesses, especially in times of depression when their cash position is likely to be weak; they may then find considerable relief in receiving from the Treasury the cash refunds from taxes paid in the previous two years. But the carry-back provisions are of no help to a *new* firm established for a new venture. Nor will the carry-forward provisions

nesses and of desirable reforms in the law. For further information the following references are useful: U.S. Treasury Department, Division of Tax Research, *Taxation of Small Business* (Washington: 1949); Smaller War Plants Corporation, *Taxation,* An Economic Report prepared by John M. Blair, Howard R. Bowen and C. C. Fichtner (Washington: Sept. 1945).

[30] Special measures designed to assist the owners of small business may well conflict with the objective of taxing individuals according to their ability to pay, inasmuch as small businesses are not infrequently owned by very wealthy men and the tax system might then have the effect of enabling such men to evade income taxes by hiding behind the privileges granted small businesses. This would be avoided if stockholders had to pay personal income taxes not only on dividends received but on their share in the total earnings of the corporations. The partners in unincorporated business firms pay personal income taxes on earnings retained or distributed.

help such a firm if the losses made force it out of business. Thus the new, small firm has neither profits from other departments, nor profits from past years, nor perhaps profits in future years, against which to offset its losses. While, through such loss offsets and consequent tax reductions, the Government shares in the venture losses of old or large firms, it does not do so in the venture losses of new small firms.[31]

If an increase in the concentration of industry in the hands of large business firms is to be prevented (and a decrease in concentration to be promoted) a high birth and survival rate of new firms and high growth rates of small firms are needed. Yet both are cut down by high income taxes. High personal income taxes reduce the capacity of individuals to accumulate funds needed to start new businesses and to nurse them through their formative stages. High corporate income taxes reduce the capacity of the new and small businesses to retain earnings to finance their development and growth, and reduce also the willingness of outsiders to furnish capital for the growth of small firms. In all these respects the small firm is severely handicapped relative to the old and established firm.[32]

In at least one industry the existence of *specific excise taxes* has worked to the disadvantage of small producers and in favor of the dominating concerns. Cigarette taxes, levied by the Federal

[31] In order to remove this bias against new, small, and venturesome business, it has been proposed that the government share in losses just as it shares, by means of the income tax, in the profits of corporations. "To assure the possibility of loss offset, the Treasury would, in fact, have to stand ready to collect cash in case of gains and to send a check in the case of losses." Alvin H. Hansen, in *Financing American Prosperity*, A Symposium of Economists, edited by Paul T. Homan and Fritz Machlup (New York: Twentieth Century Fund, 1945), p. 242.

[32] Cf. J. Keith Butters and John Lintner, *Effect of Federal Taxes on Growing Enterprises* (Boston: Harvard University, Graduate School of Business Administration, 1945).—With regard to internal financing the authors reach the following conclusion: "Since profitable small firms on the average earn a higher rate of profit and retain a larger percentage of their earnings than do profitable large firms, a high flat-rate corporate income tax would restrict the internally financed growth of small firms more severely than that of large firms" (p. 70). Regarding the availability of outside capital the authors conclude "that small companies are at a severe competitive disadvantage in comparison with large companies" (p. 90) and that this disadvantage is increased through a high flat-rate corporate income tax.

Government as well as by the states, clearly discourage price competition inasmuch as they reduce the responsiveness of demand to price changes by cigarette manufacturers and as they fall, because they are based on quantity rather than value, relatively more heavily on the cheaper brands.[33] If the abolition of cigarette taxes is not practicable because of fiscal necessity or convenience, they could at least be changed to graduated or *ad valorem* taxes in order to eliminate the present bias against the producers of cheaper products.[34]

Tax-Induced Sales of Small Business Firms

Apart from the inherent general bias of the income tax system against small business,[35] a combination of other features in the existing tax system has operated to encourage merger of small businesses with large.[36] The small corporation is frequently closely held, that is, the ownership is confined to a few men, and the equity in it very often accounts for a large proportion of the owners' assets. On the death of an owner, a tax which must be paid in cash is levied on his estate. In order to accumulate enough cash to meet the estate tax an owner, or his heirs, may have to sell his equity in the business. But there is virtually no market for the stock of small corporations, except among large corporations in the same or connected fields which frequently are willing to absorb their smaller competitors. The estate tax, therefore, puts pres-

[33] "The economy-brand cigarette today bears a Federal tax of 163 per cent of the manufacturer's selling price, compared with a tax of 104 per cent . . . [on] Lucky Strikes, Chesterfields, and Camels." House Select Committee on Small Business (Washington: 1948), quoted by William H. Nicholls, *Price Policies in the Cigarette Industry* (Nashville: Vanderbilt University Press, 1951), p. 419.

[34] See the illuminating discussion by Nicholls, *op. cit.*, pp. 415–23.

[35] Some hold that "neutrality" of the tax system with respect to the size of the business firm can be obtained only by "abolition of corporation or business taxes, for their bias against smaller firms cannot be eliminated— neither can it be compensated satisfactorily by progression and exemptions of the kind found in present laws." Henry C. Simons, *Federal Tax Reform*, p. 25.

[36] "The tax structure definitely exerts strong pressure on the owners of many closely held businesses to sell out or to merge with other larger companies; of this there can be no doubt." G. Keith Butters and John Lintner, "Taxes and Mergers," *Harvard Business Review*, Vol. XXIX (1951), p. 70.

sure upon owners of small companies to sell out to the big concerns. Alternatively, instead of a cash sale, an owner may prefer to arrange for an exchange of the stock of his firm for the much more saleable stock of the large corporation.

An owner could, of course, prepare for the payment of death duties by distributing to himself in the form of dividends more or all of the profits of his small corporation. But, apart from his desire to leave in the firm as much of his earnings as he can possibly spare, the dividends would be subject to personal income taxation, and he would be loath to pay these taxes on dividends which he takes only in order to prepare for the payment of the estate taxes. Moreover, this way of taking the profits of a corporation is much more expensive than the alternative of realizing a capital gain—which is taxed at a lower rate than dividend income. In other words, the difference between capital gains tax and ordinary income tax militates against dividend distribution and for the retention of the corporate earnings in the company and the eventual realization of the profit through the sale of the appreciated shares of stock. Hence, "the impact of the estate tax on the owners of closely held companies is reinforced by the combined effects of high income taxes and of low capital gains tax rates." [37]

The possibility of a tax advantage if business profits are taken in the form of capital gains rather than dividends may also encourage the owner of a growing but still risky business to cash in his gain at the low rate by selling out and investing in some less risky securities. In other words, he leaves the profits in the business, allowing it to grow and allowing himself to save some personal income tax, then he sells out to a large corporation and takes

---

[37] Butters and Lintner, *op. cit.,* p. 72. A recent change in the law makes it possible to provide funds needed for estate taxes through cash distributions out of the accumulated surplus of the corporations. Under the 1950 Revenue Code, distributions of cash by closely held companies need not be taxed as dividends provided the distributions are made under specified conditions and for the purpose of meeting death taxes. Thus, a closely held corporation may redeem the stock of a decedent without incurring heavy taxes. "The practical effect of this provision is to make many distributions in redemption of closely held stock entirely tax free. . . . The terms of the provision are sufficiently broad to cover a large percentage, though not all, of the cases in which the need for funds to pay estate taxes would have exerted strong pressure on the owner to sell out." Butters and Lintner, *op. cit.,* p. 73.

his profit at the lower tax rate. There is no easy answer to this problem; it would be very wrong to assume that it could or should be solved by eliminating the special treatment of capital gains; indeed, many other serious difficulties would arise if this were done. But the fact remains that the existing system works for the absorption of small business firms by big business firms and thus, indirectly, probably for the reduction of competition and the increase in monopoly power.

The Potential Bias Against Big Business

While it may be desirable to reduce as far as possible the weight of taxes on small struggling businesses, it is chimerical to think that this in itself is going to have much effect on monopoly, given the present size of the large units. A tenderness for small business can easily become a blinder preventing adequate attention being given to the continuing growth of large monopolistic business. Although the idea of special taxation of large corporate units suggests itself readily to antagonists of big business, it has never been an accepted principle of tax policy to any significant extent.[38]

A *steeply progressive income tax* has been one of the more popular proposals for reaching large corporations, but has not been adopted in the United States. The 1950 law has only two brackets: a flat normal tax of 25% on all income and an additional tax (surtax) of 22% on all income above $25,000, so that on all income in excess of $25,000 a corporation pays a tax of 47%. A really progressive income tax would have many more brackets, beginning with low rates on the lower incomes and rising steeply as income increased. The effect of such a tax would be to increase the relative profitability of small businesses as compared to large businesses. It might provide a positive incentive for large corporations to break up into independent units, and it might cause businessmen to refrain from expanding their firms to the point where they get into really high income brackets.

[38] Some hold that the excess profits tax may have tended somewhat in this direction, but it was designed to get at war and defense profits more than at "monopoly profits" or at profits of giant firms.

Undoubtedly, there would be ways of evading a progressive tax; indeed some broad avenues of evasion are obvious even to the non-expert. The taxable income of corporations is an accounting figure and a stiff tax would intensify pressures to reduce this figure, for example, by resorting to debt financing instead of equity financing (since interest payments are deductible from net income for tax purposes while dividends are paid out of taxable earnings). Similarly the earnings of one corporation might be siphoned into other corporations by means of royalty payments under patent license contracts, fees under management contracts, and similar payments deductible as "expenses" on the part of the corporation paying them. "Split ups" of large corporations into smaller corporations with control remaining in a parent company would probably be attempted. But some methods of preventing this type of evasion are also quite obvious. For example, all dividends received by one corporation from other corporations might be fully taxed, so that the income received by a parent corporation from its subsidiaries would be doubly taxed (first as income of the subsidiary and second as dividend income to the parent corporation). As a matter of fact, all dividend income was fully taxed under the Revenue Acts of 1913 and 1916. This was explained on the grounds that

> we did not want holding companies to be encouraged by the tax laws of the country. Upon the contrary, we did desire to discourage them. We also desired to discourage the system of interlocking stockholders, which has led to very much abuse.[39]

This desire to use tax measures to discourage holding companies could not stand up against the pleas of large business that they were being doubly taxed, and similar complaints from small firms with dividend income and from insurance companies and investment concerns who merely helped small stockholders diversify their risks. The law was changed, and from 1917 to 1935 intercorporate dividend income was free from taxation. In 1935, however, President Roosevelt recommended to Congress that intercorporate dividends be taxed in order to prevent evasion of

[39] Statement of Senator Williams, *Congressional Record*, Vol. 53 (1916), pp. 13333–34.

the graduated income tax he proposed.[40] Since 1935, intercorporate dividends have been taxed, but at a rate equivalent to only 15% of the rate on other corporate income.[41] Compared to the alternative of full taxation of dividend income this is only a sop to those desiring to discourage the creation of holding companies.

If intercorporate dividends were fully taxed and the income tax rates were steeply progressive, the question whether an affiliated [42] group of corporations should be allowed to present a consolidated income statement for tax purposes would become much less important than it is at present. When a group of corporations presents a consolidated income statement, it enables them to offset losses of one corporation against gains of others, so that the net income of the group is reduced by the amount of the losses, and furthermore it enables them to avoid the tax on intercorporate dividends. On the other hand, the aggregate taxable income of the group is increased—and, under a progressive scheme, would be in a much higher tax bracket.

If the tax rates are not progressive, a clear tax gain is frequently obtained by presenting a consolidated statement. At present an additional tax of 2% is imposed on the surtax net income of a group of corporations presenting a consolidated income statement.[43] This is supposed to offset the advantages offered to large groups by the consolidated return. But since corporations would not in

[40] "Provision should, of course, be made to prevent evasion of such graduated tax on corporate incomes through the device of numerous subsidiaries or affiliates, each of which might technically qualify as a small concern even though all were in fact operated as a single organization. The most effective method of preventing such evasions would be a tax on dividends received by corporations. Bona fide investment trusts that submit to public regulation and perform the function of permitting small investors to obtain the benefit of diversification of risk may well be exempted from this tax." Message to Congress, June 19, 1935.

[41] This is accomplished by allowing a deduction from taxable income of 85% of the amount received as dividends from domestic corporations.

[42] A group of corporations is considered "affiliated" if a parent corporation holds, directly or indirectly, at least 95% of the stock of the others in the group.

[43] The use of the consolidated return was denied to all corporations except railroads in 1934. Permission to use it was granted to all corporations in 1940 for purposes of the excess profits tax imposed in that year. In 1942 the permission to use consolidated returns was restored for the corporate income tax as well.

general use consolidated returns unless there were advantages in so doing, it has been suggested that such returns should either be prohibited (in which case all firms in an affiliated group would be fully taxed as separate entities) or be made compulsory (in order that the group as a unit could not escape taxation in higher income brackets). Clearly, however, if intercorporate dividends were fully taxed and tax rates were progressive, there would not be very much gained one way or the other.

All questions of administrative feasibility, possibilities of evasion, and possibilities of prevention of evasion are, however, far less significant than the question whether a steeply progressive corporation income tax is really a sensible method of controlling the size of corporations. To the extent that the amount of profit and the size of the business unit are correlated, such a tax would get at bigness, and to the extent that bigness and monopoly power are correlated, it would get at monopoly power. But we know that these correlations are far from perfect. They fail chiefly because the efficient size of the business unit is different in different industries. While it may be most desirable that taxes discourage size that is far in excess of technological or organizational requirements, it is not at all desirable that it discourage or penalize size that is necessary for efficient operations. It may be absolutely unnecessary, for example, for a flour mill to earn x million dollars a year, for this might indicate that the firm is far bigger than it has to be in order to operate efficiently. But the same x million dollars may be an impossibly small profit for a manufacturer of automobiles, who has to be big in order to be efficient.

In other words, large and small are relative terms. A large ant is appreciably smaller than a small dog. And so it is with firms. The Department of Commerce sets standards of what is to be considered large or small differently for retail and for wholesale firms. The Federal Trade Commission has gone further and set up different definitions of small companies according to whether the company is in the field of cement manufacturing, steel, petroleum, sugar, etc. A large firm, from our point of view, is a firm in a position to dominate or exercise appreciable influence over an entire industry, but the size of the firm in a position to do this in one industry may have no relation to the size of firms in similar positions in other industries. Hence, a graduated corporation income tax intended to discourage the growth of firms beyond the technically most efficient size, but imposing the same rates on all firms with the same income even though they belong to industries as diverse as retail trade and public utilities, would penalize some firms for being as big as they must be to exist at all, while permitting others to grow big enough to dominate their industries.

A steeply progressive tax would force firms to weigh the tax savings if they remained (or became) small, and therefore in the lower tax brackets, against the profitability of growing (or remaining) large. But since the profitability of growing (or being) larger includes not only the economies of large-scale production but also the monopoly profits from a greater control of the market, any tax system which deterred firms from striving for monopoly would also deter them from taking full advantage of the technical economies of large scale.

It might be a way out of this dilemma to adopt different income brackets for different industries or at least grant relief from the "prohibitive" tax rates of the high brackets to those industries where firms must needs be big and their earnings correspondingly large. But in any event it is understandable why opponents of monopoly have hesitated to propose radical progression in the rate schedule of the corporate income tax.[44]

Differential Taxes on Retained Earnings

Since a large part of the growth of business firms is financed out of retained earnings and since the present system of corporate income taxation restricts the internal financing of growth of small

[44] "The present situation, however, is not yet serious enough, or rather the prospect for sounder measures is not yet sufficiently hopeless, to warrant recourse now to radical progression in corporate taxation. It may soon be wise to invoke this last-ditch expedient, in default of a real anti-trust program—and prominent corporate executives have every reason to prefer the most progressive business tax to the far better alternative controls—but the necessity of resorting to such ill-contrived weapons against industrial syndicalism will perhaps only reveal how small is the chance of preserving economic or political liberty. When a good cause can be pursued only with such bad measures, the cause is perhaps hopeless." Henry C. Simons, *op. cit.*, p. 25.

companies much more severely than that of large ones, differential taxation of undistributed profits might be used to offset the present handicap.

Of course, the present obstacles to the growth of small firms should not be made worse and, hence, no additional taxes should be levied on the undistributed profits of corporations below a certain size, or on undistributed profits below certain amounts. But a strong case can be made for a graduated tax on retained earnings to check the sustained growth of very large corporations. These corporate giants with their easy access to the capital market do not have to rely on internal financing if they should need additional funds for profitable expansion. There is no reason why they should not distribute more of their earnings and then raise on the market the capital they need to carry out promising investment projects.[45]

Differential taxation of undistributed profits—with generous exemptions, leaving small business firms without additional tax burdens, but cutting deeply into the retained earnings of the largest corporations—would not merely equalize the effects of taxation on the financing of business growth, but might incidentally serve also as incentive for corporate split-ups. Needless to say, one would have to ensure that these split-ups of corporate concerns desiring to avoid the tax are *bona fide* and effective dissolutions and not merely sham separations to evade the tax obligation.

Tax Policy and Antimonopoly Policy

Steep progression in the corporate income tax, heavier taxation of intercorporate dividends, and graduated taxes on very large undistributed profits are not the only tax measures proposed as weapons against bigness and concentration. Other possibilities have been suggested, for example, graduated sales taxes, taxes on the number of establishments, taxes according to the number of employees.[46] But very little thought has been given to the whole subject of using tax policies to combat concentration.

[45] Corwin D. Edwards, *op. cit.*, pp. 146–47.
[46] Fred. I. Raymond, *op. cit.*, pp. 96 ff. Raymond, however, favors limitations through the corporation laws, not through tax policies.

A suggestion which is directed more against monopolistic practices than against bigness or concentration concerns the eligibility
of corporate expenses as deductions from taxable income. Expenses whose chief function is to enable the corporation to improve or maintain a monopolistic position might be made non-
deductible for income tax purposes, for example, advertising
expenses in excess of a certain percentage of sales,[47] or excessive
expenditures for certain kinds of litigation.

In certain fields, such as the cigarette industry, where advertising is "the key to the monopoly problem," taxation of advertising "would appear to offer a promising . . . line of attack." [48]
Since the main objective of such a tax would be to reduce the
handicap of small or new firms as against large national advertisers,
the tax would have to be graduated, leaving smaller amounts of
advertising outlays tax-free while levying progressively increasing rates on larger outlays. But the use of a single set of tax brackets
(in terms of dollars spent for advertising) for all industries would
not be advisable in view of the wide differences in organization,
products and markets. On the other hand, the proposal of a tax
schedule in terms of the "percentage of selling expenses to total
expenses" [49] overlooks the fact that new firms entering an industry
and small firms attempting to grow larger may have to spend a
larger percentage on advertising than firmly established companies.
Hence, "it is proposed that tax brackets [for the advertising tax]
be determined upon the basis of market control, rates varying
according to the individual firm's percentage of national sales of
each general class of product." [50]

[47] "The amount of advertising expenditures deductible as a business ex-
pense under the corporation income-tax law might be limited." George W.
Stocking and Myron W. Watkins, *Monopoly and Free Enterprise* (New
York: Twentieth Century Fund, 1951), p. 164.

[48] William H. Nicholls, *op. cit.*, pp. 201, 413. Nicholls finds it "surprising
how little attention economists have given to the use of advertising taxes as
a means of regulating monopoly" (p. 413).

[49] Henry C. Simons, *A Positive Program for Laissez Faire*, p. 34.

[50] Nicholls, *op. cit.*, p. 414. "Under such tax legislation, in an industry in
which no firm controlled as much as 5 per cent of a given product, no firm
would pay any advertising taxes. On the other hand, in industries in which
one or a few firms each accounted for more than 20–25 per cent of the national sales of a product, such firms would pay a very stiff tax on their advertising outlays while new and small firms in the same industry could ad-

That we have mentioned or discussed some of the suggested tax measures against big business or monopoly power must not be mistaken for an endorsement of these measures. All that can be endorsed at this juncture is a plea for more careful analysis of the problem of coordinating tax policy and antimonopoly policy. It has been shown that the existing tax system is not "neutral" as between small and big business, but has a bias against small business. It has further been shown that the tax system might be adapted to exercise a bias against corporate bigness and concentration, but has not been so adapted.

Most tax lawyers are horrified at the suggestion that the tax system be "misused" to combat monopoly, just as most corporation lawyers are horrified at the analogous suggestion with regard to the corporation laws. Everybody professes to be wholehearted for a campaign against monopoly, but protests against fighting it in his own field of competence.[51] The idea of using tax policy as an aid to antimonopoly policy is attractive in that it may reverse the direction in which the profit motive usually works by making it more profitable to become smaller. The incentive method has often great advantages over the prohibition method.

TRADE BARRIERS

Trade barriers, governmental measures specifically designed to restrict trade between geographic areas, are for the most part introduced for the avowed purpose of restraining competition. Import tariffs, quota restrictions, and foreign-exchange rationing are the most prominent forms of national trade barriers. When tariffs are imposed, a tax is laid on imports; when absolute quotas are established, only specified quantities of the commodities concerned are permitted to enter the country; under exchange ration-

---

vertise with little or no penalty. While such a tax would contribute little to a solution of the problem of monopoly in the heavy (producer-goods) industries which advertise relatively little, it would be very effective in helping to equalize the competitive status of large and small firms in most consumer-goods industries and in encouraging price competition as an alternative to advertising expenditures."

[51] This is the same story as with economy in the government budget: everybody is for it, provided it will not reduce the expenditures in his own bailiwick.

ing, foreign exchange cannot be obtained without special permission and each importer is allotted foreign exchange only to the extent to which his requests are approved by the appointed authorities.

Trade barriers raised within nations by provincial or local governments may be as important as national barriers. In the United States even cities and counties, as well as the individual states, have enacted laws which have the effect of creating barriers to trade between themselves and other areas.

Import Tariffs

Some tariffs are imposed primarily to raise revenue for the national government. Ordinarily, revenue tariffs are levied on the import of commodities which are not domestically produced, for example, tea and coffee in the United States. If there is some domestic production of the commodities, it too should be taxed, or the duty would be protective, stimulate domestic production and reduce the revenue from the tax on imports. A revenue tariff must be low enough to permit considerable imports, for if it restricts imports severely, not much revenue will be obtained.

Sometimes tariffs are raised for the alleged purpose of avoiding a heavy drain on a "perilously small" reserve of foreign exchange when the government is not prepared to restore an equilibrium in the balance of payments by deflation or currency depreciation. Tariffs, however, are in fact (and governments well know this) relatively permanent measures which once established are hard to get rid of. As a remedy for a temporary trade or exchange difficulty they are most inappropriate and, ordinarily, closer scrutiny will reveal that the protection of certain domestic industries, and not the protection of a foreign exchange reserve, is the real motive force behind such tariffs.

But neither the raising of funds for the treasury nor the conservation of foreign funds for the monetary authorities is of great moment in the discussions of the tariff problem. In the United States these "reasons" for import tariffs are entirely irrelevant. It is the protective tariff which dominates the economic and political discussion, and rightly so, because most tariffs have been introduced to protect domestic producers against foreign competition. In other words, not the fund-raising but the price-raising effect of tariffs was what the proponents of tariffs in the United States wanted, even if they did not talk about it. Increased prices are logically implied in any restriction of imports and protection against foreign competition, and it is the very purpose of a protective tariff to allow the domestic price of a commodity to exceed the foreign price by more than the transportation cost. If some imports are received "over the tariff wall," it is evident that the domestic price exceeds the foreign price by the transportation cost plus the tariff. Otherwise the tariff is completely prohibitive and will shut out the foreign product entirely.

Arguments for Tariff Protection

National policies designed to protect domestic industry from the competition of foreigners have been defended with a wide variety of economic arguments, most of them fallacious. Only a few of the more prominent need be mentioned here.

One of the most popular arguments in the United States rests on the assertion that protection for American workers against competition from low paid labor abroad is necessary to maintain American living standards. Despite popular acceptance this argument is unsound. The American living standard, that is, the real wage of the worker is high, partly because the American worker is very efficient, partly because labor is relatively scarce and capital relatively plentiful in the United States. This means that in the United States more capital is used per worker, which raises the productivity of labor. The importation of cheap products from abroad may compete indirectly with some particular labor group or some particular natural resource or capital equipment in the United States, but will in general contribute to higher living standards because it allows the worker to buy more goods for his wage. If tariffs exclude some of these products from the domestic market, the consumer must pay a higher price and some American workers will be retained in the production of goods which require much labor relatively to capital and could therefore more sensibly be produced in countries with a large supply of labor relative to their supply of capital. Without tariffs American workers will be employed chiefly in industries in which the larger supply of capital and the greater technical skill of American workers give the American product an advantage over foreign competitors.

Just as some American manufacturers demand tariffs pretending that these are necessary to protect the worker against the competition of low-paid workers of foreign countries, on similar grounds the manufacturers of countries with abundant cheap labor might clamor for tariffs to protect them against the "unfair" competition of American workers with skills and equipment far superior to their own. With all countries demanding tariffs to protect unsuitable industrial production, the basis for trade would be destroyed. Tariffs of this sort are, in effect, nothing but measures to enable industries which are not well suited to the American conditions of production to retain factors of production that would be much more productive in some other activity.[52]

Another prominent argument is that a tariff, by keeping out imports and thus reserving the domestic market for domestic products, helps maintain employment in the country that imposes or raises it. By restricting imports, however, tariffs necessarily restrict exports since the foreign countries can in the long run (i.e., apart from our loans or gifts) buy from us only to the extent that we buy from them. Hence, although some industries, thanks to protective tariffs, obtain domestic markets, other industries by the same token lose foreign markets. Total employment may not be greater than it would be without tariffs, but total real income will be smaller, since the country is foregoing the advantages of the specialization and division of labor afforded by international trade.

In times of depression the employment argument for tariffs is advanced with particular stress, and under these circumstances when short-run effects count a great deal, it might have some validity—provided that other countries did not retaliate by raising tariffs of their own. This proviso is utterly unrealistic; other countries will surely retaliate. Thus, if we try to combat unemployment

[52] Needless to say, such action on the part of large countries creates very serious problems for small countries who are more dependent on the international division of labor.

by shutting out imports and this incites other countries to bar our exports, unemployment is created in our export industries. This sort of tariff policy is known as "beggar-my-neighbor" policy. It leads to retaliatory commercial wars between countries, making each progressively worse off. Whenever a country attempts to improve its own position at the expense of other countries, retaliation from the other countries can be safely predicted and moreover any expected gain is more than likely to be turned into an actual loss.[53]

One important argument for the introduction of tariffs is economically defensible—the "infant industry" argument. If there are reasonable grounds for believing that a particular industry would be well suited to a country once it got a start, but that its development is hindered by established foreign competitors, then a case can be made for giving such an industry temporary assistance, perhaps through temporary tariff protection. (This situation is most likely to occur in a relatively unindustrialized country and some economists prefer to speak of the "infant country" or "underdeveloped country" argument for tariffs rather than the "infant industry" argument.) Although the infant industry argument has been fully exploited by the advocates of tariff protection, the fact that it is an argument for *temporary* protection has been ignored in practice. Many industries thus protected have, even after decades, failed to "grow up" and tariff protection has been continued and often increased long after it became abundantly clear that the industry never would be suited to the country. In other cases industries have reached a stage where they could stand on their own

[53] In general a tariff reduces the real income of the country imposing it even in the absence of retaliation. There are, however, exceptions to this. It can be shown, for example, that a country may benefit by imposing a so-called "optimum tariff" the exact height of which must be precisely calculated with reference to the various elasticities of supply and demand with respect to exports and imports. A tariff affects the terms on which marginal exports and imports are exchanged, and a country may act as a monopolist and improve its position by imposing a tariff, particularly if the elasticity of demand for exports is very low, and it can neglect the elasticity of supply. Other countries can thus be made to bear the burden of the tariff. Since, however, the validity of this argument depends on the absence of retaliation, the argument has very little general applicability in the real world, for it ignores the widespread disruption of trading relationships which competition in tariff-raising inevitably brings in its wake.

feet, but have refused to step out from behind the shelter of the tariff and face the rigors of foreign competition.

Strictly speaking, the infant-industry argument is an argument for subsidies, but not for tariffs. In exceptional circumstances a good case can be made for temporary assistance to give an industry a start it could not get without government aid although the long-run chances for its survival without aid are manifestly favorable. But this does not imply that assistance in the form of a protective tariff will be better than a cash subsidy. First, it is impossible to know how much the tariff will cost the nation. The cost of the cash subsidy is clearly stated. Secondly, most people are not aware of the fact that the tariff involves any cost at all. These are of course among the reasons why the proponents of assistance favor the tariff and say nothing about a subsidy. They fear that the voters would not approve a cash subsidy for the "infant." [54]

Pressure Group Politics

Special interests are the driving force behind the erection of tariffs. Business firms who can get the Congress to grant them tariff protection stand to gain and they not unnaturally go all out for this gain. Domestic producer groups take full advantage of the preparedness of governments to grant protection against foreign competition. Let no one think that the claims of each domestic interest group are always carefully investigated and granted only if they seem to be in the public interest. Even if we ignore the frequent cases in which the influence of a manufacturer with a Congressman, Senator or public official enabled him to slip something into the tariff schedule without others realizing what had happened,[55] we must recognize that the impossibility of obtaining data

[54] The tariff advocates are out to defeat the principle of democracy in that they present the scheme in a form that does not reveal its true nature to the voters, who might turn it down if they understood it. In this sense, we must regard the tariff as a fraud on the people in a democratic nation.

[55] F. W. Taussig reported several cases of this kind. In one case a single manufacturer was able to get a provision inserted at the last minute on the Senate floor placing a virtually prohibitive tariff on cheap white cotton gloves: "The duty was inserted in the Senate through the activity of a person well known in the trade. He had got the ear of a New England senator, a member of the Finance Committee, who had secured for his protégé the increase

about domestic or foreign costs and the enormous complexity of the tariff making process will necessarily result in arbitrary decisions in the great majority of cases. It has been estimated that under the United States tariff of 1930 some 25,000 items ordinarily imported were subject to duties.[56]

Under these circumstances, the tariff protection granted to any manufacturer is decided with reference to what he will "accept," to what other manufacturers are getting, to what he is "entitled" to on general grounds.[57] All tariff schedules contain numerous "basket clauses," for example "chemical elements, salts and compounds," the exact scope of which no one knows. It has long been accepted protectionist political doctrine that a tariff should "equalize costs of production" at home and abroad, yet domestic manufacturers do not hesitate to tell Congressional committees that their own costs are trade secrets and to present mere rumors and guesses, or even to confess complete ignorance, as to foreign costs.[58] Once tariff protection is accepted for any but very special cases (*bona fide* "infant industries" or for reasons of military security) there is no end in sight; it becomes almost impossible to draw a line and the demands of nearly every group are met in some degree.

If it was possible to persuade the public to accept extensive tariff schedules based on such flimsy evidence and obviously at the instigation and for the benefit of private interest groups, the people apparently had completely swallowed the arguments for tariffs and had come to believe in protection on the general grounds of national industrial development, maintenance of high

of duty . . . it seems tolerably clear that the moving force in bringing about the new duty was . . . pressure from the interested Mr. ———. If changes in duty such as this are made, should they not be deliberately reported and publicly considered?" F. W. Taussig, *Free Trade, the Tariff and Reciprocity* (New York: Macmillan, 1920), p. 169.

[56] E. E. Schattschneider, *Politics, Pressures and the Tariff* (New York: Prentice-Hall, 1935), p. 17.

[57] For example, the duty on poultry may be "adjusted" in line with the duty on beef, or the duty on candied fruits may be set in line with the duty on candy. The chief argument for agricultural protection has frequently been that agricultural duties should be "on a parity" with those on manufactured products. See E. E. Schattschneider, pp. 92 ff.

[58] *Ibid.*, pp. 67 ff.—The "cost equalization" argument for tariffs is, of course, logically equivalent to denying that there are any advantages at all in international trade.

living standards, and higher employment. That economists have almost unanimously pointed out the fallacies of these arguments was of little avail. The private interests have combined emotional appeals to patriotism with hard-headed lobbying and have succeeded in holding the allegiance of masses of workers, farmers, and consumers. The protectionist doctrines have achieved 'a deeply rooted and respected status in the community. There are many who even believe the allegations, promoted by protectionist propaganda, that it is socially harmful and undesirable, if not downright immoral, to buy goods from foreigners if somebody wants to produce them at home. They regard competition from foreign producers as an objectionable disturbance of national development.

Some changes in this ideology have occurred in the last fifteen years. The most important practical change was the recognition that the legislature should be relieved of some of its responsibilities in setting the tariff rates, and thus be relieved of the incessant pressures from powerful lobbies. This was accomplished through the Reciprocal Trade Agreements program under which the Administration is empowered to negotiate reductions in the tariff in return for concessions from foreign countries. Substantial tariff reductions have been made and the United States is today taking a leading part in a general international move to reduce restrictions on international trade.

Tariffs, Competition, Cartelization

Tariff protection often achieves a reduction of competition beyond that officially intended. When foreign competition is largely shut out, it may become easier for domestic producers to reduce or eliminate competition among themselves also. As long as they are fully exposed to competition from large numbers of foreign producers, no combination in restraint of trade will be of any avail to the domestic competitors. Protect them from outside competition and frequently they will be able to go ahead and protect themselves against competition from each other.

Not only are domestic cooperation and cartelization promoted by tariffs, but tariffs also play a significant role in the formation and activities of international cartels. Once domestic cartels are formed in an export industry a strong incentive is created for such cartels to get together with cartels in other countries and form an international cartel. The tariff then plays a dual role: it supports the domestic cartel and provides it with an excellent bargaining device in negotiations for a share in the world market.[59] Governments not infrequently support domestic cartels in their negotiations with foreign members of an international cartel by agreeing to impose tariffs that can be used for bargaining purposes.[60]

Import Quotas

If tariffs are costly barriers to international trade, import quotas are even more so. A tariff protects domestic producers from foreign competition to an extent that can be pre-determined; the domestic price will be raised at the most by the amount of the tariff. If domestic demand is high or domestic supply is low, imports can come in over the tariff wall and the price will be above what it would be without tariff by an amount equal to the duty. In the case of an absolute import quota, however, one cannot know by how much the domestic price can rise above the level at which foreign producers could supply us. With the quota absolutely fixed, a high domestic demand or a low domestic supply can make the domestic price go way up—by much more than any duty to which the limited imports may be subjected.

Foreign countries have made much use of import quotas, and

[59] Sir Alfred Mond, organizer of Imperial Chemical Industries in Britain, once made a statement which has become a classic quotation: ". . . in negotiation, the man behind the tariff wall always has something with which to bargain, which the man in the Free Trade country has not. Any one who has any practical experience of bargaining with continental producers knows that the first thing they say is, 'You cannot export to our country, because we have a tariff. How much of your market are you going to give us?' " Sir Alfred Mond, *Industry and Politics* (London: Macmillan, 1928), p. 246.

[60] Again a standard example comes from Britain. When the British Iron and Steel Federation joined the International Steel Cartel in 1935 and negotiations were on the verge of breaking down because of an inability to agree on the share of the British market to be allotted to foreign producers, Parliament was induced to raise the tariff from $33\frac{1}{3}$ to 50% and an agreement "exceptionably favorable to the British industry" was made. "Naturally the agreement will be hailed as a great boon for the British industry and a triumph for 'tariff bargaining.' " *The Economist*, London, June 15, 1935.

the United States has angrily denounced this unhealthy practice. But despite better intentions it has of late given in to pressures from domestic producer groups. As with many other restrictive provisions, import quotas made their appearance in the United States in the 1930's, primarily for agricultural products in connection with price-raising and production restriction programs.[61]

Sugar, wheat and cotton are now subject to absolute import quotas.[62] Occasionally the quotas are so small that domestic processors and fabricators, unable to get the needed supply from domestic sources, get into difficulties. For example, there is an annual quota of 45,656,420 pounds on long-staple cotton, some varieties of which are not obtainable from the domestic crop. Early in 1950, manufacturers requiring these varieties of cotton found that the quota was exhausted and stocks were inadequate to carry them through the year. It was necessary to get a special proclamation from the President permitting additional imports of this cotton.[63] In general, the United States Government is opposed to absolute quota and tries to resist political pressures to extend them to other commodities.[64]

[61] See C. R. Whittlesey, "Import Quotas in the United States," *Quarterly Journal of Economics*, Vol. 52 (1937–38), pp. 37–65.

[62] For a brief discussion of the sugar program see below, Chapter 8.

[63] United States Tariff Commission, *Harsh or Rough Long-Staple Cotton and Extra Long-Staple Cotton* (Washington, D.C.: 1951), Report No. 171, Second Series.

[64] The so-called "tariff quotas" which the United States has been using for certain commodities must not be confused with "absolute quotas." In contrast to the latter, "which are designed to impose greater restrictions on imports than would be effected by tariff duties alone," tariff quotas are established under the Trade Agreements Program "in connection with reductions in duties . . ." United States Tariff Commission, *Operation of the Trade Agreements Program, June 1934 to April 1948, Part III. Trade Agreement Concessions Granted by the United States* (Washington: 1949), Report No. 160. Second Series. Under this program a tariff reduction is granted on a particular commodity, but a maximum amount is set for its import at the reduced duty. Imports in excess of the tariff quota are admitted but at the regular duty. It should be clear that these tariff reductions can only be effective in lowering domestic prices if the tariff quotas are greater than the amounts that would be imported in any case. Otherwise they constitute merely gifts from the Treasury to domestic importers or foreign export cartels, without benefit to the American consumer. But if the imports permitted at the lower duty under a tariff quota are sufficiently greater than the amount that would have been imported at the higher duty, the tariff quota arrange-

Foreign Exchange Restrictions

Foreign exchange restrictions, that is, governmental controls of the price and allocation of foreign money, have not been introduced, ordinarily, for the purpose of eliminating competition in the interest of special groups. The immediate concern of the governments which introduced them was, as a rule, some serious emergency in the field of banking and international finance. But even if the initial purpose may not be the erection of new trade barriers, foreign exchange restrictions are inherently the most potent kind of trade barriers.

In addition to the normal effects of trade barriers—restriction of trade, restriction of competition, fostering of monopoly—foreign exchange restrictions also involve the exercise of administrative discretion and arbitrariness, discrimination between firms, groups, industries, and countries, personal favoritism, and often corruption. Exactly for these reasons (and herein lies the danger of even their temporary use) foreign exchange restrictions usually become a vested interest of the bureaucracy which administers them. The authorities concerned wield great power over the entire economy: by granting or refusing the foreign exchange needed by a firm for imported materials required for its operations, the authorities in effect control the prosperity or survival of the business. In countries in which foreign trade amounts to an important part of total production, the foreign-exchange control authorities can influence, by the ways in which they allocate the supply of foreign money, the growth or decline of entire industries, the distribution of real income, and the fundamental organization of the economy. Although these measures seemingly concern "only" the foreign exchange market and often have been justified as "necessary" to economize "scarce currencies," they may almost over night transform a free competitive economy into a centrally directed one.

---

ment is undoubtedly beneficial. In 1950, tariff quotas were in effect for cattle, whole milk, cream, butter, various kinds of fish, walnuts, and potatoes. Among commodities for which such quotas have been effective in the past are certain types of lumber, molasses, tobacco, silver foxes, crude petroleum and certain other fuel oils. The United States has in trade agreements also reserved the right to establish quotas for woven fabrics of wool and footwear.

Foreign exchange restrictions can restrict competition and promote monopoly in one or more of the following ways:

1. Refusal of foreign exchange to users of foreign materials or products restricts or eliminates foreign competition and thus, through administrative discretion, accords to domestic producers of the same or substitute commodities a protection in addition to any protection granted by the legislature.
2. Allocation of foreign exchange to some users of foreign materials and products, and refusal to others, may create strong domestic monopoly positions.
3. Rationing of foreign exchange for the import of necessary materials and products may make it impossible for any of the firms in an industry to compete for increased shares in the business; it thus is the equivalent of the establishment of a rigid quota cartel where competition among the members is effectively eliminated.
4. Distribution of foreign exchange to the established firms in the industry, and refusal to newcomers, effectively "closes" the industry and eliminates newcomers' competition.
5. Allocation of foreign exchange implies allocation of innumerable kinds of productive resources in a large sector of the economy, and thus replaces a more or less competitive market mechanism by governmental planning, improvisation, and direction.

The United States is one of the few nations in the world that have retained a free foreign exchange market.

Interstate Trade Barriers

Successful attempts of business groups to pursuade public authorities to restrict competition by raising trade barriers are not confined to international trade. Extensive barriers to trade between the states of the United States and even between municipalities have been created. Since the Federal Constitution forbids the imposition of duties on trade between the states, interstate trade barriers had to be more or less "indirect" in a variety of forms.

States have the power to raise revenue through taxation. For a long time the courts held that a state could not directly or indirectly lay any tax on interstate commerce. This position has been modified and although a state cannot now tax interstate commerce directly or "as such," a tax which is not specifically placed on "foreign" goods but which nonetheless hits them harder than domestic goods is permitted. The most prominent use of the state taxing power to put an indirect tariff on out-of-state goods has been the taxation of all margarine by the dairy states and the taxation of margarine made from other than locally produced oils by the cotton and cattle producing states. The purpose is frankly to protect local industry.[65]

Extensive import barriers have also been erected by individual states for the purpose of protecting local liquor industries. In this case the states can constitutionally create tariffs. The twenty-first amendment gave the states power to regulate the importation of liquor in order that states wanting to remain "dry" could do so. The opening thus created for protection of local industry was immediately seized upon: sometimes lower licence fees are charged manufacturers using local products, tax exemptions or reductions are granted producers exporting to other states, imported beverages are taxed at higher rates than local beverages, higher licence fees are charged importers, and many other special restrictions have been imposed on interstate liquor trade. Many states have special retaliatory legislation designed to get even with other states who discriminate against their products.

Serious barriers to interstate trade have resulted from regulations and taxation of motor trucking by the separate states. Most of these laws are not specifically protectionist but are attempts to

[65] For example, the Report of the South Dakota Tax Conference in 1931 stated: "The South Dakota farmers and dairymen are developing a great dairy industry which should be encouraged and protected in every legitimate way. The use of substitute dairy products, such as oleomargarine, limits the use and lowers the market of butter.

"A tax of ten cents per pound on butter substitutes will afford a measure of protection to the dairy interests and at the same time protect the general public from the use of substitutes inferior in every way to pure South Dakota butter." Quoted from *Barriers to Internal Trade in Farm Products*, A Special Report to the Secretary of Agriculture by the Bureau of Agricultural Economics, United States Department of Agriculture (Washington: 1939), p. 20.

make out-of-state trucking pay licence fees and taxes for the use of local highways. The cumulative burden on trucks running through many states is of course very heavy and has frequently stopped some kinds of interstate trucking.[66] Some of the laws, however, are clearly designed to promote exports and discourage imports. For instance

> Texas provides that nonresident owners of trucks living in an adjoining State may enter Texas without securing a license if their purpose is to buy goods, wares, and merchandise. No such exemption is made for those who take trucks into the State to sell products. Florida gives special privileges to nonresidents who come into the State to buy citrus fruit. An Arkansas law states in forthright fashion that owners of trucks may drive them into the State without securing an Arkansas permit or license if they bring the trucks in empty and for the purpose of buying or removing Arkansas products or merchandise.[67]

Several states and municipalities have found their power to protect the public health through inspections, quarantines and embargoes an extremely useful means of protecting local industry. This method of protection is particularly widespread with respect to dairy products, especially liquid milk. A local authority may decree that all dairies be inspected, it may then decide what dairies to inspect and how much to charge for the inspection. Frequently distant producers are charged much higher inspection fees than are local producers—if the authorities are willing to inspect them at all.[68] By these means milk supplies can be regulated and local dairies protected.[69] In addition, sanitary regulations may require that all processing be done within the city limits.

[66] "Thus, for example, potato growers in Colorado in August 1935 appealed to the State Public Utilities Commission to relax its requirements so that out-of-State truckers could come in and move their crop. When their petition was rejected and serious losses threatened, they offered to pay the tax themselves if outside truckers would come into the State." *Barriers to Internal Trade in Farm Products*, p. 40.

[67] *Ibid.*, p. 51.

[68] As with most legislation restricting trade, retaliation may be invited: ". . . the case is reported . . . of a Massachusetts inspector who stated he would continue to inspect the farms of those producers across the line in Connecticut who had already received licenses, but, as Connecticut was refusing to inspect dairies in Massachusetts, he would not inspect for any new Connecticut producers." *Ibid.*, p. 9.

[69] How little many of these regulations have to do with health is illus-

Embargoes under the horticultural quarantine laws are also frequently enforced to protect local industry. Thus a Georgia law permits the Governor to declare an embargo on fruits and vegetables if he thinks that domestic supplies are sufficient for the home demand, and Louisiana forbids the sale in Louisiana of products from a state which prohibits the importation of Louisiana products.[70] In order better to enforce the various laws restricting interstate trade many states have set up official "ports-of-entry," reminiscent of European customs houses, through which all motor shipments into the state must pass. It was stated in the National Conference on Interstate Trade Barriers that

> the ports-of-entry laws connected with motor vehicles constitute the most serious exercise of the State's inspection powers yet devised since the birth of our Constitution. By this method, motor vehicles transporting property across State borders are not only subject to the numerous intangible burdens exacted from them for the use of the highways, but also to tangible barriers erected upon designated highways where they are compelled to stop in order to insure full compliance with all laws and regulations.[71]

Finally, under their general regulatory powers to protect public safety and morals many states have established labeling and grading laws which require out-of-state products to be labeled in such a manner that the consumer is deterred from purchasing them or that producers are faced with extra costs. The sale of "inferior" grades is often prohibited in order to protect the market for domestic "superior" grades.

---

trated by the frank report of the Secretary of the Maryland Cooperative Milk Producers in which he expressed approval of the Baltimore regulation which prohibited the bringing of cream into the city from a distance greater than 50 miles: "Due to the high quality of our product we were able to market 3,148,574 gallons of milk in the form of cream to local ice-cream manufacturers during the past year. *Through the cooperation of the Health Department* the use of cream produced in other areas, not under their direct supervision, is prohibited at all times when this market has an ample supply. This protection to our market is very important, especially so during the past year when most eastern markets were glutted with western cream, selling at times at a low level." Quoted from *Barriers to Internal Trade in Farm Products,* p. 9. (Italics supplied.)

[70] *Trade Barriers Among the States.* Proceedings of the National Conference on Interstate Trade Barriers. (Chicago: 1939), p. 29.

[71] *Ibid.,* p. 29.

PATENT LAWS

In two fundamental respects the systems of tariff protection and patent protection bear a close resemblance to each other. First, both are designed to protect a producer from competitors: tariffs against producers competing by offering products made abroad, patents against producers, domestic or foreign, competing by imitating the same new technology. Second, both find their justification in the encouragement they give to the introduction of new industrial ventures; tariffs to foster the development of infant industries, patents to foster the development of newly born technologies. Patents, however, are made to expire automatically after a certain period—seventeen years, in the United States—while tariffs are tough perennials, hard to weed out once they are in the ground.

Justification of Patent Protection

The objective to "promote the progress of science and of the useful arts" [72] is not the only one that has been advanced by advocates of patent protection. There has been a school of thought trying to justify the patent system as the protection of a "natural property right" which an inventor is held to have in his idea. The philosophy of "natural" property rights is no longer very widely accepted. But the principle that private property must be protected for the sake of the common welfare is fundamental to our Western civilization and is, I believe, the only ground on which political freedom can thrive. Whether there should be any private property in "ideas" is a different question—which most of those who have thought about it have answered with "no." It is easy to understand why.

The institution of private property serves important social, economic, and political purposes. The economic philosophy of private property in material things is, however, not directly applicable to the problem of private property in ideas. While only a very limited number of people can at one and the same time write on

[72] This phrase is contained in the provision of the Constitution of the United States which empowers Congress to establish a patent law.

the same desk, drive the same truck, work on the same lathe, stay in the same house, till the same piece of land—an unlimited number of people can simultaneously use the same idea. The right to exclude others from the use of particular material things is necessary for their efficient use, nay for the prevention of chaos. There *must* be somebody who decides about the disposition of these things and can exclude "unauthorized" users. This is no "must" with respect to ideas. The right to exclude others from using an idea demands a justification on altogether different grounds.

Many have offered the following justification: If inventors are not otherwise rewarded for their labors, they will try to get their reward by using their inventions in complete secrecy and thus obtaining profits based on a "monopoly in the knowledge of the secret." They may even die without having revealed their secret, so that it would be permanently lost to society. But if society offers them a temporary monopoly through the grant of an exclusive right to the technology disclosed in a patent, the invention becomes publicly known and will after a brief period be available for use by all.

The trouble with this justification is that it rests on an assumption of facts which just are not so. If someone profitably exploits a secret technology which he can hope to keep secret, he would not reveal it in exchange for the doubtful security of a patent monopoly. Only if he feared that he will not be able to safeguard his secret would he be willing to disclose it and take a patent. Thus the patent system cannot be said to serve the purpose of eliciting any secrets that would not in any event become known in the near future. People patent only what they cannot hope to keep secret.

The only sound justification of the patent system, the system of granting short-lived monopoly rights in the use of new technologies, is that it can accelerate technological progress through the stimulus it provides for the financing of industrial research and development and of new industrial ventures.

This stimulus is deemed necessary because of the extraordinary risks involved in such undertakings: no one knows in advance whether they will pan out. They may cost a great deal of money and the outcome is uncertain. If after many unsuccessful tries a "hit" is made, and if others, who have not invested a cent in any of the costly tries, can quickly imitate the new invention, and compete in selling the new products or the products made by the new processes, there will not be any money even in the hit. So why risk money in invention, development and innovation? But if a patent monopoly can be expected to keep the imitators off for just a few years, it can secure the innovator a highly attractive profit. It is the hope for such temporary monopoly profits which makes people more willing to put up the venture capital for the development and exploitation of the new invention.

Extension of the Patent Monopoly

Thus, the deliberate restraint of competition which the government institutes by granting temporary patent monopolies in the use of inventions has the ultimate objective of serving the public interest. This is often forgotten by the men in charge of writing, rewriting or interpreting patent legislation. They think too much of the private interests—the inventors, the investors, and the corporations which employ the work of the former and the capital of the latter—and too little of the public interest, which is served only if the newly invented technologies are utilized as early as possible, as widely as possible, and as intensively as possible.

There are chiefly three ways in which the restraint of competition which the government intended to institute through patent protection is extended to the detriment of the public interest. One, when the control over the new technology is prolonged beyond the brief period contemplated by the law; next, when the patents through the way in which they are licensed to competitors are used to regulate competition among them and thereby to restrain competition far beyond the scope of the patent grant; finally, when individual corporations are allowed to accumulate so many patents that they can control an important part of the technology of the industry and thus can, alone or together with a few others, dominate that industry.

The prolongation of the patent monopoly can be achieved to some extent through the use of certain procedural devices provided by the patent laws, but chiefly through the practice of acquiring a succession of improvement patents that give the patentee exclusive rights to the most up-to-date developments of the original invention.[73] As long as the original patent is in force, improvements are of use only to those who hold rights under it. Therefore, improvement patents are usually sold to the holder of the first patent, extending his control by the duration of the new patents.

The extension of the scope of the patent monopoly by means of restrictive licensing has been discussed above in connection with the law of collusion. Very tight "regulations" of competition can be achieved through patent agreements restricting the output and selling policies of the licensees in several respects. An undetermined number of restrictive provisions, of patent cartels, domestic and international, may now be in force which might be declared illegal if the Government had the time and the money to prosecute them under the antitrust laws. Many of the restrictions, however, are perfectly legal uses of the monopoly conferred by the patent grant. When a patentee licenses others to use his invention, he is permitted to specify the price at which the products are to be sold, the markets in which they may be sold, the distributors through which they may be sold, and the type of product which the licensee is allowed to make. These legal restrictions may weaken or eliminate the competitive spirit of an entire industry.[74]

[73] The time extension of patent protection through certain *procedural* peculiarities can under certain conditions be very considerable; for example, the Steimer patent application on automatic glass machinery was "pending" for twenty-seven, and the Fritts patent application on photographic sound recording was pending for thirty-six years. For all practical purposes a pending patent application affords adequate protection. Since the patents run for seventeen years after they issue, the protection in these two cases lasted for forty-four and fifty-three years, respectively. Time extension through *improvement patents* is well illustrated by an example given by a patent expert from the glass container industry in a memorandum produced before an investigating committee: "The Owens basic patents expired several years ago. Nobody, however, dare use the present type of Owens machine because of improvements covered by minor patents. Likewise, if the original patent protection obtained on particular machines should not be sustained by the Courts, yet a second line of defense patents covering details and improvements may become a most valuable asset." *Hearings before the Temporary National Economic Committee*, Part 2 (Washington: 1939), p. 777.

[74] The use of patents for the elimination of competition in entire industries is best described in two court cases in which the restrictive licensing policies were held illegal. A reading of the decisions is recommended. *United States v. Masonite Corporation*, 316 U.S. 265 (1941). *United States v. Hartford-Empire Co.*, 323 U.S. 386 (1945), 324 U.S. 570 (1945).

The accumulation of patents in the hands of large corporations may secure them an almost unlimited monopoly power. When a corporation holds rights under literally thousands of patents, its domination over an industry will no longer be limited either by the duration or by the scope of any individual patent, and the degree of monopoly attained may be far out of proportion to anything the lawmakers had visualized when they wrote the laws providing for the temporary protection of inventors.[75] (According to Patent Office figures for June 1938, 174,336 patents, out of the 359,114 that were owned by corporations, were owned by firms having more than 100 patents each. One corporation, without its subsidiaries, owned as many as 8,488 patents. The nine largest patent-owners held among themselves 36,370 U.S. patents, not including patents held by their subsidiaries or patents which the corporations did not own but under which they held rights.[76])

A device which combines all three ways of extending the patent monopoly—in time, scope, and degree—beyond what had been intended by the law is the closed patent pool. Cross-licensing of patents is frequently necessary in the interest of the unobstructed use and development of technology because patents on complementary industrial techniques may be held by different firms, none of which could produce efficiently without licenses under the

[75] In the United States only the inventor, that is, only a natural person may apply for a patent. But he may assign it to a legal person. The idea that a corporation should be allowed to accumulate hundreds or thousands of patents was certainly foreign to the original sponsors of the patent law. If such accumulation is found to be undesirable from the point of view of society, the patent law could be amended to limit it. The *Oldfield* Committee in 1912, stated in its report: "Capital seeking to control industry through the medium of patents proceeds to buy up all important patents pertaining to the particular field. The effect of this is to shut out competition that would be unsuitable if the various patents were separately and adversely held. By aggregating all the patents under one ownership and control . . . a monopoly is built up that is outside of and broader than any monopoly created by the patent statutes. It is 'monopoly of monopolies' and is equivalent to a patent on the industry as such." *Revision and Codification of the Patent Statutes.* Report, Committee on Patents, House of Representatives (Washington: 1912), p. 5.

[76] *Investigation of Concentration of Economic Power,* Hearings before the Temporary National Economic Committee, Part 3 (Washington: 1939), p. 1128.

others' patents. In view of the interdependent nature of technology in many industries, patent pools are a desirable development in the patent system, provided they are open to all. They may be the most undesirable monopolistic instruments, however, if they are closed to outsiders and newcomers and if the cross-licensing restricts the price and production policies of the members. In these cases the patents serve to restrain current competition as well as future competition among the members of the pool and also potential competition by excluding the newcomers entering the industry.

Abolition or Prevention of Abuse?

The grave consequences of all these unintended restraints of competition and supports to monopoly were fully realized by many economists in the 19th century. The chief question was whether the patent system could be appropriately reformed or would have to be abolished in order to safeguard the public interest. Many economists held that abolition was the only solution compatible with a free enterprise economy.[77] Others believed that reforms, especially the introduction of compulsory licensing of all patents, would satisfy the requirements of the public interest.

The patent system was neither abolished nor seriously reformed.[78] The same arguments about the great blessings and grave costs of the patent system that were advanced one hundred years ago are still presented in academic discussions. But the proceedings in the legislative committees are usually dominated by the organizations of the patent lawyers, who successfully resist all programs of substantive patent reform. The two reforms most urgently recommended by economists are provisions for compulsory licensing and against restrictive licensing. But at present there is no in-

[77] See Fritz Machlup and Edith Penrose, "The Patent Controversy in the Nineteenth Century." *The Journal of Economic History*, Vol. X (1950), pp. 1–29.

[78] Only one country, the Netherlands, repealed its patent laws in 1869 and had no patent system from 1870 to 1912. Compulsory licensing in relatively mild forms was adopted in several countries, including England and Germany.

dication of any desire on the part of Congress to write these provisions into the law.[79]

There is no way of proving whether and to what extent the patent system achieves the acceleration of technological progress which is its official objective. There are those who contend that progress would not be the least bit slower if the patent system did not exist. But even those who attribute much of the actual advance of technology to the stimulus which the patent system provides must admit that its restraints on competition very frequently go far beyond the degree deemed necessary for the encouragement of innovation. There can be do doubt that through their patent laws governments have brought into existence and continued operation a most prolific source of monopoly power in the economy.

[79] The Temporary National Economic Committee in 1939 recommended these reforms. See *Final Report and Recommendations of the Temporary National Economic Committee*, p. 39. But Congress has not acted upon these recommendations.

CHAPTER 8

Governmental Aids to Monopoly: Licences, Regulation, Price Controls, Labor Law

Licensing and "Board Regulation": Economic Freedom Gained and Lost Again · The Public Interest and the Private Interests · The Guild System Has Returned

Public Utilities and Transportation: Protecting Competing Monopolies · Suppression of Competition in Transportation · Competition Prohibited

Conservation of Natural Resources: Private and Social Costs · Organic Natural Resources · Oil Conservation or Restriction? · Coal Conservation —a Misnomer

Price Controls: Minimum Prices and Price Supports · Output Control and Surplus Removal · Marketing Programs · International Price Programs · Subsidized Production for Destruction · Minimum-Price Controls · Prohibition of Sales Below Cost · Maximum-Price Legislation · Rent Control

Labor Legislation: Legislature versus Judiciary · The Power to Organize · The Use of Organized Power · Pruning Back · The Public Interest

W E CONTINUE OUR SURVEY of governmental aids to monopoly. This chapter will include sections on Licensing and Board Regulation, Public Utilities and Transportation, Conservation of Natural Resources, Price Control and Labor Legislation.

LICENSING AND "BOARD REGULATION"

One of the oldest and most widespread methods of government regulation is to prohibit specified activities without the express permission of the government. In the 16th century King Henry II of France carried this type of regulation to its extreme limit, at least in theory, when he declared that the right to work

[287]

was itself a *"droit royal"*—a privilege bestowed by the king.[1] In medieval and early modern times licences, charters and organized trade bodies formed the basis of a detailed government regulation of economic life in most European countries. This type of economic organization, loosely called the "guild system," became increasingly unacceptable as the mercantilistic and feudal organization of society, under the impact of more liberal conceptions of social organization, gave way to the institutions of a "free enterprise" system. Today, however, we are rapidly returning in important sectors of the economy to this older system.[2]

Economic Freedom Gained and Lost Again

The United States was established at a time when the regulatory conception of the state was on its way out in England and this conception never took deep root in America. Freedom was one of the moving ideas in the new country, and government attempts to interfere with the freedom of individuals to carry on a legitimate trade were most jealously watched.

Thus in 1885, when the New York legislature tried to regulate the manufacture of cigars by licensing, the court was blunt in its condemnation of the legislature's attempt to interfere with the right of men to pursue their occupations unmolested by government, and it clearly recognized the similarity of the provision to the pervasive restrictions of an earlier age:

> Such legislation may invoke one class of rights today and another tomorrow, and if it can be sanctioned under the Constitution, while far removed in time, we will not be far away in practical statesmanship from those ages when governmental prefects supervised the building of houses, the rearing of cattle, the sowing of seed, and the reaping of grain, and governmental ordinances regulated the movements and labor of artisans, the rate of wages, the price of food, the diet and clothing of the people, and a large range of other affairs long since in all civilized lands regarded as outside of governmental functions. Such governmental interferences dis-

[1] Needless to say, it was impossible to put such an extreme theory effectively into practice.

[2] "The gild has returned. Its purposes are the same as in the Middle Ages, although its techniques are now streamlined." J. A. C. Grant, "The Gild Returns to America," *The Journal of Politics*, Vol. 4 (1942), p. 316.

turb the normal adjustments of the social fabric, and usually de-
range the delicate and complicated machinery of industry and
cause a score of ills while attempting the removal of one.[3]

But the vigilance which is the price of freedom has been undermined by confusion of thought, and today local governments of all
kinds are permitted to regulate the right of men to practice even
the most humble trades. An unseen net of petty regulations, pegged
to local police and tax powers, has been cast over an ever expanding number of trades and professions. By and large these regulations do not stem from the Federal government and, perhaps for
this reason, the extensive use of licensing powers has not been
posed as a major political issue. The absence of the political spot-
light, however, makes even more dangerous this insidious boring
from within. Let us examine the process through which this state
of affairs has come about.

The Public Interest and the Private Interests

The simplest use of the licensing powers of the government
is for the mere raising of revenue. This creates no problems as long
as the fees are moderate and non-discriminatory and the licence is
not used as a cloak for regulatory controls. If fees are imposed by
several governmental units and are more than nominal in relation
to the profitability of the businesses licensed, their cumulative
effect may be to restrict entry into local markets or to put the
taxed businesses at a disadvantage with respect to competitors.
They may thus create local trade barriers of the kind previously
discussed.

The real problems of monopolistic exclusion arise when licensing is imposed under the police powers of local governments for
the purpose of protecting the health and safety of the public or
because the businesses concerned are otherwise "affected with the
public interest." There are clear cases where governmental intervention is necessary for the protection of the public. That certain
qualifications must be required of people calling themselves doc-

[3] *In re Jacobs*, 98 N.Y. 98, 103, 114 (1885). Today, only 65 years later,
examples of public regulations of each of the activities mentioned can be
easily cited.

tors, nurses and dentists, of those who dispense drugs or construct buildings on contract is undeniable. Similarly the importance of imposing standards of purity or safety with respect to some products may call for government intervention; that milk be adequately inspected, that buildings meet minimum safety requirements, that reasonable standards of sanitation be maintained in barber shops and restaurants is certainly closely related to the public health.

It does not follow from this, however, that licensing is the best method of obtaining these ends. Although licensing laws and "codes" which prohibit the practice of designated professions or the production of designated commodities without a licence and which lay down conditions which must be observed on penalty of revocation of the licence may be the most effective and simplest method, they are at the same time a means by which governments can arbitrarily restrict entry into legitimate occupations and discriminate between products. As we shall see, governments have frequently abused their powers and such is the force of the licensing technique that even when large numbers of the public recognize that they are being imposed upon, they have no recourse except through the courts, and the courts not infrequently refuse relief. Equivalent services or products cannot legally be obtained except from a licensed producer.[4] Hence, even when it is clear that government intervention is desirable, the licensing method may not be the best method of intervening. Even if the government wishes to insist that a "qualified" contractor should be able to build bridges, sewers and skyscrapers as well as residential houses, if all I want is a house built I should be able to hire an "unqualified" contractor as long as he knows how to build houses.[5]

[4] It is a common experience for amateur electricians or plumbers who wish to install their own fixtures in their own houses to find that they cannot do so because the local authority will not inspect and certify the installation unless it had been done by a licensed workman no matter how competently the installation had been done.

[5] ". . . there are many licensing statutes covering contractors, plumbers and others engaged in the building trades or professions which are defined so broadly that one engaging only in building houses must know how to build sewers, highways, skyscrapers and bridges." Irwin W. Silverman, L. Thompson Bennett and Irvin Lechliter, "Control by Licensing over Entry into the Market," *Law & Contemporary Problems*, Vol. 8 (1941), p. 251.

But members of the consuming public, even if they disagree with the standards set up by the government, have no alternative but to accept them when licensing is the method of regulation.

In very many, if not most cases, in which licensing is the accepted method of regulation today, certificates stating the qualifications of the holders, or "grade labeling" of the products, would be enough to protect the public without at the same time placing in the hands of local governments the power to prohibit a man from carrying on a lawful trade or selling a legitimate product. For unfortunately the concept of public health and safety is an elastic concept and, if a disposition to stretch it exists, it can be easily stretched. Members of existing trades wishing to protect themselves from the competition of newcomers frequently are able to convince their local government authority that very strict standards should be required of all new entrants into the trade or that new competitive products should be discriminated against in order that the public be protected against some alleged evils. Thus does licensing in the public interest degenerate into licensing in private interests. Sometimes the courts have ruled against the legality of such attempts, seeing through and condemning the misuse of state power:

> We are not permitted to inquire into the motive of the legislature, and yet, why should a court blindly declare that the public health is involved when all the rest of mankind know full well that the control of the plumbing business by the board and its licensees is the sole end in view.[6]

This, however, was an early decision. Nowadays courts take a more lenient (and deliberately blind) view. They have permitted extensive educational requirements to be imposed as a prerequisite to entry into the trade of a barber, ten years experience or a college degree as a prerequisite for plumbers, good moral character for photographers,[7] "sound theoretical knowledge of

---

[6] *Richey* v. *Smith*, 42 Wash. 237, 249, 84 Pac. 851, 854 (1906). Quoted from Silverman, Bennett, and Lechliter, p. 240.

[7] "Moral" and financial qualifications are very commonly imposed and are frequently interpreted in an interesting manner. In Wisconsin a watchmaker's licence may be taken away if the holder is guilty of immoral or unethical conduct. That is, among other things, if he engages in "advertising of prices on watch repairing, or the giving of watch glasses, crystals or of

watch construction" as well as technical ability for watchmakers, good reputation as well as recommendation from local property owners for contractors, nine months of college and three years' apprenticeship plus the recommendation of two funeral directors "familiar with his reputation and character" for embalmers. The list could be easily extended.[8]

The Guild System Has Returned

In addition, and here is where the resemblance to the guild method of control becomes even stronger, the administration of licensing and regulatory controls are often placed in the hands of the existing members of the trades to be controlled and are almost openly exercised for the purpose of restricting competition.[9] This is called self-government of the trade and results not only in exclusion of would-be entrants and in exploitation of the consumer but also in jurisdictional disputes reminiscent of the old disputes between medieval guilds, though carried on through the legislature. Who can cut hair, barbers or beauticians? In Utah, Connecticut, Arkansas, Illinois the feud has been furious. If barbers succeed in excluding haircutting from the terms of the beautician's licence, the beauticians retaliate by excluding barbers from curling, waving, dyeing, bleaching, etc. We can only ask in bewilderment, what has this got to do with public health? Who can remove warts, beauticians or surgeons? In Oregon beauticians can

---

any other watch parts, gratis, or at less than cost, in order to advertise or increase the watch repair business." *Ibid.*, p. 245. As every fool can plainly see (to use the immortal words of Li'l Abner) public health and safety require protection from such practices!

    [8] Twenty-four major occupations subject to statutory regulations are listed by the Marketing Laws Survey publication, *State Occupational Legislation*, Department of Commerce (Washington: 1942). This list does not include minor occupations such as watchmakers and plumbers. Maryland has tried to license paper hangers, and Washington and Illinois have tried to license horseshoers. These laws were invalidated by the courts who felt this was going a bit too far!

    [9] Such "self-government" has long been common in the medical and legal professions and it is well known that it has been used to restrict competition, particularly in medicine. The difficulties placed in the way of doctors trained in foreign countries are flagrant examples.

do so, but only on the "upper part" of the body. In Oregon also a demonstrator of cold cream must have a licence.[10]

In the name of public health we find that in Colorado meals may not be served in drug or department stores or where anything else is sold, in Philadelphia department stores cannot have an optical or optometry department, in New York one may not even be a co-partner in a drug store without being a licensed druggist. In other places bicarbonate of soda, witchhazel, epsom salts or iodine can only be sold by licensed pharmacists. In the name of public safety prefabricated housing has been hindered by legislation in favor of conventional building methods, some building materials have been arbitrarily discriminated against, and plumbing fixtures suitable for the Department of Justice building cannot be installed in private homes by a contractor wishing to keep his licence.[11]

This almost unconcealed use of licensing regulations to protect public health and welfare as a cloak for licensing to protect private wealth and welfare has apparently so blunted men's sensibilities to the implication of the use of governmental power for private purposes that a third function of licensing is becoming more and more prevalent—the openly avowed use of licensing for the direct and declared purpose of regulating prices and competitive practices. In Louisiana the legislature decided that "low prices made it impossible to support and maintain reasonably safe and healthful barbering services to the public. The result was declared by the legislature to be a menace to the health, welfare and reasonable comfort of citizens of the state and one which tended toward the transmission of disease." [12] Florida set up a price-fixing arrangement for the dry-cleaning and laundry business and it was sustained by the court on the ground that "when conditions in business become such that the welfare of the public will not be adequately protected by unrestricted competition, it is within the police power of the state to remedy the evil." [13] In Wisconsin an

[10] See J. A. C. Grant, op. cit., passim.
[11] See Silverman, Bennett and Lechliter, op. cit., pp. 248–53.
[12] Ibid., p. 260.
[13] Ibid., p. 260.

automobile dealer's licence may be revoked if he makes allowances on used car trade-ins which would tend to affect competition "adversely." [14]

Thus the fears expressed by the court in 1885 are materializing. We have so far presented only a part of the picture. Licensing is also extensively used, as we shall see later, to regulate milk prices and the prices of a large variety of other agricultural commodities. The use of licensing to protect health and safety is gradually merging into licensing to protect incomes in any case where it can be shown that competition is going to hurt somebody. Clearly professional, semi-professional, vocational, and ordinary business groups hit the jackpot when they rediscovered the old principle of licensing and "board" regulation with legislative sanction. The NRA of 1933 was based on the same principle applied on a grand scale. It went too far too fast and the courts could not take it. But the slower, piecemeal approach of state and municipal governments is in many trades reaching the same end more successfully.

Public Utilities and Transportation

Most public utilities are inevitable or "natural" monopolies and their regulation by government should not be considered as either an aid to monopoly or a restraint of competition. The production and distribution of water, gas and electricity, the provision of municipal transport services and of telephone and telegraph services can never be truly competitively organized. Not more than one set of power lines, streetcar tracks, waterpipes, etc., could economically be permitted on city streets. Where monopoly is technically unavoidable, government regulation or outright ownership of the businesses concerned is necessary in the public interest. From our point of view, therefore, this type of government regulation requires no further discussion—provided it is *true* that monopoly is inevitable.

[14] *Ibid.*, p. 245.

Protecting Competing Monopolies

It frequently happens that, although a given service cannot be competitively supplied, the service nevertheless may be subject to severe competition from substitute services. For example, electricity and gas are competitive in many uses, and streetcars and busses are alternative means of supplying city transportation. The existence of competitive means of supplying the public, and changes in public demand, may create a difficult problem for government regulatory bodies. Where rate charges are set to obtain a "fair return" on existing investment in each of the competing services and each is produced by a sole source of supply, competition cannot solve the problem and the regulatory authorities must handle it the best way they can.

If, however, one of the competing services is or could be competitively supplied, the situation becomes very different and government regulation then becomes a real restraint on competition. The history of regulation in the transportation industry provides an instructive example of the difficulties public authorities may run into when they attempt comprehensive regulation in such cases.

In 1887, when the Federal regulation of railroad rates began, railroads were in a strong monopolistic position and used this position to charge exorbitant and discriminatory rates where they could. Agricultural groups in the Middle West were particularly vulnerable and some of the Middle Western states passed regulatory acts in the 80's. Federal regulation was finally established ostensibly for the purpose of protecting the public and the customer—the shipper of goods on railroads. By 1920, however, railroads began to find themselves in difficulties and Congress was persuaded to pass the Transportation Act of that year, which was designed to improve the position of the railroads and in particular to rescue the financially weak roads.[15] The principle of regulation to protect the shipper (customer) was now coupled with the principle of regulation to protect the carrier of his goods, and the Inter-

[15] National Resources Planning Board, *Transportation and National Policy* (Washington: 1942), p. 142.

state Commerce Commission was given power to establish minimum as well as maximum rates.[16]

Suppression of Competition in Transportation

With the passage of the Motor Carrier Act of 1935 and the Transportation Act of 1940 the interests of the shipper were completely submerged in—or rather identified with—the interests of the carriers. Under pressure from railroad managements, railroad labor, railroad investors, and railroad supply industries; Congress decided that the vigorous competition of motor carriers should be restricted. It placed the motor carrier industry under a system of regulation almost as far-reaching as that covering railroads. The motor industry was a highly competitive industry. It was not necessary therefore to control it as a monopolistic public utility to prevent exploitation of the public. The demand for motor carrier regulation originated with the railroads; [17] the real purpose was to protect the railroads.[18] As a result of these acts, common carriers by motor vehicle must now obtain certificates of "pub-

[16] The Interstate Commerce Commission was directed in prescribing rates, to "initiate, modify, establish, or adjust such rates so that carriers as a whole (or as a whole in each of such rate groups or territories, as the Commission may from time to time designate) will, under honest, efficient, and economical management and reasonable expenditures for maintenance of way, structures, and equipment, earn an aggregate annual net railway operating return equal, as nearly as may be, to a fair return upon the aggregate value of the railway property of such carriers held for and used in the service of transportation." Op. cit., p. 102.

[17] Some large motor common carriers joined in the movement for Federal regulation of motor carriers, while the small operators generally opposed it. See National Resources Planning Board, op. cit., pp. 202–203.

[18] This, of course, could be, and was, interpreted as being in the public interest, as a means of providing "public relief from unsatisfactory results ascribed to widespread 'destructive and wasteful' competition, such as financial demoralization of all agencies, excess capacity, disorderly market conditions, rate and service instability, increased business risks, uncoordinated transport, and poor and undependable service . . . the contention was that the public interest required protection of stable and dependable common carriers against discrimination from other firms, especially contract carriers, and an excessive number of competitors. Shippers received rates so low as to be destructive to carriers. Hence, floors to rates must be established and limitations must be placed upon the number of firms entering transport industries." Ibid., pp. 202–203.

lic necessity and convenience" or operating permits from the Interstate Commerce Commission and their rates must be published and approved by the Commission. Even contract carriers must publish minimum rates.[19]

It is not possible even to touch on all of the many aspects of rail, road, water and air transport regulations here. They include questions of organization, finance, use of public facilities, competitive positions and practices, freedom of entry, subsidies, rates and many other lesser problems. One of the more crucial competitive questions is rate making, and here the extension of regulation from the relatively monopolistically organized railroad industry to the competitively organized trucking industry has led to a serious milking of the public.

The effect of the requirement that motor carriers must file published rates with the Interstate Commerce Commission has been to encourage the formation of private motor freight associations who act as rate making and rate publishing agents for the carriers. There are several of these associations, some of whom act in collusion with the railroads,[20] some independently. These associations recommend rate schedules to the Commission and these schedules, if approved, become binding on all truckers whether they like it or not. Individual trucking companies have the power to file individual schedules but unless the schedules are approved by the association (and therefore by their competitors), the companies filing them must defend them before the Commission, frequently against the powerful opposition of the association.[21] Even if a reduction in rates is proposed, the carrier asking the reduction

---

[19] *Common carriers* are persons who undertake "for the general public" to transport persons or property for compensation while *contract carriers* operate under special and individual contracts or agreements. See I. L. Sharfman, *The Interstate Commerce Commission*, Part 4 (New York: The Commonwealth Fund, 1937), p. 103.

[20] The railroads also have their private rate making associations.

[21] "In five important territorial-rate cases the Commission has prescribed minimum motor-carrier rates over large areas to put a stop to what it considered to be excessive rate cutting and ruinous competition. The Commission's action in these cases was to establish as minima, in most instances, the rates which the motor carriers, through their 'conferences' or 'associations' had agreed upon. Many of the rates prescribed as minima, furthermore, were the same as the rail rates or were made in definite relation thereto." National Resources Planning Board, *op. cit.*, p. 110.

must bear the burden of proof of justifying it and must show that the rates are "reasonably compensatory for the service rendered." [22]

The most common situation in which a reduction in rates is refused is where the rate requested is below full average costs of operation. Yet, it will frequently pay a trucker to pick up a cargo on a return journey even if it only covers his out-of-pocket expenses rather than return empty. Even this the Commission does not approve, because, if applied to truckers going both ways, it "might well result in a break-down of the rates in both directions." [23]

Competition Prohibited

The results of the restriction of entry and the regulation of rates in the trucking industry have been to reduce the number of trucking firms; to encourage the growth of larger size firms; to facilitate, nay, render necessary, collusive trade association activity,[24] especially with regard to rate making; to restrict independent action on the part of smaller truckers; and to increase the level of rates.[25] One important group of shippers—the farmers —was powerful enough to secure a measure of exemption. Carriers engaged in the transport of unmanufactured agricultural products are exempt from the Commission's rate.[26]

---

[22] "The compensatory or noncompensatory character of proposed rates is not always determined by consideration of costs of operation. The reasonableness of the rates may be determined by comparing them with rates of other motor carriers. They may be considered noncompensatory when out of line with rates of other motor carriers which are deemed reasonable." *Ibid.*, p. 114.

[23] *Ibid.*, p. 112.

[24] Clearly, rate making is such a complicated matter that it must be done by those very familiar with the industry. It is almost inevitable that the job will be placed in the hands of the industry itself and the industry will do it through some form of association. The reasonableness of this arrangement obscures the fact that private enterprise is conducted for profit and hence rate making by private groups will be as far as possible done in the interest of private profits.

[25] "Wherever Interstate Commerce Commission control over interstate trucking rates has been made effective, the tendency has been to raise the rates substantially and in many cases to make them roughly equivalent to railroad rates." United States Department of Agriculture, *Barriers to Internal Trade in Farm Products*, A Special Report (Washington: 1939), p. 53.

[26] ". . . in actual practice this exemption of unmanufactured agricul-

Once the protection of the economic position of the carriers is accepted as a legitimate objective of regulation, the enormous complexity of the transportation industry and the strong competitive tendencies make inevitable an increasingly extensive interference with competitive relationships. But Congress has fully accepted this, for in the Transportation Act of 1940 it declared that it is "the national transportation policy of the Congress to provide for fair and impartial regulation of all modes of transportation. . . ." In this field, therefore, it is public policy to restrain competition, to suppress it through thoroughgoing regulation by government agencies and private associations.

CONSERVATION OF NATURAL RESOURCES

Natural resources, like natural monopolies, are of peculiar concern to the public, and government interference with the private exploitation of them has in many cases been considered necessary in the public interest. If the natural resources of the nation—forests, fisheries, grasslands, soil, water, natural gas, oil, coal and other minerals—are wastefully depleted because the current cost-price relationships are such that, under unhampered private competition, it is more profitable to use them wastefully than to incur the costs of conservation, the net private gain will not reflect a similar social gain from such use of resources.

Private and Social Costs

The horizon of individuals is shorter than that of society [27] and if a given natural resource is relatively abundant with respect to

tural products has not proved so broad as was apparently anticipated by farm interests . . . the law so reads and has been so interpreted that, if strictly enforced, large numbers of farmers' trucks could not be exempted. A farmer who owns a truck often expects to do some trucking for his neighbors. But if he collects products from others and transports them to a city across the State line, he must make sure that such products are *unmanufactured*. As the law has been interpreted unless he first secures an Interstate Commerce Commission license, he cannot transport such products as pasteurized milk or cleaned rice, nor can he bring back from the city a box of corn flakes, a pound of butter, or a sack of fertilizer for a neighbor." *Ibid.*, pp. 53–54.

[27] A corporation or an individual producer who is concerned with a "family estate" may in principle be as interested in the long-term preservation

current demand, its eventual depletion may be sufficiently distant that it does not concern the immediate owners, or even the present generation, unless they take thought for future generations. Hence, when we speak of the wasteful exploitation of resources as adding to "social cost" an element that does not occur in "private costs," we are (1) contrasting the longer interests of society as a succession of generations with the shorter interests of the producer or of the generations of his lifetime; and (2) assuming that the aggregate costs over a relevant period of future time will be greater because of the wasteful exploitation than it would have been if less wasteful policies had been pursued.

In addition, social costs may be raised above private costs if private producers so conduct their operations as to cause damage in other directions. For example, if forests are destroyed or grasslands overgrazed, soil erosion or floods will result which may not affect the lumber producer or cattleman directly, but seriously harm other producers elsewhere or at a later date.

For these reasons both the state and Federal governments have adopted measures to regulate the exploitation of many natural resources. The Federal Government has reserved large areas in the public domain for national forests, parks, water power sites, reclamation, grazing, soil conservation and wild-life conservation. In addition several million acres of mineral lands have been reserved for public use. The management of these lands is in the hands of the Federal Government, which may lease to private producers the right to exploit the natural resources in accordance with conditions laid down by the Government.

Organic Natural Resources

Organic natural resources—in contrast to inorganic ones—are renewable and, if properly cared for, may be available indefinitely. Here the problem of conservation is one of ensuring that they are used in such a way that they renew themselves as rapidly as they

of natural resources under his control as is society. Nevertheless, it is impossible to rely on all producers having such a long-term interest. Furthermore, an important source of waste is ignorance and, with respect to natural resources, wastes due to ignorance may be so costly that governments feel justified in intervening.

are used. State governments, for example, regulate the taking of oysters, crabs, shrimps, sponges and other forms of marine life off their shores. A score of states regulate the use of private forest lands and in 1944 Congress passed the "Sustained-Yield Law" under which the Secretary of Agriculture or Interior can enter into agreements with a private owner of forest lands granting him the exclusive right to exploit both his land and contiguous Federal land (which he may purchase) provided he agrees to operate under the direct supervision of the Secretary on a "sustained-yield" basis.[28] A sustained-yield program may extend over more than 100 years and during this time all competition is eliminated in the exploitation of the timber included in the sustained-yield unit. There has been strong opposition from private companies to the Sustained-Yield Law since, where agreements are concluded, competition for the right to exploit Federal timber is prevented for very long periods of time.[29] Indeed, the policy implies a greater interference with private competitive relationships than would result from a direct legal requirement that all forests, private or public, be exploited on a sustained-yield basis.

Oil Conservation or Restriction?

Inorganic resources are non-renewable and here the problem of conservation is one of ensuring that physical waste is minimized within the limits set by cost factors. Of all of our non-renewable natural resources, the most spectacular waste has occurred with respect to oil. Natural conditions and inappropriate property laws have combined to maximize the potential waste of unrestrained competition in the exploitation of oil. Oil is found in vast underground pools the boundaries of which bear no relation to the artificial property lines on the earth's surface. A property owner can claim possession of the oil underneath his land only if he can bring it to the surface before his neighbors do. The oil belongs to him who captures it under the judicial "rule of capture." Hence,

[28] Only one such agreement had been made by 1949.
[29] It is complained that in principle the Government could make an agreement with a single operator to purchase and use all Federal timber lands forever.

the discovery of an oil pool may provoke a wild competitive drill-
ing of oil wells by all the owners of the land surface who completely ignore the fact that the oil pool is a unit and can be efficiently exploited only when treated as a unit. In the scramble to
get the oil itself, the natural gas which is associated with oil deposits and which is necessary to bring the oil to the surface under
its own power is frequently allowed to blow off into the air with
a double result: the gas, itself a valuable natural resource, is
irretrievably lost and large quantities, perhaps the greater part,
of the oil in the pool is rendered incapable of rising to the surface and is recoverable only at very much higher cost. Efficient
production methods and adequate protection of oil still in the
ground may be neglected in the attempt to get as much oil as
possible in the shortest possible time.

Some public regulation is clearly called for under these conditions and several states have imposed certain standards on oil
producers. But by far the most important measure taken in the
name of conservation has been the restriction of production. A
thorough-going policy of conservation in the sense of the physically efficient utilization of resources has not yet been adopted
anywhere while thorough-going restriction of production has been
almost universally adopted.[30] "Proration," the term used in the
industry to denote the distribution of "total allowable production"
among producing interests, is widely applied and the Federal Government assists the states in enforcing proration regulations by
prohibiting the movement in interstate commerce of "hot oil," i.e.,
oil in excess of the allotted quota.[31] The chief purpose of production restriction is price maintenance, which is called "stabilization" of the industry.[32] It is made possible by large-scale collusive

[30] The restriction of present use in order to save resources for future use
is widely accepted as being an appropriate conservation policy. Technological
change is so rapid, however, that this policy is highly questionable; resources
carefully saved today may be much less useful in the future. Moreover, such
restriction of production is usually introduced to maintain prices and profits
at a level considered satisfactory by existing producers. Whatever may be
said for this procedure, it should not be confused with conservation of natural
resources.

[31] The Connally "Hot Oil" Act of 1937.

[32] Thus, paradoxically, the introduction of a tariff on imports was advocated and obtained in order to help make the domestic "conservation" policy

activity between oil companies and governmental authorities. The Bureau of Mines makes monthly forecasts of demand (at current prices, of course) and the proration authorities fix quotas to limit supply to the estimated level of demand.[33] Restriction of production has probably reduced waste compared to completely unregulated private exploitation. But since it is a price maintenance program and not a conservation program, conservation is only an "accidental incident." [34] In fact proration causes avoidable waste for whether or not production from a given pool should be restricted in the interest of real conservation depends on the physical nature of the pool—which the system fails to take into account.[35] Yet, governmental restriction of output is preferred by the oil companies to a true conservation program, since it has assisted them in establishing monopolistic controls, not only over production, but over distribution as well.[36]

---

effective. See G. W. Stocking, "Stabilization of the Oil Industry: Its Economic and Legal Aspects," *American Economic Review*, Vol. XXIII (1933), Suppl., p. 62. "Much that has been done in the oil and gas industry in the name of conservation is really stablization . . . Amos L. Beaty, former president of the American Petroleum Institute, testified in the Federal oil inquiry in 1934, that stabilization was the primary aim of the oil companies in proposing Federal quota restrictions on the production of oil and gas." *Energy Resources and National Policy*, Report of the Energy Resources Committee to the National Resources Committee (Washington: 1939), p. 200.

[33] "It is doubtful if a private agency could furnish similar statistics for the oil companies for the purpose of price control and be within the law." *Control of the Petroleum Industry by Major Oil Companies*, Monograph No. 39, Temporary National Economic Committee (Washington: 1941), p. 16.

[34] This is the phrase used by the lower Federal Court in *Alfred Macmillan et al. v. The Railroad Commission of Texas et al.* District Court of the United States for the Western District of Texas, Austin Division, No. 390 Equity.

[35] See Report of the Energy Resources Committee, *op. cit.*, p. 200.

[36] Apparently, government regulation is palatable to "private enterprise" if it assists in maintaining monopoly incomes for the present owners. It is not so palatable if prices and profits are subordinate to other considerations. The attitude of the oil industry toward "conservation" has always been strongly influenced by price expectations. For example in Oklahoma "in the early part of 1926 when the Conservation Board was holding hearings, the price of oil was satisfactory and the industry optimistic, or at least indifferent; but late in the same year, when the price of oil began to decline and conditions became uncomfortable, the proration law (Oklahoma) that had been relegated to the closet by the World War again came to life. At first, a group of Oklahoma producers entered into a voluntary curtailment agreement under

Coal Conservation—a Misnomer

In the coal industry, too, price maintenance has been the chief purpose of government regulation although the necessity of regulation has frequently been justified as a "conservation" measure. For example, although the Guffey-Snyder Coal Act of 1935 had little to do with the prevention of physical waste, it was called the Bituminous Coal Conservation Act. When this act was declared unconstitutional the Bituminous Coal Act of 1937 was passed, which aimed primarily at restoring price fixing for the industry. The fact that the adoption of conservation programs was optional under the Act was considered by many to be a serious weakness.[37] There is no doubt that the story of government regulation of the coal industry belongs under price regulation and not under conservation although, as with oil, the regulatory measures may incidentally lead to the prevention of some waste.

PRICE CONTROLS

All government policies aiding or restraining competition affect prices. And since prices determine to a very large extent the allocation of resources and the distribution of incomes in our society, most of such policies are consciously designed directly or indirectly to influence prices. Clearly, much of this and the preceding chapter has been primarily concerned with governmental attempts to influence prices: patents, tariffs, licensing, public utility regulations, have their effect on the economy through prices. Prices are frankly regulated under many licensing laws and the regulation of public utility and transportation rates is direct price regulation.

In this section we are concerned with legislation in which price is the explicit and central problem and in which the expressed purpose is to prevent competitive prices from emerging.

---

a paid umpire. In 1927 the privately paid umpire was approved by the Corporation Commission, and his orders became the orders of the Commission under the 1915 act. By 1930, proration of the entire State had been thus promoted." Report of the Energy Resources Committee, *op. cit.*, p. 388.

    [37] *Ibid.*, p. 119.

There are a variety of ways in which governments may accomplish this end. Minimum prices may be set by decree, and individuals selling below these prices may be penalized. Minimum prices may be supported by government assistance to producers enabling them to withhold supplies from the market or by direct government purchase of "excess" supplies. Production may be directly restricted through quotas, or supplies may be "regulated" by marketing arrangements and discriminatory pricing policies. Maximum prices may be set by decree and individuals selling above these prices may be penalized. All of these ways of influencing prices have been used in the United States by the Federal or state governments. Frequently several of them have been used in combination since it is an extremely difficult task to maintain prices against the forces of supply and demand and the most stringent controls devisable may be required to achieve the purpose. In all cases where the government has tried directly to establish arbitrary prices it is because the supply and demand conditions in the market are such that it is feared "undesired prices" would emerge.

Minimum Prices and Price Supports

The need for minimum prices, of course, arises because the market price tends to fall below the price considered "reasonable" or "fair" by producers. But sellers will sell below the minimum prices fixed if they think that by selling more at a lower price they can do better than by selling less at a higher price. Hence, in order to sustain a minimum price above the price at which a substantial number of sellers are willing to sell, it is necessary to provide an outlet for the "surplus" goods, to prevent producers from producing as much as they would like to produce, or directly to penalize sellers who sell at lower prices. Most of the agricultural price programs depend on the first two methods; the latter, which was the central method under the National Industrial Recovery Act and the Bituminous Coal Acts, is also used in the agricultural marketing agreement and order programs. The various unfair practices laws of the states prohibiting sales below cost are another form of direct minimum price legislation.

Minimum prices for a large number of agricultural commodities are established by the Department of Agriculture.[38] These prices bear no relation to the supply of or the demand for the commodities concerned, but are calculated with reference to the prices of products that producers buy. The price support legislation is based on the belief that the prices of the agricultural commodities included in the program should have a "purchasing power" roughly equal to the purchasing power of the same commodities during some past period.[39] It is not surprising, therefore, that under these circumstances farmers persistently tend to produce more than can be sold at the prices set. Hence a complicated constellation of "programs" becomes necessary to support these prices. Farmers can obtain loans, using their produce valued at the support price as collateral, and simply turn over the collateral if they are unable to sell all of it at the support price; they can contract to sell to the Government at the support price and fulfill the contract only if they cannot get their price elsewhere; or they can sell directly to the Government.[40]

Output Control and Surplus Removal

Clearly, however, if farmers continue to produce quantities in excess of the supplies that can be marketed through normal channels at the support price, the Government is going to hold increasingly large stocks. Additional programs are therefore frequently required: "output control" programs and "surplus removal" programs enter the picture. Marketing quotas and acreage allotments have therefore been established for several commodities.[41] The

[38] Congress has made price support mandatory for corn, cotton, wheat, tobacco, rice, peanuts, wool, mohair, tung nuts, honey, Irish potatoes, milk and butterfat. Price support is permissive for other commodities and in 1949 and 1950 these included barley, dry edible beans, cottonseed, eggs, flaxseed, grain sorghums, gum naval stores, hogs, oats, dry edible peas, rye, various kinds of cover crop seed, soybeans, sweet potatoes, turkeys.

[39] For most commodities the base period is still 1909–1914. "Parity prices" are calculated by complicated formulas and support prices, which remain the same throughout the crop year, are determined at some percentage of parity as of a given date.

[40] Direct government purchasing is used to support prices only when it is not feasible to do so through loans or purchase agreements.

[41] In April 1950 corn, upland cotton, wheat, rice, peanuts, tobacco, and long staple cotton were subject to marketing quotas.

quantities which it is thought would give "adequate supplies" to the consumer are calculated and these quantities are expressed in terms of acreage allotments which are distributed by states, counties and individual farms. If these quotas are approved by two-thirds of the producers voting in a referendum they are applied to all producers, and any producer who sells more than his quota is penalized. If two-thirds of the producers do not approve the quotas, the quotas are not put into effect but very much lower support prices are paid.

Surpluses that continue to accumulate are taken care of by "surplus removal" programs. The Commodity Credit Corporation (which is the chief government agency through which purchases are made) is not permitted to sell its storable commodities in ordinary markets at less than 5% above the current support price plus carrying charges, but it can give things away for welfare purposes and it can divert commodities into other than "normal" channels of trade. The net realized losses of the CCC on price support operations in 1949 alone reached $254,761,994.

There are three broad types of surplus removal programs: export dumping, domestic welfare programs, and "diversion" into non-normal channels of trade. An amount equal to 30% of the gross receipts from duties collected under the customs laws during each calendar year is made available to the Secretary of Agriculture for these programs.

Exports have been subsidized in connection with the various foreign aid programs, but in some cases the United States engaged in outright dumping: 10¢ per bale is paid to cotton exporters, 4.5¢ per lb. or 50% of the f.a.s. price or domestic market price, whichever is lower, is paid on exports of honey to countries outside North, Central and South America. Domestic Welfare programs include subsidization of low income groups, institutions, charities and the school lunch programs. "Diversion programs" are based on the fact that it is frequently possible to sell commodities at very low prices for special uses without "spoiling" the primary market if the commodities are kept from flowing from the secondary to the primary markets. Thus almond growers are paid 14¢ per pound to sell almonds for industrial manufacture, animal feed. or other uses providing they do not include direct human consumption; cotton growers are paid to sell filberts for animal feed, export, or other outlets not competitive with direct domestic human consumption; dried-fruit growers, grain sorghum producers, honey producers, walnut producers are all paid to sell their product through diversion outlets.

Marketing Programs

But there are still other ways of raising prices to ordinary non-industrial consumers. Under the Agricultural Marketing Agreement Act of 1937, as amended, marketing agreement and order programs have been established for certain commodities. As of April 1950 these programs were in effect in a large number of production areas [42] for milk, fruits, vegetables, nuts and hops. Under these programs regulations include controls over quality, quantity and rate of shipment of the commodities; the establishment of reserve pools, the control and disposition of "surpluses"; the prohibition of "unfair trade practices"; the fixing and posting of prices. Compliance with the programs may be prescribed as a condition of eligibility for price support. Civil and criminal action can be taken against violators of marketing orders.[43] Since the growers or handlers of the commodities concerned (except milk) usually initiate the programs and administer them [44] and since

[42] Each marketing agreement or order is limited to the "smallest regional production area practicable." Hence there will be several such agreements for the same commodity. See *Price Programs of the United States Department of Agriculture*, Agriculture Information Bulletin No. 13, Production and Marketing Administration, United States Department of Agriculture, April 1950, p. 44.

[43] Marketing agreements are voluntary and affect only handlers who sign them. Marketing orders are issued by the Secretary of Agriculture and are binding on all handlers whether they sign the agreement or not. Marketing agreements that do not receive the approval of the handlers can be converted into orders by the Secretary if he finds that the issuance of an order is the only practicable means of advancing the interests of producers.

[44] "All marketing agreements and order programs for commodities other than milk provide for a committee of growers or handlers, or both, to administer the terms of the order. . . . Members of the committee are generally nominated by growers and handlers in the industry and appointed by the Secretary of Agriculture." *Price Programs of the United States Dept. of Agriculture*, p. 46.

they are openly price raising and price fixing programs, it has been necessary for them to secure specific exemption from the antitrust acts.

Federal milk programs are administered by agents appointed by the Department of Agriculture and are in general based upon the principle of maximizing monopoly returns by charging discriminating prices. Consumers of bottled milk for direct consumption will pay higher prices than manufacturers of milk products. The same milk is therefore sold at different prices depending on the use for which it is destined.[45] The milk programs are thoroughgoing control programs regulating the price of milk in great detail at every level.

In addition to the Federal milk programs are many state milk control programs. The methods of protecting the local markets from outside competition, of rewarding producers and dividing the receipts, of inspection, licensing, quota determination, price fixing and classification, etc., differ considerably and are frequently very complicated. But the purpose is always the same, to protect local milk producers.[46] Very frequently sanitary regulations provide the most efficient and flexible means of enforcing such protection and the camouflage of the "public health" only thinly conceals the real purpose.[47] Various standards of price fixing are

[45] "The classification of milk according to the use made of the milk by handlers with minimum prices to producers for each use classification, enables dairy farmers to realize the *full value* of their milk in disposing of their entire production." *Ibid.*, p. 44. (Italics supplied.) It has been said of the Federal program that "the general objective of the Federal fluid milk program has been to establish the highest producer prices in the market that could be sustained for any considerable period of time." *Economic Standards of Government Price Control*, Temporary National Economic Committee, Monograph No. 32 (Washington: 1941), p. 84.

[46] In most states milk dealers must be licensed under milk control laws and in many states a dealer's licence may be refused or revoked for action "demoralizing to price structure." See *Barriers to Internal Trade in Farm Products*, A Special Report to the Secretary of Agriculture by the Bureau of Agricultural Economics, United States Department of Agriculture (Washington: 1939), p. 15.

[47] Rhode Island at one time furnished the most spectacular method of enforcing its restrictions. In August 1937 it started adding red coloring matter to out-of-state milk delivered in violation of its law. The subsequent outcry forced the abandonment of this measure.

adopted. Cost of production plus "reasonable return" to producers are very common.[48]

International Price Programs

If all of these programs succeed in maintaining high domestic prices for agricultural products, still other difficulties arise and further action may be necessary. The United States is not an isolated economy; foreign trade, both exports and imports, must be taken into account by domestic policy makers. We have already seen that the Secretary of Agriculture has power to subsidize agricultural exports. In addition the United States has joined the International Wheat Agreement, which sets minimum and maximum prices and establishes quotas for the participating countries. This helps to keep the United States in the export field in competition with lower-cost exporters by raising the world price, thus reducing the discrepancy between United States prices and world prices.

The United States "sugar program" depends on strict control of imports. Although the welfare of consumers of sugar is placed as the first of the "prime objectives" of the sugar program, this is sheer camouflage.[49] Domestic sugar, particularly beet sugar, is produced at much higher cost than "foreign" cane sugar, and domestic production does not meet domestic requirements. Imports are necessary, but in order to keep the price high enough to protect the domestic industry, quotas are placed on imports.[50] In

[48] Thus the "standards used by the Oregon Milk Control Board in setting minimum prices are reasonable return to both producer and distributor, not unreasonable prices to the consumers, and costs of production and distribution." *Economic Standards of Government Price Control*, p. 116.

[49] "If the United States permitted sugar from Cuba, the Philippines, and other areas to come into the country in unlimited quantities, consumers, under ordinary circumstances, would benefit from lower prices. But under present wage standards in domestic producing areas, free imports, unless accompanied by an increase in the sugar tariff, would work serious hardships on producers in specialized domestic sugar-producing areas or would tend to force wage reductions on workers in such areas." *Price Programs of the United States Department of Agriculture, 1949*. Mis. Public. 683, Production and Marketing Administration, U.S. Dept. of Agriculture (March 1949), p. 39.

[50] Certain foreign areas, notably Cuba and the Philippines, are given preferential treatment.

addition, domestic producers received payments on the crops of 1942 through 1948 averaging about $2.60 per ton of beets and from 88¢ to $1.70 per ton of cane. Payments to domestic producers are conditional upon compliance with certain labor standards, marketing quotas and price regulations. They are financed out of a tax of 50¢ per hundredweight of sugar, raw value, produced or brought into the continental United States.

Subsidized Production for Destruction

The policy of thoroughgoing government intervention to protect the incomes of agricultural producers was born in the depression of the 1930's and was defended as an emergency measure. It survived the depression and has continued into periods of high economic activity. Criticism of the policy has been increasing, but for the most part the public has quietly accepted a program which fundamentally involves a transfer of income from one group in the economy to another. The income of farmers is maintained only by the subsidy given them by consumers and taxpayers. The irrational aspects of the program are clearly brought out, however, when the "surplus" removal arrangements break down and it becomes necessary to destroy food. This is especially resented if market prices are so high that many consumers consciously limit their consumption. The latest example is the 1950 potato scandal which for a time threatened to shake seriously the public's willingness to accept the price support program. While consumers were paying exorbitant prices (the basic support price was over $1 a bushel) millions of bushels of potatoes were threatened with destruction. The story is instructive.

Potatoes harvested in 1948 were supported at prices ranging from $2.15 to $3.50 a hundredweight, the 1949 crop at $1.80, and the 1950 crop at $1.68.[51] In spite of acreage restrictions potatoes poured from the farms and the Government holdings of surplus potatoes grew bigger and bigger. Part of the problem arose because Government attempts to control production by limiting the acres planted could be frustrated if farmers planted rows closer

[51] See Price Programs of the Department of Agriculture, March 1949 and April 1950, passim.

together, applied more fertilizer and insecticides, and thus increased the yield of potatoes per acre. The Secretary of Agriculture is reported to have told the Senate Agriculture Committee that the plant-industry experts in the Department of Agriculture had stated that it would be possible to treble the production of potatoes per acre in the next five years.[52] Farmers were doing well, but consumers were aggrieved at the high prices and the Government did not know what to do with the large stocks of potatoes it had been forced to purchase. The Secretary proposed that 25 million bushels of potatoes be colored blue (to prevent human beings from eating them) and given to farmers at 1¢ per 100 pounds for use as animal feed. A violent controversy immediately started. The National Potato Council protested that the entire farm program would be placed "in an untenable position insofar as public opinion and good will are concerned." It wanted the potatoes made available to industrial users.[53] But the industrial users said that the Government would have to pay the freight charges for transporting the potatoes since they could not be used profitably for industrial purposes even at a price that just covered freight rates. It was estimated that for the Government to pay the freight would have cost $15 million more than dumping potatoes. It was also proposed that the potatoes be given to charitable institutions if the latter would pay the freight. The potato dealers complained about this, arguing that it would constitute unfair competition. Apparently Congress had got the Administration into the position of having to pay farmers to produce something that could not be disposed of unless consumers were to be paid to consume it, but for which there could be no reduction of the price the housewife had to pay in the market.

Responsibility for this situation lay with the Congress and not with the Department of Agriculture since Congress had made potato price support mandatory. But when the question of whether potatoes should be destroyed was laid before the Senate Agriculture Committee, the Committee refused to commit itself; on the one side were irate consumers and on the other irate farmers. Discreetly the wary lawmakers rushed to duck the consequences

[52] *New York Times,* March 17, 1950.
[53] *New York Times,* February 1, 1950.

of their own actions. The Chairman of the Committee said that the Committee neither approved nor disapproved of the destruction of potatoes and "refused to go on record as a matter of principle"! [54]

While domestic blue potatoes were being fed to animals, Canadian potato producers found the United States market so attractive that they shipped large quantities into the country over a tariff of 75¢ per hundred pounds. This only added fuel to the fire. One might have thought that the United States legislators would suspect that if Canadian producers could make a profit after surmounting such a tariff (and after all the usual argument of low wages and living standards could not be made very convincing with regard to Canada) that there was something wrong with the United States price. But no, the United States price was not lowered. On the contrary the United States tariff was raised and since the United States had been active in a world-wide policy of reducing trade barriers and had entered certain agreements with other countries, it was necessary to persuade other countries to permit the United States to renegue on the agreements it had made.

The price of potatoes is still to be supported. The lawmakers prefer to reduce supplies and at the time of writing the extensive use of mandatory marketing agreements seems destined to be the solution for the future crops.

Minimum-Price Controls

Agricultural price legislation is by far the most extensive type of price legislation in our economy. As we have seen, it is largely a problem of *supporting* minimum prices by any means at hand, although direct price *regulation* is included in the marketing agreement and order programs, of which the milk programs are the most important. Regulation of the latter sort was also attempted for manufactured and mining products in the National Industrial Recovery Act and in the Bituminous Coal Act of 1937. The NIRA was a hasty measure to meet a widespread "emergency" and was soon declared unconstitutional. The Bituminous Coal Act, al-

[54] *New York Times,* February 2, 1950.

314   GOVERNMENT POLICIES

though it, too, had a relatively short life, expiring in 1943, is of
more importance because the price regulation which was its chief
purpose was approved by the Supreme Court.[55] Minimum prices
were provided in a code and penalties were prescribed for violation of the code by "code members" while non-members were subject to a heavy excise tax. The minimum prices were established
with reference to a weighted average of total costs. This regulation
of prices was held to be a proper exercise of the power of Congress
to regulate interstate commerce.

Prohibition of Sales Below Cost

We saw in our discussion of the antitrust laws that resale price
maintenance contracts were exempt from the antitrust laws. Nevertheless these fair trade laws, as they are called, did not cover a
sufficient number of commodities to satisfy all trade groups. Consequently nearly three-fourths of the states have been prevailed
upon to enact "unfair practices laws" or laws prohibiting sales below cost. California was the first to adopt such a law (in 1935)
and the California law has been widely copied. "Cost" is taken to
include the full cost of doing business, and cost surveys made by
industry groups or trade associations may be used as *prima facie*
evidence of cost for any particular dealer.[56] The determination of
standards by which to set legal prices and the policing of business
in order to ensure the observance of these prices are usually undertaken by trade associations, although action can also be brought
by the public authorities. Injunctions may be obtained against
violators, damages claimed if they can be proved, and sometimes
criminal actions may be brought with fines and imprisonment imposed by violations of the Act. Unfair practices acts are effective
ways of eliminating price competition, their effectiveness depending on the strength of local trade associations. They have been used
to enforce prices set on the basis of the most flimsy type of "cost

[55] *Sunshine Anthracite Coal Co.* v. *Adkins*, 310 U.S. 381 (1940).

[56] *"Prima facie* means 'at first view'; and in sales-below-cost legislation
it means that any person selling for less than the cost estimated by an industry survey or by the percentage markup specified in the law loses his case
unless he can prove to the court that his costs are actually lower." Vernon A.
Mund, *Government and Business* (New York: Harper, 1950), p. 455.

survey" evidence.[57] The constitutionality of these acts and the practices under them is still uncertain. Some of the laws have been declared unconstitutional by state courts and in several cases brought by the Department of Justice fines have been assessed or injunctions granted. The legality of the state laws as such has not yet been tested in the Supreme Court. During and after the war business did not have to be particularly concerned with the problem of low prices, but the time will certainly come when entrenched business groups will once again turn to the law to prevent price competition. A clear legal position will then become necessary.

Maximum-Price Legislation

Whereas minimum prices are usually established to protect producers, maximum prices are established to protect consumers. Minimum-price legislation is fairly common since producers groups are frequently better organized and more aware of their own immediate profit than are consumers groups. Maximum-price legislation only occurs under special conditions. In public utilities, for example, where the conditions of supply are such that effective competition is precluded, maximum-price fixing is an accepted method of regulation. During and after wars consumers are widely considered to need general protection against the power of producers to raise prices, and maximum prices are fixed for important, if not all, commodities. Thus, during the Second World War a variety of administrative agencies were created in the Federal Government to control the prices of consumers goods, raw materials and other producers goods.

However, just as minimum prices frequently cannot be maintained without supplementary controls over supply, so maximum prices frequently must be supported by supplementary controls over demand, and for the same reasons. If minimum prices are so high that producers will produce more than will be taken at those prices, the prices will be extremely difficult to maintain in face of mounting stocks. If maximum prices are so low that consumers

[57] See Federal Trade Commission, *Resale Price Maintenance* (Washington: 1945), pp. 854 ff.

will want to buy more than is available at those prices, the price
"ceilings" will be difficult to hold. One of the functions of prices
is to divide available supplies among consumers and when prices,
because of controls, are no longer an effective means of doing this,
other means must be devised. These may include "first come, first
served," favoritism of suppliers, informal rationing by suppliers,
and official rationing by the government. But the vast ramifications of administrative controls necessarily following extensive
interference with market prices makes such interference acceptable only as a last resort. Even in wartime much more could be
done than is usually done to limit the disposable income of consumers through taxation, deferred payments, etc., thus limiting
effective demand by way of fiscal and monetary controls and reducing the upward pressure upon prices without resorting to, or
relying so heavily on, direct price controls.[58]

Rent Control

The only important price control surviving the war was rent
control. It was insisted upon by the majority of voters who felt
that uncontrolled rents would result in excessive profits to landlords and serious hardship on low and medium income groups who
would find it difficult to pay higher rents. On the face of it this
seems to be simple justice. The supply of houses responds relatively
slowly to an increase in the demand for houses and in the meantime why should landlords be allowed to reap windfall profits at
the expense of poor people who have to have a roof over their
heads? On the other hand, the existing supply of housing must
be allocated in some manner. The government did not itself attempt rationing, so the landlords had to do it. Naturally friends,

[58] Since these lines were written the United States, engaged in a defense
effort financed partly by credit expansion, has again introduced maximum-
price controls. Congress resorted to price controls at a time when defense
expenditures amounted to less than a quarter of the national income and
could have been financed without serious consequences entirely through increased taxation. The failure to impose sufficient taxes coupled with the willingness to abandon the price mechanism demonstrates how little the legislature of this nation, paying lip service to the advantages of a free-enterprise
economy and of competitive markets, really appreciates the meaning of it
all.

relatives, people willing to pay good prices for furniture or in some other way to give something on the side got preference. Everybody having to move—war veterans, war workers, newly married people—bore the brunt of the housing "shortage." People already in houses who did not want to move were the only ones to gain and, since rents were kept relatively low compared to increases in incomes, they had no incentive to economize on space, to rent rooms or double up with others.

Consequently, rent control has arbitrarily favored one group against others in the community. It has not prevented the rich from getting houses, it has meant serious difficulties for those who had to move and it has not put pressure on people to use existing space to the best advantage. In addition, it reduced the profitability of building and renting and thus has retarded new building and prolonged the period of "shortage." In this case, as in many others, an interference with the price mechanism in order to ensure "justice" to some groups has repercussions in other directions that cause much more "injustice" and in the long run simply make matters worse.

Labor Legislation

Government measures assisting the cause of organized labor are designed to reduce competition among workers in the labor market. The economic consequences of labor organization are considered in the next two chapters. In this section we are not concerned with whether or not governmental support of labor organization is justified, but only with a description of the governmental measures supporting labor organization.[59] Nor are we concerned with labor legislation of the welfare sort—regulation of industrial poisons, night work, child labor, protective legislation for women, etc.—since these have only an incidental bearing on the question of monopolistic forces in the labor market.[60]

[59] We shall, however, discuss also the provisions of the Taft-Hartley Act (the Labor Management Relations Act of 1947) which were designed to *reduce* some of the support previously given to labor unions in the Wagner Act (The Labor Relations Act of 1935).

[60] Of course, the elimination of certain types of competition, e.g., competition from women and children, helped make unionization easier in some

Legislature versus Judiciary

Until recent times the history of governmental intervention with respect to labor organization was to a considerable extent a story of legislative intervention to offset the effects of court decisions. As interpreted by the courts, the common law doctrines of criminal conspiracy, restraint of trade, freedom of contract, and the 14th Amendment to the United States Constitution protecting certain basic rights, including property rights, placed serious obstacles in the way of labor organization. Combinations to raise prices were illegal under the common law and therefore, if workers combined to raise wages or shorten hours, the law of criminal conspiracy might be applied. Similarly the doctrine of restraint of trade, which rested on the right of individuals to dispose of their property or labor as they pleased, was invoked against labor actions that interfered with the rights of employers to buy in the cheapest market or of workers to sell their labor on whatever terms they wished. To be sure, the courts did not apply these doctrines in an unalloyed form; combinations to raise wages were not necessarily criminal conspiracies unless "unlawful means" were used, although, if other workers were prevented from accepting employment on whatever terms they wished, the courts tended to crack down. Similarly, the nature of the means and the "reasonableness" of the ends were taken into consideration in the application of the doctrine of restraint of trade.

Again, the 14th Amendment—originally designed to prevent racial discrimination—protecting people against deprivation of their property without "due process of law" and guaranteeing equality of treatment before the law, was applied by the courts to prevent workers from taking action that would prejudice an employer's business. Since workers could quit at will, equality of treatment demanded that employers could hire and fire at will.

Thus workers early found that the courts made few exceptions to the general rules of law for what the workers considered to be

industries and was, in fact, one of the reasons for some of the welfare legislation. Nevertheless, very different considerations are involved in the appraisal of welfare legislation, and any indirect aid to labor organization has been slight.

their special position. Combination implied power that individual members of the combination did not have and, when the possibilities of coercion inherent in such power were used for ends which conflicted with property rights and freedom of contract, the courts tended to act against the combination and its individual members. So the workers turned to the legislatures, urging them to overrule the courts and establish special rules for workers' organizations. Until recent times government aid to labor organization came from the legislative and the administrative branches of government; government restraints on labor monopoly came from the judiciary. The aid from one direction was frequently a reaction to the restraints imposed from the other.

The issues involved can be roughly divided into two groups: those connected with labor's *power to organize* and those connected with the *use of organized power*. They are not, of course, entirely separable questions, since insofar as labor organizations were restrained or penalized for taking action on behalf of their members they became less attractive to workers, and organizers faced greater difficulty in getting workers to join. Hence the first group shades into the second. Labor has always had the technical right to organize for the broad purpose of improving its working conditions, but the ability to take effective advantage of this right depends first on the strength of the resistance, in particular on the tactics employers could use to combat labor organization; and second, on the desire of workers to join, which in turn depends on what labor is permitted to do with its organized power. Thus, we must not expect that our attempt to discuss the two questions separately can be carried out with great consistency.

The Power to Organize

Labor has usually had to face bitter employer opposition to their attempts to organize, and the first interventions of the law in favor of organized labor were to place restraints on the tactics employers were permitted to use to combat labor organization. The most effective weapon in the hands of employers was the right to hire and fire at will, and thereby to discriminate against union members. In one of the earlier legislative aids to labor or-

ganization in the United States, the Federal Government in 1898
forbade interstate railroad employers to fire workers because of
union activities or membership.[61] This prohibition was declared
unconstitutional by the Supreme Court in 1908, who upheld the
employer's right to hire and fire at will, placing it in the same
category as the employee's right to quit at will.[62]

Employers took full advantage of this power, basing a large
variety of discriminatory anti-union tactics upon it. It not only
made possible discriminatory firing of workers for union activities but also the *"yellow dog"* contract (by which employees were
required to stipulate as a condition for getting a job that they
would not join a union); the *blacklist* (containing the names of
workers active in union matters, which would be widely circu-
lated among employers so that union men or union organizers
had difficulty in getting any job); the hiring of *strikebreakers;* the
use of *spies* placed among workers and in unions; and similar
tactics.

Individual states early enacted laws making it a criminal
offense for an employer to discharge workers for union activity,
but these laws were declared unconstitutional.[63] During the first
World War the Federal Government insisted that the right of
workers to organize and bargain collectively should not be interfered with in any manner, and one of the basic principles of the
National War Labor Board was that "employers should not discharge workers for membership in trade unions or for legitimate
trade union activities." [64] After the war, the Railway Labor Act
of 1926 also prohibited interference by "either party over the

[61] Erdman Act, 30 Stat. 424, 1898. The United States Strike Commission
of 1894, appointed by President Cleveland, had found that discrimination
against union leaders had caused the Chicago strike of 1894, in which there
was much rioting. The strike was broken by a Federal injunction, and Eugene
Debs and other leaders were jailed for contempt. See Carl Raushenbush and
Emanuel Stein, *Labor Cases and Materials* (New York: Crofts & Co., 1941),
p. 64.

[62] *Adair* v. *United States*, 208 U.S. 161 (1908).

[63] The leading case is that of *Coppage* v. *Kansas*, 236 U.S. 1, where a
Kansas statute outlawing yellow dog contracts was declared unconstitutional.

[64] See the discussion in W. L. McNaughton, *The Development of Labor
Relations Law* (Washington: American Council on Public Affairs, 1941), p.
31.

self-organization or designation of representatives by the other," and the prohibition was upheld by the Supreme Court, who refused to apply the decisions in the earlier cases.[65]

The first real restraint on the right of employers to impose such conditions as they saw fit in the contract of employment came in 1932, when the Norris–LaGuardia Act made "yellow dog" contracts unenforceable in the Federal Courts.[66] Later the interference of employers with employee organization was prohibited under the codes of the National Industrial Recovery Act of 1933. Finally, with the National Labor Relations Act of 1935 (The Wagner Act), the various direct methods by which employers could most effectively combat unionism were not only effectively outlawed but a positive duty to avoid all interference with unionization was placed upon employers. Interference of any kind with labor organization and any discrimination against union members were classed as unfair labor practices against which the National Labor Relations Board, established by the Wagner Act, could take action. Furthermore, company unions, i.e., unions not affiliated with any national or international unions, were ordered by the Board to be disestablished if the employers dominated or even supported them.

The following practices were listed as unfair labor practices forbidden to employers in Section 8 of the Wagner Act:

(1) to interfere with, restrain, or coerce employees in the exercise of their rights to organize and bargain collectively;

(2) to dominate or interfere with the formation or administration of any labor organization or to contribute financial or other support to it;

(3) to practice discrimination in order to encourage or discourage membership in any labor organization, although an employer shall not be precluded from making an agreement with a labor organization that union membership should be required as a condition of employment if the organization was the certified representative of the employees (i.e., the closed shop was permitted);

[65] *Texas and New Orleans Railway Co.* v. *Brotherhood of Railway and Steamship Clerks*, 281 U.S. 548 (1930).
[66] The Anti-Injunction Act, 47 Stat. 70.

(4) to discharge or otherwise discriminate against an employee because he has filed charges or given testimony under the Act;

(5) to refuse to bargain collectively with the representatives of his employees as provided in the Act.

Under the rulings of the National Labor Relations Board, bribery of workers, discrimination in assigning work, a request that the workers state their attitude toward unions, any coercive statements or derogatory remarks about unions, favoritism between different unions, and similar practices were condemned. Industrial espionage and the use of strike breakers [67] was also attacked by the NLRB.

Thus, all direct methods by which employers can interfere with the organizing activity of workers, were outlawed; the employers were required to recognize the unions and to bargain collectively with their representatives; and the unions, where they obtained closed-shop or union-shop agreements, were able to require workers to join.

Under a union-shop agreement all workers must be or become members of the union. Thus all new workers hired by the firm are required to join the union, usually after a probationary period. Under a closed-shop agreement new employees must either be hired through the union or must be members of the union when hired. These arrangements are a great help to the unions since they "automatically" increase union membership and ensure the maintenance of membership, besides giving the union full control of the supply of labor to the employer. The closed shop sanctioned by law was clearly a powerful governmental aid to organized labor against non-organized workers.[68]

[67] In addition, the Transportation of Strikebreakers Act of 1936 (The Byrnes Act) made the transportation of strikebreakers across state lines a felony. Many of the states have also passed laws bearing on the issues discussed in this section. A discussion of these laws, however, would be impossible in the short space allotted here.

[68] The immigration laws may also be regarded as government measures that helped, though indirectly, reduce the competition from labor which is not easily organized. The contract labor laws in the 1880's, which prohibited the importation of foreign labor under contract, were introduced directly in response to labor protests against the importation of Chinese coolies to work on the railroads; and the later immigration laws were also largely passed

For the most part, however, trade unions must rely on their ability to attract workers, and here the governmental interventions respecting the use by organized labor of its power has become important. If unions can make their demands effective, they are more attractive to workers and workers are more willing to pay dues than they would be if nothing were obtained. Frequently, therefore, the successful establishment of a union in a particular industry depends upon successful action against employers. Government action with respect to the purposes and methods of the use of organized power are therefore of great importance.

The Use of Organized Power

Although the right of labor to organize in order to improve its working conditions was early recognized, just what methods could it use to attain its objectives? Could it, for example, take action which would damage an employer's business, restrain trade, prevent other workers from accepting jobs offered to them, prevent or deter consumers from buying the products of an employer? How far were unions subject to the antitrust laws?

The traditional "weapons" of labor in their struggle against employers are the strike, picketing and boycotts. Violence, intimidation and coercion have always been illegal. But where does "peaceful persuasion" end and intimidation or coercion begin? The threat of physical violence is not the essence of coercion; an employer may be as much coerced by the threat of bankruptcy or severe losses as by the threat of the physical destruction of his plant; an individual worker may be as much coerced by the threat of social ostracism as by the threat of a physical attack.

It is difficult, if not impossible, to say in general terms where illegal coercion begins. Except in cases where physical violence is frankly used, whether or not certain actions constitute illegal coercion has depended on the specific circumstances of each case and upon the disposition of the courts. For a long time the courts took an extremely severe view of actions that seriously damaged an employer's business. In the notorious Danbury Hatters Case

under pressure from organized labor. (In recent years, however, some of the unions have been on the liberal side of the immigration question.)

either a primary or secondary boycott which "obstructs the free flow of commerce between the States or restricts, in that regard, the liberty of a trader to engage in business" was declared illegal and individual members of the union were held liable to the full amount of their individual property for the damage caused to the company by the boycotts.[69] In other cases, more than one picket at a factory gate was held to constitute intimidation.[70] It was even held, by an Illinois Court, that attempted coercion of employers by unions, by threatening to strike unless an agreement was signed, was unlawful.[71]

Boycotts and other labor action interfering with interstate commerce were also held by the courts to be in violation of the Sherman Antitrust Act. Under pressure from labor groups, Congress included provisions in the Clayton Act of 1914 declaring that "the labor of a human being is not a commodity or article of commerce." In addition the Clayton Act provided that the anti-trust laws should not be construed to forbid labor organizations or to interfere with the attainment of their "legitimate" objects; it limited the use of the injunction; and it provided a trial by jury for persons accused of violating injunctions by criminal acts. Yet the courts so interpreted the act that it made little, if any, difference to the position of labor under the antitrust laws. In 1940, however, the Supreme Court held that the only type of interference with interstate commerce that the Sherman Act outlaws is a monopolistic attempt to control supplies or prices of goods or to discriminate between purchasers. Hence, even though workers' actions curtail competition between employers by eliminating wage differences, interfere with the movement of goods across state lines through strikes or in other ways, or even result in the destruction of property, they are not punishable under the Sherman Act.[72] Collusive agreements between workers and employers to eliminate competition in the markets for their products are the only labor activities prohibited by the antitrust laws.

Before the Norris–LaGuardia Act, an employer could obtain a

[69] *Loewe* v. *Lawlor*, 208 U.S. 274 (1908).

[70] *American Steel Foundries* v. *Tri-City Central Trades Council*, 257 U.S. 184 (1921); *Truax* v. *Corrigan*, 257 U.S. 312 (1921).

[71] *O'Brien* v. *People*, 216 Ill. 354, 75 N.E. 108 (1905).

[72] *Apex Hosiery Company* v. *Leader*, 310 U.S. 469 (1940).

court injunction preventing workers from taking action detrimental to his business. The courts issued injunctions freely, frequently without notice to labor, without giving labor a hearing and sometimes permanently restraining unions from engaging in actions otherwise lawful. The injunction was used against unions trying to persuade workers who had signed yellow dog contracts to join the union—such persuasion being held to be an attempt to induce breach of contract. There is no doubt that the use of the injunction against labor had been abused and it was in reaction to such abuse that the Federal Anti-Injunction Act was passed in 1932, severely restricting the use of the injunction. It provided that injunctions could only be issued against those directly involved, only after open hearings and only after the court had found that unlawful acts were threatened or would continue causing substantial and irreparable injury to the complainant's property; that the denial of relief would inflict greater injury on the complainant than the granting of relief would inflict on the defendant; that the complainant had no adequate remedy at law and that the officers charged with protecting complainant's property were unable or unwilling to furnish adequate protection. Personal notice of the hearings had to be given to all parties. (Subsequently many states passed similar acts.)

The use of the organized power of labor was given wider scope and greater effectiveness by the Wagner Act of 1935. This act specifically set out to strengthen the position of organized labor in order to put it in an "equal bargaining position" with employers. It imposed no restrictions or obligations on labor unions, provided no dispute machinery, but did impose restrictions and obligations on employers; it was an act "in favor of" organized labor and designed to offset as far as possible all of the disadvantages purportedly existing when labor did not have strong unions to match the "bargaining strength" of their employers. The National Labor Relations Board could issue cease-and-desist orders against employers charged with violating the Act; one of its primary functions was to designate bargaining units and determine the proper representatives of those units; it had no concern with the terms of the collective bargaining contract.

Not only was collective bargaining laid down as basic public policy (this was in itself not new, the desirability of collective bargaining having been affirmed in the Norris–LaGuardia Act) but the assumption was implicit in the Act that for collective bargaining to be effective unions must be strong. The possibility of collective bargaining was supported by the prohibitions laid upon employers against 'interfering with labor organization and the duty laid on them to bargain in good faith; and by the provisions for the supervision of free elections whenever employees requested it (although not oftener than once a year). The strength of the union was supported by the approval of "union security" arrangements, which expressly included the closed shop and, through the absence of limitations, also included many other techniques of assisting an established union to maintain its organized strength, such as preferential hiring and the "check-off" arrangement under which the employer deducts union dues from wages on behalf of the union.

All in all, every practicable support was given to the growth of trade unions and the effective use of their power, while no restraints or obligations were placed upon them. The tactics unions could use and the purposes they could use them for were in no way limited by the Act, but the tactics and purposes of employer action were restricted.

Pruning Back

It was felt by many that Congress had gone "too far" in the Wagner Act; that unions were in "too strong" a position because of it; that something needed to be done now to "equalize" the bargaining power of employers. In particular it was charged that unions took advantage of their position to gouge employers, that is, that unions themselves sabotaged the collective bargaining process by refusing to bargain reasonably and in good faith.

And so the Labor Management Relations Act of 1947, the Taft-Hartley Act, was passed. This Act did not deny that collective bargaining was in the public interest, but it did implicitly deny that strong and protected trade unions were necessary to the successful functioning of a collective bargaining regime.[73]

[73] For an admirably clear analysis of the premises and implications of both the Wagner Act and the Taft-Hartley Act see Donald H. Wollett, *Labor*

Collective bargaining was supported by a reaffirmation of the rights of labor to organize and bargain collectively without employer interference. The unfair labor practices of employers listed in the Wagner Act were maintained (except that employers were now permitted to express their opinion about unions "unless it contains a threat of reprisal, threat of force, or a promise of benefit"). But from certain provisions of the law one can infer that the lawmakers no longer believed in the "need" for collective bargaining. For example, there were provisions giving employees the right to refuse to join a union and the right to get rid of their union, through so-called "de-certification" proceedings, without replacing it by another.

In an attempt to reduce the strength of trade unions the closed shop was prohibited. Closed-shop agreements are now unenforceable, and action can be brought against employers and unions who enter into them. The only permissible union security arrangement is a special kind of union shop which can be established only if a majority of those eligible to vote approve of it. In addition employers and unions who agree to certain kinds of check-off and welfare fund arrangements can be prosecuted. In these respects the Taft-Hartley Act for the first time establishes a government regulation over the terms of the collective bargaining contract.

It is in the provisions regarding "unfair labor practices" that the Taft-Hartley Act differs most conspicuously from the Wagner Act. While the 1935 statute was only concerned with protecting the unions from unfair practices of employers, the 1947 statute concerns itself also with the protection of employers from unfair practices of unions. Indeed, the fact that the new law requires that some unfair union practices be given "priority" before the National Labor Relations Board has been regarded as evidence of partiality for the employers.[74]

Relations and Federal Law (Seattle: University of Washington Press, 1949), especially pp. xxii–xxiii and Chapter IV.

[74] In view of the fact that the NLRB has more work than it can handle and is always very far behind, the priority provision forces them to hear certain employer complaints before dealing with other matters that may have come up earlier. No union complaints have the same priority. Furthermore, the Board is required to request injunctive relief to employers in the case of some union practices and may request injunctions in others. No employer practices are subject to mandatory injunctions.

The following practices are listed as unfair labor practices of unions:

(1) to restrain or coerce employees in the exercise of their right not to join a union;

(2) to restrain or coerce employers in the selection of their representatives for the purposes of collective bargaining;

(3) to attempt to force an employer to discriminate against employees who are not union members (except under a union-shop agreement and then only if the employee has been denied union membership for failure to pay dues or initiation fees);

(4) to refuse to bargain collectively in good faith;

(5) to conduct strikes or boycotts in order to (a) force any employer or self-employed person to join an organization or to cease doing business with any other person; (b) to force an employer to bargain with any other than a certified union; or (c) to discriminate in favor of any particular labor organization in the assignment of work unless the employer is failing to conform to an order of the Board regarding the certified bargaining representative for the employees;

(6) to require employees of organizations covered by a union-shop agreement to pay excessive or discriminatory initiation fees; and

(7) to cause or attempt to cause an employer to pay for services which are not performed or are not to be performed (featherbedding).

The duty to bargain collectively includes the duty to file a sixty-day notice ("cooling-off period") before the termination or proposed modification of an agreement. During this time no strikes are permitted and the union must discuss the problems with employers at reasonable intervals.

There is no way of evaluating partisan complaints that the Taft-Hartley Act pruned back too far the advantage which the Wagner Act had given to trade unions, or to the opposite complaints that the pruning was insufficient and left the unions with bargaining strength far superior to that of employers. The basic assumption of such conflicting complaints, as well as the basic justification of the legislation in question—the notion that there is such a thing as an "equalization of bargaining power"—will have to be examined before more can be said. This will be done in the next chapter, but we may reveal here that the results will be disappointing.

The Public Interest

Ordinarily the public sees these conflicts of views and interests only as conflicts between labor and management, or labor and capital; and the "public's" interest is believed to be chiefly in the "fair" and "peaceful" settlements of the conflicts. The public realizes that it may be injured by labor disputes, but it believes that such injury lies only in the loss of output and the disturbance of the economy through strikes and lock-outs. That permanent injury to the public may ensue from a peaceful and seemingly fair settlement—injury because of monopolistic wage determination—is commonly overlooked.

The government has assisted in the creation of monopoly power of unmeasured magnitude wielded by hundreds of trade unions. When the government creates monopolies in the hands of businessmen, economists are almost unanimous in evaluating adversely the economic effects. Is there a similar consensus regarding the economic effects of the monopoly controls in the hands of labor organizations? Or is the creation and exercise of trade union control over the price and the supply of labor to the employer widely regarded as desirable from the point of view of the public interest? To these questions the next two chapters will address themselves.

PART IV—LABOR POLICIES

CHAPTER 9

Monopolistic Labor Policies: Bargaining Power

Labor and Society: The Size of the Group Called "Labor" · "Pro-Labor" Sentiment · Approval of Labor Monopoly · Arguments for Strong Trade Unions · Two Points of Romantic Semantics

Equalizing the Bargaining Power: The Meaning of Bargaining Power · "Labor—the Most Perishable Commodity" · Workers Must Eat—They Cannot Wait · No Visible Competition for Labor · Conspiracies among Employers · Immobility of Labor · Immobility and Isolated Markets · Profits at the Expense of Wages · Immobility and General Unemployment · Immobility and Nonwage Competition · Corporations as Combinations of Capital · Redressing the Balance · Dealing with Isolated Labor Markets · Dealing with Employers' Collusion · Dealing with "Employer Differentiation"

A DISCUSSION OF governmental labor policies was part of our general survey of governmental aids to monopoly, which included governmental supports of business monopoly and governmental restraints of competition in agricultural markets. But because there are very essential differences between labor and "other commodities" regarding the nature of what is sold and the markets in which it is sold, and because of the social objectives which guide the evaluation of the results of competition and monopoly in the labor markets, the question of "labor monopoly" and monopolistic wage determination calls for further discussion.

LABOR AND SOCIETY

The word "labor" has many different meanings. As used in economic, sociological and political discussions it may refer, among other things, to
1. the labor services actually or potentially supplied, demanded, employed, or sold (i.e., man-hours of work, labor effort);

[333]

2. the actual or potential suppliers (sellers) of labor services (i.e., the workers, owners of labor power);
3. the people who live for the most part on labor income (i.e., the labor income recipients and their dependents);
4. the people who work for compensation or without compensation (i.e., the suppliers of marketed or non-marketed labor, such as housewives, students, as well as gainfully employed workers);
5. the persons who work or seek work for compensation or gain (i.e., the labor force);
6. any specified subdivision of the previous three, for example, non-agricultural wage earners, non-supervisory employees, or workers employed in manufacturing, mining and construction;
7. employee organizations, their leaders, or members (i.e., organized labor, trade unions);
8. the people who regard themselves as members of the "proletariat" exploited by the bourgeois class (i.e., the "labor class" in the Marxian sense).

The Size of the Group Called "Labor"

The relation of "labor" to society depends very much on which of the meanings of labor is referred to. Even the purely quantitative relationships vary elastically with the meanings. Labor in the sense 3—the labor income recipients—is almost identical with the total population, since nearly all of the 150 million people in the United States live for the most part on labor income, as wage and salary workers, as self-employed workers, or as their dependents.[1] Labor in the sense 4—the people who work with or without compensation—is probably identical with the "working-age population," or about 113 million people in 1950; housewives and students often work harder than gainfully employed workers.

Labor in the sense 5, the total labor force, included in 1950

[1] If the incomes from pensions and old-age annuities are regarded as postponed payments for past labor services, the exceptions to the above statement are truly negligible: only a fraction of one percent of the population receive the larger part of their income in the form of interest, dividends or rents.

about 65 million persons.[2] Labor in the sense 6 is a large or small group, depending on the subdivisions included; for example, there were in 1950 over 46 million non-agricultural wage and salary workers in the labor force,[3] there were about 32 million wage and salary workers employed in non-agricultural establishments outside of finance, service, and government,[4] and over 18 million in mining, manufacturing and construction alone.[5] Labor in the sense 7, organized labor, was estimated to run to 15 million.

It is a very special sense in which Marxians speak of the "labor class": a feeling of solidarity on the part of each comrade, of "belonging" to the "proletariat," of being exploited by and opposed to the bourgeois class,—these are essential criteria for this sociological concept. If they are taken seriously, not more than a few million Americans belong to the labor class in this extremely narrow sense; for it was found by an opinion poll that 88 percent of all Americans consider themselves as members of the "middle class" and only 6 percent as members of the "lower class." [6]

"Pro-Labor" Sentiment

The multiplicity of meaning has given rise to much confusion, especially in political discussions. Almost everybody is "on the side of labor" if the widest of the concepts is accepted, since labor is almost the same as the entire society. But only few in the United States are "on the side of labor" if this is interpreted as an endorsement of class war with the destruction of the capitalist order as the major objective. Many are "on the side of labor" if the improvement

[2] The total labor force includes the armed forces. The average civilian labor force was 63 million in 1950. *Annual Report on the Labor Force, 1950.* Bureau of the Census, *Current Population Reports, Labor Force* (Washington: 1951), p. 2.

[3] *Ibid.*

[4] Included in this group are manufacturing, construction, trade, transportation, public utilities, and mining. Finance, service and government employed about 13 million workers. Source: Department of Labor. See *Economic Indicators, February 1951*, prepared for the Joint Committee on the Economic Report by the Council of Economic Advisers (Washington: 1951), p. 8.

[5] *Ibid.*

[6] William A. Lydgate, *What America Thinks* (New York: Thomas Y. Crowell, 1944), p. 159.

of working conditions in industry is under discussion. The number of people "on the side of Labor"—with a capital L—varies with the particular trade union policies or with the particular trade union leaders of the moment.

The interests of these different groups of labor may or may not coincide. What then is "the interest of labor"? The pro-labor sentiment of an economist—thinking of the welfare of the nation; the pro-labor sentiment of a politician—thinking of the votes in his constituency; the pro-labor sentiment of a student of the labor movement—thinking of the progress in the battle for the right to organize; the pro-labor sentiment of a social worker—thinking of the poverty of particular workers' families; and the pro-labor sentiment of a communist organizer—thinking of the overthrow of the government and the rule of the proletariat; these are very different things and one will do well to distinguish them.

I know of no economist of our time who would not accept a higher living standard (real income) of the entire people as the most desirable, or among the most desirable, of social objectives. There may be differences of opinion regarding the importance of equality of income, although I believe that the overwhelming majority of economists would agree that greater equality is preferable to lesser equality, provided total income is not reduced in consequence of the change in relative shares. If one includes in "labor" all the people who obtain the greater part of their livelihood from labor income, the interest of labor can almost be identified with the national interest.

If labor is more narrowly defined, a discrepancy between the interests of labor and of the rest of society may arise. For example, if only unionized workers or only industrial workers (according to some specified definition) were to be called "labor," then most economists would refuse to be partial and to put the interest of "labor" thus defined above the interest of the rest of society. They would judge the desirability of any action affecting the income of "labor" according to what it may do to the size of the total income of the nation and, given that size, to the equality of its distribution. This remark will become relevant in some phase of the discussions of collective bargaining and trade union wage policy.

Approval of Labor Monopoly

The evaluation of monopolistic attempts to increase the real income of labor will likewise vary according to what group is meant by "labor." Assume for a moment that by collective bargaining labor could increase its share of the national income without affecting, in either the short or the long run, the size of the national income. If labor includes almost the whole of society, the gain it achieves would be at the expense of a negligible minority, and if the share of the minority was sufficiently large, the shift in the distribution of income would be applauded by those who considered the rich minority to be expropriators and exploiters; others might deplore and denounce it as the result of black-mail and extortion. But, strictly within the given assumptions, a "welfare economist," applying his test—total income unchanged, inequality reduced— could only welcome the effect of the monopolistic action, provided that inequality within the labor group was not enhanced.

The evaluation is different if "labor" is a smaller group and the "rest of society" not merely a rich "upper crust." For in this case there is no presumption that the inequality of income is reduced when the share of labor increases. If the rest of society includes many who are worse off than the members of the group called "labor," then the monopolistic action that increases labor's share may injure others who are less prosperous. The economist, therefore, would not be able to agree that matters are improved by this change in distribution.

It is a fact, however, that most economists in the last one hundred and fifty years have been decidely sympathetic to the "combination" of workers and to the collective utilization of the improved market position thereby attained. However opposed they were to monopoly in general and to monopolistic price determination by businessmen's coalitions, they approved of workingmen's coalitions and their attempts to change the wage bargain in labor's favor. Although John Stuart Mill, the great classical economist, could write that ". . . monopoly, in all its forms is the taxation of the industrious for the support of indolence, if not plunder," [7] he was not

[7] John Stuart Mill, *Principles of Political Economy* (First edition, 1848;

afraid of labor monopolies. Although convinced that competition was beneficial in the labor market as elsewhere, he believed that combinations of workers through trade unions would not effectively limit competition, but would rather be an aid to a "free market for labor." [8]

The laws against combination of workmen were abolished in England in 1825 and Mill expressed satisfaction with the repeal of anti-union legislation, which he called "a government interference in which the end and the means are alike odious." [9] He added a statement, to which nearly every economist probably subscribes: "If it were possible for the working classes, by combining among themselves, to raise or keep up the general rate of wages, it needs hardly be said that this would be a thing not to be punished, but to be welcome and rejoiced at." [10]

What Mill in his later years, and many others after him, had in mind was that workers' combinations, if they were effectual, might succeed in obtaining a moderate increase in real wages at the expense of profits, perhaps that part of profit which the employers could make only because of certain advantages they had over unorganized workers. Some of Mill's contemporaries and successors formulated the theory of "unequal bargaining power" and of the consequent exploitation of the workers and corresponding profits of the employers, and stressed the need for a redress of the balance by an equalization of bargaining power. If this, and only this, is what the combination of workers in unions achieves, "labor monopoly" is different from almost all other kinds of monopoly and its promotion by government is surely indicated.

third edition, 1852; seventh edition, 1871; London: Longmans Green, 1926), p. 792.

[8] *Ibid.*, p. 937.

[9] *Ibid.*, p. 933.

[10] *Ibid.*, p. 934. But Mill reasoned that the masses of workers are "too numerous and too widely scattered to combine at all, much more to combine effectually. If they could do so," they might be able to obtain "an increase of general wages at the expense of profits. But the limits of this power are narrow; and were they to attempt to strain it beyond those limits, this could only be accomplished by keeping a part of their number permanently out of employment." In this formulation the statement appeared only in the seventh edition of Mill's work, published in 1871. The formulation in earlier editions did not concede the possibility that wage increases might be obtained at the expense of profits without leading to unemployment.

Arguments for Strong Trade Unions

Although it would be useless and silly to use these pages to justify or denounce, attack or defend, support or criticize labor coalitions, it may be useful and sensible to present in an orderly fashion the main issues of the controversy about the economic function and social desirability of strong labor unionism. An attempt to unscramble the mixture of arguments may do some injustice to some, since it is so easy through slight twists in the formulation to make appear nonsensical what would make good sense in another wording or context. Nevertheless we shall be able to think more clearly if we take to pieces and reduce to their logical elements the composite arguments that are usually presented.

1. *Arguments relating to inequality of bargaining strength.*

(a) Unorganized workers are at a disadvantage because labor is the most perishable of commodities.

(b) Unorganized workers are at a disadvantage because they have no reserve funds and cannot hold out as long as the employers.

(c) Unorganized workers are at a disadvantage because of their limited mobility which prevents them from leaving inferior jobs in areas or fields in which competition among employers is limited.

(d) Unorganized workers are at a disadvantage because employers combine to restrain competition for labor and to keep wages down.

(e) Unorganized workers are at a disadvantage because chronic unemployment makes it hard for employed labor to change jobs and this immobility reduces employers' competition for labor.

(f) Unorganized workers are at a disadvantage because non-wage attractions and attachments to individual employers reduce labor mobility as well as employers' competition for labor.

(g) Unorganized workers are at a disadvantage because of the combination of capital and the organization of owners in corporations.

2. *Arguments relating to certain technical defects of the labor market.*

(a) An unorganized labor market cannot determine wage differentials in accordance with exact job differences.

(b) An unorganized labor market tends to produce either inadequate adjustments or over-adjustments to changes in demand.

(c) An unorganized labor market tends to generate upward and downward spirals of wage levels.

3. *Arguments relating to real wages and national income.*

(a) Unions can raise the workers' real wages by bringing about increases of total production.

(b) Unions can raise the workers' real wages entirely at the expense of profits without adverse effects upon total production.

(c) Unions can raise the workers' real wages, the effect upon total production being undetermined but unimportant compared with the improvement of the workers' share.

(d) Unions cannot raise the real wages of all workers, but can change relative wages of different labor groups in favor of organized labor.

4. *Arguments relating to ethics, justice, and workers' morale.*

(a) The contrast between the poverty and insecurity of workers and the affluence of their employers is morally wrong and such unequal sharing in the fruits of their combined efforts can be corrected with the help of strong unions.

(b) The large profits of enterprise are evidence of rank exploitation of the workers, who should combine to secure fairer wages.

(c) Justice demands recognition of the rights of individual workers in their jobs, and only strong unions can secure these rights.

(d) In the interest of justice and of workers' morale it is necessary to provide a machinery for the redress of grievances, and only a strong union can provide it.

(e) The worker must be provided with a sense of participation in the affairs of the enterprise in which he works, and this is made possible by membership in a strong union.

(f) Workers should acquire class-consciousness in order to be better prepared for the class war and the political struggle against capitalism; trade unions are important instruments in the political struggle and have a significant role in preparing for the "expropriation of the expropriators."

Of the arguments relating to ethics, justice, and workers'

morale, the first two, 4 (a) and 4 (b), merely reaffirm the existence of an unequal distribution of income and affirm that it is due to the existence of "exploitation"—and hence could be removed by removing the inequality in the market position of workers and employers. In this respect they are merely other ways of putting the básic assumptions of the first group of arguments we have listed. Insofar, however, as they are meant to be conclusive arguments for strong unions, requiring no further analysis, they are purely emotional in character resting only on sympathy for the underdog, and are beyond the pale of economic reasoning. Argument 4 (f) is part of the Marxian doctrine, assigning to trade unions chiefly a political role.[11] This argument is categorically rejected by almost all American trade unions. Arguments 4 (c), 4 (d) and 4 (e) are of great significance everywhere, but they are largely irrelevant to our discussion [12] which concerns only the economics of monopolistic or competitive wage determination and, at the moment, the question why many stern opponents of monopoly approve monopolistic labor organization. These three arguments point to highly important functions of trade unions apart from wage determination.

Two Points of Romantic Semantics

The economic arguments for collective rather than competitive participation of workers in wage determination will be discussed in the pages that follow. But before we enter upon this discussion we must recall and take care of two problems of semantics lest they hinder our understanding of the problems in question.

First, it is insisted by some that one ought not to use the words "monopoly" and "monopolistic" in connection with labor unions and their practices.[13] This is chiefly a matter of sensitiveness about

[11] Marx did not believe that trade unions could succeed in securing higher wage rates in the long run. Trade unions should be supported, according to him, as instruments of class war.

[12] Improvements of workers' morale may increase productivity and thus become relevant to the discussion of efficiency wage rates.

[13] Complaining about the increasingly widespread application of these terms to labor organizations and warning against "superficial analogies that stimulate namecalling," Richard A. Lester charges that "Economists sometimes seem to overlook the fact that unions do not 'sell labor,' are not profit-

words that have acquired unpleasant connotations. If employers
are much better off than workers, even after everything unions
have done, how can the workers' coalition be called a monopoly?
If labor organization is good, how can it be called monopolistic
—which makes it appear bad? We have considered this argument
in an earlier chapter—at the end of Chapter 2—and shall not repeat here what was said there. It should be clear that the elimination of competition among workers in their bargaining with employers is the first and major objective of trade unions.[14] One may,
of course, deny that certain unions have *much* monopoly power, or
make *excessive* use of their monopoly power, but to deny that
union wage policy is a part of the general problem of monopoly
would be sheer wilfulness—or romantic sentimentality.

Second, it is insisted that "labor is not a commodity" and that,
therefore, any generalizations about commodities and about the
markets in which and the prices at which they are sold do not apply to labor, the labor market and wage rates. The proposition that
labor is not a commodity was not originally meant either as a
statement of fact or as a definition or classification for purposes of
economic analysis; it was meant to be normative, its significance
was moral, religious, political, and legal. It had a special bearing
on the discussion of slavery and slave labor—on the purchase and
sale of human beings. But also in the discussion of wage labor

---

making institutions, and are as much political as they are economic." Richard
A. Lester, "Reflections on the 'Labor Monopoly' Issue," *Journal of Political
Economy*, Vol. LV (1947), pp. 513, 517. Exactly the same could be said,
and has been said, about cartels and trade associations. Cartels and trade associations, ordinarily, do not sell anything either. Some of them have even
less direct contact with actual price making than the unions have with wage
making. Nonetheless, any influence they exercise on price making is clearly
monopolistic in intent as well as in effect. Yet, there are those who declare
that "it is unscientific and unfair to treat trade unions in the same way as
combinations of capitalists." Forrest Revere Black, "How Far is the Theory
of Trust Regulation Applicable to Labor Unions?" *Michigan Law Review*,
Vol. XXVIII (1929), p. 980.

[14] "By trial and error, they [the workers] have discovered that to serve
their own self-interest, they would have to stop competing against each other,
and act in concert. Only in this way could they obtain some measure of control over the labor supply." Report and Recommendations of the Labor Committee of the Twentieth Century Fund, in S. T. Williamson and Herbert
Harris, *Trends in Collective Bargaining* (New York: Twentieth Century
Fund, 1945), p. 222.

the normative statement was important, particularly in connection with the law against combination in restraint of trade. In the United States this last issue was much debated.

Although since 1842 no court of final jurisdiction in the United States had held labor organizations to be illegal combinations in restraint of trade, and the Sherman Antitrust Act was not generally considered to be applicable to labor, nevertheless several of the first cases decided under the Act had to do with labor disputes. The severe application of the law to trade unions raised a widespread fear on the part of labor leaders that the courts would so interpret the law that trade unions would be greatly restricted.[15] Organized labor, therefore, pressed Congress strongly for action and the Congress, in the Clayton Act of 1914, attempted to make it clear that the "legitimate" activities of labor were exempted from the antitrust laws. This was done in Section 6, which provided "that the labor of a human being is not a commodity or article of commerce." These words, according to Samuel Gompers, President of the American Federation of Labor, "are sledgehammer blows to the wrongs and injustice so long inflicted upon the workers." This statutory declaration, according to him, is "the industrial magna charta upon which the working people will rear their structure of industrial freedom." [16]

Although the declaration that labor was not a "commodity" was designed merely as a direction to the courts for the interpretation of the law,[17] many have read into it a meaning for economic analysis, and there it does not make much sense. We shall not enlarge on the fact that most of these semantic controversies are utterly futile [18] and that definitions and classifications can be judged only in relation to the purpose for which they are used. The way

[15] Alpheus T. Mason, *Organized Labor and the Law* (Durham, N.C.: Duke University Press, 1925), p. 173.

[16] Samuel Gompers, "The Charter of Industrial Freedom," *The American Federationist*, Vol. XXI (1914), p. 971.

[17] Alpheus T. Mason, *op. cit.*, pp. 175–202. The hopes of the labor leaders were soon dashed by the courts which interpreted the important provisions of the Act as having made no changes in the law.

[18] Similar examples: "money is not a commodity," "bank deposits are not money," "stocks of consumers goods are not capital," "economics is not a science," "tomatoes are not vegetables," "poker is not gambling," "applesauce is not a dessert," "water is not a beverage."

most economists have defined "commodity" and have used this concept, it certainly covers human labor sold at a price. It would be difficult to improve on the following observation about the point at issue: "unless we understand clearly that labor *is* a commodity, in spite of all pious pronouncements to the contrary, we shall never understand the phenomena of industrial relations. But we shall also not understand industrial relations unless we realize that labor is much *more* than a commodity, and that the labor-bargain involves a complex set of psychological, sociological, even theological relationships out of which the commodity aspect is abstracted."[19]

EQUALIZING THE BARGAINING POWER

The first set of arguments supporting the desirability of replacing a system of individual wage "bargaining"[20] by a system of collective bargaining relates to the inequality of the bargaining power of individual workers competing with one another for jobs, and that of their employers.

The Meaning of Bargaining Power

The theories explaining "labor's natural bargaining disadvantage" and the "employer's superior bargaining strength" have been concerned with the reasons for the inequality, but have rarely attempted to explain the *meaning* of "bargaining power." Apparently it has been assumed that everybody knows intuitively what it is or perhaps knows from personal experience in shopping, selling and bargaining what it means to be at a distinct disadvantage. Unfortunately, it is a most difficult task to give precise meaning to the concept even if one only wants to know what it is and has no ambition to measure it.[21]

[19] Kenneth E. Boulding, *Religious Perspectives of College Teaching in Economics.* (New Haven: Edward W. Hazen Foundation, 1950), p. 21.

[20] Of course, the individual worker standing alone rarely has a chance to "bargain" in the sense of negotiating. All he can do, as a rule, is to accept the bargain offered by the employer. Individual bargaining means nothing but entering into the wage contract without union aid.

[21] Analyses relevant to the issue were attempted by A. C. Pigou, *Principles and Methods of Industrial Peace* (London: Macmillan, 1905), Ap-

The few definitions that were attempted stressed different aspects of bargaining. For example, one writer regarded the "power to withhold" as the essential thing; [22] another held that it was more important to ask which of the parties would suffer a greater loss from such withholding, and consequently defined bargaining power as the cost of imposing a loss upon the other party.[23] It was objected to this definition that the purpose of bargaining was not to impose a loss on the other party but to gain an advantage for oneself, whereas "the ability to gain an advantage is not always commensurate with the ability to impose a loss with a given disadvantage to one's self." [24] In an attempt to emphasize the advantage which it could yield, bargaining power was then defined as the ability to obtain the best possible price obtainable under all the circumstances prevailing, including the preferences of all parties concerned and the conditions of all markets directly or indirectly involved.[25] In other words, not merely the degrees of competition to which each party is exposed, but all resistances and repercussions they both may have to face in all related markets are regarded as important determinants of "bargaining power."

Perhaps we can get at these complex concepts with some simpler reasoning and simpler formulations. If we are out to measure either the potential gains or the actual gains which a seller

---

pendix A; and *The Economics of Welfare* (London: Macmillan, 4th ed., 1938), pp. 451–61; also by Sumner H. Slichter, "Impact of Social Security Legislation upon Mobility and Enterprise," *American Economic Review*, Vol. XXX (1940), Suppl. p. 57, and by John T. Dunlop and Benjamin Higgins, " 'Bargaining Power' and Market Structures," *Journal of Political Economy*, Vol. L (1942), pp. 1–26, reproduced in John T. Dunlop, *Wage Determination under Trade Unions* (New York: Macmillan, 1944), pp. 74–94.

[22] John R. Commons and J. B. Andrews, *Principles of Labor Legislation* (New York: Harper and Brothers, 4th ed., 1936), p. 372.

[23] Sumner H. Slichter, *op. cit.*, p. 57.

[24] Dunlop and Higgins, *op. cit.*, p. 2.

[25] Dunlop and Higgins, *op. cit.*, pp. 4–5, 23. Although no definition in words is offered, the following definition can be synthesized from the glossary given for the symbols used in the algebraic definition: "the bargaining advantage of a factor" is equal to the ratio of the excess of "the actual price paid for the factor" over "the supply price of the factor that would rule under pure competition in all relevant markets, for the number of units actually taken," to "the demand price of the commodity that would rule under pure competition in all relevant markets, for the number of units actually taken." *Op. cit.*, p. 5.

could make because of his "bargaining power," we must compare
the highest price he could get, or the price he actually gets, with
the price he would get if he had no bargaining power at all. To
have no bargaining power at all means to have no alternative other
than to take or leave the price that is offered. Bargaining power
would then imply the ability to get more than is first offered.[26]
But the ability to get more implies not merely a power to ask for
more, hold out for more, or fight for more, but also an ability of
the other party to give more. Here lies the root of the complications, because the bargaining strength or weakness of the worker,
if it is defined by his ability or inability to insist on and obtain a
better wage, is then a hybrid between his strategic position and
the economic position of the employer. This comprehensive concept of bargaining power may serve the purpose of comparing the
positions of different worker groups with one another, but is of
no use in comparing the strengths of the worker with that of his
employer.[27]

Assume a certain group of workers has had no bargaining
power at all and always has accepted whatever wage the employer
was offering. Now the workers form a union, secure a closed-shop
agreement, and possess unlimited strike funds. In other words,
they now have what it ordinarily takes to achieve substantial bargaining advantages. Yet, the employer may not be able to pay
another cent because if he paid it he would be forced out of busi-

[26] Since power may be either fully or only partially exercised, the price
actually obtained need not measure the full power. Bargaining power as a
"*potential*" would be measured by the difference between the price the seller
could obtain if he used all the power at his command and the price he would
get if he had no alternative but to take or leave what he is offered. *Utilized*
bargaining power would be measured by the difference between the price the
seller actually obtains and the price he would get if he had no alternative but
to take or leave what he is offered.

[27] If W_1 and W_2 are two groups of workers and E_1 and E_2 are their employers, three kinds of comparisons of bargaining strength are possible, assuming that each party uses all the strength it has and that we know the
wages that would be paid if workers did not have any strength at all: (1)
Compare the gains of W_1 and W_2 if E_1 and E_2 are exactly alike in every respect; (2) compare the gains of W_1 and W_2 if E_1 and E_2 are in very different
positions; (3) compare the strength of W_1 with that of E_1 and the strength of
W_2 with that of E_2. How this last comparison—which is the relevant one for
our purposes—can be made is unanswered.

ness. The increased power of the workers would be of no avail. Expressed in the most drastic and unpolished form: "Even if you wrest from the other fellow all he has got, you won't get much if he hasn't got anything."

This shows why we need the comprehensive concept of bargaining power, which includes the position of the other party in all relevant markets, if we wish to explain the results of a bargain. The potential improvement of the wage bargain for the workers will depend to a large extent on the potential increase in the prices the employers may get for their products without losing too much business, and on the potential reduction in prices the employers may be able to force upon the suppliers of materials and other means of production.[28] The extended or comprehensive concept of bargaining power can throw light on why labor monopolies which by all institutional standards may be equally strong will have to accept relatively low wages in one sector of the economy and can obtain relatively high wages in another. On the other hand, this comprehensive concept cannot be the thing people are talking about when they say that workers have less bargaining power than their employers. For this discussion a concept of bargaining strength which includes all circumstances that bear on the demand for labor includes too much. A narrower concept is needed, which concentrates on the positions of the two parties in relation to each other.

Since the matter is so intricate, we may try to put it in still another way. There are two different issues involved in the claim that collective bargaining be substituted for the inequitable wage bargain between the individual helpless worker and his powerful employer. One is the question whether workers in competition with one another are at a disadvantage relative to their employers, a disadvantage that calls for correction. The other question is how much the elimination of inter-worker competition can do to increase their wages. For the second question, which allows also for the possibility of an over-correction of any disadvantage that

[28] In technical language, the bargaining strength of the workers acting in concert (e.g., through a union) depends on the elasticity of demand for their labor, which in turn depends among other things on the elasticity of demand for the product and on the elasticity of supply of complementary and substitutable factors of production.

may have initially existed, the extended, comprehensive concept
of bargaining power will be relevant. But the first question is not
directed at the entire possible gain but only at such part of that
gain as would be needed to compensate for an initial disadvantage
in bargaining strength. But what is this initial disadvantage? We
still have not ascertained just what that bargaining power is which
is so unequal, according to the arguments set forth. The point
is that we shall not be able to establish a meaning of the terms
before we examine the arguments. Only by going into the arguments can we find out what their proponents may have had in
mind.

"Labor—the Most Perishable Commodity"

One of the most widely repeated arguments is that workers
have an inferior bargaining position because the commodity they
have to sell is the most perishable of all commodities. There are
commodities that last at least a day or two, while labor will not
even last a minute. Any labor hour not sold is forever lost; "to-morrow, to-day's labor will no longer exist." [29]

Literally interpreted, the idea that labor is the most perishable of all commodities is nonsense. All services are perishable.
Yesterday's services, whether of land, labor, or capital are gone
with yesterday and can never be recovered. Consider, for example,
the services of a commodity that has infinite life for all practical
purposes. If the services which land, a tunnel, a national park, are
capable of yielding to-day are not used to-day, they are forever lost,
even though the physical asset is still there to yield new services
to-morrow. Of course, some things are more perishable than others
in the sense that the service-yielding life of some assets is relatively fixed and limited whether or not the services are used. If a
piece of capital equipment will hold for another twenty years of
service and is not used this year, it may still be used for the twenty

[29] "What he withholds to-day cannot be sold to-morrow, for labour is
more perishable than cut flowers. To-morrow, to-day's labour will no longer
exist." R. G. Hawtrey, *The Economic Problem* (London: Longmans, Green,
1925), p. 29. The idea was first advanced in W. T. Thornton's *On Labour*
(Second edition, 1870). See W. H. Hutt, *The Theory of Collective Bargaining* (London: King & Son, 1930), pp. 42–45.

years thereafter, provided that technological change does not make it obsolete.[30] But if a worker has twenty more years of work in him and he is not employed this year, one year of his service life is gone—there are only nineteen more years left. Labor is of course not unique in this respect. The services of any commodity the length of whose service life is not dependent on use are equally perishable in this sense. This is equally true of land and, as we have seen, of anything with an infinite service life; it is true of capital funds; it is true also of capital equipment if obsolescence is the determining factor of its useful life; it is true of buildings or equipment whose wear and tear does not depend on use but just on the passage of time.

In any event, while labor is perishable, although not necessarily more perishable than other services, it is not for this reason that workers can be held to be in an inferior bargaining position. Indeed, it would not help if labor could be stored. It is absurd to think that wage rates would be higher if labor were not perishable and could be stored. (Imagine the crash on the labor market if large stocks of non-perishable labor, withheld and stored for a certain time, were suddenly dumped on the market.)

The perishability argument for labor's bargaining disadvantage is probably an illogical offshoot of a very real and hard fact, namely, that workers often cannot wait, that they cannot hold out for higher wages, because they have inadequate financial reserves and their families must eat.

Workers Must Eat—They Cannot Wait

This hard fact, undeniable as it is, is not of itself an explanation for a bargaining disadvantage. But it may be part of such an explanation when other facts are added. We shall see the role that it really plays, but first we must, for the sake of clarity, distinguish several ideas that are here confounded.

That workers are poor and must sell their labor in order to sur-

[30] Some pieces of capital equipment deteriorate faster if they are *not* used; some call for maintenance regardless of use, or even in excess of the outlays needed when used. One speaks in these instances of "negative user cost." John Maynard Keynes, *The General Theory of Employment, Interest and Money* (New York: Harcourt, Brace, 1936), p. 53.

vive is, of course, a fundamental reason why the supply of labor is what it is. If workers were not so poor, if everyone had a home, a piece of land, some chickens, rabbits, or even a cow, they would surely offer less labor for sale than they do without these "reserves." Or if each worker were paid a weekly minimum by the government, say in the form of family allowances or unemployment benefits, his eagerness to sell his labor would be smaller than without such aid. In other words, any income that he has apart from the wages he earns for his labor will affect his supply of labor. Thus the amounts of labor supplied (i.e., offered for sale) at various wage rates tend to be smaller if the workers have "outside income" or wealth. And if the supply of labor is smaller, the wage rate will be higher. Now, if this is all that the argument about the workers' "inability to wait" means to affirm, there is nothing wrong with it. One might call it confusing to speak of "bargaining power" when really a change in the "offer curve" of labor is involved, and might reserve the terms "bargaining power" for the ability to obtain better wages, given the workers' preferences for work and leisure. Furthermore, one might note that the effect of financial reserves on the daily or weekly supply of labor is probably not the thing that people had in mind when they wrote or talked about the individual workers' bargaining disadvantage and tried to explain it by the employers' "ability to wait" compared with that of the workers.

Labor, according to this view, is in a disadvantageous bargaining position because of the difference in financial reserves which allows the employer to wait longer for labor than the workers can wait for wages.[31] If this theory—that prices are affected by the comparative ability to wait—were correct, for commodities as well as for services, the prices of foodstuffs and medicines would always be excessive just because consumers could not wait for them. If some of these necessities are in fact over-priced and others are not, it is because the degree of competition among the producers is low with respect to some and high with respect to others. A medicine for which there is no substitute as a cure for a fatal disease will probably be very expensive if there is only one pro-

[31] An excellent survey of this and many related ideas is contained in Hutt's book cited in footnote 29 above.

ducer who can make it. Its price will come down quickly when the number of producers becomes large. The ability to wait for the medicine may be no greater than before: the sick still would die without it. Yet, competition among producers would pull down the price. (And incidentally, the financial reserves of the producers would also be irrelevant to the story.)

The argument, in its naive form, says in effect that employers will pay workers much less than they could profitably pay, because they can get away with it. The worker has to accept the wage offered or starve. While we may accept the statement that unorganized workers frequently have little alternative than to accept the wage offered, we must ask why this wage should be below the competitive one, that is, below the wage that would equate the cost of hiring a worker to the value of the product he could produce. In other words, why should it be below the wage the worker could get even if he did hold out?

If unlimited competition existed among employers—and the financial straits of the workers *per se* would be no sufficient reason for the absence of such competition among employers—every profit-seeking employer would be anxious to hire more workers when he could get them at a cost below what they are worth to him, and any worker receiving from one employer less than the net value of his product would be able to get a job with another employer at a higher wage. It would not be necessary for the worker to withhold his labor and hold out for the higher wage; employers would hang out their signs "Help Wanted" as long as help was so cheap that they could make money by hiring more. Now, if you should doubt that this would really happen in the world we live in, if you should think that all this is "pure theory" —you may be right, though not because workers are poor and cannot wait, but because employers may not compete so vigorously with one another as was assumed in the theory.

The lack of competition for workers among the employers and the lack of financial reserves on the part of workers *may* be connected facts—and this is why there is truth in this argument. The worker's lack of financial reserves may make it difficult if not impossible for him to move to better jobs, even if they are available. The employer may know that his workers cannot quit even if he pays them a relatively low wage. At the same time he may also know that he cannot get more workers at that low wage, that he would have to pay more to attract them; but this he may be unwilling to do Thus we see this possible, though not necessary link: The lack of funds reduces the workers' mobility, and the lack of workers' mobility may be one of several factors reducing employers' competition for labor. It is the latter, the lack of employers' competition for labor, which must be regarded as the necessary condition of labor's disadvantage in individual wage bargains.

No Visible Competition for Labor

Reduced workers' mobility, due to lack of funds or other reasons, is only one of several factors behind the lack of employers' competition for labor. We shall presently discuss it more fully and discuss also some other possible causes of lacking or restrained competition for labor. But before we do so we ought to pause a little and reflect whether and how unlimited competition can be "seen" by an observer and, furthermore, whether the absence of certain kinds of "competitive" acts would indicate the absence of competition.

A popular misconception associates competition always with active rivalry and with positive efforts on the part of the competitor to keep his rivals from getting something that he wants to get. Such forms of competition, however, are rare. Incidentally, they would not exist in purely competitive markets, neither in the model nor in reality. They do not normally exist in the labor market. Not often do we hear of employer A approaching John Smith, trying to persuade him to quit work with employer B and take a job with him at higher wages and better conditions. If these were the only forms of active competition, it would mean that there is no competition between you and me as buyers of meat or oranges or handkerchiefs. I have never tried to talk the storekeeper into selling his wares to me instead of to you. Our competition takes a very different form. At the present prices of oranges you and I buy certain amounts. We compete for the available supply simply by our willingness to buy, and if together we want to buy more oranges than are on the market the price will rise. Our competition is unrestricted as long as we buy all we want at the price. We could restrict competition, for example, if we conspired to buy less than we would be inclined to buy at the present price, for the purpose of depressing the price.

Whether it is oranges or labor: competition among buyers is unrestricted, although "invisible," as long as the buyers do not restrict their purchases in an attempt to influence the price or in the knowledge that larger quantities could be had only at a higher price.

Conspiracies among Employers

The buyers of labor may restrict their purchases as a result of explicit or implicit understandings among themselves. Such downright conspiracies or tacit understandings can surely put workers who are bargaining individually at a serious disadvantage. Employers, being few in numbers and in the same social group, can easily act in concert to keep down wages while workers, being numerous and each desperately in need of a job, are helpless—with- union—against the solid employer front.

It is reported that conspiracies among employers to restrict employment in order to keep wage rates down have always existed. Adam Smith in 1776 claimed that "Masters are always and everywhere in a sort of tacit, but constant and uniform combination, not to raise the wages of labour above their actual rate." [32] In modern times attempts of employers and employers' associations to influence the labor market have been notorious chiefly in combating collective actions of trade unions and, in particular, in discriminating against individual workers who were known as "agitators" or "trouble makers." But we also have reports about employers' combinations to restrict competition for local labor. In a recent study of the movement of factory workers in a New England industrial community, for example, the investigators found that "there was relatively little active competition among employers for labor because of the gentlemen's agreement between a considerable number of the firms not to hire labor away from each

[32] Adam Smith, *An Inquiry into the Nature and Causes of the Wealth of Nations* (1st ed., 1776, Routledge edition 1903), Book I, Chapter VIII, p. 51.

other." [33] If a worker applied for a job in one firm, that firm even checked with his previous employer to see if the worker was wanted back; if so, he was not hired. If new firms came into town and offered higher wages in order to attract labor, pressure was brought through the Chamber of Commerce to force the new firms into line. "Pirating" of workers was a severely frowned upon practice.

Restrained competition, short of collusion, may also exist if each employer refrains from doing certain things because he expects retaliatory actions by others. The economist uses the term "noncollusive oligopsony" to denote the situation in which each buyer, in making his offer or in determining the amount of his purchases, takes account of expected retaliatory reactions on the part of his competitors in the buying market. There is every reason to believe that this situation may at times exist in many a local labor market.[34]

[33] Charles A. Myers and W. Rupert Maclaurin, *The Movement of Factory Workers* (New York: Wiley and Sons, 1943), p. 40.

[34] We have no knowledge of the frequency of actual conspiracy or of noncollusive oligopsony among employers, and I doubt that we can really find out. In order to indicate the kind of information we should need for diagnosing a case of collusive or noncollusive oligopsony, I shall sketch an imaginary hearing with an employer and assume that all answers are truthful.

> Q. Would you be able—if you wanted—to find more labor of the same quality as you are employing and at the same wage rate as you are paying?
> A. No. (If the answer is "Yes," the employer is in a position of pure competition in the labor market. He apparently does not employ more workers, either because it would cost too much to produce more—increasing cost of production—or he does not "need" any more workers, that is, he is in a monopolistic position in the selling of his product—in other words, he sees the limitations of his selling market.)
> Q. If you were able to obtain more labor of adequate quality and at the same wage rate, would you find it profitable and would you be willing to hire?
> A. Yes. (If the answer were "No" it would fit in with a "Yes" to the first question.)
> Q. Would you be able to find some more labor of adequate quality if you paid a higher wage rate than you are paying?
> A. Yes. (If the answer were "No," I would doubt its accuracy.)
> Q. Why don't you pay higher wages and get more workers?
> A_1 It would not be profitable; my labor cost would be too high.
> A_2 Other employers would be mad at me.

On the other hand, there is also every reason to believe that these restraints of competition for labor, collusive or noncollusive, will not last long in periods of rising demand. In the New England study mentioned it was found that under the impact of a wartime labor shortage, these agreements became weaker and tended to be maintained only between firms holding war contracts. In general, the probability is great that, when demand increases, each employer would be so eager to obtain workers that he would violate such agreements and offer higher wages anyway.

In periods of unemployment, on the other hand, the presumption would be that agreements to keep down wages would not be necessary, since employers could get all the labor they needed at the going wage rates. There may be exceptions for certain categories of skilled labor which may be somewhat scarce even during periods of unemployment. Employers may agree among themselves not to compete for these more qualified workers. Employers may thus succeed in keeping labor costs down in times of slack business and at the same time they may not be seriously inconvenienced so long as they can get enough of these skilled workers to carry on their limited operations.

A_3 Other employers would also start paying higher wages, so that I should not get many more workers and yet would have to pay much more to keep what I have.

Diagnosis   I (based on A_1): The case is a "monopsonistic" one: the employer restricts employment because he does not wish to pay higher wages.

Diagnosis   II (based on A_2): The case is one of "collusive oligopsony": the employer has some explicit or tacit understanding with other employers to avoid wage increases.

Diagnosis III (based on A_3): The case seems to be one of "noncollusive oligoposony": the employer wants to avoid a tug-of-war for scarce labor in which each tries to outbid the other.

I have no opinion about the frequency of these "findings" if we could obtain them in reality. In making this statement I am retracting one that I made a few years ago when I said: "I venture the opinion that neither of the two cases [of oligopsony] occurs frequently in reality." Fritz Machlup, "Monopolistic Wage Determination as a Part of the General Problem of Monopoly," in *Wage Determination and the Economics of Liberalism,* Economic Institute of the Chamber of Commerce of the United States (Washington: 1947), p. 58. Large parts of the present chapter and the next are based on this paper.

We conclude that restraints by employers of competition for
common labor (unskilled or of moderate skills) are unnecessary—
and thus without effect—in times of unemployment, and evaded
and transgressed—and thus again without effect—in times of over-
employment, and therefore significant only in times where demand
is neither slack nor booming and labor, thus, is neither plentiful
nor especially scarce. This leaves the periods of "normalcy" as
the only times in which the restraints may become important;
whether this means "most of the time" or only relatively brief
periods we do not know. With regard to some highly skilled labor
the restraints may be effective in slack as well as normal times.

Immobility of Labor

From the discussion of "deliberate" restrictions by employers
of competition for workers we return now to the theme previously
introduced: the "natural" limitations of employers' competition
which are due to labor immobility. By immobility of labor we
mean the failure of workers to take advantage of better job opportunities because of lack of information, lack of funds to pay
the costs of moving, lack of housing facilities at the new places,
lack of necessary permits, licences, initiations, or because of any
other institutional obstacles to transfer.

The workers' failure to move because of their unwillingness
to move, that is, their failure to be attracted by what to the outside observers may appear as better job opportunities is a different story. For some problems, aversion to moving and obstacles to
moving may be treated alike because they have the same consequences. But for other problems it is essential to make a difference between "I-am-not-willing-to-move" and "I-am-not-able-to-
move," and where this difference is significant we should reserve
the term immobility for the latter. All of these concepts, incidentally,—"movement," "mobility" and "immobility"—may refer
to transfers between geographic regions or between different occupations or both.

Ordinarily we speak of immobility only if the obstacles to movement are "institutional," in the sense of being subject to social
control or conceivably avoidable or removable. In a literal sense,

land is immobile; but for purposes of economic analysis it is usually preferable to regard land at significantly different locations
as land of different kind or quality. Applying the same reasoning
to labor, we should speak of occupational immobility only if the
obstacles to the occupational change were artificial, temporary, or
somehow removable (for example, if they could be removed by
defraying the cost of re-training). If an occupational transfer of
workers is impossible because of their innate abilities and disabili-
ties, it is analytically preferable to regard the workers as being of
different kinds or qualities. After all, labor is not a homogeneous
commodity, and it would make little sense to deal with differences in quality as "immobility." Differences in the workers' personal *preferences* (tastes), in their innate *abilities* (quality) and
in their *opportunities* (access) should be distinguished. The last
differences are remediable or at least conceivably remediable.
Remediable but not yet remedied differences in workers' opportunities are what is essentially referred to in economic analysis by
the term "immobility." [35]

Despite the definition of mobility in terms of personal desires
and difficulties, the mobility of a *group* of workers is neither the
aggregate nor the average of the mobility of its individual members. A sufficiently large *fringe* with sufficiently large mobility
makes the group highly mobile even if the majority of its members
are more or less immobile. For it will hardly ever be necessary for
all members of the group to move. How large a fringe has to be
mobile in order to permit us to say that the group of workers is
mobile will depend on the problem under discussion, for example,
on the exact change in demand or technology and on the size of
adjustment needed to restore "equilibrium." One may, for many
practical purposes, speak of *perfect* mobility of labor if ten or
fifteen out of a hundred workers find it possible to move when
preferred job opportunities elsewhere open up or when their

---

[35] Immobility in this analytical sense cannot be measured statistically.
One can observe and count *movement,* but not *mobility.* For neither the
magnitude of the stimulus—the attraction to movement—nor the magnitude
of the friction—the obstacles to movement—can be ascertained. Mobility
may be perfect while no actual movement occurs (e.g., there may be no
stimulus to move); or actual movements may be considerable despite small
mobility (e.g., it may take inordinate stimuli to overcome excessive obstacles).

old jobs become less desirable than jobs elsewhere. Furthermore, perfect mobility in this sense can often bring about the required wage adjustments without any actual movement occurring. A rise in the competitive wage level, that is, rise in the rates paid for labor in jobs to which some of their workers could move, might be sufficient to cause employers to adjust their wages in order to keep their workers from moving. It is necessary to bear these points in mind because of the naive views sometimes expressed by sociologists and writers on labor problems who believe that an assumption of perfect mobility in economic analysis means that all the workers everywhere actually move from their jobs and homes at the slightest provocation.

Immobility and Isolated Markets

Immobility may create relatively isolated labor markets. It isolates groups of workers in localities or occupations in which the number of employers may be too small to permit effective competition. Labor markets which are either geographically or occupationally isolated are certainly not the norm, but they are not too rare exceptions. We all know of company towns where workers have no chance of alternative employment and only an expensive chance of moving away. We know of many places where skilled laborers have only one possible employer in their trade and where alternative employment means either work in much less valuable occupations or, again, work in far-away places. In such cases competition among employers is naturally limited.

But it would be rash and superficial to speak of the lack of workers' mobility and the lack of employers' competition for labor as if the link between the two were a necessary one. It is in fact only a possible one. To understand this we must embark on a bit of rather subtle analysis, to examine the nature of the deviations from competition, one or more of which will be found in an isolated labor market.[36] We must distinguish at least four such deviations: (1) The obstacles preventing workers from moving from a

[36] Unfortunately I shall not be able to avoid the use of technical jargon. Those who are not equipped with the skill necessary to understand it, will either have to bear with me for a few pages or skip them.

poor to a better area of employment opportunities. (2) The limitations on competition among the existing enterprises for the available labor in the low-wage area. (3) The absence of competition
from new enterprise (new employers) moving into the area. (4)
The elimination of competition among the workers in the area
through the formation of a trade union. The fourth element of non-
competition will be introduced only later, because we wish to
understand the position of labor in this isolated market if workers
are not unionized and each man must shift for himself.

The existence of obstacles to the migration of workers—e.g.,
high transfer costs and lack of funds to defray them—creates an
isolated area of undetermined size.[37] It may be a very large area
with hundreds of different employers or a very small area with only
a few employers or perhaps only one. Thus the position of employers in the isolated labor market may be one of pure competition
(if there are very many small firms among whom workers readily
move around from job to job), "monopsonistic competition" (if
there are very many small firms, but workers will not too easily
and readily change jobs), "oligopsonistic competition" (if there
are only a smaller number of firms, or a few big ones, either in
collusion concerning hiring and wages, or inhibited in their hiring practices and wage policies by fear of retaliation), or complete "monopsony" (only one firm in the labor market). Hence,
the fact that a labor market is isolated because emigration from it
is difficult or impossible is not *per se* a sufficient cause for limitations in the competition among the existing employers for the
available labor supply. Nor is it a cause for the absence of newcomers' competition of firms moving into the area to take advantage of cheap labor.

What are the effects of the first element of non-competition—
the "exit-barrier" for workers—if it is not combined with any of

[37] The entire analysis runs in terms of an isolated "area," which may be
understood to be a geographical or occupational area. In the latter case,
however, we must assume that the workers in the isolated occupational area
would be willing to move into other occupations and would after re-training
be equally qualified for them. Otherwise we shift the analysis from one of
immobility of labor to one of quality differences of labor. We are concerned
here only with possible disparities between the earnings of potentially
homogeneous labor in different occupations in the absence of mobility.

the other elements, that is, if there are many employers in the isolated area in unlimited competition among themselves as well as
exposed to latent competition from newcomers? If there is a relative over-supply of labor in the area—relative to other areas—
there will develop a spread between the (lower) wage in the
area and the (higher) wage outside. This spread will continue
even if employers outside are willing to hire more workers, for the
low-paid workers cannot afford the cost of moving away. And
it will continue although each employer in the area pays workers all they are worth to him. Neither the "pure" competition
among the existing firms nor the "perfect" competition from newcomers will eliminate the regional (or occupational) wage differential, because the differential will be determined by the difference in the marginal productivity of labor within the area and
outside.[38]

This difference in labor productivity is implied in the fact that
the area is one of relative over-supply of labor. It may be due to a
lower quality of natural resources or a smaller amount of resources
per worker in the area, compared with other areas. In other words,
because of relatively unfavorable conditions of production the
cheap labor cost per unit of input (hour of work) will not be
cheap labor cost per unit of output and/or the cheap labor may
be just an offset to other cost items that are higher in the labor-
surplus area than elsewhere. The low wage, therefore, will not
be bid up by competing employers in the area—each of whom
employs as many workers as it is profitable to employ (i.e., up to
the amount at which the marginal revenue product of labor is

[38] The expression "marginal productivity" throughout this discussion
stands for "marginal value productivity" or "marginal net revenue productivity." Incidentally, our analysis here and in the passages that follow violates
the rule of economic theory that interdicts the promiscuous meandering between the analyses of the individual firm, the industry, the area, and the
whole economy. "Marginal productivity," for example, means different things
on these different levels of analysis. But it would take several times the space
that we are devoting to this discussion if we were to make all the distinctions
and qualifications required by adherence to the rule. I believe that the results
of an analysis which carefully avoids the identification of "marginal productivity from the point of view of the individual firm" with "marginal productivity within the whole area" would not in any essential respect differ from
our rougher kind of reasoning.

equal to the wage rate)—nor by any new firms—since the lower wage does not promise a higher profit rate than is obtained elsewhere and thus will not attract any new firms to the area.

We are entitled to consider the case described as a deviation from competition, for labor in the surplus area produces less than it could be producing outside: the workers are willing to move to better jobs outside and they are capable of doing the work required, but because of the lack of funds to finance the transfer they cannot move and must stay in their less productive and correspondingly less well paid jobs.

Let us now introduce the second deviation from competition: limited competition among the employers in the isolated area. Although there will now be a tendency on the part of the employers to restrict employment in order to depress the wage rate, the wage rate cannot in fact be depressed as long as newcomers' competition is perfect, that is, as long as new firms will move into the labor-surplus area when the wage is below the level commensurate with net productivity.[39] Hence, to close the argument we must introduce also the third deviation from competition: the absence of newcomers' competition, the failure of new employers to move into an area of really cheap labor despite the profits they could thus make. This could be the case, for example, if only one employer, or a very few employers, dominated the labor market in the area, so that a potential newcomer would know that the present "favorable" labor market would disappear as soon as he invaded the area.[40]

Now we have isolated the kind of conditions that would enable the existing employers to pay still lower wages—and get away with it. It is the combination of three conditions—an exit-restriction for workers, a restriction of competition among exist-

[39] For the sake of completeness we might mention the possibility that the general tendency of employers under monopsonistic competition to restrict employment may result in less efficient plant operation and less efficient use of labor, and consequently in a further reduction of wage rates without an increase in rates of profit.

[40] A labor-surplus area, incidentally, is not necessarily a densely populated one. The over-supply of labor is relative to other resources. Hence, a small local labor force may constitute an "over-supply" of labor, just as there may be a "labor scarcity" despite a large local labor force.

ing employers, and an entry-restriction for new employers,—which produces a three-fold deviation from the model of pure and perfect competition: (1) a difference between the marginal productivity of labor in the isolated area and outside; (2) a difference between the wage rates paid by employers in the area and the marginal productivity of the labor they employ, and (3) a difference between the wage rates and the average net productivity of labor in the area, which implies a monopsony profit margin accruing to the employer.[41]

Profits at the Expense of Wages

The foregoing analysis has established the possibility of "profits at the expense of wages" and brought out the conditions under which the possibility can be realized. A few more propositions can be formulated to generalize our results:

(i) While immobility of labor is a necessary condition for the differences between the marginal productivities of labor within and outside an area, such differences need not arise if no relative over-supply of labor develops. In other words, an isolated area is not necessarily a labor-surplus area. It is therefore conceivable that even in the absence of labor mobility the marginal productivity of labor in an isolated area is the same as that outside—though this would be a sheer coincidence.

(ii) It follows that, if labor is immobile and cannot move out, and enterprise is "immobile" and will not move in, a differential between the wages in an isolated area and those outside can exist which is not conditioned by a difference in the marginal productivity of labor, but entirely due to "monopsonistic pressure" in the isolated labor market.

(iii) It follows further that wage rates in an isolated area may be the same as those outside and nevertheless be relatively depressed through monopsonistic restrictions. For there may be a relative scarcity, rather than over-supply, of labor within the area, making the internal marginal productivity of labor higher than that

---

[41] For further discussion of the relationship between mobility and profit see Fritz Machlup, *The Economics of Sellers' Competition: Model Analysis of Sellers' Conduct* (Baltimore: Johns Hopkins Press, 1952), Chapter 7.

outside, while the wage rates in the area—owing to the absence of employers', and especially newcomers', competition—may be depressed to the level of wages elsewhere.

(iv) Hence, neither the presence nor the absence of actual differences in wage rates will in any way indicate the existence or non-existence of effective monopsonistic pressures in the labor market. The wage rates in the isolated area may be the same as those outside and yet depressed below the level that would prevail if there were unlimited competition among employers, old and new, but no mobility of labor between areas. The wage rates in the isolated area may be below those outside and yet not depressed by monopsonistic influence but entirely in line with the differential productivity maintained by the immobility of labor. The wage rates in the isolated area may be below those outside partly because of differences in productivity maintained by the immobility of labor and partly because of the combined effects of labor immobility and employers' monopsony.

In any event, in order to understand the possibility of "profits at the expense of labor" we must be clear about this general proposition: immobility of labor is a necessary but not a sufficient condition for the existence of employers' "monopsony profits"; to permit such profits to prevail there must also be immobility of enterprise, that is, lack of newcomers' competition for labor.

Immobility and General Unemployment

The analysis of labor immobility in terms of isolated areas is perhaps unduly narrow. Is it not possible that the mobility of labor "all around" is insufficient to permit any reliance on the existence and effectiveness of competition among the buyers of labor?

The following line of reasoning seems to suggest that the existence of the "industrial reserve army" (as the pool of unemployed was called by Marx) constantly reduces employers' competition for labor. Just as competition among sellers of goods implies that the buyers have a choice among various sellers and can easily transfer their patronage from one to another, competition among buyers of labor might presuppose that the sellers—that is, the workers—have a choice among various buyers and can easily move from one employer to another. Now, one can readily see that, under conditions of serious unemployment, workers do not have such a choice and cannot move from one employment to another. Since under modern conditions periods of serious unemployment seem to be hardly more exceptional than periods of full employment, one could infer that as a rule labor is not mobile enough to assure effective competition among employers. And from this one could conclude that, in an economy with long stretches of unemployment, workers, not organized but competing with one another (and especially the unemployed striving to get the jobs of the employed), will be at a distinct disadvantage vis-à-vis employers.

The conclusion follows from the premises, but one of the premises is false. It is not necessary that workers can easily transfer from one job to another for competition among buyers of labor to exist: the existence of a pool of unemployed is sufficient to put each employer in a position of pure competition as a buyer of labor. When labor is not scarce but easily available at the going wage, employers have no reason to restrict employment for the purpose of lowering the wage rate. In other words, employers, in times of general unemployment, have no monopsonistic choice or leeway concerning the wage rate they may pay. They can get as many workers as they may wish to hire at the rock-bottom rate of pay. No degree of immobility of labor can secure any special bargaining power to employers who buy labor under conditions of pure competition.[42]

It is in times of rising demand, when labor becomes scarce and firms can secure more workers only by paying higher wage rates, it is then that firms may prefer to forego some potential profits of increased operations in order to avoid reducing the profits they make in their current operations at the current wage rates. It is then that they take advantage of any labor immobility that exists. But exactly then the geographical and occupational mobility of workers increases markedly. Exactly then workers have little difficulty in finding other jobs.

In brief, in periods of unemployment the immobility of labor is severe, but the employers are practically in positions of pure

[42] To be sure, this argument applies only where the pool of unemployed includes the type of labor demanded.

competition in hiring because each firm is faced with a practically unlimited supply of labor. In periods of full employment the employer's position in the labor market becomes more monopsonistic as he becomes aware of the limitations of the supply available to him, but the mobility of labor is then substantially increased.

Immobility and Nonwage Competition

Employers compete for labor not merely by the wages they offer but also by offering several kinds of nonwage advantages. Workers are attracted by many considerations—vacations with pay, retirement and other welfare benefits, company housing schemes, pleasant working conditions, etc.,—and employers will attempt to attract and keep a work force with such devices as well as with good wages.

The fact that the nonwage benefits that go with the job may be valued very differently by old workers and new, old and young, single men and family men, old men and young, local and out-of-state workers, and so forth, may make it less likely that employers are in positions of pure competition in buying labor. The differentiation of employers and of jobs in the eyes of the workers, the different attachment that workers may have to their jobs, causing some of them to quit and others to stay on when their wages are reduced or wages elsewhere are raised, the different attraction that the nonwage benefits have for different job seekers, and above all the realization of these different attitudes by the employer, create for each firm a position of monopsonistic competition in the labor market. In the absence of workers' organization the firm will count on losing some but not all workers if it reduces wage rates, and on obtaining more workers only through offering wage increases.

Under such conditions any increase in employment will cost the firm more than the wage it pays to the new workers, for it will probably be necessary for the firm to pay the increased wage rates to its old workers also. (Most industrial firms know that wage discrimination against its more or less permanent work force undermines workers' morale and does not pay in the long run.) [43] Since

[43] I have restricted this statement to industrial firms. It certainly would

the cost of an increase in the amount of labor employed exceeds the wage paid to the additional workers (by the wage increase granted to the old ones) and since the firm will undertake such increase in its work force only when the revenue expected from it covers the entire increase in cost, the revenue produced by the new workers must naturally exceed the wages they are paid.[44]

The result of all this is sometimes called "monopsonistic exploitation" of labor.[45] The idea is that, in a firm which offers equal pay for equal work, the worker is paid less than what he produces, that is, less than the increase in revenue that his employment brings forth. Of course, he cannot be paid more, because the difference between this increase in revenue and his wage has to be paid to his fellow workers who get a wage increase at the same time as new workers are hired.[46] But is it not possible that the difference is greater than the increased wage payments to other workers and contains a fat margin of profit? Is it certain that the entire difference between his wage and the additional net revenue which he

---

not hold for private schools and universities. They regularly discriminate in favor of new appointees and against the old guard, except if one of the latter is just about to quit for a better paying position.

[44] In technical lingo this is expressed as follows: Under monopsonistic competition the marginal labor cost to the firm exceeds the wage rate it pays; since profit is maximized when employment is so adjusted that marginal labor cost is equal to (or just below) the marginal net revenue productivity of labor, the latter must of course exceed the wage rate.

[45] Joan Robinson, *The Economics of Imperfect Competition* (London: Macmillan, 1932), p. 282. Gordon F. Bloom, "A Reconsideration of the Theory of Exploitation," *Quarterly Journal of Economics,* Vol. LV (1941), pp. 413–42. Reprinted in *Readings in the Theory of Income Distribution* (Philadelphia: Blakiston, 1946), pp. 245–77. See also Gordon F. Bloom and Herbert R. Northrup, *Economics of Labor and Industrial Relations* (Philadelphia: Blakiston, 1950), pp. 317–47.

[46] There may be a large difference between the price of labor and the value of its marginal physical product. This difference is due to (a) the reduction in product price that the firm must grant to its customers in order to dispose of an increased output and (b) the increase in factor price that the firm must grant to its employees in order to acquire an increased input. These two parts of the spread between the price of the factor and the value of its marginal physical product are called (a) "monopolistic exploitation" and (b) "monopsonistic exploitation" of the factor. These terms, misleading in several respects, are merely to remind the student of the fact that the spread would not exist if the firm were (a) selling its products under pure competition and (b) buying its factors under pure competition.

produces goes into the pay envelopes of other workers, rather than into the employer's pocket? The answer rests on a technicality.[47] But the question whether the firm gets "profits at the expense of workers" depends on very real circumstances: on the readiness of other firms to take advantage of profit opportunities afforded by the availability of cheap labor wherever it exists. The monopsonistic positions which firms can acquire through nonwage competition are not by themselves sufficient to secure or maintain a profit position by the firm. But they will induce firms to limit the employment of labor to some extent and may thus result in less employment at given wage rates. And this, in the absence of unions, may mean slightly lower money wage rates than if employers' competition for labor were unlimited and not deflected by nonwage considerations.

Corporations as Combinations of Capital

We turn now to the last of the arguments that we have encountered concerning labor's bargaining disadvantage. The Wagner Act of 1935 stated that wage rates were depressed and "the stabilization of competitive wage rates" was prevented by "the inequality of bargaining power between employees who do not

[47] We must distinguish between *marginal* cost of labor and *marginal* net revenue productivity of labor, on the one hand, and *average* cost of labor and *average* net revenue productivity of labor on the other. The marginal labor cost—the increase in total labor cost when more workers are hired—exceeds the wage rate or average labor cost exactly by the wage increases going to the rest of the workers when the additional workers are employed. If the firm equalizes marginal labor cost and marginal net revenue productivity, the latter exceeds the wage rate by exactly the additional pay going to the other workers. If the marginal net revenue productivity at a certain volume of employment should exceed the wage rate by more than the relevant increment of wage going to other workers, the firm has failed to make the right adjustment of the volume of employment, that is, it is not making as much money as it could. Thus, if the marginal net revenue productivity of labor exceeds the marginal labor cost, the firm is not making a profit at the expense of labor but instead it is making a smaller profit than it could make. Matters are quite different with regard to average productivity and average cost of labor. The difference between these is of course the profit margin per unit of labor. The existence of such a profit margin is not dependent on, and perhaps not even affected by, the existence of monopsonistic instead of pure competition in buying labor.

possess full freedom of association or actual liberty of contract, and employers who are organized in the corporate or other forms of ownership association. . . ." [48]

This implies that the combination or union of several capitalists in corporations or other forms of "ownership association" gives them as employers a bargaining advantage over workers unless the latter also are organized in a combination or union of workers. A sole proprietor, apparently, need not possess bargaining strength superior to that of an individual worker, but if several owners "organize" in partnerships or corporations their bargaining power is enlarged, and workers also must organize in order to remove an otherwise unavoidable inequality in bargaining power.

To the extent that this represents more than the mere verbiage prefacing the substantive provisions of the statute, we may give it two possible interpretations. (1) The association of several owners or capitalists in corporations—we may, I suppose, forget the partnerships—strengthens their position in the labor market because of the concentration of financial power which it implies. (2) The formation of large corporations controlling several potentially independent establishments reduces the number of employers and therefore the degree of employers' competition for labor.

The first interpretation is nothing but the familiar argument that identifies financial strength, or the size of financial reserves, with market position and infers from differences in financial strength the existence of unequal bargaining power. We have not been able to discover any validity in this argument except to the extent that financial strength is exercised to restrict competition either by forcing other employers into conspiracies or by keeping other employers out of the labor market. In other words, this argument is untenable unless it is so interpreted that it is transformed into the logically different argument referred to by our second interpretation.

The second interpretation makes better economic sense. There can be no doubt that the corporation laws have permitted a degree of concentration of industry which is incompatible with

[48] National Labor Relations Act of 1935, Section 1.

effective competition. But we must not confuse competition in the sale of products with competition in the purchase of labor. If corporate concentration has succeeded in reducing or eliminating competition in particular "industries" defined by the product sold, this concentration need not mean anything regarding competition in the labor market. For, at least with respect to unskilled labor, *all* industries in the sense referred to above compete for the same kind of labor. Hence, the "concentration of economic control" in *particular* "industries" is not relevant to our discussion (except in relation to highly specialized labor needed by only one industry).

There is still the possibility that the growth of corporations has seriously reduced the number of independent employers in any given geographic area. If it has, the argument has some validity. But it is doubtful that the competition among employers in any area is really much less effective than it would be in the absence of the corporate form of business enterprise. In its effect upon newcomers' competition the argument is perhaps more relevant. But to the extent that it is, we have discussed it in earlier sections and need not repeat our findings here.

Redressing the Balance

Our survey and analysis of the various arguments contending that unorganized labor is at a disadvantage and that the employer holds an advantage in the wage bargain has revealed some unsound and some sound averments. And, incidentally, it has, I believe, cleared up the meaning of the concept of bargaining power as it is employed in propositions referring to the inequality of the bargaining positions of the two parties of the wage contract.

Bargaining power in this context simply means control over price or, in the labor market, the power to influence the determination of the wage rate. A party has no bargaining power at all if its only choice is to "take it or leave it." This is the situation of a buyer or seller under pure competition. A party has bargaining power if it has some "leeway" or some alternatives besides the mere acceptance or non-acceptance of the one price that is put before it. If one party, say, the employer, has a choice between hiring fewer workers at a lower wage or more at a higher wage, while the other party, the worker, has no other choice but to take or refuse the job at the wage named by the employer, the bargaining strength of the parties is unequal. Workers not acting in concert and not organized in a union acting for them are typically in a position of pure competition, that is, without any bargaining power whatsoever. Employers, on the other hand, may be in a position to influence the wage rate at which they hire. They may have a large leeway and set the wage rate high or low as they deem wise or profitable. Or they may have only little leeway, or none at all. Their bargaining power, in other words, may be substantial, small or nil.

What was called bargaining power in this context is nothing but monopoly or monopsony power. Any deviation from pure and perfect competition gives a seller or buyer that control over price which is called monopoly or monopsony power in general economic discussion, and bargaining power in discussions of the special problem of wage determination.

Workers not acting in concert and not organized in a union acting for them will be at a disadvantage *vis-à-vis* employers whenever the latter are not exposed to unlimited competition. We must therefore recognize the validity of those assertions of labor's disadvantage that claim and explain limitations in employers' competition in the buying of labor. The arguments based on the extreme perishability of labor and on labor's inability to wait were found to be untenable. The argument based on labor's immobility due to general unemployment was found to be weak. But three other arguments were found to be more or less valid: monopsonistic competition due to the nonwage aspects of different jobs may have some, though limited, significance; reduced employers' competition for labor in relatively isolated areas may be of very real significance; and restricted employers' competition due to collusive or cooperative (oligopsonistic) practices may be a most serious matter.[49]

[49] The two most significant arguments are in a sense merely two aspects of one argument. For employers' conspiracy to be effective, labor markets will have to be somewhat isolated; otherwise employers would not be few,

Now that the inequality has been shown to exist, what can be done to redress the balance? There are essentially two ways of approaching the task. One is for the government to take measures to create competition where it appears to be lacking and to remove all obstacles to competition that are removable. The other is to compensate for the limitations on employers' competition for labor, and for the monopsony power which it implies, by measures limiting workers' competition for jobs and creating monopoly power on the part of labor. We know, of course, that the first approach has never been tried, whereas the second was adopted. We shall, however, discuss briefly the potential effectiveness of the two alternative approaches to dealing with the inequities in question.

Dealing with Isolated Labor Markets

Are there any measures by which government could reduce or remove labor's disadvantage in isolated labor markets by reducing or removing the underlying limitations to competition? We have distinguished three kinds of limitations: those on the mobility of labor, those on competition among existing employers in the isolated area, and those on the entry of new enterprise as new competition for labor.

The basic defect, of course, is immobility of labor. Remove it, and the area, be it geographical or occupational, is no longer isolated. Government measures to deal with this problem might include labor information services (about job opportunities, wage rates and living conditions), employment agencies (labor exchange services), and loans or subsidies to help finance the cost of the transportation, relocation or retraining of workers. Such measures are more easily listed than carried out. But we are usually inclined to exaggerate the size of the task, to exaggerate the lack of mobility of labor. If job opportunities elsewhere are plentiful

would always be exposed to newcomers' competition, and labor could avoid the effects of local monopsony power by moving away. Since limited mobility of labor and limited competition from new employers is thus implicitly assumed, employers' oligopsony operates only in relatively "isolated" labor markets. We continue, nevertheless, to discuss the oligopsonistic aspects separately.

and well advertised, workers prove to be remarkably mobile even without any special governmental measures to aid mobility. Migrations of workers on an unheard-of scale took place in the United States both at the beginning and at the end of the second World War: it is reported that the mere existence of job opportunities, apart from wage differentials, was often sufficient to induce wholesale migration into places where new industries had sprung up.

It is said that occupational immobility is much harder to correct than geographical immobility. Of course, insofar as the failure to change occupations is due to differences in the tastes or to the innate abilities of workers, there is nothing to be corrected. But insofar as occupational immobility is due to the financial barriers that interfere with the possibility of workers' changing jobs or acquiring new skills, it may be remediable. If remedied, a better allocation of the economy's labor resources will result as they are shifted from relatively overcrowded fields to others that are less well worked.[50]

Turning to the alternative approach, the organization of labor, we ask what the trade unions have done to deal with the same problem. To say that they have rarely tried to attack the basic

[50] The relative over-supply of labor in particular occupations may be the result of original "mistakes" or of changes in demand or technology. A worker's original choice of occupation may be restricted because of lack of knowledge or because of the difficulties in the way of his acquiring proficiency in the trade he would like to enter. Already skilled workers may find that their skills are no longer in demand because technological change has rendered them redundant, or that they have entered an industry in an expanding phase only to discover when they have finished their training that they cannot get jobs at those wages because too many others have done the same thing. (This is, of course, simply the way in which the pricing mechanism normally operates. An increase in demand leads to higher prices, which are gradually pulled down as the supply increases in response.) But entry may be easier than exit and, once attached to an industry and having invested in the acquisition of particular skills, a worker may have trouble leaving. He may not be able to afford the loss of income incident to a new period of apprenticeship or he may no longer be young enough to be adaptable. Whatever is the cause of his immobility, the result is that wages will tend to fall because some workers cannot move on to better paid jobs even if they want to. Whether governmental financing of retraining can much alleviate this situation is questionable, and the danger of mistakes in the direction of "occupational reconversion" is great. Often time will be the only real cure, no replacements being made of those in the overcrowded occupation who leave the labor force for good.

problem—the immobility of workers—is not to reproach them, for there is not much that they could have done. In the main, their approach was restrictive. To relieve workers from the unfortunate results of restricted mobility preventing an exodus from depressed or distressed areas (geographical or occupational) the unions have introduced restrictions of other types: they have restricted the supply of workers to the firms or industries in the area, for example, through closed shops with restricted membership, thereby creating unemployment for the workers frozen out, or through spread-the-work devices with a shortened work week, thereby creating part-time unemployment for all workers. And they have attempted to obtain higher wage rates for their members. If they succeed in raising wage rates or in keeping them at a level above the marginal productivity of the amount of labor available, while doing nothing to reduce the over-supply, they create a condition of chronic unemployment in the area.[51]

Labor immobility alone, as we have seen, does not explain a disadvantage of labor in the wage bargain. The reduced wage rates which in the absence of union restrictions would be associated with an over-supply of labor in an isolated area might well be the outcome of pure and perfect employers' competition for labor. Hence, if trade union action succeeds in raising wages above this "competitive" level, not through facilitating the transfer of labor out of the overcrowded area, but through the exercise of collective bargaining strength, such action is not in compensation of any bargaining disadvantage, not an attempt to offset monopsony power by monopoly power, but a unilateral use of the latter.

Matters are different when competition among the employers in the area and from potential newcomers to the area is limited. In this case the exercise of union strength in wage bargaining could be regarded as genuine redress of the balance—if it is not a reversal of the imbalance. But are there no possibilities for the

[51] This should not be interpreted to mean that improvements in the organization of the labor market, for example, hiring halls in casual labor markets, are not desirable or that unions have not done some very useful things of this kind. It simply means that, so far as the problem is basically one of labor immobility, unions have been ineffective in remedying it and that, as a result of their wage policy, the one useful competitive remedy, the migration of industry into the area, is given less opportunity to help matters.

other approach, for the restoration or re-invigoration of employers' competition?

As far as the existing employers in the area are concerned, there is not much that can be done to invigorate competition among them if their number is very small. If there are no more than two or three, the chances for making them compete without pulling any punches are not much better than the chances for making a single firm compete with itself. There may be more scope for policies to make newcomers' competition more perfect. Suggestions of measures the government could take toward this end have included the "systematic informing of enterprisers about areas of labor redundancy." [52] Although this might help a little, it would be naive to assume that lack of information is the chief impediment to competition among enterprisers. Fully informed firms will abstain from moving into a cheap-labor area if the employers that have been dominating it are their own affiliates, members of the same corporate empire; or if the minimum scale of operations in new production units would require so much labor that the cheap-labor area might be expected to become a dear-labor area almost over night. Nothing can be done if the latter reason prevails. And nothing short of the dismemberment of corporate empires would help to remove the first obstacle to competition.

Bringing new industries into labor-surplus areas is a widely favored proposal: If labor cannot move out, if workers are unable to transfer to jobs elsewhere, the jobs may be moved to them. Does this mean that the government should go into business and open establishments in areas where private firms refuse to go? Or that government should subsidize private business firms to settle in labor-surplus areas? If the potential effectiveness of a governmental policy of increasing newcomers' competition for labor, that is, the mobility of enterprise taking advantage of cheaper labor, is appraised, not by itself, but in conjunction with a policy of increasing the mobility of labor taking advantage of better job opportunities, the conclusions may well be encouraging. Attacks on both these fronts may have considerable success in lifting

[52] Henry C. Simons, "Some Reflexions on Syndicalism," *Journal of Political Economy,* Vol. LII (1944), p. 15.

the barriers to the movement of labor to jobs and of jobs to labor
and in thus merging a hitherto isolated labor market with that of
the rest of the economy.[53]

The union approach to the problem tends toward the opposite
direction: Unionization will more often reduce than increase the
mobility of labor: and by artificially raising the wage rates in the
isolated area it will reduce any attraction which the area may have
had for new enterprise. With regard to the objective of compensating for the employers' monopsony power, unionization may be
fully successful. But there is no reason why unions should limit
the exercise of their bargaining power carefully to the dose just
needed to neutralize the employers' bargaining power. And if they
not merely recoup the profits which the employers, in the absence
of labor's collective strength, might have made at the expense of
labor, but try to get more, the effect may be a misallocation or
under-utilization of resources, especially labor, more serious than
that which would result without any redress of the balance.

Dealing with Employers' Collusion

Little can be done to compel a small group of employers to
compete with each other when they are not exposed to competition from the outside. Whether it is simple self-restraint in expectation of reciprocal treatment from the other gentlemen,
whether it is an informal understanding not to "spoil" the labor
market, or whether it is a downright conspiracy to maintain the
wage level and avoid "pirating" of labor—one way or another employers will contrive to restrain their competition in a labor market
in which (a) labor is not plentiful enough to meet their unrestricted demand, (b) labor is not scarce enough to make them
forget their gentlemanly restraint, (c) labor is not mobile enough
to leave the market, and (d) outside employers are not dynamic
enough to move in and spoil their game.

No antitrust agency of the government will be able to do anything about it. The only chances for the competitive approach to

[53] Needless to point out, the degree of communication and interfusion
that makes "one" market out of several partial markets is a matter of judgment and analytical convenience.

the problem lie in increasing the number of individual firms in any local market and in increasing the aggressive spirit of potential invaders of local markets, who would raid the local labor market by offering aid to workers moving to jobs in their establishments elsewhere or would themselves move into the area and open new establishments there. Both the increase in the number of firms and the increase in their dynamic aggressiveness cannot be accomplished under the present system of corporate concentration. Only the dismemberment of corporate combines into their component parts—that is, economic autonomy of establishments that can be independently operated without great loss of efficiency— may achieve the reduction or elimination of monopsony and oligopsony in local labor markets.

There is nothing that trade unions can do to reinforce employers' competition for labor or break up employers' conspiracies. On the contrary, the formation of labor unions and the introduction of collective bargaining will frequently induce employers to formalize their cooperative activities with regard to wage determination. The trade union approach to the problem is to set bargaining strength against bargaining strength, monopoly power against monopsony power. The official theory of the equalization of bargaining strength serves as a moral and economic basis for the policy of government aid to the creation and increase of union power. The moral basis is firm and solid. The economic basis is shaky, if only because we know from the theory of bilateral monopoly that there is no way of telling the point at which the opposing powers are of "equal" strength and just "neutralize" each other. No attempt is made in theory or in practice to limit the exercise of labor's collective bargaining power to what it would take to offset employers' collusion or restraint of competition.

Dealing with "Employer Differentiation"

We still have to deal with the phenomenon of so-called "monopsonistic exploitation" due to the differentiation of jobs or employer desirability causing various degrees of workers' attraction and attachment to the particular employer. We have found that this phenomenon is probably of small practical significance, but as the logical counterpart of "monopolistic competition due to product differentiation" the abstract model of "monopsonistic competition due to employer differentiation" has been given considerable attention in theoretical analysis. Now, assuming that in the absence of trade unions many firms would be confronted with such individualized labor supply conditions that they could pay low wage rates if their work force were small and would have to pay higher wage rates if their work force were larger—the greater the work force the higher the wage rate—could the government do anything to change the conditions?

If we wish to remain in the realm of practical reality, we had better admit that the government would not be able to alter the situation. If we stepped "through the looking-glass" into an economic wonderland, we could readily prescribe the measures to repair the situations and transform the state of monopsonistic competition into one of pure competition on the part of each employer. We could do it by progressive subsidies to each employer who increases his work force, where the rate of progression precisely offsets his rising wage costs; or we could do it through public labor supply agencies guaranteeing each employer to furnish any amount of labor of given quality and at a uniform wage rate.[54]

Trade unions can sometimes do in reality what a government could do only in our fantasy. If a union in its wage contract with an employer has set a wage rate and can actually furnish him any amount of labor that he may want to employ at this rate, it has done the trick and created for him a state of pure competition in buying his labor. (This presupposes that he trusts the union to stick to the agreement and not to demand wage increases just because he consistently hires a large number of workers.) Here then we find an instance where the union is able to remove a limitation of the employers' competition for labor; and where it might

[54] This would be a case of "counter-speculation" by the government to prevent monopolistic and monopsonistic restrictions in Abba Lerner's model economy. Abba P. Lerner, *The Economics of Control* (New York: Macmillan, 1946), pp. 55 and 84.

even succeed in inducing them to employ more labor at an increased wage rate.[55]

The idea is most intriguing, for it combines results that are not usually compatible with one another: The creation of monopoly control over the labor supply through a trade union and the exercise of this control achieve here at the same time the elimination of the monopsony positions of the employers covered by the contract, an increase in the wage rate, a reduction of the employers' profit, and an increase in employment. Unfortunately the case is not easily found in reality. It would presuppose, among other things, that every single firm in the industry or area to which this union contract applies must have been making abnormal profits; that is, they must have been in a sheltered position, well-protected from newcomers' competition. Otherwise the increase in wages will force some of the firms out of business and, although the employment in the surviving firms might be greater than before, the employment in the industry or area as a whole will be reduced.[56]

There is again no way of telling what the unionization of labor will do to the balance or imbalance of bargaining power of the two parties. That each individual employer, as a result of the union policy, may under the wage contract act as a pure competitor in buying labor does not mean that the bargaining power of the employers as a whole is reduced to nil. We must not confuse the market position of the individual firm after it has accepted the wage contract with the union with the bargaining position which it, or the group of employers, has while it negotiates the contract. (Similarly, the collective bargaining strength of the organized workers must not be confused with the position of an

---

[55] If without a union the firm must count on having to pay higher wage rates as it employs more workers, its marginal labor cost will include the increments of wages paid to those of its workers whom it could pay less if it employed fewer men, but to whom it must pay the higher wage rate paid to attract additional workers. Under a union contract fixing a uniform wage rate regardless of the amount of employment, the marginal labor cost of the firm will be the same as the wage rate. Hence, for a certain range the marginal labor cost may be reduced as a result of the union contract even if the wage rate is increased, and the firm may employ more rather than less labor. See Joan Robinson, *op. cit.*, p. 295.

[56] Joan Robinson, *op. cit.*, p. 299.

individual worker under the contract.) What the relative strength of the parties will be in any particular case under any particular conditions cannot be determined. The hope that they be exactly or approximately "equal" has absolutely no foundation.[57]

[57] For an application of the theory of bilateral monopoly, with indifference maps, contract curves, and all the rest to labor market and collective bargaining, see William Fellner, "Prices and Wages under Bilateral Monopoly," *Quarterly Journal of Economics,* Vol. LXI (1947), pp. 503–532.

CHAPTER 10

Monopolistic Labor Policies:
Wage Rates and Income

Correcting Defects of the Labor Market: Wage Differentials and Job
Evaluation · Incorrect Adjustments to Changes · Upward and Downward
Spirals

Raising the National Income: The Purchasing Power Argument · Increasing the Propensity to Consume · Shocking the Employers into Increased
Efficiency · Energizing the Workers into Increased Efficiency

Redistributing the National Income: Gaining—at Whose Expense? · Real
Wages and Labor's Relative Share · Wage Increases Paid Out of Profits? ·
Getting a "Cut" in Monopoly Profits · Squeezing all Profits in a Changing
Economy · Raising Wages as Productivity Rises · The Unorganized Ma-
jority · There Will Always Be a Short Run

The Wage Structure: Restricting the Supply · "No Help Wanted" · "Natural" and "Artificial" Wage Differentials · Wages in General Are Too Low

Wages, Employment, Inflation: The Hidden Connection · Wage Policies
of Trade Unions · "Full Employment Policy" · Political Freedom in Jeop-
ardy · Restraint or Self-Restraint? · Governmental Regulation of Wage
Rates · Reducing the Monopoly Power of Unions · The Problems of
Poverty and Insecurity · The Wage Problem under Socialism

W E CONTINUE IN THIS CHAPTER the discussion of the wage-
bargaining function of trade unions and the effects of
monopolistic wage determination. Having examined, in the preceding chapter, the "arguments relating to the inequality of bargaining strength," we shall proceed to an examination of the
"arguments relating to certain technical defects of the labor market" and the "arguments relating to real wages and national income." Let us recall that our discussion is not intended to lead to
a general appraisal of trade unionism. The fact that we omit from
this discussion the "arguments relating to ethics, justice, and
workers' morale"—because they do not directly bear on our theme
—should make it clear that no over-all appraisal of unions and

union policies can here be attempted. Only the unions' role in the determination of wages and allocation of resources can properly concern us within the framework of this book.

CORRECTING DEFECTS OF THE LABOR MARKET

It is argued that there are serious technical defects inherent in a free competitive labor market, difficulties which to explain as "frictions" may be "formally permissible but beautifully irrelevant and even vicious." [1] These technical defects, if left uncorrected, are believed to result either in intolerable inequities for particular groups or in serious injury to the economy as a whole; they can be corrected, it is held, through the appropriate use of trade union control over wage rates. Three separate arguments have been advanced along such lines. We shall discuss them in turn.

Wage Differentials and Job Evaluation

Under modern conditions of industrial mass production there are hundreds of operations within a single establishment which require the setting of hundreds of different wage rates for which the market pricing mechanism is hopelessly inadequate. There just is not enough "supply and demand" to enable a market rate to be set. In other words "the market process is too rough a tool to make the distinctions that the enterprise and wage earners have found useful. The caprice of a foreman or supervisor is a mutually unsatisfactory means of settling differentials. Some rules of thumb must be devised, particularly when style and engineering changes would otherwise create added opportunity for bickering and debate. The job-evaluation plans require a rigorous definition of the elements of a task . . . The economist must recognize that these schemes fulfill the important function of providing a definite, well-known, and relatively impersonal mechanism for settling differentials within rather wide ranges in an area where

[1] John T. Dunlop, *Wage Determination under Trade Unions* (New York: Macmillan, 1944), p. 219.

the pricing mechanism in any conceivable institutional form would prove utterly inadequate." [2]

Since labor is not homogeneous, and the demands that different tasks make on human skill and effort are very different, the need for job evaluation is apparent. It has always existed, but in small-scale establishments the "boss" did what in large-scale establishments became a big administrative affair. Whether or not unions exist, modern large-scale management will find it useful to employ "job evaluation experts" to assist in setting rates for the finer gradations of tasks to be performed in the factory. If union representatives also assist in the process, the men may be more satisfied than otherwise. But certainly the necessity for administrative determination of job differentials is no particular economic argument for the formation of a strong labor union. (It is no more an argument for a cooperative solution than the heterogeneity of houses or apartments would be an argument for cooperative house evaluation to correct a "technical defect" of the housing market whose pricing mechanism proves "utterly inadequate" for settling the differentials within a wide range of different values. Of course, the less competition in the market the greater the contribution of "objective" evaluation.)

Job evaluation is in essence nothing but the evaluation of technical differences in services needed by a producer and the appropriate interpolation of intermediate wage rates between the rates for various kinds of "standard labor." Lest this be misunderstood, let us state emphatically that union participation in job evaluation may be thoroughly desirable from the point of view of everybody concerned, including management, which may find it most important for maintaining workers' morale.

Incorrect Adjustments to Changes

While no mechanism provides instantaneous adjustments, the time lags in the reaction of the supply of labor to changes in demand are held to be particularly long and this is said to have disruptive effects upon a free labor market without trade union control. The disruptive effects may be seen in unnecessarily large

[2] *Ibid.*, p. 215.

fluctuations in wages or in unnecessarily poor adjustments of labor supply to demand.

The argument apparently does not apply to short-run adjustments. With or without trade unions, the wages of particular workers do not in general tend to fluctuate closely in sympathy with fluctuations in the demand for the products they help to produce, even though such fluctuations cause fluctuations in the demand for labor.[3] Such fluctuations in demand are 'more commonly met by fluctuations in employment, with some workers totally or partially unemployed for a time. Whether or not it would be better, from some point of view, if all day-to-day fluctuations in demand were reflected in fluctuating wage rates, rather than in fluctuating employment, is beside the point—since neither the presence nor the absence of trade union control over wages can create such a market.

It is therefore to long-run adjustments that the argument must refer. No doubt, changes in the demand for particular types of labor may fail to cause appropriate changes in the supply of this labor: an increase in demand may cause an "overadjustment" of supply while a decrease in demand may fail to be met by any decrease, or by a sufficient decrease, in supply until wages have fallen very low—and then the supply may decrease too much. It is argued that because workers are relatively immobile, very large wage differentials are necessary to induce significant movements of workers into or out of industries, areas or occupations. In other words, workers do not respond to small differentials, but respond in large blocks to large differentials. Thus wage fluctuations of an excessively wide and uneconomic nature occur.

It is very doubtful whether there are many types of occupations in which this type of situation exists; nor is it likely to be very common with regard to geographic movements. Where it exists, the chief remedy is obviously to improve the information services avail-

---

[3] "Both buyers and sellers soon recognize that the price of labor is incapable of rapid and successful adjustments to every change in the orders received or products sold by the firm . . . In the light of the very many adjustments that would be constantly required of an exactly compensating system and the cumulative uncertainties of the lags, the tendency for all parties in the labor market (organized or unorganized) to prefer rates that are definitely and assuredly settled, save for infrequent (longer-run) changes, is not difficult to understand." Dunlop, *op. cit.*, p. 218.

able to workers and to take the type of measure mentioned earlier to help them overcome their immobility. Of course, if there is an increase in demand for workers in some field, no one can say with any certainty how many workers will eventually be required. It may, however, become clear after a while that too many workers are coming into that field—more than will be employed at the wage rate attracting them. In such cases, there is no doubt that a system by which workers were informed of this fact would be desirable. If an attempt were made, however, to prevent "overcrowding" by enabling a trade union to restrict the number of workers, the union would quite naturally be inclined to restrict numbers to whatever extent appeared necessary to maintain the wages of existing workers at the highest possible level—a procedure that would merely freeze out other workers who would be more than glad to enter at lower rates.

Similarly, if the demand for labor has fallen in a certain field and downward pressures on wages are created, no amount of wage bargaining is going to get around the hard fact that too many workers are attached to the industry or the occupation. Again the problem is one of lacking mobility. As a rule, trade union policies are designed to prevent or at least delay the economically necessary adjustments. Where the demand for particular specialized labor increases, unions will not often prevent the wage rates from rising, but frequently through barriers to entry they prevent the supply from adjusting itself. Where the demand for particular kinds of labor decreases, they try to prevent the wage rates from falling and thereby aggravate unemployment in the affected industries. Sometimes they have attempted to avoid both the wage reductions and the unemployment by compelling employers to hire more workers than are needed for the particular tasks. This so-called "feather-bedding" was often applied where workers were displaced because of technological changes.

This is not to deny that unions may sometimes prevent hardship to workers without preventing economically necessary adjustments. Sometimes employers can alter their production arrangements to maintain a more even level of employment without incurring higher labor costs, and may do so under union pressure whereas otherwise they would not. Sometimes workers are put to considerable inconvenience through the sheer inconsiderateness of employers, and union pressure may prevent such inconsiderate behavior.[4]

Upward and Downward Spirals

"Another technical difficulty with the price mechanism, regarded as a set of institutions, arises from the tendency of corrective price movements to set in motion others that may be non-equilibrating."[5] For example, when a shift in demand calls for a shift of resources from one industry to another, an increase in wages in the industry now favored should, according to the model mechanism, change the wage structure in favor of labor employed in and transferring to that industry. But, instead, the wage increase, according to the argument, is likely to "spill over" because the workers in all industries will demand and obtain wage increases. What was supposed to be an adjustment in the wage structure ends up as a maladjustment in the structure as well as the level of wages in the form of an inflationary movement. "In much the same way, a decrease in wage rates, entirely required in one sector, may initiate a downward spiral elsewhere."[6]

The argument—if it is to demonstrate that a labor market with trade union control over wages is superior to one with unorganized labor—had better be divided, inasmuch as it may have merits with regard to downward spirals while it has none with regard to upward spirals. Inflationary "rounds of wage increases" are extremely unlikely without trade unions. Workers, when they see wage rates go up in other industries, may of course wish to have theirs increased too, but if there is no increased demand for their labor, their wishes, in the absence of union pressure, would remain unanswered. Unless an inflationary fiscal or monetary policy is causing an increase in effective demand all around and is pulling up product prices in general, a wage increase in selected industries in which more labor is demanded cannot in an unorganized labor market initiate a "round of increases." Strong trade unions, however, may succeed in forcing employers to grant parallel raises

[4] For examples see Clinton S. Golden and Harold J. Ruttenberg, *The Dynamics of Industrial Democracy* (New York: Harper, 1942), pp. 28 ff.

[5] John T. Dunlop, *op. cit.*, p. 218.

[6] *Ibid.*, p. 219.

(though this cannot go very far unless the supply of credit is elastic or the government is prepared to use fiscal policy to prevent unemployment).

Deflationary wage spirals are more likely to develop in the absence of trade union resistance, and there is some support for the argument that a "downward inflexibility" of wage rates enforced by strong unions is a "stabilizing" influence in an economy threatened by deflation. The issue is controversial. On the one side are those who fear that wage flexibility may allow a recession to degenerate into a severe depression and who therefore prescribe downward rigidity of wages as preventive medicine. On the other side are those who hold that depression and stagnation can be more reliably treated through readjustment in the wage structure, which requires wage flexibility, and that income deflation, if it is not remedied by the cost-price adjustment, must be halted through monetary and fiscal policy. According to the first view, wage inflexibility will stop the increase in unemployment; according to the second, wage inflexibility will cause further unemployment. Depending on which of these views is accepted, strong trade unions will be hailed or blamed for their role during a decline of general business activity.

Raising the National Income

For resisting the downward pressures on wage rates when effective demand declines, trade unions are credited, as we have just seen, with performing a "stabilizing" function in an economy threatened by deflation. Others go further and credit trade unions with even more positive performances in combating depressions. Through successful insistence on wage increases they can, it is argued, bring about an increase in effective demand and employment; that is, they can raise the national income.

The Purchasing Power Argument

There are those who have a rather primitive conception of the relationship between wage rate changes and total demand (or "purchasing power," as they often prefer to say). In their view, an increase in wage rates is identified with an increase in the total of wages paid out; and the resulting increase in demand for goods is identified with increased production and employment. Neither of these two postulates, however, may be taken for granted. An increase in wage rates may cause employers to use so much less labor that total wage payments fall rather than rise. And an increase in the demand for goods may cause an increase in prices rather than output. In bad times an increase in wage rates may well fail to raise wage payments, and in good times an increase in demand may well fail to increase output and employment.

The purchasing power theory of wage rate boosts is an illegitimate extension of the theory of the effects of increased investment outlays upon consumption and employment. Increased investment outlays imply additional pay envelopes and, as their contents are spent, producers of consumers goods will decide to increase output and to hire more workers to produce it. If *additional* pay envelopes can do this, why should *enlarged* pay envelopes not have the same effect?

There are at least two important differences. Additional pay envelopes to newly employed workers imply increased wage payments, while enlarged pay envelopes to workers hitherto employed may be smaller in number. If employers reduce the number of workers relatively less than wages rates are increased, they have to finance the increased pay roll, and may have to borrow. It is not at all certain that they are always willing and able to do this. To finance an increase in expenses is not as attractive as to finance promising investment expenditures. To disburse funds in acquiring assets is one thing; it is another to disburse funds in incurring expenses which encroach on profit or even spell loss. This explains why businessmen may at times be loath to finance a wage increase and may decide to reduce employment sufficiently to avoid increased wage payments. Only in times of expanding business activity will businesses be disposed to raise the funds for wage increases, because then they expect to be able to raise selling prices to make up for the higher production cost.

In the effect on selling prices we find the second difference

between the spending of wages received from increased investment and the spending of wage increases due to a raise secured by
the union. While in both cases the demand for consumers goods
is increased, in the first case cost conditions remain unchanged,
in the second case production cost is increased. The combined
effect of increased cost and increased demand, as a result of the
raise in wages, will more likely be a higher level of selling prices
than a higher level of production and employment.

The crude purchasing power theory of wage rate increases is
rarely expounded by professional economists. But it has wide currency in popular discussions.

Increasing the Propensity to Consume

A somewhat more sophisticated and yet similar argument for
wage rate increases through trade union pressures is built upon
the fact that poorer people usually spend a larger part of their
income than rich people. The rich usually save more. Hence, if
more dollars are channeled into the pay envelopes of the workers
and less into the coffers of the corporations and the pockets of
the capitalists, the total spending for consumers goods will increase.

If the investment expenditures of business and the expenditures
of government do not fall, increased expenditures by consumers
may result in an increase in employment. A change in income
distribution in favor of the workers and at the expense of profit
recipients reduces the general "propensity to save." If the "incentives to invest" remain the same, or at least are not reduced, the
national income may be increased.

The big "ifs" in this case are not much different from those in
the previous argument. First, an increase in wage rates forced by
the unions need not imply an increase in wage payments. Second, an increase in wage rates may be accompanied by an increase
in product prices. Third, the income distribution may therefore
not be changed in favor of more eager consumers. Fourth, even if
it should be so changed, the incentives to invest may be reduced
as much or more than the propensity to save. Consequently, it is
neither necessary nor likely that trade union pressures for higher

wages result in raising the national income through increasing the propensity to consume.[7]

Shocking the Employers into Increased Efficiency

The argument that trade unions through strong wage bargaining can succeed in raising real wages together with the total product of the economy is not always based on the effect of wage increases upon effective demand and employment. It is sometimes based on the effects of wage increases upon the productivity of labor due to improved equipment, technology, and management of the firms affected. In discussing these induced advances of productivity we shall duly distinguish the three paths of advance: the use of more capital per worker, the use of novel methods of production, and the use of greater solicitude and alertness on the part of management.

The increase in labor productivity through the use of more and better equipment is, of course, one of the ways in which capital is "substituted" for labor as the latter becomes relatively more expensive. Such substitution implies the employment of more capital per worker or, what is another aspect of the same thing, the employment of less labor per unit of capital.[8] If we assume that capital is scarce and labor fully employed, the substitution of capital for labor in the industries in which wage rates are raised can mean only one thing: the availability of less capital and more labor in all other fields of economic activity.[9] The result may be

[7] Since the term "propensity to consume" was proposed by J. M. Keynes it may be well to note that neither Keynes himself nor his more distinguished disciples have endorsed wage increases as a means for raising employment.

[8] Substitution of capital for labor need not mean more or better equipment—it may mean less labor with given equipment. There may also be substitution between different kinds of labor, for example, through the use of more supervisory personnel per worker or of less workers per supervisor. The various substitutions induced by wage increases have sometimes been mistaken for "improved" production methods or "improved" technology when they were in fact only movements along given production functions to economize a factor of production that had become more expensive.

[9] The situation would be different if we were to start from the assumption of unemployment of labor and over-abundance of capital. If capital went begging, the induced substitution of capital for labor might open up new investment opportunities and lead to new investment expenditures, increased

unemployment of labor or a reallocation of labor with more labor employed in fields where it can be employed only with reduced productivity. In other words, the increased productivity in the industries where wages are increased is more than offset by reduced productivity in the rest of the economy.[10]

Increases of labor productivity through the use of novel methods of production occur constantly as the technical arts develop. New technology is invented, developed, and put into practice; and the product obtainable from given resources is thereby increased. The thesis that the wage pressures by trade unions will speed up the development of new technology is accepted by some, rejected by others. Those who accept it believe in a special theory of "induced inventions." This theory contends that the increased wage costs will put a premium on all research and development work leading to "labor-saving inventions." The use of such inventions will raise output per unit of labor.

Those who reject the thesis hold that the flow of new inventions will not be increased by increased production costs, but at best may be directed into other channels. The tasks that are set for inventors and research laboratories may of course be changed when the economizing of expensive labor is made a more important objective of management. But this does not mean that these induced inventions will be any more instrumental in raising the nation's product than any other inventions would be. If

---

employment, and all the rest. This is indeed a possibility. But there is no evidence that businessmen are normally inclined to increase the aggregate rate of investment outlays when labor costs are increasing. We must not forget, moreover, that the substitution of capital for labor in the affected industries means reduced employment in these industries and perhaps reduced investment opportunities elsewhere. In any event, the increased-productivity thesis was not designed as another increased-employment case; it was meant to be a separate thesis that would hold also under conditions other than under-employment and over-saving. Yet, if neither labor nor capital is redundant, the wage-induced substitution of capital for labor can increase productivity in the affected industries only, but not in the whole economy. In the whole economy productivity will be reduced through the induced reallocation of resources.

[10] The induced transfer of labor from the high-wage industry to lower-wage industries and the induced withdrawal of capital from the latter for investment in the former must involve a reduction in average and total productivity in the use of resources.

the redirection of inventive efforts should be successful and thus bring forth more "very labor-saving inventions," the ultimate effects upon the marginal productivity of labor and upon the relative share that labor can obtain of the national income would not be favorable, but rather adverse.[11]

There is no empirical evidence that would support the improved-technology-through-increased-wage-rate thesis. And the weight of reasoning is against rather than for it.

There remains the third method of raising the productivity of labor in enterprises that are confronted with the necessity of paying higher wage rates: pinched by the increased production cost, the management may be shaken out of its "usual" indolence and shocked into greater alertness and solicitude.

This theory is at variance with one of the assumptions of pure theory, namely, that firms always attempt to maximize their pecuniary profits and, hence, always do their best to minimize the cost of production. But, after all, this assumption is not made on the basis of strong empirical evidence, but chiefly on grounds of expediency in theorizing. It is quite likely that some managements are easy-going, complacent, inefficient as long as they can afford it, but can be shocked into alertness, assiduity, efficiency under the impact of wage increases encroaching upon profits. Perhaps under the shelter of some monopoly position they may have been able to take it easy; the disappearance of profits may now make them hustle and bustle to make up by other economies for the cost increase caused by the new union wages.

To generalize this possibility into a statement of a general tendency is not permissible. If firms have been in a sheltered position before the wage increase, why should they be more exposed to competition after the wage increase? If all firms in the industry are confronted with the same wage increase, will they not all take the easy way of raising their selling prices rather than suddenly make exertions they have customarily avoided in the past? The thesis might be plausible if the wage increase were forced only upon those firms who had obviously been slack and sluggish and would then be forced to pull up when confronted with a wage increase which, since other firms in the industry are not affected,

[11] J. R. Hicks, *The Theory of Wages* (London: Macmillan, 1932), p. 122.

cannot be translated into a price increase. This would be a plan to "pin-point" particular firms in an industry in a selective wage-raising attack.[12] But as a general theory of the effects of wage increases under union pressure the thesis is untenable.[13]

Energizing the Workers into Increased Efficiency

Increased productivity of labor because of increased efficiency of management is one thing; increased productivity because of increased effort and efficiency of labor is another. There is also a theory that the efforts and efficiency of workers will increase in consequence of increased wages and that these wage increases will therefore pay for themselves.

If workers are undernourished, sick and weak, their physical efforts will surely be inferior to those of well-fed, healthy and strong people. Where a wage increase means the difference between an insufficient and an adequate diet, the workers' efficiency can evidently be increased in consequence of a higher wage. This was certainly true in the early beginnings of the industrial era and is true today in some of the less developed countries where the standards of living of most workers are below the necessary minimum to maintain their physical efficiency. Under these circumstances a firm paying high enough wages to enable its workers to eat decently (and sometimes meals are provided free by the firm) may be able actually to reduce its labor costs. If, however, the total output of the country is very low in comparison with the number of people to be fed, increased money wages for all workers would surely not help. For such countries the improvement of workers' efficiency is primarily a question of increasing per capita output and is a very long-run affair. In any case, for the

---

[12] We are also told that certain trade unions under "union-management cooperation" plans have functioned as efficiency experts advising employers how to operate more economically. The rendering of technical assistance may in actual practice be linked with wage bargaining, but this establishes no inherent connection between wage increase and productivity increase.

[13] If forced increases in cost could be relied upon to induce increases in efficiency, we ought to argue for excise taxes on production. There is surely no reason why one cost increase should induce greater efficiency while another should not. Trade union spokesmen oppose excise taxes because they are sure that the consumer must pay most of these taxes.

labor problem in the industrial countries of our time the argument that increased wages would improve physical efficiency has no relevance.[14]

There is still another possibility. An increase in wage rates may raise the workers' morale and their willingness to do their best. An increase in labor effort per hour proportional to an increase in the wage rate per hour might of course pay for the wage increase. But again no general theory can be based on this possibility. There have been cases where labor effort increased drastically from one week to the next. There have probably been instances when such increased effort was induced by a pay raise that raised the workers' morale. But there is no evidence that such increases in labor effort are permanent. The enthusiasm which inspires them wears off rather quickly and the labor effort soon falls back to the previous level.[15] Moreover, the wage increase may just as easily produce a reduction in labor effort. Workers may be disappointed by the raise, which may be smaller than the raise they had hoped to get. Or the raise may permit the workers to have a better time—which may take some of their energy and leave less for their labor effort.

Practically no support for the argument that forced wage increases can be paid out of a wage-boost-induced increase in labor productivity has been derived from the theses reviewed.

REDISTRIBUTING THE NATIONAL INCOME

Perhaps the most common claim of trade unions is that they have effected a redistribution of the national income.[16] Undoubtedly they have; but have they succeeded—can they succeed—in changing the distribution in favor of labor?

[14] A qualification may perhaps be in order with regard to a few very isolated areas or in particularly poor slum conditions in big cities. But even there wage increases would not "pay for themselves" through increased worker efficiency.

[15] We have not discussed incentive wage schemes, under which extra labor effort is separately paid for.

[16] "A prime objective of collective bargaining is the redistribution of the proceeds of production." Clinton S. Golden and Harold J. Ruttenberg, *op. cit.*, p. 151.

Gaining—at Whose Expense?

No one, of course, questions the ability of particular trade unions by driving powerful wage bargains to effect a change in income distribution in favor of their members, or at least of those of their members who stay employed. But the essential question is at whose expense this change will be accomplished. Will it be, in the long run, at the expense of profits and property incomes or will it be at the expense of other labor groups? This question has been debated for over a century, but no agreement has been reached. The one side is just as firmly convinced that strong bargaining increases the workers' share in the national product at the expense of capitalists as the other side is convinced that in the long run the workers in unions with greater bargaining power obtain their gains at the expense of workers in weaker unions or no unions.

The "visible evidence" seems to be all in support of the union argument. For example, we see, or read about, a great union victory, achieved after a hard struggle against strong resistance of management, the wage contract thus obtained providing for a substantial increase in wage rates and the workers thereafter receiving higher wages. This takes place all the time, one week in that industry, next week in another, and everywhere about the same pattern: a union victory against an unwilling management, a new wage contract, higher wages. How can one doubt, in view of this record, that collective bargaining obtains for the workers more than they would get had they to take what employers offered them voluntarily, moved by nothing but the invisible hand of competition?

Economists on the other side of the argument would not deny the "evidence." But the evidence refers only to *money* wages of particular labor *groups* in the *short* run. One may go beyond the visible record and may credit trade union action with gaining increases in money wages even for all workers and even in the long run; or with gaining increases in real wages for some labor groups in the short and long run. But this is still not the issue. The issue is whether one may legitimately ascribe to trade union action an increase in the *real* wages of labor *as a whole* in the *long* run.

The question of short versus long run is pertinent chiefly because of the rate of capital investment. Some of the wage increases may be at the expense of the owners of the immobile capital sunk in particular enterprises. In the long run capital cannot be "exploited" by labor, since liquid capital may simply shy away from investments that do not promise the competitive rate of return—after reserving a safety margin for future union wage demands. And the competitive rate of return on new investment will not be lower because of trade union wage policies.

The question of particular labor groups versus labor as a whole is pertinent because relative wage rates determine the amounts of employment in different industries. Some trade unions have more monopoly power than others and pursue more aggressive wage policies. They are able to keep ahead of the game and maintain "monopolistic" wage differentials over other labor groups.[17] This will mean that fewer workers find employment in the industries that pay the monopolistic wage rates; that in other industries, which absorb some of the workers who cannot get the more attractive jobs, wage rates are lower than they would be otherwise; that some workers may remain unemployed who would otherwise contribute to the national product; and that as consumers the workers have to pay higher prices for the products made with dearer labor.

The last point indicates why the question of real wages versus money wages is pertinent. The prices of consumers goods are unquestionably higher than they would be if money wage rates were not pushed up by trade union pressures. This implies that the increased money wages do not buy correspondingly increased amounts of goods, and probably buy no more than could have been bought with money wages not raised at all. (The phenomenon of the wage-price spiral since the Second World War has made this point common knowledge.)

Real Wages and Labor's Relative Share

But further evidence is presented to support the thesis that trade union action has been successful in raising labor's share in

[17] For a discussion of "monopolistic wage differentials" see below, pp. 414 ff.

the national income. Firstly, the absolute share of labor—total real wages—as well as real wages per worker have markedly increased in the United States since the beginning of the labor movement. Secondly, the relative share of labor—the portion of wage and salary incomes in the total national income—has increased also.

However, the evidence can be explained differently and, therefore, does not prove what it is supposed to prove. The remarkable increase in real wages per worker can be explained as the result of increased productivity, partly due to improved technology, partly due to an increase in the supply of capital; and the same increase in real wages may also have occurred without any collective bargaining.[18] The increase in the relative share of wage and salary incomes [19] can be explained by the rapid growth of capital per worker, which drastically reduced the scarcity of capital relative to labor, and by a few statistical quirks, such as the shift of many persons from the category of self-employed into the category of salary recipients.

Careful consultation of the statistical record of money wage rates, real wage rates, total money wage income, total real wage income, and relative share of wage income in the national income gives no support to the argument that union wage pressures have succeeded in redistributing the national income in favor of labor. At some times money wages and real wages moved together, at other times they moved in opposite directions. Increased real

[18] "It is neither wise nor necessary to attempt to make a case for collective bargaining in terms of an alleged failure for wages to rise when individuals bargain with large corporations.

"Between 1880 and 1930 the percentage of workers in the United States who were organized into unions was rather low. Business was in the saddle and ran the country pretty much as it wished to run it. During this period, however, real per capita incomes rose about two and one-half fold. The amount of capital per worker increased nearly three-fold." Sumner H. Slichter, Reservation to the "Report and Recommendations of the Labor Committee" of the Twentieth Century Fund. *Trends in Collective Bargaining.* (New York: Twentieth Century Fund, 1945), p. 219.

[19] For the thirty years prior to 1928 the relative share of wages and salaries in the national income varied between 59.5 percent (in the decade 1899–1908) and 65.1 percent (in the decade 1919–1928). Since 1930 the variations were between 59.44 percent (in 1941) and 72.73 percent (in 1933).

wage rates were in some years associated with increased total wage income, in other years with reduced total wage income. A higher total wage income represented in some years a higher relative share, in other years a lower relative share of the national income. By and large, the annual changes in the relative share of labor income are associated most closely with changes in business activity and corporation profits—labor's share being highest in the worst depression years with serious unemployment, and lowest in prosperity years with high levels of employment and profits. Thus, the years when money wage rates, total money wage income, and total real wage income were most depressed yielded some of the highest relative shares of labor.

Wage Increases Paid Out of Profits?

In view of the inconclusiveness of the record we must examine the arguments of the spokesmen for trade union wage policies as far as they relate to the distribution of income. When they present their demands for wage increases, they repeatedly point to the large profits in the industries with whose representatives they start bargaining, and state that these profits are large enough to absorb the wage increases demanded. And they conclude that employment need not be reduced nor prices increased in consequence of the wage raise they propose. This argument tallies with the original thesis that trade unions through collective bargaining could achieve their aims entirely at the expense of profits.

If trade unions based a wage demand on the existence of high average or aggregate profits in an "industry," they would soon find when they started bargaining with individual firms that some firms might be making large profits while others were making little or none at all. Unless the industry is concentrated in a very few monopolistic firms, the existence of high aggregate profits or of high profits in a few of the lower-cost firms would be no indication of whether all firms across the board were making sufficient profits to meet a wage demand based upon the average level of profits.[20]

[20] The argument of trade unions basing their wage demands on high profits of the "industry" has sometimes been referred to as the "statistical fallacy."

LABOR POLICIES

But even if firms *could* meet wage demands entirely out of profits, one must ask the further question whether they *would* do so. Here the analysis of the different effects of excise taxes and lump sum taxes furnishes an illuminating analogy. If a lump sum tax equal to the increase in labor cost that would result from an increase in wage rates for a given work force were imposed on the firm, it might be able to pay this sum out of profits and would have no incentive to reduce employment or make any other adjustments. But if the cost increase is imposed as an additional expense of the firm for each hour of labor that it uses, it is hardly conceivable that the firm would fail to make appropriate adjustments, for example by employing less labor and by charging higher prices for the product.[21]

The notion of forced wage increases payable out of profits must therefore be analysed with a view to the adjustments firms typically make when wage demands are made upon them. We shall undertake this analysis, first, for the case where workers attempt to get a "cut" in the *monopoly* profits of their employers and, second, for the case when workers even in *competitive* industries attempt to "squeeze" profits whenever they appear as a result of changes in demand or technology.

Getting a "Cut" in Monopoly Profits

Where a firm enjoys a high degree of monopoly in the sale of its products and can reap monopoly profits, the thought that the workers employed in the firm might appropriate a large share in the profits is very attractive. As a matter of fact, labor unions can be most successful in such situations.

Unions do not attempt to break the business monopolies of the firms with which they deal; they avoid doing anything to reduce the degree of monopoly that the firms have in their selling markets. On the contrary, unions may seek to increase and con-

[21] The argument basing wage demands on the firms' *ability to pay*—stressing their ability to pay the increase out of their profits without raising their selling prices—appears to count on the firms' *inability to act* in response to the increased labor cost. As a rule, firms that have acquired some ability to pay have had ability to act and adjust. Why should they suddenly be paralysed and fail to adjust to the increase in an important cost item?

solidate these monopolistic positions. We know of many cases where a union has succeeded in "organizing" the employers, in limiting competition among them and in protecting them from "chiseling" newcomers. This is sometimes done by making sure that no potential competitor can obtain the necessary supply of labor or materials. Successful union-management cooperation in restraining competition among business firms has been described in many court cases in which the Government charged violations of the antitrust laws.[22]

But the aid which a union may give to established business firms in their efforts to limit competition need not take such sensational forms. Much less conspicuous methods will often be even more effective. For example, the adoption by a national trade union of a uniform wage standard for the entire industry can effectively eliminate new competition from areas in which the competitive wage level is lower because of differences in labor efficiency, natural resources, or capital endowment. Through such wage standards the unions protect the established business firms from newcomers' competition. That trade unions frequently also give political aid to the maintenance of monopolistic positions of their industries through supporting high protective tariffs is an old story.

The effect of such interplays between business monopoly and labor monopoly are not compensatory but additive. The output restriction by the monopolistic enterprise will usually be more drastic after the labor union accomplishes its objective. The protection which the union secures for the monopoly position of the firm will permit the latter to pursue a bolder price policy. In

[22] In order to strengthen the competitive position of local manufacturers, Chicago carpenters combined with millwork manufacturers and contractors to refuse to install material made by non-union mills located outside of Illinois. *United States* v. *Brims*, 272 U.S. 549 (1926). In order to protect manufacturers, electrical workers in New York City combined with their employers to boycott out-of-city and non-union electrical products. *Allen Bradley Co.* v. *Local #3, Brotherhood of Electrical Workers*, 325 U.S. 797 (1944). In the "Chicago Milk Case" a labor union was charged with combining with distributors and producers to prevent milk being brought into Chicago by persons who refused to maintain illegally fixed prices. *The Meadowmoor Dairies, Inc.* v. *The Milk Wagon Drivers' Union*, 371 Ill. 377; 21 N.E. (2nd) 308 (1939).

addition, whatever the demand situation, the increased labor cost will be an incentive to still sharper output restriction and higher prices. True, the workers employed in the firm will have become sleeping partners sharing in the monopoly profits of their employer; but the restriction of production, at the expense of other workers and consumers, will be more serious than before.[23]

Some exceptional situations have received much attention in recent literature. Economists have developed hypothetical cases in which business firms would swallow wage increases without reducing employment and without raising selling prices. These are cases where all of the following four conditions prevail: (1) There is no way of introducing labor-saving methods, that is, of producing the same output with less labor; (2) all firms concerned are making monopoly profits, that is, there is no marginal firm which could not stand the increased cost; (3) the firms sell at prices fixed by conspiracy, collusion, or in fear of retaliation; and (4) the firms, despite such concerted actions or group spirit and despite the higher labor cost due to the union wage increase, do not dare to make any upward revision of their selling prices. This is a conjuncture of conditions which furnishes intellectual satisfaction to the student of economic theory but which cannot be found often in reality. In general, while it will be relatively easy for trade unions to obtain wage increases where business makes high monopoly profits, there will be a restrictive effect of the monopolistic wage rates in addition to the restrictive effects of the monopolistic selling prices. That is to say, the raise which the workers can force upon the monopolistic employers will not be all at the expense of monopoly profits but will be partly at the expense of other labor groups.

Squeezing all Profits in a Changing Economy

Thus, when labor monopolies "cut in" on the profits of monopolistic enterprises, existing output restrictions will be aggravated. But when labor monopolies try to appropriate all super-

[23] As Joan Robinson says, ". . . monopolistic exploitation cannot be removed by raising wages." *The Economics of Imperfect Competition* (London: Macmillan, 1932), p. 290.

normal profits of competitive businesses, a progressive paralysis may afflict the economy.

In an economy steered by the profit motive the emergence of profits—due to increased demand for an industry's products or to its improved methods of production—has a definite function. It is to attract additional resources to that industry. If, however, an alert trade union quickly appropriates these profits in the form of increased wages, it sabotages the functioning of the system. "Where labor resources are not much specialized, the proper correction for inordinate rates of return on investment is not higher wages but larger investment, larger employment, larger output, and lower relative product prices. . . . Temporary increases in relative wages are justified if necessary to attract additional supplies of labor from other industries. If attained by collusive, collective action of workers where supply is adequate or redundant, increases will serve, not to facilitate expansion of output, but to prevent it." [24]

Profits which properly fulfill their function of attracting additional resources—natural resources, capital, enterprise, and labor —will be only temporary because, after these resources are put to work in the profitable industries and the new output is available, the prices of the products must fall. If, instead, the workers in the profitable industries through expeditious action of strong unions can by way of pay increases seize the profits, the re-allocation of resources will not take place. These wage increases are then paid, ultimately, not at the expense of profits—which sooner or later would have been dissipated in the form of lower prices to consumers—but at the expense of all other workers, who as consumers are deprived of the income increase they would have had through the reduction of prices.

---

[24] Henry C. Simons, "Some Reflexions on Syndicalism," *Journal of Political Economy*, Vol. LII (1944), p. 16. Simons was a liberal economist. A socialist economist may be quoted on the same subject coming to the same conclusion: "If profits are kept at the normal level by changes in wages . . . the mechanism by which resources are directed from one use to another breaks down . . . A system of uncontrolled private enterprise in which wages are more plastic than profits must entail the misdirection of resources and the waste of potential wealth on an extensive scale." Joan Robinson, *op. cit.*, p. 291.

Thus, what on the surface appears to be a wage increase at the expense of profits, and nothing but profits, turns out upon examination to be an increase for some workers at the expense of the rest of the people. Rather than the successful transfusion of income from capitalists to workers that it was believed to be, the redistribution is in effect one from the mass of workers (and other consumers) to a privileged group of workers. Moreover, it is not merely a *redistribution* of national income but a *preclusion* of a potential increase. An increase in national income would have been brought about through the reallocation of resources under the stimulus of the supernormal profits, but is precluded as a result of the seizure of the profits through the successful collective bargaining.

Raising Wages as Productivity Rises

The problem of redistributing the national income is complicated, as we have seen, when the economy is growing, first, because the redistribution is then often confined to the increment of national income, so that the groups deprived of income do not lose what they have had, but only what they would have had in the absence of the redistributing measures; and secondly, because these measures may prevent some of the potential increase in national income from being realized at all and may thus inflict on some or on everybody an additional loss that is not offset by anybody's gain.

This insight is helpful when we examine the question of the distribution of the fruits of increased productivity in a growing economy. There are many possible ways in which the benefits of increased productivity may be distributed among the people. For example, they may accrue to consumers, through price reductions of goods produced; to all labor, through increases in wages, salaries, and incomes of the self-employed; to all wage labor, through increases of all wage rates; only to organized workers, through increases in union wage rates; only to the workers employed in the industries in which the increase in productivity takes place, through increases in their pay; or only to the owners of the capital invested in these industries, through increases in their profits and through protection of these profits by means of barriers to expansion and to the entry of newcomers. The last of these methods of distribution is universally rejected and competition is supposed to prevent it from occurring. The first is generally among economists regarded as the most equitable one, although it is opposed by those who doubt the smooth functioning of an economy with a steadily falling price level and a constant wage level. A number of economists advocate a continually rising wage level, provided the wage increases are general and not excessive, so that they can be met out of the continual rise in productivity without an increase in the price level.

The case for a slowly rising wage level, advancing in step with the productivity of labor, is sometimes presented as a case for strong trade union wage pressures. This might theoretically result in a distribution of the benefits of progress to organized workers alone—or to less than one-fourth of the labor force in the United States. In practice, some of the wage increases would probably spill over to some of the unorganized labor groups (chiefly *via* the increase in effective demand financed through the credit or fiscal expansion needed to avoid the unemployment which the union wage increases would otherwise create). Real trouble, however, may come from an interpretation of the case for "wages rising with productivity" that would reserve the benefits of advancing productivity to the workers in the industries in which the advance takes place.

Indeed, such interpretation is sometimes made, and the call for wage increases in proportion to the increase in productivity is taken to justify union demands in those industries which, because of improved technology and consequent cost reductions, can afford to pay higher wages without charging higher prices for their products. This proposition is thoroughly unsound. It misses completely the economic function of prices and wages; its realization would sabotage the economic allocation of resources without serving any purpose that could be justified from any ethical or political point of view.

A sensible allocation of resources, including labor, requires that they not be used for less urgently demanded products if they could be used for products more urgently demanded. The competitive market is supposed to accomplish this allocation by making the same goods or services available to all potential users at the same prices; price differentials for the same services do however have a function within an economic system, namely, to induce a transfer of resources to superior use-opportunities where the transfer itself is costly. Clearly, then, to propose that firms or industries in which productivity has increased should be forced to pay higher wages for the same kind of work that rates lower wages elsewhere, is sheer foolishness from an economic point of view.[25]

One might accept an economically unsound arrangement if it were ethically much superior. But no one could claim that the proposition in question satisfied any ethical norm. If five industries, let us call them A, B, C, D, and E, employ the same type of labor; if one of them, say Industry A, develops a new production process and is now able to make the same product as before with half the amount of labor; then this Industry A could afford to raise its wage rates without raising its selling prices. Should now workers in Industry A get a wage increase of 100 percent while their fellow workers in Industries B, C, D, and E get nothing? Should the coincidence that the technological advance took place in A give the workers there the windfall of the entire benefit, raising them above the rest of the people? I can see no ethical argument that could be made in favor of such a scheme.

But as a matter of practical fact, apart from economics and ethics, the scheme could never be consistently applied, because the workers in other industries would not stand for it, if they also had any monopoly power. Recent history has shown this quite clearly. When the first wage adjustments were made after the

[25] This would be as unreasonable as to charge different prices of coal to different industries according to their ability to pay; or to sell cotton more cheaply to inefficient spinning mills and charge more to those who can afford to pay more; or to sell steel at a higher price to those who produce goods that are urgently demanded and therefore can be made and sold with profit, but to give low-priced steel to those who produce goods that are less urgently demanded and therefore cannot be profitably produced. Of course, for a monopolist, practicing price discrimination in order to exploit consumers as thoroughly as possible, the scheme would be sensible. As a general principle—if the nation's resources are to be used economically—the scheme is fatuous.

last World War, difficult wage negotiations between strong trade unions and large corporations were aided by "impartial and objective fact-finding": experts studied what would be the particular firm's ability to pay higher wages without raising prices. Yet as soon as the first fact-finding was completed, unions came demanding the same or similar wage increases in other firms and other industries, one after another, wherever the bargaining power of the unions was up to the task, and similar wage increases had to be given in all of these firms and industries regardless of their ability to pay, regardless of whether their selling prices would remain stable or go up slightly or a great deal. It simply would not be fair if a favored group were to be the sole beneficiary of progress while the rest of the population would have to sit back and wait for better luck.

Under these circumstances we ought to realize that a rule of granting wage increases commensurate with productivity increases is not easily translated into practice. It will be difficult to make people understand that it does *not* mean wage increases in the firms or industries that could afford to pay higher wages, but that it means, instead, wage increases all over the lot approximating the average increase in productivity of the economy. Over the past fifty years the productivity of the economy has increased on the average by something between 2½ and 3 percent a year. If it is proposed to advance the wage level without pushing up the price level, the wage increases will have to stay within the 2½ and 3 percent per year.

Even this would mean that the benefits of progress were distributed exclusively to the employed members of the labor force. The pensioners and annuitants, the people living on past savings and those who cannot obtain a raise in pay, because their employers could not stand it, would be excluded from the benefits of progress. And as a matter of practical fact, it is probably out of the question to expect trade unions to exercise the moderation essential to the plan. A union would hardly be so modest as to ask for only a three percent increase if it thinks it could get ten percent. As soon as one union obtains a greater raise, the race is on and the consequence is a distribution of the benefits of increasing productivity which is not in favor of "labor," but in favor of the particular labor groups that have greater monopoly power, to the disadvantage of the rest of the people.

The Unorganized Majority

While some advocates of the argument for redistribution of income through collective bargaining deny that such redistribution may be at the expense of unorganized labor, others are willing to admit it, adding the advice, however, that these workers had better get organized. The implication, and sometimes the explicit contention, is that trade unions and collective bargaining would do for these as yet non-unionized labor groups what it has done for union labor: it would give them the bargaining power they now lack and secure them higher wages.

The advice—to the extent to which it is practicable—may be good. A labor group that has fallen behind other groups in the scramble for an increased share in the total product may well eliminate some of the handicap if it organizes and attains bargaining power. But whatever it thus obtains will reduce the advantage which the earlier organized labor groups have attained through the use of their collective bargaining power. The advice, therefore, is disinterested and indeed self-sacrificing. (It is as if a winning player in a card-game taught the other players the techniques by which he has gained superiority over them.) Of course, as long as only a minority of workers is organized, the unionization of additional labor groups need not seriously hurt the members of existing unions, since the gains which the new union can win for the newly organized workers will probably still come to a greater extent out of the potential earnings of the unorganized majority. It is not practically possible for all members of the labor force to be organized in unions that could collectively bargain for them.[26]

[26] Only three-fourths of the civilian labor force are "non-agricultural wage and salary earners." The rest are self-employed and agricultural workers. For the self-employed to attain "bargaining power" that could raise the value of their labor would mean attaining monopoly power in the sale of the products of their labor. Farmers—though not farm workers—are probably now receiving monopoly prices for their labor thanks to government measures. Since less than one-fourth of the civilian labor force is unionized, more than two-thirds of all non-agricultural wage and salary earners (that

But if it were possible and all workers were organized, the bargaining power (in the wider sense of the word) [27] of the unions would surely be unequal, and collective bargaining would still yield relative wages different from those that would emerge without any unions. The consequent redistributions of income from the members of unions with less bargaining power to the members of those with more would however imply that the gains and losses would be relatively smaller than they were when an organized minority had an unorganized majority to feed on.

The thesis that any gains which the organized minority of workers have made thanks to collective wage bargaining have in effect been losses of the unorganized majority of workers can be neatly demonstrated in the form of syllogistic reasoning.

(1) The unions have secured increases in real wages for their members beyond what they would have received otherwise;

(2) The union wage pressures have not induced increases in efficiency or productivity beyond what would have occurred in any case;

(3) The union wage pressures have not over long periods reduced the profitability of industry below what it would have been;

(4) It follows that the gains referred to in (1) must have been chiefly at the expense of unorganized workers.

Are the premises "true"? The first premise is an assertion by the advocates of hard collective bargaining and is not contested by the opposition. The second premise is probably false and must be qualified; there have undoubtedly been some induced advances in productivity, though perhaps not of substantial size. To the extent to which the increases in real wages secured by union pressures have been greater than the increases in productivity induced by them, the conclusion remains valid. The validity of the third premise is difficult to appraise. As regards the actual profitability of industry, statistical profit data, although not reliable, convey the impression that over long periods profits have not diminished relatively to other types of income. Indeed, the continued existence of profits of "excessive" magnitude is regularly cited by union

---

is, more than one-half of the civilian labor force) receive wages not set by collective bargaining.

[27] See above, Chapter 9, pp. 344–48.

representatives when they justify their periodic wage demands. Now there is still the possibility that profits as a share of total income would have much increased had it not been for the trade unions. I do not know of any economists so arguing. If we, then, take the three premises to be acceptable, the conclusion follows, with a qualification—which was expressed above by the adverb "chiefly"—to take account of the possibility that a third class of income recipients might have paid for the gain of the union workers. Yet, that interest and rent incomes should have been permanently reduced as a result of the wage increases secured by unions does not appear very plausible.[28]

There Will Always Be a Short Run

Most of the theorizing about the effects of collective bargaining by strong unions upon the distribution of the national income refers to the "long run." Temporary effects are usually disregarded and only permanent effects are stressed.

This kind of theorizing may yield results not applicable to the affairs of the real world. Assume, for example, that the wage increases secured by collective bargaining can temporarily encroach upon profits; that the adjustments, which eventually shift the incidence from the owners of enterprise to consumers and unorganized workers, take time; and that, before this time is over, the unions act again and secure another advance in wage rates; would this not invalidate the theory? If the trade unions never allow the economy enough time for the adjustments to work themselves out, if they move again and again and always stay ahead

---

[28] National income statistics in the United States indeed show that the relative shares of wages and salaries as well as profits have increased, while the relative shares of interest and of rent have decreased, in the last twenty years. The large supply of loanable funds, augmented by bank credit expansion under a conscious easy-money policy of the monetary authorities, fully explains the relatively lower interest income Rent controls can explain the relatively lower rent income. To the extent that the large increases in the prices of goods and services should be attributed to union wage policies, while rents have been kept down through rent controls, one might "credit" the trade union wage pressures with the relative reduction of rent income. But this would imply charging the trade unions with the responsibility for the inflation.

of the game, is it not the short-run theory that should be applied? Since there will always be a short run, are not the short-run effects the ones that really count?

These are highly suggestive questions and one is easily persuaded to answer them affirmatively. But what they really call for is an examination of the meaning of "long-run" adjustments in this context. Probing into this, we can see that it covers very different things, some of which may take a life-time of a plant while others may take no more than the reaction-time of an alert businessman. We can see, moreover, that adjustment periods have no fixed clock-time or calendar time, but may become shorter and shorter as the same sort of stimulus recurs and the pattern of response remains essentially the same. The stimuli are the wage pressures by trade unions, the responses are investment decisions and price decisions by businessmen. At first it could be assumed that it would take many years—namely, until the replacement of deteriorated equipment becomes necessary—for the forced wage cost increases to be followed by reduced investment in the affected industries. As time goes on, however, one will have to assume that entrepreneurs include trade union wage pressures in their expectations, so that their investment decisions reflect, not past "disappointments," but rather "anticipations" of future cost increases. In other words, investments may be adjusted or even overadjusted to union wage pressures long in advance. Price decisions, which first are assumed to wait for the determination of the exact effects upon production cost or even for the emergence of inflated demands for products, may later have to be assumed to be coincident with, if not anticipatory of, the acceptance of a new wage contract fixing increased rates of pay.

In brief, what in an analytical model is regarded as the short run may be without relevance to reality, and what in the model is called the long run may refer to adjustments which in reality may not be long delayed but, instead, may be practically instantaneous or even in advance of the impulse that "causes" them. No one knows to what extent this may have happened with regard to the adjustments to union wage pressures in our economy. No one knows whether short-run theory or long-run theory is more applicable to the appraisal of the effects of union wage determination upon income distribution. I am inclined to regard long-run theory as the one that is really relevant for the point at issue.

THE WAGE STRUCTURE

Bargaining power (monopoly power) has been defined in terms of control or influence over *price* or in terms of control or restriction of *supply*. The same difficulties that exist with respect to the relationship between the two criteria in the discussion of business monopoly confront us in the discussion of labor monopoly.

Restricting the Supply

When we say that a seller has control over price this may refer to a different good or service than is referred to when we say that he has control over supply. In order to obtain control over the price of a service it may be necessary that control over supply extend to a competing service. Full control over the supply of a certain kind of labor, for example, means little or nothing if the supply of a competing kind of labor, of an almost perfect substitute, cannot be controlled at all. In this case some degree of control over price can only be established—either by extending the control over supply to the competing labor group or by reducing the substitutability between the two kinds of labor. The latter can be done through many devices, for example, by making the use of the competing labor less desirable through the withholding of complementary services. Sometimes different "kinds" of labor are not different because of differences in skill, experience, physical strength, intelligence, location, etc., but merely because workers possess or do not possess membership cards in a particular trade union or trade union local.[29] On the other hand, the natural differences may be sufficiently great, the substitutability of other kinds of labor sufficiently imperfect, to make it unnecessary to resort to artificial reductions of substitutability or to extend the control over supply to other labor groups. The meaning of control over supply

[29] The differentiation of labor in the building industry is most remarkable. Because of union definitions up to 19 different "crafts" are required for the building of a house.

then becomes unambiguous. Where we are sure what "supply" is controlled, "control" means essentially that every individual worker will refuse to supply any labor (a) at a wage below that agreed in the union contract and (b) whenever the union leadership orders a concerted withholding of all labor, that is, a strike.

The objective of the exercise of bargaining power is to obtain a higher *price* for the labor of the union members and this presupposes that the union can control the *supply*. For otherwise employers may get labor from other "sources of supply" or from disloyal members of the union, at a lower price, and the fixing of a union wage is ineffective. While thus the restrictions on the amounts of labor available to employers are prerequisite for the exercise of control over price, the determination of the price determines the amounts of labor the employers will employ. This may give the appearance of a fixed number of jobs in the firm or industry and, although it reflects the limitation of demand, it may by itself act, as we shall presently see, as an effective deterrent to potential suppliers of labor.

The greater the number of unemployed job seekers in a particular field, the harder it becomes for the union to "control" the supply of labor. In order to maintain its bargaining position, therefore, the union will often find it desirable to restrict the number of persons who might become aspirants for jobs. In craft unions this is often done through apprenticeship rules by which the ratio of apprentices to old hands is held down and the period of apprenticeship is extended.[30] Sometimes the unions charge exorbitant initiation fees, which may operate as a deterrent for would-be members of the craft.[31] There may be all sorts of ritualistic or

[30] Examples: electricians have allowed no more than one apprentice for every three workers; plasterers sometimes only one apprentice for every ten workers; bricklayers in some states got the legislature to restrict the number of apprentices to one apprentice for every eight journeymen; carpenters have varied the ratio between 1:4 and 1:10, and in some states require four years of apprenticeship with low beginners' wages and strict rules for the kind of tasks they are allowed to do.

[31] The union initiation fees for airline pilots have been up to $100, for stage hands up to $150, for hod carriers up to $250, for theatrical agents up to $500. By contrast, the initiation fees charged by large industrial unions are very low. The United Textile Workers, a few years ago, charged only $1, the United Steel Workers $3.

legalistic barriers to entry, prohibitive "hiring hall rules," and other devices to restrict the long-run supply of labor controlled by the union.

The "keeping out of substitute labor" is often not enough, especially if the substitute labor can compete indirectly through its products. In such cases a union may refuse to permit the use of intermediate products made elsewhere.[32] Sometimes they permit the use of competing labor or of competing intermediate products provided the employer also hires union members to "stand-by" or to perform unnecessary tasks.[33] Some unions undertake to fight the substitution of machinery for the labor of their members, or even the use of more efficient working methods if they result in the replacement of labor.[34]

Some of the devices by which the competition of non-union members, out-of-town labor, or not-on-the-spot labor is excluded may with equal logic be regarded as means of restricting the supply of labor (where "supply" comprises the substitutes) or as means of enhancing the demand for labor (where "labor" means only the employment of local union members). The same two ways of looking at the problem suggest themselves with regard to slow-down rules. If a union sets maximum standards for their members' hourly or daily performance, one may regard this as a device for restricting the supply (of labor effort per man) or as a device

[32] For example, the carpenters have refused to permit the use of lumber that was cut in the lumber yards to the exact sizes needed for a building and have insisted that the carpenters do the cutting or trimming at the site. Likewise, plumbers have insisted that certain plumbing units be fitted-together "on the job." Or the hanging of factory-glazed windows or the installation of factory-painted kitchen cabinets have been forbidden by unions in the building trades.

[33] Teamsters' unions have required trucks entering a city to hire a member of the local in addition to the out-of-town driver on the truck. Musicians' unions have required the employment of stand-by musicians when recorded music was performed. Under typographical union law, advertising plates and matter set up in outside print shops may be accepted by newspaper composing rooms only if duplicates are set up in the newspaper plant and discarded.

[34] The painters' union has prohibited the use of spray guns and they have prescribed the maximum width of brushes to be used by union painters. A Chicago building trade union prevented the use of ready-mixed concrete and insisted on the use of the obsolete "puddle-method."

for increasing the demand (for workers). Maximum performance
rules of this sort have been customary in several trades.[35]

"No Help Wanted"

·All the restrictive devices for controlling the supply of labor
are probably less important in their effects than the restriction of
the amount of labor employed that is inherent in the wage bargain itself. The bargain, if it fixes monopolistic wage rates, restricts the number of jobs in the trades or industries concerned.[36]

The sign "no help wanted" is the most effective barrier to entry. The firms, having agreed by contract with the union to pay
certain minimum rates, may not be aware of any "restriction" of
the labor supply; they can get all the workers for the jobs they
wish to fill. But the number of jobs is restricted by the high price
of labor.

If the wage rates fixed between the union and the employers
are in excess of the competitive rates, the attractive wage differential might make workers who are employed elsewhere at lower
wages more than willing to seek employment in the firms paying
the better wages. But, alas, all jobs there are filled and applicants
are turned away. These underprivileged who are crowding the occupations that are still open, will never know that it was a monopolistic wage bargain that excluded them from the jobs they
desired; all they ever know is that the industry had all the men
that were "needed" and that all jobs were held by more fortu-
nate people who had been there first and had a sort of squatter's
right.

The number of workers which an industry "needs" depends on
the wage rate it has to pay. A monopolistic wage rate determination restricts the number of workers who find work in that industry and excludes a large number of others, who are compelled
to seek employment elsewhere at less satisfactory wages.

This exclusion of willing and able workers from better jobs is

[35] Best-known examples: typesetters, bricklayers, shinglers.

[36] As Hicks has said, "a man ignorant of economics nearly always feels
the regulation of prices to be more justifiable than the limitation of supply—
although they come to the same thing." *The Theory of Wages,* p. 166.

deplorable not merely from the point of view of equity and justice; it reduces the performance of the whole economic system in a most crucial respect. The "economic principle" calls for an allocation of resources in such a way that more valuable tasks get a priority before less valuable tasks. The total national product is reduced whenever resources are shut out from more valuable uses and diverted to less valuable ones. Monopolistic pricing of goods or labor does exactly this. It restricts the employment of labor in the production of goods that are more desired and forces the excluded labor into less desired uses or into idleness.

"Natural" and "Artificial" Wage Differentials

If all work were equally unpleasant and all workers equally skilled, any existing wage differentials would be due to lack of mobility and lack of competition. Enduring deviations from the "normal" wage level would be due to monopsony or monopoly. Now, of course, the unpleasantness of work and the quality of labor are not equal in all occupations and industries, and this accounts for considerable wage differentials. How can these "natural" differentials be distinguished from the "artificial" ones, that is, from those caused by restraints of competition?

The workers themselves are the sole judges of differences in the unpleasantness of work and they are reasonably good judges of their own qualifications. If a worker seeks to transfer to a certain job, he is usually convinced that he is capable of doing the job and he will have appraised the differences in unpleasantness. If the wage rate in an occupation or industry is so high that workers in large numbers prefer employment there to the alternatives that are open to them, and if they cannot get the preferred employment, that wage rate is monopolistic.

If a certain job pays $1.50 per hour while another pays only $1.10 and if this differential of 40 cents were just enough to pay for the greater unpleasantness or for the rarer qualification, there would not be large numbers of workers desirous of shifting from the $1.10 job to the $1.50 job. If many, however, would like to shift but find that no more workers are wanted where the better wage is paid, then the better wage is not the result of a naturally scarce supply but of monopolistic wage determination.

A wage higher than that paid in other industries or occupations is monopolistic if it prevents, and it is proper if it permits, the "maximum transfer of workers from less attractive, less remunerative, less productive employments." [37]

Wages in General Are Too Low

This discussion should make it clear that the complaint against monopolistic wage rates does not imply that wage rates "in general" are too high. The exact opposite is true. Since monopolistic wage rates mean that the access to preferred jobs is restricted, they also mean that more people are forced into poorer jobs. These poorer jobs are made still poorer through the oversupply of labor excluded from employment that is monopolistically controlled. An elimination of monopolistic wage determination would open up the better jobs—which would then, of course, be somewhat less attractive than they are now—and would relieve the congestion in the low-wage industries and occupations. As a result, *real wages in general would be higher* if the low wage rates were permitted to rise in consequence of mass migrations of workers into the higher-wage jobs that would open up when these high wages were appropriately reduced.

The increase in the general level of real wages that would result from the change in the wage structure—from the reduction of monopolistic wage rates—would be chiefly a matter of increased employment and output in industries where operations are now restricted because of the artificially increased labor cost. The argument relates essentially to relative wages, not to the money wage level, and is based on the real output produced in the economy and on the real wages received by workers.[38]

[37] Simons, *op. cit.*, p. 14.

[38] I am fully aware of the fact that persons not well trained in economic theory will be skeptical concerning such pronouncements. Believing only in what they can see immediately and as "concrete reality," they will take only the wage cuts as real and regard the promise of an increase in the general real wage level as a pious hope, if not as a false front. But they are

The reduction of "monopolistic" wage rates can be regarded as "appropriate" when it increases the number of jobs and reduces the number of job seekers in the particular industry and area sufficiently to establish equilibrium of supply and demand. Trade unions could exercise important functions in establishing labor markets designed to achieve these equilibria of supply and demand for all areas and industries and to increase the mobility of workers between them. But these functions would not be compatible with the traditional concept of collective bargaining for the purpose of securing the highest possible wage rates for the members of large and strong unions. The present concept of collective bargaining—based on wage rate determination according to all the bargaining power the parties can obtain—cannot be reconciled with the idea of unrestricted access of workers to the jobs they want.

The problem of an economic wage determination is completely misunderstood by the public and the significance of the wage structure is not appreciated. While the notions of supply and demand are at least vaguely understood in relation to commodity prices, there does not seem to be even a faint suspicion that supply and demand could possibly have something to do with the determination of appropriate wage rates—except perhaps that supply should be controlled and demand somehow expanded to sustain the wage rates fixed on the basis of relative bargaining power. The announced objectives of legislation are always to "improve" collective bargaining—meaning that the possibilities of disputes be reduced and the chances for their settlement be increased—and to provide for "orderly and peaceful procedures" and cooperation between employers and employees. In short, society does not seem to be in the least interested in what wage rates are agreed upon between strong labor combinations and strong corporate combines, as long as they are the result of peaceful collective bargaining. "Peaceful

---

mistaken at least in the motives of my own considerations. I have no aspirations of talking any union leader into any wage concessions. If strong unions are permitted and furthered by legal and administrative institutions, the members and leaders of such unions should, I believe, get for themselves what they can get. The law is supposed to fix the rules of the game and the citizens should play it as well as they can. As long as society believes in *large and strong* combinations of labor, the leaders of these combinations have a responsibility chiefly to their own members.

labor-management relations" have assumed so great a significance in the minds of the public and the legislators that the question of competitive or monopolistic wage rates is completely ignored.

WAGES, EMPLOYMENT, INFLATION

Economists have always emphasized the relationship between wage rates and employment and have, in particular, stressed the fact that wage increases under union pressure may result in unemployment. As some say, labor can easily price itself out of the market. But although earlier economists had expected that trade union leaders would soon learn this important fact,[39] it has become reasonably clear to most observers that those in charge of union wage policy do not fully appreciate the connection between increased wage rates and reduced employment.

The Hidden Connection

If economists have been so sure about the connection between monopolistic wage increases and unemployment, how was it possible that this "fact" could have been overlooked by labor leaders? The answer is that in some cases the connection is hidden and has not become visible to the trade union men who forced substantial pay raises upon their employers, and in others the connection is short-circuited, as it were, for the wage increases need not cause unemployment, but may cause inflation instead.

1. Several industries in which wage increases were obtained through union pressure enjoy a relatively inelastic demand for their products and, therefore, were able to shift most of the higher labor cost to the consumer through increased product prices. Thus the particular union could gain a conspicuous wage increase while suf-

---

[39] John Stuart Mill, after explaining that unemployment will be caused by forced wage increases, stated: "Experience of strikes has been the best teacher of the laboring classes on the subject of relation between wages and the demand and supply of labor; and it is most important that this course of instruction should not be disturbed." John Stuart Mill, *Principles of Political Economy* (first edition, 1848; third edition, 1852; seventh edition, 1871. Longmans Green & Co., 1926), p. 936. This statement appeared in the third edition, published in 1852, and in all later editions.

fering only an inconspicuous reduction in employment. (It should
be understood that increased prices of products with relatively
inelastic demand imply that consumers must spend more money on
the products in question and have less to spend on other products.)

2. Even in industries with relatively elastic demand it usually
takes some time for the effects of wage increases to materialize.
The increase in product prices may be delayed; the response of the
market to the increase may not be instantaneous; and the response
of the firms to the decline in orders may not be immediate. Hence,
the reaction of employment to the wage increase may be long delayed.

3. If the union did not previously have a complete monopoly of
the labor supply to the particular firm or industry, but gained closed
shop or union shop rights together with the wage increases, any
reduction in employment would occur in the ranks of non-union
workers, while the unions could actually experience an increase in
membership and member employment.

4. If the general trend was favorable to the industry concerned,
permitting an expansion of employment and production, the wage
increases would not cause an absolute reduction in employment
but merely retard its growth. Employment in that industry would
increase in spite of the wage increases and nobody could see that
employment was lower than it could be without the monopolistic
wage differential.

5. While the restriction of the growth of the industry which
had to grant the wage increases may have aggravated the unemployment problem in other fields or areas of the economy, even this
effect could be compensated by credit expansion or expansionary
fiscal policies, permitting demand to absorb higher prices without
decline in aggregate employment.

6. When the restrictive effects of increased wage rates were
not offset by the expansionary effects of an inflated money supply,
and mass unemployment occurred, one could always seek its explanation on other grounds, such as "underconsumption," "over-
saving" "insufficient purchasing power," "strikes of capital," or
what not.

Since the causal connection between forced wage increases, on
the one side, and reduced employment or inflation, on the other, is

usually either indirect and subject to time lags or so generalized that it is hard to demonstrate a direct connection between the actions of an individual union and the reactions throughout the economy, how can one expect the rank and file of union members to ·recognize the connection? Can one expect under these circumstances that individual unions should make it an important consideration in their wage bargaining?

Wage Policies of Trade Unions

The connection between forced wage increases and general unemployment might concern the leaders of an imaginary nationwide union comprising all workers in all trades and industries. But the leaders of any union of workers of only a *particular* industry are at best concerned with unemployment of their members, not with unemployment in general. It is unreasonable to expect the leader of any particular union to assume responsibility for the state of employment in the nation; he is chiefly responsible for the wages of his union's members. The rank and file of a union may want their leader to obtain for them the largest possible pay envelopes, but not to sell them down the river in the interest of a fancy "deflated gross national product" which can hardly mean anything to them. The members of, say, the steel workers union do not pay their leaders for promoting maximum employment either in the steel industry or in the total economy; and if the leaders do what they are appointed to do, they will fight for bigger pay envelopes of their members, regardless of the "unproven" effects upon the economy which academic economists may ascribe to these policies.

Of course, it will be good strategy for union leaders to assert that higher wage rates mean increased purchasing power, and that increased purchasing means higher employment; this may win for their wage policies the sympathy of the public. And it will also be good strategy to plug for so-called full employment policies through fiscal measures of the government; this may win for their wage policies easier acceptance by employers. But they would be unfaithful to their members if they sacrificed a possible wage gain to the "patriotic" objective of greater employment. To expect the union leader to act as a responsible statesman in the interest of the nation is to expect him to do what his followers would consider "selling out to the bosses." Since almost every group of sellers can improve its position by combining to restrict supply and to raise the price of its product or service, the organized sellers of labor services should not be expected to forego these advantages of combination permitted under the law.

We frequently hear about some "exceptional" trade union leaders who have exhibited an exemplary degree of responsibility and moderation.[40] With all due respect for the wisdom and sincerity of these men, I believe that their moderation was conditioned by the particular circumstances of their trades. The trades in question were characterized by exceptionally high elasticities of demand and of technological, occupational and regional substitution. "Moderation" in these instances was in the interest of the members of the union.[41] Where monopoly power, because of the circumstances of the situation, cannot be strong, the fullest exploitation of that power will yield results which may appear to prove remarkable self-restraint. Full exploitation of a union's bargaining position (in the wider sense) may appear as "irresponsible highway robbery" or as "responsible statesmanship" depending on whether the union's monopoly power is strong or weak.

According to current opinion, almost generally accepted, it is the main purpose of a trade union to bargain collectively for its members and obtain for them whatever advantages it can get on the basis of its bargaining power. It is one of the paradoxes of our time that most people will praise the existence of an institution but quickly condemn it when it carries out its functions.

"Full Employment Policy"

Mass unemployment is intolerable. During recent years most industrial nations have charged their governments with the responsibility of preventing mass unemployment and of taking ap-

[40] The Ladies Garment Workers appear to have had such responsible leadership.

[41] Examples of trade unions keenly aware of the relation between wage rates and employment were the glass bottle blowers, the molders, and the hosiery workers; they were impressed with the ease of substitution of machinery for labor or of substitution of non-union labor for union labor. See John T. Dunlop, op. cit., pp. 48 and 64.

propriate measures to secure a high level of employment, if possible, "full employment." [42] What kind of measures should be considered appropriate for this purpose is controversial. But what has become known as "the" full-employment policy consists chiefly of fiscal measures, particularly of increased government expenditures. Since unemployment will usually decline when "effective demand" increases, some economists have chosen to ascribe unemployment, no matter what brought it on, to a "deficiency of effective demand." [43] The cure of such "deficiency" is then seen primarily in loan expenditures of the government.

If it is the recognized responsibility of the government to combat unemployment by providing more "effective demand"; if it is the recognized function of trade unions to use their bargaining power to force up wage rates; and since, with any given amount of effective demand, increased wage rates tend to reduce employment, an unending chase between union wage policy and government fiscal policy must develop. The continual expansion of total demand allows the unions to force wages up whenever a contract expires or can be terminated; the permanent responsibility for maintaining full employment in the face of a total demand that always tends to become insufficient forces the government to continual budget expansions. The result is a continual inflation of the money flow and of commodity prices.

The maintenance of a "sufficient demand"—sufficient to pre-

[42] Full employment, according to one of the more widely used definitions, exists when the number of unemployed job seekers does not exceed the number of vacant jobs. Since there is continuous change, some employment opportunities disappearing while new ones open up; since adjustments take time and the transfer of workers to new jobs cannot take place without friction; and since some jobs as well as some job seekers are available only at certain seasons, a state of full employment will ordinarily involve unemployment of between three and six percent of the labor force. Another, though related, definition of full employment regards it as "a situation in which employment cannot be increased by an increase in effective demand." *National and International Measures for Full Employment*, Report by a Group of Experts appointed by the Secretary General, United Nations (Lake Success, N.Y.: 1949), p. 13.

[43] Commenting on various "causes of unemployment" and on "the main reason" why displaced workers may remain unemployed, the Report of Experts to the United Nations points to "the lack of alternative employment opportunities, which in turn is due to a deficiency of effective demand." *Op. cit.*, p. 13.

vent the emergence of underemployment—implies an expansion of total demand (a) to take care of the regular growth of the labor force and (b) to take care of the regular increase in money wage rates insisted upon by the unions. Not all of the "new spending" that is needed to avoid an "insufficiency" of demand has to be done by the government, for business will often be willing to expand investment outlays at a greater rate than the savings out of current income increase; business may even be willing, in such periods of investment expansion, to finance the increase in working capital needed to pay the increased wages. But these contributions of new business spending to the total expansion of demand cannot always be sufficient. There will be times when business outlays are too small even to provide enough outlays for all the saving that is done out of a "full-employment" income, let alone to finance the increments to the wage bill needed to employ an expanding labor force at increasing wage rates. During such times the government contributions to aggregate spending would have to be particularly heavy.

If government and business spending together were just large enough to provide a complete offset to all the saving that is done out of income, and to provide also employment for the expanded labor force, the money flow would expand, but the level of prices would not be driven up. But if the spending must also allow payment of wage increases exceeding any simultaneous increases in labor productivity, then such spending will drive up the prices of commodities. Continually rising prices can have disruptive effects on the structure of the economy. Quite apart from the injustice which price inflation inflicts upon savers, pensioners and other recipients of relatively fixed incomes, its effects on the economy can be deleterious. Direct price controls cannot permanently suppress such an inflation. They can only add to the damages by reducing the productive efficiency of the system and the standards of morality of the people and their respect for law.

Political Freedom in Jeopardy

We want to avoid price inflation as well as unemployment. But if we allow trade unions to pursue their wage policies while we instruct the government to maintain full employment, we cannot avoid inflation. If we abandon the full-employment policy, we may not be able to avoid serious unemployment. Must the inference be drawn that the double goal of full employment and approximate price stability can be attained only if we destroy the trade unions or restrain them from following the policies they choose? To draw this inference is to forget that society has other goals besides full employment and price stability; it is to forget political freedom as a goal of even superior importance. Abolishing the right of workers to combine and to pursue wage policies of their own choosing would be an odious abrogation of a freedom for which democratic society has long striven. Should it give up this freedom because of a fear of the effects of either inflation or unemployment?

The dilemma, however, is even more serious because political freedom is also in danger if we allow either unemployment or inflation to assume serious dimensions. Mass unemployment over extended periods, apart from its economic and social implications, breeds political upheaval which may well terminate political freedom. Serious inflation, although the reasons are less widely appreciated, may likewise wreck the existing social and political system. Indeed, a historical study of totalitarian revolutions could demonstrate that inflations played a more important role than unemployment in preparing the ground for the fascist or communist revolutions and the establishment of authoritarian regimes.

Political freedom is thus jeopardized from all three sides of our problem. An attempt to smash the trade unions could probably be undertaken only as part of an attempt to set up an authoritarian regime.[44] (Fascism, Nazism and Communism all did away with free trade unionism. Formally, certain labor organizations were allowed to exist, but they were deprived of any powers regarding wage rates.) An attempt to maintain full employment with unrestrained union powers to bargain for higher wage rates would re-

[44] On the problem of controlling or destroying labor monopolies Henry Simons wrote: "Government, long hostile to other monopolies, suddenly sponsored and promoted widespread organization of labor monopolies, which democracy cannot endure, cannot control without destroying, and perhaps cannot destroy without destroying itself." Henry C. Simons, "Hansen on Fiscal Policy," *Journal of Political Economy*, Vol. L (1942), p. 162.

sult in continual inflation, eventually terminated by a totalitarian regime. (This is recognized by many advocates of full employment policy, who therefore propose centralized wage controls.) [45] An attempt to avoid inflation by resisting the fiscal and monetary expansion that would finance the maintenance of employment in the face of increased union wage rates would result in unemployment, eventually bringing on a totalitarian regime. (The thesis that unemployment is a fertile breeding ground for communism or national socialism is so firmly accepted that no references are required either to historical evidence or to authorities.)

This is too dark, too hopeless a picture to be accepted. We refuse to accept the inevitability of the loss of freedom. It may be true that of the three objectives or semi-objectives—full employment, stable price levels, unrestrained labor unions—only two can be attained at the expense of the third. It may be true that a full-employment policy with unrestrained trade unions will lead to continual inflation; that a stable price level, with trade unions unrestrained, can be maintained only at the risk of serious unemployment; and that both full employment and price stability can be maintained only if trade unions are restrained in acquiring or exercising their bargaining power. But it is not true that such re-

---

[45] "A policy of full employment will require, therefore, that the present system of wage-bargaining by trade unions and employers' federations in *individual industries* should be replaced by a system of wage determination on a national basis." M. Joseph and N. Kaldor, *Economic Reconstruction after the War* (Handbooks published for the Association for Education in Citizenship by the English Universities Press), p. 18. Sir William Beveridge wrote in a similar vein: "Irresponsible sectional wage bargaining may lead to inflationary developments which bestow no benefits upon the working class; . . . and which endanger the very policy of full employment whose maintenance is a vital common interest of all wage earners . . . Two suggestions may be made for dealing with this problem. First, the central organizations of labor . . . should devote their attention to the problem of achieving a unified wage policy which ensures that the demands of individual unions will be judged with reference to the economic situation as a whole . . . The second suggestion relates to arbitration. In the new conditions of full employment, wages ought to be determined by reason, in the light of all the facts and with some regard to general equities and not simply by the bargaining power of particular groups of men." William H. Beveridge, *Full Employment in a Free Society* (New York: W. W. Norton & Co., 1945), pp. 199–200.

straint of trade union powers is either equivalent to or inseparable from an abrogation of political liberty.

Restraint or Self-Restraint?

There is a widespread belief that it will not be necessary to restrain labor organizations and to enjoin them from acquiring or exercising monopoly power, because they will learn to exercise sufficient self-restraint. We could cite scores of statements to this effect, although it is not always clear whether they are meant as safe predictions, confident expectations, pious hopes, or mere exhortations directed at the labor leaders. For example, "we must have an enlightened policy against wage inflation," and harm can be avoided if the powerful groups "develop a sense of responsibility in the exercise of their power, and something approaching economic statesmanship." [46]

We know that such economic statesmanship exists during national emergencies, when appeals to patriotism are heeded and self-restraint is practiced by the majority, leaders as well as rank and file. We believe that responsible leadership can also develop in times when no national emergency exists. But we doubt that such leadership can long survive against strong pressures from the rank and file incited by the criticisms and promises of opposition leaders. Moral suasion will not for long induce organized labor to refrain from utilizing the bargaining power which they have and know that they have.

There are those who do not hope that *individual* trade unions will exercise the desired self-restraint in wage policy, but do hope that in time *national* labor organizations will assume "the responsibility of protecting the total volume of employment opportunities from being narrowed by the policies or actions of any given union. The federations of unions have an interest in a well-balanced wage structure, in contrast with the interests of certain strong unions which may push the wages of their members too high for

---

[46] The first remark was Alvin H. Hansen's, the second John Maurice Clark's, both in their contributions to *Financing American Prosperity*, ed. by Paul T. Homan and Fritz Machlup (New York: Twentieth Century Fund, 1945), pp. 260 and 116, respectively.

the good of labor as a whole."[47] Does this hope imply that individual trade unions will give up their autonomy and let the national federation determine the wage rates which they should ask from employers? Does it imply that national labor federations will exercise disciplinary power over the wage policies of all trade unions, and yet will not exercise the economic and political powers which this implies within the nation and *vis-à-vis* the government? This is more than one is allowed to hope.[48]

If self-restraint is not a likely solution of the problem of monopolistic wage determination, what kinds of restraints can be imposed on trade unions that would not abrogate, reduce or compromise any rights essential to a truly liberal democracy? The right to form voluntary associations is a fundamental right in a democratic nation and the law must not interfere with such associations so long as they do not become potentially dangerous to the freedom or survival of society. Moreover, while collective wage bargaining is probably the chief function of labor unions, we must not forget that they have also other functions which are of great importance to the welfare and morale of the working men.

It is sometimes suggested that permanent governmental wage regulation would provide the needed and appropriate restraint on monopolistic wage determination. There is some measure of

[47] Sumner H. Slichter, in his contribution to *Financing American Prosperity*, p. 320.

[48] If such a complete monopoly of all labor in the country were managed in the interest of all members and could be kept from falling into the hands of particular group leaders, one might conceive of results far superior to those of the economic warfare conducted by unions fighting for their group interests. The leadership of the Central Union of All Labor, conscientiously acting in the interest of all members, would have to avoid unemployment as well as exploitation of one group by another, and thus would have to eschew the high wage differentials which independently acting craft or industrial unions obtain for their members. No one can expect such a thing to happen. Particular groups or personalities within the omnibus union could easily usurp the power and wield it in their own interest. The leader of the omnibus union might possibly promote himself to be the all-powerful Leader of the Union now known as the United States of America. It is interesting to speculate which is the shorter road to totalitarianism: the one-union system of labor, constituting a government of labor by labor (for labor?), or the syndicalist system of strong industry-unions independently and militantly exploiting the less strongly organized or unorganized workers and disrupting the economy through a series of paralysing strikes.

consistency in this suggestion. For where monopoly is regarded as inevitable and the monopolized service is of great importance to the public, government regulation of prices has been resorted to. Rate regulation in transportation and public utilities was the American solution of the problem of monopolistic pricing where it was impossible to eliminate the monopoly positions by legal fiat. Hence, since monopolistic wage determination is inevitable once trade unions have attained substantial power, regulation of wage rates by the government would seem to be the "logical" solution.

Governmental Regulation of Wage Rates

Neither organized labor nor management want the government permanently in the business of wage rate setting, and most economists also reject the idea, though for different reasons. Management has always been distrustful of governmental regulation and, in this case, fears that the government might fall under the dictation of organized labor. Labor leaders fear that the government might be too much under the influence of big business; and, more importantly, they do not want to abdicate their chief function. Many economists are apprehensive of expanding government intervention in economic life, and doubt that the government would do a better job than the market, however imperfect and monopolistic.

In addition, grave dangers to the democratic system may arise if wage rate setting, or the control over wage rate setting, is permanently entrusted to the government. The wage rate might become an essential part of the promises and platforms on which political parties would win or lose elections and governments would stand or fall. The consequences to our political life might be serious, to say the least.

It would be worse than meaningless to hand wage controls over to an administrative agency with wide administrative discretion, and without definite principles or criteria for its decisions. The results would be little different from those under the present system of bilateral monopoly. The practice of the Wage Control Board would probably be to set the wage rates a little lower than the trade unions asked, while the practice of the unions would be to ask for wage rates somewhat higher than they thought would be accepted. Among the criteria of the Wage Board would probably be the employers' ability to pay what the unions ask, a criterion which we have shown should be largely irrelevant to the problem of economic pricing. The application of this criterion may seriously aggravate the monopolistic distortions of the wage structure and obstruct the development of those industries that ought to expand on the basis of comparative social costs (opportunity costs of resources) and social benefits (as measured by effective demand). But, in lieu of such uneconomic criteria as the employers' ability to pay, could we not devise a set of rules to be used for governmental wage rate regulation designed to establish a wage structure conforming to the economic principle and a wage level consistent with stability of the price level?

Such rules, I believe, could be designed. Inasmuch as a competitive wage structure would call for a lowering of some of the monopolistic wage rates, and inasmuch as absolute reductions of any wage rates would meet with such a resistance as perhaps could not be overcome by democratic means, the rules might provide only for *relative* reductions of these rates by keeping them unchanged while other wages are increased. The increases in the general wage level must be held down to a rate of approximately three percent a year in order to avoid unemployment or price inflation. Thus, the wage structure could undergo gradual and continual adjustments if the rules were to provide that all wage rates would rise by three percent a year except that (a) the wage rates for jobs (industries, occupations, areas) for which there is an oversupply would not be allowed to increase (and there would be an oversupply of labor wherever wage rates were at monopolistic levels and no barriers to entry existed), and (b) the wage rates for jobs for which supply is relatively small would be increased faster. The trade unions, losing their collective bargaining functions,[49] should assume new functions in administering, super-

[49] Suggestions for such a solution of the problem of wage rate determination were made by me in "Monopolistic Wage Determination as a Part of the General Problem of Monopoly," in *Wage Determination and the Economics of Liberalism* (Washington: Chamber of Commerce of the United

vising and enforcing the rules, especially in the necessary "local wage boards." Their participation in job evaluation schemes in individual establishments or firms would also be important. The administratively most difficult part of any such program of wage regulation of an "artificial free market," [50] would be the objective determination of excessive and scarce supply of labor for particular jobs, industries, occupations, areas.[51] The politically most difficult part would be to win the support of the trade unions, for it would hardly be possible to get the program adopted against the resistance of organized labor. To most experts in labor economics the program looks utterly fantastic, and perhaps it is.

Reducing the Monopoly Power of Unions

If governmental wage regulation according to sound principles is impossible or unacceptable; if self-restraint of trade unions is contrary to all reasonable expectations; if the monopoly power of trade unions has become so great that the wage structure is badly distorted and the wage level steadily pushed up far in excess of the rise in productivity, it is imperative to search for means and

States, January 1947), p. 76, and by Abba P. Lerner, "Money as a Creature of the State," *American Economic Review*, Vol. XXXVII (1947), Suppl., pp. 316–17. Lerner added the following comment: "The side-stepping of collective bargaining will undoubtedly be denounced as an attack on labor. It is important to note that it will appear so only to those who in their thinking have completely substituted the labor unions for the workers, raising these instruments for improving the economic welfare of labor to the status of ends in themselves. We should remember that an end in itself is nearly always a means for some end which one does not like to mention aloud, such as the maintenance of the positions, prestige, and salary of a union bureaucrat." *Ibid.*, p. 317.

[50] Abba P. Lerner, *op. cit.*, p. 316.

[51] Lerner, in his latest book, proposes that each worker, employed or unemployed, should express his preference for an occupation for which he is qualified. From this information an "index of relative attractiveness" would be computed for each occupation. Wage rates in occupations for which this index is more than twice the national average would remain constant while other wages are increased; in occupations for which the index is less than half the national average wage rates would be increased by six percent a year; in occupations for which the index falls between these limits wage rates would be increased by three percent a year. Abba P. Lerner, *Economics of Employment* (New York: McGraw-Hill, 1951), pp. 214–15.

ways of reducing the monopoly power of trade unions without impairing their non-wage functions.

Proposals for the reduction of union monopoly power have been directed at particular trade union practices, at the closed shop, and at the size of the bargaining unit and at inter-union combination. Regarding monopolistic labor practices, some attention has been given to the possibilities of prohibiting mass picketing and other forms of intimidation. But it would probably be futile to legislate against such practices as long as public opinion sympathizes with those acting in violation of the law, for the chances are that it could not be enforced.

Closed-shop agreements may be undesirable for different reasons. For example, one may dislike the requirement that, as a condition of employment in a firm, a worker must join a union not of his own choosing; one may on general grounds oppose the idea of involuntary membership in non-public associations. But the relationship between the closed shop and the monopoly power of the union is not entirely what many believe it is. For, although closed-shop agreements may be important to a union for the purpose of *acquiring* monopoly power, they are not essential for the purpose of *keeping* the power that it has acquired. Prohibition of the closed shop may keep weak unions from growing stronger, but it can probably do little to reduce the strength of now powerful unions.

Those who associate the degree of monopoly with the size of the union, propose measures to split large trade unions into smaller groups. The idea is simple: If the bargaining group cannot comprise more than the workers of the particular firms or in a particular area (state), and cannot combine with other bargaining groups in the industry, it may not have the power to bring the whole industry to a standstill. For example, the union of the miners employed by a particular mine operator or in a particular area (state) is less apt to tyrannize the nation than are the United Mine Workers of America.

Proposals against Big Labor, meaning trade unions of large size, are sometimes formulated as proposals against "industry-wide bargaining." This is technically wrong. In the technical sense of the word, as used by the expert in labor problems and industrial relations, industry-wide bargaining is comparatively rare in the United States. In this technical sense it refers to instances in which the national union negotiates and concludes a wage contract for all local unions, covering all or most workers of the particular industry or craft in the country; preferably with an employers' association comprising all the firms which employ members of these unions. In a wider and looser sense, however, industry-wide bargaining need not imply that one single contract is negotiated by a national union and covers all or most workers of the industry. Where individual bargaining units and locals follow the pattern suggested by the national union, the results are practically the same as if one all-inclusive contract were made by one industry-wide bargaining unit. When the representative of the national union "sits in" at the bargaining between a "small" bargaining unit and an employer, or even when he "advises" the bargaining group, this may be, for most practical purposes, "industry-wide" bargaining. The adoption of a national wage standard for all locals in the country is certainly one of the techniques of industry-wide bargaining in this wider sense.

Proposals to outlaw industry-wide bargaining have been called nonsensical, because they were taken to refer to the technical sense of the term.[52] Referring, however, to the wider and looser sense, they are not meaningless at all. A union bargaining only for the workers in a small area and controlling only these workers, can eliminate only the direct competition among workers for jobs in the area, but not the indirect competition through the products made by workers in other areas. If the bargaining group is expanded to comprise the workers in all areas, or if the separate

---

[52] Outlawing industry-wide collective bargaining only in the technical sense of the word would do nothing to reduce the monopoly power of unions. Whether a national union negotiates and signs a wage contract for the whole industry, or whether each local or each bargaining unit signs a separate wage contract with each employer in the industry, makes a difference primarily regarding clerical procedures; but it makes no difference regarding wage determination as long as the terms of the contracts are the result of industry-wide combination and each local group is backed by the power of the national union. As long as there is such industry-wide combination among local unions, the resort to industry-wide collective bargaining in the technical sense of the word may be even an organizational improvement and may conceivably facilitate the maintenance of industrial peace.

bargaining groups act in concert, then indirect competition through the products made in different parts of the country is limited along with the direct competition of workers for jobs. In other words, the local union officials bargaining for higher wages need no longer fear that producers elsewhere may be able to produce more cheaply with cheaper labor.

If the control of trade unions were limited to the workers of individual firms [53] or to workers in particular areas (e.g., states) and if inter-union combination were prevented, the monopoly power of unions would certainly be much reduced. Limitations of the size of unions would, however, be ineffective in industries dominated by a few giant firms. In these industries labor unions comprising "only" the workers of individual firms would still have the power to monopolize the industry and incidentally to paralyse the economy. Hence, if we are serious about the prevention of inordinate monopoly power and excessive concentration of power in private hands, the size of corporate combines would have to be cut down together with the size of labor combinations.

The simultaneous attack on size in business organization and in labor organization is also indicated for political reasons as well as on grounds of justice. Not that labor monopolies are in any sense an "offset" to business monopolies. Not that the latter can be at all neutralized or mitigated or made more tolerable by the existence of labor monopolies. (On the contrary, the combined effects are worse, and the interests of most labor groups, which are badly injured in consequence of the operation of business monopolies, suffer additional injury as a result of the operation of labor monopolies.) But as long as the majority of workers *believe* that they are benefited by the wage policies of powerful trade unions, it would neither be politically feasible nor morally tolerable to proceed against concentration of trade union power and continue to condone the corporate combination of industrial establishments which could be operated independently without excessive loss of efficiency.[54]

[53] Company unions in the sense of company-dominated labor organizations could nevertheless be avoided.

[54] The basic principle of a really liberal democracy is the dispersion of power. No individual's decisions should affect many people. What a business executive or a labor leader decides might always be of consequence to a

The Problems of Poverty and Insecurity

In several places in this discussion we have reminded ourselves of the fact that any adverse conclusions about the effects of collective bargaining and the wage policies of strong trade unions must not be allowed to reflect on the appraisal of the social desirability of trade unions as such and of their various functions other than wage bargaining. Some of these functions are of great significance for the workers' welfare and for the social acceptability of the industrial system.

Another reminder should be added. We have been concerned in this discussion with monopolistic wage determination as a part of the general problem of monopoly and, hence, with the problem of pricing as a cause and effect of the allocation of resources in the economy. We have analysed the probable effects of trade union wage policies upon the size and distribution of the national income, and we have found that collective bargaining by strong unions, although advocated as a means of effecting greater equality of distribution, was more likely to produce greater inequality among different labor groups. These conclusions might be regarded as merely negative—as refutations of erroneous theories.

To establish that trade unions cannot solve the problems of inequality, poverty, and insecurity does not bring us any nearer to a solution of these problems. We have not, of course, set out to find such a solution. But it may be appropriate to remark that our findings are not inconsistent with other attempts to mitigate poverty and insecurity. Although we are satisfied that wage rates which reflect competitive supply and demand rather than monopolistic bargaining power will contribute to the reduction of poverty, we may state that the functioning of a competitive price system need not be impaired by measures to help the poor and to provide more security to the worker and his family. A rich society, such as the United States, can afford to secure a minimum standard to its members, provided it does it in ways that do not interfere

small group of employees, customers, suppliers, but should be of little consequence to hundreds of thousands or even millions. On the basis of this political philosophy one may oppose Big Business and Big Labor, even apart from the question of monopoly, prices, wages, and national income.

with the price mechanism and therefore with the efficiency in the use of the available resources.

The Wage Problem under Socialism

The preservation of a wage structure conducive to an economic allocation of resources is a problem not only for a capitalist system. More or less the same problem exists in a socialist economy.

A socialist system may also rely on the price mechanism to steer productive factors and intermediate goods into the most desired uses. In such a system the significance of a competitive wage structure is exactly the same as in a capitalist economy. If the socialist economy uses other methods of resource allocation besides or in lieu of the price mechanism, it will still find that appropriately determined wage rates have important functions as economic incentives, as distributors of income, as determinants of production cost, and as generators of demand. With regard to any of these functions it may be vital for the socialist economy not to leave the determination of wage rates to the bargaining strength or skill of individual labor organizations. It will be necessary either to impose restraints on the policies and actions of these organizations or to take wage rate setting completely out of their hands.

Totalitarian socialism does not stand for such things as trade union wage policies. The state cannot permit such syndicalist sabotage of the plans of society. These plans, on the other hand, cannot be carried out either, if the wage structure is determined by egalitarian sentimentalists. The incentive function of wage rate differentials is fully appreciated by the totalitarian planners and they inveigh against the "leftist leveling of wages." [55]

[55] "In order to insure our enterprises the necessary manpower, it is essential to attract the workers to the enterprises, so as to turn them into a more or less constant force. . . . Fluctuation of labor power has become a scourge to production. . . . It is due to incorrect organization of the system of wages, to an incorrect wage scale, to a leftist leveling of wages. . . . Leveling results in that the unskilled worker has no interest to become skilled. . . . Marx and Lenin say that the difference between skilled and unskilled labor will exist even under Socialism, even after the abolition of classes, that only under Communism will this difference disappear, because even under Socialism 'wages' would be paid according to work done and not according to one's needs." Joseph V. Stalin, *The New Russian Policy* (New York: John Day Company, 1931), pp. 6–8.

Democratic socialism, as represented by the British Labor Government of the Postwar Years, is politically supported by the trade unions and therefore cannot relieve them of the control they have over wage determination. On the other hand, the government could not leave them an entirely free hand in their wage policies, and had to insist on some measure of coordination of union policy with national plans. In many instances appeals to solidarity and patriotism succeeded in inspiring them to exercise great moderation in their wage demands. From time to time heavier moral suasion was applied. In a good many instances the strongest appeals to party discipline were of no avail and the trade unions insisted on wage demands which gave impetus to a general wage inflation and aggravated the nation's price level and foreign exchange problems.

This is mentioned here merely in order to demonstrate that the difficulties created through collective bargaining by powerful trade unions are not only problems for a capitalist, free-enterprise system; and that the concern about the problem is not, as some may be inclined to think, the capitalist's anxiety to protect his profits. The problem exists in any kind of economic system where wage determination has become "monopolistic" or "syndicalistic."

PART V—FACTS, THEORIES, MEASUREMENTS

CHAPTER 11

Economic Fact and Theory

Variations in Method: Conceptual Framework (Part I) · Taxonomic Approach (Part II) · Historical Approach (Part III) · Theoretical Approach (Part IV)

Abstraction, Theory, and Fact: "It's a Fact" · "It's Just a Theory" · Facts or Implied Theories?

Explanation, Prediction, Evaluation: Prediction versus Explanation · Hypothetical Predictions · Evaluation · Implied Value Judgments · An Illustration · Conflicting Values

Measurement: "Science is Measurement" · Some Implications of Measurement · Fictitious Accuracy

I PROPOSE TO PAUSE here and look back along the way we have traveled in this book, not in order to muse contentedly on our achievements, but in order to see in a different perspective the kind of approach we have taken in pursuit of our problems. Discussions of practical economic issues are commonly, and perhaps inevitably, mixtures of fact and fiction, logic and preconception, history and theory, political philosophy and plain common sense. What have been the mixtures chosen for the discussions of the various topics in this book?

VARIATIONS IN METHOD

We set out with the preparation of a "conceptual framework" appropriate for the description, analysis and appraisal of the phenomena referred to by the terms monopoly and competition. Part I was devoted to this task. Part II dealt with business policies, and attempted to describe monopolistic business practices in general terms, using a rather "taxonomic" approach. Part III, the discussion of government policies concerning monopoly and competition, was more "historical" in nature than any of the other parts of the book. Part IV treated the implications of labor policies and their probable effects on organized bargaining power, wage determination and income distribution in a more deliberately "theoretical" analysis than was employed in the rest of the book. Thus, these four parts are rather different as to the methods of discourse practised. It seems worth our while to ask whether these variations in method were appropriate in view of the problems examined.

Conceptual Framework (Part I)

It would be pretentious if I claimed that it was absolutely necessary to begin with the construction or justification of a conceptual framework for our discussions, or that this was the only intelligent thing to do. After all, there are enough books on our subject that do not follow this procedure. Can the subject perhaps be treated without any conceptual framework at all? Of course not. A writer surely "means" something when he uses such words as monopoly and competition, and what he means is usually rather involved; nevertheless he often assumes that his readers will know what he means even if he does not bother with definitions and with attempts to ascertain the place of his concepts in his universe of discourse.

Such a confidence in the possibility of achieving a meeting of minds without the benefit of "preliminary negotiations" may be based on one of three presuppositions: (1) all of the words used are part of the common vocabulary in every-day parlance and have clear unambiguous meanings; (2) the terms and concepts used have been satisfactorily discussed, explained and consistently defined in previous writings by the same or other authors with which one may assume most of the readers to be familiar; or (3) the terms and concepts used are such that the reader, even if he is not at the outset familiar with their precise meanings and connotations, can be expected to grasp the ideas as the discussion proceeds.

It is the last of these presuppositions on which many writers in economics count when they choose not to bother with a discussion of their conceptual framework. Many a writer proceeds on the assumption: "You will get what I mean as I go on." This is a very sensible procedure in many instances. But I felt it was not reasonable to follow it for this book. In the very first pages we found that most of the popular notions of monopoly and competition were vague, ambiguous, confusing; and that we had to clear the ground and start with some simple idealized "models" if we wanted to obtain manageable tools of reasoning. Moreover, we found that there was little point in talking about competition and monopoly if we had not a pretty clear idea of their effects on the performance of the economy. These effects are obviously connected with the price mechanism. It follows that competition and monopoly have to be understood in the light of the insight gained from working with a model of an economic system in which productive resources are steered to their uses by a price mechanism whose functioning is affected by the more or less "monopolistic" market positions of sellers and buyers. Thus, the concepts of competition and monopoly are firmly "bound up" with the concepts of price mechanism, resource allocation, consumer preferences, productive efficiency, total output—in short, they are part and parcel of a conceptual framework which had to be introduced and exhibited if the whole discussion was to make good sense.

There are of course many central and side issues that had to be dealt with in this connection. If one were to appraise monopolistic "deflections" and "deviations" of the performance of the economic system only in the light of standards developed from mental experimentations with an abstract "model economy" with the very "simplest" set of assumptions, serious errors of judgment would be inevitable. For example, the simplest assumptions would postulate a much greater degree of divisibility of resources than exists in reality. But one can understand the problem of "natural monopolies" only by using models providing also for indivisible resources; and thus the conceptual framework appropriate for the tasks for which we were preparing had to include certain special assumptions. This enabled us to discuss in Part I the inevitability and desirability of monopoly in certain fields or under certain conditions before embarking in Parts II and III on descriptions of the policies of businessmen and of governments with regard to the creation, reinforcement, maintenance, and exploitation of monopoly positions. Descriptions of these policies would have been

largely meaningless without the benefit of findings about their
probable effects and at least some presumptive appraisals of these
effects. Why should we ever care to describe a "policy" or "practice" if we did not suspect that it had some significant effects or
implications? Descriptive accounts, therefore, are more illuminating if they are preceded by an exposition of the conceptual framework that enables us to sense or check the suspected or asserted
effects or implications of the phenomena described.

Taxonomic Approach (Part II)

It is impossible to describe anything without the use of general categories. Even so, it would be possible to take these categories for granted and to give a description of monopolistic business practices by telling what certain companies have done at
certain times at certain places. Indeed, such "case histories" are
very important, if not indispensable, to our understanding of the
issues involved. Fortunately numerous good case studies of monopolistic business policies are available, and students of industrial
organization and control are always adding to our knowledge of
"cases."

An alternative approach to the description of business policies
is to omit names, dates, and places, and to classify the reported
actions according to some significant aspects. This is the classificatory or taxonomic approach; it is the one that I have chosen
in Part II of this book. Just as the case approach presupposes some
prior classificatory attempt, however tentative, the taxonomic approach presupposes some prior case studies, however incomplete.
In other words, the two approaches are interdependent, each
being based on some previous steps along the other. But where
the number of cases is very large and the main purpose is to arrive
at generalizations, the taxonomic approach will be more manageable.

Classifications must be on the basis of some principles, and one
may well argue about their selection. But any such argument can
be meaningful only in view of the explicit or implicit purposes the
classification is to serve. Speaking of monopolistic business practices a lawyer will most probably group them according to the

major provisions of the laws actually or potentially violated, while economists may choose among several possible distinguishing criteria. In the discussions of Part II we favored some of the classificatory principles that had suggested themselves in the course of the discussions of the conceptual framework in Part I. But we felt it necessary to engage also in cross-classifications according to other characteristics more commonly selected for emphasis.[1]

It probably goes without saying that classifications not only serve analysis but also presuppose analysis. For example, it would surely not be possible to group certain actions according to their effects if we did not have a theory to help us. The theories prerequisite to various classificatory principles are of different degrees of complexity. Thus it takes less analysis to sort types of conduct according to technique employed than according to purposes served.

Historical Approach (Part III)

When I say that I followed a historical approach in discussing government policies regarding monopoly and competition, I am exaggerating, perhaps more than is legitimate, in order to bring out a contrast. The contrast that I wish to point up is this: while we spoke in Part II of the actions of unidentified business firms, without regard to time or place, we discussed in Part III the actions of particular governments—chiefly the United States, but also some individual states—as particular events in time.

The exaggeration involved in my suggestion does not consist in the fact that the discussion in the three chapters of Part III was systematically subdivided according to different kinds (classes) of governmental measures; such systematic subdivisions are perfectly compatible with historical accounts. The exaggeration lies in the fact that the emphasized features of the treatment—the

---

[1] At one point I enumerated more than twenty different types of price discrimination. (Chapter 5, pp. 135–63.) This may look as if I had allowed my taxonomic zeal to go to some extremes. But the stringing together of this large number of "types" was not excessive taxonomy—but too little. Separate classifications according to different principles, such as according to techniques employed, purposes served, effects achieved, or special conditions required, would each distinguish only a handful of categories. But a cross-classification could yield many more "types" than I had the space to present.

selection and presentation of individual, unique events and the placing of these events in time—are, though necessary, not sufficient characteristics of historical work. Although it is often done, one should not regard dates as the essence of history, or a writer of chronology as a historian. Some of the main tasks of the historian— the search for and evaluation of documents, the interpretation of evidence, the linking of events in time by detailed analysis of causes, conditions, motives, and effects, and the presentation of the findings in the whole "historical setting"—were not brought into play in our account of government restraints of and aids to monopoly. There was no need, in the chapters of Part III, for first-hand historical research or for new critical historical analysis. For our purposes we were able to rely on accepted accounts of governmental actions in our field of interest and we could be satisfied with a recapitulation of the highlights or, in certain areas, of some representative instances.

But why did we choose to make the treatment of this phase of our theme as historical as it was? Would it not have been neater to continue with the taxonomic approach used in the preceding part? It certainly would have been possible to do so. We could have described in general terms the economically significant features of the different kinds of measures which government in general may take to foster competition and restrain monopoly, and to aid monopoly and restrict competition,—any government, at any time, anywhere. Instead, we reported on particular acts passed by the United States Congress or on particular decisions pronounced by the Supreme Court of the United States in certain years and under specific circumstances. The reason, of course, is that the historical approach is preferable where it does not unduly lengthen the account.[2] The chief advantage of the taxonomic approach is that it eliminates masses of details and boils down enormous num-

---

[2] This should not be misunderstood as an endorsement of the so-called "historical method," or of the doctrine of the "historical school" in economics, according to which history was prior to theory—if theory was to be recognized at all. This methodological view was untenable and all attempts to support it have failed. "There is no reason to regard this failure as less than definitive." Thorstein Veblen, "Gustav Schmoller's Economics," *Quarterly Journal of Economics*, Vol. XVI (1901), p. 7.

bers of individual cases to a small number of types or classes. Where we were dealing with millions of business firms and billions of business actions, we availed ourselves of the space-saving distillation accomplished by the taxonomic process. Most of the color and of the flavor of the individual stories are lost in such distillation, and the reader was advised to sample some of the case histories in order to make up for the loss. But even if only one representative case for each type of monopolistic business practice mentioned in Part II had been selected for illustration, the reports on these cases would have filled several volumes.

Dealing with government actions to *restrain competition* we were also faced with too large a number of instances to make it practical to use historical reporting. This is the field where local and state governments have been so terribly active, and where laws, decrees and ordinances have poured forth in such profusion, that the taxonomic method is the only feasible one. The same is true of the actions of national governments to restraint competition in international trade and in other respects. It is in the fight *against monopoly* that the actions of individual governments become sufficiently unique, and the number of significant measures or decisions sufficiently small to enable us to use the historical approach. Thus it was chiefly in the chapter on the antitrust policy of the United States that we could present an account more historical in nature than the treatment of other topics.

The historical approach, where it can be used without undue demands on space, has many advantages over taxonomic distillation. We have only to imagine how an entirely unhistorical, taxonomic treatment of the American antitrust policy would look, and we can readily sense what it would lack. Indeed, the present state of the antitrust law and the possibilities of its further development could not be understood without the benefit of the insight gained by a historical review.

On the other hand, there is no lack of "implicit analysis" in a historical account of economic policies. When reasons, motives, purposes, and effects are discussed in connection with specific measures, economic theory must be used. Frequently, however, the writer of a historical account has so much confidence in the theoretical analysis which he or others have employed, that he announces the results of the analysis as if they were findings of fact.

Theoretical Approach (Part IV)

When it came to the discussion of labor policies, there was no widely accepted body of theory that could be taken for granted and relied on with confidence. The examination of the conceptual framework in Part I may have prepared us sufficiently for the discussions of business policies in Part II and of government policies in Part III, but not for the discussion of labor policies. One should think that the analytical models employed as aids in visualizing the effects of cartel price determination for industrial products or of increased concentration of industry control by corporate mergers would be equally helpful in visualizing the effects of union wage determination for industrial labor or of increased union control over the labor market through industry-wide collective bargaining. Yet, whether because of differences in the kinds of analysis employed, or because of differences in the effects inferred from the same kind of analysis, or because of differences in the evaluation of the same effects, at the present state of professional thinking the problems of competition and monopoly in the labor market cannot be meaningfully discussed without first laying a more solid foundation of economic analysis suitable to these problems.

Awareness of this situation led me to use in Part IV of this book an explicitly theoretical approach, abstracting from all descriptive and historical material. After all that I have said about the advantages of the historical approach wherever it is practicable, I need hardly emphasize that by not following it we sacrificed valuable familiarity with trade union development and a great deal of information about things worth knowing. But a history that cannot say anything about the most significant relationships among the events which it reports is not very meaningful. Before one has an idea, for example, how changes in union membership, in money wages rates, product prices, real wage rates, and employment can be connected with one another, a historical, or rather chronological, approach to these matters cannot enlarge our understanding.[3] Likewise, a taxonomic treatise of trade union practices would not be very revealing before we have more confidence in our ability to judge the various types of practices according to their economic effects.

Can abstract theorizing help us here, can it do for us what we need? The reader who has had the patience to struggle through Part IV may have some idea about this: I hope he has come to share my appreciation of the fact that "reality" is much too complex to be understood unless we abstract from most of it and break the rest down into a few crucial elements the relationships among which we can examine in isolation. In reality too many things happen at once, so that we can never "observe" what causes what. If by some magic we could arrange that absolutely everything in the world remained unchanged while we experimented with a single change, say, an increase in the wage rates paid in a particular industry, and watched what happened—then reality could become a laboratory for experimental research in economics. In want of such magic we must resort to mental experiments with abstract models where we can move one thing at a time. This is what the "theoretical approach" tries to do, and I believe it is the only approach that can lead to answers, however tentative, where we still lack understanding of fundamental relationships.

Nevertheless, I know that many will find the analysis presented in Part IV "too abstract" and "too unrealistic." Quite possibly it can be shown to be deficient; its validity or applicability may well be questioned. But I hope those who do so will point to the flaws and make the corrections instead of confining themselves to the complaint that there was "too much theory and not enough facts." About this complaint and the relationship between economic fact and theory some further comments are in order at this point.[4]

[3] This is not to deny that the inspection of different time series may give the investigator an idea for the development of a theory, although of course he must have some hunch about relevant connections before he selects his series.

[4] For an excellent exposition of the relationship between fact and theory in the natural and social sciences see Morris R. Cohen, *Reason and Nature*

ABSTRACTION, THEORY, AND FACT

Theorizing means abstracting from many things and isolating a few things with a view to grasping an otherwise hidden connection between the latter. Few people are given to this kind of mental exercise, chiefly because of a lack of training in abstract thinking. Some dislike high degrees of abstraction because, not used to it and unable to participate, they find it tedious, others, because they distrust it when they see how the theorist comes out with conclusions they cannot check. More often than not, he who distrusts and disparages theory will regard as "theory" anything that calls for his mental effort or disagrees with his prejudices, while he will uncritically accept as an axiom, if not as "fact," many an old theory which others have long abandoned as invalid or inapplicable.

"It's a Fact"

When a trusted theory is considered as a "fact," this is merely a naive misunderstanding by an unschooled mind. All of us have heard people say "it's a fact" when they merely meant "it's true" and were referring, not to observation, but to hypothetical propositions and presumed "rules" of experience, or even to exploded theories and plain superstitions. This indiscrimination in the popular use of language is mentioned here only because we shall find that it is part of a much broader and yet more subtle problem of confusing facts and theories. Any number of intelligent people, well trained in some branch of knowledge, are wont to accept as "fact" what on inspection turns out to be merely the result of inferences resting on rather special if not specious theories.

In the strictest sense of the word, a fact is an event in time that has been *observed*, that is, for which we have evidence, based on sensory perception, which is accepted as conclusive. But there is a large category of *"inferred facts"* and, depending on the methodological point of view, some kinds of inferred facts are given the full status of facts.[5] There are, for example, events in

(New York: Harcourt, Brace & Co., 1931), especially the chapters on "Reason and Scientific Method" (pp. 76–146) and on "The Social and the Natural Sciences" (pp. 333–68).

[5] To many, however, a fact is strictly "a datum of experience as dis-

time, certain particular occurrences, which—although occurrences
of the type are observable—have not been directly observed but
merely inferred from other observations, yet where (because of an
established one-to-one relationship, or perfect correlation, between the class of the facts observed and the class of the facts
inferred) the occurrence is regarded as just as certain as if it had
been directly observed. There is another kind of inferred "facts"
—which may be denied the status of fact—where the certified
observations plus inferences do not guarantee that the inferred
event has actually taken place. This is the kind of conclusion which
in law cases is referred to by "circumstantial evidence": the observed facts are taken as strong indication, but not as absolutely
incontrovertible evidence, of the suspected occurrence. If other
interpretations of the observed facts are possible, the "fact" that
is inferred from the observed ones is surely not as good a fact as
one directly observed.

A third kind of "inferred fact" relates to occurrences that are
never directly observable. They are facts by construction only, but
a one-to-one relationship may have been postulated between a
certain kind of observation and a certain "construct." The impossibility of direct observation may be inherent in the construct, yet
scientists may be satisfied that the construct is no less part of
"reality" than the results of direct observation based on sense
perception.[6]

It has been denied that there are in the world of human actions
—and, hence, in the social sciences—any facts in the strict sense
of the word. Whatever may be called a fact in the social sciences
is certainly of a nature rather different from that of the fact of
the natural sciences. The latter is concerned mostly with physical
properties and, indeed, the bulk of the facts of physics are "data"

tinguished from conclusions." *Oxford Universal English Dictionary* (Oxford
University Press, 1937), Vol. III, p. 667.

[6] For example, the atom "is evidently a construct, because no one ever
experienced an atom, and its existence is entirely inferential." But, although
first "a pure invention, without physical reality," we have accumulated so
much "information all pointing to the atom, until now we are as convinced
of its physical reality as of our hands and feet." This and similar "constructs"
are regarded as "good" because "there is a unique correspondence between it
and the physical data in terms of which it is defined." P. W. Bridgman, *The
Logic of Modern Physics* (New York: Macmillan, 1927), pp. 59 and 55.

read from the indicators of scientific instruments. The social sciences are concerned with human actions, or with certain aspects of the results of human actions, which may have real existence (as "social" phenomena) only in the minds of the actors and of other parties concerned.[7] Thus, there is a serious difficulty in establishing what it really is that economists (or historians or sociologists) can "observe."

But we need not here go into these profound questions of methodology.[8] Perhaps we can be satisfied for our purposes with the simple device of regarding as facts those data of direct observation or of "record" which are so firmly established that they cannot reasonably be questioned. Anything that looks substantially different to different observers or from different points of view, or that lends itself to different "interpretations" should not be called a fact.

"It's Just a Theory"

The question how two or more separately observed facts hang together, whether some may be causes or effects of others, is tentatively answered by a mental scheme of interrelationships which we call theory. Often the validity of a theory is distinguished from its applicability. For it may happen that a theory "explains" the relationships between certain "hypothetical facts" which are so different from and incomparable with any actually observed facts that it can never be applied to anything. Most controversies among economists concern the applicability of theories, and especially their applicability to particular ("concrete") situations. The chief disagreements are matters of judgment: whether the facts are such that the theory applies.

[7] "Action" is defined as "human behavior when and insofar as the acting individual attaches a subjective meaning to it." An action is a "social action" when and "insofar as, by virtue of the subjective meaning attached to it by the acting individual (or individuals), it takes account of the behavior of others and is thereby oriented in its course." Max Weber, *The Theory of Social and Economic Organization*, ed. by Talcott Parsons (London: Hodge, 1947), p. 80.

[8] For an excellent and brief exposition of the essential problem involved see Friedrich A. Hayek, "The Facts of the Social Sciences," *Ethics*, Vol. LIV (1943), pp. 1–13. Reprinted in Friedrich A. Hayek, *Individualism and Economic Order* (Chicago: University of Chicago Press, 1948), pp. 57–76.

According to the degree of abstraction we may distinguish general theories, special theories, applied theories, and implied theories. In the latter two forms, theory is sometimes not identified as theory and may pass as description, historical narrative, purely factual account, statistical data. This is particularly so in the case of implied theory, where concrete cases, events or situations are discussed as if they were nothing but objective facts, while upon close inspection these so-called facts turn out to be inferences based on theories and would look quite different from the point of view of other theories. Let us illustrate this by an example.

Facts or Implied Theories?

The following statement looks to most people like a straight-forward account of historical facts: "From January 1946 to December 1952 the steel workers union, in a strong bargaining position, aided by government policies, was able to obtain for its members wage increases of x percent; and the steel companies, using their monopolistic position in the market, boosted steel prices by y percent."

This statement is chockful of theories, some of rather questionable validity. Let us examine the assertions made in the statement and see to what extent they are facts or implied theories. (a) That the union was or is in a "strong bargaining position" cannot be established by direct observation, but only inferred from certain impressions on the basis of some very special theories, most of which have not even succeeded in defining the main concepts employed. (See above Chapter 9, pp. 344–48.) It is possible to question the assertion. (b) That the union was "aided by government policies" is an assertion that can be supported only by theories concerning the effect of certain kinds of government measures upon trade union strength. The assertion implies that in the absence of certain government policies the union would have been weaker. It is not impossible to assert the contrary and make a plausible case for such an assertion. (c) That steel workers' wages increased by x percent can be said only on the basis of a considerable number of conceptual and statistical conventions which in turn are based upon certain propositions of wage theory, index

number theory, etc.[9] (d) That the union "obtained" these wage
increases for its members is an assertion which rests on the hypothesis that there would have been no wage increase had it not
been for union pressure. The statement gives no justification for
this hypothesis. (e) That the steel companies were in a "monopolistic position" is an assertion the very meaning of which depends
on the theory held. The particular theories used to support the
assertion are rejected by many, including the steel companies. (f)
That the companies "used" their monopolistic position is equally
questionable, especially if it is argued that they used it for boost-
ing steel prices. The opposite may be argued. (g) That steel prices
rose by y percent can be said only on the basis of certain conceptual
and statistical conventions which in turn are based upon certain
propositions of price theory, index number theory, etc.[10] (h) That

[9] "Wages" may refer to contractual wage rates, average hourly earnings,
average weekly earnings, total weekly payroll, average hourly labor cost
(including the cost of fringe benefits), and perhaps other things. Which of
these figures is considered relevant depends on several questions (including
the theory of collective bargaining). It should be clear that these different
wage data may change not only by different percentages but also in different directions. For example, when contractual wage rates increase average
hourly earnings may decline if the percentage of unskilled labor employed
becomes much larger; or average weekly earnings may fall as contractual
wage rates rise if the number of hours worked is reduced. For want of an
index of contractual wage rates, we must usually consult the published
statistics of average hourly earnings, although this is affected by the amount
of overtime worked as well as by the composition of the work force. Since
the fringe benefits granted the workers during the period in question would
figure among the obtained improvements of the wage contract, the cost of
these concessions to the companies must be added to the wages paid. From
all this it will be clear that there may be an indefinite number of findings
for the "wage increase."

[10] For each steel product and each steel producer there are differences
between base prices, mill net prices, and delivered prices, and the choice
between these depends on certain theoretical considerations. There is also
the difficulty in computing an average price increase. If an average price were
calculated by dividing total sales proceeds for all steel products by total
tonnage sold, one might find the average price reduced if the composition
had changed from more expensive to less expensive products—even while
every single steel product were sold at an increased price. This explains the
need of using "appropriate" index number methods which make "adequate"
allowance for changes in the composition of the product mix, for differences
in specifications and qualities, for differences in transport costs and distances
of deliveries, etc.

the companies "boosted" the steel prices is an assertion which, to be meaningful in the context, implies the hypothesis that steel prices would not have increased in a perfectly competitive market. One may argue differently and, indeed, we shall presently do so.

While it may now be patent that not one of the eight assertions is a simple fact directly ascertainable by observation,—that, instead, every one involves inferences linking, through implied theories, the asserted facts to other facts presumably established by observation or casual impression,—the most essential points of the statement can be found to rest on the weakest hypotheses, not even conceivably amenable to empirical tests or observation of any sort. I refer to the assertions (d) and (h) that increases in steel wages and steel prices are attributable to the particular policies and actions of steel workers unions and steel companies, respectively, in the sense that the increases would not have occurred if unions and companies had had no control over wages and prices, respectively. These assertions are open to question; a very strong case can be made against the theories on which they rest.

I am willing to argue that the existence of unions and of union contracts running for periods such as a whole year was, during 1946–1952, a stabilizing factor and that wage rates in these years would have risen more often and more sharply if the labor market had been more competitive.[11] I should argue with even more conviction that unrestricted competition in steel products would have driven steel prices higher than they were "set" by the companies. These were times of distinct "excess demand" with deferred deliveries, customer rationing and allocations; unrestricted competition would have driven prices to levels at which enough would-be buyers were squeezed out of the market to reduce total demand to the scarce supply. The steel companies used their control over prices to hold them below the competitive levels.[12] If my reasoning and my judgment of the actual facts are correct, any monopoly

---

[11] Cf. Albert Rees, "Postwar Wage Determination in the Basic Steel Industry," *American Economic Review*, Vol. XLI (1951), pp. 389–404.

[12] Whether this was "good" or "bad" for society can be decided only on the basis of a whole system of theory and valuation. I regard it as "bad," on the basis of my scheme of social values. But there is no agreement on this.

power possessed by unions and companies was used to keep steel wages and prices from rising as much as they would have in free competitive markets.

Surely, I am not presenting these counter-assertions as facts. They are conclusions based on hypotheses which happen to be different from those·on which the original assertions rested. But, I submit, that this theorizing is better than the implied theorizing of the pseudo-factual statement under examination, first, in that it admits the hypothetical character of the findings and discloses the underlying hypotheses and, second, in that it is more consistent with the concepts used in the rest of the statement. For the references to "bargaining position" and "monopolistic position" are meaningful only in (implied) comparison with a situation where the parties concerned are not enjoying such positions, that is, in comparison with a more competitive situation, if not with a state of pure and perfect competition. Such a comparison is carried through in the counter-assertions, but is disregarded in the original assertions.

We shall not take more space to illustrate the contention that most of the so-called facts in economics are really "implied theory." [13] But we should demand that theory be made explicit whenever it can be done without undue effort. If this were done, people would become more critical of "facts" and less averse to "theory"; at least they would know that the so-called facts cannot be better than the theories implied.

EXPLANATION, PREDICTION, EVALUATION

Theory, the schematic linking of hypothetical facts in our minds, is used for purposes of fact finding, explanation, prediction, and evaluation. In fact finding, theory is a means of establishing "inferred facts" from observed facts. In explanations, theory leads us from certain given facts to others that are regarded as their "causes" and are selected out of the vast array of facts observed or inferred. In predictions, theory goes from given facts to their

[13] For another example of implied theory in an historical statement—on the effects of merger upon concentration in industry—see above Chapter 4, p. 115.

future "effects." In evaluation, theory links facts with systems of values or "ends."

Prediction versus Explanation

If it is as easy as all that, one might wonder why scientists and philosophers have been puzzling throughout the ages about the logical and methodological relationships in question. Let us admit then that we are indulging in great simplifications. But it is better to have vaguely correct ideas about these matters than downright false ones or none at all.

In predictions of future events we believe that we know the conditions and factors at work and can tell what the outcome will be; in explanations of past events what we know is the outcome and we are called upon to tell what were the responsible conditions and the significant factors at work. Thus, logically there is little difference: in the one case, we go forward from causes to effects, in the other, backward from effects to causes. Practically, the difference may be great: it is easy to show that a prediction was wrong —at least, if the timing of the effect was included in the prediction and we can wait long enough—while it may be difficult, if not impossible, to disprove an explanation.

For example, if I make a diagnosis of the situation in the tin industry and then, on the basis of my judgment about all observed, inferred, and anticipated facts and on the basis of my theoretical insight, make the prediction that the price of tin will be at least 20 percent higher within six months, all it takes to prove me wrong is—six months and reliable reports on tin prices. On the other hand, if I observe that tin prices have increased by 20 percent in the last six months and now give an explanation for it, pointing to increased demand and increased production costs, it would not be easy to prove me wrong. It might be possible to prove that production costs have not increased,—which would throw out half of my explanation—but it would be difficult to disprove the asserted increase in demand. If someone should find evidence of a price fixing agreement among the largest tin producers, he could point to it as another explanation of the price increase. But it would be hard to present conclusive proof that the agreement, rather than the demand or cost increase, was the "real" cause and would have caused the price increase in the absence of any increase in demand or cost.[14]

The word "prediction" is often used for merely hypothetical statements. In a real prediction the forecaster assumes the responsibility for all the conditions on which his prediction depends; he says not merely what will happen *if* . . . , but what will happen, *period*. Not so in hypothetical predictions. The practical value of such "iffy" predictions depends on how many ifs are included and how hard it is to find out whether they are actually realized.

Hypothetical Predictions

To say, for example, that sugar prices will fall by at least fifteen percent within a year if the quota restrictions on imports are abolished, may be very helpful advice because it states only one condition, and an easily ascertainable one at that. Less helpful, on the other hand, would be a "prediction" that enumerates many of the conditions on which it depends and leaves it to the "clients" —legislature, administration, business management, general public—to judge for themselves how likely it is that all the listed conditions will be fulfilled. Something like this: "If the quota restrictions on sugar imports are abolished, if the import tariff and the sugar tax are left unchanged, if no great changes occur in the conditions of foreign cane production and of domestic sugar beet production, if transport costs remain the same, if the domestic fruit crops are not substantially increased, if national income does not rise by more than ten percent, and if the income tax structure is not markedly altered, then we may expect sugar prices to fall by at least fifteen percent within a year." Yet this is still a modest

---

[14] If in the natural sciences more stress is laid upon prediction than upon explanation, the reason is that they are so much concerned with controlled experiments. Explanations of past events where no checks are possible as to the actual circumstances and operative factors are equally difficult and controversial in the natural and social sciences. To establish beyond doubt or controversy the causes responsible for the explosion of a boiler or a tank or for the collapse of a structure is sometimes as impossible as it is to establish the causes responsible for explosion or collapse in the economy. Several different explanations may fit the data and there is no way of knowing for sure what may have caused things to come out as they did.

example of a conditional prediction; we could easily expand the list of ifs to several times its present length. Moreover, all of the stated conditions are of the ascertainable, or approximately ascertainable, sort, while we could easily add a few where no one could possibly know how to go about finding out whether they were fulfilled or not.

There is a good reason for denying that hypothetical predictions are predictions at all. For we may go on adding necessary conditions until no doubt remains and the outcome is absolutely assured. The last condition to be added, making the "forecast" 100 percent certain, might read: ". . . and if nothing else happens that could interfere with the predicted outcome." This, of course, transforms the statement into a pure tautology, that is, it becomes equivalent to saying that a certain event must occur if and when it occurs. Between a real forecast, or unconditional prediction, on one end and, on the other end, a tautological statement enumerating all the conditions that would make the predicted outcome an absolute certainty, there is a long scale of hypothetical statements and it is a matter of methodological taste where one wishes to draw the line between propositions one agrees to call predictions and propositions one refuses to call predictions.[15]

But if the difference between real and hypothetical predictions, or unconditional and conditional forecasts, consists in whether the forecaster bears the responsibility for the fulfillment of all conditions on which the prediction rests or whether he leaves some of them to his "clients" to judge for themselves, one will quickly appreciate that, from the "clients'" point of view, the difference is more or less a formality. For in the end it does not help the "clients" if the forecaster has the self-confidence or the gambling spirit that it takes to assume responsibility for an uncondi-

---

[15] Some reasonable points for drawing the line:

(a) immediately after the unconditional prediction and before the stipulation of any conditions at all;

(b) between conditional predictions providing only for such conditions as are under our control and propositions providing also for conditions we cannot control;

(c) between conditional predictions providing only for conditions whose realizations we can clearly ascertain before the event and propositions providing also for conditions whose realization we cannot ascertain at all or only after the event.

tional forecast. If it is uncertain whether all the conditions will be satisfied, the cocksureness of the forecaster making an unconditional prediction will not reduce the risk of anybody acting on the basis of this prediction. The really important question is whether we can rely on the forecaster's judgment or our own that all the conditions implied in the unconditional prediction or spelled out in the conditional prediction, respectively, are going to be fulfilled. And this depends on the degree of control we have over the conditions and on the degree of certainty or measure of probability that the conditions we cannot control will nevertheless be realized. Neither of the two is very great in economic affairs. And it is for this reason that economists are better in explaining than in predicting. Nevertheless, any policy recommendations that are made by economists presuppose some degree of confidence in their ability to predict.[16]

Evaluation

Policy recommendations presuppose more than some ability to predict that certain "effects" will follow from certain measures; they presuppose also some ability to compare alternative effects and to know which are preferable. In other words, political economists must also seek to formulate guiding principles for the comparative evaluation of alternative states of affairs.

This statement will be protested by many who have fought hard to keep economics pure, free from "value judgments," cleanly segregated from politics. Their idea is that the economist should merely present his list of probable effects to be expected from alternative policies and let the politician choose from the list. Working under such directives an economist must refrain from saying that free trade or low tariffs are better than high protective tariffs and import prohibitions; that free access to trades and occupations

---

[16] Perhaps it should be mentioned that prediction in economics is rarely concerned with the actions of *particular* consumers or firms. There is much confusion on this point because we speak of theories of the "individual" consumer and the "individual" firm. But these theories presuppose merely that there are *enough* people who will act in such a way that the results will correspond to the results of the "model action" of the idealized individual.

is preferable to a system of franchises and licences; that a scheme of subsidized production of potatoes with fixed price supports and destruction of the .surplus output is undesirable; that price-fixing combinations and industrial monopolies are against the public interest. Of course, the purists who oppose the admission of value judgments into economics will not deny that the economist has the right as a citizen to have and express his ideas about what he likes and what he dislikes—provided that he makes it clear that he speaks as a citizen, not as an economist.

I have much sympathy with this view and with the demand that the economist in his professional work should maintain objectivity and not "take sides." Yet I am not convinced that it can be done with full consistency. Perhaps complete freedom from value judgments in economics can be achieved if a great many things remain unsaid which ought to be said and which only an economist is qualified to say. Many economists, incidentally, believe they have avoided value judgments when they have skirted the words "good" and "bad," "desirable" and "undesirable," or "superior" and "inferior," and instead have spoken only about optimum allocation and misallocation of resources, efficient and wasteful use of resources, or economic and uneconomic organization of production.[17] The implications are that everybody agrees society ought to work economically, efficiently, optimally; that economists need not evaluate this objective but can impartially analyse and report on the ways of approaching it; and that there are standards, not subject to diverse interpretation, by which the optimum and the deviations therefrom can be ascertained. All this, however, is controversial.

Implied Value Judgments

The controversy extends even to such seemingly simple things as an "increase in aggregate real income." According to most economists, the idea of an increase in real income can be distinguished from the idea of an increase in welfare. For any change in income

---

[17] "Misallocation," "inefficient" and "uneconomic" use of resources are understood here to be synonymous. A few writers have developed narrower meanings of "efficiency."

there will probably be *some* members of society who are worse off while others are better off and, hence, a judgment about *total welfare* implies either that we can measure, compare and add up the utilities or satisfactions of different persons, or that we have some objective standards by which to weigh the importance of changes in income distribution for the total welfare of the community. If we can do neither and if we thus cannot "objectively" say that an increase in total real income is equivalent to an increase in total welfare, we might omit statements about welfare and be satisfied with the "objectivity" of statements about total real income. But even this is denied by some economists. For there will probably be *some* products in the total real income of society of which less is produced while more is available of others and, hence, a judgment that *total output* on balance has increased implies that we accept some weights, such as market prices, by which to measure, compare and add up the values of different goods and services. But the acceptance of market prices for this purpose involves, according to these dissenters, certain conventions or hypotheses that rest on value judgments.[18]

[18] The majority of economists is quite willing to accept market prices for the purpose of real income measurements without admitting that this implies any value judgments. However, since market prices change over time, they would employ a double test for the comparison of the incomes of two periods: the bundle of goods and services of the second period, in order to deserve a plus sign in the comparison with the first period, must be bigger in value both on the basis of the prices prevailing in the first period and on the basis of the prices prevailing in the second period.

Yet, even this test cannot satisfy everybody for it fails to take account of the effects of income distribution upon prices. The following argument will explain one of the difficulties. Assume that the value of total output (goods and services) of Situation II is greater than the value of total output of Situation I, no matter whether it is calculated in terms of prices of Situation II or in terms of prices of Situation I. But the change in the composition of total output may have been associated with a change in the distribution of income such that some groups of people receive, not only a smaller relative share of the total, but actually less than before. One might be satisfied with the "imaginary-compensation test," that is, with estimating whether compensation payments from those who have gained to those who have lost (in comparison with Situation I) would leave the former still better off after the latter were fully compensated for their losses. But assume now that such compensation payments are actually enforced through a system of taxes and bonuses; that this redistribution of income leads to shifts in demand and, consequently, changes in prices; and that calculated in terms of these prices

The bearing of all this on the subject matter of this book is probably clear.[19] Are we entitled to say in scientific objectivity that the abolition or reduction of monopoly will lead to a more efficient use of resources and thus to an increase in real income? Or does such a statement depend on value judgments? A verdict confirming the suspicion that value judgments are involved would not, however, weaken the case against monopolies, provided the implied value judgments can be ferreted out, made explicit, and shown to be generally accepted; at least the case would hold for all those who are willing to subscribe to the postulated value judgments—as well as to the theories on which the particular argument is based.

An Illustration

Perhaps we should offer an illustration showing how closely pure "causal" analysis and "welfare" analysis are connected in the comparative evaluation of two situations. Assume that a locally produced building material has been generally used by all contractors in a city; that a less expensive out-of-state product becomes available and threatens to replace the local product; that, in order to protect the business of the local producer and the employment of his workers, the use of the substitute material in local building construction is prevented through appropriate "safety regulations"

---

the bundle of goods and services produced in Situation II would be worth less than the output in Situation I. In other words, the comparison between the two bundles of output would depend on whether the changes in income distribution that were associated with the change in output were or were not "undone" through income transfers; output would appear to have decreased in the one case, but increased in the other. To measure real income in terms of prices prevailing without compensation payments to losers is to accept an implicit value judgment to the effect that the subjective valuations by the beneficiaries of a change should win out over the subjective valuations by the losers.

Quite apart from such sophisticated arguments, the use of market prices as weights in the aggregation of heterogeneous goods and services is rejected by most Marxist economists as based on a "bourgeois-capitalist prejudice."

[19] For a thorough and refined treatment of the subject from the point of view of modern welfare analysis see Tibor Scitovsky, *Welfare and Competition* (Chicago: Richard D. Irwin, 1951). His book appeared after my book was completed in manuscript.

in the building code of the city or by the refusal of local building unions to handle the imported material. If these "monopolistic" interventions by the local government or local trade unions are dropped, benefits will accrue to certain groups of people while others will be harmed. On balance, what will be the effects? How can the economist justify his recommendation that the monopolistic restraints be abolished?

His argument will have to be divided according to several points of view: (1) taking account of all people concerned, those in the state where the new material is produced as well as those in the city; (2) taking account of the city people only; (A) taking account of the long-run effects; (B) taking account of the near future only. Moreover, he will have to consider the possibilities (a) that the displaced city workers will easily find other jobs, almost as good as the ones they lost; (b) that they will find employment only on much less favorable terms; or (c) that they are unfit for any other employment. (All this, incidentally, will be relevant only upon the assumption that the new building material is so much cheaper or better than the city product that the latter, if the new material may be used, could not be sold even at a price barely above direct costs.[20])

Most economists would have no difficulties in recommending against the monopolistic interventions from any points of view if assumption (a) can be made concerning reemployment opportunities. Difficulties begin with assumptions (b) and (c), where serious losses of income to the displaced workers (in addition to the long-run income losses of landlords owing to rent reductions resulting from an increased supply of housing) must be set against the gains of builders, contractors, building laborers, tenants and new home owners in the city, and of workers employed in the production of the new building material outside the city. Theorizing on the basis of (2A)—the long-run interests of the city people alone—will be complicated by the fact that, deducing from balance-of-payments principles, one may anticipate eventually the development and production of some "export item" in the

---

[20] This assumption is necessary because the city plant ordinarily would not be shut down as long as by continuing operations more than all variable costs (inclusive of "user cost") could be earned.

city, which may help to outweigh the losses involved in the displacement of workers. Arguing on the basis of (2Bb) or (2Bc)—only the city, only the short run, with reemployment trouble—the economist may have to concede much to the advocates of restriction, though of course the argument would be explicitly narrow and short-sighted, that is, confined to the effects upon local interests in the near future.

It must be left to the reader to figure out for himself the possibilities and probabilities of the case from the different points of view and upon different assumptions. But it is probably sufficiently clear that all relevant arguments will involve comparisons of alternative situations for different groups of people over different periods of time, comparative evaluations which can be made comprehensive only with the help of economic theories linking changes in prices, production and incomes with changes in the welfare of different people, communities, and generations.

Conflicting Values

Welfare analysis solely in terms of consumable goods and services is not enough. There are also other considerations for the evaluation of the performance of the economic system, and for the comparison of alternative states of affairs. But society is not unanimous with regard to the objectives of its economic organization. As we said before (Chapter 3, pp. 71–72) it is not possible for society to strive at the same time for the attainment of a maximum of consumable income, of progress, of stability, of employment, of equality, of security, and of freedom. To the extent to which these social goals conflict with one another, compromises will be necessary. But different people attach different degrees of importance to these social goals, and compromises on these matters cannot be reached solely in the market place. These compromises are made through political machinery, though in a very rough and inefficient way.[21] Political scientists and economists have to collaborate on

[21] To illustrate this point: Theoretically it is possible to let the conflict between current consumable income and rate of progress be solved by the savings decisions of individual households and business firms, guided by relative prices and interest rates in conjunction with income anticipations and personal time preferences. But society is not satisfied with such an ar-

the task of evaluating the machinery by which conflicts in the hierarchy of social objectives are ironed out or compromised. The tools of economic theory can to good advantage be applied in the analysis of issues of this sort.

MEASUREMENT

The difference between scientific knowledge and knowledge acquired and used in the ordinary business of every-day life is that the former always strives to be clearer, more systematic, more definite and more exact where the latter is vague, unsystematic, indefinite and approximate. From the emphasis on the ideal of greater accuracy has developed a boastful slogan: "Science is Measurement."

"Science is Measurement"

This slogan has had some good and some bad consequences. The good ones are too obvious to call for discussion. The bad ones

---

rangement and interferes in a variety of ways on behalf of faster progress, that is, on behalf of higher future incomes relative to current consumption. These interventions are through the patent system, by which resources are lured into research and development work; through conservation measures, by which natural resources are kept from current use under the pretense that more should be left for future generations; through inflationary monetary policies, by which credit is created to finance additional investment; through fiscal policies designed (not as counter-cyclical measures, but) to finance government investment in generous amounts and in areas in which competitive enterprise could adequately function (and, paradoxically, at the same time to reduce private saving through sharply progressive tax rates); through direct controls allocating strategic materials for selected investments; etc., etc. The merits and demerits of such policies must be analysed by economists and explained to the public, which in its "selection" of political leaders may exert a modicum of influence on governments.

Perhaps the present author should be allowed to express a value judgment in opposition to most government interventions in the operation of competitive markets. He is an old-fashioned liberal who prefers to leave as much as possible to the anonymous decisions in competitive markets, and as little as possible to decisions by men in power, partly because he is convinced that the interventions are necessarily clumsy and wasteful (and, as a rule, exploited for the benefit of private interests at the expense of the public and almost without regard to social costs), partly because he fears that they seriously encroach upon individual freedom—which in his scale of values holds top place in the hierarchy of objectives.

are that, in an attempt to be "more scientific," people have tried to measure where there was nothing to measure, have slighted important studies where numerical relationships were not of the essence, and have promoted an excessive allocation of intellectual resources to "measurement at all cost" at the expense of other kinds of research and analysis.[22]

To be sure, where a description involves discrete units of any kind of object, it is desirable that they be counted; where a description or a theory involves comparisons of extensive or intensive magnitudes,[23] they should be made in numerical terms; and where a theory involves quantitative relationships, numerical ratios ought to be developed if possible. Yet there are descriptions or theories where none of these operations is relevant or meaningful and attempted measurements are useless or inappropriate.[24]

Some Implications of Measurement

In certain fields of inquiry measurement affects the measured objects or even annihilates them.[25] To what extent, if any, does

[22] "We cannot refuse the name *science* to logic or to the non-quantitative branches of mathematics such as analysis situs, projective geometry, etc. Nor is there good reason for refusing the adjective *scientific* to such works as Aristotle's *Politics* or Spinoza's *Ethics* and applying it to statistical 'investigations' or 'researches' that do not advance the understanding of anything." Morris R. Cohen, *op. cit.*, p. 89.

[23] Extensive magnitudes can be meaningfully added, subtracted, multiplied, and divided; intensive magnitudes cannot. The usual examples of the former are length or weight, and of the latter temperature or hardness. The term "measurement" is used for both, though in somewhat different senses.

[24] "There has been a lot of foolishness connected with this attempt to measure everything. There is, for example, this statement of Lord Kelvin's . . . : 'If you cannot measure, your knowledge is meagre and unsatisfactory.' Its practical meaning tends to be: 'If you cannot measure, measure anyhow.'" Frank H. Knight, on "Quantification: The Quest for Precision" in *Eleven Twenty-Six: A Decade of Social Science Research*, ed. by Louis Wirth (Chicago: University of Chicago Press, 1940), p. 169.

[25] The "Heisenberg principle of uncertainty," concerned with the effects of observation upon the observed, relates to quantum mechanics in physics and the impossibility of determining "position" as well as "momentum" simultaneously. Analogous principles may apply in other fields. Examples of victims of destruction by measurement are photons, mesons, neutrinos. Cf. Henry Margenau, *The Nature of Physical Reality: A Philosophy of Modern Physics* (New York: McGraw-Hill, 1950), p. 373.—Margenau believes that

this apply to economics? One thing seems unavoidable: measurement in economics presupposes that many individuals and organizations make disclosures about their private affairs; hence, their privacy is interfered with and the freedom of the individual may thereby be encroached upon. Often, however, the disclosures are obtained in connection with government interventions that are undertaken for other purposes, so that data for measurement are "by-products" available without any *additional* encroachment upon individual freedom.

Most of the phenomena that are significant for problems of competition and monopoly are *conceivably* measurable, but measurements are practically impossible. Measurements of propensities, preferences and anticipations are surely not feasible on a sufficiently large scale to be helpful in the solution of our problems. But even the most essential magnitudes—prices, costs, sales, profits —cannot be measured with any degree of accuracy.[26] Some of this will become apparent in the next chapter on "Measuring the Degree of Monopoly."

Measurement is sometimes believed to be independent of theory. Some others regard measurement as a prerequisite of theory. This reverses the true roles of the two. Measurement *presupposes theory*, although the latter may be primitive, should be tentative, and frequently is implicit rather than explicit.[27] Of course, measurement may result in the revision, qualification, or disqualification of a theory, but this does not modify the fact that, quite apart from the obvious theoretical foundation of all *indirect* measurements, even "the simplest direct measurements depend upon theoretic assumptions." [28]

this applies also to the social sciences: "perfectly good measurement in atomic physics (as well as in biology and in the social sciences) may 'kill' or annihilate a system. . . ." *op. cit.*, p. 377.

[26] On the inherent difficulties in obtaining price and cost data see Fritz Machlup, *The Economics of Sellers' Competition: Model Analysis of Sellers' Conduct* (Baltimore: Johns Hopkins Press, 1952), Chapter 1.

[27] For an illuminating discussion of this issue see Tjalling C. Koopmans, "Measurement Without Theory," *Review of Economics and Statistics*, Vol. XXIX (1947), pp. 161–172.

[28] Morris R. Cohen, *op. cit.*, p. 97.

Fictitious Accuracy

Concepts must be adapted to the purposes for which they are constructed. Revisions of theories may compel re-adaptations of the concepts to which they relate. Moreover, different questions asked about seemingly the same set of phenomena may require slightly different concepts. For example, prices paid by consumers (that is, "delivered prices") may be relevant for one problem while another may refer to prices received by producers (that is, mill-net prices, net of transportation and distribution cost). Clearly, if we need statistical data about prices of certain products, it will make a difference whether they are to be used in one context or another, and theory must be applied in making the choice.

The relativity of the relevance of concepts, and hence of statistical data, is often overlooked; especially when statistics are regularly published, the temptation is great to mistake the data for accurately measured facts. The following example may serve as a warning against such a mistake. A few years ago the Department of Commerce revised several basic concepts and methods of estimation for its statistics of the United States national income (in current dollars, not "real income"). Evidently it had been felt that the concepts previously employed were not relevant to the sort of problems for which national income figures were most frequently demanded and that the changed concepts were more relevant. As a result of the revision, the "national income" of 1945, which had been reported at 161 billion dollars, was raised to 182.8 billion, that is, by 21.8 percent. And while the 1946 "national income" had been above that of 1945 on the basis of the old method, it was below the 1945 income on the basis of the new method.

Even apart from differences in basic definitions and classifications, the discrepancies in the results of repeated or simultaneous measurements of the same so-called economic facts are embarrassingly large.[29] Thus, two different methods of measuring the size of the labor force—both methods used by the U.S. Bureau of the Census for April 1950—resulted in a discrepancy of 3½ mil-

[29] For a veritable chamber of horrors in this class of "statistical findings" see Oskar Morgenstern, *On the Accuracy of Economic Observation* (Princeton: Princeton University Press, 1950), pp. 50–64.

lion people.[30] In the absence of similar control measurements in
most of the areas of statistical investigation we do not know the
extent to which gross inaccuracies exist in the data available for
empirical research and naively regarded as "the facts."

[30] Clarence D. Long, "Discussion: Statistical Standards and the Census,"
The American Statistician, Vol. 6 (1952), p. 11.

CHAPTER 12

Measuring the Degree of Monopoly

Purposes, Obstacles, Criteria: The Desirability of Measurement · Degree of Monopoly versus Monopoly Power · The Basic Difficulties of Measurement · The Possible Criteria for Measurement

Numbers and Concentration: The Number of Firms · The Concentration of Control · Definitions of Firm and Industry · The Size of the Market · Competition from Outside the Industry · The Index of Divergence

The Rate of Profit: The Accounting Rate of Profit · An Adjusted Rate of Profit

Price Inflexibility: The Rigidity of Administered Prices · Frequency and Amplitude of Changes · Comparing the Indexes · Margin Inflexibility

The Gap Between Marginal Cost and Price: Inequality Between Marginal Cost and Price · Objections and Limitations · Changes in the Degree of Monopoly

Other Measurement Proposals: Gross Profit Margin and Aggregate Monopoly Income · Industry Control and the Slope Ratios of Demand Curves · Cross-Elasticities of Demand · Penetration and Insulation

A Monopolist's Self-Analysis

Conclusion

H OW CAN MONOPOLY power be measured? Considerable effort has in recent years been devoted to answering this question. But why do we want to measure monopoly power? Is it worth while spending much effort on the question?

PURPOSES, OBSTACLES, CRITERIA

It is easier to justify the efforts devoted to the question of measurement than it would be to justify a failure to attempt an answer. Sheer intellectual curiosity compels us as economic theorists to work on this problem, for we could not with good conscience

[469]

go on talking about "great" or "little" monopoly power, or about various degrees of monopoly, without trying to ascertain the meaning of these words. And this implies at least the possibility of "conceivable" measurement, even if practical measurement were to remain impossible.

The Desirability of Measurement

But apart from any interest in intellectual exercises and in the niceties of theoretical systems, we are anxious to know the facts about the economy in which we live, and we want to learn which industries are more monopolistic than others and which firms have more monopoly power than others. Some practical methods of measurement are needed for this purpose. Finally, if we want the government to succeed in its policy of restraining monopoly, we must look for ways and means of pointing out just what degree of monopoly obtains in this industry or that; government measures to check monopoly could undoubtedly be more intelligent and more effective if the measurement of monopoly power were practicable.

Some lawyers would not agree with the statement that measurements of the degree of monopoly could be of much use in the antimonopoly policies of the government. They hold that the most important task for the government is to prevent business practices by which monopoly power is increased, regardless of how big this power has been before or would be afterwards. This view deserves our respect, especially since we have not thus far been able to devise an index of the degree of monopoly, and it would surely not have been wise for the government to defer all action and wait until economists succeeded in devising such an index.

One may agree with this legal policy of proceeding against monopolistic practices regardless of the monopoly power involved, and nevertheless may hold that it would be desirable to have ways of measuring the degree of monopoly and to adopt a policy —complementary with the other, not replacing it—of proceeding against monopoly wherever it goes beyond a certain point.

We conclude that we must try hard to learn how to measure monopoly, not only for the intellectual satisfaction of solving a difficult problem and for the gratification of our desire to have more intelligence about the facts of economic life, but also for the development and application of intelligent governmental policies.

Degree of Monopoly versus Monopoly Power

We have not thus far explicitly distinguished between "monopoly power" and "degree of monopoly," although we have preferred to use the former expression when the monopolistic position of a firm or small group of firms was under discussion, while the latter expression has been used chiefly with reference to the monopolistic situation of a whole industry. The difference is perhaps not of great importance, but may be worth pointing out.

"Power" cannot well be separated conceptually from a subject "having" or "exercising" power. Power, the ability to achieve certain effects, must be somebody's ability. Hence, when we speak of monopoly power we think of a firm, or specific group of firms, capable of exercising some influence over others or some control over the supply of a commodity in the market, or having some discretion with regard to the prices charged. On the other hand, it would be somewhat confusing to attribute "monopoly power" to an entire industry consisting of many firms not acting collectively. To be sure, the industry may be in a sheltered position or may include powerful firms who restrict supply and exclude potential newcomers; and the industry may thereby be able to sell at monopoly prices. But we should prefer to speak in this connection of the high "degree of monopoly" in the industry.

If an industry consists of a few large firms with a great deal of monopoly power and several small firms with little or no monopoly power, the "industry" will surely be described as monopolistic, and one may perhaps attempt to evaluate the degree of monopoly in the industry. But no one will say that the "industry"—the group of strong and weak firms—possesses "monopoly power." Or take an industry in which no individual firm has any monopoly power whatsoever, but which through pressure group politics has succeeded in obtaining governmental restrictions on new investment, entry, or total output. We can then speak only of the degree of monopoly, caused by the restrictive measures and effecting increased product prices, but we cannot well speak of monopoly power.

Having made the distinction, I do not regard it as imperative to observe it too pedantically. While I shall avoid speaking of the monopoly power of an industry, I feel justified in speaking of the degree of monopoly of firms as well as of industries.

The Basic Difficulties of Measurement

The chief difficulty of our task of measuring "monopoly" lies in the fact that monopoly never becomes perceptible except by its causes or its effects. It has this in common with many other concepts, such as force, power, strength, potential, capacity; none of these is *directly* measurable.[1] One may have theories about what causes monopoly and may hope that all these causes are measurable; or one may have theories about what effects monopoly can have and, assuming that the monopoly is exploited to its fullest extent, may try to measure the effects.

Any measurement of monopoly depends thus, first of all, on whether we are satisfied that our theories are valid; second, on whether they are complete; third, on whether the phenomena selected as the relevant ones can be discerned in reality; fourth, on whether they lend themselves to numerical description; and fifth, whether such numerical descriptions of all relevant phenomena are actually available.

Assume, for example, that we have prepared a catalogue of all the factors which we know *cause* or contribute to monopoly, and that we are satisfied that our theory is valid in the sense that all the factors selected are really sufficient or accessory conditions of monopoly. But can we ever be sure that our catalogue is complete?

---

[1] When we say that Mr. A. has great or little physical strength, we judge it either from his appearance, inferring it from his build, weight, muscles, or other things "known" in general to "cause" physical strength, or from his performance, assuming that what we observed was really the effect of his application and assuming furthermore that he applied all the strength that he has. Needless to say, we may be badly mistaken in our judgment. If we try to judge monopoly power, we are still worse off regarding both observation and interpretation.

If we have overlooked some other factors that may create or increase monopoly power, a measurement based only on the ones included in the catalogue may be grossly incorrect. Among the factors that are included there may be some that cannot be made objects of observation and whose presence or absence cannot be directly ascertained; or, if they are all discernible by observation, some may not be suitable for numerical description (such as collusion, whose existence may be ascertained but whose "magnitude" cannot be measured); finally, certain factors may be numerically describable, but we may lack any kind, or the right kind, of statistical information.

Assume next that we have listed all the *effects* which we know the use of monopoly power may have, and that we are confident that our theory is valid. Further, assume, for the sake of simplicity, that the phenomena possibly affected or produced by the use of monopoly power can be ascertained and numerically described, and that statistical information is actually available. There would still remain two difficulties that cannot be overcome: in the first place, we can never know whether all of the monopoly power was used or whether much more power exists than was used; secondly, the phenomena selected as affected or conditioned by monopoly may possibly be also affected or conditioned by other factors and it may not be feasible to separate the effects of the exercise of monopoly power from the effects of other forces.

The Possible Criteria for Measurement

Having indicated the kind of difficulties that may frustrate any attempts to measure monopoly, we may proceed to see whether such difficulties actually exist when we try to list, examine, and measure either the causes or the effects of monopoly.

Beginning with an account of the causes, and assuming that our task is to measure the degree of monopoly in the production and sale of a commodity narrowly defined in terms of its physical properties, we run immediately into the difficulty of discovering whether or not the various sellers compete vigorously and effectively with one another. We know that evidence of collusion is hard to come by, and that it is impossible to assess its effectiveness in

numerical terms. Even if we were able to read the minds of each
of the competitors, we would not know how to "grade," "add," or
"average" our findings. Assume that one of the producers, or a firm
outside the group, holds patent rights under which all producers
are licensed, how can the restriction of competition be measured?
Assume that there are various sorts of "ties" between some of the
competing companies—interlocking stock-holding, interlocking
office-holding, common ownership of the community-of-interest
type, influence by minority stock holders—how can they be discovered, how can their effects on competition be appraised, and
how can the appraisals be reduced to numerical terms, to make
them additive or comparable with other relevant factors?

The situation seems a bit easier with regard to other relevant
factors, such as the number of firms and the degree of concentration of control over the supply of a product. Here descriptions in
numerical terms appear practicable. These possibilities will be
reviewed presently in greater detail. But the results will be vitiated
by the fact that the effects of geographic differentiation (local
versus regional versus national markets), competition from other
products (the elasticity of substitution between the commodity
in question and competing commodities), and competition from
abroad may be important elements in the total picture, but are difficult to ascertain and, thus far, impossible to measure. And there
are various kinds of barriers against entry, giving an industry protection from newcomers' competition, and thereby a degree of
monopoly that may not show as monopoly "power" in the hands
of any firm; but, again, there is no way of measuring these barriers
in any practical sense.

Turning to the possibilities of measurement by effects, price
relationships seem to offer the only basis for any sort of test. The
most "obvious" object of inquiry is the relationship between average cost and price because the gap between the two determines
profits, and profits have long been regarded as the monopoly index
par excellence. In lieu of historical profit margins and profit rates,
some adjusted or corrected profit computations, however, may be
more suitable for an attempted measurement of monopoly. From
another point of view, the gap between marginal cost and price
has been judged to be more significant for the purpose. And, be-

cause of the practical impossibility of obtaining the necessary data, it has been suggested that one should look for the effects of monopoly in the relative movements of the prices of products and the prices of the major means of production, for which approximate data can be found. These are movements over time. Movements of selling prices over time have also been looked upon as revealing the effects of monopoly because of the fact that, ordinarily, it takes monopoly power to keep prices from moving widely and frequently. Thus, measurements of price flexibility over time have been made in order to detect the presence and degree of monopoly. All of these attempts will be discussed in this chapter. But in view of what we have said about the basic difficulties inherent in the problem of measurement, we cannot have high hopes concerning the reliability or even relevance of the results obtained by the alternative methods.

Some of the criteria to be used for the attempted measurement of monopoly relate only to individual firms, and all the pertinent data would have to come from individual firms. This is true, for example, for marginal or average cost figures, selling prices, profits, investment values. Other criteria, however, refer to relationships among different firms, and the data coming from any one firm must be viewed in combination with and in relation to data from all the other firms that are regarded as members of the same "industry." This is especially true for most of the "causes" of monopoly, such as the control of one firm over others, a firm's relative share in a market, the degree of concentration of control over total supply.

NUMBERS AND CONCENTRATION

We are first turning our attention to those criteria of monopoly which relate to "causal" or contributing factors, are subject to "numerical" description, and presuppose the existence of a group of firms that can be meaningfully described as an "industry."

The Number of Firms

Since the number of firms in an industry is frequently mentioned as one of the chief factors determining whether or not the

individual firms are in a monopolistic position, the simplest
method of getting an idea of the amount of monopoly in each industry might be to count the number of firms.

For this purpose we must distinguish between firms and establishments. The Census of Manufactures lists the number of establishments in each industry—the individual plants, mills, factories,
shops; but several such establishments can be owned by one firm.
The 74 establishments, for example, in the beet sugar industry are
by no means 74 separate firms nor are the 2,153 establishments
in the wholesale meat packing industry.

If, in fact, the 2,153 meat packing establishments were all
separate and independent firms of equal size, one such firm would
"control" an output of 0.046 percent of the supply of the whole
industry, and four of them together would produce 0.18 percent.
(The actual situation is different; the four largest meat packers
produce more than 40 percent of the nation's supply.) On the other
hand, the 19,223 establishments in the general saw mills and planing mills industry are really 18,190 separate companies.[2]

Unfortunately, however, the number of firms actually tells us
very little. Firms are not of equal size. The mere number of firms,
even if they all produce an identical commodity and sell it in the
same undivided market, does not by itself indicate the degree of
control of any one of them. One firm may have a lion's share of
the market while a large number of small businesses may share
the insignificant remainder. If a hundred firms of equal size compete in the market, the large number may mean something; but
if a few of the hundred firms are very large and some 70 or 80
percent of the total output is concentrated in their hands, then
the large number in the industry does not mean much as a measure
of the degree of competition.

The Concentration of Control

To overcome this difficulty it is possible to measure the degree
to which production is concentrated in a few hands in the industry by calculating the percentage of the total physical or value
product that is produced by the largest producers. The size of

[2] See Table I.

firms and the concentration of control in the industry may be measured, apart from total product and sales, in terms of productive capacity, value of assets, number of employees, or some other characteristics. The results of the computation will differ according to the criterion chosen and sometimes the difference will be substantial. In particular, if the figures are used to compare one industry with another, sales figures will be distorted by the differences in the degree of vertical integration in different industries, and figures based on value of assets or any of the other measures will not reflect the different ratios of assets (or other measures) to sales in different industries.

The Department of Commerce produced a special report, based on the 1947 Census of Manufactures, showing for 452 narrowly defined industries the ratios of total output produced by the largest four, largest eight, largest twenty, and largest fifty companies. Where the corresponding figures from the 1935 Census (which had used many different industry classifications) were comparable, they were also shown in the 1947 concentration report.[3] From this report I have selected 60 industries for Table I. The Table gives first the number of establishments in each industry according to the 1935 and 1947 Census of Manufactures and then the "concentration percentage" for the largest four and largest eight producers respectively. ("Producer" means here the individual firm regardless of the number of establishments that it owns.) This concentration percentage does not represent the proportion of establishments owned, but the proportion of the total value of the industry's product that was contributed by the largest firms in the industry, their size being measured by "total value of shipments," except in a few industries in which serious duplication made it preferable to use "value added by manufacture."

[3] The report on "Concentration of Output in Largest Manufacturing Companies," prepared by the Department of Commerce and transmitted to the Monopoly Subcommittee of the House, is published as Appendix II of the Hearings. *Study of Monopoly Power*, Hearings before the Subcommittee on Study of Monopoly Power of the Committee on the Judiciary, House of Representatives, 81st Congress, 1st Session, Serial No. 14, Part 2-B (Washington: 1950), pp. 1436–56.

Concentration ratios based on the 1935 Census of Manufactures were computed by the National Resources Committee and published in *The Structure of the American Economy*, Part I (Washington: 1939), pp. 239–63.

TABLE I

CONCENTRATION OF OUTPUT IN LARGEST MANUFACTURING COMPANIES, 1935 AND 1947

Industry	Value of Annual Shipments, 1947, in Millions of Dollars	Number of Establishments 1935	Number of Establishments 1947	Number of Companies 1947	1947 Concentration Ratio: Companies First Four	1947 Concentration Ratio: Companies First Eight	1935 Concentration Ratio: Companies First Four	1935 Concentration Ratio: Companies First Eight
Primary aluminum	161.0	4 [1]	11	3	100		100	
Telephone & telegraph equipment	689.2	43 [1]	90	50	95.7	98.3		
Aluminum rolling and drawing	404.8	13 [1]	29	15	94.2	98.5		
Locomotives and parts	354.7	14	36	33	90.7	94.9		
Cigarettes	1,131.9	29	28	19	90.4	99.7	89.7	99.4
Matches	56.7	24	29	18	82.7	93.7	70.3	91.3
Cork products	30.1	34 [2]	36	34	81.9	91.1	76.9	90.2
Salt	46.1	39 [3]	38	25	80.5	90.5		
Soap and glycerin	1,085.8	238	249	223	79.0	85.9	73.5	83.1
Synthetic fibers	705.3	32	38	22	78.4	94.4	74.3	90.2
Tin cans and other tinware	679.9	204	217	102	77.8	85.9	80.8	85.6
Corn products	460.0	36	55	47	77.2	94.6		
Tires and inner tubes	1,547.0	42	57	35	76.6	89.6	80.9	90.4
Cereal preparations	284.7	110	64	55	74.9	89.4	68.1	82.2
Distilled liquors except brandy	870.2	391	226	144	74.6	86.4	51.2	71.4

Aircraft engines	463.4	20 [1]	57	54	71.5	88.2		
Biscuits, crackers and pretzels	540.2	348	326	249	71.5	77.7		
Cane-sugar refining	818.4	18	25	17	69.9	87.6	69.6	88.3
Beet sugar	262.9	77	74	17	68.4	93.8	68.8	89.4
Blast furnaces	1,713.9	72	86	33	67.3	82.1	66.0	82.8
Oleomargarine	214.6	14	27	17	63.7	89.6	79.1	96.0
Glass containers	422.6	80 [3]	87	41	62.9	79.2		
Photographic equipment	440.1	118	366	346	61.2	70.2		
Shortening and cooking oils	884.7	48 [2]	100	68	59.2	80.9	69.0	85.9
Motor vehicles and parts	3,577.4 [4]		963	779	55.7	63.6		
Metal barrels, drums and pails	173.1	64	70	49	52.1	73.9	37.0	56.9
Wire drawing	912.1	88	134	103	45.0	61.9	40.2	54.0
Steelworks and rolling mills	2,275.7 [4]		215	111	44.7	62.8		
Paper bags	320.5	107	193	160	44.2	58.6	34.8	48.7
Cottonseed oil mills	518.1	458	315	172	43.3	55.3	32.9	43.5
Motorcycles & bicycles	163.7	23	76	75	42.3	67.9	60.6	90.1
Meatpacking—wholesale	977.0 [4]	1,223	2,153	1,999	41.3	53.6		
Cigars	311.4	746	822	765	40.6	57.1	38.5	50.7
Petroleum refining	6,623.7	395	437	277	37.3	58.8	38.2	58.9
Electrical appliances	466.0	118 [1]	326	310	35.8	46.9		
Mattresses and bedsprings	331.1	824	879	842	35.7	42.0	25.8	31.2
Needles, pins and fasteners	147.2	79 [1]	277	273	33.8	49.3	63.4	76.2
Textile machinery	403.4	349 [2]	489	470	30.2	43.5	29.4	45.9
Cement hydraulic	408.9	153	155	73	29.5	45.1		
Flour and meal	2,511.5	2,193	1,243	1,084	29.0	40.6	29.4	37.0
Pulp mills	939.6	188	226	132	27.8	38.5	22.7	34.5

TABLE I
(cont.)

CONCENTRATION OF OUTPUT IN LARGEST MANUFACTURING COMPANIES, 1935 AND 1947

Industry	Value of Annual Shipments, 1947, in Millions of Dollars	Number of Establishments		Number of Companies	1947 Concentration Ratio: Companies		1935 Concentration Ratio: Companies	
		1935	1947	1947	First Four	First Eight	First Four	First Eight
Leather tanning & finishing	1,070.1	384	561	500	26.5	38.6	22.5	34.3
Radios and related products	606.0 [4]	305 [1]	857	799	25.6	35.3		
Toilet preparations	371.9	558	718	692	23.8	38.2	25.3	40.7
Malt liquors	1,317.9	666 [2]	440	404	21.4	30.0	11.8	17.7
Newspapers	1,917.3	6,728	8,339	8,115	20.9	26.0		
Sheet metal work	424.3	1,400 [2]	1,708	1,665	20.5	28.5		
Bolts, nuts, washers, rivets	463.8	219 [1]	364	339	20.1	31.4		
Paving mixtures and blocks	50.2	132	263	182	19.1	29.1	48.9	63.5
Paperboard boxes	1,475.4	1,214 [2]	1,522	1,323	17.9	27.4	14.1	20.7
Confectionery products	944.9	1,314	1,686	1,620	17.2	24.9	12.5	19.9
Bread & other bakery products	2,416.9	10,325 [1]	6,797	5,985	16.4	25.9		
Paper and board mills	2,812.0		665	453	15.6	23.7		
Cotton broad-woven fabrics	3,294.6	670 [2]	602	422	13.1	22.2		
Commercial printing	1,521.7	10,295 [1]	11,932	11,810	9.1	13.4		
Men's and boys' suits & coats	1,411.6	1,848 [1]	1,816	1,761	8.8	15.3		

TABLE I
(*cont.*)

CONCENTRATION OF OUTPUT IN LARGEST MANUFACTURING COMPANIES, 1935 AND 1947

Industry	Value of Annual Shipments, 1947, in Millions of Dollars	Number of Establishments		Number of Companies 1947	1947 Concentration Ratio: Companies		1935 Concentration Ratio: Companies	
		1935	1947		First Four	First Eight	First Four	First Eight
Sawmills and planing mills, general	2,526.9		19,223[5]	18,190[5]	5.4	7.2		
Women's suits and coats	1,003.8	1,753[1]	2,477	2,464	4.8	7.9		
Dresses, unit price	1,353.1	2,422[3]	4,202	4,165	2.6	4.7		
Fur goods	357.0	2,438	2,229	2,227	2.6	4.5	2.6	4.5

[1] 1939 figure.
[2] Not precisely comparable with 1947.
[3] 1937 figure.
[4] Value added by manufacture.
[5] For a correction of an error in the Census figures for this industry I am indebted to Dr. John Blair, Bureau of Industrial Economics, Federal Trade Commission.

Sources: Department of Commerce, "Concentration of Output in Largest Manufacturing Companies," published in Appendix II, *Study of Monopoly Power*, House of Representatives, Serial No. 14, Part 2-B (Washington: 1950), pp. 1436–56.
Bureau of the Census, Census of Manufactures, 1947.
Bureau of the Census, Census of Manufactures, 1935.

The concentration of production in the hands of the four largest producers in the industries listed in Table I ranges from nearly 100% in the aluminum industry to slightly more than 2½% in a branch of the clothing industry. To be sure, there is undoubtedly a high degree of monopoly in the one industry and very little in the other. Hence the index of concentration may give a general idea of the existence of monopoly power in an industry. But in many cases it will be seriously wrong.

The index of concentration and the statistics of the number of firms in an industry are open to much the same objections: they fail to take account of the arbitrary elements in the definition of a firm and of the classification of firms into industries; since they are compiled on a national basis, they relate to concentration only with respect to the national market and fail to take account of the subdivision of the national market into local markets; and they cannot make allowance for the effect of competition from other products (including imported products) on the monopoly power of the producers of given products.

Definitions of Firm and Industry

From the point of view of monopoly power, a firm that is a legal entity but not an economically independent unit (e.g., a subsidiary of a corporation) should not be counted as a separate firm. But it is not always easy to decide over how many legal units the control of a particular firm extends, i.e., just what group of firms should, from an economic point of view, be called one firm. Both the number of firms counted and any index of concentration depend on where the lines are drawn. The figures shown in Table I are based upon "consolidated" data, that is, a "company" is the parent corporation together with subsidiaries in which it owns more than a 50% interest.

The existence of large corporations with a diversified production also reduces the significance of the "industry" concept as a basis for the classification of firms. An industry may be broadly defined to include a large group of products, for example, "electrical machinery apparatus and supplies," or narrowly defined to include a smaller group such as "electrical generating and transmission apparatus," and the concentration index for each "industry" will be very different. But almost any "industry" will include a large variety of products some of which may be sold to quite different groups of consumers, serving totally different purposes, and thus constituting no direct substitutes for one another. It may be that almost every firm in the "industry" makes the whole set of products (which may be "joint products") so that all products are offered by many firms; but, on the other hand, it may be that each firm is specialized in one article and enjoys a complete monopoly of that article.

If the broad industrial classifications are taken for measuring the degree of concentration, concentration in industries more narrowly defined is hidden, for the chances are greater that firms which control only a negligible proportion of the whole production of the broadly defined industry produce a large proportion of the output of one particular article, which may not directly compete with any other product of the industry. The broader the definition of industry, the greater the likelihood that the group includes some specialized firms. The concentration index for the broader industry would never reveal this monopoly power.

If, however, the narrow definition is taken, corporations which produce a substantial part of that product, but whose chief line of activity is something else, are, under present practices of the Census Bureau, excluded from the narrow classification entirely. For example, although the chief product of General Motors Corporation is automobiles and the company is therefore included in the automobile industry, it is also an important producer of electrical machinery such as refrigerators, and of locomotives, where it does not appear in the statistics. It is not possible at present to classify such firms in several industries in proportion to their sales in each industry, because the figures are not available.

In Table I, total sales are represented by total shipments, which in turn are supposed to represent total output. But they include only total sales of the end products; interdepartmental transactions and intercompany transactions within consolidated concerns are not shown. Hence, if the large firms in one industry are highly integrated while the other firms are not, all of the transactions between the subsidiaries or departments of the large concern do not appear in the sales statistics of the industry; similar transactions do, however, appear as sales for the non-integrated section of the industry. Thus, insofar as the transactions within the integrated concerns relate to products which would otherwise be classed as part of the output of the industry, an index of concentration based on sales will clearly be too low, and, in particular, will not be comparable with a similar index in another industry where all the firms are equally integrated.

For this reason, among others, a basis of measurement more widely accepted than total output is total assets. If concentration is measured in terms of capital assets, this difficulty is avoided, although the objection remains that all the assets of a large firm will, under present practice, be included in the statistics of the "industry" to which its major product belongs, and thus the importance of the firm in that industry will be overstated, and understated in other industries. No matter what measurements are tried, the fact that many corporations are producing in a large number of fields which according to accepted statistical definitions are considered separate industries, together with the fact that corporate financial data are at present available only on a consolidated basis make it "impossible to make any type of adjustment for the inevitable resultant over- and under-statements of concentration." [4]

The Size of the Market

The second important objection to these measures of the degree of monopoly is the failure to distinguish between firms serving the national market and those serving only regional or even local markets. An industry with ten thousand firms in the country may be much less competitive than one with only fifty firms; the fifty firms may compete with each other in the national market, whereas the market of the populous industry may be locally divided and each of the ten thousand firms may be a local monopolist.

In order to make clear why national concentration of control need not add to the power of local monopolies let us imagine for

[4] *Report of the Federal Trade Commission on the Concentration of Productive Facilities 1947* (Washington: 1949), p. 8.

a moment that transportation is still so undeveloped (or expensive) that each community in the country has its local bakery. The number of establishments in the country would, of course, be enormous. If each establishment were owned by a separate firm, the index of concentration would be a minute fraction of a percent. Yet each firm would enjoy a local monopoly. If now, for some fabulous reason and under some fabulous legal provision, all bakery firms were merged into one national corporation, the concentration index would jump to one hundred percent, yet no change would occur in the monopoly power of the local branches of the national concern.

Mental experiments like this, despite the palpably "unrealistic" assumptions on which they rest, can give us more insight and understanding. If we are permitted to continue our speculation for another moment, let us return to the assumption of independent, local producers, each serving his local market as a perfect monopolist—although the index of concentration is next to zero. Let us then introduce some development in transportation: with lower transport costs larger-scale production will begin, the number of establishments and firms will fall and regional competition between firms may develop. But the index of concentration will now be higher than before because the largest firms will produce a larger percentage of the total industry's product. The widening of the market may thus have caused a reduction in the degree of monopoly power and at the same time an increase in the "concentration of control" in the industry. Surely, with the concentration of control and the degree of monopoly moving (in this example) in opposite directions, one cannot expect the former to be a reliable measure of the latter.

Competition from Outside the Industry

The degree of foreign competition is undoubtedly an important factor determining the degree of monopoly of domestic producers in the home market. Yet, the concentration index includes only the shares of domestic producers in the supply from domestic sources. An industry with a high degree of concentration may be much exposed to competition from importers and, as a result, be much more competitive than another industry with less concentration of control but less competition from abroad. Incidentally, the inclusion of exports in the sales figures (or output, assets, employment, etc.) of the firms and industries may also distort the concentration index as a measure of the degree of monopoly in the national market. For example, the four largest producers may be largely exporters and have only small shares in the domestic market.

The most serious defect of a concentration index as an index of the degree of monopoly is its failure to reflect competition from "other industries." We have already commented on the arbitrariness of the definition of the industry. The mere statistical operation of breaking up a more broadly defined industry into more narrowly defined industries may increase the index of concentration to a multiple of what it was under the broader classification, without any change in the actual market positions of any of the firms involved. But there is no way of defining industry groups so as to equalize the degree to which they are exposed to competition from products of other industries. For example, Venetian blinds and window shades are defined as separate industries; likewise, leather dress gloves and fabric dress gloves; creamery butter and oleomargarine, or household furniture upholstered, wood house furniture, metal house furniture, metal office furniture, public buildings furniture and professional furniture. Inter-industry competition may be of importance in the markets in question. On the other hand, typewriters, photographic equipment, surgical and medical instruments, dental equipment and supplies are probably not much exposed to direct competition from products of other industries.

These observations may be generalized by stating that the elasticities of substitution between the products of different industries may be very different for any kind of classification adopted by the statistician. An industry with a very high concentration index may nevertheless have a very low degree of monopoly if the elasticity of substitution between its products and the products of other industries is high. An industry with a smaller degree of concentration of control may be more monopolistic than industries with higher concentration if no good substitutes for its products are produced by others.

The elasticity of substitution between products is the chief determinant of the elasticity of demand for any one of them. But sometimes the elasticity of demand for a product is relatively high even though we do not know which products are in direct competition with it. A price increase for such a product may result in a drastic decline in sales although we may not be able to tell to what products the buyers turn who are driven away by the higher price. If the elasticity of demand for the product of the industry is very high, even a one-hundred-percent concentration of control over that industry cannot give it a high degree of monopoly. A wide dispersion of supply over many producers makes the elasticities of demand faced by the individual producers very high, regardless of what the composite elasticity of demand for the product of the industry may be. Concentration of control over the supply of the industry may reduce the elasticities of demand for the output of the large producers, and thus increase their control over price. But these elasticities cannot fall any lower than that of the demand for the product of the industry. Hence, the contribution which concentration of control can make to the degree of monopoly is limited by the elasticity of demand for the product of the industry.

If all industries were alike with respect to the elasticity of consumers' demand, the degree of competition from abroad, the size of the domestic market (local, regional, national), the differentiation of the product offered by different producers, the absence or presence of collusion and cooperation among the producers, and in all other respects, then the concentration of control over output would be a good index of the relative degrees of monopoly. The concentration index alone, when all other things are different, cannot tell us much. To be sure, if we are able to obtain all the information needed to classify industries such that each class contains only firms competing for the same buyers, the concentration index might be the most important single indication of the degree of monopoly. As long as this is not the case, the concentration index can be only one of several other bits of information, highly significant in some instances, less significant in others, and sometimes quite irrelevant.[5]

[5] All these reservations and warnings are designed to urge caution in the

The Index of Divergence

Where the degree of concentration of control over output is a significant factor for the degree of monopoly, it becomes interesting to find out whether this concentration is the result of large-scale production or rather the result of a combination of control over separate productive facilities. In other words, is production concentrated in a few plants or is control over the production of many separate plants concentrated in a few hands?

An answer to this question has been attempted—by John Blair of the Federal Trade Commission—through the development of an "index of divergence" between "concentration on a plant basis" and "concentration on a company basis." [6] If the total output of an industry is produced in a few plants, the "plant concentration curve"—showing vertically the cumulative percentage of the total output of the industry and horizontally the number of the largest plants that account for it—will rise sharply indicating that a few plants produce a large share of the output of the industry. If production is widely dispersed over several establishments, the plant concentration curve will rise only slowly. If each establishment is controlled by a separate firm, the "company concentration curve" will coincide with the plant concentration curve. If some companies own more than one plant, the company concentration curve must lie above the plant concentration curve. The divergence between the two curves indicates to what extent the concentration of control over output exceeds the concentration of production. In other words, it indicates in which industries the existing degree

use and interpretation of concentration indexes, but not to discourage empirical researchers from using them at all. Where no action depends on the use of concentration indexes as sole indicators of monopoly and only the correctness of general impressions is at stake, there should be little objection to the procedure. Thus, in a recent study on monopolistic conditions in manufacturing all "census industries" in which the four largest firms account for at least half the total value of output, or the producers of "census products" for which the four largest firms account for at least three-fourths, were regarded as monopolistic. G. Warren Nutter, *The Extent of Enterprise Monopoly in the United States, 1899–1939* (Chicago: University of Chicago Press, 1951).

[6] *Report of the Federal Trade Commission on the Divergence Between Plant and Company Concentration, 1947* (Washington: 1950).

of concentration of control is not conditioned by the technological economies of large-scale production. (The method takes no account of economies of large-scale organization or management of separate establishments. Whether such economies are important is a controversial issue.[7])

The method has many limitations, most of which are inherent in the kind of data available and have been discussed on the preceding pages. Additional limitations refer to the problem of measuring the divergence between two curves in such a way that the results are meaningful for comparisons between different industries. This restricts, for example, the application of the method to industries with at least 50 companies (because the divergence between the two curves, measured by a planimeter, would be smaller for an industry with only a few firms than for an industry with many firms, even if the few firms control many separate plants while only some of the many firms control more than one establishment).

Several "divergence patterns" emerged from the study.[8] A high divergence index was shown for industries with small-scale operations but multiple-plant control. This was, of course, the very thing that the index was supposed to show. But high divergence indexes were shown also by industries with large-scale

---

[7] See above Chapter 3, pp. 51–53.

[8] *Ibid.*, pp. 29–35. According to the study, "the different divergence patterns suggest different types of public policy. Thus in those industries with low plant and low company concentration . . . the task of protecting the public interest appears to be primarily that of preventing collusive agreements and arresting any such increase in company concentration as may tend to lessen competition. Among those industries with high company concentration and high divergences . . . there is need to guard against not merely collusive agreement but also monopoly; and *if monopoly should be found to exist,* the available remedies include the possibility of reducing the size of the largest business concerns. Finally, in those industries with high company concentration and low divergence . . . , monopolistic concentration cannot readily be corrected by dissolution of monopolistic business firms but must be remedied instead by appropriate correction or, if necessary, by regulation of business behavior." *Ibid.,* p. 35. I have added the emphasis in the above quotation in order to show that the Federal Trade Commission regards neither high concentration of control nor high divergence between company and plant concentration as an indication of monopoly, but only as a sort of warning signal.

production if "company concentration" exceeded "plant concentration" by a substantial margin, and by industries with small-scale production and moderate multiple-plant control. Low divergence indexes were shown for industries where the number of companies was only slightly greater than the number of plants, regardless of whether large-scale or small-scale production prevailed in the industries.

The purpose of the divergence index may perhaps be best characterized by the statement that a high "divergence" combined with a high "company concentration" may point to instances of concentration of control that are not technologically conditioned, and, to the extent to which the concentration contributes to monopoly, to instances of monopoly not related to large-scale production.

THE RATE OF PROFIT

Of all the possible effects of monopoly, high profits of the firms in monopolistic industries are probably the most notorious,[9] although our "empirical knowledge" of monopolistic profit rates is casual and unsystematic. This is not surprising, since the necessary information must come from individual business firms who are firm believers in the inviolability of business secrets. Moreover, there are disturbing differences between accounting profits and returns on capital invested, short-run profits and long-run profits, natural-scarcity rents and monopoly profits, book-values of existing assets and economic values of necessary assets, and other matters that confuse the issue.

[9] The importance of "monopoly profits" as a guide to the discovery of cases where the exercise of monopoly power interferes with the economic use of resources was emphasized by the National Resources Committee: "Only those administrative controls over price which are sufficiently strong to allow the making of monopoly profits are significant to the long-run problem of securing a balanced use of resources." National Resources Committee, *The Structure of the American Economy*, Part I, p. 140. By "administrative controls over price" is meant the sellers' power of choosing between several possible prices as distinct from the sellers' passive acceptance of "market-dominated prices."

The Accounting Rate of Profit

Neither the profit margin on each unit of output sold or on each dollar of sales, nor the sum total of profits of the firm is directly relevant for our purposes. What counts is the *rate* of profits, that is the percentage return on capital. And since the form in which firms have raised their capital—through stock issues, bond sales, or other ways of finance—is not relevant for an evaluation of the monopoly position they may have in the sale of their products, we must not treat interest payments different from the earnings on equity capital. This means either that we must calculate a "normal profit rate" (competitive annual cost of new investible funds) on the entire investment as a cost to the business and regard only the "excess profit rate" as relevant to our problem, or that we must calculate the entire earnings, before deduction of interest paid or imputed, as a percentage rate on the entire capital invested and compare it with the rates of earnings obtained in all other branches of the economy. The latter procedure is much simpler since it does not require the determination of the "normal profit rate."

We have no current statistical data on profits or earnings of business by industry groups or individual industries in the United States. Only for two years, 1921 and 1928, have industrial profit rates been calculated—by Ralph C. Epstein—for representative samples of firms in a large number of industries.[10] I present in Table II a brief extract of the "percentage earnings to capitalization, 1921 and 1928," chiefly in order to show what profit rates statistics would look like and how nice it would be to have them on a year-by-year basis.

Although some of the industries selected for Table II approximately correspond to those included in Table I, we must warn that the classifications used are not the same. The fact that the profit rate data do not refer to the entire industry, that is, to all the firms in each industry, but only to a representative sample of firms, should not be regarded as a defect. Such a sample may be more indicative of the position of the industry than any average

[10] Ralph C. Epstein, *Industrial Profits in the United States* (New York: National Bureau of Economic Research, 1934).

of all firms could. The briefest examination of Table II reveals
that a large number of industries had fluctuating profit rates, most
of them making low profits or even losses in 1921, a depression
year, and high profits in 1928, a prosperity year. (Bolts and nuts,
metal products, tools, and sheet metal show the greatest recovery
from 1921 to 1928.) Some industries had lower profit rates in 1928
than in 1921. (Remarkable declines occurred in textile machinery,
miscellaneous textiles, carpets, weaving woolens.) A few industries had consistently high profit rates. (Newspapers and periodi-
cals, toilet preparations, bakery products, printing and publishing.) Others had consistently low profit rates. (Planing mills,
bituminous coal.) But, apart from the fact that profits statistics
for only two years are of little use for almost anything, is there
any light that profits data of this sort can throw on our problem,
the measurement of the degree of monopoly?

TABLE II

PERCENTAGE EARNINGS TO CAPITALIZATION, 1921 AND 1928

Industry	1921	1928
Scientific instruments	13.1	27.3
Newspapers and periodicals	21.5	26.5
Toilet preparations	29.2	25.4
Proprietary preparations	11.4	21.8
Firearms	2.1	19.6
Bolts and nuts	− 1.8	19.0
Miscellaneous chemicals	5.3	17.8
Bakery products	15.0	17.5
Miscellaneous clay and stone	1.5	17.1
Printing and publishing	24.4	17.1
Electrical machinery	6.4	16.5
Motor vehicles	8.4	16.1
Miscellaneous metal products	− 2.9	15.6
Tobacco	13.1	15.6
Tools	− 3.1	15.2
Confectionery	6.6	15.2
Non-ferrous metals	1.9	14.8
Textile machinery	22.6	14.6
Job printing	13.1	13.9
Wire and nails	− .4	13.8

TABLE II
(cont.)

Industry	1921	1928
Miscellaneous machinery	− 2.6	13.5
Portland cement	8.1	12.8
Cardboard boxes	.8	12.8
Miscellaneous clothing	4.3	12.4
Flour	8.9	12.0
Sheet metal	−12.4	11.8
Glass	9.5	11.8
Men's clothing	6.7	11.4
Miscellaneous lumber products	8.0	10.1
Petroleum refining	14.5	9.8
Planing mills	9.9	8.5
Millwork	1.8	8.3
Miscellaneous textiles	12.2	7.7
Groceries	2.6	7.4
Carpets	15.9	6.7
Gas and oil wells	1.1	5.8
Blank paper	1.9	5.1
Meat packing	− 7.0	4.6
Bituminous coal	9.0	4.5
Weaving woolens	11.4	1.5
Rubber products	−12.6	1.3

Source: Ralph C. Epstein, *Industrial Profits in the United States* (New York: National Bureau of Economic Research, Inc., 1934), pp. 75–78.

Although many monopolistic firms may make profits, there are several fundamental pitfalls in the idea that the accounting rate of profit can show the degree to which monopoly power is exercised. For example, total profits will necessarily rise when there is an increase in demand, and these profits will persist until new productive resources flow into the industry. If profit rates are calculated on the basis of book values of assets or historical money investment, profit rates must necessarily rise. Suppose there is an increase in the demand for farm products. (Agriculture is usually regarded as a sector of the economy where monopoly power—apart from government-made monopoly—is almost completely absent.) The increase in demand will raise the prices of farm products. The book values of the land would adjust themselves only in the course of many years to the increased earnings. Hence, there will be a conspicuous rise of the "percentage earnings to capitalization," and this rate will stay high for many years (provided demand stays up). Will anybody suggest that this rise is due to the farmers' monopoly power? It is not difficult to see that the higher "profit rate" is the combined result of accounting practice and of the natural scarcity of land, with higher demand leading to higher implicit economic rent.

This example shows that high statistical profit rates need not be high economic profit rates: the income in question may be rent of naturally scarce resources, hence neither profit in the narrower sense of the word, nor profit or rent associated with monopoly power.[11] On the other hand the statistics may show "normal" or even low profit rates which conceal a goodly measure of monopoly. A variety of items may have cut in on the *amount* of net profit: there may be expenditure items that are merely outlays for the maintenance of the monopoly position; there may be expenditure items or allowances from selling prices by which parts of the earnings are transferred to other (controlling or subsidiary) firms or individuals; there may be depreciation or depletion items which are based on a valuation of assets already implying capitalized monopoly profits; or some other "reducing diets" may have been prescribed for the accounting profits of the firm. Another variety of things may have blown up the capitalization figures that serve as the base for the computation of the *rate* of profit: assets may appear in the books at historical costs in excess of eventual replacement costs; the valuation of some assets may include capitalization of expected excess profits; assets may be carried which are not necessary for the production of the actual output of the industry (excess capacity, unused real property, idle cash balances, etc.). All these and similar things may account for a heavy swelling of the capital figures of firms and, consequently, for slim profit rates.[12]

[11] For a discussion of the differences between rent and profit and between natural and artificial scarcities see Fritz Machlup, *The Economics of Sellers' Competition: Model Analysis of Sellers' Conduct* (Baltimore: Johns Hopkins Press, 1952), Chapter 8.

[12] For an elaboration of some of these points see Joe S. Bain "The Profit

The statistical rates of profit, if calculated by comparing the accounting figures of net profit with the accounting figures of capitalization, are thus incapable of indicating the degree of monopoly.

An Adjusted Rate of Profit

That the accounting rates of profit, the only ones that may be available to the statistician, are such unreliable indices of economic excess profits and monopoly situations is unfortunate, since the relationship between supernormal profits and monopolistic barriers against potential entrants into the industry is highly significant. Firms sheltered against newcomers' competition are likely to earn higher returns on their investments than firms in industries wide open to anybody willing to start a new business. Insofar as closed entry or difficult entry is regarded as an element of monopoly, or even as its essence, a rate of profit adjusted and corrected for the defects mentioned would be an important index of monopoly in this sense.

It has been suggested by Joe S. Bain that all the necessary corrections and adjustments of accounting data be made and a "theoretical profit rate" be calculated, which in comparison with the normal, competitive profit rate (or interest rate for industrial capital) would be indicative of monopoly power. The accounting figure of profit would be replaced by an adjusted "theoretical profit," and the accounting figure of net assets would be replaced by an adjusted value of "necessary net assets." [13]

We need not discuss in detail all the corrections and adjustments which the accounting data would have to undergo. From the list of possible defects to which we referred before, it must be clear that the "adjuster" would have to examine revenues, operating expenses, fixed charges, depreciation, the type and amount of assets really necessary for the production of the actual output volume, and the valuation of these required assets at a "replacement-cost-of-service-value." The examination would be a frightfully

---

Rate as a Measure of Monopoly Power," *Quarterly Journal of Economics,* Vol. LV (1941), pp. 271–93.

[13] Joe S. Bain, *op. cit.,* p. 290.

laborious task and the adjustment, even if well-defined principles were agreed upon, would leave an embarrassingly wide leeway to the judgment and the imagination of the investigator.

Even with all figures scrupulously corrected, the emerging "adjusted rates of profit"—the "Bain measures" of the degree of monopoly—might still be the combined effect of several forces, not easily disentangled. An excessive adjusted rate of profit might be the result of normal returns on excessive investment or of excessive returns on necessary investment; and the sources of these returns would not be revealed by the examination.[14] It might be interesting to know whether excessive profits could be attributed to monopolistic selling prices of the products or, on the other hand, to monopsonistic buying or hiring prices of factors of production. And it would certainly be interesting to know to what extent an excessive "theoretical profit rate" would be due to the downward adjustment of such excessive investment as might have resulted from easy entry of actual newcomers into an industry where producers are in monopolistic positions owing to product differentiation (and where the investment of older firms is rendered excessive through the encroachment on their business by newcomers); [15] or to the downward adjustment of excessive investment undertaken to forestall entry of potential newcomers; [16] or to excessive returns on "necessary" investment under the shelter of other barriers to the entry of potential newcomers. There are probably many other possibilities of excessive theoretical profit rates.

Even if excessive profit rates could definitely be attributed to difficulties of entry, the underlying conditions would still be in need of investigation. The difficulties of expansion and entry may lie in the natural scarcity of "specific" resources—which often have no market prices or no flexibly adjusted prices so that (since

[14] *Ibid.*, p. 288.
[15] In this case the "actual" profit rate of the firms would be normal. It is the Chamberlinian case of monopolistic competition (product differentiation) with perfect ease of entry, resulting in excess capacity without monopoly profits. See Fritz Machlup, *op. cit.*, Chapter 10.
[16] Firms often build up excess capacity in order to deter potential newcomers; frequently firms increase their capacity in order to gain higher quotas under cartel agreements.

"implicit rents" appear in business accounts in the form of profit) even the adjusted rate of profit may look excessive. Or the expansion of productive capacities and the entry of firms into the industry may be delayed by frictions and obstacles which one may wish to consider as "normal" rather than "monopolistic." If one regards the existence of "artificial barriers" against the competition of potential newcomers to the industry as the essence of monopoly proper, the real task of examining the monopoly situation would begin when the analysis of the rate of profit is finished.[17]

Before results of investigations of "adjusted profit rates" become available we cannot say whether and how it will be possible to separate monopoly elements from non-monopoly elements. But we know for certain that such a separation is not possible on the basis of the unadjusted accounting rates of profit and that these rates cannot be accepted as measurement of the degree of monopoly.

PRICE INFLEXIBILITY

During the Great Depression of the thirties a new—or hitherto overlooked—phenomenon received much emphasis: inflexibility of certain prices despite depressed business activity. The phenomenon was ascribed to the price policies of firms in strong monopolistic positions. If price inflexibility was an effect of the exercise of monopoly power, could one not devise ways of measuring relative inflexibilities and use the results as measures of the degrees of monopoly?

The Rigidity of Administered Prices

Most of the "market-dominated" prices (such as farm product prices) showed serious price declines during the depression period while a number of "administered" prices rigidly maintained their

[17] It has been objected to Bain's measure that "it lumps together the effects of monopoly, monopsony, limit to entry, and . . . also to some extent the effects of frictional forces in a competitive system, like ignorance and special degrees of uncertainty . . . But why call it a measure of monopoly power?" K. W. Rothschild, "A Further Note on the Degree of Monopoly," *Economica*, New Series, Vol. X (1943), p. 69.

level. Most of the market-dominated prices change continuously
and follow every impulse, however slight, of changing market conditions, whereas many administered prices change only infrequently. An industry that can hold its prices for long intervals,
adjusting them only infrequently to changing market conditions,
is apparently in a monopolistic position.

In particular, if in the face of dwindling demand some industries can resist the general tendency toward lower prices and can
hold their selling prices at or near the prosperity level, that power
of resistance cannot be anything but monopoly power. Thus the
small downward-flexibility or small depression-sensitivity of certain prices suggests itself as a measurement of the degree of monopoly of those who administer these prices.

For a measurement of the general flexibility of the prices of
different commodities, or products of different firms, three sets of
data might be observed, and firms or industries ranked according
to the findings: (1) the frequency of price changes, (2) the extent
or amplitude of price changes, and (3) the timing of price changes
compared with price adjustments in other industries. The third
criterion is not really practicable. The "order" in time cannot
reasonably be separated from the frequency and degree of change.
(For example: which industry could be said to have lowered its
prices earlier, one which made a two percent price cut in May
and another ten percent cut in September, or one which made a
fifteen percent cut in June?) Furthermore, it would not be possible
to separate time lags of impacts from time lags of adjustments.
(The slack in demand does not occur simultaneously in all markets, hence the order of price changes does not tell anything about
the order in which industries adjust their prices to changed market
conditions.)

Frequency and Amplitude of Changes

The frequency of price changes and the degree of change are
ascertainable for many commodities, although statistical information on prices and price changes is vitiated in part by the fact
that true selling prices can usually not be obtained by the statistician. (More or less secret discounts, rebates and other forms of

allowances are not always shown in the material available to the statistician. The problem of changes in quality complicates matters still further.)

A comprehensive study of price flexibility was made by the National Resources Committee—under the direction of Gardiner C. Means—and figures on 617 wholesale price items were published. Table III below contains 52 of these items, more or less at random. The figures for frequency of change refer to monthly averages during the years 1926 to 1933 inclusive, hence 96 months. The highest number of changes is, therefore, 95. Several commodities with the maximum frequency of price change were included in the table, which on the other hand contains also some price items with as little as four or five changes.[18]

The amplitude of price change is expressed by an "index of depression sensitivity." This index is supposed to show the depth of the price trough in the depression year 1932 as compared with the surrounding prosperity years of 1929 and 1937; the difference between the 1932 price and the average of the 1929 and 1937 prices is considered "as the drop in price attributable to the depression," all prices being "expressed as a percent relative of the 1929 price."[19] Thus, a large "index of depression sensitivity" indicates a deep price trough in 1932 as compared with 1929 and 1937. (For example, the corn prices in 1932 were 71.5 percent below the average of 1929 and 1937). A negative "index of depression sensitivity" indicates that the 1932 price was above the average of 1929 and 1937. (For example, the prices of plaster showed such a perverse behavior.)[20]

[18] Information on monthly average prices cannot really tell much about the frequency of price changes. Prices that change several times a day, once a day, once a week, or once a month are all lumped together in the group of maximum frequency of change if the study starts from monthly average prices. For further criticism leveled against this procedure see Tibor Scitovszky, "Prices under Monopoly and Competition," Journal of Political Economy, Vol. XLIX (1941), p. 681.

[19] National Resources Committee, op. cit., pp. 131 and 187.

[20] The price data used in the study were the monthly averages published by the Bureau of Labor Statistics. These data have been shown to be unreliable, especially for depression periods when the divergence between prices actually received and prices quoted or reported is apt to increase drastically. For example, while the BLS reported a 5 percent price decline for aluminum between 1929 and 1933, the Census Bureau reported an actual price drop by

TABLE III

PRICE FLEXIBILITY OF VARIOUS WHOLESALE PRICE ITEMS

Commodity	Frequency of Change 1926–1933 [1]	Index of Depression Sensitivity [2]
Farm Products		
Corn	95	71.5
Rye No. 2	95	59.5
Wheat	95	54.1
Cows	94	48.9
Hogs	94	63.0
Lambs, western	94	46.0
Poultry, live	95	28.4
Cotton, middling	95	46.3
Tobacco, leaf	95	68.0
Potatoes	94	45.8
Manufactures		
Bread Chicago	14	− 4.9
Bread New Orleans	16	34.0
Bread New York	5	10.3
Bread San Francisco	6	− 1.8
Beef, fresh	74	35.8
Bacon	72	53.1
Cured hams	95	42.8
Poultry, dressed, Chicago	85	27.4
Salt	14	1.6
Men's shoes	16	19.4
Crome leather	20	32.8
Men's 3 piece suits	10	33.2
Cotton goods: Print cloth, 27″	93	46.0
Knit goods: Men's cotton hose	24	40.4
Anthracite, chestnut	38	− 3.9
Bituminous, soft coal, mine run	24	12.3
Gasoline, eastern	94	24.8
Kerosene, Standard	43	16.5
Bar iron, Chicago	28	26.4
Bar iron, Pittsburgh	4	.6
Steel plates	40	25.7

TABLE III
(*cont.*)

Commodity	Frequency of Change 1926–1933 [1]	Index of Depression Sensitivity [2]
Manufactures (cont.)		
Steel rails	4	.1
Portland Cement	15	17.4
Douglas fir lath	91	28.8
Yellow pine lath	89	52.8
Chestnut	12	29.2
Plate glass	6	− 6.1
Window glass	13	23.0
Plaster	8	−20.6
Gravel	13	12.6
Stone, crushed	7	.3
Fertilizer	42	14.8
Electric iron, plain	8	9.8
Vacuum cleaners	8	4.4
Book paper	11	25.6
Newsprint paper	8	3.0
Wood pulp, sulphite	22	51.5
Wood pulp, mechanical	24	22.1
Matches, regular	22	−10.2
Laundry soap, pound	14	31.6
Laundry soap, 100 cakes	4	− 1.4
Cigarettes	9	−10.9

[1] Comparing the monthly averages of the 96 months from 1926 to 1933 the maximum frequency of change is 95.

[2] Taking an average of the prices in 1929 and 1937 (the two years of relative prosperity) and using the difference between this figure and the price in 1932 as the drop in price attributable to the depression (with all prices expressed as a percent relative of the 1929 price), the index shows the relative price cut which 1932 prices represent as against the average of 1929 and 1937.

Source: National Resources Committee, *The Structure of the American Economy* (Washington: 1939), Part I, pp. 188–99.

The usefulness of the "index of depression sensitivity" is impaired not only by the doubtful reliability or known unreliability of many price data, but also by a defect inherent in its conception. The index might be low, and thus give the impression of a relatively inflexible price, not because of any failure of the price to fall during the depression, but because of a failure of the price to recover after the depression. A low 1937 price would depress the prosperity average of 1929 and 1937 and make the depression trough deceptively shallow.

An examination of the two flexibility indexes shows that frequency of price change and depression sensitivity are roughly correlated. This is somewhat reassuring, for matters would be further complicated if alternative measures of price flexibility gave drastically inconsistent results; but it does not as such prove anything about the correlation between price inflexibility and the degree of monopoly.[21] We still have nothing beyond the theoretical proposition that price maintenance must be the result of monopoly because the exercise of monopoly power or the application of monopolistic arrangements are the most plausible and most consistent explanations of relative price stability. However, they are not the only possible explanations. In principle it is conceivable that a price would remain stable even without any monopoly; and in principle it is possible that a monopolist changes his prices frequently and drastically. To be sure, neither of these possibilities seems particularly likely. And especially in cases of collective monopoly—collusive oligopoly—the reasons for price stability in the face of changing conditions are most understandable.

There is no doubt that price inflexibility *may* be the result of

35 percent. Cf. Lloyd Reynolds, "Producers' Goods Prices in Expansion and Decline," *Journal of the American Statistical Association*, Vol. 34 (1939), p. 33.

[21] Theoretically, a monopolist may find it to his advantage to make frequent changes in his selling price. Moreover, he may find it profitable to increase the price while his direct costs fall. The frequency of price change would in this case wrongly indicate absence of monopoly power and, of course, would be inconsistent with the index of depression sensitivity. Cf. D. H. Wallace, "Monopoly Prices and Depression," in *Explorations in Economics*, ed. Edward S. Mason (New York: McGraw-Hill, 1936), p. 347.

monopolistic policies.[22] Nevertheless, price inflexibility cannot without further evidence be taken as a sure indication, and still less as a measurement, of the sellers' monopoly power.[23]

Comparing the Indexes

The various indirect "measurements" of monopoly power discussed in the preceding sections are not easily comparable with one another, because of shortcomings in the statistical material and in the way the material has been put together. Classifications of industries are highly arbitrary, and firms classified in one industrial group in the profits figures may well be classified in another sector for concentration data or price data. But even if entirely satisfactory and comparable data were available, it is not to be expected that the measures of "monopoly" in terms of profit rates, price rigidity, and concentration would rank industries in any more consistent order than a ranking in the available tabulations yields. A look into the tables reproduced above will easily show that some industries are on the bottom of the profitability roster but high up on the concentration roster, and *vice versa;* and a similar lack of correlation will be found between the price inflexibility index and any of the other two tables.

In order to see whether the inconsistent results were due to incomparability of the data, the National Resources Committee made an attempt to calculate price indexes for the products of the industries as classified by the 1935 census of manufactures. For many of these classes no price index could be constructed, either

[22] A pure monopolist would not have much reason to keep his prices inflexible. While he would avoid the day-to-day fluctuations that are characteristic of perfectly competitive markets, he would surely adjust his prices to all but the most temporary changes in demand or cost conditions. Apart from regulated monopoly it is chiefly in oligopolistic positions that sellers prefer to "leave the market undisturbed." In the majority of cases "monopolistic policies" are oligopolistic policies. For a discussion of oligopolistic price rigidity see Fritz Machlup, *op. cit.*, Chapter 14. On the erroneous belief that oligopolistic price rigidity is incompatible with marginalist theory of price see Chapter 2 of the same book.

[23] For an excellent survey of various concepts of price flexibility and difficulties of measurement see Edward S. Mason, "Price Inflexibility," *Review of Economic Statistics*, Vol. XX (1938), pp. 53–64.

because adequate price data were not available or because prices were not comparable as a result of changes in the quality of the products or for other reasons. But for some industry classes the National Resources Committee did compute a "depression-price index," so that some index of price flexibility could be shown side by side with a concentration index. In Table IV the two indexes are reproduced for 27 selected industries. The industries are listed in the order of decreasing concentration.

The depression-price index in Table IV must not be confused with the depression-sensitivity index of Table III. While the latter indicates the price fall from a prosperity level (comparing the difference between the low 1932 and the high 1929 and 1937 prices) the depression-price index shows the depression (1932) price itself in relation to the pre-depression (1929) level. Thus, (neglecting the fact that one of the indexes includes 1937 prices while the other index does not) a high depression-sensitivity index expresses a severe price fall and corresponds to a low depression-price index. The industries or products which, in Table IV, are shown with depression-price indexes around 90 or 100 are, of course, those with relatively inflexible prices.

After what has been said about the relationships between concentration and monopoly power on the one hand, and between monopoly power and price inflexibility on the other hand, nobody will expect to find a high correlation between the concentration index and the depression-price index. Only after the various industrial groups were carefully sorted from many points of view and a small list selected of those industries which were assumed to produce for a national or international market, did the National Resources Committee believe that "a rough relation . . . between concentration and price insensitivity" could be detected from the statistical figures.[24] Since concentration is one among several possible causes of monopoly, and monopoly policy is one among several possible causes of price inflexibility, the "rough relation" is theoretically plausible. But one cannot claim that this relation has been statistically "verified."

[24] *Op. cit.*, p. 142.

TABLE IV
Concentration and Depression-Price-Fall

Industry	Concentration Index [1]	Depression-Price Index [2]
Cigarettes	89.7	111.0
Motor vehicles (not incl. motorcycles)	87.3	88.9
Tin cans (& other tinware)	80.8	91.7
Soap	73.5	76.2
Matches	70.3	120.3
Salt	60.3	104.5
Meat packing, wholesale	55.6	50.8
Steel-works and rolling mill products	49.3	82.3
Glass	44.9	91.4
Cigars	38.5	93.6
Petroleum refining	38.2	61.7
Cement	29.9	67.1
Boots and shoes (other than rubber)	26.0	70.1
Fertilizers	25.9	72.2
Pulp (wood and other fiber)	22.7	64.3
Leather	22.5	59.4
Clay products (other than pottery)	19.3	82.8
Pottery, incl. porcelain ware	19.0	80.1
Bread and other bakery products	18.2	90.6
Paper	14.7	84.4
Concrete products	10.2	80.8
Cotton manufactures	8.4	57.8
Men's cotton garments	7.5	71.4
Knit goods	5.3	55.5
Men's, youths' and boys' clothing	5.1	72.3
Lumber and timber products	4.7	64.3
Planing mill products	4.6	72.6

[1] This concentration index is the percentage of total value product of the industry produced by the largest four producers (largest in terms of value product).

[2] This depression-price index is the percentage ratio of 1932 prices to 1929 prices.

Source: National Resources Committee, *The Structure of the American Economy*, Part I, pp. 265–69.

Margin Inflexibility

One of the most serious defects of the conception of price inflexibility as an indication of the degree of monopolistic control over price in an industry lies in the failure to take account of the flexibility or inflexibility of the *cost* elements that enter into the prices of the products in question. Is it the gross selling price of the product, or is it rather the price net of direct costs that is relevant for an estimate of the discretion or leeway the seller has in pricing his product? Although the answer seems self-evident, a simple illustration may be helpful.

Assume that the producers of product A have reduced its selling price from 100 to 95, that is, by 5 percent, while the producers of B have reduced the price from 100 to 70, that is, by 30 percent. Those who see in the amplitude of price movements the essence of price flexibility will say that the price of A is relatively inflexible, the price of B relatively flexible. But assume further that the direct unit cost of A has declined from 90 to 88, while the direct unit cost of B has come down from 60 to 32. Simple arithmetic will reveal that the margin over direct cost—that is, the gross margin to cover indirect costs and profit—has decreased from 10 to 7 for product A, and from 40 to 38 for product B. This reduction in the margin is 30 percent for A and only 5 percent for B, exactly the reverse of the relationship of the changes in selling prices.[25]

Thus, the suspected inflexibility in the price of A turns out to be an inflexibility in the direct cost of A, while the producer's margin is very flexible. Conversely, the supposed flexibility in the price of B is merely the result of a substantial reduction in the direct cost of B, while the producer's margin is relatively inflexible. If the difference in the reduction of this "mark-up" is to be interpreted in terms of the sellers' "monopoly power," one will undoubt-

[25] Written in a more convenient form:

	Period 1.	Period 2.	Change
Price of A	$100	$ 95	— 5%
Direct cost of A	90	88	— 2.2%
Margin	$ 10	$ 7	—30%
Price of B	$100	$ 70	—30%
Direct Cost of B	60	32	—46.7%
Margin	$ 40	$ 38	— 5%

edly have to conclude that the producers of A have been under the pressure of vigorous competition while the producers of B have been in a more monopolistic position and therefore much more successful in maintaining the net value of their services.

After this simple reconsideration of the inflexibility problem it appears strange that so much attention should have been given to prices instead of cost-price margins. The focus should not have been on price inflexibility but on margin inflexibility if the results were to indicate monopolistic control. Of course, instead of emphasizing the margin or mark-up over direct cost, one may point to greater or smaller co-variations between selling prices and direct costs.

A study of this kind was made by Alfred C. Neal, who calculated direct costs for 106 industries for the period 1929 to 1933 and compared them with the selling prices.[26] He called these prices "flexible" when they exceeded direct costs by a constant absolute margin, because then they reflected the full change in direct cost. But flexible prices, in this terminology, would imply inflexible margins. If, during a depression, margins decreased in absolute amounts, the prices in question were considered hyper-flexible even if they declined relatively less than direct costs and thus left larger percentage margins. The main purpose of Neal's study was to test the importance of industrial concentration for price inflexibility, and the author was satisfied that "differential price behavior among industries . . . is to be explained for the most part by differential unit direct cost behavior rather than by concentration" and that "concentration does not even explain the *difference* between actual price declines and those which could be expected on the basis of changes in direct cost." [27] Strangely enough, these negative conclusions seemed to the author worth emphasizing although he had also found that "concentration did have a small but significant influence upon the decline in the difference between unit price and unit direct cost—the overhead-plus-profits margin. This margin tended to decline least where concen-

---

[26] Alfred C. Neal, *Industrial Concentration and Price Inflexibility* (Washington: American Council on Public Affairs, 1942).—Neal used Census data, which are more pertinent to studies of this kind than BLS price statistics.

[27] *Ibid.*, p. 165. (Italics in the original.)

tration was high; most where it was low." [28] This, of course, is the point that should have been stressed.

An industrial enterprise buys materials, intermediate products and services from other enterprises; it buys labor services; and it adds its own (managerial and capital) services. The difference between its sales proceeds and its purchases from other enterprises is called "value added by manufacture"; the difference between this and its labor cost is the gross margin over direct cost or the payment received for the services of the enterprise itself.[29] In a study of the monopoly power of the enterprise and its workers taken together, we should want to look at the relative flexibility of the "value added." In a study of the monopoly power of enterprise only, it is the flexibility of the margin, or the "selling price of its own services," in which we should be interested.

The question of margin flexibility received more attention in a study by John T. Dunlop, who compared price changes with changes in direct cost in percentage rather than absolute terms.[30] "Price flexibility" in this terminology implies that margins change relatively as much as direct costs. Not the amplitude of price changes, but its ratio to that of changes of direct costs characterizes this price flexibility. In view of the fact that this modified concept of flexibility is related to another measure, which is plainly designated as an index of the "degree of monopoly," we shall defer the report on the Dunlop study until a little later.

The Gap Between Marginal Cost and Price

The concentration index, the profit rate, or the price inflexibility prevailing in an industry are at best "circumstantial evidence" of the presence and exercise of monopoly power but can never be accepted as sufficient proof. This is clear particularly in cases

---

[28] *Ibid.*, pp. 165–66.

[29]

$$\text{Sales proceeds} \begin{cases} \text{Direct cost} \begin{cases} \text{paid to other enterprises} \\ \text{paid to wage labor} \end{cases} \\ \text{Gross margin for management and capital} \end{cases} \left. \begin{array}{c} \\ \\ \\ \end{array} \right\} \text{Value added by manufacture}$$

[30] John T. Dunlop, "Price Flexibility and the 'Degree of Monopoly'," *Quarterly Journal of Economics,* Vol. XLVII (1939), pp. 522–33.

where such "evidence" is contradictory. Economists have long searched for a more satisfactory way of establishing the existence and measuring the degree of monopoly as they conceive of it. If several of their recent suggestions are as yet not practicable with the scant information available, they are at least logically consistent with some fundamental ideas about the nature and significance of "monopoly power," or at least one sense of monopoly power.

Inequality Between Marginal Cost and Price

One of the essential ideas about monopoly is undoubtedly that output is somehow restricted and that selling price is higher "than it might be"—might be, of course, if the model of pure competition were realized with everything else unchanged. If pure competition prevailed everywhere, production in each line would be pushed to the point where the incremental cost of increased output equaled the selling price. The inequality and, especially, the degree of inequality of marginal cost and selling price might then serve, it seems, as evidence of the presence and extent of monopolistic pricing. (Note, however, that "monopolistic" has here an arbitrarily specific meaning. It refers only to one type of output restriction—namely, to that inherent in the firm's policy of taking account of the elasticity of demand for its product; it does not refer to monopolistic barriers against newcomers' competition.)

The seller's knowledge that an increased output could be disposed of only at reduced prices operates to restrict production. The actual output of such a seller is, therefore, in most cases smaller than that "ideal" output whose marginal cost would equal the selling price. The marginal cost of his output is lower than the selling price of the product. This is probably true for all industries and for all single firms within each industry, but to varying degrees. In some firms the excess of price over marginal cost will be small, while in others it will be considerable. Where the gap between marginal cost and price is very small, the deviation of actual output from "ideal" output is likely to be small too. An increase in output would lower the selling price and, in many of these cases, increase marginal cost. Where the gap between marginal cost and selling price is wide, output might perhaps be increased considerably before the gap would disappear.

The relative size of the gap between the marginal cost and the selling price of current output was suggested by Abba P. Lerner as a measure of the degree of monopoly and has become known as the Lerner formula.[31] The excess of selling price over marginal cost (P–MC) is divided by the selling price (P) so that a ratio (expressible as a percentage deviation) is obtained. Thus, $\dfrac{P–MC}{P}$ is the Lerner index of the degree of monopoly. If the marginal cost is equal to the selling price, as it will be under pure competition, the numerator will be zero and therefore the fraction will be zero. The fraction will rise toward 1 as the relative gap between price and marginal cost increases. But it could reach unity only if the price were infinite or the marginal cost zero. Hence, the index will show the "degree of monopoly" as a relative deviation from pure competition.

The Lerner formula bears a close relationship to the elasticity of demand which the seller envisages for his product. The reason sounds technical but is fairly simple. We know that profits in a firm are a maximum when the additional receipts for a further slight increase in output would no longer cover the incremental costs of its production. In other words, profit is maximized when marginal cost is equal to marginal revenue. Thus, when the seller makes as much profit as he believes he can possibly make under prevailing conditions, the gap between selling price and marginal cost is the same as the gap between selling price and marginal revenue. Hence, if the seller maximizes profits, Lerner's formula for the degree of monopoly will be the ratio of the gap between price and marginal revenue to the price. But one of the several expressions for the elasticity of demand is the ratio of price to the gap between price and marginal revenue.[32] Thus, if the firm is in equilibrium, Lerner's formula is the reciprocal of the elasticity of demand.

[31] Abba P. Lerner, "The Concept of Monopoly and the Measurement of Monopoly Power," *Review of Economic Studies*, Vol. 1 (1934), pp. 157–75.
[32] See Fritz Machlup, *op. cit.*, Appendix to Chapter 5.

Objections and Limitations

If the essence of monopoly is seen in the restriction of output, the Lerner formula gives at best a very indirect indication of it. For the deviation of price from the marginal cost of the output produced does not indicate by how much the volume of actually produced output falls short of the so-called competitive output. This substitution of a price-cost discrepancy for a difference between actual and "ideal" output is probably the greatest weakness of a formula which is supposed to measure deviation from the "optimum allocation of resources." [33]

Several other objections were raised against the Lerner measurement of monopoly power. Price may differ from marginal cost for reasons other than "monopoly," or price may be close to marginal cost in spite of considerable monopoly power. The latter objection was anticipated by Lerner's statement that his formula would not measure the potential degree of monopoly but, instead, the degree of "monopoly in force," that is, the degree to which monopoly power is exercised. And, as to the first objection, if a price-marginal-cost discrepancy were due to reasons other than the search for monopoly profits—for instance, to inertia, incompetence, high cost of change, etc.—the Lerner formula would still give a measure of the degree of monopoly in a wider sense, for it is not the "intentional" monopoly *policy* but the actual deviation from the competitive norm in which the economist is chiefly interested.

Another objection lies in the ambiguity of the marginal-cost concept and, consequently, the difficulty of using it for actual measurements. The marginal cost of a certain output will show considerable differences according to the various ways in which

[33] According to Lerner the allocation of resources is a "relative optimum" if no change in the use of resources could put any individual "in a preferred position without putting another individual in a worse position" (*ibid.*, p. 162). In order to measure all deviations from the optimum allocation of resources, the formula for the "degree of monopoly" must be supplemented by the formula for the "degree of monopsony." This is necessary because the marginal cost figures of a firm reflect not only the average prices of productive factors but also the increased factor costs due to rising factor supply curves to the firm. Lerner suggests measuring the degree of monopsony by the relative gap between average cost and marginal revenue (*ibid.*, p. 161).

changes in output are engineered; these differences are usually
dealt with (and simplified) under the heading of long-run versus
short-run changes. For different problems different marginal-cost
values may be relevant. But which of the values of marginal cost
would be relevant for the measurement of the degree of monopoly
if short-run marginal cost and long-run marginal cost are quite
different? It would not disturb me to find two different degrees
of monopoly for a particular firm, one referring to short-run considerations, the other to the long run. Lerner regards the short-
run cost as the appropriate figure for his formula.[34]

The chief objection to this concept of the degree of monopoly
is that the lack of data and the difficulties of measurement make
it out of the question to apply it practically to a large number of
firms. However, the existing difficulties of measuring, insurmount-
able as they may seem at the moment, should not lead us to dis-
card a theoretical tool which may serve to open the way for fruit-
ful discussions of the theoretical and statistical aspects of the problem, if to nothing else.

Incidentally, by way of contrast to a later development, it
should be noted that the Lerner formula was designed to apply
to the individual firm and only with many qualifications to entire
industries, but not at all to the economy as a whole. Indeed, if every
supplier of goods and services "enjoyed" the same "degree of
monopoly power," there would not be any deviation from the
optimum allocation of resources in the economy.[35] Only *differ-*

---

[34] *Ibid.*, p. 171. Lerner recommends that "the very shortest period" be
taken for the determination of marginal cost. This would be the variation
of total cost if all fixed equipment remained unchanged with a small variation of output. It ought to be clear that long-run marginal cost can never
be relevant—for any problem whatever—when it is higher than short-run
marginal cost. Long-run marginal cost included new investment outlays
while short-run marginal cost does not include any part of investment cost.
But new investment outlays are made only when the cost of increased output with the given capacity would be too high, that is, when long-run marginal cost—the additional cost of producing additional output with increased
productive capacity—is *less* than short-run marginal cost. It follows that a
rule to use only short-run marginal cost for calculations of the degree of
monopoly may sometimes—namely, when capacity is utilized almost to the
limit—result in a lower monopoly index than if long-run marginal cost were
used.

[35] *Ibid.*, p. 172. Two qualifications are necessary, one concerning the

ences in the "degrees of monopoly" in the production of different goods and services matter; these differences would point to relative under-utilization of resources in the fields showing higher-than-average degrees of monopoly.

Changes in the Degree of Monopoly

For a few selected industries (steel, cement, hosiery, leather belting) studies have been made to find out how production costs changed when output volumes changed.[36] All cost data were corrected for changes in the prices of the means of production so that the data would reflect only the effects of the changes in the volumes of output. In other words, an attempt was made to compute marginal cost from statistical and accounting data. The findings, which are not unquestioned and certainly must not be generalized, have a distinct bearing on the matter of measuring the degree of monopoly.

Economists have sometimes assumed that marginal costs vary significantly with changes in output; that they first fall as output increases from smallest to larger volumes, and then rise as output increases further to optimum capacity and above. In other words, the marginal cost curve was assumed to be U-shaped. On the other hand, conditions may be such that the U of the marginal cost curve has a flat bottom. That is, marginal costs in existing plants can be

"degrees of monopsony" (see footnote 33) and another concerning the "production of leisure." In order to have optimum allocation, the "price" of leisure would have to bear the same ratio to its "marginal cost" that prevails in the production of goods and services.

[36] Kurt Ehrke, *Die Übererzeugung in der Zementindustrie von 1858–1913* (Jena: Gustav Fischer, 1933); United States Steel Corporation, *T.N.E.C. Papers,* Comprising the Pamphlets and Charts Submitted by United States Steel Corporation to the Temporary National Economic Committee (United States Steel Corporation, 1940), Vol. I, pp. 223–301, (prepared by Theodore O. Yntema); Joel Dean, *Statistical Determination of Costs, with Special Reference to Marginal Costs* (Chicago: University of Chicago Press, 1936) especially Chapter II; Joel Dean, *Statistical Cost Functions of a Hosiery Mill* (Chicago: University of Chicago Press, 1941); Joel Dean, *The Relation of Cost to Output for a Leather Belt Shop* (New York: National Bureau of Economic Research, 1941).

For a convenient summary of these and other studies see National Bureau of Economic Research, *Cost Behavior and Price Policy* (New York: 1943), pp. 90–116.

almost completely constant for a considerable range of possible outputs. Precisely this was the result of the studies just mentioned. For all the various outputs which the investigated firms have produced over a number of years—and they had substantial variations in output—marginal costs, when corrected for changes in the prices of material and labor, were nearly constant.[37] Hence, changes in the prices of material and in wage rates have been the only factors changing the marginal cost of production.[38]

If this were so for *all* industries, one distressing conclusion would follow. It would be distressing from the point of view of political economy that no industry was even approaching "optimum utilization of capacity," not even when output was relatively large. (For, at "optimum utilization," marginal costs *must* be rising.) [39] On the other hand, universally constant marginal costs would be helpful to the statistician, because measuring changes in the degree of monopoly would become a good deal easier: changes in the prices of labor and material can be compared with changes in the prices of products.

It therefore becomes important to ask whether marginal costs are likely to remain constant over considerable ranges of output in all, or a major part of, industry. This would appear possible under two conditions: (1) when plants are not operated every day of the week and every hour of the day, so that another working day, another shift or longer working hours permit an increase in production without any change in efficiency of any of the equipment, material or men; or (2) when plants have enormous excess capacity

[37] This surely does not disprove the modern equilibrium theory of the firm, as was believed by some of its critics. According to that theory marginal costs must be rising at the chosen volume of output *if* pure competition prevails. If competition is not pure, outputs may move in a range where marginal costs are constant or even decreasing.

[38] That is to say, price and wage changes would have caused parallel shifts of the horizontal marginal cost curves.

[39] One speaks of optimum utilization of capacity if an output is produced at which *average* cost is lowest. Average cost can be a minimum only at an output below which marginal cost must have been *lower* than average cost (because only then could average cost have decreased) and beyond which marginal cost must be *higher* than average cost (because only then could average cost be rising after having reached its minimum); hence, by logical necessity, marginal cost must be rising in the range around minimum average cost.

in all their equipment, the idle equipment being as efficient as that in use, so that operation of the unused equipment permits an increase in production without any changes in efficiency. It is possible that both these conditions have by and large been realized in many branches of American industry; this is probably the result of the development of an economy of expensive labor and cheap capital, and of an industry accustomed to business fluctuations. An industrial firm faced with fluctuating business tries to achieve flexibility in the use of its productive equipment mostly by subdividing the plant into separate units so that changes in the volume of output can be made without severe changes in variable unit cost.[40]

If marginal cost is really constant with respect to changes in output, one may take changes in the prices of labor and material as representative of all changes in marginal costs except those due to improved production techniques. If such technological changes are disregarded for short-run comparisons, a properly weighted index of cost-prices can be meaningfully compared with an index of product-prices, and the result, according to a proposal by John T. Dunlop, can be taken as a measure of changes in the degree of monopoly in particular industries—provided, of course, that the gap between marginal cost and price is accepted as a measure of the degree of monopoly.[41] Of course, *changes* in the degree of monopoly need not tell anything about the degree of monopoly itself. An industry in which the degree of monopoly power has increased may still be highly competitive, and an industry in which the degree of monopoly power has diminished may still be highly monopolistic. Nevertheless, interesting suggestions can be obtained from such a study.

According to Dunlop's findings the "degree of monopoly" tended to increase rather markedly during the depression period (1929–1933) in numerous industries, notably in Tobacco, Paper Manufacturing, Agricultural Machinery, Automobiles; and to a lesser extent in Boots and Shoes, and Iron and Steel. The tobacco

[40] For example, a steel mill will have ten separate furnaces and auxiliary equipment making it possible to shut down part of the plant without causing the inefficiencies in production that would result from operating an "indivisible" plant at a fraction of its full capacity.

[41] John T. Dunlop, *op. cit.*

industry showed the most marked increase. In contrast to the experience of these industries, Cotton Manufacturing, Woolen and Worsted, and Leather tended to show almost no change (or slight decreases) in the "degree of monopoly." Conversely, in the upswing period (after 1933) the first group tended to show rather marked declines in monopoly power compared with the relative stability of the "degree of monopoly" in Cotton Manufacturing and Woolen and Worsted.[42]

These admittedly tentative and provisional results may suggest —though not more than suggest—that the industries with the relatively *stable* "degree of monopoly" enjoy relatively *little* monopoly power: their selling prices rise only with their costs, and are forced down as soon and as much, in percentage terms, as costs are reduced; in other words, their margins are as *flexible* as their costs. The marked cyclical changes in the "degree of monopoly" in the other groups of industries seem to point to the existence of a more monopolistic position of firms in these fields; at least, they seem to have the power of resisting price reductions proportional to their cost reductions; their margins are relatively inflexible and, hence, relatively larger in depression than in prosperity. The decline of their monopoly power during the business upswing is perhaps due to higher elasticities of demand for the particular products in prosperity periods.[43] Or perhaps (and more likely) a policy of "price stability" throughout the cycle (which may recommend itself for other reasons) might for some industries explain the cyclical changes in the relative gap between price and marginal cost, appropriately or inappropriately named the "degree of monopoly."

[42] *Ibid.*, p. 530 ff.—The use of notoriously unreliable statistical data reduces the value of the findings. See footnote 20 above on the defects of the BLS price indexes during depression years.

[43] This conclusion would be contrary to Harrod's "Law of diminishing elasticity of demand." This "law" asserts that demand elasticities diminish in the course of the upswing. R. F. Harrod, *The Trade Cycle* (London: Oxford University Press, 1936), pp. 86–97. Also in Harrod, "Imperfect Competition and the Trade Cycle," *Review of Economic Statistics,* Vol. XVIII (1936), pp. 84–88. An argument to the contrary was advanced by John K. Galbraith, "Monopoly Power and Price Rigidities," *Quarterly Journal of Economics,* Vol. L (1936), p. 463. For a discussion of this issue see John D. Sumner, "A Note on Cyclical Changes in Demand Elasticity," *American Economic Review,* Vol. XXX (1940), pp. 300–308.

OTHER MEASUREMENT PROPOSALS

The Lerner formula for the measurement of the degree of monopoly inspired numerous economists to work on this problem and to come forth with proposals of "improved" or alternative solutions or applications. Proposals not yet discussed in the preceding sections will now be surveyed—even if they do not look promising.

Gross Profit Margin and Aggregate Monopoly Income

The Lerner formula was reduced to an absurdity when it was transformed into the so-called Kalecki formula,[44] which supposedly would measure the degree of monopoly of the whole economy [45] and would even explain the distribution of income between the labor and non-labor classes.

The assumption of constant marginal cost, acceptable for selected industries and over short periods, was adopted as if it were valid in all industries and over all periods. (To generalize this assumption is to *assume*—not to prove—that monopoly exists everywhere; for, as was explained earlier, marginal cost must be increasing in the relevant range of output if competition is pure.) Constant marginal cost would usually mean that each successive increase in output could be produced with a proportional increase in total prime cost: the outlay for labor and material would always be the same per unit of output, no matter how production volumes were changed. With this assumption marginal cost becomes equal to average prime cost; and with the additional assumption that the depreciation of equipment is independent of the use that is made of it, the gap between selling price and marginal cost becomes a gap between selling price and labor-and-material cost per unit of output. This gap, in business language, is nothing but the gross profit margin.

[44] M. Kalecki, "The Distribution of the National Income," *Econometrica*, Vol. VI (1938), pp. 97–112, reprinted in revised form in *Essays in the Theory of Economic Fluctuations* (London: Allen and Unwin, 1939), pp. 13–41, and in *Readings in the Theory of Income Distribution*, ed. W. Fellner and B. F. Haley (Philadelphia: Blakiston, 1946), pp. 197–217.

[45] Lerner had stated that if we apply his idea of measurement "to the whole economy we get the appropriate *reductio ad absurdum*." *Op. cit.*, p. 175.

The ratio of the gross profit margin to the price is, of course, the same as the ratio of total gross profit to total gross receipts. Thus, the Lerner formula has been transformed by Kalecki into another formula—the "ratio of sales going to gross profit" [46]— which is still supposed to measure the degree of monopoly. Gross profit, according to Kalecki, can be subdivided into executives' salaries (S), depreciation (D) and capitalists' income (C), and thus his formula for the degree of monopoly reads $\frac{C + D + S}{T}$, where the numerator contains all three parts of gross profit and the denominator is the gross turnover (T), the sales, of the firm.

The figures for all individual firms in an industry can be easily added together and the resulting ratio is supposed to express the average degree of monopoly for the industry. And if the figures of the whole economy are added together, they are supposed to tell us the average degree of monopoly of the whole economy. (This is exactly the inference against which Lerner had warned. See above p. 512.) When finally the inter-industry payments for materials are eliminated and total turnover of the economy is reduced to net national income, the average degree of monopoly of the economy is supposed to "determine" the distributive shares going to labor, on the one hand, and to capitalists and executives, on the other.

The major fault of this whole line of reasoning, apart from the question-begging assumption of generally constant marginal cost, is that a substitution of a new *name* for an old ratio is offered as a plausible *explanation* of that ratio. The ratio between gross profits and total turnover is given the name "degree of monopoly," and then the degree of monopoly is said to determine the distributive share going to gross profits. The implication of this whole business is, of course, that all income except that of common labor is characterized as monopoly profit or income derived from the exploitation of monopoly power. Unfortunately, our insight into economic processes is not increased by this attempt to offer names and definitions in the place of explanations.

The Kalecki formula is misleading also if applied to individual firms or industries. Take, for example, the case of an industry with

[46] Roswell H. Whitman, "A Note on the Concept of 'Degree of Monopoly'," *Economic Journal*, Vol. LI (1941), pp. 261–69.

alternative ways of producing its product, one firm using expensive
equipment and relatively less labor, another firm using more modest equipment and a larger labor force. The two firms may produce at the same unit cost, sell at the same price, and make the
same net profit as well as the same rate of return on total investment. But one firm, having larger overhead and smaller direct cost,
will show a greater ratio of gross profits to turnover. According
to the Kalecki formula this firm would possess a much higher degree of monopoly power than the other firm with smaller capitalization and larger labor cost.[47] The least that can be said about this
odd result is that the name "degree of monopoly" is in this case
anything but descriptive of the comparative market positions of
the firms. The search for the sources of deviations from the optimum allocation of resources is not helped by this peculiar index
of the "degree of monopoly."

Industry Control and the Slope Ratios of Demand Curves

While the Kalecki formula supposedly measures the degree
of monopoly of the economy as a whole, and while the Lerner formula is designed to measure the degree of monopoly exercised
by the individual firm (which as a rule is in inverse proportion to
the elasticity of demand for its product), the so-called Rothschild
formula is intended to measure the monopoly control of the individual firm within the industry to which it belongs.[48] In order
to see "how far a particular firm controls the market for a certain
commodity," [49] the slope of the demand curve for the product
of the firm—the so-called "species" demand curve—is compared
with the slope of the demand curve for the product of the industry
—the so-called "genus" demand curve—or, to facilitate the comparison, with the slope which the demand curve for the product of
the firm would have if the prices for the products of the entire industry always moved in unison with the prices charged by the firm.
In other words, the slope of the species demand curve "provided

[47] Whitman, op. cit., p. 264.
[48] K. W. Rothschild, "The Degree of Monopoly," Economica, New Series,
Vol. IX (1942), pp. 24–39.
[49] Ibid., p. 33.

the competing firms do not change their price"[50] is divided by the slope of the species demand curve assuming "that all the firms increase or decrease their prices by the same absolute amount, or in the same ratio" or in some other determined fashion depending "on the merits of the case."[51]

If a firm "controls" the output of the entire industry, the two curves coincide, the slope ratio is 1:1, and the Rothschild formula yields 1, or complete monopoly control. If a firm controls only a very small part of the total supply of "the commodity" and if its product is not differentiated from that of other suppliers, the slope of the demand curve for the firm will be zero and, regardless of the slope of industry demand curve, the Rothschild index will be zero; that is to say, the firm has no monopoly control whatever. In all other cases the Rothschild formula will yield values greater than zero and less than unity.[52]

Contrasting his formula with Lerner's, Rothschild grants that the Lerner index "is probably the ideal measure if we want to deal with problems like the social cost of monopoly, the allocation of resources under monopoly, the divergence from optimum output, and similar questions," but he submits that it cannot indicate the

[50] *Ibid.*, p. 24.—The terms, "species demand curve" and "genus demand curve" were proposed by Morris A. Copeland, "The Theory of Monopolistic Competition," *Journal of Political Economy,* Vol. XLII (1934), p. 531.

[51] Rothschild, *op. cit.*, p. 25. The basic idea of the Rothschild index was expressed by John Maurice Clark when he said that "an 'element of competition' . . . begins at the point where the demand schedule for the product of an individual producer is more elastic than the total demand schedule in the market or market area." J. M. Clark, "Basing Point Method of Price Quoting," *The Canadian Journal of Economics and Political Science,* Vol. IV (1938), p. 481. Rothschild can speak of slope where Clark speaks of elasticity because he reduces the industry demand curve to a demand curve for the product of the firm assuming that all prices in the industry move in unison, and thereby he obtains two curves intersecting in one point, namely, at the output sold at the current price. Clark compares two curves that have very different positions on the graph, one curve referring to the firm's output, the other to the industry's output; this would make a comparison of slope meaningless.

[52] Rothschild discusses some exceptional cases, such as the case of the rising demand curve, but we may dismiss them without misgivings. Rothschild obviously uses slopes rather than elasticities because the latter vary inversely with the former, and the resulting ratios would not be suitable for indexes; for example, where the slope ratio is zero, the elasticity ratio would be infinite.

firm's control over the market. Precisely this is what he claims his own formula can do. On the other hand, the "potential monopoly power" which the Rothschild formula supposedly measures is control over a "commodity" or "industry" which is clearly delimited from other commodities or industries. Where the "group" of products or firms whose prices are assumed to change in unison with the prices of the firm in question cannot be clearly delimited, the "calculation" of this index "will break down." [53]

But even where such delimitation would be meaningful, it is hard to see how calculations should be made in view of the fact that the underlying estimates are so manifestly out of the analyst's reach. The Lerner index calls only for estimates of marginal costs. The Rothschild index calls for slopes of curves under highly hypothetical assumptions, namely, for the numerator, that no changes of other prices occur and, for the denominator, that certain other prices change simultaneously in a predetermined way. What other prices and in what way? Let us not forget that neither of the two demand curves whose slopes enter the Rothschild formula may be equivalent to the demand as seen by the seller, for in actual fact the seller may neither expect all other relevant prices to remain unchanged nor all other relevant prices to move in step with his own.[54] Hence, firms will hardly ever make estimates of the sort required by the Rothschild formula and outside observers will rarely be equipped to make the estimates for them.[55]

[53] *Ibid.*, pp. 33–34.

[54] In criticism of Rothschild's index it has been said that "if a seller's monopoly power is to be measured in terms of the *ex ante* demand schedules for his product and for his 'market,' we must admit first that his monopoly power is what he thinks it is, and second that neither he nor we will probably be able to find out exactly what he thinks." Joe S. Bain, "Measurements of the Degree of Monopoly: A Note," *Economica*, New Series, Vol. X (1943), p. 68. In reply Rothschild stated: "In my index of monopoly power it is not the subjective (*ex ante*) seller's demand curve that matters, but the objective (*ex post*) curve." But he admitted that "the difficulties of quantitative measurement remain," K. W. Rothschild, "A Further Note on the Degree of Monopoly," *Economica*, p. 69.

[55] This does not mean that a firm may not actually reflect about the demand for its products under various hypothetical conditions including the ones prescribed for the Rothschild formula. The United States Steel Corporation once compared the (highly elastic) demand for the steel products of an individual supplier, assuming his competitors would not respond to his price changes, with the (very inelastic) demand for steel in general, that is,

The Rothschild formula makes sense under certain circumstances. Under other circumstances it makes little or no sense. For example, if a firm is a party to a price fixing agreement, the demand curve on the assumption of unchanged prices charged by rivals would have practically infinite elasticity, or a zero slope. The demand curve based upon consonant changes of rivals' prices might be relatively steep. But the Rothschild formula, with zero in the numerator, would show a zero degree of monopoly. In this situation as in many others, a measurement of monopoly power by the Rothschild formula, apart from practical difficulties, would be even theoretically inconceivable.

Cross-Elasticities of Demand

The major weakness of the Rothschild formula, its dependence on the possibility of delimiting the industry—the group of competitors whose prices are relevant for determining the demand for the production in question—is seemingly overcome by an analysis which explicitly eliminates the industry concept and concentrates on the interrelationships between individual firms. These interrelationships can be numerically expressed by the cross-elasticities of demand, the ratios between the relative changes in the quantity demanded of the product concerned and the relative changes in the price of another firm's product. A firm, according to this formulation, has a "pure monopoly" if all cross-elasticities of demand for its product with respect to the prices of all products offered by other firms are zero.[56]

This so-called Triffin criterion of monopoly, which incidentally implies the group concept (which he has previously explicitly

---

assuming all steel prices moving together. Cf. United States Steel Corporation. *T.N.E.C. Papers*, Vol. III, pp. 24–26; also *Hearings before the Temporary National Economic Committee*, Part 27 (Washington, 1941), pp. 14634–35. The comparison was made in order to explain why the individual supplier would not act without regard for the market as a whole and for the probable reactions of their competitors. Incidentally, the monopoly power of a price leader would never show in the Rothschild index even if the industry produced a homogeneous product and if all the required estimates and calculations could be properly made.

[56] Robert Triffin, *Monopolistic Competition and General Equilibrium Theory* (Cambridge: Harvard University Press, 1940), p. 103.

rejected) in the selection of the products in regard to which cross-elasticities are estimated and in the list of the products in regard to which positive cross-elasticities are established, fails to furnish any single index of the degree of monopoly. There is no meaningful way in which the individual cross-elasticities can be aggregated, averaged, or otherwise combined in a numerical value indicative of the monopoly power of any particular firm. For product A there may be high cross-elasticities with respect to three (competing) products while for product B there may be eight, but not quite as high. For which of the two products should the seller's position be called less monopolistic, more competitive? The Triffin criterion obviously holds only for defining the limit, but not for evaluating any intermediate positions.

Penetration and Insulation

Even for the description of the degree of competition between only two single-product firms the cross-elasticity of demand would not suffice. The cross-elasticity would show the relative shift of demand to or from one of the products in response to an increase or reduction in the price of the other product. But the shiftability of demand is not enough; the firm favored by the shift has to be able to meet an increase in demand by increased production; that is, it has to have the capacity to expand its output if it wants to make an inroad into the market of its rival. Thus, in order to express a producer's power to penetrate his rival's market, Andreas G. Papandreou proposes a "coefficient of penetration," combining the cross-elasticity of demand with an index of the "capacity to expand output to match the increases in the quantity demanded following a price cut." [57]

Moreover, power shows itself not only in aggression but also in defense. A firm's "monopoly power *vis-à-vis* its competitors is not limited to its capacity to penetrate their markets. Its capacity to withstand attacks on their part is equally important." [58] Papan-

---

[57] Andreas G. Papandreou, "Market Structure and Monopoly Power," *American Economic Review*, Vol. XXXIX (1949), pp. 883–97, esp. p. 891.— Papandreou expresses his "coefficient of penetration" in a long formula, which I do not have the courage to reproduce here.

[58] *Ibid.*, p. 893.

dreou recommends expressing the latter by a "coefficient of insulation which will measure the degree of non-responsiveness of the actual volume of sales of [a] firm . . . to price cuts initiated by its competitors." [59] When more than two firms, producing differentiated products, are competing in the market, the coefficients of penetration and insulation will not bear simple inverse relationships. As a matter of fact, the merely formal derivation of these coefficients becomes very complex and their actual measurement becomes hopeless.

Papandreou admits this, but he proposes that his coefficients "be employed in an *ordinal* sense to describe the structure of the balance of power in an industry or market. . . . Exact cardinal measures would not add substantially to our knowledge." [60]

A MONOPOLIST'S SELF-ANALYSIS

Of the many indexes and measurements discussed here, the Lerner formula is probably the most sensible, although it is rather arbitrary to call the ratio measured the "degree of monopoly." Executives of individual firms who have never dreamed of possessing any monopoly power at all, will surely be taken by surprise when they learn that monopoly power is attributed to them by the economists.

However, it will be easy for sellers to apply the Lerner method of measurement to their own position. They may ask themselves how much it would cost them to produce slightly more (or slightly less) than they actually do, say a carload more (or less), or whatever may be a proper unit of their output. When they find that this differential cost of production is considerably below the current selling price, they may know for themselves that they possess a considerable degree of "monopoly power."

This comparison of price and marginal cost will probably appear very silly to the business executive if he does not know its implications. It is not implied that selling prices should be reduced

[59] *Ibid.* In this point Papandreou's proposal goes back to an earlier suggestion by Theodore Morgan, "A Measure of Monopoly in Selling," *Quarterly Journal of Economics*, Vol. LX (1946), pp. 461–63.—Again, the "coefficient of insolution" is shown in a long formula with many symbols.

[60] Papandreou, *op. cit.*, pp. 894–95.

to the marginal cost figures of his present output. The real implications can perhaps be made clear through a little self-analysis:
one may guess for oneself the degree of output restrictions that
goes with the exercise of that monopoly power (of which the
guesser probably has been unconscious hitherto). This can be
done by answering the following questions:

(1) If you were offered a contract for your product over a
year (and renewable thereafter) for any quantity which you might
care to produce at a price equal to your present selling price; how
much would you produce? (Don't forget that you would not have
any selling expenses; advertising, etc., could be stopped; you need
not have any misgivings as to the future, for you will have an
option to renew the contract for an indefinite period.)

(2) If you received the same contract for unlimited quantities, but at a price 10 percent below the present price, how much
would you produce?

(3) If the same contract for unlimited quantities were at a
price of 15 percent below the present price, how much would you
produce?

(4) The same at a price 20 percent below present price?

(5) Etc., etc.

The executive of the industrial firm answering these questions
for himself may find that the production figures which he chooses
for the various imaginary contracts exceed his present output by
large amounts. Under the first hypothesis—unlimited quantities at
unchanged price—the chosen output might even be a multiple of
his present production. The same might be true for a few less
attractive offers at lower prices. At certain reduced prices, however, he might choose to produce no more than he does at present,
or he might find that he would rather not produce at all, the losses
of a completely idle plant being smaller than those of production
at such terribly low prices.

The list of hypothetical outputs compared with his present output may give the executive of the industrial firm an idea of the
"output restriction" due to "monopoly,"—monopoly in the sense
that the seller's knowledge that an increased supply would not
sell, or sell only at lower prices, causes him to produce no more
than he does. The imaginary contracts for unlimited quantities of

product, implying perfect elasticities of demand for the firm's product, make cost conditions the sole cause for limiting its output; and this, indeed, is the essence of the assumption of "pure competition." The hypothetical outputs produced for an unlimited market at the current price, that is, the quantities which the executive of our industrial firm will have put down in the top row of his list, may appear to him fantastically high. He need not think, however, that these huge quantities would really be produced if pure competition were suddenly to prevail in his industry. For, since under pure competition marketability seems unlimited only to the individual seller while total demand on the market is just as limited as under monopoly, the price would obviously be lower than the current price in the top row of this list. The price might be so low that several of the existing plants would not produce at all, and only the more efficient firms would work. What the price would be, nobody could tell, not even the shrewdest market expert, because most conditions would be totally different.

CONCLUSION

When the gap between price and marginal cost is suggested as a measure of the "degree of monopoly," the word monopoly is used only in a special meaning: as deviation from "pure" competition. The restriction of production which presumably is revealed by that gap may be regarded as that output restriction which is due to imperfect elasticity of demand as seen by the individual seller. But there are other sorts of output restrictions.

It is conceivable that competition in a certain market is pure while entry into the industry is curbed by some artificial barriers. In such cases there would be no "monopolistic restriction" in the sense discussed above—but there would obviously be monopolistic restriction in another sense. Output would not be restricted by any one firm operating in the industry, but it would be restricted by the fact that the number of firms would be smaller than under perfect freedom of entry. There would be no gap between marginal cost and price, but there would probably be a margin between average cost and price, that is, a profit margin giving rise to a profit rate above normal. The supernormal profit rate, resulting from imperfect entry into the trade, may however not be capable of statistical verification because of the difficulties described earlier in this chapter.

There are some reasons to believe that an output restriction evidenced by a gap between marginal cost and price could never be very serious as long as entry into the industry is free and easy enough to prevent supernormal profits; that the gap can be large only in cases where the demand as seen by the seller is of low elasticity, and that this imperfect elasticity is often connected with imperfect entry into the industry. (The easier the entry the greater the number of sellers and, usually, the more substitutable their products.) Since measurements of the ease of entry into an industry appear still more difficult than price and cost measurements within a single firm, the relative price-marginal-cost gap is not an unreasonable first approximation to the problem of measurement. Theoretically, the measurement of the relative price-marginal-cost gap should be supplemented in each case by an analysis of the adjusted profit rate.[61] Practically, we should admit that, with the information now available, no measurement at all is possible.

Perhaps it should be stated that so many different elements enter into what is called a monopolistic position and so complex are their combined effects that a measurement of "the" degree of monopoly is even conceptually impossible. We may be able to measure one element or another, but would still not know how to combine them in a single measure. The conceptual difficulties of measuring *the* degree of monopoly have been likened to those of measuring *the* degree of health or *the* degree of sinfulness.[62] These concepts likewise cover numerous deviations from standards, where the degree of each single deviation might possibly be subject to numerical expression, but where no unique value can be attached to the combination.

[61] These two "fundamental" measurements of the degree of monopoly look at the first blush rather similar. The one starts from the excess of price over marginal cost, the other from the excess of price over average cost. These two differences, however, are brought into relation to very different things: the former is made a ratio of the selling price, the latter is multiplied by the yearly output and made a ratio of the necessary capital.

[62] Edward H. Chamberlin, in a round table discussion on "Monopoly and Competition and their Regulation" held by the International Economic Association at Talloires, France, September 1951.

One may question the need for measurements as long as there are clearly ascertainable practices or institutions which obstruct entry into particular industries or occupations and reduce competition among those within the fields. Measurement is no substitute for good judgment, whereas good judgment may often do without measurement. If we can see barriers to entry, obstacles to mobility, and other restrictions of competition we can proceed to remove them even if we cannot "measure" their effects.

Index

Ability to pay, as criterion for government wage fixing, 428; increased wages out of profit, 398n, 405; wage rate discrimination based on, 404n
Absentee ownership, 58n
Adair v. *U.S.*, 320n
Adams, Walter, 82n
Addyston Pipe and Steel Co. v. *U.S.*, 105n, 188, 200n, 202n, 228
Advertising, a barrier to entry, 124-26; and delivered prices, 142n; deceptive, 160, 174; for brand names, 142n, 160, 173; not under pure competition, 16; of lower prices, 291n; taxes on, 264; to gain business, 5; to reduce demand elasticity, 10
Agglomeration, 110
Agricultural Adjustment Act, 211n
Agricultural Marketing Agreement Act, 211n, 308
Agricultural monopoly policies, 42, 56-57, 59, 158, 210-12, 271n, 304-12
Allocation of resources, 3, 20, 21, 30, 32, 36, 163, 276, 304, 372, 381, 401-02, 403-04, 414, 433, 434, 441, 459, 511, 512, 519, 520
Aluminum case, 192, 224n
Aluminum Corporation, 83, 157, 192, 224n
American Agricultural Chemical Company, 131
American Column & Lumber Co. v. *U.S.*, 189, 202n
American Economic Association, 214n
American Federation of Labor, 343
American Steel Foundries v. *Tri-City Central Trades Council*, 324n
American Sugar Refining Company, 188, 219
American Tobacco Company, 107, 147, 188, 219
American Tobacco Co. v. *U.S.*, 124n, 192, 203n, 225n
Andrews, J. B., 345n
Anonymous ownership, 238
Anti-Injunction Act, 321n
Antimonopoly policies, 6, 176, 263-65; critics of, 69-70, 204
Antitrust laws, and trade unions, 191,

210-11, 323, 342n, 343; appraisal of, 226-36; basic statutes, 193-98; complaints about, 205; exemptions from, 189-93, 194, 198, 210-17, 229, 309; interpretation of, 153, 183-84, 188-93, 199-209, 219-21, 222-26, 227, 232; on collusion, 199-217; on monopolization through merger, 217-226; philosophy of, 226, 232
Antitrust prosecutions, against cartels, but not trusts, 232; against farmers or workers, 210, 318, 343; complaints about, 205; criminal versus civil, 206, 207n, 230; needed to secure respect for the law, 231n; reduce evasion, 210; reduce uncertainty, 205; suspended, 217; tardy, 184, 194, 206, 208, 214, 229
Apex Hosiery Company v. *Leader*, 324n
Apprenticeship rules, 411
Appropriations, 184, 194, 210, 227
Aristotle, 185, 465n
Arkansas, 278, 292
Arnold, Thurman W., 82n, 88n, 184n, 229n, 230
Arrow-Hart and Hegeman Electric Co., v. *Federal Trade Comm.*, 223n
Asset Valuation, 490, 494-97
Assets versus stocks, 109, 190, 193, 196, 198, 221-24
Atom, 449n
Authoritarian regime, 74-78, 423, 424, 434
Automobile industry, 65, 126n, 139, 159, 294, 515
Average-price cartel, 97

Backward-rising supply curve, 60
Bain, Joe S., 494n, 495-96, 497n, 521n
Balance of payments, 266, 273, 462
Ballinger, W. J., 128n
Banking, 213, 275
Bargaining power, and financial strength, 350, 368; and labor mobility, 370; and perishability, 339, 348-52, 370; and unemployment, 364-65, 367; equalization of, 34, 325, 326, 328, 338-39, 367-71, 375, 376, 378, 379; exploitation of, 420, 424n; labor

Bargaining power (*continued*)
  slow in acquiring, 45; meaning of,
  344-48, 351, 369; of different unions
  unequal, 407, 424n; requires control
  of supply, 410-12; under price dis-
  crimination, 138-39, 151
Basing-point system, 55n, 90, 120, 129,
  132n, 145, 147, 166, 167, 189, 192,
  203
Beard, Charles A. and Mary R., 184
Beaty, Amos L., 303n
Beechnut Packing Company v. *U.S.*,
  93n
Beggar-my-neighbor policy, 269
Bennett, L. Thompson, 290n, 293n,
  294n
Berge, Wendell, 94n
Bethlehem Steel Corporation, 115n
Beveridge, Sir William, 424n
Bilateral monopoly, 34, 376, 379n, 427
Bituminous Coal Act, 216n, 304, 313
Black, Forrest Revere, 342n
Blair, John M., 254n, 481n
Bloom, Gordon F., 366n
Bogus, independents, 100, 175; patents,
  130
Bolen, George L., 122n
Boonstra, Earl R., 215n
Boulding, Kenneth E., 34n, 62n, 344n
Bowen, Howard R., 254n
Boycott, 176, 324, 328
Bradley Co. v. *Local #3, Brotherhood
  of Electrical Workers*, 399n
Bribery, 168, 176, 322
Bridgman, P. W., 449n
Buffer stocks, 57, 59
Building industry, 410n, 412n, 462
Building ordinances, 182, 462
Bureau of Corporations, 188
Bureau of Labor Statistics, 499n
Burns, Arthur Robert, 82n, 132n
Business cycle, 34, 57, 60, 253
"Business Limitation Act," 246n
Butters, J. Keith, 255n, 256n, 257n
Byrnes Act, 322n

California, 314
Canada, 313
Capital and small business, 253-63; by-
  passing the market, 243; "exploited"
  by labor, 395, 408; for new ventures,
  65, 67-69, 282; heterogeneous factors
  lumped as, 20n; income from, 334n;
  increased supply of, 396; needs for
  large-scale production, 238; or-

ganized, 339, 368; per worker, 267,
  389-90, 396; perishable services of,
  348; versus labor, 329
Capitalism, 238, 335, 340, 401n, 434-35,
  461n
Capper-Volstead Act, 211n
Carry-back provisions, 254-55
Cartels, agricultural, 212; based on patents, 92-93, 119, 156-57, 207-10, 282-
  83; checked by law, 228-32; compared with trade unions, 44, 342n;
  criminal or beneficial, 231; defined,
  28, 85n; enforcement policies, 91-94;
  exports by, 149, 189, 214, 273n, 274n;
  forms of, 86-98; international, 91-93,
  214, 272-73; promotes by tariffs, 273-
  74; quota, 58, 96, 214, 276, 303, 307,
  309; versus trusts, 98-99, 105, 200n,
  232
Carter, William A., 82n
Case studies, 81, 442
Cassady, Ralph, Jr., 138n, 141n
Cease-and-desist orders, 188, 189, 196,
  197, 222, 325
Celler Anti-Merger Act, 197-98, 223-
  24, 232
Cement cases, 129, 130, 133, 145n, 189,
  192, 196n, 204n, 229
Cement Manufacturers Protective Assn.
  v. *U.S.*, 189, 229
Census Bureau, 335n, 476-81, 483, 499n
Chain-store law, 197
Chamberlin, Edward Hastings, 29n,
  496n, 527n
Chemical industry, 65
Cigarette industry, 41, 54, 122, 124, 219,
  233, 256-57, 264
Civil Aeronautics Act, 212
Clark, John Maurice, 425n, 520n
Clark, Tom C., 207n
Clayton Act, 103, 109, 113, 147, 176,
  188-92, 195-98, 204, 210-11, 221-24,
  232, 244, 324, 343
Cleveland, Grover, 320n
Closed shop, 27, 71, 321, 322, 326, 327,
  328, 346, 373, 418, 430
Coal, 18, 31, 42, 56, 131, 154, 304, 313-
  14
Cobweb cycles, 60
Coffee, 56, 143n, 266
Cohen, Morris R., 447n, 465n, 466n
Collective bargaining, at expense of un-
  organized majority, 407; combined
  with union-management cooperation,
  392n; credited with improved labor

income, 396; inducing employers' coalition, 376; not sole function of unions, 426, 429n; promoted by law, 322, 325-29; unrestricted access to jobs inconsistent with, 416; versus competition among workers, 44

Collusion, among buyers, 35n; among employers, 45, 339, 353-56, 359, 368, 370, 375-76; among workers, 338; among unions, 430; and cartels, 28, 85-98; and identical prices, 163-68; as proof of absence of monopoly, 220; between workers and employers, 324; during emergencies, 217; evidence of, 135, 202-03; illegal under Sherman law, 184, 194; implied in "fair price" view, 26; in banking, 213; in insurance, 213; in oil industry, 302-03; in price leadership, 11, 127-36; in retailing, 93-94, 215-16; in transportation, 212-13, 297, 298; law of, 199-217; not measurable, 473-74; novel forms of, 206; reduces demand elasticity, 10; through patent licenses, 190-91, 207-10, 229, 282-85; to fix prices, 87-91, 164, 166-68, 188-93, 200-09, 216, 220, 502, 522; to restrain competition among sellers, 36-37, 55, 88-89; to restrict output, 28, 96, 202; versus "cooperation," 86-87

Collusive oligopsony, 354n, 502

Colorado, 278n, 293

Commodity Credit Corporation, 307

Commons, John R., 345n

Communism, 336, 423, 434n

Community of interests, 242

Company unions, 321, 432n

Compensation test, 20-21, 460n

Competition, affected by concentration, 116, 258, 482-87; among employers, 339, 352-67, 368, 373, 375, 377; among trade unions, 431-32; among workers, 342, 347, 359, 375; and foreign exchange restrictions, 276; and identical prices, 163-67; and patent protection, 105, 119, 207-10, 280-86; and price discrimination, 139, 163; and resource allocation, 20; degree versus kinds of, 4-5; enforced, 226; for consumer's dollar, 6; for labor, 339, 352-69; from abroad, 486; from newcomers, 27, 36, 117-26, 276, 285, 291, 360, 361, 371n, 373, 377, 495-97; from "other industries," 486; in foreign trade, 214, 265-

76; in retail trade, 93, 169-70, 182, 191, 215, 229, 314-15; in steel, 453; invisible, 352, 394; monopsonistic, 35n, 168, 355n, 359, 361n, 362, 365, 377; negative or positive, 170; perfect, 12, 19, 20, 70, 360, 369; pure, 14-19, 22-23, 137n, 163-68, 345n, 352, 359, 364-65, 366n, 377-78; quasi-pure, 131, 134; regulated, 4; restrained by government, 182-83, 235, 265-79, 280-86, 287-317; "soft," 233; the "virtues" of, 4; to end competition, 175-76; unfair, 102-04, 148, 168-77, 188, 190, 196, 203, 215, 216, 305, 312, 314; versus public regulation, 295; vigorous versus predatory, 101

Concentration, affecting competition, 7-8, 116-17; against public interest, 235; aided by corporation laws, 239-49, 368; and degree of monopoly, 484-87; and employers' competition, 368; and price rigidity, 503-07; and taxation, 253-65; caused by merger, 52, 105-17, 234, 239-40; in terms of assets, 484; measured in terms of output, 478-82; measurement of, 114, 475-85; necessary because of technology, 239-40, 488-89; number of firms and, 475-76; of financial power, 368; on plant and company basis, 488-90

Conceptual framework, 439, 440-42

Conduct versus behavior, 85n

Conglomeration, 110-11, 198

Connally Hot Oil Act, 302n

Connecticut, 278n, 292

Consent decree, 230n

Conservation, 56, 299-304, 464n

Consolidated Steel Corporation, 225

Consolidation, 106-07, 188, 232, 260

Construct, 449

Cooperation, among banks, 213; to restrain competition, 4, 37; versus collusion, 85-86; versus domination, 99

Cooperatives, 42, 43, 45, 157, 211-12

Copeland, Morris A., 520n

Coppage v. *Kansas*, 320n

Copper, 18, 56, 154, 157

Copyright, 140, 172

Corn Products Refining Company, 131, 192, 230n

Corn Products Refining Co., v. *Federal Trade Comm.*, 192

Corporate merger, see Merger

Corporation, and labor, 339, 367-68; law, 182, 184, 187, 234-35, 237-49, 367-68; tax, 249-65
Cotton, 14, 17, 18, 56, 274, 306n, 307
Counterspeculation, 377n
Credit supply, 386
Cross-elasticity of demand, 9, 162n, 522-23
Cross-hauling, 54
Cross-licensing, 284
Crown Zellerbach Corporation, 131
Cummins, Senator, 175n
Cut-throat competition, 27, 60, 99-100, 103, 120, 176
Cyclical fluctuations, 57, 58

Damocles Sword clause, 230
Danbury Hatters Case, 324-25
Darcy v. Allin, 186
Dean, Joel, 171n, 513n
Debits and credits to monopoly, 69-74
Debs, Eugene, 320n
Deception, 169, 173, 177
Deflation, 34, 34n, 62, 266, 386
Delivered prices, 90, 144, 165-68, 203, 142n, 452n, 467
Democracy, 74-79, 270n, 426, 427, 432n
Depreciation, of currency, 266; of durable assets, 253
Depression, 58, 171, 216, 254, 268-69, 355, 386, 387, 397, 497
Dier's case, 186
Direct controls, 77, 122, 304-17, 422, 464n
Direct costs, 462
Director, Aaron, 122n
Diseconomies of scale, 52n
Dissolution, 147, 184, 188, 189, 190, 219, 220, 231, 232, 233, 235, 258, 263, 374, 376, 430-32
Distribution channels, 27, 122-23, 124-25, 175
Divergence, index of, 488-90
Diversification, 110, 482-83
Divestiture, 109, 222, 223, 231
Divisibility, of productive facilities, 123-26; of resources, 441
Division of markets, 28, 93, 95, 202, 214, 233
Domar, Evsey D., 252n
Domination, 37-39, 99, 104-05, 117, 190, 192, 219, 242
Douglas, William O., Justice, 199n, 215n

Dumping, 141, 148, 307
Dunlop, John T., vii, 345n, 381n, 382n, 383n, 385n, 420n, 508, 515-16
Duopoly, 48
Du Pont, 239n
Dynamic analysis, 30

Economies of scale, 51, 52, 116, 162, 238-40, 261-62, 489-90
Economist, 273n
Eddy, Arthur Jerome, 89n
Edwards, Corwin D., 52n, 53n, 82n, 86n, 111n, 112n, 113n, 206n, 242n, 244n, 263n
Efficiency versus power, 102
Ehrke, Kurt, 513n
Elasticity of demand, and degree of monopoly, 10, 487, 509, 510, 516, 520n, 527; and effects of wage boosts, 417-18; attempts to reduce, 10, 28, 36; defined, 9; discrimination determined by, 139, 152-53; for glass jars and plastics, 156; for labor, 347n, 420; for plate glass, 157; in interdependent markets, 162n; in regional markets, 149n; of railroad shippers, 154-55; output restriction determined by, 25, 509; tariff making according to, 269n; under pure competition, 12, 22
Elasticity of substitution, 9n, 486-87
Elasticity of supply, and the tariff, 269n; as seen by buyers, 40; of complementary factors, 347n; of primary commodities, 57; taken account of by employers, 35n
Empire-building, 52
Employment, and tariffs, 268, 272; and union policy, 377; and wage rates, 19, 338n, 378, 387, 398, 417-29; due to increased investment, 387; fluctuations in, 383; increased by greater consumption, 388-89; reduced through wage increase, 378, 387, 398; restriction of, 355; wage increase consistent with greater, 378, 387; wage increases, inflation and, 417-29
Employment agencies, 371
Entry, 12, 19, 24, 26-27, 29, 33, 36, 38, 44, 57, 117-26, 173, 276, 285, 288-94, 296-99, 361, 362, 371, 372n, 377, 378, 384, 412, 413, 495-97, 526-27
Epstein, Ralph C., 491, 493n
Equality, 336, 433, 463
Equilibrium, 357
Erdman Act, 320n

Estate tax, 256
Ethics, 37, 88, 98, 130, 140, 168-70, 231, 340, 380, 404
Ethyl Gasoline Corp. v. *U.S.*, 130n, 191, 229
Evaluation, 458-64
Excess capacity, 60-62, 296n
Excess-profits tax, 251, 258n, 260n
Excise taxes, 251, 255, 392n, 398
Exclusion, 117-26, 281, 289; see Entry
Exclusive-dealer arrangements, 112, 125, 175, 202, 247n
Explanation versus prediction, 454-56
Exploitation, by discrimination, 162, 163; monopolistic, 366n; monopsonistic, 366; of bargaining power, 420, 424n; of consumers, 3, 404n; of inventions, 65, 281-82; of monopoly position, 84, 471, 511; of natural resources, 55-56, 299-304; of workers, 3, 340, 341, 361-64, 366, 376-79
Export cartels, 149, 189, 214, 273-74
External expansion, 115, 128
Evans, G. H., Jr., 116n

Fact, meaning of, 448-68
Fair price or profit, 26, 88, 169, 170, 183, 204, 210, 305
Fair return, 295, 296n
Fair-trade laws, 94, 169-72, 182, 191, 193, 215, 229, 314
Featherbedding, 328, 384
Federal Reserve Act, 213
Federal Reserve Board, 196n
Federal Trade Commission, 74n, 89n, 94n, 105n, 106n, 110n, 115n, 116n, 129n, 132n, 150n, 151n, 160n, 175, 189, 196, 198, 205, 214, 222-23, 230, 232, 247n, 261, 315n, 481n, 484n, 488n, 489n
Federal Trade Commission Act, 188, 191, 192, 196, 203, 215
Federal Trade Comm. v. *Cement Institute*, 129n, 133n, 145n, 192, 196n, 197n, 204n, 229
Federal Trade Comm. v. *Staley Mfg. Co.*, 192
Federal Trade Comm. v. *Western Meat Co.*, 190, 223n
Fellner, William, 379n, 517n
Fetter, Frank A., 82n, 100n, 110n, 145n, 164n, 185n
Fichtner, C. C., 254n
Finance, of growing firms, 253-65; of increased pay roll, 387, 422; of new

investment, 387, 422, 464; of transfer of labor, 351, 361, 371-72; of ventures, 65, 67-69, 282; out of retained profits, 243, 248, 253-55, 257-58, 262-63; withheld from competitors, 27, 112, 123
Fiscal policy, 34, 249-50, 316, 385-86, 403, 418, 419, 421, 464n
Fishery Cooperatives and Marketing Act, 211n
Florida, 278, 293
Folk, George E., 184n, 208n
Food and Drug Law, 176
Food Stamp Plan, 141, 157
Ford, Henry, 65
Forecasting, 455-58
Foreign-exchange restrictions, 265, 275-76
Forestalling, 186, 187
Formula pricing, 88, 145
Franchises, 27
Freedom, and privacy, 466; as a social goal, 71-72, 463, 464n; from state intervention, 288-89; in danger, 74-78, 422-25; of association, 426; private property a requisite of, 280; requires dispersion of power, 432n; the aim of liberalism, 237n
Freight absorption, 90, 120, 142, 144, 165, 167
Fringe benefits, 452n
Full employment, as social goal, 72, 463; defined, 421n; labor market under, 365; policy, 419, 420-22, 424
Full-line forcing, 112, 247n

Galbraith, John K., 516n
Gary, Elbert H., 87n
General Electric Company, 209n, 229
Gentlemen's agreement, 86-87, 353, 375
Geographic discrimination, 142, 149
Georgia, 192, 213, 279
Georgia v. *Pennsylvania Railroad Co.*, 192, 213n
Glass container industry, 88n, 149, 156, 283n
Golden, Clinton S., 385n, 393n
Gompers, Samuel, 343
Goodyear Tire and Rubber Company, 150n
Gordon, Robert A., 245n
Gotschal, Sylvan, 177n
Graham, Frank D., 238n
Grant, J. A. C., 288n, 293n

Growth of business firm, 51, 53, 109, 115, 128, 224, 234, 238n, 237-49, 253-65, 298, 369; of economy, 30, 49, 62; of employment, 418; of labor force, 422; of market, 51; of monopoly, 218, 221, 225, 227-35
Guilds, 183, 185, 288, 292-94

Haley, Bernard F., 517n
Hamilton, Walton H., 82n
Hand, Learned, Judge, 224n
Handler, Wilton, 171n, 173n, 199n, 200n
Hansen, Alvin H., 255n, 423n, 425n
Hardwood Lumber Assn. v. *U.S.*, 164n, 189
Harlan, John M., Justice, 201n
Harris, Herbert, 342n
Harrod, R. F., 516n
Hawtrey, R. G., 348n
Hayek, Friedrich A., 30n, 53n, 70n, 76n, 77n, 450n
Heisenburg, Werner, 465n
"Help Wanted," 351
Heterogeneity, as cause of monopoly, 29n, 33, 53; of buyers, 40; of employers, 365, 376, 377; of houses, 382; of labor, 382
Hicks, John R., 391n, 413n
Higgins, Benjamin, 345n
Hiring halls, 373n, 412
Hiring practices, 35n, 373n
Historical approach, 65, 81, 115, 185, 440, 443-46
Historical school, 444n
Holding company, 100, 107, 187, 188, 223, 242, 247n, 248, 259-60
Homan, Paul T., 67n, 255n, 425n
Homogeneity, of commodities, 15, 33; of factors of production, 19-20, 357, 359n
Homogenizing of products, 54
Hoover, Edgar M., Jr., 171n
Horizontal integration, 110, 116-17
Hutt, W. H., 348n, 350n

Ideal type, 17, 18
Identical prices, 90, 146, 163-68, 192, 203
Illinois, 187, 292, 292n, 324
Imitation, 64, 169, 172, 177, 280-86
Immobility, 20, 72n, 339, 352, 356-63, 365-67, 370, 375, 383-84
Import quotas, 265, 273-74

Import restrictions, 266-79, 310
Income distribution: see National income
Income elasticity of demand, 57
Index, of concentration, 114n, 475-90; of depression-sensitivity, 499-502; of divergence, 488-90; of monopoly, 469-528; of price inflexibility, 497-503; of relative attractiveness, 429n
Indivisibility, 123-26, 441
Industrial Commission, 122n
Industrial reserve army, 363
Industry, and inter-industry competition, 485-87; and size of market, 484-85; concentration of control of, 475-82; degree of monopoly in, 471-72; delimitation of, 7, 114n, 369, 482-84; demand for product of firm versus, 519-22; integration within, 483-84; number of firms in, 475-76; unions and average profits of, 397
Industry-wide bargaining, 71, 430-32
Infant industry argument, 33, 269-71, 280
Inflation, and wage increases, 417-29, 249, 316, 385, 408n, 418, 421-24, 435, 464n; repressed by price controls, 422
Initiation fees, 27, 411n
Innovation, 63-64, 280-86, 390
Instability, 56-62, 385-86, 423
Insulation, coefficient of, 524
Insurance, 191, 213-14
Integration, 110-11, 198, 246, 483-84, 488-89
Interest and rent income, 334n, 408
Interlocking directorates, 106, 189, 195, 242, 244, 248, 251n; stock holding, 187, 195, 241-42, 244, 248, 259
Internal economies, see Economies of scale
Internal expansion, 114, 128
International cartels, 92-93, 214, 272-73
International commodities agreements, 310
International Harvester Company, 131, 132n, 190, 220n
International Paper Company, 131
Interstate Commerce Act, 153n, 154, 187, 213n
Interstate Commerce Commission, 192, 196n, 213, 295-99
Interstate trade barriers, 276-79
Inventions, 65, 176-77, 187, 280-86, 390

Investment financed by earnings, 243; in small firms, 254; incentives, 67-69, 388, 389, 409; promoted through restrictions, 63; reduced through business taxes, 68, 251
Isolated labor market, 358-62, 363, 371-75

Jacobs, in re, 289n
Jastram, Roy W., vii
Job evaluation, 339, 381-82, 429
Joseph, M., 424n
Judiciary Committee (House or Senate), 108n, 113n, 116n, 195n, 224n, 248n, 477n

Kaldor, Nicholas, 424n
Kalecki, M., 517-19
Kansas, 320n
Keim, Walter G., 143n, 160n
Kelvin, Lord William Thomas, 465n
Keynes, John Maynard, 349n, 389n
Knight, Frank H., 78n, 237n, 465n
Knit Goods Weekly, 160n
Koopmans, Tjalling C., 466n

Labor, and anti-trust law, 191, 210-11, 323, 342n, 343; and corporations, 339, 368; competition for, 340, 351-69; exploitation of, 361-64, 366; groups versus labor as a whole, 395; lack of funds of, 351, 361; meanings of, 333-34; mobility of, 72n, 339, 352, 356-67, 371-75; "not a commodity," 324, 342, 343, 344; perishability of, 339, 348-49, 371; share of national income, 391, 394, 395-97; shortage of, 355
Labor disputes, 329, 416
Labor force, 334, 335, 422, 467
Labor law, 182, 191, 210-11, 317-29, 338, 416
Labor market, artificially free, 429; employers' collusion in, 353-56, 370; invisible competition in, 352-53, 394; isolated through labor immobility, 356-62, 365, 370, 371-75; lacking stability unless organized, 382-86; made more competitive through unions, 338; monopsonistic because of isolation, 358-62; monopsonistic through employer differentiation, 365-67, 376-78; monopsony reduced through dissolving corporations, 376; pure competi-
tion in, 345n, 359, 364, 377-78; technical defects in, 381-86
Labor monopoly, approval of, 337-38; legislation and, 317; needed for security, 72n; no offset to business monopoly, 432; objections to term, 45, 341; of all labor in nation, 424n, 426n; reducing power of, 428-32; restraints on, 318-19, 425-27
Labor productivity, distribution of benefits from increased, 402-03; increased by wage increase, 389-93; increased through improved technology, 390; increased through large capital supply, 267, 360; influenced by workers' morale, 341, 393; regional differences in, 360
Labor relations, 329, 416-17
Labor Relations Act, 317n, 321, 368n
Labor-saving inventions, 390
Labor supply, guaranteed to employer, 377-78; ill adjusted to demand, 382-85; made perfectly elastic, 377-78; smaller if workers have other incomes, 350
Ladies Garment Workers, 420n
Lag between impact and price change, 498; between stimulus and response, 409
Land, immobility of, 357
Larcom, R. C., 240n
Large-scale production, see Economies of scale
Lavarello, Angela, viii
Lechliter, Irvin, 290n, 293n, 294n
Leitch Mfg. Co. v. *Barber Co.,* 209n
Lenin, Nikolai, 434n
Lerner, Abba P., 377n, 429n, 510-12, 517, 518, 520-21, 524
Lester, Richard A., 341-42n
Lewis, W. Arthur, 50n
Libby-Owens-Ford, 231n
Liberalism, 50n, 118n, 236-37n, 280, 288-89, 401n, 422-25, 426, 432n, 464n
Licences, governmental, 27, 287-94, 309; under patents, 92-93, 282-86
Li'l Abner, 291n
Lindahl, Martin L., 82n
Lindley, Judge, 193n, 194n
Lintner, John, 255n, 256n, 257n
Lippmann, Walter, 242n
Litigation, 27, 52n, 112, 119-20, 129, 176, 177, 264

Livermore, Shaw, 95n
Lobbying, 52n, 119, 216n, 229, 270-72
Local price cutting, 100, 147, 148, 202, 218
Location, and price uniformity, 165; as basis for price discrimination, 141, 142, 149; may imply product differentiation, 15, 53
Loewe v. *Lawlor*, 324n
Long, Clarence D., 468n
Louisiana, 279, 293
Lydgate, William A., 335n
Lynch, David, 82n

Machlup, Fritz, 12n, 39n, 67n, 85n, 91n, 104n, 116n, 121n, 132n, 166n, 230n, 255n, 285n, 355n, 362n, 420n, 425n, 466n, 494n, 496n, 503n, 510n
Maclaurin, W. Rupert, 119n, 354n
Macmillan v. *Railroad Commission of Texas*, 303n
Maple Flooring Manufacturers Assn. v. *U.S.*, 89n, 164n, 189, 229
Margarine, 277
Margenau, Henry, 465n
Margin inflexibility, 506-08
Marginal cost, decreasing, 49; flat or U-shaped, 513-15, 517; exceeded by selling price, 22, 32; in definition of monopoly, 39n
Marginal labor cost, 366n, 367n, 378n
Marginal productivity, 360n, 362, 363, 366n, 373, 391
Marketing agreements, 211, 305, 308
Marx, Karl, 341n, 363, 434n
Marxian theory, 118n, 334, 335, 341, 363, 461n
Maryland, 278n, 292n
Mason, Alpheus T., 343n
Mason, Edward S., 502n, 503n
Massachusetts, 187n, 278n
Maximum prices, 305, 315-17
Maximum profit, 13, 19, 309, 366n, 391
Maximum size of firm, 246, 247n
McCarran Act, 191, 214n
McGrath, J. Howard, 220n
McNaughton, W. L., 320n
Meadowmoor Dairies, Inc. v. *The Milk Wagon Drivers' Union*, 399n
Means, Gardiner C., 499
Measurement, and theory, 466; conceivable versus practical, 466, 470; desirability of, 470-71; difficulties of, 472-73; in social sciences, 464-68; of degree of monopoly, 469-528; of im-

mobility, 357n; of price flexibility, 498-505; of propensities, 466; of wage increase, 452n
Mellon, Andrew William, 239n
Merchant Marine Act, 213n
Merger, aided by corporation law, 238-40; behind price leadership, 128-30; causing concentration, 52, 55, 114, 115, 234, 239-40; double effect of, 29; legality of, 187, 189, 193, 196, 198, 221-26; methods of arranging, 105-13, 221-24; not checked by antitrust laws, 184, 189, 190, 196, 221-26, 232-34; promoted by tax system, 256-58; reduces demand elasticity, 11; size and intent of, 220-21; waves of, 106; versus cartel, 98-99, 105, 200n, 232
Merrill Foundation, 115n
Methodology, 439-40, 444n, 446-51, 454-67
Middle class, 335
Milk, 45, 51, 154, 158, 182, 275n, 278, 290, 294, 306n, 308-09, 313
Mill, John Stuart, 337, 338, 417n
Miller-Tydings Fair-Trade Act, 191, 193, 213
Minimum prices, 215-16n, 297, 305, 313
Minimum size of firm, 117, 123-24, 238-39, 374
Mining, 56
Mises, Ludwig von, 236-37n
Misrepresentation, 160, 173, 174,
Mitchel v. *Reynolds,* 186
Mobility, and trade unions, 372-73, 375; of enterprise, 360-63, 371, 374; of labor, 72n, 339, 352, 356-63, 364, 371-73
Model, abstract, 441, 446; analytic, 24; an ideal construction, 18, 24, 441; of pure and perfect competition, 12-15, 22, 38
Mogul Steamship Co. v. *McGregor, Gow et al.*, 186-87
Mommsen, Theodor, 185n
Mond, Sir Alfred, 273n
Monopolistic business practices, 81-177; classified, 35, 36, 38-39, 85; harmful by definition, 3; judged in court cases, 188-93; lobbying included, 119; to raise competitors' costs, 104
Monopolization, 194, 198, 199n, 217-26, 232-35
Monopoly, aided by government, 182-83, 236-329; and price discrimination, 136-37, 164, 404n; and price inflexi-

bility, 497-508; a prerequisite of progress, 70; as artificial delay of newcomers, 70; as consciousness of limitation of market, 83; as imperfect demand elasticity, 9-10, 35, 38, 509-13, 516, 527; as imperfect entry, 26, 36, 38, 495-97, 509, 527; by secret knowhow, 281; charges against, 4, 72-73; controlling supply or price, 410-11; criteria for measuring, 473-75; definitions of, 38-39; degree of, 220, 471-72, 485-87, 508-28; due to product differentiation, 29n, 53; expansion of meaning of, 29, 82-83; expenses to maintain, 264; four categories of business, 35-37; government action against, 181-235; granted by Crown, 186; "in and of itself," 109, 220, 233; indicated by profits, 474, 490-97; inevitable or desirable, 46, 47, 294, 441; legal concept of, 84, 99, 199n, 217-18, 220, 225, 233; narrow sense of, 95, 104, 228, 233; natural, 48, 294, 441; of labor, 43-45, 72n, 317-19, 337-38, 341, 344-79, 386-435; popular criteria of, 3; public versus private, 48, 49, 50; size and, 123-26, 189, 226, 235, 246-48, 251, 261, 430-32; tax policy and, 249-65; through patented inventions, 280-86; trade barriers and, 265-79; versus restraint of trade, 199-201, 217
Monopoly Inquiry and Control Act, 187
Monopoly power as control over price or wage, 370; as penetration and insulation, 523-24; judged by seller's self-analysis, 524-26; of unions reduced, 428-32; or degree of monopoly, 471-72; to oppose monopsony, 376; unused or exploited, 471, 473, 511
Monopoly prices, above competitive norm, 21, 27, 29, 31-32; below competitive norm, 32-33, 453; necessarily arbitrary, 204, 225n
Monopoly profits, as sympton of monopoly, 11, 474, 490-97; shared with workers, 398-400
Monopsonistic competition, 35n, 168, 355n, 359, 361n, 362, 365-67, 376-78
Monopsonistic exploitation, 366, 376
Monopsony, 40-41, 45, 359, 362, 363, 365-67, 371n, 375, 376-78, 496, 511n
Moody, John, 122n
More, Sir Thomas, 186

Morgan, J. P. Comp., 239n
Morgan, Theodore, 524n
Morgenstern, Oscar, 467n
Morton Salt Co. v. G. S. Suppiger Co., 191, 229
Motor Carrier Act, 296
Motor transport, 183, 277-79, 296-99
Mund, Vernon A., 82n, 216n, 314n
Munn v. Illinois, 187
Musgrave, Richard A., 252n
Myers, Charles A., 354n

National Bureau of Economic Research, 513n
National Income, affected by redistribution, 388-89; and by reduction of monopoly, 461; and by wage increase, 386-93, 402; compared for two periods, 460n; dependent on resource allocation, 21; distribution of, 21, 304, 336, 341, 460; distribution of increment of, 402; equality of distribution of, 336, 341, 433, 463; other goals conflicting with maximization of, 71-72, 463; prices affecting measurement of, 460n; redistribution of, 388, 393-410, 460; share of labor in, 391, 394, 395-97; statistical measurement of, 467; unequal distribution of, 341, 433; versus total welfare, 459-63
National Industrial Recovery Act, 171, 190, 216, 305, 313, 321
National Labor Relations Board, 321, 325, 327
National Recovery Administration, 157n, 171, 190, 216, 294
National Resources Committee, 239n, 303n, 304n, 477n, 490n, 499, 501n, 503, 504, 505n
National Resources Planning Board, 295n, 296n, 297n, 298n
National Tax Association, 249-50n
Nationalization, 50
National War Labor Board, 320
Natural monopolies, 48, 294, 441
Neal, Alfred C., 507, 508n
Nelson, Saul, 143n, 160n
Neutrino, 465n
New Jersey, 147, 187n, 242
New York, 187, 288, 293
New York Times, 312n, 313n
N.Y. v. North River Sugar Ref. Co., 187
Nicholls, William H., 124n, 256n, 264n
"No help wanted," 413
Non-ferrous metals, 7, 42, 132

Norris-LaGuardia Act, 321, 324-25, 326
Northern Securities Co. v. *U.S.*, 188
Northrup, Herbert R., 366n
Nourse, Edwin G., vii
Nutter, G. Warren, 488n

O'Brien v. *People,* 324n
Oil industry, 131, 132n, 148, 301-03; see also Standard Oil Comp.
Oklahoma, 303n
Old-age annuities, 334n
Oligopoly, 104, 502, 503n
Oligopsony, 354, 359, 370, 376
O'Mahoney, Joseph C., 222n
Open-price system, 89, 189, 191, 204
Oppressive practices, 36-37, 98-104, 129-30, 134-35, 136, 147-48, 175-76, 219; see also Predatory practices
Optimum, allocation of resources, 4, 21, 102, 243; size of firm, 51, 123, 261
Optimum tariff, 269n
Oregon, 292-93, 310n
Over employment, 356

Papandreou, Andreas G., 523-24
Parity prices, 306n
Parsons, Talcott, 450n
Patent licence agreements, 92-93, 191, 207-10, 229, 259, 282-86
Patent litigation, 27, 176, 177
Patents, accumulations of, 119, 284; and antitrust laws, 207-10, 228; compulsory licensing of, 192, 285; discrimination based on, 140, 157; domination through, 105, 119, 192, 283-84; enlarging scope of, 191, 207-10; extension of, 282-85; leasing machines protected by, 140, 189, 191, 209; philosophy of—laws, 176-77, 280-82; pooling agreements, 119, 190, 284-85; promoting progress, 33, 65-67, 71, 176-77, 182, 280, 285-86, 464; reform of—law, 209-10, 234-35, 285-86; restricting entry, 27, 33, 119, 182, 280-86; restrictive licensing of, 207-10, 282-85; under Statute of Monopolies, 186; used for price fixing, 190, 191, 207-10, 229
Patents Committee (House or Senate), 88n, 92n, 156n, 284n
Paul, Randolph E., 251n
Penalties for antitrust violations, 194, 206-07, 230, 233
Penetration, coefficient of, 523
Penrose, Edith, vii, 285n

Percale, 17, 40
Perfect competition, 12, 19, 20, 70, 360, 369
Perfect market, 13-14, 163, 166
Perishability, 339, 348-49, 370
Phantom freight, 145-48
Philadelphia and Reading Company, 131
Pigou, A. C., 344n
Pittsburgh Plus, 145, 189
Planned economy, 75, 76-77, 275-76
Plinius, 185
Politics, in public monopolies, 49, 112, 118; in tariff making, 270-72, 274
Pool, 92, 187, 212, 285; see also Cartel
Potatoes, 275n, 278n, 306n, 311-13
Predatory practices, 188, 218, 219, 221, 224, 225; see Oppressive practices
Prediction versus explanation, 454-58
Price controls, 77, 304-16, 422
Price discrimination, 135-63; a monopolistic practice, 37, 137, 404; as unfair competition, 176; by railroads, 153-55, 159, 213, 295; by vertically integrated concerns, 111; cartels pooling receipts from, 97; classified, 443; defined, 135-36; for farm products, 157-58, 309; for goods with interdependent demand, 162n; illegal under Clayton Act, 188, 190, 195, 197; implied in price uniformity, 166; in buying, 168; to discourage newcomers, 27; types of, 137-63; under basing-point system, 144-47, 189, 192, 203-04
Price-elasticity of demand, defined, 9; see Elasticity
Price inflexibility, a symptom of monopoly, 11, 475, 497-508; and competition, 134n, 166-67; as stabilizer of economy, 62-63; versus margin inflexibility, 506-08
Price leadership, and monopoly index, 522n; collusive or non-collusive, 11; domination and, 104-05, 127-36, 190; four types of, 134; informal, 100
Price policy, monopolistic by definition, 83
Price stability, 423, 428; see also Stability
Price supports, 58-59, 305-13
Price System, disturbances of, 31; function of, 20, 316, 372n, 403, 433, 441
Price war, 120, 129, 163
Private property, 177n, 280, 281

Product differentiation, gives more choice, 33, 53; implying monopoly, 30-31, 33, 53, 496; to aid price discrimination, 158; to reduce demand elasticity, 10

Product discrimination, 138, 154n, 155, 156, .158, 161

Productivity of labor, 267, 341n, 360

Profits, accounting rate of, 491-95; adjusted rate of, 495-97; attracting newcomers, 19; business size and, 261; capital gain and, 257-58; capitalization of, 494-97; difficult to calculate, 11, 32, 251, 493-97; from monopsony, 362, 363, 375, 496; from temporary monopoly, 282; function of, 401; indicating monopoly, 11, 474, 490-97; "loss offset" to, 254; maximization of, 13, 19, 309, 366n, 391; of innovators, 67-68, 282; of landlords, 316; pools, 96-97; taxation of, 68, 250-63; through exploiting workers, 340, 362, 366, 375; undistributed, 243, 247n, 248, 253-55, 257-58, 262-63; wages encroaching on, 339n, 340, 378, 388, 391, 397-402

Progress, 30, 33, 49, 64, 71-72, 463

Proletariat, 334, 335, 336

Propensity, not measurable, 466; to consume, 388; to save, 388; to spend, 58n

Proration, 302

Prostitution, 121

Protection, against competing workers, 44, 399; against deception, 173; against high prices, 315-17; against imitation, 33, 64-65, 72, 170-78, 280-86; by dominating firm, 104; by racketeers, 121; from damage by competitors, 170; from foreign competition, 33, 149n, 265-76; from newcomers, 20, 27, 38, 55, 64, 70, 119, 125-26, 276, 378, 399; of health and safety, 182, 278, 289, 291n; of high-cost producers, 59-60; of local producers, 279, 309; of employers from unions, 327; of trade-marks, 172; through tariffs, 33, 149n, 265-74

Public corporations, 50n

Public relations, 52n, 112, 118

Public safety and health, 182, 278, 289, 291n

Public utilities, 37, 48, 155, 161, 294-95, 315

Public v. private monopolies, 48-50

Purchasing power theory, 386-88

Purdy, Harry L., 82n

Pure competition, 14-19; and identical prices, 163-68; as a standard of comparison, 22-23, 139n, 345n; in buying labor, 345n, 359, 364-65, 366n, 377-78; no active rivalry under, 18, 352

Quantity discounts, 141, 150-52, 190-91, 197, 247n

Quasi-pure competition, 131, 134

Quota cartels, 58, 96, 214, 276, 303, 307, 309

Radio industry, 119n

Railroads, 50n, 122, 141, 153-55, 159, 187, 188, 192, 213, 245, 260n, 294-99, 321, 322n

Railway Labor Act, 320

Rationing, 33, 265, 276, 316, 453

Raushenbush, Carl, 320n

Raymond, Fred, I., 246-47n, 263n

Real wages, 267, 338, 340, 415; versus money wages, 394-95

"Realism" and "Reality," 12, 17, 18, 19-20, 84-85, 447, 449

Reasonable restraint, 109, 183, 186, 190, 200-02, 220, 225, 318

Reciprocal Trade Agreements, 272

Reed-Bulwinkle Act, 192, 213

Rees, Albert, 453n

Regional monopolies, 55n

Regulation, of farm prices, 313; of insurance, 213; of motor transport, 277-78, 296-99; of natural resources, 302-04; of public utilities, 294-95, 315; of railroads, 187, 192, 294-99; of union wage rates, 427-29; of widely held corporations, 245; private vs. public, 229

"Relativity of relevance," 467

Rent control, 316-17, 408

Rent versus profit, 494

Republic Steel Corporation, 115n

Resale price maintenance, 93, 143, 153, 190, 191, 193, 208-09, 215-16, 229, 314-15

Restrictions, in agriculture, 41-43, 56-62, 305-07, 309-12; of acreage, 311-12; of capacity, 202; of employment, 355, 361, 363; of entry, 20, 25, 26, 33, 117-26, 173, 296-99; of imports, 265-76, 310; of labor supply, 372n, 410-13, 421; of oil production, 301-04; of operations, 24-26, 28-29, 33, 285; of

Restrictions (*continued*)
output, 21-29, 33, 57-59, 96, 202, 301-12, 399-400; of purchases, 353; of sales, 86-98; of size of firm, 246-48
Retail outlets, 122-23, 124-25, 175
Revenue tariffs, 266
Reynolds, Lloyd, 502n
Rhode Island, 309n
Richey v. *Smith*, 291n
Robinson, E. A. G., 82n
Robinson, Joan, 366n, 378n, 400n, 401n
Robinson-Patman Act, 103, 152, 190, 195, 197
Rockefeller, John D., 239n
Rockefeller Foundation, viii
Roosevelt, Franklin D., 259-60
Roosevelt, Theodore, 184, 229n
Rosenthal Fund, viii
Rothschild, K. W., 497n, 519-22
Rubber, 56, 57
Rule of reason, 109n, 184, 188, 199, 200-02, 220
Ruttenberg, Harold J., 385n, 393n

Sales tax, 251, 263
Saving, 388, 422, 463n, 464n
Schattschneider, E. E., 271n
Schechter Poultry Corporation v. *U.S.*, 190
Schmoller, Gustav, 444n
Schoolmasters' Case, 170n
Schroeder, Gertrude Guyton, 115n
Schumpeter, Joseph A., 64n, 66n, 73n, 76n
Schwegmann Brothers v. *Calvert Distillers Corp.*, 193, 216n
Scitovsky, Tibor, 461n, 499n
Sears, Roebuck and Co., 150n
Security, 34, 69, 71-72, 463
Selling below cost, 103, 170, 175, 305, 314-15
Selling cartel, 98
Servicing and repair, 125
Sharfman, I. L., 297n
Sharing the market, 202, 212, 214
Sherman Act, 108, 176, 183-85, 187-92, 193-95, 199-235, 324, 343
Shipping Act, 212
Short run, versus long run, 394, 408-10, 462, 512
Silverman, Irwin W., 290n, 293n, 294n
Simons, Henry C., 50n, 77n, 247n, 252n, 256n, 262n, 264n, 374n, 401n, 415n, 423n

Slichter, Sumner H., 68n, 345n, 396n, **426n**
Slope ratio of demand curves, 519-22
Small Business Committee, 111n, 184n, 195n, 207n, 230n, 231n, 233, 256n
Small Business Mobilization Act, 217n
Smith, Adam, 87n, 353
Smullyan, Emile Benoit, vii
Social goals, 71-72, 250, 336, 423, 463-64
Social versus natural sciences, 449-50, 456n, 466n
Socialism, 50, 83n, 401n, 434-35
Sociology, 85n, 118, 335, 344, 358, 450
South Dakota, 277n
Species and genus demand curves, 519-22
Speculation, 60
Spinoza, Baruch, 465n
Squeezability, 141
Stability, 34, 56-62, 71-72, 386, 423, 428, 463
Stalin, Joseph V., 434n
Standard Fashion Co. v. *Magrane-Houston Co.*, 122n
Standard of living, 267, 272, 313, 336, 392
Standard Oil Company, 81, 100, 107, 109n, 122, 131, 132n, 147, 148, 219, 232
Standard Oil Company of New Jersey v. *U.S.*, 188, 199n, 201n, 219n, 232n
Static analysis, 30
Statistical estimates, of concentration, 475-85; of labor force, 335, 467; of labor income, 396; of labor mobility, 357n; of national income, 396-97, 467; of price flexibility, 498-505; of prices, 467; of profit rates, 491-95; of wages and earnings, 452n
Statistical services, 86, 88, 189, 203
Statute of monopolies, 183, 186
Steel industry, 87, 115n, 129, 145, 146, 147, 154, 273n, 451-53, 515
Steel syndicate, German, 97n
Steel trust case, 189, 220, 232
Stein, Emanuel, 320n
Stigler, George J., 116n
Stocking, George W., 82n, 92n, 235n, 264n, 303n
Stocks versus assets, 109, 190, 193, 196, 198, 221-24
Streetcar transport, 47-48, 161, 294, 295
Strikes, 75, 320, 322, 324, 328, 329, 411, 417n, 426n

Subsidies, for distressed industries, 58; for employers, 377; for exports, 307; for farmers, 311; for industry in distressed areas, 374; for infant industries, 270; for moving workers, 371; for private monopolies, 49; through discrimination, 163

Substitutability, among products, 8-9, 36, 486-87; between union labor and non-union labor, 410-11, 420

Substitution of capital for labor, 389

Sugar, 18, 56, 118, 147, 274, 310

Sugar Institute v. *U.S.*, 191, 203n, 229

Sugar trust case, 188, 219n, 232

Sumner, John D., vii, 516n

Sunshine Anthracite Coal Co. v. *Adkins*, 314n

Suppression of technology, 64-65

Surplus Commodities Administration, 157

Surplus removal, 306-08, 311-13

Sutton, C., 72n

Swift & Co. v. *Federal Trade Comm.*, 190, 223n

Swift and Co. v. *U.S.*, 219n

Syndicalism, 426n, 435

Syndicates, 43, 44, 98

Taft, William Howard, 183, 184, 200n, 201n

Taft-Hartley Act, 317n, 326-29

Tariff Commission, 274n

Tariff quotas, 274n

Tariffs, 33, 149n, 182, 265-75, 310n, 313

Taussig, Frank W., 270-71n

Tautologies, 41, 457

Tax policies, 67-69, 234-35, 249-65, 316

Taxes, evasion of, 239, 247n, 259-61; monopoly props compensating for high, 68-69; on advertising, 264; on corporations, 249-65; on excess profits, 251, 258n, 260n; reducing investment, 68; reducing saving, 464n; to avoid inflation, 316; to redistribute income, 21-22n, 250, 460n; to restrict interstate trade, 277

Taxonomic approach, 439, 442-43, 444, 445, 447

Tea, 56, 143n, 266

Technological inevitability of monopoly, 51, 117, 239

Technological integration, 110-11, 117, 238-40, 246, 483-84, 488-90

Technology, change of, 51, 357, 372n; cross-licensing and, 284; induced change of, 389, 390; necessitates concentration, 47, 51; progress of, 30, 33, 49, 63-64, 70, 286, 302n, 396; protected by patents, 280-86; requiring large capital, 238; suppression of, 64-65

Telephone, 47, 161, 245, 294

Temple Anthracite Coal Co. v. *Federal Trade Comm.*, 222n

Temporal discrimination, 161

Temporary National Economic Committee, 17n, 73n, 74n, 75n, 82n, 94n, 117n, 128n, 129n, 143n, 149n, 151n, 156n, 160n, 164n, 185n, 191n, 199n, 200n, 206n, 209, 222n, 248, 249n, 283n, 284n, 286n, 303n, 309n, 310n, 513n, 522n

Terminology, confusion in, 12; motives behind, 83n

Texas, 149, 278, 303n, 321n

Texas and New Orleans Railway Co. v. *Brotherhood of Railway and Steamship Clerks*, 321n

Thatcher Mfg. Co. v. *Federal Trade Comm.*, 190, 223n

Theoretical analysis, 440, 443, 445, 446-47, 448-68

Thornton, W. T., 348n

Timberg, Sigmund, vii, 201n, 205n

Tin, 56

Tippetts, Charles S., 95n

Tobacco, 41, 100, 107, 188, 275n, 306n, 515

Tobacco cases, 81, 107, 124n, 147, 188, 192, 201n, 203n, 219, 225, 228, 233

Trade associations, 88ff, 189, 191, 203, 204, 206, 216, 229, 314, 342n

Trade barriers, 265-79, 313; see also Tariffs

Trade-mark agreements, 93

Trade-marks, 93, 171, 172, 173, 215

Trade unions, administering government wage rules, 428; and antitrust laws, 191, 210-11, 324, 341n, 343; and class war, 340; and competition among workers, 342, 347, 359; and democratic society, 423, 426, 432-33n; and labor supply, 373, 377; and mobility, 372-73, 375; arguments for, 339-41; assist in job evaluation, 382, 429; bar adjustments of labor supply, 384; cause upward spiral of wages, 385; compared with cartels, 44, 342n; consider elasticity of demand for product, 420; control competition from non-

Trade unions (*continued*)
  union labor, 412; control labor supply, 411-12; could equilibrate labor supply and demand, 416; cut in on monopoly profits, 398-400; effect change in income distribution, 393-410; eliminating monopsony, 377; exercising self-restraint, 425-27; exploiting their bargaining power, 420; favor employers' monopoly power, 398; free labor market and, 340; gain benefits for members from other workers, 394-95, 405, 407-08; gain wage increase and greater member employment, 378, 418; have functions besides wage bargaining, 426, 429; in nation-wide combination, 430, 432; labor laws and, 317-29; making labor supply perfectly elastic, 377-78; merged in national union, 419, 429n; preventing downward spiral of wages, 386; preventing hardship to workers, 384-85; preventing indirect competition through products, 431-32; reduction of power of, 428-32; regarded as "Labor," 334; responsible to members versus nation, 416n, 419-20, 425-27; restrained, destroyed or split up, 423-32; sabotaging the function of profit system, 401; split in smaller groups, 430-32; unable to enforce employers' competition, 376; unequal bargaining strength of, 347, 407, 424n; with closed shop, 27, 71, 321, 322, 326, 327, 328, 346, 373, 418, 430
Transportation, and antitrust laws, 192, 212-13; competing means of, 295-99; cost of, 15, 142, 144, 145-46, 165, 267, 452n; motor-, 183, 277-78, 296-99; of strike breakers, 322n; of surplus commodity, 312; of workers, 371; protected from competition, 183, 295-99; public monopoly of, 50n; rate discrimination in, 141, 153-55, 159; regulated, 50n, 187, 192, 277-78, 294-99
Triffin, Robert, 522-23
Truax v. *Corrigan*, 324n
Trust agreement, 106, 187, 242
Tying clauses, 112, 176, 188, 189, 195, 202, 247n

Uncertainty, 204-05, 465n
Underdeveloped country, 269

Undistributed profits, 243, 247n, 248, 253-55, 257, 262-63
Unemployment aggravated by wage rigidity, 384, 386; caused by union wage increase, 338n, 390; creates industrial reserve army, 363; creates pure competition for labor, 355-56; due to excessive product prices, 31; due to excessive wage rates, 31, 373; mitigated by wage rigidity, 386; most serious when labor share greatest, 397; prevented by fiscal expansion, 403, 418, 420-22, 423-24; reduces labor mobility, 339, 363-65, 370
Unfair competition, 102-04, 148, 168-77, 188, 190, 196, 203, 215, 305, 312, 314
Unfair labor practices, 321, 327
Uniform prices, 90, 163-68
Union-management cooperation, 392n, 399
Union shop, 322, 327, 328, 418
United Mine Workers, 430
United Nations, 421n
United States Alkali Export Assn. v. *U.S.*, 214n
United States Industrial Alcohol Company, 131
United States Maltsters Assn. v. *Federal Trade Comm.*, 203n
United States Steel Corporation, 81, 87n, 107, 109n, 115n, 164n, 189, 220, 225, 513n, 521-22n
U.S. v. *Aluminum Co. of America*, 192, 224n, 225n
U.S. v. *American Linseed Oil Co.*, 189, 203n
U.S. v. *American Tobacco Co.*, 188, 201n, 219n
U.S. v. *Brims*, 399n
U.S. v. *Columbia Steel Co.*, 225-26
U.S. v. *Corn Products Refining Co.*, 143n
U.S. v. *E. C. Knight Co.*, 188, 219n, 232
U.S. v. *General Electric Co.*, 189, 208n, 229
U.S. v. *Hartford-Empire Co.*, 89n, 192, 283n
U.S. v. *International Harvester Co.*, 132n, 190, 220n
U.S. v. *Masonite Corp.*, 133n, 191, 209n, 283n
U.S. v. *N.Y. Great Atlantic and Pacific Tea Co.*, 193n, 194n

U.S. v. Socony-Vacuum Oil Co., 199n, 202n
U.S. v. South Eastern Underwriters Assn., 191, 213n
U.S. v. Standard Oil Co. (Indiana), 190
U.S. v. Standard Oil Co. (New Jersey), 148n
U.S. v. Trenton Potteries Co., 190, 202n, 204
U.S. v. United Shoe Machinery Co., 189
U.S. v. United States Steel Corporation, 87n, 189, 220, 232
U.S. v. Univis Lens Co., 191, 229
U.S. v. William L. Hutcheson, 191, 211n
United Steel Workers, 411n
United Textile Workers, 411n
University salaries, 366n
Unorganized majority, 406-08
Unreasonable restraint, 109, 183, 186, 190, 200-02, 220, 225, 318
Unstable industries, 56, 62-64
User cost, 349n, 462n
Utah, 292

Value added, 508
Value judgment, 458-64
Veblen, Thorstein, 444n
Venture capital, 65-67, 282
Vertical integration, 110-11, 198, 240, 246n, 483-84
Virginia-Carolina Chemical Company, 131

Wage differentials according to job evaluation, 381-82; between isolated markets, 358-63, 371; definition of monopolistic, 414-15; incentive function of, 435; necessary to induce movement of workers, 358, 383, 404; no evidence for monopsony, 363; supervised by central union, 426n; through monopolistic union policy, 395
Wage discrimination, 365
Wage flexibility, 386
Wage increase, and employment, 378, 387, 398, 417-29; and inflation, 417-29; and induced inventions, 390; at expense of capital incomes, 394, 408; at expense of profit, 378, 391, 394, 397-402; by fixed annual percentage, 428; causing greater management effort, 389, 391-92; causing greater national income, 386-93; causing substitution of capital for labor, 389-90;

consistent with greater employment, 378, 387, 418; faster than rise of productivity, 422; inducing greater labor effort, 392-93; inelastic product demand helps, 417-18; in money versus real terms, 394-95; in step with productivity, 402-06; measurement of, 452n; preventing expansion of output, 401-02; raising labor productivity, 389; reduced earnings despite, 452n; resulting from increased productivity, 396; resulting in higher prices, 388, 391, 398, 400; selective as to particular firms, 392; versus total payroll, 387; with unchanged prices and employment, 400
Wage level, 403, 415, 428
Wage-price spiral, 395
Wage rates, and capital supply, 267, 396; and employers' collusion, 353-56, 370, 375-76; and employment, 19, 338n, 387, 398, 417-29; and exploitation, 341, 362-65, 376-79; and labor mobility, 19, 356-63, 371-75; and union strength, 44, 344-48, 368-70, 373, 376-79, 380-435, 451-54; below marginal labor cost, 366n, 367n; definition of monopolistic, 414; employment restricted to reduce, 353, 355n, 361, 364; fluctuating, 383; in isolated areas, 358-62, 363, 371-75; raised at expense of profit, 338, 391, 394, 397-402; regulated by government, 427-29; restricting entry, 27, 373, 395, 413-14, 415; versus earnings and payroll, 452n
Wage spirals, 340
Wage structure, 410-17, 386, 428, 434
Wage uniformity, 399, 431
Wagner Act, 317n, 321-22, 325-27, 328, 367
Wallace, Donald H., 502n
War emergency measures, 122, 217
War Production Board, 217
Washington, 292n
Watkins, Myron W., 82n, 92n, 157n, 235n, 264n
Webb-Pomerene Act, 189, 214
Weber, Max, 450n
Welfare economics, 20, 337, 459-64
Welfare programs, 141, 157, 307, 317, 433
Wheat, 14, 18, 19, 56, 59, 274, 306n, 310
White, Edward D., Justice, 199n, 201n

Whitman, Roswell H., 518n, 519n
Whittlesey, C. R., 274n
Wickersham, Attorney General, 184n
Wilcox, Clair, 73n, 74n, 82n, 117n
Williams, Senator, 259n
Williamson, S. T., 342n
Wirth, Louis, 465n

Wisconsin, 291n, 293-94
Wollett, Donald H., 326n

Yellow-dog contract, 320, 325
Yntema, Theodore O., 513n

Zone prices, 90, 143-44